Unsexing Gender, Engendering Activism
Readings in Gender Studies

Edited By

Danielle M. DeMuth
Julia M. Mason
Grand Valley State University

Kendall Hunt
publishing company

Kendall Hunt
publishing company

www.kendallhunt.com
Send all inquiries to:
4050 Westmark Drive
Dubuque, IA 52004-1840

Printed in the United States of America
10 9 8 7 6 5 4 3 2 1

CONTENTS

FOREWORD

Unsexing Gender, Engendering Activism: Readings in Gender Studies is an exciting introduction to the study of gender in the contemporary world. Its goal is to provide students the means to describe and analyze how gender stereotypes develop and their importance in shaping everyday decisions. The readings are interdisciplinary, drawing on a wide range of authors, including novelists, journalists, sociologists, psychologists, and historians.

The reader lays a firm foundation for understanding *gender*, with articles and essays that explore how we define and talk and write about gender. Subsequent sections examine gender in social institutions like schools, the workplace, and the family, and focus on the ways in which gender has an impact on bodies. The final section develops an understanding of activism and its significance for ending the inequality embedded in our culture. Coming to grips with these important topics will ground you in the major concepts in the field of women and gender studies and will permit you to rethink your own individual and social environments.

Unsexing Gender, Engendering Activism grew out of the collaborative approach that characterizes feminist teaching. Both Dr. Danielle DeMuth and Dr. Julia Mason have studied and taught about women and gender for almost ten years, and at several institutions. While they bring unique interests to their teaching—DeMuth's graduate work was in English, Mason's in American Culture Studies—they share a commitment to providing students a common foundation for understanding and analyzing *gender* that will serve for future study. Their decisions about what to include in this Reader were also shaped by the hundreds of students with whom they have shared classrooms over many semesters.

In seriously engaging with the materials in *Unsexing Gender, Engendering Activism: Readings in Gender Studies,* not only will you gain significant new knowledge and strengthen your analytical skills, you will influence the students who follow.

Kathleen Underwood
Director, Women and Gender Studies
Associate Professor, History
Grand Valley State University

PREFACE

Unsexing Gender, Engendering Activism emerged from our desire to bring foundational concepts, questions, and methods in Gender Studies together with new research in this interdisciplinary field. We chose the title *Unsexing Gender, Engendering Activism* to highlight four important aspects of the field of Gender Studies: the study of gender as a pervasive social construct; "nature vs. nurture" debates on gendered traits and differences; the intersection of gender with other social and cultural identities (such as class, race, age, ethnicity, nationality and sexuality); and an emphasis on activism meant to show what you can *do* with this emergent research and information.

While it is relatively easy to locate an excellent text that introduces the field of Women's Studies, finding a text that represents the study of gender across the disciplines is much more difficult. This collection includes work by fiction writers and poets, journalists, essayists and activists as well as articles from academics in Gender Studies, African and African American Studies, Education, Cultural Studies, Social and Political Science, Sociology, Biology, History, Anthropology, Social Work, Economics, and Business.

Some of the readings collected here are read each semester by tens of thousands of students across the U.S. in classes similar to this one. In addition to some foundational feminist essays, such as Peggy McIntosh's essay "Unpacking the Invisible Knapsack," Adrienne Rich's "Claiming an Education" and Audre Lorde's "Uses of the Erotic," this collection includes readings gathered from *Feminist Teacher*, *Signs: Journal of Women in Culture and Society*, *Gender and Society*, and *The Journal of Men's Studies*—journals publishing cutting-edge research in feminism and gender studies.

Each section of this reader is accompanied by a list of key concepts. Not all the terms are actually defined in the readings; instead, they will be defined in class and in the course textbook. Some of the terms repeat across sections and are listed as key concepts to review. Concepts such as *gender*, *sex* and *sex-gender system*, for example, are highlighted in each section, and as you read each new section, your definition of these terms and their significance will grow.

WOMEN'S STUDIES, MEN'S STUDIES, GENDER STUDIES

The first courses in Women's Studies appeared at colleges in the United States in the 1960s. These courses were taught throughout the university curriculum and were aimed at looking specifically at the experience of women in literature, history and the social sciences. Initially these courses corrected a gap in their respective disciplines; for example, history curriculum lacked women's history, while English classes lacked literature by women. The voices and experience of women were missing throughout the curriculum. By 1970, when it became clear that the various classes about women throughout the curriculum formed a more cohesive study, the first program in Women's Studies was founded at San Diego State University. The interdisciplinary study of women grew from one program in 1970 to 276 Women's Studies programs in 1977 and by 1989 that number had nearly doubled to 525.[1]

---

[1]Reynolds, Michael, Shobha Shagle and Lekha Venkataraman. "A National Census of Women's and Gender Studies Programs in U.S. Institutions of Higher Education." Chicago, IL: National Opinion Research Center. December 26, 2007, 3.

The field grew in important ways. Men's Studies emerged as a field in the 1980s. While some might suggest that the entire university curriculum outside of Women's Studies departments was already "men's studies," research in most fields was androcentric, generalizing from men to the rest of humanity, and little research was being done on the specific experience of being male. Some programs maintained an emphasis on "Women's Studies," whereas other programs expanded their emphasis to "Gender Studies" in order to emphasize femininity and masculinity in relationship to each other—as concepts that rely on each other for meaning. Thus, "Gender Studies," rooted in the study of women and feminism, necessarily includes Lesbian, Gay, Bisexual and Transgender Studies (LGBT) and queer theory. In 2007, the National Women's Studies Association (NWSA), reported 650 diverse women and gender studies programs in community colleges, four-year colleges, and universities nationwide.[2]

ORGANIZATION OF THE READINGS

The reader is organized into eight sections. The first three sections of the reader—*Gendered Identities*, *Discourses of Gender* and *Explanations of Gender*—highlight foundational questions in the field of Gender Studies. These sections complement traditional ways of studying gender and suggest the new directions taken in the last several years.

The readings in *Gendered Identities* show that gender is much more complicated than the simple and rather stereotypical ideas of femininity and masculinity that most people envision. The selections unpack the ways that gender, race, sexuality, and class shape social location and are designed to help each reader examine her/his own position, which is the first step in examining the role of gender in shaping our lives, institutions, and interactions, and also the first step in working toward social change.

The brief section *Discourses of Gender* provides readers with tools and examples for looking at popular culture. How is gender socially constructed through cultural representations, such as music, advertising, film, video, and magazines? How do these representations of gender shape our knowledge?

Research is beginning to show a much more complicated relationship than the simple opposition "nature vs. nurture" might suggest. *Explanations of Gender* tackles these debates and foregrounds new research. Initially, many argued that women's behaviors, achievements and desires were both driven and constrained by biology. Early gender theorists challenged those ideas and instead argued that *women were made, not born*. To put it more simply, female and male behavior was not determined by biology but was instead shaped by culture. Rather than assume that male/masculine and female/feminine are natural, essential and biologically determined, gender theorists assert that we live in a "sex-gender system"—a system that divides labor differently and grants gendered meanings to the relatively meaningless biological categories of "male" and "female," and ascribes to these categories differing values, behaviors and desires. More recently, some theorists have challenged the idea that sex and gender are connected—suggesting instead that the cultural categories of gender are not linked to the biological categories of sex. Rather than the simple analogy, "male is to masculine as female is to feminine," new gendered categories have emerged—like "female masculinity." Readings in anthropology, sociology, and psychology further challenge biological explanations of gender by suggesting that what we often assume to be gendered behavior is neither natural nor universal. Instead, different cultures sometimes exhibit gender relationships very different than what we might assume to be stereotypical

---

[2]Ibid, 3.

behaviors. Readings in sociology suggest that gender is one category used, in combination with race, class, ethnicity, sexual orientation, able-bodiedness and national citizenship, to maintain social inequalities.

Gender in Education and *Reworking Labor and the Family* explore the three most significant cultural institutions that play a part in socializing us to race, gender and class expectations throughout our lifespan: education, family and the workplace. These sections offer explanations of how these institutions work and examples of activism meant to improve these institutions, including challenging the gender pay gap, sexual harassment, and homophobic bullying. The sections also highlight alternatives—including gay families, stay at home fathers, innovative workplaces, and radical heterosexuality.

Gendered Bodies emphasizes the ways in which our experience of our bodies is shaped by the culture and politics of gender, race, class, ethnicity and sexuality. Topics include: body image, sex education, uses of pleasure and the erotic, and historical perspectives on changing standards of beauty. *Gender, Violence and Anti-Violence Activism* focuses on ending gender-based violence and highlights campus-based initiatives to end sexual assault, including men's efforts to educate other men. The final section of the book, *Feminisms and Gender Justice*, weaves together the history, lived experiences, and activism that has created more than 150 years of feminist activism in the United States.

CLAIMING AN EDUCATION

What do you have a right to expect from your professor or instructor, your program of study, and your university? First and foremost to be taken seriously. To be challenged, to be treated fairly, to be heard. Crucial to each student's success in this class is what Adrienne Rich calls "claiming an education." *Claiming* rather than "receiving" an education requires a contract between you (the student) and your professor or instructor, your program of study, and the university itself. In order to hold up your end of this contract, you must take yourselves seriously, come prepared, and take advantage of the opportunities offered by this class. This book and our classrooms are designed to offer diverse perspectives in order to support you in developing a critical stance and informed opinion on foundational ideas and current trends in Gender Studies. Students say that courses in Gender Studies are challenging, exciting and transformative.

Danielle M. DeMuth
Assistant Professor, Women and Gender Studies
Grand Valley State University

ABOUT THE EDITORS

Danielle M. DeMuth is Assistant Professor of Women and Gender Studies at Grand Valley State University, where in addition to Introduction to Gender Studies she teaches courses on global feminism, Arab and Arab-American Feminism, feminist theory, and lesbian, gay and queer literature. Her research interests include lesbian and queer literature and feminism in the Arab world. She started teaching Introduction to Gender Studies in 1997 while working on her PhD in English at the University of Toledo. She is grateful to more than ten years of students in Women and Gender Studies who have claimed their education and continue to inspire her as they apply their knowledge and activism in the world.

Julia M. Mason is Assistant Professor of Women and Gender Studies at Grand Valley State University where she teaches: Introduction to Gender Studies; Women, Health and Environment; Women's Community Collaborative and Foundations of Feminism. She earned her doctorate in American Culture Studies, with graduate certificates in Women's Studies and Ethnic Studies, from Bowling Green State University. She also has a Master of Arts in American Indian Studies from The University of Arizona. She has been teaching gender studies courses since 2001. Her research interests include: breast cancer in the media; ecofeminism; and feminist activism.

SECTION I

Gendered Identities

Key Concepts for Section I: Gendered Identities

Ageism
Androcentrism
Classism
Dichotomy/Dichotomous
Doing Gender
Dominance/Domination
Double Standards
Femininity/Femininities
Gender
Gender Neutral Pronouns
Gender Studies
Heterosexism
Hierarchy
Homophobia
Homosexuality
Internalized Oppression
Intersectionality
Intersex
Marginalization
Masculinity/Masculinities

Men's Studies
Misogyny
Myth of Meritocracy
Mythical Norm
Oppression
Patriarchy
Power
Privilege
Queer Theory
Racism
Sex
Sex-Gender System
Sexism
Socialization
Subordinance/Subordination
Tokenism
Transgender
Transphobia
Unearned Entitlement
Women's Studies

X: A Fabulous Child's Story

Lois Gould

Lois Gould's *"X: A Fabulous Child's Story"* first appeared in Ms. *Magazine in December 1972 and was published as a book in 1978. Gould is well known for her best selling novel* Such Good Friends *(1970) and her memoir* Mommy Dressing *(1998). She was also a contributor to* The New York Times. *Lois Gould died in 2002.*

Once upon a time, a baby named X was born. This baby was named X so that nobody could tell whether it was a boy or a girl. Its parents could tell, of course, but they couldn't tell anybody else. They couldn't even tell Baby X, at first.

You see, it was all part of a very important Secret Scientific Xperiment, known officially as Project Baby X. The smartest scientists had set up this Xperiment at a cost of Xactly 23 billion dollars and 72 cents, which might seem like a lot for just one baby, even a very important Xperimental baby. But when you remember the prices of things like strained carrots and stuffed bunnies, and popcorn for the movies and booster shots for camp, let alone 28 shiny quarters from the tooth fairy, you begin to see how it adds up.

Also, long before Baby X was born, all those scientists had to be paid to work out the details of the Xperiment, and to write the *Official Instruction Manual* for Baby X's parents and, most important of all, to find the right set of parents to bring up Baby X. These parents had to be selected very carefully. Thousands of volunteers had to take thousands of tests and answer thousands of tricky questions. Almost everybody failed because, it turned out, almost everybody really wanted either a baby boy or a baby girl, and not Baby X at all. Also, almost everybody was afraid that a Baby X would be a lot more trouble than a boy or a girl. (They were probably right, the scientists admitted, but Baby X needed parents who wouldn't *mind* the Xtra trouble.)

There were families with grandparents named Milton and Agatha, who didn't see why the baby couldn't be named Milton or Agatha instead of X, even if it *was* an X. There were families with aunts who insisted on knitting tiny dresses and uncles who insisted on sending tiny baseball mitts. Worst of all, there were families that already had other children who couldn't be trusted to keep the secret. Certainly not if they knew the secret was worth 23 billion dollars and 72 cents—and all you had to do was take one little peek at Baby X in the bathtub to know if it was a boy or a girl.

But, finally, the scientists found the Joneses, who really wanted to raise an X more than any other kind of baby—no matter how much trouble it would be. Ms. and Mr. Jones had to promise they would take equal turns caring for X, and feeding it, and singing it lullabies. And they had to promise never to hire any baby-sitters. The government scientists knew perfectly well that a baby-sitter would probably peek at X in the bathtub, too.

The day the Joneses brought their baby home, lots of friends and relatives came over to see it. None of them knew about the secret Xperiment, though. So the first thing they asked was what kind of a baby X was. When the Joneses smiled and said, "It's an X!" nobody knew what to say. They couldn't say, "Look at her cute little dimples!" And they couldn't say, "Look at his husky little biceps!" And they couldn't even say just plain "kitchy-coo." In fact, they all thought the Joneses were playing some kind of rude joke.

But, of course, the Joneses were not joking. "It's an X" was absolutely all they would say. And that made the friends and relatives very angry. The relatives all felt embarrassed about having an X in the family. "People will think there's something wrong with it!" some of them whispered. "There *is* something wrong with it!" others whispered back.

"Nonsense!" the Joneses told them all cheerfully. "What could possibly be wrong with this perfectly adorable X?"

Nobody could answer that, except Baby X, who had just finished its bottle. Baby X's answer was a loud, satisfied burp.

Clearly, nothing at all was wrong. Nevertheless, none of the relatives felt comfortable about buying a present for a Baby X. The cousins who sent the baby a tiny football helmet would not come and visit any more. And the neighbors who sent a pink-flowered romper suit pulled their shades down when the Joneses passed their house.

The *Official Instruction Manual* had warned the new parents that this would happen, so they didn't fret about it. Besides, they were too busy with Baby X and the hundreds of different Xercises for treating it properly.

Ms. and Mr. Jones had to be Xtra careful about how they played with little X. They knew if they kept bouncing it up in the air and saying how *strong* and *active* it was, they'd be treating it more like a boy than an X. But if all they did was cuddle it and kiss it and tell it how *sweet* and *dainty* it was, they'd be treating it more like a girl than an X.

On page 1,654 of the *Official Instruction Manual*, the scientists prescribed: "plenty of bouncing and plenty of cuddling, *both*. X ought to be strong and sweet and active. Forget about *dainty* altogether."

Meanwhile, the Joneses were worrying about other problems. Toys, for instance. And clothes. On his first shopping trip, Mr. Jones told the store clerk, "I need some clothes and toys for my new baby." The clerk smiled and said, "Well, now, is it a boy or a girl?" "It's an X," Mr. Jones said, smiling back. But the clerk got all red in the face and said huffily, "In *that* case, I'm afraid I can't help you, sir." So Mr. Jones wandered helplessly up and down the aisles trying to find what X needed. But everything in the store was piled up in sections marked "Boys" or "Girls." There were "Boys' Pajamas" and "Girls' Underwear" and "Boys' Fire Engines" and "Girls' Housekeeping Sets." Mr. Jones went home without buying anything for X. That night he and Ms. Jones consulted page 2,326 of the *Official Instruction Manual*. "Buy plenty of everything!" it said firmly.

So they bought plenty of sturdy blue pajamas in the Boys' Department and cheerful flowered underwear in the Girls' Department. And they bought all kinds of toys. A boy doll that made pee-pee and cried, "Pa-pa." And a girl doll that talked in three languages and said, "I am the Pres-i-dent of Gen-er-al Mo-tors." They also bought a storybook about a brave princess who rescued a handsome prince from his ivory tower, and another one about a sister and brother who grew up to be a baseball star and a ballet star, and you had to guess which was which.

The head scientists of Project Baby X checked all their purchases and told them to keep up the good work. They also reminded the Joneses to see page 4,629 of the *Manual*, where it said, "Never make Baby X feel *embarrassed* or *ashamed* about what it wants to play with. And if X gets dirty climbing rocks, never say 'Nice little Xes don't get dirty climbing rocks.'"

Likewise, it said, "If X falls down and cries, never say 'Brave little Xes don't cry.' Because, of course, nice little Xes *do* get dirty, and brave little Xes do cry. No matter how dirty X gets, or how hard it cries, don't worry. It's all part of the Xperiment."

Whenever the Joneses pushed Baby X's stroller in the park, smiling strangers would come over and coo: "Is that a boy or a girl?" The Joneses would smile back and say, "It's an X." The strangers would stop smiling then, and often snarl something nasty—as if the Joneses had snarled at *them*.

By the time X grew big enough to play with other children, the Joneses' troubles had grown bigger, too. Once a little girl grabbed X's shovel in the sandbox, and zonked X on the head with it. "Now, now, Tracy," the little girl's mother began to scold, "little girls mustn't hit little—" and she turned to ask X, "Are you a little boy or a little girl, dear?"

Mr. Jones who was sitting near the sandbox, held his breath and crossed his fingers.

X smiled politely at the lady, even though X's head had never been zonked so hard in its life. "I'm a little X," X replied.

"You're a *what*?" the lady exclaimed angrily. "You're a little b-r-a-t, you mean!"

"But little girls mustn't hit little Xes, either!" said X, retrieving the shovel with another polite smile. "What good does hitting do, anyway?"

X's father, who was still holding his breath, finally let it out, uncrossed his fingers, and grinned back at X.

And at their next secret Project Baby X meeting, the scientists grinned, too. Baby X was doing fine.

But then it was time for X to start school. The Joneses were really worried about this, because school was even more full of rules for boys and girls, and there were no rules for Xes. The teacher would tell boys to form one line, and girls to form another line. There would be boys' games and girls' games, and boys' secrets and girls' secrets. The school library would have a list of recommended books for girls, and a different list of recommended books for boys. There would even be a bathroom marked BOYS and another one marked GIRLS. Pretty soon boys and girls would hardly talk to each other. What would happen to poor little X?

The Joneses spent weeks consulting their *Instruction Manual* (there were 249½ pages of advice under "First Day of School"), and attending urgent special conferences with the smart scientists of Project Baby X.

The scientists had to make sure that X's mother had taught X how to throw and catch a ball properly, and that X's father had been sure to teach X what to serve at a doll's tea party. X had to know how to shoot marbles and how to jump rope and, most of all, what to say when the Other Children asked whether X was a Boy or a Girl.

Finally, X was ready. The Joneses helped X button on a nice new pair of red-and-white checked overalls, and sharpened six pencils for X's nice new pencil box, and marked X's name clearly on all the books in its nice new book bag. X brushed its teeth and combed its hair, which just about covered its ears, and remembered to put a napkin in its lunchbox.

The Joneses had asked X's teacher if the class could line up alphabetically, instead of forming separate lines for boys and girls. And they had asked if X could use the principal's bathroom, because it wasn't marked anything except BATHROOM. X's teacher promised to take care of all those problems. But nobody could help X with the biggest problem of all—Other Children.

Nobody in X's class had ever known an X before. What would they think? How would X make friends?

You couldn't tell what X was by studying its clothes—overalls don't even button right-to-left, like girls' clothes, or left-to-right, like boys' clothes. And you couldn't guess whether X had a girl's short haircut or a boy's long haircut. And it was very hard to tell by the games X liked to play. Either X played ball very well for a girl, or else X played house very well for a boy.

Some of the children tried to find out by asking X tricky questions, like "Who's your favorite sports star?" That was easy. X had two favorite sports stars: a girl jockey named Robyn Smith and a boy archery champion named Robin Hood. Then they asked, "What's your favorite TV program?" And that was even easier. X's favorite TV program was "Lassie," which stars a girl dog played by a boy dog.

When X said that its favorite toy was a doll, everyone decided that X must be a girl. But then X said that the doll was really a robot, and that X had computerized it, and that it was programmed to bake fudge brownies and then clean up the kitchen. After X told them that, the other children gave up guessing what X was. All they knew was they'd sure like to see X's doll.

After school, X wanted to play with the other children. "How about shooting some baskets in the gym?" X asked the girls. But all they did was make faces and giggle behind X's back.

"How about weaving some baskets in the arts and crafts room?" X asked the boys. But they all made faces and giggled behind X's back too.

That night, Ms. and Mr. Jones asked X how things had gone at school. X told them sadly that the lessons were okay, but otherwise school was a terrible place for an X. It seemed as if Other Children would never want an X for a friend.

Once more, the Joneses reached for their *Instruction Manual*. Under "Other Children," they found the following message: "What did you Xpect? *Other Children* have to obey all the silly boy-girl rules, because their parents taught them to. Lucky X—you don't have to stick to the rules at all! All you have to do is be yourself. P.S. We're not saying it'll be easy."

X liked being itself. But X cried a lot that night, partly because it felt afraid. So X's father held X tight, and cuddled it, and couldn't help crying a little, too. And X's mother cheered them both up by reading an Xciting story about an enchanted prince called Sleeping Handsome, who woke up when Princess Charming kissed him.

The next morning, they all felt much better, and little X went back to school with a brave smile and a clean pair of red-and-white checked overalls.

There was a seven-letter-word spelling bee in class that day. And a seven-lap boys' relay race in the gym. And a seven-layer-cake baking contest in the girls' kitchen corner. X won the spelling bee. X also won the relay race. And X almost won the baking contest, except it forgot to light the oven. Which only proves that nobody's perfect.

One of the Other Children noticed something else, too. He said: "Winning or losing doesn't seem to count to X. X seems to have fun being good at boys' skills *and* girls' skills."

"Come to think of it," said another one of the Other Children, "maybe X is having twice as much fun as we are!"

So after school that day, the girl who beat X at the baking contest gave X a big slice of her prize winning cake. And the boy X beat in the relay race asked X to race him home.

From then on, some really funny things began to happen. Susie, who sat next to X in class, suddenly refused to wear pink dresses to school any more. She insisted on wearing red-and-white checked overalls—just like X's. Overalls, she told her parents, were much better for climbing monkey bars.

Then Jim, the class football nut, started wheeling his little sister's doll carriage around the football field. He'd put on his entire football uniform, except for the helmet. Then he'd put the helmet *in* the carriage, lovingly tucked under an old set of shoulder pads. Then he'd start jogging around the field, pushing the carriage and singing "Rock-a-bye Baby" to his football helmet. He told his family that X did the same thing, so it must be okay. After all X was now the team's star quarterback.

Susie's parents were horrified by her behavior, and Jim's parents were worried sick about his. But the worst came when the twins, Joe and Peggy, decided to share everything with each other. Peggy used Joe's hockey skates, and his microscope, and took half his newspaper route. Joe used Peggy's needlepoint kit, and her cookbooks, and took two of her three baby-sitting jobs. Peggy started running the lawn mower, and Joe started running the vacuum cleaner.

Their parents weren't one bit pleased with Peggy's wonderful biology experiments, or with Joe's terrific needlepoint pillows. They didn't care that Peggy mowed the lawn better, and that Joe vacuumed the carpet better. In fact, they were furious. It's all that little X's fault, they agreed. Just because X doesn't know what it is, or what it's supposed to be, it wants to get everybody *else* mixed up, too!

Peggy and Joe were forbidden to play with X any more. So was Susie, and then Jim, and then *all* the Other Children. But it was too late; the Other Children stayed mixed up and happy and free, and refused to go back to the way they'd been before X.

Finally, Joe and Peggy's parents decided to call an emergency meeting of the school's Parents' Association, to discuss "The X Problem." They sent a report to the principal stating that X was a "disruptive influence." They demanded immediate action. The Joneses, they said, should be *forced* to tell whether X was a boy or a girl. And then X should be *forced* to behave like whichever it was. If the Joneses refused to tell, the Parents' Association said, then X must take an Xamination. The school psychiatrist must Xamine it physically and mentally, and issue a full report. If X's test showed it was a boy, it would have to obey all the boys' rules. If it proved to be a girl, X would have to obey all the girls' rules.

And if X turned out to be some kind of mixed-up misfit, then X should be Xpelled from the school. Immediately!

The principal was very upset. Disruptive influence? Mixed-up misfit? But X was an Xcellent student. All the teachers said it was a delight to have X in their classes. X was president of the student council. X had won first prize in the talent show, and second prize in the art show, and honorable mention in the science fair, and six athletic events on field day, including the potato race.

Nevertheless, insisted the Parents' Association, X is a Problem Child. X is the Biggest Problem Child we have ever seen!

So the principal reluctantly notified X's parents that numerous complaints about X's behavior had come to the school's attention. And that after the psychiatrist's Xamination, the school would decide what to do about X.

The Joneses reported this at once to the scientists, who referred them to page 85,759 of the *Instruction Manual*. "Sooner or later," it said, "X will have to be Xamined by a psychiatrist. This may be the only way any of us will know for sure whether X is mixed up—or whether everyone else is."

The night before X was to be Xamined, the Joneses tried not to let X see how worried they were. "What if—?" Mr. Jones would say. And Ms. Jones would reply, "No use worrying." Then a few minutes later, Ms. Jones would say, "What if—?" and Mr. Jones would reply, "No use worrying."

X just smiled at them both, and hugged them hard and didn't say much of anything. X was thinking. What if—? And then X thought: No use worrying.

At Xactly 9 o'clock the next day, X reported to the school psychiatrist's office. The principal, along with a committee from the Parents' Association, X's teacher, X's classmates, and Ms. and Mr. Jones, waited in the hall outside. Nobody knew the details of the tests X was to be given, but everybody knew they'd be *very* hard, and that they'd reveal Xactly what everyone wanted to know about X, but were afraid to ask.

It was terribly quiet in the hall. Almost spooky. Once in a while, they would hear a strange noise inside the room. There were buzzes. And a beep or two. And several bells. An occasional light would flash under the door. The Joneses thought it was a white light, but the principal thought it was blue. Two or three children swore it was either yellow or green. And the Parents' Committee missed it completely.

Through it all, you could hear the psychiatrist's low voice, asking hundreds of questions, and X's higher voice, answering hundreds of answers.

The whole thing took so long that everyone knew it must be the most complete Xamination anyone had ever had to take. Poor X, the Joneses thought. Serves X right, the Parents' Committee thought. I wouldn't like to be in X's overalls right now, the children thought.

At last, the door opened. Everyone crowded around to hear the results. X didn't look any different; in fact, X was smiling. But the psychiatrist looked terrible. He look as if he was crying! "What happened?" everyone began shouting. Had X done something disgraceful? "I wouldn't be a bit surprised!" muttered Peggy and Joe's parents. "Did X flunk the *whole* test?" cried Susie's parents. "Or just the most important part?" yelled Jim's parents.

"Oh, dear," sighed Mr. Jones.

"Oh, dear," sighed Ms. Jones.

"*Sssh,*" ssshed the principal. "The psychiatrist is trying to speak."

Wiping, his eyes and clearing his throat, the psychiatrist began, in a hoarse whisper. "In my opinion," he whispered—you could tell he must be very upset—"in my opinion, young X here—"

"Yes? Yes?" shouted a parent impatiently.

"*Sssh!*" ssshed the principal.

"Young *Sssh* here, I mean young X," said the doctor, frowning, "is just about—"

"Just about *what*? Let's have it!" shouted another parent.

". . . just about the *least* mixed-up child I've ever Xamined!" said the psychiatrist.

"Yay for X!" yelled one of the children. And then the others began yelling, too. Clapping and cheering and jumping up and down.

"*SSSH!*" SSShed the principal, but nobody did.

The Parents' Committee was angry and bewildered. How *could* X have passed the whole Xamination? Didn't X have an *identity* problem? Wasn't X mixed up at *all*? Wasn't X *any* kind of a misfit? How could it *not* be, when it didn't even *know* what it was? And why was the psychiatrist crying?

Actually, he had stopped crying and was smiling politely through his tears. "Don't you see?" he said. "I'm crying because it's wonderful! X has absolutely no identity problem! X isn't one bit mixed up! As for being a misfit—ridiculous! X knows perfectly well what it is! Don't you, X?" The doctor winked, X winked back.

"But what *is* X?" shrieked Peggy and Joe's parents. "*We* still want to know what it is!"

"Ah, yes," said the doctor, winking again. "Well, don't worry. You'll all know one of these days. And you won't need me to tell you."

"What? What does he mean?" some of the parents grumbled suspiciously.

Susie and Peggy and Joe all answered at once. "He means that by the time X's sex matters, it won't be a secret any more!"

With that, the doctor began to push through the crowd toward X's parents. "How do you do," he said, somewhat stiffly. And then he reached out to hug them both. "If I ever have an X of my own," he whispered, "I sure hope you'll lend me your instruction manual."

Needless to say, the Joneses were very happy. The Project Baby X scientists were rather pleased, too. So were Susie, Jim, Peggy, Joe, and all the Other Children. The Parents' Association wasn't, but they had promised to accept the psychiatrist's report, and not make any more trouble. They even invited Ms. and Mr. Jones to become honorary members, which they did.

Later that day, all X's friends put on their red-and-white checked overalls and went over to see X. They found X in the back yard, playing with a very tiny baby that none of them had ever seen before. The baby was wearing very tiny red-and-white checked overalls.

"How do you like our new baby?" X asked the Other Children proudly.

"It's got cute dimples," said Jim.

"It's got husky biceps, too," said Susie.

"What kind of baby is it?" asked Joe and Peggy.

X frowned at them. "Can't you tell?" Then X broke into a big, mischievous grin. *"It's a Y!"*

My Life as a Man

Elizabeth Gilbert

Elizabeth Gilbert is a journalist and writer of fiction, biography and memoir, including her bestselling Eat, Pray, Love: One Woman's Search for Everything Across Italy, India and Indonesia *(2006). She has been a frequent contributor to both* GQ *and* Variety. *Her memoir of her years as a bartender was the basis for the film* Coyote Ugly. *"My Life as a Man" originally appeared in* GQ *in 2001.*

The first time I was ever mistaken for a boy, I was 6 years old. I was at the county fair with my beautiful older sister, who had the long blond tresses one typically associates with storybook princesses. I had short messy hair, and I had scabs all over my body from falling out of trees. My beautiful sister ordered a snow cone. The lady at the booth asked, "Doesn't your little brother want one, too?"

I was mortified. I cried all day.

The last time I was mistaken for a boy was only a few weeks ago. I was eating in a Denny's with my husband, and the waitress said, "You fellas want some more coffee?"

This time I didn't cry. It didn't even bother me, because I've grown accustomed to people making the mistake. Frankly, I can understand why they do. I'm afraid I'm not the most feminine creature on the planet. I don't exactly wish to hint that Janet Reno and I were separated at birth, but I do wear my hair short, I am tall, I have broad shoulders and a strong jaw, and I have never really understood the principles of cosmetics. In many cultures, this would make me a man already. In some very primitive cultures, this would actually make me a king.

But sometime after the Denny's incident, I decided, *Ah, to hell with it. If you can't beat 'em, join 'em.* What would it take, I began to wonder, for me to actually transform into a man? To live that way for an entire week? To try to fool everyone? . . .

Fortunately, I have plenty of male friends who rally to my assistance, all eager to see me become the best man I can possibly be. And they all have wise counsel to offer about exactly How to Be a Guy:

"Interrupt people with impunity from now on," says Reggie. "Curse recklessly. And never apologize."

"Never talk about your feelings," says Scott. "Only talk about your accomplishments."

"The minute the conversation turns from something that directly involves you," says Bill "let your mind wander and start looking around the room to see if there's anything nearby you can have sex with."

"If you need to win an argument," says David, "just repeat the last thing the guy you're fighting with said to you, but say it much louder."

So I'm thinking about all this, and I'm realizing that I already do all this stuff. I always win arguments, I'm shamefully slow to apologize, I can't imagine how I could possibly curse any more than I already goddamn do, I've spent the better part of my life looking around to see what's available to have sex with, I can't shut up about my accomplishments, and I'm probably interrupting you right this moment.

Another one of my friends warns, "You do this story, people are gonna talk. People might think you're gay." Aside from honestly not caring what people think, I'm not worried about this possibility at all. I'm worried about something else entirely: that this transformation thing might be *too* easy for me to pull off.

What I'm afraid I'll learn is that I'm *already* a man.

My real coach in this endeavor, though, is a woman. Her name is Diane Torr. Diane is a performance artist who has made her life's work the exploration of gender transformation. As a famous drag king, she has been turning herself into a man for twenty years. She is also known for running workshops wherein groups of women gather and become men for a day.

I call Diane and explain my goal, which is not merely to dress up in some silly costume but to genuinely pass as male and to stay in character for a week.

"That's a tough goal," Diane says, sounding dubious. "It's one thing to play with gender for the afternoon, but really putting yourself out there in the world as a man takes a lot of balls, so to speak. . . ."

Diane agrees to give me a private workshop on Monday. She tells me to spend the weekend preparing for my male life and buying new clothes. Before hanging up, I ask Diane a question I never thought I would ever have to ask anybody:

"What should I bring in terms of genitalia?"

This is when she informs me of the ingredients for my penis.

"Of course," I say calmly.

I write *birdseed* on my hand, underline it twice and make a mental note to stay away from the aviary next week.

I SPEND THE WEEKEND INVENTING MY CHARACTER

One thing is immediately clear: I will have to be younger. I'm 31 years old, and I look it, but with my smooth skin, I will look boyish as a man. So I decide I will be 21 years old for the first time in a decade.

As for my character, I decide to keep it simple and become Luke Gilbert—a midwestern kid new to the city, whose entire background is cribbed from my husband, whose life I know as well as my own.

Luke is bright but a slacker. He really doesn't give a damn about his clothes, for instance. Believe me, I know—I'm the one who shopped for Luke all weekend. By Sunday night, Luke owns several pairs of boring Dockers in various shades of khaki, which he wears baggy. He has Adidas sneakers. He has some boxy short-sleeve buttondown shirts in brown plaids. He has a corduroy jacket, a bike messenger's bag, a few baseball caps and clean underwear. He also has, I'm sorry to report, a really skinny neck.

I haven't even met Luke yet, but I'm beginning to get the feeling he's a real friggin' geek.

THE TRANSFORMATION BEGINS PAINLESSLY ENOUGH

It starts with my hair. Rayya, my regular hairdresser, spends the morning undoing all her work of the past months—darkening out my brightest blond highlights, making me drab, brownish, inconsequential; chopping off my sassy Dixie Chick pixie locks and leaving me with a blunt cut.

"Don't wash it all week," Rayya advises. "Get good and greasy; you'll look more like a guy."

Once the hair is done, Diane Torr gets to work on me. She moves like a pro, quick and competent. Together we stuff my condom ("This is the arts-and-crafts portion of the workshop!"), and Diane helps me insert it into my Calvins. She asks if I want my penis to favor the left or right side. Being a traditionalist, I select the right. Diane adjusts me and backs away; I look down and there it is—my semierect penis, bulging slightly against my briefs. I cannot stop staring at it and don't mind saying that it freaks me out to no end. Then she tries to hide my breasts. To be perfectly honest, my breasts are embarrassingly easy to make disappear. Diane expertly binds them down with wide Ace bandages. Breathing isn't easy, but my chest looks pretty flat now—in fact, with a men's undershirt on, I almost look as if I have well-developed pectoral muscles.

But my ass? Ah, here we encounter a more troublesome situation. I don't want to boast, but I have a big, fat, round ass. You could lop off huge chunks of my ass, make a nice osso buco out of it, serve it up to a family of four and still eat the leftovers for a week. This is a woman's ass, unmistakably. But once I'm fully in costume, I turn around before the mirror and see that I'm going to be OK. The baggy, low-slung pants are good ass camouflage, and the boxy plaid shirt completely eliminates any sign of my waist, so I don't have that girlie hourglass thing happening. I'm a little pear-shaped, perhaps, but let us not kid ourselves, people. There are pear-shaped men out there, walking among us every day.

Then Diane starts on my facial transformation. She has brought crepe hair—thin ropes of artificial hair in various colors, which she trims down to a pile of golden brown stubble. I elect, in homage to Tom Waits, to go with just a small soul patch, a minigoatee, right under my bottom lip. Diane dabs my face with spirit gum—a kind of skin-friendly rubber cement—and presses the hair onto me. It makes for a shockingly good effect. I suggest sideburns, too, and we apply these, making me look like every 21-year-old male art student I've ever seen. Then we muss up and darken my eyebrows. A light shadow of brown under my nose gives me a hint of a mustache. When I look in the mirror, I can't stop laughing. *I am a goddamn man, man!*

Well, more or less.

Diane looks me over critically. "Your jaw is good. Your height is good. But you should stop laughing. It makes you look too friendly, too accessible, too feminine." I stop laughing. She stares at me. "Let's see your walk."

I head across the floor, hands in my pockets.

"Not bad," Diane says, impressed.

Well, I've been practicing. I'm borrowing my walk from Tim Goodwin, a guy I went to high school with. Tim was short and slight but an amazing basketball player (we all called him "Tim *God*win"), and he had an athletic, kneeknocking strut that was very cool. There's also a slouch involved in this walk. But it's—and this is hard to explain—a *stiff* slouch. Years of yoga have made me really limber, but as Luke, I need to drop that ease of motion with my body, because men are not nearly as physically free as women. Watch the way a man turns his head: His whole upper torso turns with it. Unless he's a dancer or a baseball pitcher, he's probably operating his entire body on a ramrod, unyielding axis. On the other hand, watch the way a woman drinks from a bottle. She'll probably tilt her whole head back to accommodate the object, whereas a man would probably hold his neck stiff, tilting the bottle at a sharp angle, making the bottle accommodate *him*. Being a man, it seems, is sometimes just about not budging.

Diane goes on to coach my voice, telling me to lower the timbre and narrow the range. She warns me against making statements that come out as questions, which women do constantly (such as when you ask a woman where she grew up and she replies, "Just outside Cleveland?").

But I don't do that begging-for-approval voice anyway, so this is no problem. As I'd suspected, in fact, all this turning-male stuff is coming too easily to me.

But then Diane says, "Your eyes are going to be the real problem. They're too animated, too bright. When you look at people, you're still too engaged and interested. You need to lose that sparkle, because it's giving you away."

The rest of the afternoon, she's on me about my eyes. She says I'm too flirtatious with my eyes, too encouraging, too appreciative, too attentive, too *available*. I need to intercept all those behaviors, Diane says, and erase them. Because all that stuff is "shorthand for girl." Girls typically flirt and engage and appreciate and attend; men typically don't. It's too generous for men to give themselves away in such a manner. Too dangerous, even. Granted, there are men in this world who are engaging, attentive and sparkly eyed, but Luke Gilbert cannot be one of them. Luke Gilbert's looks are so on the border of being feminine already that I can't afford to express any behavior that is "shorthand for girl," or my cover is blown. I can only emit the most stereotypical masculine code, not wanting to offer people even the faintest hint that I'm anything but a man.

Which means that gradually throughout Monday afternoon, I find myself shutting down my entire personality, one degree at a time. It's very similar to the way I had to shut down my range of physical expression, pulling in my gestures and stiffening up my body. Similarly, I must not budge emotionally. I feel as if I'm closing down a factory, silencing all the humming machines of my character, pulling shut the gates, sending home the workers. All my most animated and familiar facial expressions have to go, and with them go all my most animated and familiar emotions. Ultimately, I am left with only two options for expression—boredom and aggression. Only with boredom and aggression do I truly feel male. It's not a feeling I like at all, by the way. In fact, I am amazed by how much I don't like it. We've been laughing and joking and relating all morning, but slowly now, as I turn into Luke, I feel the whole room chill.

Toward the end of the afternoon, Diane gives me her best and most disturbing piece of advice.

"Don't look at the world from the surface of your eyeballs," she says. "All your feminine availability emanates from there. Set your gaze back in your head. Try to get the feeling that your gaze originates from two inches behind the surface of your eyeballs, from where your optic nerves begin in your brain. Keep it right there."

Immediately, I get what she's saying. I pull my gaze back. I don't know how I appear from the outside, but the internal effect is appalling. I feel—for the first time in my life—a dense barrier rise before my vision, keeping me at a palpable distance from the world, roping me off from the people in the room. I feel dead eyed. I feel like a reptile. I feel my whole face change, settling into a hard mask.

Everyone in the room steps back. Rayya, my hairdresser, whistles under her breath and says, "Whoa . . . you got the guy vibe happenin' now, Luke."

Slouching and bored, I mutter a stony thanks.

* * *

Diane finally takes me outside, and we stroll down the street together. She has dressed in drag, too. She's now Danny King—a pompous little man who works in a Pittsburgh department store. She seems perfectly at ease on the street, but I feel cagey and nervous out here in the broad daylight, certain that everyone in the world can see that my face is covered with fake hair and rubber cement and discomfort. The only thing that helps me feel even remotely relaxed is the basketball I'm loosely carrying under my arm—a prop so familiar to me in real life that it helps put me at ease in disguise. We head to a nearby basketball court. We have a small crowd following us—my hairdresser, the makeup artist, a photographer. Diane and I pose for photos under the hoop. I set my basketball down, and almost immediately, a young and muscular black guy comes over and scoops it off the pavement.

"Hey," he says to the crowd. "Whose basketball is this?"

Now, if you want to learn how to define your personal space as a man, you could do worse than take lessons from this guy. His every motion is offense and aggression. He leads with his chest and chin, and he's got a hard and cold set of eyes.

"I said, whose basketball is this?" he repeats, warning with his tone that he doesn't want to have to ask again.

"It's hers," says my hairdresser, pointing at me.

"Hers?" The young man looks at me and snorts in disgust. "What are you talkin' about, *hers*? That ain't no *her*. That's a *guy*."

My first gender victory!

But there's no time to celebrate this moment, because this aggressive and intimidating person needs to be dealt with. Now, here's the thing. Everyone on the court is intimidated by this guy, but I am not. In this tense moment, mind you, I have stopped thinking like Luke Gilbert; I'm back to thinking like Liz Gilbert. And Liz Gilbert always thinks she can manage men. I don't know if it's from years of tending bar, or if it's from living in lunatic-filled New York City, or if it's just a ridiculous (and dangerously naive) sense of personal safety, but I have always believed in my heart that I can disarm any man's aggression. I do it by paying close attention to the aggressive man's face and finding the right blend of flirtation, friendliness and confidence to put on my face to set him at ease, to remind him: *You don't wanna hurt me, you wanna like me*. I've done this a million times before. Which is why I'm looking at this scary guy and I'm thinking, *Give me thirty seconds with him and he'll be on my side*.

I step forward. I open up my whole face in a big smile and say teasingly, "Yeah, that's my basketball, man. Why, you wanna play? You think you can take me?"

"You don't know nothin' about this game," he says.

In my flirtiest possible voice, I say, "Oh, I know a *little* somethin' about this game. . . ."

The guy takes a menacing step forward, narrows his eyes and growls, "You don't know *shit* about this game."

This is when I snap to attention. This is when I realize I'm on the verge of getting my face punched. What the hell am I doing? This guy honestly thinks I'm a man! Therefore, my whole cute, tomboyish, I'm-just-one-of-the-guys act is not working. One-of-the-guys doesn't work when you actually *are* one of the guys. I have forgotten that I am Luke Gilbert—a little white loser on a basketball court who has just challenged and pissed off and *flirted* with an already volatile large black man. I have made a very bad choice here. I've only been on the job as a male for a few minutes, but it appears as though I'm about to earn myself a good old-fashioned New York City ass-kicking.

He takes another step forward and repeats, "You don't know shit about nothin'."

"You're right, man," I say. I drop my eyes from his. I lower my voice, collapse my posture, show my submission. I am a stray dog, backing away from a fight, head down, tail tucked. "Sorry, man. I was just kidding. I don't know anything about basketball."

"Yeah, that's right," says the guy, satisfied now that he has dominated me. "You don't know shit."

He drops the ball and walks away. My heart is slamming. I'm angry at my own carelessness and frightened by my newfound helplessness. Luke didn't know how to handle that guy on the court, and Luke almost got thrown a beating as a result (and would have deserved it, too—the moron). Realizing this makes me feel suddenly vulnerable, suddenly aware of how small I've become.

My hands, for instance, which have always seemed big and capable to me, suddenly appear rather dainty when I think of them as a man's hands. My arms, so sturdy only hours before, are now the thin arms of a weenie-boy. I've lost this comfortable feeling I've always carried through the world of being strong and brave. A five-foot-nine-inch, 140-pound woman can be a pretty tough character, after all. But a five-foot-nine-inch, 140-pound man? Kinda small, kinda wussy. . . .

* * *

My world-famously tolerant husband seems to have no trouble with my transformation at first. He unwinds my breast bandages every night before bed and listens with patience to my complaints about my itching beard. In the mornings before work, he binds up my breasts again and lends me his spice-scented deodorant so I can smell more masculine. We vie for mirror space in the bathroom as he shaves off his daily stubble and I apply mine. We eat our cereal together, I take my birth control pills, I pack my penis back into my slacks. . . .

It's all very domestic.

Still, by Wednesday morning, my husband confesses that he doesn't want to hang around with me in public anymore. Not as long as I'm Luke. It's not that he's grossed out by my physical transformation, or threatened by the sexual politics at play, or embarrassed by the possibility of exposure. It's simply this: He is deeply, emotionally unsettled by my new personality.

"I miss you," he says. "It's seriously depressing for me to be around you this way."

What's upsetting to Michael is that as a man, I can't give him what he has become accustomed to getting from me as a woman. And I'm not talking about sex. Sex can always be arranged, even this week. (Although I do make a point now of falling asleep immediately after it's over, just to stay in character.) What Michael hates is that I don't engage him anymore. As Luke, I don't laugh at my husband's jokes or ask him about his day. Hell, as Luke, I don't even have a husband—just another drinking buddy whose jokes and workday concerns I don't really care about. Michael, still seeing his wife under her goatee, keeps thinking I'm mad at him, or—worse—bored by him. But I can't attend to him on this, can't reassure him, or I risk coming across like a girl.

The thing is, I don't like Luke's personality any more than Michael does. As Luke, I feel completely and totally bound—and not just because of the tight bandage wrapped around my chest. I keep thinking back to my drag-king workshop, when Diane Torr talked about "intercepting learned feminine habits." She spoke of those learned feminine habits in slightly disparaging terms. Women, she said, are too attentive, too concerned about the feelings of others, too *available*. This idea of women as lost in empathy is certainly a standard tenet of feminism (Oprah calls it the Disease to Please), and, yes, there are many women who drown in their own overavailability. But I've never personally felt that attentiveness and engagement are liabilities. As a writer—indeed, as a *human being*—I think the most exciting way you can interact with this fantastic and capricious world is by being completely available to it. Peel me wide open; availability is my power. I would so much rather be vulnerable and experience existence than be strong and defend myself from it. And if that makes me a girlie-girl, then so be it—I'll be a goddamn girlie-girl.

Only, this week I'm not a girl at all. I'm Luke Gilbert. And poor Luke, I must say, is completely cut off from the human experience. The guy is looking at the world from a place two inches behind his eyeballs. No wonder my husband hates being around him. I'm not crazy about him myself.

* * *

[Wednesday], I'm walking home alone. Just ahead of me, a blond woman steps out of a bar, alone. She's screamingly sexy. She's got all the props—the long hair, the tiny skirt, the skimpy top, the wobbly stiletto heels, the eternal legs. I walk right behind this woman for several blocks and observe the tsunami she causes on 23rd Street in every man she passes—everyone has to react to her somehow. What amazes me, though, is how many of the men end up interacting with *me* after passing *her*. What happens is this: She saunters by, the guy stares at her in astonishment and then makes a comment about her to me because I'm the next man on the scene. So we have a little moment together, the guy and me, in which we share an experience. We get to bond. It's an icebreaker for us.

The best is the older construction worker who checks out the babe, then raises his eyebrows at me and declares: "Fandango!"

"You said it!" I say, but when I walk on by, he seems a little disappointed that I haven't stuck around to talk more about it with him.

This kind of interaction happens more than a dozen times within three blocks. Until I start wondering whether this is actually the game. Until I start suspecting that these guys maybe don't want to talk to the girl at all, that maybe they just desperately want to talk to *one another*.

Suddenly, I see this sexy woman in front of me as being just like sports; she's an excuse for men to try to talk to one another. She's like the Knicks, only prettier—a connection for people who otherwise cannot connect at all. It's a very big job, but I don't know if she even realizes she's doing it.

* * *

[Friday] night, taking a friend's advice, I go out drinking in the East Village, where seven out of ten young men look just like Luke Gilbert. I end up at a bar that is crawling with really cute pierced-nosed girls. I'm wondering whom I should try to pick up when an opportunity falls into my lap. A pretty red-haired girl in a black camisole walks into the bar alone. She has cool tattoos all over her arms. The bouncer says to her, "Hey, Darcy, where's your crowd tonight?"

"Everyone copped out," Darcy says. "I'm flying solo."

"So lemme buy you a drink," I call over from the bar.

"Rum and Coke," she says, and comes over to sit next to me.

Fandango!

We get to talking. Darcy's funny, friendly, from Tennessee. She tells me all about her roommate problems. She asks me about myself, but I don't share—Luke Gilbert is not available for sharing. Instead, I compliment Darcy on her pretty starfish necklace, which Darcy tells me was a gift from a childhood neighbor who was like a grandmother to her. I ask Darcy about her job, and she tells me she works for a publishing house that prints obscure journals with titles like *Catfish Enthusiast Monthly*.

"Damn, and here I just let my subscription to *Catfish Enthusiast Monthly* run out," I say, and she laughs. Darcy actually does that flirty thing girls do sometimes where they laugh and touch your arm and move closer toward you all at the same time. I know this move. I've been doing this move my whole life. And it is with this move and this touch and this laugh that I lose my desire to play this game anymore, because Darcy, I can tell, actually likes Luke Gilbert. Which is incredible, considering that Luke is a sullen, detached, stiff guy who can't make eye contact with the world. But she still likes him. This should feel like a victory, but all I feel like is a complete shitheel. Darcy is nice. And here I'm lying to her already.

Now I really *am* a guy.

"You know what, Darcy?" I say. "I have to go. I'm supposed to hook up with some friends for dinner."

She looks a little hurt. But not as hurt as she would look if, say, we dated for a month and then she found out the truth about me.

I give her a little kiss good-bye on the cheek.

"You're great," I tell her.

And then I'm done.

UNDOING IT ALL TAKES A FEW DAYS

Rubbing alcohol gets the last of the spirit gum and fake hair off my face. I pluck my eyebrows and put on my softest bra (my skin has become chafed from days of binding and taping). I scatter my penis across the sidewalk for the pigeons. I make an appointment to get my hair lightened again. I go to yoga class and reawaken the idea of movement in my body. I cannot wait to get rid of this gender, which I have not enjoyed. But it's a tricky process, because I'm still walking like Luke, still standing like Luke, still thinking like Luke.

In fact, I don't really get my inner Liz back until the next weekend. It's not until the next Saturday night, when I am sitting at a bar on my own big fat ass, wearing my own girlie jeans, talking to an off-duty New York City fireman, that I really come back into myself. The fireman and I are both out with big groups, but somehow we peel off into our own private conversation. Which quickly gets serious. I ask him to tell me about the crucifix around his neck, and he says he's been leaning on God pretty hard this year. I want to know why. The fireman starts telling me about how his beloved father died this winter, and then his fiancée left him, and now the pressures of his work are starting to kill him, and there are times when he just wishes he could cry but he doesn't want people to see him like that. My guy friends are all playing darts in the corner, but I'm the one sitting here listening to this fireman tell me about how he never cries because his dad was such a hard-ass Irish cop, don'tcha know, because he was raised to hang so tough.

I'm looking right into this guy. I'm not touching him at all, but I'm giving him my entire self. He needs me right now, to tell all this to. He can have me. I've got my eyes locked on him, and I can feel how bad he wants to cry, and with my entire face I am telling this man: *Tell me everything*.

He says, "Maybe I was hard on her, maybe that's why she left me, but I was so worried about my father. . . ."

The fireman digs at his eye with a fist. I hand him a bar napkin. He blows his nose. He keeps talking. I keep listening. He can talk to me all night because I am unbound and I am wide-open. I'm open around the clock, open twenty-four hours a day; I never close. I'm really concerned for this guy, but I'm smiling while he spills his story because it feels so good to catch it. It feels so good to be myself again, to be open for business again—open once more for the rewarding and honest human business of complete *availability*.

We are all Works in Progress

Leslie Feinberg

Leslie Feinberg *is a journalist and transgender, peace, labor, socialist and anti-racist activist. This essay comes from a compiled volume of hir speeches,* Trans Liberation: Beyond Pink or Blue *(1998). Ze has written two novels.* Stone Butch Blues *(1993), hir first novel, received the Lambda Literary Award as well as the American Library Association Award for Gay and Lesbian Literature. Hir other books include* Drag King Dreams *(2006), and* Transgender Warriors: Making History from Joan of Arc to Rupaul *(1996).*

The sight of pink-blue gender-coded infant outfits may grate on your nerves. Or you may be a woman or a man who feels at home in those categories. Trans liberation defends you both.

Each person should have the right to *choose* between pink or blue tinted gender categories, as well as all the other hues of the palette. At this moment in time, that right is denied to us. But together, we could make it a reality.

And that's what this book is all about.

I am a human being who would rather not be addressed as Ms. or Mr., ma'am or sir. I prefer to use gender-neutral pronouns like *sie* (pronounced like "*see*") and *hir* (pronounced like "*here*") to describe myself. I am a person who faces almost insurmountable difficulty when instructed to check off an "F" or an "M" box on identification papers.

I'm not at odds with the fact that I was born female-bodied. Nor do I identify as an intermediate sex. I simply do not fit the prevalent Western concepts of what a woman or a man "should" look like. And that reality has dramatically directed the course of my life.

I'll give you a graphic example. From December 1995 to December 1996, I was dying of endocarditis–a bacterial infection that lodges and proliferates in the valves of the heart. A simple blood culture would have immediately exposed the root cause of my raging fevers. Eight weeks of' round-the-clock intravenous antibiotic drips would have eradicated every last seedling of bacterium in the canals of my heart. Yet I experienced such hatred from some health practitioners that I very nearly died.

I remember late one night in December my lover and I arrived at a hospital emergency room during a snowstorm. My fever was 104 degrees and rising. My blood pressure was pounding dangerously high. The staff immediately hooked me up to monitors and worked to bring down my fever. The doctor in charge began physically examining me. When he determined that my anatomy was female, he flashed me a mean-spirited smirk. While keeping his eyes fixed on me, he approached one of the nurses, seated at a desk, and began rubbing her neck and shoulders. He talked to her about sex for a few minutes. After his pointed demonstration of "normal sexuality," he told me to get dressed and then he stormed out of the room. Still delirious, I struggled to put on my clothes and make sense of what was happening.

The doctor returned after I was dressed. He ordered me to leave the hospital and never return. I refused. I told him I wouldn't leave until he could tell me why my fever was so high. He said, "You have a fever because you are a very troubled person."

This doctor's prejudices, directed at me during a moment of catastrophic illness, could have killed me. The death certificate would have read: Endocarditis. By all rights it should have read: Bigotry.

As my partner and I sat bundled up in a cold car outside the emergency room, still reverberating from the doctor's hatred, I thought about how many people have been turned away from medical care when they were desperately ill–some because an apartheid "whites only" sign hung over the emergency room entrance, or some because their visible Kaposi's sarcoma lesions kept personnel far from their beds. I remembered how a blemish that wouldn't heal drove my mother to visit her doctor repeatedly during the 1950s. I recalled the doctor finally wrote a prescription for Valium because he decided she was a hysterical woman. When my mother finally got to specialists, they told her the cancer had already reached her brain.

Bigotry exacts its toll in flesh and blood. And left unchecked and unchallenged, prejudices create a poisonous climate for us all. Each of us has a stake in the demand that every human being has a right to a job, to shelter, to health care, to dignity, to respect.

I am very grateful to have this chance to open up a conversation with you about why it is so vital to also defend the right of individuals to express and define their sex and gender, and to control their own bodies. For me, it's a life-and-death question. But I also believe that this discussion will have great meaning for you. All your life you've heard such dogma about what it means to be a "real" woman or a "real" man. And chances are you've choked on some of it. You've balked at the idea that being a woman means having to be thin as a rail, emotionally nurturing, and an airhead when it comes to balancing her checkbook. You know in your guts that being a man has nothing to do with rippling muscles, innate courage, or knowing how to handle a chain saw. These are really caricatures. Yet these images have been drilled into us through popular culture and education over the years. And subtler, equally insidious messages lurk in the interstices of these grosser concepts. These ideas of what a "real" woman or man should be straightjacket the freedom of individual self-expression. These gender messages play on and on in a continuous loop in our brains, like commercials that can't be muted.

But in my lifetime I've also seen social upheavals challenge this sex and gender doctrine. As a child who grew up during the McCarthyite, Father-Knows-Best 1950s, and who came of age during the second wave of women's liberation in the United States, I've seen transformations in the ways people think and talk about what it means to be a woman or a man.

Today the gains of the 1970s women's liberation movement are under siege by right-wing propagandists. But many today who are too young to remember what life was like before the women's movement need to know that this was a tremendously progressive development that won significant economic and social reforms. And this struggle by women and their allies swung human consciousness forward like a pendulum.

The movement replaced the common usage of vulgar and diminutive words to describe females with the word *woman* and infused that word with strength and pride. Women, many of them formerly isolated, were drawn together into consciousness-raising groups. Their discussions–about the root of women's oppression and how to eradicate it–resonated far beyond the rooms in which they took place. The women's liberation movement sparked a mass conversation about the systematic degradation, violence, and discrimination that women faced in this society. And this consciousness raising changed many of the ways women and men thought about themselves and their relation to each other. In retrospect, however, we must not forget that these widespread discussions were not just organized to *talk* about oppression. They were a giant dialogue about how to take action to fight institutionalized anti-woman attitudes, rape and battering, the illegality of abortion, employment and education discrimination, and other ways women were socially and economically devalued.

This was a big step forward for humanity. And even the period of political reaction that followed has not been able to overturn all the gains made by that important social movement.

Now another movement is sweeping onto the stage of history: Trans liberation. We are again raising questions about the societal treatment of people based on their sex and gender expression. This discussion will make new contributions to human consciousness. And trans communities, like the women's movement, are carrying out these mass conversations with the goal of creating a movement capable of fighting for justice–of righting the wrongs.

We are a movement of masculine females and feminine males, cross-dressers, transsexual men and women, intersexuals born on the anatomical sweep between female and male, gender-blenders, many other sex and gender-variant people, and our significant others. All told, we expand understanding of how many ways there are to be a human being.

Our lives are proof that sex and gender are much more complex than a delivery room doctor's glance at genitals can determine, more variegated than pink or blue birth caps. We are oppressed for not fitting those narrow social norms. We are fighting back.

Our struggle will also help expose some of the harmful myths about what it means to be a woman or a man that have compartmentalized and distorted your life, as well as mine. Trans liberation has meaning for you–no matter how you define or express your sex or your gender.

If you are a trans person, you face horrendous social punishments–from institutionalization to gang rape, from beatings to denial of child visitation. This oppression is faced, in varying degrees, by all who march under the banner of trans liberation. This brutalization and degradation strips us of what we could achieve with our individual lifetimes.

And if you do not identify as transgender or transsexual or intersexual, your life is diminished by our oppression as well. Your own choices as a man or a woman are sharply curtailed. Your individual journey to express yourself is shunted into one of two deeply carved ruts, and the social baggage you are handed is already packed.

So the defense of each individual's right to control their own body, and to explore the path of self-expression, enhances your own freedom to discover more about yourself and your potentialities. This movement will give you more room to breathe–to be yourself. To discover on a deeper level what it means to be your self.

Together, I believe we can forge a coalition that can fight on behalf of your oppression as well as mine. Together, we can raise each other's grievances and win the kind of significant change we all long for. But the foundation of unity is understanding. So let me begin by telling you a little bit about myself.

I am a human being who unnerves some people. As they look at me, they see a kaleidoscope of characteristics they associate with both males and females. I appear to be a tangled knot of gender contradictions. So they feverishly press the question on me: woman or man? Those are the only two words most people have as tools to shape their question.

"Which sex are you?" I understand their question. It sounds so simple. And I'd like to offer them a simple resolution. But merely answering woman or man will not bring relief to the questioner.

As long as people try to bring me into focus using only those two lenses, I will always appear to be an enigma.

The truth is I'm no mystery. I'm a female who is more masculine than those prominently portrayed in mass culture. Millions of females and millions of males in this country do not fit the cramped compartments of gender that we have been taught are "natural" and "normal." For many of us, the words *woman* or *man*, *ma'am* or *sir*, *she* or *he*–in and of themselves–do not total up the sum of our identities or of our oppressions. Speaking for myself, my life only comes into focus when the word *transgender* is added to the equation.

Simply answering whether I was born female or male will not solve the conundrum. Before I can even begin to respond to the question of my own birth sex, I feel it's important to challenge the assumption that the answer is always as simple as either-or. I believe we need to take a critical look at the assumption that is built into the seemingly innocent question: "What a beautiful baby–is it a boy or a girl?"

The human anatomical spectrum can't be understood, let alone appreciated, as long as female or male are considered to be all that exists. "Is it a boy or a girl?" Those are the only two categories allowed on birth certificates.

But this either-or leaves no room for intersexual people, born between the poles of female and male. Human anatomy continues to burst the confines of the contemporary concept that nature delivers all babies on two unrelated conveyor belts. So are the birth certificates changed to reflect human anatomy? No, the U.S. medical establishment hormonally molds and shapes and surgically hacks away at the exquisite complexities of intersexual infants until they neatly fit one category or the other.

A surgeon decides whether a clitoris is "too large" or a penis is "too small." That's a highly subjective decision for anyone to make about another person's body. Especially when the person making the arbitrary decision is scrubbed up for surgery! And what is the criterion for a penis being "too small"? Too small for successful heterosexual intercourse. Intersexual infants are already being tailored for their sexuality, as well as their sex. The infants have no say over what happens to their bodies. Clearly the struggle against genital mutilation must begin here, within the borders of the United States.

But the question asked of all new parents: "Is it a boy or a girl?" is not such a simple question when transsexuality is taken into account, either. Legions of out-and-proud transsexual men and women demonstrate that individuals have a deep, developed, and valid sense of their own sex that does not always correspond to the cursory decision made by a delivery-room obstetrician. Nor is transsexuality a recent phenomenon. People have undergone social sex reassignment and surgical and hormonal sex changes throughout the breadth of oral and recorded human history.

Having offered this view of the complexities and limitations of birth classification, I have no hesitancy in saying I was born female. But that answer doesn't clear up the confusion that drives some people to ask me "Are you a man or a woman?" The problem is that they are trying to understand my gender expression by determining my sex–and therein lies the rub! Just as most of us grew up with only the concepts of *woman* and *man*, the terms *feminine* and *masculine* are the only two tools most people have to talk about the complexities of gender expression.

That pink-blue dogma assumes that biology steers our social destiny. We have been taught that being born female or male will determine how we will dress and walk, whether we will prefer our hair shortly cropped or long and flowing, whether we will be emotionally nurturing or repressed. According to this way of thinking, masculine females are trying to look "like men," and feminine males are trying to act "like women."

But those of us who transgress those gender assumptions also shatter their inflexibility.

So why do I sometimes describe myself as a masculine female? Isn't each of those concepts very limiting? Yes. But placing the two words together is incendiary, exploding the belief that gender expression is linked to birth sex like horse and carriage. It is the social contradiction missing from Dick-and-Jane textbook education.

I actually chafe at describing myself as masculine. For one thing, masculinity is such an expansive territory, encompassing boundaries of nationality, race, and class. Most importantly, individuals blaze their own trails across this landscape.

And it's hard for me to label the intricate matrix of my gender as simply masculine. To me, branding individual self-expression as simply feminine or masculine is like asking poets: Do you write in English or Spanish? The question leaves out the possibilities that the poetry is woven in Cantonese or Ladino, Swahili or Arabic. The question deals only with the system of language that the poet has been taught. It ignores the words each writer hauls up, hand over hand, from a common well. The music words make when finding themselves next to each other for the first time. The silences echoing in the space between ideas. The powerful winds of passion and belief that move the poet to write.

That is why I do not hold the view that gender is simply a social construct—one of two languages that we learn by rote from early age. To me, gender is the poetry each of us makes out of the language we are taught. When I walk through the anthology of the world, I see individuals express their gender in exquisitely complex and ever-changing ways, despite the laws of pentameter.

So how can gender expression be mandated by edict and enforced by law? Isn't that like trying to handcuff a pool of mercury? It's true that human self-expression is diverse and is often expressed in ambiguous or contradictory ways. And what degree of gender expression is considered "acceptable" can depend on your social situation, your race and nationality, your class, and whether you live in an urban or rural environment.

But no one can deny that rigid gender education begins early on in life—from pink and blue color-coding of infant outfits to gender-labeling toys and games. And those who overstep these arbitrary borders are punished. Severely. When the steel handcuffs tighten, it is human bones that crack. No one knows how many trans lives have been lost to police brutality and street-corner bashing. The lives of trans people are so depreciated in this society that many murders go unreported. And those of us who have survived are deeply scarred by daily run-ins with hate, discrimination, and violence.

Trans people are still literally social outlaws. And that's why I am willing at times, publicly, to reduce the totality of my self-expression to descriptions like masculine female, butch, bulldagger, drag king, cross-dresser. These terms describe outlaw status. And I hold my head up proudly in that police lineup. The word *outlaw* is not hyperbolic. I have been locked up in jail by cops because I was wearing a suit and tie. Was my clothing really a crime? Is it a "man's" suit if I am wearing it? At what point—from field to rack—is fiber assigned a sex?

The reality of why I was arrested was as cold as the cell's cement floor: I am considered a masculine female. That's a *gender* violation. My feminine drag queen sisters were in nearby cells, busted for wearing "women's" clothing. The cells that we were thrown into had the same design of bars and concrete. But when we—gay drag kings and drag queens—were thrown into them, the cops referred to the cells as bull's tanks and queen's tanks. The cells were named after our crimes: gender transgression. Actual statutes against cross-dressing and cross-gendered behavior still exist in written laws today. But even where the laws are not written down, police, judges, and prison guards are empowered to carry out merciless punishment for sex and gender "difference."

I believe we need to sharpen our view of how repression by the police, courts, and prisons, as well as all forms of racism and bigotry, operates as gears in the machinery of the economic and social system that governs our lives. As all those who have the least to lose from changing this system get together and examine these social questions, we can separate the wheat of truths from the chaff of old lies. Historic tasks are revealed that beckon us to take a stand and to take action.

That moment is now. And so this conversation with you takes place with the momentum of struggle behind it.

What will it take to put a halt to "legal" and extralegal violence against trans people? How can we strike the unjust and absurd laws mandating dress and behavior for females and males from the books? How can we weed out all the forms of trans-phobic and gender-phobic discrimination?

Where does the struggle for sex and gender liberation fit in relation to other movements for economic and social equality? How can we reach a point where we appreciate each other's differences, not just tolerate them? How can we tear down the electrified barbed wire that has been placed between us to keep us separated, fearful and pitted against each other? How can we forge a movement that can bring about profound and lasting change–a movement capable of transforming society?

These questions can only be answered when we begin to organize together, ready to struggle on each other's behalf. Understanding each other will compel us as honest, caring people to fight each other's oppression as though it was our own.

This book is one of my contributions to this societal discussion. Many of the chapters are adaptations of talks I gave in the spring of 1997, as I set out on the rocky road to recover my health. In the weeks after the last intravenous tubes were removed from my arms and chest, I emerged from illness like a resistance fighter climbing up from a sewer into the sunlight. I faced a calendar filled with opportunities to speak with people at universities, conferences, and rallies. That particular spring was a precious gift I could not take for granted. I'd fought so hard to live.

I remember the enormous physical effort it took to lug my suitcase off a conveyorbelt, to walk long distances through crowded airports. But I also remember amazing conversations I had with many wonderful individuals. I found people were ready to talk about sex and gender liberation in every part of the United States I visited–from Manhattan to Tallahassee, from Birmingham to Denver. I was moved by the emotional and enthusiastic responses I received from audiences in Berlin, Leipzig, Köln, and Hamburg, Germany.

Some of those speeches are included in this book. I've prefaced them with a description of the circumstances, audiences, and surroundings, so that you can feel yourself a part of it. I've also included the voices of other trans people–each of whom I deeply respect. These trans people have different identities, experiences, and viewpoints from mine, so you can hear the wider conversation that is now underway.

The poet Rainer Maria Rilke wrote, "Be conversant with transformation." This book is my voice in this conversation. I look forward to hearing yours.

White Privilege
Unpacking the Invisible Knapsack

Peggy McIntosh

Peggy McIntosh is a Senior Research Scientist and Associate Director of the Wellesley College Centers for Women, where she is also currently the Director of the Gender, Race and Inclusive Education Project. She has taught English, American Studies and Women's Studies. McIntosh's work focuses on feminism, anti-racism and education. This was originally presented at a Virginia Women's Studies Conference in 1986 and has since been widely anthologized.

"I was taught to see racism only in individual acts of meanness, not in invisible systems conferring dominance on my group"

Through work to bring materials from women's studies into the rest of the curriculum, I have often noticed men's unwillingness to grant that they are overprivileged, even though they may grant that women are disadvantaged. They may say they will work to women's statues, in the society, the university, or the curriculum, but they can't or won't support the idea of lessening men's. Denials that amount to taboos surround the subject of advantages that men gain from women's disadvantages. These denials protect male privilege from being fully acknowledged, lessened, or ended.

Thinking through unacknowledged male privilege as a phenomenon, I realized that, since hierarchies in our society are interlocking, there are most likely a phenomenon, I realized that, since hierarchies in our society are interlocking, there was most likely a phenomenon of while privilege that was similarly denied and protected. As a white person, I realized I had been taught about racism as something that puts others at a disadvantage, but had been taught not to see one of its corollary aspects, white privilege, which puts me at an advantage.

I think whites are carefully taught not to recognize white privilege, as males are taught not to recognize male privilege. So I have begun in an untutored way to ask what it is like to have white privilege. I have come to see white privilege as an invisible package of unearned assets that I can count on cashing in each day, but about which I was "meant" to remain oblivious. White privilege is like an invisible weightless knapsack of special provisions, maps, passports, code-books, visas, clothes, tools, and blank checks.

Describing white privilege makes one newly accountable. As we in women's studies work to reveal male privilege and ask men to give up some of their power, so one who writes about having white privilege must ask, "having described it, what will I do to lessen or end it?"

After I realized the extent to which men work from a base of unacknowledged privilege, I understood that much of their oppressiveness was unconscious. Then I remembered the frequent charges from women of color that white women whom they encounter are oppressive. I began to understand why we are just seen as oppressive, even when we don't see ourselves that way. I began to count the ways in which I enjoy unearned skin privilege and have been conditioned into oblivion about its existence.

My schooling gave me no training in seeing myself as an oppressor, as an unfairly advantaged person, or as a participant in a damaged culture. I was taught to see myself as an individual whose moral state depended on her individual moral will. My schooling followed the pattern my colleague Elizabeth Minnich has pointed out: whites are taught to think of their lives as morally neutral, normative, and average, and also ideal, so that when we work to benefit others, this is seen as work that will allow "them" to be more like "us."

DAILY EFFECTS OF WHITE PRIVILEGE

I decided to try to work on myself at least by identifying some of the daily effects of white privilege in my life. I have chosen those conditions that I think in my case attach somewhat more to skin-color privilege than to class, religion, ethnic status, or geographic location, though of course all these other factors are intricately intertwined. As far as I can tell, my African American coworkers, friends, and acquaintances with whom I come into daily or frequent contact in this particular time, place and time of work cannot count on most of these conditions.

1. I can if I wish arrange to be in the company of people of my race most of the time.
2. I can avoid spending time with people whom I was trained to mistrust and who have learned to mistrust my kind or me.
3. If I should need to move, I can be pretty sure of renting or purchasing housing in an area which I can afford and in which I would want to live.
4. I can be pretty sure that my neighbors in such a location will be neutral or pleasant to me.
5. I can go shopping alone most of the time, pretty well assured that I will not be followed or harassed.
6. I can turn on the television or open to the front page of the paper and see people of my race widely represented.
7. When I am told about our national heritage or about "civilization," I am shown that people of my color made it what it is.
8. I can be sure that my children will be given curricular materials that testify to the existence of their race.
9. If I want to, I can be pretty sure of finding a publisher for this piece on white privilege.
10. I can be pretty sure of having my voice heard in a group in which I am the only member of my race.
11. I can be casual about whether or not to listen to another person's voice in a group in which s/he is the only member of his/her race.
12. I can go into a music shop and count on finding the music of my race represented, into a supermarket and find the staple foods which fit with my cultural traditions, into a hairdresser's shop and find someone who can cut my hair.
13. Whether I use checks, credit cards or cash, I can count on my skin color not to work against the appearance of financial reliability.

14. I can arrange to protect my children most of the time from people who might not like them.
15. I do not have to educate my children to be aware of systemic racism for their own daily physical protection.
16. I can be pretty sure that my children's teachers and employers will tolerate them if they fit school and workplace norms; my chief worries about them do not concern others' attitudes toward their race.
17. I can talk with my mouth full and not have people put this down to my color.
18. I can swear, or dress in second hand clothes, or not answer letters, without having people attribute these choices to the bad morals, the poverty or the illiteracy of my race.
19. I can speak in public to a powerful male group without putting my race on trial.
20. I can do well in a challenging situation without being called a credit to my race.
21. I am never asked to speak for all the people of my racial group.
22. I can remain oblivious of the language and customs of persons of color who constitute the world's majority without feeling in my culture any penalty for such oblivion.
23. I can criticize our government and talk about how much I fear its policies and behavior without being seen as a cultural outsider.
24. I can be pretty sure that if I ask to talk to the "person in charge", I will be facing a person of my race.
25. If a traffic cop pulls me over or if the IRS audits my tax return, I can be sure I haven't been singled out because of my race.
26. I can easily buy posters, post-cards, picture books, greeting cards, dolls, toys and children's magazines featuring people of my race.
27. I can go home from most meetings of organizations I belong to feeling somewhat tied in, rather than isolated, out-of-place, outnumbered, unheard, held at a distance or feared.
28. I can be pretty sure that an argument with a colleague of another race is more likely to jeopardize her/his chances for advancement than to jeopardize mine.
29. I can be pretty sure that if I argue for the promotion of a person of another race, or a program centering on race, this is not likely to cost me heavily within my present setting, even if my colleagues disagree with me.
30. If I declare there is a racial issue at hand, or there isn't a racial issue at hand, my race will lend me more credibility for either position than a person of color will have.
31. I can choose to ignore developments in minority writing and minority activist programs, or disparage them, or learn from them, but in any case, I can find ways to be more or less protected from negative consequences of any of these choices.
32. My culture gives me little fear about ignoring the perspectives and powers of people of other races.
33. I am not made acutely aware that my shape, bearing or body odor will be taken as a reflection on my race.
34. I can worry about racism without being seen as self-interested or self-seeking.
35. I can take a job with an affirmative action employer without having my co-workers on the job suspect that I got it because of my race.
36. If my day, week or year is going badly, I need not ask of each negative episode or situation whether it had racial overtones.
37. I can be pretty sure of finding people who would be willing to talk with me and advise me about my next steps, professionally.
38. I can think over many options, social, political, imaginative or professional, without asking whether a person of my race would be accepted or allowed to do what I want to do.

39. I can be late to a meeting without having the lateness reflect on my race.
40. I can choose public accommodation without fearing that people of my race cannot get in or will be mistreated in the places I have chosen.
41. I can be sure that if I need legal or medical help, my race will not work against me.
42. I can arrange my activities so that I will never have to experience feelings of rejection owing to my race.
43. If I have low credibility as a leader I can be sure that my race is not the problem.
44. I can easily find academic courses and institutions which give attention only to people of my race.
45. I can expect figurative language and imagery in all of the arts to testify to experiences of my race.
46. I can chose blemish cover or bandages in "flesh" color and have them more or less match my skin.
47. I can travel alone or with my spouse without expecting embarrassment or hostility in those who deal with us.
48. I have no difficulty finding neighborhoods where people approve of our household.
49. My children are given texts and classes which implicitly support our kind of family unit and do not turn them against my choice of domestic partnership.
50. I will feel welcomed and "normal" in the usual walks of public life, institutional and social.

ELUSIVE AND FUGITIVE

I repeatedly forgot each of the realizations on this list until I wrote it down. For me white privilege has turned out to be an elusive and fugitive subject. The pressure to avoid it is great, for in facing it I must give up the myth of meritocracy. If these things are true, this is not such a free country; one's life is not what one makes it; many doors open for certain people through no virtues of their own.

In unpacking this invisible knapsack of white privilege, I have listed conditions of daily experience that I once took for granted. Nor did I think of any of these perquisites as bad for the holder. I now think that we need a more finely differentiated taxonomy of privilege, for some of these varieties are only what one would want for everyone in a just society, and others give license to be ignorant, oblivious, arrogant, and destructive.

I see a pattern running through the matrix of white privilege, a patter of assumptions that were passed on to me as a white person. There was one main piece of cultural turf; it was my own turn, and I was among those who could control the turf. My skin color was an asset for any move I was educated to want to make. I could think of myself as belonging in major ways and of making social systems work for me. I could freely disparage, fear, neglect, or be oblivious to anything outside of the dominant cultural forms. Being of the main culture, I could also criticize it fairly freely.

In proportion as my racial group was being made confident, comfortable, and oblivious, other groups were likely being made unconfident, uncomfortable, and alienated. Whiteness protected me from many kinds of hostility, distress, and violence, which I was being subtly trained to visit, in turn, upon people of color.

For this reason, the word "privilege" now seems to me misleading. We usually think of privilege as being a favored state, whether earned or conferred by birth or luck. Yet some of the conditions I have described here work systematically to over empower certain groups. Such privilege simply confers dominance because of one's race or sex.

EARNED STRENGTH, UNEARNED POWER

I want, then, to distinguish between earned strength and unearned power conferred privilege can look like strength when it is in fact permission to escape or to dominate. But not all of the privileges on my list are inevitably damaging. Some, like the expectation that neighbors will be decent to you, or that your race will not count against you in court, should be the norm in a just society. Others, like the privilege to ignore less powerful people, distort the humanity of the holders as well as the ignored groups.

We might at least start by distinguishing between positive advantages, which we can work to spread, and negative types of advantage, which unless rejected will always reinforce our present hierarchies. For example, the feeling that one belongs within the human circle, as Native Americans say, should not be seen as privilege for a few. Ideally it is an unearned entitlement. At present, since only a few have it, it is an unearned advantage for them. This paper results from a process of coming to see that some of the power that I originally say as attendant on being a human being in the United States consisted in unearned advantage and conferred dominance.

I have met very few men who truly distressed about systemic, unearned male advantage and conferred dominance. And so one question for me and others like me is whether we will be like them, or whether we will get truly distressed, even outraged, about unearned race advantage and conferred dominance, and, if so, what we will do to lessen them. In any case, we need to do more work in identifying how they actually affect our daily lives. Many, perhaps most, of our white students in the United States think that racism doesn't affect them because they are not people of color; they do not see "whiteness" as a racial identity. In addition, since race and sex are not the only advantaging systems at work, we need similarly to examine the daily experience of having age advantage, or ethnic advantage, or physical ability, or advantage related to nationality, religion, or sexual orientation.

Difficulties and angers surrounding the task of finding parallels are many. Since racism, sexism, and heterosexism are not the same, the advantages associated with them should not be seen as the same. In addition, it is hard to disentangle aspects of unearned advantage that rest more on social class, economic class, race, religion, sex, and ethnic identity that on other factors. Still, all of the oppressions are interlocking, as the members of the Combahee River Collective pointed out in their "Black Feminist Statement" of 1977.

One factor seems clear about all of the interlocking oppressions. They take both active forms, which we can see, and embedded forms, which as a member of the dominant groups one is taught not to see. In my class and place, I did not see myself as a racist because I was taught to recognize racism only in individual acts of meanness by members of my group, never in invisible systems conferring unsought racial dominance on my group from birth.

Disapproving of the system won't be enough to change them. I was taught to think that racism could end if white individuals changed their attitude. But a "white" skin in the United States opens many doors for whites whether or not we approve of the way dominance has been conferred on us. Individual acts can palliate but cannot end, these problems.

To redesign social systems we need first to acknowledge their colossal unseen dimensions. The silences and denials surrounding privilege are the key political surrounding privilege are the key political tool here. They keep the thinking about equality or equity incomplete, protecting unearned advantage and conferred dominance by making these subject taboo. Most talk by whites about equal opportunity seems to me now to be about equal opportunity to try to get into a position of dominance while denying that systems of dominance exist.

It seems to me that obliviousness about white advantage, like obliviousness about male advantage, is kept strongly inculturated in the United States so as to maintain the myth of meritocracy, the myth that democratic choice is equally available to all. Keeping most people unaware that freedom of confident action is there for just a small number of people props up those in power and serves to keep power in the hands of the same groups that have most of it already.

Although systemic change takes many decades, there are pressing questions for me and, I imagine, for some others like me if we raise our daily consciousness on the perquisites of being light-skinned. What will we do with such knowledge? As we know from watching men, it is an open question whether we will choose to use unearned advantage, and whether we will use any of our arbitrarily awarded power to try to reconstruct power systems on a broader base.

Just Walk On By
A Black Man Ponders His Power to Alter Public Space

Brent Staples

Brent Staples earned a PhD in Psychology from The University of Chicago. He is an editorial writer for The New York Times *and has published a memoir* Parallel Time: Growing up in Black and White *(1994). "Just Walk on By" first appeared in* Ms. Magazine *in 1986.*

My first victim was a woman—white, well dressed, probably in her early twenties. I came upon her late one evening on a deserted street in Hyde Park, a relatively affluent neighborhood in an otherwise mean, impoverished section of Chicago. As I swung onto the avenue behind her, there seemed to be a discreet, uninflammatory distance between us. Not so. She cast back a worried glance. To her, the youngish black man—a broad six feet two inches with a beard and billowing hair, both hands shoved into the pockets of a bulky military jacket—seemed menacingly close. After a few more quick glimpses, she picked up her pace and was soon running in earnest. Within seconds she disappeared into a cross street.

That was more than a decade ago. I was 22 years old, a graduate student newly arrived at the University of Chicago. It was in the echo of that terrified woman's footfalls that I first began to know the unwieldy inheritance I'd come into—the ability to alter public space in ugly ways. It was clear that she thought herself the quarry of a mugger, a rapist, or worse. Suffering about of insomnia, however, I was stalking sleep, not defenseless wayfarers. As a softy who is scarcely able to take a knife to a raw chicken—let alone hold it to a person's throat—I was surprised, embarrassed, and dismayed all at once. Her flight made me feel like an accomplice in tyranny. It also made it clear that I was indistinguishable from the muggers who occasionally seeped into the area from the surrounding ghetto. That first encounter, and those that followed, signified that a vast, unnerving gulf lay between nighttime pedestrians—particularly women—and me. And I soon gathered that being perceived as dangerous is a hazard in itself. I only needed to turn a corner into a dicey situation, or crowd some frightened, armed person in a foyer somewhere, or make an errant move after being pulled over by a policeman. Where fear and weapons meet—and they often do in urban America—there is always the possibility of death.

In that first year, my first away from my hometown, I was to become thoroughly familiar with the language of fear. At dark, shadowy intersections in Chicago, I could cross in front of a car stopped at a traffic light and elicit the *thunk, thunk, thunk, thunk* of the driver—black, white, male, female—hammering down the door locks. On less-traveled streets after dark, I grew accustomed to but never comfortable with people who crossed to the other side of the street rather than pass me. Then there were the standard unpleasantries with police, doormen, bouncers, cab drivers, and others whose business it is to screen out troublesome individuals *before* there is any nastiness.

I moved to New York nearly two years ago and I have remained an avid night walker. In central Manhattan, the near-constant crowd cover minimizes tense one-on-one street encounters. Elsewhere—visiting friends in SoHo, where sidewalks are narrow and tightly spaced buildings shut out the sky—things can get very taut indeed.

Black men have a firm place in New York mugging literature. Norman Podhoretz in his famed (or infamous) 1963 essay, "My Negro Problem—And Ours," recalls growing up in terror of black males; they "were tougher than we were, more ruthless," he writes—and as an adult on the Upper West Side of Manhattan, he continues, he cannot constrain his nervousness when he meets black men on certain streets. Similarly, a decade later, the essayist and novelist Edward Hoagland extols a New York where once "Negro bitterness bore down mainly on other Negroes." Where some see mere panhandlers, Hoagland sees "a mugger who is clearly screwing up his nerve to do more than just *ask* for money." But Hoagland has "the New Yorker's quick-hunch posture for broken-field maneuvering," and the bad guy swerves away.

I often witness that "hunch posture," from women after dark on the warrenlike streets of Brooklyn where I live. They seem to set their faces on neutral and, with their purse straps strung across their chests bandolier style, they forge ahead as though bracing themselves against being tackled. I understand, of course, that the danger they perceive is not a hallucination. Women are particularly vulnerable to street violence, and young black males are drastically overrepresented among the perpetrators of that violence. Yet these truths are no solace against the kind of alienation that comes of being ever the suspect, against being set apart, a fearsome entity with whom pedestrians avoid making eye contact.

It is not altogether clear to me how I reached the ripe old age of 22 without being conscious of the lethality nighttime pedestrians attributed to me. Perhaps it was because in Chester, Pennsylvania, the small, angry industrial town where I came of age in the 1960s, I was scarcely noticeable against a backdrop of gang warfare, street knifings, and murders. I grew up one of the good boys, had perhaps a half-dozen fist fights. In retrospect, my shyness of combat has clear sources.

Many things go into the making of a young thug. One of those things is the consummation of the male romance with the power to intimidate. An infant discovers that random flailings send the baby bottle flying out of the crib and crashing to the floor. Delighted, the joyful babe repeats those motions again and again, seeking to duplicate the feat. Just so, I recall the points at which some of my boyhood friends were finally seduced by the perception of themselves as tough guys. When a mark cowered and surrendered his money without resistance, myth and reality merged—and paid off. It is, after all, only manly to embrace the power to frighten and intimidate. We, as men, are not supposed to give an inch of our lane on the highway; we are to seize the fighter's edge in work and in play and even in love; we are to be valiant in the face of hostile forces.

Unfortunately, poor and powerless young men seem to take all this nonsense literally. As a boy, I saw countless tough guys locked away; I have since buried several, too. They were babies, really—a teenage cousin, a brother of 22, a childhood friend in his mid-twenties—all gone down in episodes of bravado played out in the streets. I came to doubt the virtues of intimidation early on. I chose, perhaps even unconsciously, to remain a shadow—timid, but a survivor.

The fearsomeness mistakenly attributed to me in public places often has a perilous flavor. The most frightening of these confusions occurred in the late 1970s and early 1980s when

I worked as a journalist in Chicago. One day, rushing into the office of a magazine I was writing for with a deadline story in hand, I was mistaken for a burglar. The office manager called security and, with an ad hoc posse, pursued me through the labyrinthine halls, nearly to my editor's door. I had no way of proving who I was. I could only move briskly toward the company of someone who knew me.

Another time I was on assignment for a local paper and killing time before an interview. I entered a jewelry store on the city's affluent Near North Side. The proprietor excused herself and returned with an enormous red Doberman pinscher straining at the end of a leash. She stood, the dog extended toward me, silent to my questions, her eyes bulging nearly out of her head. I took a cursory look around, nodded, and bade her good night. Relatively speaking, however, I never fared as badly as another black male journalist. He went to nearby Waukegan, Illinois, a couple of summers ago to work on a story about a murderer who was born there. Mistaking the reporter for the killer, police hauled him from his car at gunpoint and but for his press credentials would have tried to book him. Such episodes are not uncommon. Black men trade tales like this all the time.

In "My Negro Problem—And Ours," Podhoretz writes that the hatred he feels for blacks makes itself known to him through a variety of avenues—one being his discomfort with that "special brand of paranoid touchiness" to which he says blacks are prone. No doubt he is speaking here of black men. In time, I learned to smother the rage I felt at so often being taken for a criminal. Not to do so would surely have led to madness—via that special "paranoid touchiness" that so annoyed Podhoretz at the time he wrote the essay.

I began to take precautions to make myself less threatening. I move about with care, particularly late in the evening. I give a wide berth to nervous people on the subway platforms during the wee hours, particularly when I have exchanged business clothes for jeans. If I happen to be entering a building behind some people who appear skittish, I may walk by, letting them clear the lobby before I return, so as not to seem to be following them. I have been calm and extremely congenial on those rare occasions when I've been pulled over by the police.

And on late-evening constitutionals along streets less traveled by, I employ what has proved to be an excellent tension-reducing measure: I whistle melodies from Beethoven and Vivaldi and the more popular classical composers. Even steely New Yorkers hunching toward nighttime destinations seem to relax, and occasionally they even join in the tune. Virtually everybody seems to sense that a mugger wouldn't be warbling bright, sunny selections from Vivaldi's *Four Seasons*. It is my equivalent of the cowbell that hikers wear when they know they are in bear country.

Beyond Bean Counting

JeeYeun Lee

JeeYeun Lee is a Korean American woman born in Japan and raised in Chicago. Her writing has been published in Q&A: Queer in Asian America *(1998),* Queer Studies: A Lesbian, Gay, Bisexual and Transgender Anthology *(1996) and* Witness Aloud: Lesbian, Gay and Bisexual Asian/Pacific American Writings *(1993). This article appeared in* Listen Up: Voices from the Next Feminist Generation *edited by Barbara Findlen (2001).*

I came out as a woman, an Asian American and a bisexual within a relatively short span of time, and ever since then I have been guilty of the crime of bean counting, as Bill Clinton oh-so-eloquently phrased it. Every time I am in a room of people gathered for any reason, I automatically count those whom I can identify as women, men, people of color, Asian Americans, mixed-race people, whites, gays, lesbians, bisexuals, heterosexuals, people with disabilities. So when I received the call for submissions for this anthology, I imagined opening up the finished book to the table of contents and counting beans; I then sent the call for submissions to as many queer Asian/Pacific American women writers as I knew.

Such is the nature of feminism today: an uneasy balancing act between the imperatives of outreach and inclusion on one hand, and the risk of tokenism and further marginalization on the other. This dynamic has indelibly shaped my personal experiences with feminism, starting from my very first encounter with organized feminism. This encounter happened to be, literally, Feminist Studies 101 at the university I attended. The content of the class was divided into topics such as family, work, sexuality and so forth, and for each topic we studied what various feminist paradigms said about it: "liberal feminism," "socialist feminism," "radical feminism" and "feminism and women of color."

Taking this class was an exhilarating, empowering and very uneasy experience. For the first time I found people who articulated those murky half-formed feelings that I could previously only express incoherently as "But that's not fair!" People who agreed, sympathized, related their own experiences, theorized, helped me form what I had always known. In seventh grade, a teacher made us do a mock debate, and I ended up arguing with Neil Coleman about whether women or men were better cooks. He said more men were professional chefs, therefore men were better. I responded that more women cooked in daily life, therefore women were better. He said it was quality that mattered, not quantity, and left me standing there with nothing to say. I knew there was something wrong with his argument, something wrong with the whole issue as it was framed, and felt extremely betrayed at being made to consent to the inferiority of my gender, losing in front of the whole class. I could never defend myself when arguments like this came up, invariably with boys who were good at debates and used to winning. They left me seething with resentment at their manipulations and frustrated at my speechlessness. So to come to a class that addressed these issues directly and gave me the words for all those pent-up feelings and frustrations was a tremendously affirming and empowering experience.

At the same time, it was an intensely uncomfortable experience. I knew "women of color" was supposed to include Asian American women, but I could not find any in the class readings. Were there no Asian American feminists? Were there none who could write in English? Did there even exist older Asian American women who were second or third generation? Were we Asian American students in the class the first to think about feminism? A class about women, I thought, was a class about me, so I looked for myself everywhere, and I found nothing. Nothing about Asian American families, immigrant women's work patterns, issues of sexuality and body image for Asian women, violence against Asian American women, Asian American women in the seventies feminist movement, nothing anywhere. I wasn't fully conscious then that I was searching for this, but this absence came out in certain feelings. First of all, I felt jealous of African American and Chicana feminists. Their work was present at least to some degree in the readings: They had research and theories, they were eloquent and they *existed*. Black and Chicana women in the class could claim them as role models, voices, communities—I had no one to claim as my own. My emerging identification as a woman of color was displaced through the writings of black and Chicana women, and I had to read myself, create my politics, through theirs; even now, to a certain extent, I feel more familiar with their issues than those of Asian American women. Second, I felt guilty. Although it was never expressed outright, I felt that there was some pressure on me to represent Asian American issues, and I could not. I felt estranged from the Asian American groups on campus and Asian American politics and activism in general, and guilty about this ignorance and alienation.

Now mind you, I'm still grateful for this class. Feminism was my avenue to politics: It politicized me; it raised my consciousness about issues of oppression, power and resistance in general. I learned a language with which I could start to explain my experiences and link them to larger societal structures of oppression and complicity. It also gave me ways that I could resist and actively fight back. I became interested in Asian American politics, people of color politics, gay/lesbian/bisexual politics and other struggles because of this exposure to feminism. But there is no excuse for this nearly complete exclusion of Asian/Pacific American women from the class. Marginalization is not simply a politically correct buzzword, it is a material reality that affects people's lives—in this case, my own. I would have been turned off from feminism altogether had it not been for later classes that dealt specifically with women of color. And I would like to name names here: I went to Stanford University, a bastion of privilege that pretends to be on the cutting edge of "multiculturalism." Just under twenty-five percent of the undergraduate population is Asian/Pacific American, but there was no mention of Asian/Pacific American women in Feminist Studies 101. All the classes I took on women of color were taught by graduate students and visiting professors. There was, at that time, only one woman of color on the feminist studies faculty. I regret that I realized the political import of these facts only after I left Stanford.

I understand that feminists in academia are caught between a rock and a hard place—not too many of us hold positions of decision-making power in universities. And I must acknowledge my gratitude for their struggles in helping to establish feminist studies programs and produce theories and research about women, all of which create vital opportunities and affirmation. But other women's organizations that are not constrained by such explicit forces are also lily-white.

This obviously differs from group to group, and I think many of them are very conscientious about outreach to historically marginalized women. But, for instance, in 1992 and 1993, at the meetings I attended of the Women's Action Coalition (WAC) in New York City, out of approximately two hundred women usually fewer than twenty women of color were present.

But this is not a diatribe against feminism in general. I want to emphasize that the feminism that I and other young women come to today is one that is at least sensitive to issues of exclusion. If perhaps twenty years ago charges of racism, classism and homophobia were not taken seriously, today they are the cause of extreme anguish and soul-searching. I am profoundly grateful to older feminists of color and their white allies who struggled to bring U.S. feminist movements to this point. At the same time, I think that this current sensitivity often breeds tokenism, guilt, suspicion and self-righteousness that have very material repercussions on women's groups. I have found these uneasy dynamics in all the women's groups I've come across, addressed to varying degrees. At one extreme, I have seen groups that deny the marginalizing effects of their practices, believing that issues of inclusion really have nothing to do with their specific agendas. At the other extreme, I have seen groups ripped apart by accusations of political correctness, immobilized by guilt, knowing they should address a certain issue but not knowing how to begin, and still wondering why "women of color just don't come to our meetings." And tokenism is alive and well. Those of us who have been aware of our tokenization often become suspicious and tired of educating others, wondering if we are invested enough to continue to do so, wondering if the overall goal is worth it.

In this age when "political correctness" has been appropriated by conservative forces as a derogatory term, it is extremely difficult to honestly discuss and confront any ideas and practices that perpetuate dominant norms—and none of us is innocent of such collusion. Many times, our response is to become defensive, shutting down to constructive critiques and actions, or to individualize our collusion as solely a personal fault, as if working on our individual racist or classist attitudes would somehow make things better. It appears that we all have a lot of work to do still.

And I mean *all*. Issues of exclusion are not the sole province of white feminists. I learned this very vividly at a 1993 retreat organized by the Asian Pacifica Lesbian Network. It has become somewhat common lately to speak of "Asian and Pacific Islanders" or "Asian/Pacific Americans" or, as in this case, "Asian Pacifica." This is meant to be inclusive, to recognize some issues held in common by people from Asia and people from the Pacific Islands. Two women of Native Hawaiian descent and some Asian American allies confronted the group at this retreat to ask for more than lip service in the organization's name: If the group was seriously committed to being an inclusive coalition, we needed to educate ourselves about and actively advocate Pacific Islander issues. And because I don't want to relegate them to a footnote, I will mention here a few of these issues: the demand for sovereignty for Native Hawaiians, whose government was illegally overthrown by the U.S. in 1893; fighting stereotypes of women and men that are different from those of Asian people; decrying U.S. imperialist possession and occupation of the islands of Guam, the Virgin Islands, American Samoa, the Marshall Islands, Micronesia, the Northern Mariana Islands and several others.

This was a retreat where one would suppose everyone had so much in common—after all, we were all queer API women, right? Any such myth was effectively destroyed by the realities of our experiences and issues: We were women of different ethnic backgrounds, with very different issues among East Asians, South Asians, Southeast Asians and Pacific Islanders; women of mixed race and heritage; women who identified as lesbians and those who identified as bisexuals; women who were immigrants, refugees, illegal aliens or second generation or more; older women, physically challenged women, women adopted by white families, women from the

Midwest. Such tangible differences brought home the fact that no simplistic identity politics is *ever* possible, that we had to conceive of ourselves as a coalition first and foremost; as one woman on a panel said our identity as queer API women must be a *coalitional* identity. Initially, I thought that I had finally found a home where I could relax and let down my guard. This was true to a certain degree, but I discovered that this was the home where I would have to work the hardest because I cared the most. I would have to be committed to push myself and push others to deal with all of our differences, so that we *could* be safe for each other. And in this difficult work of coalition, one positive action was taken at the retreat: We changed the name of the organization to include "bisexual," thus becoming the Asian Pacifica Lesbian and Bisexual Network, a name that people started using immediately.

All this is to say that I and other young women have found most feminist movements today to be at this point, where there is at least a stated emphasis on inclusion and outreach with the accompanying risk of tokenism. I firmly believe that it is always the margins that push us further in our politics. Women of color do not struggle in feminist movements simply to add cultural diversity, to add the viewpoints of different kinds of women. Women of color feminist theories challenge the fundamental premises of feminism, such as the very definition of "women," and call for recognition of the constructed racial nature of *all* experiences of gender. In the same way, heterosexist norms do not oppress solely lesbians, bisexuals and gay men, but affect all of our choices and non-choices; issues posed by differently abled women question our basic assumptions about body image, health care, sexuality and work; ecofeminists challenge our fundamental ideas about living on and with the earth, about our interactions with animals, plants, food, agriculture and industry. Many feminists seem to find the issues of class the most difficult to address; we are always faced with the fundamental inequalities inherent to twenty-first-century multinational capitalism and our unavoidable implication in its structures. Such an overwhelming array of problems can numb and immobilize us, or make us concentrate our energies too narrowly. I don't think that we have to address everything fully at the same time, but we *must* be fully aware of the limitations of our specific agendas. Progressive activists cannot afford to do the masters' work for them by continuing to carry out oppressive assumptions and exclusions.

These days, whenever someone says the word "women" to me, my mind goes blank. What "women"? What is this "women" thing you're talking about? Does that mean me? Does that mean my mother, my roommates, the white woman next door, the checkout clerk at the supermarket, my aunts in Korea, half of the world's population? I ask people to specify and specify, until I can figure out exactly what they're talking about, and I try to remember to apply the same standards to myself, to deny myself the slightest possibility of romanticization. Sisterhood may be global, but who is in that sisterhood? None of us can afford to assume anything about anybody else. This thing called "feminism" takes a great deal of hard work, and I think this is one of the primary hallmarks of your feminists' activism today: We realize that coming together and work together are by no means natural or easy.

Toward a New Vision
Race, Class, and Gender as Categories of Analysis and Connection

Patricia Hill Collins

Patricia Hill Collins is a Distinguished University Professor of Sociology at the University of Maryland. She has examined the intersections of race, gender, class, sexuality and nation in several books includ-ing Black Feminist Thought: Knowledge, Consciousness, and the Politics of Empowerment *(1990),* Black Sexual Politics: African Americans, Gender, and the New Racism *(2004),* Fighting Words: Black Women and the Search for Justice *(1998), and From* Black Power to Hip Hop: Racism, Nationalism, and Feminism *(2005). This piece was delivered as the keynote address at the Workshop on Integrating Race and Gender into the College Curriculum at Memphis State University in 1989 and appeared in* Race, Sex & Class: an Interdisciplinary Journal *in 1993.*

The true focus of revolutionary change is never merely the oppressive situations which we seek to escape, but that piece of the oppressor which is planted deep within each of us.

—AUDRE LORDE, *Sister Outsider*, 123

Audre Lorde's statement raises a troublesome issue for scholars and activists working for social change. While many of us have little difficulty assessing our own victimization within some major system of oppression, whether it be by race, social class, religion, sexual orientation, ethnicity, age or gender, we typically fail to see how our thoughts and actions uphold someone else's subordination. Thus, white feminists routinely point with confidence to their oppression as women but resist seeing how much their white skin privileges them. African-Americans who possess eloquent analyses of racism often persist in viewing poor White women as symbols of white power. The radical left fares little better. "If only people of color and women could see their true class interests," they argue, "class solidarity would eliminate racism and sexism." In essence, each group identifies the type of oppression with which it feels most comfortable as being fundamental and classifies all other types as being of lesser importance.

Oppression is full of such contradictions. Errors in political judgment that we make concerning how we teach our courses, what we tell our children, and which organizations are worthy of our time, talents and financial support flow smoothly from errors in theoretical analysis about the nature of oppression and activism. Once we realize that there are few pure victims or oppressors, and that each one of us derives varying amounts of penalty and privilege from the multiple systems of oppression that frame our lives, then we will be in a position to see the need for new ways of thought and action.

To get at that "piece of the oppressor which is planted deep within each of us," we need at least two things. First, we need new visions of what oppression is, new categories of analysis that are inclusive of race, class, and gender as distinctive yet interlocking structures of oppression. Adhering to a stance of comparing and ranking oppressions—the proverbial, "I'm more oppressed than you"—locks us all into a dangerous dance of competing for attention, resources, and theoretical supremacy. Instead, I suggest that we examine our different experiences within the more fundamental relationship of domination and subordination. To focus on the particular arrangements that race or class or gender takes in our time and place without seeing these structures as sometimes parallel and sometimes interlocking dimensions of the more fundamental relationship of domination and subordination may temporarily ease our consciences. But while such thinking may lead to short-term social reforms, it is simply inadequate for the task of bringing about long-term social transformation.

While race, class and gender as categories of analysis are essential in helping us understand the structural bases of domination and subordination, new ways of thinking that are not accompanied by new ways of acting offer incomplete prospects for change. To get at that "piece of the oppressor which is planted deep within each of us," we also need to change our daily behavior. Currently, we are all enmeshed in a complex web of problematic relationships that grant our mirror images full human subjectivity while stereotyping and objectifying those most different than ourselves. We often assume that the people we work with, teach, send our children to school with, and sit next to . . . will act and feel in prescribed ways because they belong to given race, social class or gender categories. [These judgments by category relationships that transcend the legitimate differences created by race, class and gender as categories of analysis.] We require new categories of connection, new visions of what our relationships with one another can be. . . .

[This discussion] addresses this need for new patterns of thought and action. I focus on two basic questions. First, how can we reconceptualize race, class and gender as categories of analysis? Second, how can we transcend the barriers created by our experiences with race, class and gender oppression in order to build the types of coalitions essential for social exchange? To address these questions I contend that we must acquire both new theories of how race, class and gender have shaped the experiences not just of women of color, but of all groups. Moreover, we must see the connections between the categories of analysis and the personal issues in our everyday lives, particularly our scholarship, our teaching and our relationships with our colleagues and students. As Audre Lorde points out, change starts with self, and relationships that we have with those around us must always be the primary site for social change.

HOW CAN WE RECONCEPTUALIZE RACE, CLASS AND GENDER AS CATEGORIES OF ANALYSIS?

To me, we must shift our discourse away from additive analyses of oppression (Spelman, 1982; Collins, 1989). Such approaches are typically based on two key premises. First, they depend on either/or, dichotomous thinking. Persons, things and ideas are conceptualized in terms of their opposites. For example, Black/White, man/woman, thought/feeling, and fact/opinion are defined in oppositional terms. Thought and feeling are not seen as two different and interconnected ways of approaching truth that can coexist in scholarship and teaching. Instead, feeling is defined as antithetical to reason, as its opposite. In spite of the fact that we all have "both/and" identities (I am both a college professor and a mother—I don't stop being a mother when I drop my child off at school, or forget everything I learned while scrubbing the toilet), we persist in trying to classify each other in either/or categories. I live each day as an African-American woman—a race/gender specific experience. And I am not alone. Everyone has a race/gender/class specific identity. Either/or, dichotomous thinking is especially troublesome when applied to theories of oppression because every individual must be classified as being either oppressed or not oppressed. The both/and position of simultaneously being oppressed and oppressor becomes conceptually impossible.

A second premise of additive analyses of oppression is that these dichotomous differences must be ranked. One side of the dichotomy is typically labeled dominant and the other subordinate. Thus, Whites rule Blacks, men are deemed superior to women, and reason is seen as being preferable to emotion. Applying this premise to discussions of oppression leads to the assumption that oppression can be quantified, and that some groups are oppressed more than others. I am frequently asked, "Which has been most oppressive to you, your status as a Black person or your status as a woman?" What I am really being asked to do is divide myself into little boxes and rank my various statuses. If I experience oppression as a both/and phenomenon, why should I analyze it any differently?

Additive analyses of oppression rest squarely on the twin pillars of either/or thinking and the necessity to quantify and rank all relationships in order to know where one stands. Such approaches typically see African-American women as being more oppressed than everyone else because the majority of Black women experience the negative effects of race, class and gender oppression simultaneously. In essence, if you add together separate oppressions, you are left with a grand oppression greater than the sum of its parts.

I am not denying that specific groups experience oppression more harshly than others—lynching is certainly objectively worse than being held up as a sex object. But we must be careful not to confuse this issue of the saliency of one type of oppression in people's lives with a theoretical stance positing the interlocking nature of oppression. Race, class and gender may all structure a situation but may not be equally visible and/or important in people's self-definitions. In certain contexts, such as the antebellum American South and contemporary South America, racial oppression is more visibly salient, while in other contexts, such as Haiti, El Salvador and Nicaragua, social class oppression may be more apparent. For middle-class White women, gender may assume experiential primacy unavailable to poor Hispanic women struggling with the ongoing issues of low-paid jobs and the frustrations of the welfare bureaucracy. This recognition that one category may have salience over another for a given time and place does not minimize the theoretical importance of assuming that race, class and gender as categories of analysis structure all relationships.

In order to move toward new visions of what oppression is, I think that we need to ask new questions. How are relationships of domination and subordination structured and maintained in the American political economy? How do race, class and gender function as parallel and interlocking systems that shape this basic relationship of domination and subordination? Questions such as these promise to move us away from futile theoretical struggles concerned with ranking oppressions and towards analyses that assume race, class and gender are all present in any given setting, even if one appears more visible and salient than the others. Our task becomes redefined as one of reconceptualizing oppression by uncovering the connections among race, class and gender as categories of analysis.

1. The Institutional Dimension of Oppression

Sandra Harding's contention that gender oppression is structured along three main dimensions—the institutional, the symbolic and the individual—offers a useful model for a more comprehensive analysis encompassing race, class and gender oppression (Harding 1986). Systemic relationships of domination and subordination structured through social institutions such as schools, businesses, hospitals, the workplace and government agencies represent the institutional dimension of oppression. Racism, sexism, and elitism all have concrete institutional locations. Even though the workings of the institutional dimension of oppression are often obscured with ideologies claiming equality of opportunity, in actuality, race, class and gender place Asian-American women, Native American men, White men, African-American women and other groups in distinct institutional niches with varying degrees of penalty and privilege.

Even though I realize that many . . . would not share this assumption, let us assume that the institutions of American society discriminate, whether by design or by accident. While many of us are familiar with how race, gender and class operate separately to structure inequality, I want to focus on how these three systems interlock in structuring the institutional dimension of oppression. To get at the interlocking nature of race, class and gender, I want you to think about the antebellum plantation as a guiding metaphor for a variety of American social institutions. Even though slavery is typically analyzed as a racist institution, and occasionally as a class institution, I suggest that slavery was a race, class, gender specific institution. Removing any one piece from our analysis diminishes our understanding of the true nature of relations of domination and subordination under slavery.

Slavery was a profoundly patriarchal institution. It rested on the dual tenets of White male authority and White male property, a joining of the political and the economic within the institution of the family. Heterosexism was assumed and all Whites were expected to marry. Control over affluent White women's sexuality remained key to slavery's survival because property was to be passed on to the legitimate heirs of the slave owner. Ensuring affluent White women's virginity and chastity was deeply intertwined with maintenance of property relations.

Under slavery, we see varying levels of institutional protection given to affluent White women, working class and poor White women and enslaved African women. Poor White women enjoyed few of the protections held out to their upper class sisters. Moreover, the devalued status of Black women was key in keeping all White women in their assigned places. Controlling Black women's fertility was also key to the continuation of slavery, for children born to slave mothers themselves were slaves.

African-American women shared the devalued status of chattel with their husbands, fathers and sons. Racism stripped Blacks as a group of legal rights, education and control over their own persons. African-Americans could be whipped, branded, sold, or killed, not because they were poor, or because they were women, but because they were Black. Racism ensured that Blacks would continue to serve Whites and suffer economic exploitation at the hands of all Whites.

So we have a very interesting chain of command on the plantation—the affluent White master as the reigning patriarch, his White wife helpmate to serve him, help him manage his property and bring up his heirs, his faithful servants whose production and reproduction were tied to the requirements of the capitalist political economy and largely propertyless, working class White men and women watching from afar. In essence, the foundations for the contemporary roles of elite White women, poor Black women, working class White men and a series of other groups can be seen in stark relief in this fundamental American social institution. While Blacks experienced the most harsh treatment under slavery, and thus made slavery clearly visible as a racist institution, race, class and gender interlocked in structuring slavery's systemic organization of domination and subordination.

Even today, the plantation remains a compelling metaphor for institutional oppression. Certainly the actual conditions of oppression are not as severe now as they were then. To argue, as some do, that things have not changed all that much denigrates the achievements of those who struggled for social change before us. But the basic relationships among Black men, Black women, elite White women, elite White men, working class White men and working class White women as groups remain essentially intact.

A brief analysis of key American social institutions most controlled by elite White men should convince us of the interlocking nature of race, class and gender in structuring the institutional dimension of oppression. For example, if you are from an American college or university, is your campus a modern plantation? Who controls your university's political economy? Are elite White men overrepresented among the upper administrators and trustees controlling your university's finances and policies? Are elite White men being joined by growing numbers of elite White women helpmates? What kinds of people are in your class-rooms grooming the next generation who will occupy these and other decision-making positions? Who are the support staff that produce the mass mailings, order the supplies, fix the leaky pipes? Do African-Americans, Hispanics or other people of color form the majority of the invisible workers who feed you, wash your dishes, and clean up your offices and libraries after everyone else has gone home?

If your college is anything like mine, you know the answers to these questions. You may be af-filiated with an institution that has Hispanic women as vice-presidents for finance, or substantial numbers of Black men among the faculty. If so, you are fortunate. Much more typical are colleges where a modified version of the plantation as a metaphor for the institutional dimension of oppression survives.

2. The Symbolic Dimension of Oppression

Widespread, societally sanctioned ideologies used to justify relations of domination and subor-dination comprise the symbolic dimension of oppression. Central to this process is the use of stereotypical or controlling images of diverse race, class and gender groups. In order to assess the power of this dimension of oppression, I want you to make a list, either on paper or in your head, of "masculine" and "feminine" characteristics. If your list is anything like that compiled by most people, it reflects some variation of the following:

Masculine	Feminine
aggressive	passive
leader	follower
rational	emotional
strong	weak
intellectual	physical

Not only does this list reflect either/or dichotomous thinking and the need to rank both sides of the dichotomy, but ask yourself exactly which men and women you had in mind when compil-ing these characteristics. This list applies almost exclusively to middle class White men and women. The allegedly "masculine" qualities that you probably listed are only acceptable when exhibited by elite White men, or when used by Black and Hispanic men against each other or against women of color. Aggressive Black and Hispanic men are seen as dangerous, not power-ful, and are often penalized when they exhibit any of the allegedly "masculine" characteristics. Working class and poor White men fare slightly better and are also denied the allegedly "mas-culine" symbols of leadership, intellectual competence, and human rationality. Women of color and working class and poor White women are also not represented on this list, for they have never had the luxury of being "ladies." What appear to be universal categories representing all men and women instead are unmasked as being applicable to only a small group.

It is important to see how the symbolic images applied to different race, class and gender groups interact in maintaining systems of domination and subordination. If I were to ask you to repeat the same assignment, only this time, by making separate lists for Black men, Black women, Hispanic women and Hispanic men, I suspect that your gender symbolism would be quite different. In comparing all of the lists, you might begin to see the interdependence of symbols applied to all groups. For example, the elevated images of White womanhood need devalued images of Black womanhood in order to maintain credibility.

While the above exercise reveals the interlocking nature of race, class and gender in structuring the symbolic dimension of oppression, part of its importance lies in demonstrating how race, class and gender pervade a wide range of what appears to be universal language. Attending to diversity in our scholarship, in our teaching, and in our daily lives provides a new angle of vision on interpretations of reality thought to be natural, normal and "true." Moreover, viewing images of masculinity and femininity as universal gender symbolism, rather than as symbolic images that are race, class and gender specific, renders the experiences of people of color and of nonprivileged White women and men invisible. One way to dehumanize an individual or group is to deny the reality of their experiences. So when we refuse to deal with race or class because they do not appear to be directly relevant to gender, we are actually becoming part of someone else's problem.

Assuming that everyone is affected differently by the same interlocking set of symbolic images allows us to move forward toward new analyses. Women of color and White women have different relations to White male authority and this difference explains the distinct gender symbolism applied to both groups. Black women encounter controlling images such as the mammy, the matriarch, the mule and the whore, that encourage others to reject us as fully human people. Ironically, the negative nature of these images simultaneously encourages us to reject them. In contrast, White women are offered seductive images, those that promise to reward them for supporting the status quo. And yet seductive images can be equally controlling. Consider, for example, the views of Nancy White, a 73-year-old Black woman, concerning images of rejection and seduction:

> My mother used to say that the black woman is the white man's mule and the white woman is his dog. Now, she said that to say this: we do the heavy work and get beat whether we do it well or not. But the white woman is closer to the master and he pats them on the head and lets them sleep in the house, but he ain't gon' treat neither one like he was dealing with a person. (Gwaltney, 148)

Both sets of images stimulate particular political stances. By broadening the analysis beyond the confines of race, we can see the varying levels of rejection and seduction available to each of us due to our race, class and gender identity. Each of us lives with an allotted portion of institutional privilege and penalty, and with varying levels of rejection and seduction inherent in the symbolic images applied to us. This is the context in which we make our choices. Taken together, the institutional and symbolic dimensions of oppression create a structural backdrop against which all of us live our lives.

3. The Individual Dimension of Oppression

Whether we benefit or not, we all live within institutions that reproduce race, class and gender oppression. Even if we never have any contact with members of other race, class and gender groups, we all encounter images of these groups and are exposed to the symbolic meanings attached to those images. On this dimension of oppression, our individual biographies vary tremendously. As a result of our institutional and symbolic statuses, all of our choices become political acts.

Each of us must come to terms with the multiple ways in which race, class and gender as categories of analysis frame our individual biographies. I have lived my entire life as an African-American woman from a working class family and this basic fact has had a profound impact on my personal biography. Imagine how different your life might be if you had been born Black, or White, or poor, or of a different race/class/gender group than the one with which you are most familiar. The institutional treatment you would have received and the symbolic meanings attached to your very existence might differ dramatically from that you now consider to be natural, normal and part of everyday life. You might be the same, but your personal biography might have been quite different.

I believe that each of us carries around the cumulative effect of our lives within multiple structures of oppression. If you want to see how much you have been affected by this whole thing, I ask you one simple question—who are your close friends? Who are the people with whom you can share your hopes, dreams, vulnerabilities, fears and victories? Do they look like you? If they are all the same, circumstance may be the cause. For the first seven years of my life I saw only low income Black people. My friends from those years reflected the composition of my community. But now that I am an adult, can the defense of circumstance explain the patterns of people that I trust as my friends and colleagues? When given other alternatives, if my friends and colleagues reflect the homogeneity of one race, class and gender group, then these categories of analysis have indeed become barriers to connection.

I am not suggesting that people are doomed to follow the paths laid out for them by race, class and gender as categories of analysis. While these three structures certainly frame my opportunity structure, I as an individual always have the choice of accepting things as they are, or trying to change them. As Nikki Giovanni points out, "we've got to live in the real world. If we don't like the world we're living in, change it. And if we can't change it, we change ourselves. We can do something" (Tate 1983, 68). While a piece of the oppressor may be planted deep within each of us, we each have the choice of accepting that piece or challenging it as part of the "true focus of revolutionary change."

HOW CAN WE TRANSCEND THE BARRIERS CREATED BY OUR EXPERIENCES WITH RACE, CLASS AND GENDER OPPRESSION IN ORDER TO BUILD THE TYPES OF COALITIONS ESSENTIAL FOR SOCIAL CHANGE?

Reconceptualizing oppression and seeing the barriers created by race, class and gender as interlocking categories of analysis is a vital first step. But we must transcend these barriers by moving toward race, class and gender as categories of connection, by building relationships and coalitions that will bring about social change. What are some of the issues involved in doing this?

I. Differences in Power and Privilege

First, we must recognize that our differing experiences with oppression create problems in the relationships among us. Each of us lives within a system that vests us with varying levels of power and privilege. These differences in power, whether structured along axes of race, class, gender, age or sexual orientation, frame our relationships. African-American writer June Jordan describes her discomfort on a Caribbean vacation with Olive, the Black woman who cleaned her room:

> . . . even though both "Olive" and "I" live inside a conflict neither one of us created, and even though both of us therefore hurt inside that conflict, I may be one of the monsters she needs to eliminate from her universe and, in a sense, she may be one of the monsters in mine (1985, 47).

Differences in power constrain our ability to connect with one another even when we think we are engaged in dialogue across differences. Let me give you an example. One year, the students in my course "Sociology of the Black Community" got into a heated discussion about the reasons for the upsurge of racial incidents on college campuses. Black students complained vehemently about the apathy and resistance they felt most White students expressed about examining their own racism. Mark, a White male student, found their comments particularly unsettling. After claiming that all the Black people he had ever known had expressed no such beliefs to him, he questioned how representative the viewpoints of his fellow students actually were. When pushed further, Mark revealed that he had participated in conversations over the years with the Black domestic worker employed by his family. Since she had never expressed such strong feelings about White racism, Mark was genuinely shocked by class discussions. Ask yourselves whether that domestic worker was in a position to speak freely. Would it have been wise for her to do so in a situation where the power between the two parties was so unequal?

In extreme cases, members of privileged groups can erase the very presence of the less privileged. When I first moved to Cincinnati, my family and I went on a picnic at a local park. Picnicking next to us was a family of White Appalachians. When I went to push my daughter on the swings, several of the children came over. They had missing, yellowed and broken teeth, they wore old clothing and their poverty was evident. I was shocked. Growing up in a large eastern city, I had never seen such awful poverty among Whites. The segregated neighborhoods in which I grew up made White poverty all but invisible. More importantly, the privileges attached to my newly acquired social class position allowed me to ignore and minimize the poverty among Whites that I did encounter. My reactions to those children made me realize how confining phrases such as "well, at least they're not Black," had become for me. In learning to grant human subjectivity to the Black victims of poverty, I had simultaneously learned to demand White victims of poverty. By applying categories of race to the objective conditions confronting me, I was quantifying and ranking oppressions and missing the very real suffering which, in fact, is the real issue.

One common pattern of relationships across differences in power is one that I label "voyeurism." From the perspective of the privileged, the lives of people of color, of the poor, and of women are interesting for their entertainment value. The privileged become voyeurs, passive onlookers who do not relate to the less powerful, but who are interested in seeing how the "different" live. Over the years, I have heard numerous African-American students complain about professors who never call on them except when a so-called Black issue is being discussed. The students' interest in discussing race or qualifications for doing so appear unimportant to the professor's efforts to use Black students' experiences as stories to make the material come alive for the White student audience. Asking Black students to perform on cue and provide a Black experience for their White classmates can be seen as voyeurism at its worst.

Members of subordinate groups do not willingly participate in such exchanges but often do so because members of dominant groups control the institutional and symbolic apparatuses of oppression. Racial/ethnic groups, women, and the poor have never had the luxury of being voyeurs of the lives of the privileged. Our ability to survive in hostile settings has hinged on our ability to learn intricate details about the behavior and world view of the powerful and adjust our behavior accordingly. I need only point to the difference in perception of those men and women in abusive relationships. Where men can view their girlfriends and wives as sex objects, helpmates and a collection of stereotypes categories of voyeurism—women must be attuned to every nuance of their partners' behavior. Are women "naturally" better in relating to people with more power than themselves, or have circumstances mandated that men and women develop different skills?. . .

Coming from a tradition where most relationships across difference are squarely rooted in relations of domination and subordination, we have much less experience relating to people as different but equal. The classroom is potentially one powerful and safe space where dialogues among individuals of unequal power relationships can occur. The relationship between Mark, the student in my class, and the domestic worker is typical of a whole series of relationships that people have when they relate across differences in power and privilege. The relationship among Mark and his classmates represents the power of the classroom to minimize those differences so that people of different levels of power can use race, class and gender as categories of analysis in order to generate meaningful dialogues. In this case, the classroom equalized racial differences so that Black students who normally felt silenced spoke out. White students like Mark, generally unaware of how they had been privileged by their whiteness, lost that privilege in the classroom and thus became open to genuine dialogue. . .

2. Coalitions around Common Causes

A second issue in building relationships and coalitions essential for social change concerns knowing the real reasons for coalition. Just what brings people together? One powerful catalyst fostering group solidarity is the presence of a common enemy. African-American, Hispanic, Asian-American, and women's studies all share the common intellectual heritage of challenging what passes for certified knowledge in the academy. But politically expedient relationships and coalitions like these are fragile because, as June Jordan points out:

> It occurs to me that much organizational grief could be avoided if people understood that partnership in misery does not necessarily provide for partnership for change. When we get the monsters off our backs all of us may want to run in very different directions (1985, 47).

Sharing a common cause assists individuals and groups in maintaining relationships that transcend their differences. Building effective coalitions involves struggling to hear one another and developing empathy for each other's points of view. The coalitions that I have been involved in that lasted and that worked have been those where commitment to a specific issue mandated collaboration as the best strategy for addressing the issue at hand.

Several years ago, masters degree in hand, I chose to teach in an innercity parochial school in danger of closing. The money was awful, the conditions were poor, but the need was great. In my job, I had to work with a range of individuals who, on the surface, had very little in common. We had White nuns, Black middle class graduate students, Blacks from the "community," some of whom had been incarcerated and/or were affiliated with a range of federal anti-poverty programs. Parents formed another part of this community, Harvard faculty another, and a few well-meaning White liberals from Colorado were sprinkled in for good measure.

As you might imagine, tension was high. Initially, our differences seemed insurmountable. But as time passed, we found a common bond that we each brought to the school. In spite of profound differences in our personal biographies, differences that in other settings would have hampered our ability to relate to one another, we found that we were all deeply committed to the education of Black children. By learning to value each other's commitment and by recognizing that we each had different skills that were essential to actualizing that commitment, we built an effective coalition around a common cause. Our school was successful, and the children we taught benefited from the diversity we offered them.

. . . None of us alone has a comprehensive vision of how race, class and gender operate as categories of analysis or how they might be used as categories of connection. Our personal biographies offer us partial views. Few of us can manage to study race, class and gender simultaneously. Instead, we each know more about some dimensions of this larger story and less about others . . . Just as the members of the school had special skills to offer to the task of building the school, we have areas of specialization and expertise, whether scholarly, theoretical, pedagogical or within areas of race, class or gender. We do not all have to do the same thing in the same way. Instead, we must support each other's efforts, realizing that they are all part of the larger enterprise of bringing about social change.

3. Building Empathy

A third issue involved in building the types of relationships and coalitions essential for social change concerns the issue of individual accountability. Race, class and gender oppression form the structural backdrop against which we frame our relationship—these are the forces that encourage us to substitute voyeurism . . . for fully human relationships. But while we may not have created this situation, we are each responsible for making individual, personal choices concerning which elements of race, class and gender oppression we will accept and which we will work to change.

One essential component of this accountability involves developing empathy for the experiences of individuals and groups different than ourselves. Empathy begins with taking an interest in the facts of other people's lives, both as individuals and as groups. If you care about me, you should want to know not only the details of my personal biography but a sense of how race, class and gender as categories of analysis created the institutional and symbolic backdrop for my personal biography. How can you hope to assess my character without knowing the details of the circumstances I face?

Moreover, by taking a theoretical stance that we have all been affected by race, class and gender as categories of analysis that have structured our treatment, we open up possibilities for using those same constructs as categories of connection in building empathy. For example, I have a good White woman friend with whom I share common interests and beliefs. But we know that our racial differences have provided us with different experiences. So we talk about them. We do not assume that because I am Black, race has only affected me and not her or that because I am a Black woman, race neutralizes the effect of gender in my life while accenting it in hers. We take those same categories of analysis that have created cleavages in our lives, in this case, categories of race and gender, and use them as categories of connection in building empathy for each other's experiences.

Finding common causes and building empathy is difficult, no matter which side of privilege we inhabit. Building empathy from the dominant side of privilege is difficult, simply because individuals from privileged backgrounds are not encouraged to do so. For example, in order for those of you who are White to develop empathy for the experiences of people of color, you must grapple with how your white skin has privileged you. This is difficult to do, because it not only entails the intellectual process of seeing how whiteness is elevated in institutions and symbols, but it also involves the often painful process of seeing how your whiteness has shaped your personal biography. Intellectual stances against the institutional and symbolic dimensions of racism are generally easier to maintain than sustained self-reflection about how racism has shaped all of our individual biographies. Were and are your fathers, uncles, and grandfathers really more capable than mine, or can their accomplishments be explained in part by the racism members of my family experienced? Did your mothers stand silently by and watch all this happen? More importantly, how have they passed on the benefits of their whiteness to you?

These are difficult questions, and I have tremendous respect for my colleagues and students who are trying to answer them. Since there is no compelling reason to examine the source and meaning of one's own privilege, I know that those who do so have freely chosen this stance. They are making conscious efforts to root out the piece of the oppressor planted within them. To me, they are entitled to the support of people of color in their efforts. Men who declare themselves feminists, members of the middle class who ally themselves with anti-poverty struggles, heterosexuals who support gays and lesbians, are all trying to grow, and their efforts place them far ahead of the majority who never think of engaging in such important struggles.

Building empathy from the subordinate side of privilege is also difficult, but for different reasons. Members of subordinate groups are understandably reluctant to abandon a basic mistrust of members of powerful groups because this basic mistrust has traditionall been central to their survival. As a Black woman, it would be foolish for me to assume that White women, or Black men, or White men or any other group with a history of exploiting African-American women have my best interests at heart. These groups enjoy varying amounts of privilege over me and therefore I must carefully watch them and be prepared for a relation of domination and subordination.

Like the privileged, members of subordinate groups must also work toward replacing judgments by category with new ways of thinking and acting. Refusing to do so stifles prospects for effective coalition and social change. Let me use another example from my own experiences. When I was an undergraduate, I had little time or patience for the theorizing of the privileged. My initial years at a private, elite institution were difficult, not because the coursework was challenging (it was, but that wasn't what distracted me) or because I had to work while my classmates lived of family allowances (I was used to work). The adjustment was difficult because I was surrounded by so many people who took their privilege for granted. Most of them felt entitled to their wealth. That astounded me.

I remember one incident watching a White woman down the hall in my dormitory try to pick out which sweater to wear. The sweaters were piled up on her bed in all the colors of the rainbow, sweater after sweater. She asked my advice in a way that let me know that choosing a sweater was on of the most important decisions she had to make on a daily basis. Standing kneedeep in her sweaters, I realized how different our lives were. She did not have to worry about maintaining a solid academic average so that she could receive financial aid. Because she was in the majority, she was not treated as a representative of her race. She did not have to consider how her classroom comments or basic existence on campus contributed to the treatment her group would receive. Her allowance protected her from having to work, so she ws free to spend her time studying, partying, or in her case, worrying about which sweater to wear. The degree of inequality in our lives and her unquestioned sense of entitlement concerning that inequality offended me. For a while, I categorized all affluent White women as being superficial, arrogant, overly concerned with material possessions, and part of my problem. But had I continued to classify people in this way, I would have missed out on making some very good friends whose discomfort with their inherited or acquired social class privileges pushed them to examine their position.

Since I opened with the words of Audre Lorde, it seems appropiate to close with another of her ideas. . . .

Each of us called upon to take a stand. So in these days ahead, as we examie ourselves and each other, our works, our fears, our differences, our sisterhood and survivals, I urge you to tackle what is most difficult for us all, self-scrutiny of our complacencies, the idea that since each of us believes she is one the side of right, she need not examine her position (1985).

I urge you to examine your position.

REFERENCES

1. Acker, Joan. 1994a. The Gender Regime of Swedish Banks. *Scandinavian Journal of Management* 10, no. 2: 117–30.
2. Acker, Joan, and Donald Van Houston. 1974. Differential Recruitment and Control: The Sex Structuring of Organizations. *Administrative Science Quarterly* 19 (June, 1974): 152–63.
3. Amott, Teresa, and Julie Matthaei. 1996. *Race, Gender, and Work: A Multi-cultural Economic History of Women in the United States*. Revised edition. Boston: South End Press.
4. Benería, Lourdes. 1999. Globalization, Gender and the Davos Man. *Feminist Economics* 5, no. 3: 61–83.
5. Bremner, Robert H. 1956. *From the Depths: The Discovery of Poverty in the United States*. New York: New York University Press.
6. Brodkin, Karen. 1998. Race, Class, and Gender: The Metaorganization of American Capitalism. *Transformine Anthropology* 7, no. 2: 46–57.
7. Brown, Michael K., Martin Carnoy, Elliott Currie, Troy Duster, David B. Oppenheimer, Marjorie M. Shultz, and David Wellman. 2003. *White-Washing Race: The Myth of a Color-Blind Society*. Berkeley: University of California Press.
8. Burris, Beverly H. 1996. Technocracy, Patriarchy and Management. In *Men as Managers, Managers as Men*, ed. David L. Collinson and Jeff Hcarn. London: Sage.
9. Cockburn, Cynthia. 1983. *Brothers* London: Pluto Press.
10. _____. 1991. *In the Way of Women: Men's Resistance to Sex Equality in Organization*. Ithaca, N.Y.: ILR Press.
11. Cohn, Samuel. 1985. *The Process of Occupational Sex-Typing: The Femininization of Clerical Labor in Great Britain*, Philadelphia: Temple University Press.
12. Collins, Patricia Hill. 2000. *Black Feminist Thought*, second edition, New York and London: Routledge.
13. Collinson, David L., and Jeff Hearn. 1996. Breaking the Silence: On Men, Masculinities and Managements. In *Men as Managers, Managers as Men*, ed. David L. Collinson and Jeff Hearns. London: Sage.
14. Connell, R. W. 2000. *The Men and the Boys*. Berkeley: University of California Press.
15. _____. 1995. *Masculinities*, Berkeley: University of California Press.
16. _____. 1987. *Gender & Power*, Stanford, Calif.: Stanford University Press.
17. Figart, Deborah M., Ellen Mutarl, and Marilyn Power. 2002. *Living Wages, Equal Wages*. London and New York: Routledge.
18. Foner, Philip S. 1947. *History of the Labor Movement in the United States*. New York: International Publishers.
19. Frankel, Linda. 1984. Southern Textile Women: Generations of Survival and Struggle. In *My Troubles Are Going to Have Trouble with Me*, ed. Karen Brodkin Sacks and Dorothy Remy. New Brunswick, N.J.: Rulgers University Press.

20. Glenn, Evelyn Nakano. 2002. *Unequal Freedom: How Race and Gender Shaped American Citizenship and Labor*. Cambridge: Harvard University Press.

21. Goldin, Claudia. 1990. *Understanding the Gender Gap: An Economic History of American Women*. New York and Oxford: Oxford University Press.

22. Gutman, Herbert G. 1976. *Work, Culture Society in Industrializing America*. New York: Alfred A. Knopf.

23. Hartmann, Heidi. 1976. Capitalism, Patriarchy, and Job Segregation by Sex. *Sigus* 1, no. 3, part 2: 137–69.

24. Hearn, Jeff. 1996. Is Masculinity Dead? A Critique of the Concept of Masculinity/Masculinities. In *Understanding Masculinities: Social Relations and Cultural Arenas*, ed. M. Mac an Ghaill. Buckingham: Oxford University Press.

25. _____. 2004. From Hegomonic Masculinity to the Hegemony of Men. *Feminist Theory* 5, no. 1: 49–72.

26. Hearn, Jeff, and Wendy Parkin. 2001. *Gender, Sexuality and Violence in Organizations*. London: Sage.

27. Janiewski, Dolores. 1996. Southern Honour, Southern Dishonour: Managerial Ideology and the Construction of Gender, Race, and Class Relations in Southern Industry. In *Feminism & History*, ed. Joan Wallach Scott. Oxford: Oxford University Press.

28. Kanter, Rosabeth Moss. 1977. *Men and Women of the Corporation*. New York: Basic Books.

29. Keister, Lisa. 2000. *Wealth in America: Trends in Wealth Inequality*. Cambridge: Cambridge University Press.

30. Kessler-Harris, Alice. 1982. *Out to Work: A History of Wage-Earning Women in the United States*, New York: Oxford University Press.

31. Kilbourne, Barbara, Paula England, and Kurt Beron 1994. Effects of Individual, Occupational, and Industrial Characteristics on Earnings: Intersections of Race and Gender. *Social Forces* 72: 1149–76.

32. McDowell, Linda. 1997. A Tale of Two Cities? Embedded Organizations and Embodied Workers in the City of London. In *Geographies of Economies*, ed. Roger Lee and Jane Willis, 118–29. London: Arnold.

33. Middleton, Chris. 1983. Patriarchal Exploitation and the Rise of English Capitalism. In *Gender, Class and Work*, ed. Eva Gamarnikow, David H. J. Morgan, June Purvis, and Daphne E. Taylorson. London: Heinemann.

34. Milton, David. 1982. *The Politics of U.S. Labor: From the Great Depression to the New Deal*. New York: Monthly Review Press.

35. Omi, Michael, and Howard Winant. 1994. *Racial Formation in the United States*. New York: Routledge.

36. Padavic, Irene, and Barbara Reskin. 2002. *Women and Men at Work*, second edition. Thousand Oaks, Calif.: Pine Forge Press.

37. Perrow, Charles. 2002. *Organizing America*. Princeton and Oxford: Princeton University Press.

38. Read, Rosslyn. 1996. Entrepreneurialism and Paternalism in Australian Management: A Gender Critique of the "Self-Made" Man. In *Men as Managers, Managers as Men*, ed. David L. Collinson and Jeff Hearn. London: Sage.

39. Reskin, Barbara F., Debra B. McBrier, and Julie A. Kmec. 1999. The Determinants and Consequences of Workplace Sex and Race Composition. *Annual Review of Sociology* vol. 25: 335–61.

40. Royster, Deirdre A. 2003. *Race and the Invisible Hand: How White Networks Exclude Black Men from Blue-Collar Jobs*. Berkeley: University of California Press.

41. Seidler, Victor J. 1989. *Rediscovering Masculinity: Renson, Language, and Sexuality*. London and New York: Routledge.

42. Taylor, Paul F. 1992. *Bloody Harlan: The United Mine Workers in Harlan County, Kentucky, 1931–1941*. Lanham, Md.: University Press of America.

43. Wacjman, Judy. 1998. *Managing Like a Man*. Cambridge: Polity Press.

44. Williams, Eric. 1944. *Capitalism and Slavery*. Chapel Hill: University of North Carolina Press.

Toward a Theory of Disability and Gender

Thomas J. Gerschick

Thomas J. Gerschick earned his PhD from the University of Michigan. He is an Associate Professor of Sociology at Illinois State University, where he teaches about social inequality. His research focuses on the intersection of gender and disability, especially how people with disabilities create self-satisfying gender identities. His most recent publication is "Masculinity and the Degrees on Bodily Non-Normativity in Western Culture" in the Handbook of Men and Masculinities *(2004). This essay appeared in* Signs: Journal of Women in Culture and Society *in 2000.*

As feminist theory has developed, scholars increasingly have attended to how gender intersects with other social characteristics, including sexual orientation, class, and race and ethnicity, to shape the perceptions, experiences, and life chances of women and men. More recently, activists and scholars have applied feminist insights, theory, and methods to the intersection of disability and gender.[1] However, comprehensive theories about the relationship between disability and gender remain elusive. This essay contributes to the development of such theory by addressing the following questions: How does disability affect the gendering process? How does it affect the experience of gender? How does having a disability affect women's and men's abilities to enact gender? In what ways are the experiences of women and men with disabilities similar and different?[2]

Developing a theory of disability and gender provides insight into the lives of a large number of people. The U.S. Census Bureau estimates that in 1994 more than 20.6 percent of the U.S. population, or about fifty-four million people, had some level of physical or mental disability; for 9.9 percent of the population, or twenty-six million people, this disability was severe (McNeil 1997, 1).[3] After women, then, people with disabilities represent the largest minority population in the United States. Given that the likelihood of developing a disability increases with age, and given that the baby-boom generation is aging, the proportion of the U.S. population with disabilities will likely continue to increase. Moreover, accounting for the experiences of women and men with disabilities makes feminist theories of gender more inclusive, complex,

---

This essay is dedicated to the memory of Adam S. Miller (1971-99), friend and frequent coauthor. I would like to thank Bob Broad and Georganne Rundblad for their comments on previous drafts of this essay and Ryan Hieronymous for research assistance.
[1]See Fine and Asch 1988; Hillyer 1993; Morris 1993a, 1993b; Gerschick and Miller 1995; Wendell 1996, 1997; Gerschick 1998.
[2]Space limitations necessitate that I focus on disabilities primarily in the United States in this essay. See Lynn and Wilkinson 1993 for a number of international perspectives on women and disability.
[3]McNeil 1997 provides Census Bureau definitions and measures of disability.

and nuanced. Finally, a theory of the relation between gender and disability provides another tool that people with disabilities can use to understand and challenge their oppression.

In order to contextualize the experiences of women and men with physical disabilities, we need to attend to three sets of social dynamics: the stigma assigned to disability, gender as an interactional process, and the importance of the body to enacting gender.

To have a disability is not only a physical or mental condition; it is also a social and stigmatized one (Goffman 1963). As anthropologist Robert Murphy observes, "Stigmatization is less a by-product of disability than its substance. The greatest impediment to a person's taking full part in this society are not his physical flaws, but rather the tissue of myths, fears, and misunderstandings that society attaches to them" (1990, 113). Thus, stigmatization is embedded in the daily interactions between people with disabilities and the temporarily able-bodied.[4] In order to enact gender, people with disabilities must be recognized by others as "appropriately" masculine or feminine (West and Zimmerman 1987). Much is at stake in this process, as one's sense of self rests precariously on others' validation or rejection of one's gender performance. Successful enactment bestows status and acceptance; failure invites embarrassment and humiliation (West and Zimmerman 1987). Thus, people with disabilities are engaged in an asymmetrical power relationship with their temporarily able-bodied counterpars.

Bodies are central to achieving recognition as appropriately gendered beings. Bodies operate socially as canvases on which gender is displayed and kinesthetically as the mechanisms by which it is physically enacted. Thus, the bodies of people with disabilities make them vulnerable to being denied recognition as women and men. The type of disability, its visibility, its severity, and whether it is physical or mental in origin mediate the degree to which the body of a person with a disability is socially compromised. For instance, a severe case of the Epstein-Barr virus can lead to disability; however, typically the condition is not readily apparent and, as a consequence, does not trigger stigmatization and devaluation. Conversely, having quadriplegia and using a wheelchair for mobility is highly visual, is perceived to be severe, and frequently elicits invalidation.[5] Moreover, the degree to which a person with a disability is legitimized or delegitimized is context-specific and has both material and nonmaterial consequences.

Disability affects the gendering process in many ways. My current research suggests that the age of onset combines with the type, severity, and visibility of a person's disability to influence the degree to which she or he is taught and subjected to gendered expectations. As C. West and D. H. Zimmerman (1987) note, no one escapes being gendered, including people with disabilities. However, all people do not experience the same degree and type of gender socialization and expectations. For instance, if an infant has a congenital disability and if that disability is severe, as in the case of spina bifida, parents and others in the infant's social world will assign her or him to sex and gender categories but will likely hold fewer gender expectations than for an infant who has a milder disability, such as a visual impairment. Conversely, when the onset of a disability occurs later in a child's life, she or he already will have experienced a significant amount of gender socialization and internalized many gendered expectations. Thus, her or his struggles for social

---

[4]I intentionally use the term *temporarily able-bodied* to highlight the facts that aging is often disabling and that many of us will develop a disability during our lifetime. In 1994, e.g., the disability rate among the U.S. population ages 65–79 years was 47.3 percent, for those ages 80 years and older, it rose to 71.5 percent (McNeil 1997).

[5]Of course, the degree to which one's body is compromised is also affected by other social characteristics, including race and ethnicity, social class, age, and sexual orientation. Unfortunately, exploring these other characteristics is beyond the scope of this essay.

validation as a woman or man will begin with a different level of awareness and commitment to gender. For people with disabilities, then, gendering is conditional.

Furthermore, theories of gender presume that everyone has the same ability to learn, understand, respond to, and be held accountable for gendered expectations. However, for people with a mental disability, these abilities are compromised to different degrees. For example, a person with profound mental retardation may not be able to comprehend many aspects of gender and consequently would largely be beyond the reach of sanctions, while the same does not hold true for a person with a learning disability. Additionally, mental illness can vary individuals' gender enactment. Kay Redfield Jamison (1995), for instance, eloquently describes how her gender performance varied depending on whether she was manic or depressed.

Although women and men with disabilities share similar experiences of devaluation, isolation, marginalization, and discrimination, their fortunes diverge in important ways. Two stigmatized statuses converge in the lives of women with disabilities, further diminishing their already devalued gender status. As M. Fine and A. Asch note, they experience "sexism without the pedestal" (1988, 1). Conversely, for men with physical disabilities, masculine gender privilege collides with the stigmatized status of having a disability, thereby causing status inconsistency, as having a disability erodes much, but not all, masculine privilege.

Although there is much that we do not know regarding the extent of violence that people with disabilities experience, research suggests that children with disabilities are 70 percent more likely to be physically or sexually abused than their able-bodied counterparts (Crosse, Kaye, and Ratnofsky 1993). This abuse is likely to be chronic rather than episodic and to be perpetuated by someone the victim knows, such as a family member or personal attendant (Sobsey and Doc 1991). Furthermore, this abuse is gendered; females with disabilities are more likely to be sexually assaulted, whereas males with disabilities are more likely to experience other forms of physical abuse (Sobsey, Randall, and Parrila 1997). Thus, having a disability exacerbates one of the worst, most direct elements of oppression.

In the contemporary United States, to be perceived as physically attractive is to be socially and sexually desirable. As a result of their invalidated condition, women and men with disabilities are constrained in their opportunities to nurture and to be nurtured, to be loved and to love, and to become parents if they so desire (Fine and Asch 1988, 13). Writer Susan Hannaford explains, "I discovered on becoming officially defined as 'disabled' that I lost my previous identity as a sexually attractive being" (1985, 17). This dynamic, in addition to being mediated by degree, type, and severity of disability, may also be gendered. For example, Hannaford maintains that women are four times as likely as men to divorce after developing a disability (18) and only one-third to one-fourth as likely to marry (76). Fine and Asch (1988, 12–23) provide a range of supporting evidence. Ironically, this may also mean that women with disabilities are less likely than their able-bodied counterparts to be limited by many of the gendered expectations and roles that feminists have challenged.

Women and men with physical disabilities are also economically more vulnerable than nondisabled people. Among people of working age, women with disabilities are less likely to participate in the labor force than both nondisabled women and men with disabilities. This gap varies by gender and the severity of the disability. For instance, according to the U.S. Census Bureau, nondisabled women's labor force participation rate in 1994 was 74.5 percent. For women with a mild disability, the percentage dropped to 68.4 percent, and it plunged to 24.7 percent for women with severe disabilities. For men, the respective numbers were 89.9 percent, 85.1 percent, and

27.8 percent (McNeil 1997). Women with disabilities are also more susceptible to being tracked into low-wage service-sector jobs.

Similarly, gender and the severity of one's disability affect median monthly earnings. Among women 21–64 years of age in 1994, median monthly earnings were S1,470 among those with no disability, $1,200 among those with a nonsevere disability, and $1,000 among those with a severe disability. Comparable figures for men were $2,190, $1,857, and $1,262 (McNeil 1997). As a consequence, women and men with disabilities are poorer than their able-bodied counterparts, and women with disabilities fare worst of all (LaPlante et al. 1999).

In brief summary, disability has a profound effect on the material and nonmaterial experience of gender. Yet, there is still much we do not know about this dynamic: How and under what conditions do social characteristics such as race, class, age, and sexual orientation further mediate the relationship between gender and disability? How does gender affect the experience of disability? How do the dynamics identified in this essay vary by culture in a global context? How might the stigmatization and marginalization that women and men with disabilities face contribute to the creation of alternative gender identities? As we enter a new millennium, I encourage the readers of *Signs* to take up these questions and to add further inquiries of their own so that we can soon develop more comprehensive theories about the relationship between disability and gender.

REFERENCES

Crosse, S. B., E. Kaye, and A. C. Ratnofsky. 1993. *Report on the Maltreatment of Children with Disabilities.* Washington, D.C.: National Center on Child Abuse and Neglect.

Fine, M., and A. Asch. 1988. "Introduction: Beyond Pedestals." In *Women with Disabilities: Essays in Psychology, Culture, and Politics*, ed. M. Fine and A. Asch, 1–37. Philadelphia: Temple University Press.

Gerschick, T. J. 1998. "Sisyphus in a Wheelchair: Men with Physical Disabilities Confront Gender Domination." In *Everyday Inequalities: Critical Inquiries*, ed. J. O'Brien and J. A. Howard, 189–211. Oxford: Blackwell.

Gerschick, T. J., and A. S. Miller. 1995. "Coming to Terms: Masculinity and Physical Disability." In *Men's Health and Illness: Gender, Power, and the Body*, 183–204. Thousand Oaks, Calif.: Sage.

Goffman, E. 1963. *Stigma: Notes on the Management of Spoiled Identity.* New York: Touchstone.

Hannaford, S. 1985. *Living Outside Inside: A Disabled Woman's Experience.* Berkeley, Calif.: Canterbury.

Hillyer, B. 1993. *Feminism and Disability.* Norman: University of Oklahoma Press.

Jamison, K. R. 1995. *An Unquiet Mind.* New York: Knopf.

LaPlante, M. P., J. Kennedy, H. S. Kaye, and B. L. Wenger. 1999. *Disability and Employment.* Available on-line at http://dsc.ucsf.edu/default.html.

Lynn, M., and S. Wilkinson, eds. 1993. "Women and Disability," special issue of *Canadian Woman Studies*, vol. 13, no. 4.

McNeil, J. M. 1997. *Americans with Disabilities, 1994–95.* Current Population Report No. P70-61. Washington, D.C.: Bureau of the Census.

Morris, J. 1993a. "Feminism and Disability." *Feminist Review*, no. 43 (Spring): 57–70.

———. 1993b. "Gender and Disability." In *Disabling Barriers—Enabling Environments*, ed. J. Swain, V. Finkelstein, S. French, and M. Oliver, 85–92. Thousand Oaks, Calif.: Sage.

Murphy, R. F. 1990. *The Body Silent.* New York: Norton.

Sobsey, D., and T. Doe. 1991. "Patterns of Sexual Abuse and Assault." *Sexuality and Disability* 9(3):243–59.

Sobsey, D., W. Randall, and R. K. Parrila. 1997. "Gender Differences in Abused Children with and without Disabilities." *Child Abuse and Neglect* 21(8):707–20.

Wendell, S. 1996. *The Rejected Body: Feminist Philosophical Reflections on Disability.* New York: Routledge.

_____. 1997. "Toward a Feminist Theory of Disability." In *The Disability Studies Reader,* ed. L. Davis, 260–78. New York: Routledge.

West, C., and D. H. Zimmerman. 1987. "Doing Gender." *Gender & Society* 1(2):125–51.

SECTION II

Discourses of Gender

Key Concepts for Section II: Discourses of Gender

Chronotype
Content Analysis
Cult of True Womanhood
Cultural Context
Dehumanization
Dreamworld
Discourse
Emphasized Femininity
Filmic techniques from *Dreamworlds*
Gaze
Hegemonic Masculinity
Ideology
Infantilization
Male Gaze
Meaning
Media Activism
Media Literacy
Metaphor
Motif
Objectification
Pink Think
Popular Culture
Pornographic Imagination
Problem with No Name
Rhetorical Triangle
Sexual Object
Sexual Subject
Symbol
Theme
Tough Guise
Tropes

Concepts to Review

Ageism
Androcentrism
Classism
Dichotomy/Dichotomous
Doing Gender
Dominance/Domination
Double Standards
Femininity/Femininities
Gender
Heterosexism
Homophobia
Internalized Oppression
Intersectionality
Marginalization
Masculinity/Masculinities
Misogyny
Mythical Norm
Oppression
Power
Privilege
Racism
Sex
Sex-Gender System
Sexism
Socialization
Subordinance/Subordination
Tokenism

Pink Think 101

Lynn Peril

Lynn Peril is an essayist. She earned an M.A. in History with a concentration in Gender from San Francisco State University. In her research and writing, she focuses on gender prescriptions in historical popular culture. Her column "The Museum of Femoribilia," appears in Bust *magazine. She has written two books* College Girls: Bluestockings, Sex Kittens and Coeds, Then and Now *(2006) and* Pink Think: Becoming a Woman in Many Uneasy Lessons *(2002) from which this essays comes.*

AN INTRODUCTION

Long before it's time for Mom to help plan the wedding dress or Dad to give the bride away, it's time to be raising a future wife in your home. Because wives aren't born—they are made. Your daughter is born a female, but she has to learn how to be feminine.

CONSTANCE J. FOSTER, *"Raise Your Girl to Be a Wife,"* Parents *magazine*, 1956

The full-page ad that graced women's magazines in 1958 was so discreet as to be mysterious: a pink-suited socialite posed atop San Francisco's Russian Hill, while her servants carried a bevy of pink gift-wrapped boxes from her car to her fashionable apartment building. "Pink is a very special mood" read the large and flowing type beneath the picture. One had to investigate the smaller print to discover that the ad was for "Serena, the luxury sanitary napkin" by Modess. In addition to its other fancy attributes, Serena was "softly pink to please" the most discriminating woman, its pastel color as much an homage to femininity as the use to which it was put. Serena was not the only pink pad to grace drugstore shelves: the "soft pink covering" on Kotex's Miss Deb napkins made sixties-era preteens "feel feminine and dainty—just the way a young lady wants to feel."

With such strong associations between femininity and the color pink, it may come as a surprise to discover that pink was not originally considered a "girl color" at all. Until the nineteenth century, most babies wore white; and if baby clothing incorporated color, boys were just as likely to wear pink as girls. The identification of girls with pink and boys with blue was apparently a French innovation, the exact origins of which remain unclear.[1] It soon found its way into popular culture on this side of the Atlantic, however. In 1868, Louisa May Alcott included a scene in her phenomenally

---

[1] Valerie Steele, "Appearance and Identity," in *Men and Women: Dressing the Part*, Claudia Brush Kidwell and Valerie Steele, eds. (Washington, D.C.: Smithsonian Institution Press, 1989), 15.

successful novel *Little Women* wherein Amy March (the artsy sister, remember?) puts "a blue ribbon on the boy and a pink on the girl, French fashion," to differentiate between newborn twins.[2] But color-coding babies pink and blue according to their gender didn't become widespread until the post–World War II baby boom, when the arbitrary color assignment of a century or so before turned into a new mass habit and established a modern "fact." By the time a 1952 series of poise and beauty booklets called *The Charming Woman* urged readers to "Ask yourself why a baby has to wear pink and blue," its answer suggested that the conflation of color and gender sprang directly from the womb: "[T]hese are the young delicate colors which actually *look like* the baby."[3]

There's more to the story of pink than baby booties and blankets. A 1948 fad among coeds for pink Brooks Brothers shirts assumed such proportions that a year later the venerable menswear retailer began manufacturing a version specifically for women. The new shirt was only slightly modified from the original (or, as a *New Yorker* article smirkingly noted, "the body of the shirt is—ah—fuller") and immediately clicked with the college crowd.[4]

The shirt craze was just the tip of the iceberg, however. The sight of so many girls and women clamoring for that particular item, cash clenched in sweaty fists, buoyed the hope of manufacturers everywhere. Then again, maybe we were simply a nation literally "in the pink" with postwar prosperity, giddy that the war was over and ready for some serious shopping. Responding to the resounding demand of consumers, pink products became more and more visible in magazine ads and on the shelves of all manner of stores. Did you want to coordinate an outfit around your Brooks Brothers shirt? Start from the inside out with a Playtex "Pink-Ice" girdle, packaged in a "slim, shimmering pink tube." It was guaranteed to be both "cool as a frosty drink" and "invisible beneath your briefest swimsuit"—though a look at the size of the garment quickly confirms that "brief was a relative term. Were you tired of your antiseptic hospital-white kitchen and bathroom? Then the newly popular pastel lines of appliances and plumbing fixtures were for you! Little did pink-crazed shoppers realize they'd actually been available since the late 1920s.

It was Mamie Eisenhower's passion for pink that brought the color a new prominence. From the rhinestone-spattered, pink silk ball gown she wore to hubby Ike's inaugural in 1953 to the decor of her White House boudoir and vacation cabin, Mamie surrounded herself with a pale shade soon marketed as "First Lady Pink." A few short years later, Americans were in the throes of what can only be described as pinkmania. Pink-besotted consumers could purchase pastel products ranging from pots, pans, and hand mixers to automobiles and golf balls. Housewives washed their Tickled Pink cups and plates in Dreft, a dishwashing powder that turned the water a gentle shade of pink while leaving the suds a fluffy white. Up-to-date gals got "fashion's fresh, young 'in the pink' look" by using one of three shades of Pond's powdered makeup, each available in an "adorable pink Date Case." A 1955 fashion layout devoted to Pink Party Dresses got to the heart of the color's appeal: "It makes the stag line giddy, it's the toast of gala occasions . . . and it's a legitimate feminine wile."[5]

TURNING PINK INTO PINK THINK

From the moment she's wrapped in a pink blanket, long past the traumatic birthday when she realizes her age is greater than her bust measurement, the human female is bombarded with advice on how to wield those feminine wiles. This advice ranges from rather vague proscriptions

[2]Louisa May Alcott, *Little Women* (Boston: Little, Brown and Company, 1898), 313.

[3]"How to Wear Hats," by Mr. John, in *The Charming Woman*, No. 10, Helen Fraser, ed. (New York: The Charming Woman, Inc., 1950, 1952), 300.

[4]"For Women Only," *The New Yorker*, September 17, 1949, 26–27.

[5]"Pink Party Dresses," *Tempo & Quick*, July 18, 1955, 46–47.

along the lines of "nice girls don't chew gum/swear/wear pants/fill-in-the-blank," to obsessively elaborate instructions for daily living. How many women's lives, for example, were enriched by former Miss America Jacque Mercer's positively baroque description of the proper way to put on a bathing suit, as it appeared in her guide *How to Win a Beauty Contest* (1960)?

> [F]irst, roll it as you would a girdle. Pull the suit over the hips to the waist, then, holding the top away from your body, bend over from the waist. Ease the suit up to the bustline and with one hand, lift one breast up and in and ease the suit bra over it. Repeat on the other side. Stand up and fasten the straps.[6]

Instructions like these made me bristle. I formed an early aversion to all things pink and girly. It didn't take me long to figure out that many things young girls were supposed to enjoy, not to mention ways they were supposed to behave, left me feeling funny—as if I was expected to pound my square peg self into the round hole of designated girliness. I didn't know it at the time, but the butterflies in my tummy meant I had crested the first of many hills on the roller coaster ride of femininity—or, as I soon referred to it, the other f-word. Before I knew what was happening, I was hurtling down its track, seemingly out of control, and screaming at the top of my lungs.

After all, look what I was up against. The following factoids of femininity date from the year of my birth (hey, it wasn't *that* long ago):

- In May of 1961, Betsy Martin McKinney told readers of *Ladies' Home Journal* that, for women, sexual activity commenced with intercourse and was completed with pregnancy and childbirth. Therefore, a woman who used contraceptives denied "her own creativity, her own sexual role, her very femininity." Furthermore, McKinney asserted that "one of the most stimulating predisposers to orgasm in a woman may be childbirth followed by several months of lactation." (Mmm, yes, must be the combination of episiotomy and sleep deprivation that does it.) Politely avoiding personal examples, she neglected to mention how many little McKinneys there were.
- During the competition for the title of Miss America 1961, five finalists were given two questions to answer. First they were asked what they would do if "you were walking down the runway in the swimsuit competition, and a heel came off one of your shoes?" The second question, however, was a bit more esoteric: "Are American women usurping males in the world, and are they too dominant?" Eighteen-year-old Nancy Fleming, of Montague, Michigan, agreed that "there are too many women working in the world. A woman's place is in the home with her husband and children." This, along with her pragmatic answer to the first question ("I would kick off both shoes and walk barefooted") and her twenty-three-inch waist (tied for the smallest in pageant history), helped Nancy win the crown.
- In 1961, toymaker Transogram introduced a new game for girls called Miss Popularity ("The True American Teen"), in which players competed to see who could accrue the most votes from four pageant judges—three of whom were male. Points were awarded for such attributes as nice legs, and if the judges liked a contestant's figure, voice, and "type." The prize? A special "loving" cup, of course! Who, after all, could love an unpopular girl?

These are all prime examples of "pink think." Pink think is a set of ideas and attitudes about what constitutes proper female behavior; a groupthink that was consciously or not adhered to by advice writers, manufacturers of toys and other consumer products, experts in many walks of life, and the public at large, particularly during the years spanning the mid-twentieth century—but

---

[6]Quoted in Frank De Ford, *There She Is: The Life and Times of Miss America* (New York: The Viking Press, 1971), 72.

enduring even into the twenty-first century. Pink think assumes there is a standard of behavior to which all women, no matter their age, race, or body type, must aspire. "Femininity" is sometimes used as a code word for this mythical standard, which suggests that women and girls are always gentle, soft, delicate, nurturing beings made of "sugar and spice and everything nice." But pink think is more than a stereotyped vision of girls and women as poor drivers who are afraid of mice and snakes, adore babies and small dogs, talk incessantly on the phone, and are incapable of keeping secrets. Integral to pink think is the belief that one's success as a woman is grounded in one's allegiance to such behavior. For example, a woman who fears mice isn't necessarily following the dictates of pink think. On the other hand, a woman who isn't afraid of mice but pretends to be because she thinks such helplessness adds to her appearance of femininity is toeing the pink think party line. When you hear the words "charm" or "personality" in the context of successful womanhood, you can almost always be sure you're in the presence of pink think.

While various self-styled "experts" have been advising women on their "proper" conduct since the invention of the printing press, the phenomenon defined here as pink think was particularly pervasive from the 1940s to the 1970s. These were fertile years for pink think, a cultural mindset and consumer behavior rooted in New Deal prosperity yet culminating with the birth of women's liberation. During this time, pink think permeated popular books and magazines aimed at adult women, while little girls absorbed rules of feminine behavior while playing games like the aforementioned Miss Popularity. Meanwhile, prescriptions for ladylike dress, deportment, and mindset seeped into child-rearing manuals, high school home economics textbooks, and guides for bride, homemaker, and career girl alike.

It was almost as if the men and women who wrote such books viewed proper feminine behavior as a panacea for the ills of a rapidly changing modern world. For example, myriad articles in the popular press devoted to the joys of housewifery helped coerce Rosie the Riveter back into the kitchen when her hubby came home from the war and expected his factory job back. During the early cold war years, some home economics texts seemed to suggest that knowing how to make hospital corners and a good tuna casserole were the only things between Our Way of Life and communist incursion. It was patriotic to be an exemplary housewife. And pink-thinking experts of the sixties and seventies, trying to maintain this ideal, churned out reams of pages that countered the onrushing tide of both the sexual revolution and the women's movement. If only all women behaved like our Ideal Woman, the experts seemed to say through the years, then everything would be fine.

You might even say that the "problem with no name" that Betty Friedan wrote about in *The Feminine Mystique* (1963) was a virulent strain of pink-thinkitis. After all, according to Friedan, "the problem" was in part engendered by the experts' insistence that women "could desire no greater destiny than to glory in their own femininity"—a pink think credo.

"Let's Face It"

Pink think assumed not only that the "average American woman" was Caucasian but that those who weren't white aspired to be. This was especially apparent in *Let's Face It,* a 1959 "Guide to Good Grooming for Negro Girls." While some of the book's illustrations portrayed girls with vaguely African-American features, other sketches might well have come from any other guide aimed at white teens. Juxtaposed over chapter titles that appealed directly to the reader herself ("The Clothes You Wear," "The Way You Act"), the images strongly suggested that the way "you" wanted to be was white.

BECOMING A WOMAN IN MANY UNEASY LESSONS

Pink think was, and remains, an active agent in the lives of many women who internalized its contradictory messages and struggled to meet its illusory goals. Even I, a pants-wearing, dress-hating tomboy, was not immune to its tyranny. Miss Popularity and Miss America failed to imprint a big pink "G"-for-girl on my forehead, but still, trying to hold myself up to the rigid standards of pink think caused me no end of distress.

Long Before Pink Think, There Was True Womanhood

Experts have long expounded on what makes an ideal woman. As defined by historian Barbara Welter in an influential 1966 essay, the True Woman was a nineteenth-century paradigm of feminine virtues described in women's magazines, gift annuals, religious literature, and cookbooks.

The True Woman was pious. Not only was she responsible for her own spiritual life, but her "purifying, passionless love" could bring "an erring man back to Christ."[*] She was pure and virtuous. "Sit not with another in a place that is too narrow; read not out of the same book; let not your eagerness to see anything induce you to place your head close to another person's," wrote Mrs. Eliza Farrar in *The Young Lady's Friend* (1842).[†]

Above all, she was submissive. Welter quoted a Mrs. Sandford on the subject of womanly self-abnegation: "A really sensible woman feels her dependence. She does what she can, but she is conscious of inferiority...."[‡] Finally, she cherished the domestic state. As Mrs. S. E. Farley wrote in 1846, "the true dignity and beauty of the female character seem to consist in a right understanding and faith and cheerful performance of social and family duties."[§]

According to Welter, the "cult of True Womanhood" flourished from 1820 to 1860. But as one contemplates twentieth-century pink think, it's obvious that the True Woman has had a long-lasting influence.

[*] Barbara Welter, "The Cult of True Womanhood," *American Quarterly* 18 (Summer 1966), 153.
[†] Ibid., 155.
[‡] Ibid., 159.
[§] Ibid., 162.

It all started with an incident in kindergarten when we girls made Easter bonnets out of paper plates and fabric scraps. My mom's contribution to the project was a couple of yards of pink net leftover from a beautiful Barbie ball gown she had made a few weeks before. I imagined a beautiful hat with the net covering my face, and tried my best to convey this desire to the adult in charge of the pointy scissors and stapler. I don't remember why I wanted a veil, an item of apparel generally associated with nuns and widows—perhaps pink think had already compromised my fashion sense. More likely, I had seen a veiled woman on the street and wanted to claim some of her mysterious sophistication for myself. But the word "veil" was not yet in my vocabulary, and the resulting monstrosity resembled nothing so much as a puffy pink cloud. Instead of a veil, the hat sported a couple of fake violets the scissors lady had thrown in for good measure. I was mortified. And when one of my teachers referred to me and my hideous hat as "dainty," I resolved I would never be that again—whatever it meant.

Over thirty years have passed since that unfortunate incident, and I have grown up to be many things, but dainty sure as hell isn't one of them. Instead, inspired by the many absurdities and contradictions of pink think, I have become a connoisseur and collector of what *Bust* magazine editor Debbie Stoller describes as "femoribilia": books, games, and other objects infused with pink think expectations and proscriptions—what an anthropologist might call the material culture of femininity.

Some of these artifacts are easy to spot, even by amateurs. Would anyone really disagree that a certain eleven-and-a-half-inch fashion doll packs a pink think wallop with her pneumatic breasts, minuscule waist, and pointed feet just waiting for tiny stiletto heels? Other objects are more subtle in their approach—the box for a Modess sanitary belt, for example.[7] Not only does the little pink box contain a remnant of an age gone by, it features a photo of a statuesque beauty, elegantly coiffed and gowned in pink. In her gloved hand she holds a feather fan (which uncannily resembles a giant pink mop head), and she stands against an ethereal painted backdrop of grand stairway and chandelier. In short, she is a picture of poised perfection even while having her period. "You there," the little box seems to say, "you in the baggy jeans and the stained underpants, you too could be this woman. In fact, you *should* be this woman. She isn't bothered by cramps or swollen with bloat, and she certainly didn't throw the toilet brush at her husband or boyfriend this morning in a fit of PMS-induced frenzy. What's wrong with you? Buy me, and be like her." The belt itself is—of course!—a tender shade of pink.

My own collection of femoribilia started with the purchase of a 1962 text called *Health and Safety for Teen-Agers* in a Seattle used-book store. Its cover featured wonderful mid-century modern graphics and typography, as well as a photo of two studious teens conscientiously poring over a textbook. Tucked inside were plastic transparencies of the human body—the kind that always reminded me of the cadaver slices on display at Chicago's Museum of Science and Industry, which amazed and terrified me as a little girl. What delighted me now were the book's beautiful, color-saturated illustrations of stylishly dressed teens in vintage clothing, every last one of them beset by either the quaintest of problems ("I'm not sure how to act at a class party") or the smarmiest of personalities ("Our group has prepared a summary of our best ideas about how you can learn to concentrate. We'll have copies mimeographed later so each of you can have one").

It was the section devoted to dating do's and don'ts that really rang my bell, as it carefully outlined behavior for both girls and boys. "As a rule, a girl does not ask a boy for a date—even though she would very much like to do so." "When you are 'eating out' on a date, the girl's order is always given first." Such regulations seemed absolutely bizarre, especially since my own experiences with a long line of musician boyfriends rather uncomfortably resembled the book's examples of dating don'ts. After a long day at work, I found it comforting to follow along with "Dick" and "Gretchen" as they bumbled their way through an ice-skating date, or commiserate with "Vic Schultz," who "became very much discouraged" a few weeks after his transfer to Lake High School. When I found an old home economics textbook in a thrift store several weeks later I bought it immediately. Chock-full of antiquated instructions on cooking, sewing, and clean living, the book mesmerized me with its audacious assumptions about female behavior. I was hooked. Before I knew it, I was actively seeking out items that were prime examples of pink think pedantry.

During the golden age of pink think, the ideal of femininity was so deeply interwoven in the American psyche that even seemingly genderless items were marketed specifically to women. By simply affixing the word "lady" in front of its product's name, a manufacturer created a whole

---

[7]For those too young or of the wrong sex to remember, a sanitary belt was an elastic device worn around the waist from which dangled, fore and aft, two metal clips to hold your sanitary napkin in place. They were an uncomfortable yet necessary nuisance, one which women eagerly abandoned in the early 1970s when self-stick pads became available.

new set of expectations. For example, according to a 1962 catalogue, Papermate's Lady Capri pen had a soft pastel finish and was "practical for women who demand heavy duty pen elegance." Other Papermate Capri pens were guaranteed to write over greasy spots. But only the "completely feminine" Lady Capri could write—elegantly, one surmises—"even over cold cream," just the thing for the gal hastily scribbling down important phone numbers during her nightly beauty ritual.

With some products, though, manufacturers went even further to impress feminine suitability on the public. Razors and shaving were by and large considered the domain of men, despite the fact that women, too, had been removing their unwanted hair since time immemorial. So when Norelco introduced a new product in the early 1960s, it went for the one-two punch of feminizing prefix plus color: no one could possibly mistake a woman's pastel pink Lady Norelco for the more "masculine" (i.e., beige) version sold to her husband.

Using the color pink as a symbol of femininity didn't work as well for the Lionel Toy Company in 1957, when, hankering after a whole new group of consumers, it tried to market a toy train to little girls. Their solution—and imagine, if you will, the board meetings that led up to this decision—was to manufacture a train identical in all respects to their regular models, except for its color. After all, how could it lose? The Lady Lionel featured not only real smoke and a working headlight, but what the company's 1958 catalogue referred to as "a beautiful pink frosted locomotive." The rest of the train was done up in the equally "fashion-right" colors of robin's egg blue and buttercup yellow. The boys in marketing assumed that girls would flock to the color pink like moths to a flame, but sales were meager. The pink train was in production for only two years—leading, of course, to its present-day status as a highly valued collectible.

What worked for products also worked for people. The color pink could always be trusted to help those women engaged in activities not traditionally associated with their gender to maintain an aura of femininity. Donna Mae Mims, a driver who won a Sports Car Club of America National Championship in 1964, dubbed herself the "Pink Lady." She drove a pink Austin Healey Sprite with the words "Think Pink" emblazoned on the rear deck, and wore pink coveralls and a pink crash helmet. Ms. Mims may have had the audacity to compete against men and win, but pink helped to deflect criticism and reminded observers that she was, at heart, a girl like any other. (Her appearances in a provocative men's magazine, *The Millionaire*, didn't hurt either.)

THE PATRON SAINT OF PINK THINK

Perhaps no one used the color pink as effectively as fifties movie star and patron saint of pink think, Jayne Mansfield. "Pink was my color," she later reflected, "because it made me happy":

> [Pink] is bright and gay. "Mansfield pink" will become famous, I'd tell anyone who called it "Mansfield Madness." Now I had something to intrigue the photographers. Come up for a drink and paint me pink. I'd invite anyone who had a camera. I'd add I would be happy to pose for any layouts they'd like. I was desperate.[8]

But not for long. As her star rose in the Hollywood firmament, she indulged her penchant often. She owned a pink Jaguar and was married in a skin-tight pink lace gown. Her Sunset Boulevard home was called the "Pink Palace" in honor of its decorating scheme. When Mansfield invited all and sundry to a party celebrating her new pink swimming pool, it was filled to the brim with pink champagne for the occasion. But pink was more than a chromatic theme for Mansfield. It was a visual shorthand for her ideas of femininity and female sexuality. "Men want

---

[8]Guus Luuters and Gerard Timmer, *Sexbomb: The Life and Death of Jayne Mansfield* (Secaucus, N.J.: Citadel Press), 114.

women to be pink, helpless and do a lot of deep breathing," she advised. "If a girl has curviness, exciting lips and a certain breathlessness, it helps. And it won't do a bit of harm if she has a kittenish, soft cuddly quality."[9]

Eventually, however, Mansfield was trapped by this very philosophy. Losing her bikini top was a playful way of calling attention to her sexy self. But ten years later an unending series of broken bra straps, split dresses and errant boobs that leapt out when least expected seemed pathetic and, worse yet from Mansfield's publicity-loving point of view, boring. As Mansfield biographer Martha Saxon pointed out, there was a sea change in attitudes toward female sexuality from the not-before-you're-married 1950s to the Pill-fueled coffee-tea-or-me 1960s, and Mansfield's leering, innuendo-filled approach to sex was passé before she knew what hit her.[10]

Mansfield clung to the precepts of pink think even as they proved a shaky scaffold for public acceptance. Yet her instincts were unerring in at least one way: surrounding herself with the color pink was an effective confirmation of her hyper-feminine status. Mansfield, of course, pushed femininity far past its natural boundaries. A frequently married mother of five, there was little question of her public devotion to women's most traditional roles. But even her beloved pink couldn't help her out when Mr. Blackwell, naming her as one of the worst dressed women of 1964, called her a "stuffed sausage" whose "baby pink look—the baby doll shorties and darling pink bows for her multicolored hair"—was more suitable for her young daughter. No one came to Mansfield's defense when Paul McCartney, riding high on the Beatles' successes of 1965, called her "an old bag" right in the middle of a Playboy interview.[11] It was, after all, only what everybody else had been thinking for years. Mansfield was only thirty-four in June 1967, when she was reputedly decapitated in a horrendous car wreck on her way from a nightclub engagement.

A Few Helpful Words from the Patron Saint of Pink Think

The following rules to "help a girl be physically attractive" are listed in *Jayne Mansfield's Wild, Wild World* (1963):

1. Yes, think sexy, that is important. It makes you walk, talk and be sexier.
2. Dress sexy—not obvious, but teasing.
3. Create sexy incidents and conversations. Again not obvious but subtle. [Of course, subtlety—just what Jayne was known for!]
4. Be careful who you are with and where. They are your frame.
5. Never hurry.
6. Work towards good health.
7. Stay away from competition that's too rugged.
8. Learn all you can about the subject of being attractive.
9. Use artificial devices if necessary.
10. If you build a better man-trap, you'll catch a better man.

---

[9]Martha Saxon, *Jayne Mansfield and the American Fifties* (Boston: Houghton Mifflin, 1975), 98.
[10]Ibid., xv–xvi.
[11]Ibid., 180, 177.

FEMININITY: THE OTHER F-WORD

One of pink think's supreme ironies is that even so-called experts couldn't agree on what constituted femininity—while all the while they preached the imminent fall of western civilization if women wore pants on the street. Not that femininity has ever been easy to define. Even a 1987 dictionary I consulted fell into pink think when it followed up its definition of feminine ("having qualities characteristic of or suitable to women") with the words "gentle, delicate, etc."

When it came right to down to it, women in the golden age of pink think were bombarded from all sides with conflicting advice. Consider, for example, the origin of femininity. Was it something women were born with or something learned as they grew up? Teen advice doyenne Evelyn Millis Duvall briefly touched on both sides of this question in her *Facts of Life and Love for Teenagers*, a teen advice classic that went into multiple editions throughout the 1950s and 1960s. My copy is a pink-and-black beauty from 1957, but you'll find one at your neighborhood thrift or used-book store with little difficulty. Duvall wrote:

> Girls are born female. Nature endows girls with the physical potentialities of becoming women. The basic physical characteristics that make girls forever different from boys and women different from men . . . these things are her essential *femaleness.*
>
> *Femininity*, on the other hand, is learned. Most of what goes into making a woman act and behave and feel like a woman is learned as she grows up—as a little girl, as a budding young woman, and as the mature, full-grown woman.[12]

Of course, Duvall was not immune to pink think (among other things, she advised menstruating girls to "Dress just a little more prettily [and] smile a little wider than usual"), but her definition got straight to what she thought was the crux of the matter: femininity needed to be learned.

Conversely, *Good Housekeeping* magazine told readers in a 1960 article called "How to Know When You're Really Feminine" that the "grass-roots fact about woman [on] which experts agree" was that her psychology was based firmly on her biology. According to one of the fourteen specialists in feminine behavior consulted by *Good Housekeeping*, woman's real character was by nature "womb-centered"—a description that brings to mind the pesky wandering uterus held responsible for so many female troubles centuries before *Good Housekeeping*'s panel reached its conclusions. At any rate, women couldn't avoid being feminine any more than they could avoid blood pressure or urine production.

Whether they thought femininity innate or learned, the experts agreed that proper feminine behavior required constant, vigilant reinforcement. Women who didn't follow the experts' rules—whether through inattention or wanton disregard—were often assigned to the gulag of gender nonconformity as malcontents and deviants. *Good Housekeeping*'s experts darkly hinted at the unnamed "emotional penalty" paid by women who tried to avoid their biological destiny. Juvenile delinquency and lesbianism were but two of the outcomes for women (if you could even call them that) who ignored the standards of femininity. Even married women who were otherwise impeccably feminine in their appearance and behavior could become suspect if they didn't "fulfill" their sexuality by bearing children. The key to avoiding such tragedies, of course, was found between the covers of the latest guides to charm, beauty, and personality.

---

[12]Evelyn Millis Duvall, *Facts of Life and Love for Teen-Agers* (New York: Association Press, 1956), 27–28.

ALWAYS ASK A MAN

Red-haired former B-movie actress (*Journey to the Center of the Earth*) Arlene Dahl is perhaps best known as the mother of Fabio-like studmuffin Lorenzo Lamas, but she was also a firm believer in the "delicacy and refinement" of female behavior. "Shocked" at the discovery that some women dressed for themselves or other women and not for men, Dahl wrote *Always Ask a Man*, a 1965 beauty guide and pink think classic. Beauty for beauty's sake served no purpose, Dahl maintained. Instead, her book was for women who longed "to be beautiful for and be loved by a man." To that end, she cautioned women against wearing pants; men "with few exceptions . . . do not like them." As for cosmetics, Dahl wore "a touch of lipstick to bed . . . a pale peach or pink to match my sheets." Perhaps there's truth to the rumor that husband Fernando Lamas never saw her naked face during their marriage.

Ladylike behavior was at least as important as, if not more so than, ladylike appearance. Dahl laid down some specific rules (emphasis is hers):

> NEVER upstage a man. Don't top his joke even if you have to bite your tongue to keep from doing it. Never launch loudly into your own opinions on a subject—whether it's petunias or politics . . .
>
> If you don't give a man a chance to look after you, he'll soon give up and let you look after yourself! Men have a naturally protective attitude about women, so don't keep trying to prove how self-sufficient you are.
>
> Keep your femininity in focus and you can overcome all handicaps. Let yourself be frankly and fabulously female and you'll have men fighting for your smiles. Remember the secret ingredient of fascination—*femininity*.

Among the many celebrities whose thoughts on femininity Dahl went on to quote, the professionally tan George Hamilton had the most—ahem—interesting take on the subject: "A woman is often like a strip of film—obliterated, insignificant—until a man puts the light behind her." Beginning to get the picture?

As we shall see in the coming pages, the pink think of the 1940s to 1970s held that femininity was necessary for catching and marrying a man, which was in turn a prerequisite for childbearing—the ultimate feminine fulfillment. This resulted in little girls playing games like Mystery Date long before they were ever interested in boys. It made home economics a high school course and college major, and suggested a teen girl's focus should be on dating and getting a boyfriend. It made beauty, charm, and submissive behavior of mandatory importance to women of all ages in order to win a man's attention and hold his interest after marriage. It promoted motherhood and housewifery as women's only meaningful career, and made sure that women who worked outside the home brought "feminine charm" to their workplaces lest a career make them too masculine.

Not that pink think resides exclusively alongside antimacassars and 14.4 modems in the graveyard of outdated popular culture. Shoes, clothing, and movie stars may go in and out of style with astounding rapidity, but attitudes have an unnerving way of hanging around long after they've outlived their usefulness—even if they never had any use to begin with.

How Do You Rate as a Girl?

What's your pink appeal? Take this simple test, courtesy of the February 1960 issue of *Seventeen* magazine. (My score? Let's just say there's room for improvement.)

1. Do you wait for a boy to open a car door, even though you both know you are quite capable of managing it yourself?
2. Do you listen responsively to a story you have heard before rather than squash the pleasure of the boy who is telling it?

3. If you are going to the movies with another girl, do you look presentable enough to cope with an unexpected encounter?
4. If your bureau drawers or closets were open to view without warning, could you stand the inspection without apologies?
5. In a serious discussion which includes both sexes, can you keep from being overpowering even though you know a great deal on the subject?
6. If a boy forgets his manners, can you restrain yourself from correcting him?
7. Are you able to refuse a kiss without hurting a boy's pride and sending him home in a huff?
8. If that special boy told you he liked your long hair, would you keep it long to please him?
9. Have you the courage to be nice to a boy whom the other girls consider a bore?
10. In stores, are you apt to moon over pretty lingerie and perfume?

Scoring: Seven or more yeses: you are a veritable flower of femininity! Five to seven yeses: there are a few thorns. Under five: ouch!

The Male Consumer as Loser
Beer and Liquor Ads in Mega Sports Media Events

Michael A. Messner
Jeffrey Montez de Oca

Michael Messner is a Professor of Sociology and Gender Studies at the University of Southern California. Messner's primary research is in the social construction of gender and sport. His most recent book is It's All For the Kids: Gender, Families and Youth Sports *(2009).* **Jeffrey Montez de Oca** *is a Visiting Assistant Professor of Sociology at Franklin and Marshall College. He earned his PhD at the University of Southern California. His research is focused on sport during the cold war period. This essay appeared in* Signs: Journal of Women in Culture and Society *in 2005.*

The historical development of modern men's sport has been closely intertwined with the consumption of alcohol and with the financial promotion and sponsorship provided by beer and liquor producers and distributors, as well as pubs and bars (Collins and Vamplew 2002). The beer and liquor industry plays a key economic role in commercialized college and professional sports (Zimbalist 1999; Sperber 2000). Liquor industry advertisements heavily influence the images of masculinity promoted in sports broadcasts and magazines (Wenner 1991). Alcohol consumption is also often a key aspect of the more dangerous and violent dynamics at the heart of male sport cultures (Curry 2000; Sabo, Gray, and Moore 2000). By itself, alcohol does not "cause" men's violence against women or against other men; however, it is commonly one of a cluster of factors that facilitate violence (Koss and Gaines 1993; Leichliter et al. 1998). In short, beer and liquor are central players in "a high holy trinity of alcohol, sports, and hegemonic masculinity" (Wenner 1998).

This article examines beer and liquor advertisements in two "mega sports media events" consumed by large numbers of boys and men—the 2002 and 2003 Super Bowls and the 2002 and 2003 *Sports Illustrated* swimsuit issues. Our goal is to illuminate tropes of masculinity that prevail in those ads. We see these ads as establishing a pedagogy of youthful masculinity that does not passively teach male consumers about the qualities of their products so much as it encourages consumers to think of their products as essential to creating a stylish and desirable lifestyle. These ads do more than just dupe consumers into product loyalty; they also work with consumers to construct a consumption-based masculine identity relevant to contemporary social conditions. Drawing on insights from feminist cultural studies (Walters 1999), we argue that these gendered tropes watched by tens of millions of boys and men offer a window through which we can broaden our understanding of contemporary continuities, shifts, and strains in the social construction of masculinities.

GENDER, MEN'S SPORTS, AND ALCOHOL ADS

Although marketing beer and liquor to men is not new, the imagery that advertisers employ to pitch their product is not static either. Our analysis of past Super Bowls and *Sports Illustrated* beer and liquor ads suggests shifting patterns in the gender themes encoded in the ads. Consistently, over time, the ads attempt not to simply "plug" a particular product but to situate products within a larger historically specific way of life. Beer and liquor advertisers normally do not create product differentiation through typical narratives of crisis and resolution in which the product is the rescuing hero. Instead, they paint a series of images that evoke feelings, moods, and ways of being. In short, beer and liquor advertising engages in "lifestyle branding." Rather than simply attaching a name to a product, the brand emanates from a series of images that construct a plausible and desirable world to consumers. Lifestyle branding—more literary and evocative than simple crisis/resolution narratives—theorizes the social location of target populations and constructs a desiring subject whose consumption patterns can be massaged in specific directions. As we shall see, the subject constructed by the beer and liquor ads that we examined is an overtly gendered subject.

Beer and alcohol advertising construct a "desirable lifestyle" in relation to contemporary social conditions, including shifts and tensions in the broader gender order. Ads from the late 1950s through the late 1960s commonly depicted young or middle-aged white heterosexual couples happily sharing a cold beer in their suburban backyards, in their homes, or in an outdoor space like a park.

In these ads, the beer is commonly displayed in a clear glass, its clean, fresh appearance perhaps intended to counter the reputation of beer as a working-class male drink. Beer in these ads symbolically unites the prosperous and happy postwar middle-class couple. By the mid-1970s, women as wives and partners largely disappeared from beer ads. Instead of showing heterosexual couples drinking in their homes or backyards, these ads began primarily to depict images of men drinking with other men in public spaces. Three studies of beer commercials of the 1970s and 1980s found that most ads pitched beer to men as a pleasurable reward for a hard day's work. These ads told men that "For all you do, this Bud's for you." Women were rarely depicted in these ads, except as occasional background props in male-dominated bars (Postman et al. 1987; Wenner 1991; Strate 1992).

The 1950s and 1960s beer ads that depicted happy married suburban couples were part of a moment in gender relations tied to postwar culture and Fordist relations of production. White, middle-class, heterosexual masculinity was defined as synonymous with the male breadwinner, in symmetrical relation to a conception of femininity grounded in the image of the suburban housewife. In the 1970s and early 1980s, the focus on men's laboring bodies, tethered to their public leisure with other men, expressed an almost atavistic view of hegemonic masculinity at a time when women were moving into public life in huge numbers and blue-collar men's jobs were being eliminated by the tens of thousands.

Both the postwar and the postindustrial ads provide a gendered pedagogy for living a masculine lifestyle in a shifting context characterized by uncertainty. In contrast to the depiction of happy white families comfortably living lives of suburban bliss, the postwar era was characterized by anxieties over the possibility of a postwar depression, nuclear annihilation, suburban social dislocation, and disorder from racial and class movements for social justice (Lipsitz 1981; May 1988; Spigel 1992). Similarly, the 1970s and 1980s beer ads came in the wake of the defeat of the United States in the Vietnam War, the 1972 gas crisis, the collapse of Fordism, and the turbulence in gender relations brought on by the women's and gay/lesbian liberation movements.

All of these social ruptures contributed to produce an anxious white male subject (Connell 1995; Lipsitz 1998). Therefore, there is a sort of crisis/resolution narrative in these beer ads: the "crisis" lies broadly in the construction of white masculinities in the latter half of the twentieth century (Kimmel 1987), and the resolution lies in the construction of a lifestyle outside of immediate anxieties. The advertisements do not straightforwardly tell consumers to buy; rather, they teach consumers how to live a happy, stress-free life that includes regular (if not heavy) consumption of alcoholic beverages.

The 2002 and 2003 ads that we examine here primarily construct a white male "loser" whose life is apparently separate from paid labor. He hangs out with his male buddies, is self-mocking and ironic about his loser status, and is always at the ready to engage in voyeurism with sexy fantasy women but holds committed relationships and emotional honesty with real women in disdain. To the extent that these themes find resonance with young men of today, it is likely because they speak to basic insecurities that are grounded in a combination of historic shifts: deindustrialization, the declining real value of wages and the male breadwinner role, significant cultural shifts brought about by more than three decades of struggle by feminists and sexual minorities, and challenges to white male supremacy by people of color and by immigrants. This cluster of social changes has destabilized hegemonic masculinity and defines the context of gender relations in which today's young men have grown toward adulthood.

In theorizing how the loser motif in beer and liquor ads constructs a version of young white masculinity, we draw on Mikhail Bakhtin's (1981) concept of the chronotope. This is especially relevant in analyzing how lifestyle branding goes beyond the reiteration of a name to actually creating desirable and believable worlds in which consumers are beckoned to place themselves. The term *chronotope*—literally meaning "time-space"—describes how time and space fuse in literature to create meaningful structures separate from the text and its representations (Bakhtin 1981). The ads that we looked at consistently construct a leisure-time lifestyle of young men meeting in specific sites of sports and alcohol consumption: bars, television rooms, and stadiums. This meeting motif gives a temporal and spatial plane to male fantasy where desire can be explored and symbolic boundaries can simultaneously be transgressed and reinscribed into the social world.

TWO MEGA SPORTS MEDIA EVENTS

This article brings focus to the commercial center of sports media by examining the gender and sexual imagery encoded in two mega sports media events: the 2002 and 2003 Super Bowls and the 2002 and 2003 *Sports Illustrated* swimsuit issues. (See the appendix for a complete list of the ads and commercials).[1]

Mega sports media events are mediated cultural rituals (Dayan and Katz 1988) that differ from everyday sports media events in several key ways: sports media actively build audience anticipation and excitement throughout the year for these single events; the Super Bowl and the swimsuit issue

---

[1]We first conducted a content analysis of the Super Bowl tapes and the *Sports Illustrated* swimsuit issues to determine how many beer and liquor ads there were and where they were placed in the texts. Next, we employed textual analysis to identify common thematic patterns in the ads. We also sought to identify tensions, discontinuities, and contradictory gender themes in the ads. Finally, we examined the ways that the advertisements meshed with, respectively, the actual Super Bowl football game broadcast and the *Sports Illustrated* swimsuit issue text. We sought to understand how the intertextual cross-referencing of beer and liquor ads' gender themes with the game or the swimsuit models might variously create tensions in the dominant gender codings of the texts, reinforce these tensions, or both. In the absence of a systematic study of the various ways that audiences interpret and use these texts, our textual analysis is obviously limited.

are each preceded by major pre-event promotion and hype—from the television network that will broadcast the Super Bowl to *Sports Illustrated* and myriad other print and electronic media; the Super Bowl and the swimsuit issue are used as marketing tools for selling the more general products of National Football League (NFL) games and *Sports Illustrated* magazine subscriptions; the Super Bowl and the swimsuit issue each generate significant spin-off products (e.g., videos, books, "making of" TV shows, calendars, frequently visited Web pages); the Super Bowl and the swimsuit issue generate significantly larger audiences than does a weekly NFL game or a weekly edition of *Sports Illustrated*; and advertisements are usually created specifically for these mega sports media events and cost more to run than do ads in a weekly NFL game or a weekly edition of *Sports Illustrated*.

To be sure, the Super Bowl and the *Sports Illustrated* swimsuit issue are different in some fundamental ways. First, the Super Bowl is a televised event, while the swimsuit issue is a print event. Second, the Super Bowl is an actual sporting contest, while the swimsuit issue is a departure from *Sports Illustrated*'s normal coverage of sports. However, for our purposes, we see these two events as comparable, partly because they are mega sports media events but also because their ads target young males who consume sports media.

Super Bowl Ads

Since its relatively modest start in 1967, the NFL Super Bowl has mushroomed into one of the most expensive and most watched annual media events in the United States, with a growing world audience (Martin and Reeves 2001), the vast majority of whom are boys and men. Increasingly over the past decade, Super Bowl commercials have been specially created for the event. Newspapers, magazines, television news shows, and Web sites now routinely run pre–Super Bowl stories that focus specifically on the ads, and several media outlets run post–Super Bowl polls to determine which ads were the most and least favorite. Postgame lists of "winners" and "losers" focus as much on the corporate sponsors and their ads as on the two teams that—incidentally?—played a football game between the commercials.

Fifty-five commercials ran during the 2003 Super Bowl (not counting pregame and postgame shows), at an average cost of $2.1 million for each thirty-second ad. Fifteen of these commercials were beer or malt liquor ads. Twelve of these ads were run by Anheuser-Busch, whose ownership of this Super Bowl was underlined at least twenty times throughout the broadcast, when, after commercial breaks, the camera lingered on the stadium scoreboard, atop which was a huge Budweiser sign. On five other occasions, "Bud" graphics appeared on the screen after commercial breaks, as voice-overs reminded viewers that the Super Bowl was "brought to" them by Budweiser. This represented a slight increase in beer advertising since the 2002 Super Bowl, which featured thirteen beer or malt liquor commercials (eleven of them by Anheuser-Busch), at an average cost of $1.9 million per thirty-second ad. In addition to the approximately $31.5 million that the beer companies paid for the 2003 Super Bowl ad slots, they paid millions more creating and testing those commercials with focus groups. There were 137.7 million viewers watching all or part of the 2003 Super Bowl on ABC, and by far the largest demographic group watching was men, aged twenty-five to fifty-five.

Sports Illustrated Swimsuit Issue Ads

Sports Illustrated began in 1964 to publish an annual February issue that featured five or six pages of women modeling swimsuits, embedded in an otherwise normal sixty-four-page magazine (Davis 1997). This modest format continued until the late 1970s, when the portion of the magazine featuring swimsuit models began gradually to grow. In the 1980s, the swimsuit issue morphed into a special issue in which normal sports coverage gradually disappeared. During this decade, the issue's average length had grown to 173 pages, 20 percent of which were focused on swimsuit models. By the 1990s the swimsuit issue averaged 207 pages in length, 31 percent of which featured swimsuit models. The magazine has continued to grow in recent years. The 2003 issue was 218 pages in length, 59 percent of which featured swimsuit models. The dramatic growth in the size of the swimsuit issue in the 1990s, as well as the dropping of pretence that the swimsuit issue had anything to do with normal "sports journalism," were facilitated by advertising that began cleverly to echo and spoof the often highly sexualized swimsuit imagery in the magazine. By 2000, it was more the rule than the exception when an ad in some way utilized the swimsuit theme. The gender and sexual themes of the swimsuit issue became increasingly seamless, as ads and *Sports Illustrated* text symbiotically echoed and played off of each other. The 2002 swimsuit issue included seven pages of beer ads and seven pages of liquor ads, which cost approximately $230,000 per full page to run. The 2003 swimsuit issue ran the equivalent of sixteen pages of beer ads and thirteen pages of liquor ads. The ad space for the 2003 swimsuit issue sold for $266,000 per full-page color ad.

The millions of dollars that beer and liquor companies spent to develop and buy space for these ads were aimed at the central group that reads the magazine: young and middle-aged males. *Sports Illustrated* estimates the audience size of its weekly magazine at 21.3 million readers, roughly 76 percent of whom are males.[2] Nearly half of the male audience is in the coveted eighteen- to thirty-four-year-old demographic group, and three quarters of the male *Sports Illustrated* audience is between the ages of eighteen and forty-nine. A much larger number of single-copy sales gives the swimsuit issue a much larger audience, conservatively estimated at more than 30 million readers.[3]

The Super Bowl and the *Sports Illustrated* swimsuit issue are arguably the biggest single electronic and print sports media events annually in the United States. Due to their centrality, size, and target audiences, we suggest that mega sports media events such as the Super Bowl and the swimsuit issue offer a magnified view of the dominant gender and sexual imagery emanating from the center of the sports-media-commercial complex. Our concern is not simply to describe the stereotypes of masculinity and femininity in these ads; rather, we use these ads as windows into the ways that cultural capitalism constructs gender relationally, as part of a general lifestyle. In this article, we will employ thick description of ads to illuminate the four main gender relations themes that we saw in the 2002 and 2003 ads, and we will follow with a discussion of the process through which these themes are communicated: erotic and often humorous intertextual referencing. We will end by discussing some of the strains and tensions in the ads' major tropes of masculinity.

LOSERS AND BUDDIES, HOTTIES AND BITCHES

In the 2002 and 2003 beer and liquor ads that we examined, men's work worlds seem mostly to have disappeared. These ads are less about drinking and leisure as a reward for hard work and more about leisure as a lifestyle in and of itself. Men do not work in these ads; they recreate.

---

[2] *Sports Illustrated*'s rate card claims 3,137,523 average weekly subscribers and additional single-copy sales of 115,337. The company then uses a multiplier of 6.55 readers per issue to estimate the total size of its audience at 21,306,468.

[3] In addition to *Sports Illustrated*'s 3,137,523 average weekly subscribers, the company's rate card claims 1,467,228 single-copy sales of the swimsuit issue. According to the same multiplier of 6.55 readers per magazine that *Sports Illustrated* uses for estimating the total size of its weekly audience, the swimsuit issue audience is over 30 million. More than likely, the multiplier for the swimsuit issue is higher than that of the weekly magazine, so the swimsuit issue audience is probably much larger than 30 million.

And women are definitely back in the picture, but not as wives who are partners in building the good domestic life. It is these relations among men as well as relations between men and women that form the four dominant gender themes in the ads we examined. We will introduce these four themes by describing a 2003 Super Bowl commercial for Bud Lite beer.

Two young, somewhat nerdy-looking white guys are at a yoga class, sitting in the back of a room full of sexy young women. The two men have attached prosthetic legs to their bodies so that they can fake the yoga moves. With their bottles of Bud Lite close by, these voyeurs watch in delight as the female yoga teacher instructs the class to "relax and release that negative energy . . . inhale, arch, *thrust* your pelvis to the sky and exhale, *release* into the stretch." As the instructor uses her hands to push down on a woman's upright spread-eagled legs and says "focus, focus, focus," the camera (serving as prosthesis for male spectators at home) cuts back and forth between close-ups of the women's breasts and bottoms, while the two guys gleefully enjoy their beer and their sexual voyeurism. In the final scene the two guys are standing outside the front door of the yoga class, beer bottles in hand, and someone throws their fake legs out the door at them. As they duck to avoid being hit by the legs, one of them comments, "*She's* not very relaxed."

We begin with this ad because it contains, in various degrees, the four dominant gender themes that we found in the mega sports media events ads:

1. Losers: Men are often portrayed as chumps, losers. Masculinity—especially for the lone man—is precarious. Individual men are always on the cusp of being publicly humiliated, either by their own stupidity, by other men, or worse, by a beautiful woman.
2. Buddies: The precariousness of individual men's masculine status is offset by the safety of the male group. The solidity and primacy—and emotional safety—of male friendships are the emotional center of many of these ads.
3. Hotties: When women appear in these ads, it is usually as highly sexualized fantasy objects. These beautiful women serve as potential prizes for men's victories and proper consumption choices. They sometimes serve to validate men's masculinity, but their validating power also holds the potential to humiliate male losers.
4. Bitches: Wives, girlfriends, or other women to whom men are emotionally committed are mostly absent from these ads. However, when they do appear, it is primarily as emotional or sexual blackmailers who threaten to undermine individual men's freedom to enjoy the erotic pleasure at the center of the male group.

To a great extent, these four gender themes are intertwined in the Super Bowl "Yoga Voyeurs" ad. First, the two guys are clearly not good-looking, high-status, muscular icons of masculinity. More likely they are intended to represent the "everyman" with whom many boys and men can identify. Their masquerade as sensitive men allows them to transgress the female space of the yoga class, but they cannot pull the masquerade off and are eventually "outed" as losers and rejected by the sexy women. But even if they realize that they are losers, they do not have to care because they are so happy and secure in their bond with each other. Their friendship bond is cemented in frat-boy-style hijinks that allow them to share close-up voyeurism of sexy women who, we can safely assume, are way out of these men's league. In the end, the women reject the guys as pathetic losers. But the guys do not seem too upset. They have each other and, of course, they have their beers.

Rarely did a single ad in our study contain all four of these themes. But taken together, the ads show enough consistency that we can think of these themes as intertwined threads that together make up the ideological fabric at the center of mega sports media events. Next, we will illustrate how these themes are played out in the 2002 and 2003 ads, before discussing some of the strains and tensions in the ads.

REAL FRIENDS, SCARY WOMEN

Five twenty-something white guys are sitting around a kitchen table playing poker. They are laughing, seemingly having the time of their lives, drinking Jim Beam whiskey. The caption for this ad reflects the lighthearted, youthful mood of the group: "Good Bourbon, ice cubes, and whichever glasses are clean." This ad, which appeared in the 2002 *Sports Illustrated* swimsuit issue, is one in a series of Jim Beam ads that have run for the past few years in *Sports Illustrated* and in other magazines aimed at young men.[4] Running under the umbrella slogan of "Real Friends, Real Bourbon," these Jim Beam ads hail a white, college-age (or young college-educated) crowd of men with the appeal of playful male bonding through alcohol consumption in bars or pool halls. The main theme is the safety and primacy of the male group, but the accompanying written text sometimes suggests the presence of women. In one ad, four young white guys partying up a storm together and posing with arms intertwined are accompanied by the caption, "Unlike your girlfriend, they never ask where this relationship is going." These ads imply that women demand levels of emotional commitment and expression undesirable to men, while life with the boys (and the booze) is exciting, emotionally comfortable, and safe. The comfort that these ads suggest is that bonding and intimacy have clear (though mostly unspoken) boundaries that limit emotional expression in the male group. When drinking with the guys, a man can feel close to his friends, perhaps even drape an arm over a friend's shoulder, embrace him, or tell him that he loves him. But the context of alcohol consumption provides an escape hatch that contains and rationalizes the eruption of physical intimacy.

Although emotional closeness with and commitment to real women apparently are to be avoided, these ads also do suggest a role for women. The one ad in the Jim Beam series that includes an image of a woman depicts only a body part (*Sports Illustrated* ran this one in its 2000 swimsuit issue in 3-D). Four guys drinking together in a bar are foregrounded by a set of high-heeled legs that appear to be an exotic dancer's. The guys drink, laugh, and seem thoroughly amused with each other. "Our lives would make a great sitcom," the caption reads, and continues, "of course, it would have to run on cable." That the guys largely ignore the dancer affirms the strength and primacy of their bond with one another—they do not need her or any other women, the ad seems to say. On the other hand—and just as in the "Yoga Voyeurs" commercial—the female dancer's sexualizing of the chronotopic space affirms that the bond between the men is safely within the bounds of heterosexuality.

Although these ads advocate keeping one's emotional distance from women, a commitment to heterosexuality always carries the potential for developing actual relationships with women. The few ads that depict real women portray them consistently as signs of danger to individual men and to the male group. The ads imply that what men really want is sex (or at least titillation), a cold beer, and some laughs with the guys. Girlfriends and wives are undesirable because they push men to talk about feelings and demonstrate commitment to a relationship. In "Good Listener," a 2003 Super Bowl ad for Budweiser, a young white guy is sitting in a sports bar with his girlfriend while she complains about her best friend's "totally self-centered and insensitive boyfriend." As he

---

[4]Most of the Jim Beam "Real Friends" ads discussed here did not appear in the two *Sports Illustrated* swimsuit issues on which we focus. However, it enhances our understanding of the gender themes in the Jim Beam ads to examine the thematic consistencies in the broader series of Jim Beam "Real Friends" ads.

appears to listen to this obviously boring "girl talk," the camera pulls to a tight close-up on her face. She is reasonably attractive, but the viewer is not supposed to mistake her for one of the model-perfect fantasy women in other beer ads. The close-up reveals that her teeth are a bit crooked, her hair a bit stringy, and her face contorts as she says of her girlfriend that "she has these *emotional* needs he can't meet." Repelled, the guy spaces out and begins to peer over her shoulder at the television. The camera takes the guy's point of view and focuses on the football game while the speaking woman is in the fuzzy margins of his view. The girlfriend's monologue gets transposed by a football announcer describing an exciting run. She stops talking, and just in time his gaze shifts back to her eyes. She lovingly says, "You're such a great listener." With an "aw-shucks" smile, he says "thanks," and the "Budweiser TRUE" logo appears on the screen. These ads suggest that a sincere face and a bottle of beer allow a guy to escape the emotional needs of his partner while retaining regular access to sex. But the apparent dangers of love, long-term commitment, and marriage remain. The most overtly misogynist ad in the 2003 Super Bowl broadcast was "Sarah's Mom." While talking on the phone to a friend, a young, somewhat nerdy-looking white guy prepares to meet his girlfriend's mother for the first time. His friend offers him this stern advice: "Well, get a good look at her. 'Cause in twenty years, that's what Sarah's gonna look like." The nerd expresses surprised concern, just as there is a knock on the door. Viewed through the door's peep-hole, the face of Sarah's mother appears as young and beautiful as Sarah's, but it turns out that Sarah's mother has grotesquely large hips, thighs, and buttocks. The commercial ends with the screen filled mostly with the hugeness of the mother's bottom, her leather pants audibly stretching as she bends to pet the dog, and Sarah shoveling chips and dip into her mouth, as she says of her mother, "Isn't she incredible?" The guy replies, with obvious skepticism, "yeah."

The message to boys and men is disturbing. If you are nerdy enough to be thinking about getting married, then you should listen to your male friends' warnings about what to watch out for and what is important. If you have got to have a wife, make sure that she is, and always will be, conventionally thin and beautiful.

In beer ads, the male group defines men's need for women as sexual, not emotional, and in so doing it constructs women as either whores or bitches and then suggests ways for men to negotiate the tension between these two narrow and stereotypical categories of women. This, we think, is a key point of tension that beer and liquor companies are attempting to exploit to their advantage. They do so by creating a curious shift away from the familiar "madonna-whore" dichotomy of which Western feminists have been so critical, where wives/mothers/girlfriends are put on a pedestal and the women one has sex with are put in the gutter. The alcohol industry would apparently prefer that young men not think of women as madonnas. After all, wives and girlfriends to whom men are committed, whom they respect and love, often do place limits on men's time spent out with the boys, as well as limits on men's consumption of alcohol. The industry seems to know this: as long as men remain distrustful of women, seeing them either as bitches who are trying to ensnare them and take away their freedom or as whores with whom they can party and have sex with no emotional commitment attached, then men remain more open to the marketing strategies of the industry.

WINNERS AND LOSERS

In the 2002 and 2003 Super Bowls, Budweiser's "How Ya Doin'?" ads featured the trope of a country bumpkin, or hick, in the big city to highlight the rejection of men who transgress the symbolic boundaries of the male peer group. These ads also illustrate the communication and emotional processes that police these boundaries. Men may ask each other "how's it goin'," but they do not want to hear how it's *really* goin'. It is these unspoken limits that make the group bond feel like an emotionally safe place: male buddies at the bar will not ask each other how the relationship is going or push each other to get in touch with their feminine sides. But men who transgress these boundaries, who do not understand the unwritten emotional rules of the male group, are suspect, are branded as losers, and are banished from the inner circle of the group.

REVENGE OF THE REGULAR GUYS

If losers are used in some of these ads to clarify the bounds of masculine normality, this is not to say that hypermasculine men are set up as the norm. To the contrary, overly masculine men, muscle men, and men with big cars who flash their money around are often portrayed as the real losers, against whom regular guys can sometimes turn the tables and win the beautiful women. In the ads we examined, however, this "regular guy wins beautiful fantasy woman" outcome was very rare. Instead, when the regular guy does manage to get the beautiful fantasy woman's attention, it is usually not in the way that he imagined or dreamed. A loser may want to win the attention of—and have sex with— beautiful women. But ultimately, these women are unavailable to a loser; worse, they will publicly humiliate him if he tries to win their attention. But losers can always manage to have another beer.

If white-guy losers risk punishment or humiliation from beautiful women in these ads, the level of punishment faced by black men can be even more severe. Although nearly all of the television commercials and print ads that we examined depict white people, a very small number do focus centrally on African Americans.[5] In "Pick-Up Lines," a Bud Lite ad that ran during the 2002 Super Bowl, two black males are sitting at a bar next to an attractive black female. Paul, the man in the middle, is obviously a loser; he's wearing a garish shirt, and his hair looks like an Afro gone terribly wrong. He sounds a bit whiny as he confides in his male friend, "I'm just not good with the ladies like you, Cedric." Cedric, playing Cyrano de Bergerac, whispers opening pickup lines to him. The loser turns to the woman and passes on the lines. But just then, the bartender brings another bottle of beer to Cedric, who asks the bartender, "So, how much?" Paul, thinking that this is his next pickup line, says to the woman, "So, how much?" Her smile turns to an angry frown, and she delivers a vicious kick to Paul's face, knocking him to the floor. After we see the Budweiser logo and hear the voice-over telling us that Bud Lite's great taste "will never let you down," we see a stunned Paul rising to his knees and trying to pull himself up to his bar stool, but the woman knocks him down again with a powerful backhand fist to the face.

This Bud Lite "Pick-Up Lines" ad—one of the very few ads that depict relations between black men and black women—was the only ad in which we saw a man being physically beaten by a woman. Here, the African American woman as object turns to subject, inflicting direct physical punishment on the African American man. The existence of these very few "black ads" brings into relief something that might otherwise remain hidden: most of these ads construct a youthful white masculinity that is playfully self-mocking, always a bit tenuous, but ultimately lovable. The screwups that white-guy losers make are forgivable, and we nearly always see these men, in the end, with at least a cold beer in hand. By contrast, the intersection of race, gender, and class creates cultural and institutional contexts of suspicion and punishment for African American boys and men (Ferguson 2000). In the beer ads this translates into the message that a black man's transgressions are apparently deserving of a kick to the face.

---

[5]Of the twenty-six beer and malt liquor ads in the two Super Bowls, twenty-four depicted people. Among the twenty-four ads that depicted people, eighteen depicted white people only, three depicted groups that appear to be of mixed race, and three focused on African American main characters. Thirteen of the twenty-four beer and liquor ads in the two *Sports Illustrated* swimsuit issues depicted people: twelve depicted white people only, and one depicted what appears to be the silhouette of an African American couple. No apparent Latino/as or Asian Americans appeared in any of the magazine or television ads.

EROTIC INTERTEXTUALITY

One of the dominant strategies in beer and liquor ads is to create an (often humorous) erotic tension among members of a "threesome": the male reader/viewer, a woman depicted as a sexy fantasy object, and a bottle of cold beer. This tension is accomplished through intertextual referencing between the advertising text and the sport text. For instance, on returning to live coverage of the Super Bowl from a commercial break, the camera regularly lingered on the stadium scoreboard, above which was a huge Budweiser sign. One such occasion during the 2003 Super Bowl was particularly striking. Coors had just run its only commercial (an episode from its successful "Twins" series) during this mega sports media event that seemed otherwise practically owned by Anheuser-Busch. Immediately on return from the commercial break to live action, the handheld field-level camera focused one by one on dancing cheerleaders (once coming so close that it appears that the camera bumped into one of the women's breasts), all the while keeping the Budweiser sign in focus in the background. It was almost as though the producers of the Super Bowl were intent on not allowing the Coors "twins" to upstage Anheuser-Busch's ownership of the event.

Omnipresent advertising images in recent years have continued to obliterate the already blurry distinction between advertising texts and other media texts (Goldman and Papson 1996). This is surely true in the world of sport: players' uniforms, stadium walls, the corner of one's television screen, and even moments within telecasts are regularly branded with the Nike swoosh or some other corporate sign. Stephanie O'Donohoe argues that "popular texts have 'leaky boundaries,' flowing into each other and everyday life. . . . This seems especially true of advertising" (1997, 257–58). The "leakiness" of cultural signs in advertising is facilitated, O'Donohoe argues, "by increasing institutional ties between advertising, commercial media, and mass entertainment. . . . Conglomeration breeds intertextuality" (257–58). When ads appropriate or make explicit reference to other media (e.g., other ads, celebrities, movies, television shows, or popular music), they engage in what Robert Goldman and Stephen Papson call "cultural cannibalism" (1998, 10). Audiences are then invited to make the connections between the advertised product and the cultural meanings implied by the cannibalized sign; in so doing, the audience becomes "the final author, whose participation is essential" (O'Donohoe 1997, 259). As with all textual analyses that do not include an audience study, we must be cautious in inferring how differently situated audiences might variously take up, and draw meanings from, these ads. However, we suspect that experiences of "authorship" in the process of decoding and drawing intertextual connections are a major part of the pleasure of viewing mass media texts.

The 2002 and 2003 *Sports Illustrated* swimsuit issues offer vivid examples of texts that invite the reader to draw intertextual connections between erotically charged ads and other non-ad texts. Whereas in the past the *Sports Illustrated* swimsuit issue ran ads that were clearly distinct from the swimsuit text, it has recently become more common for the visual themes in the ads and the swimsuit text to be playfully intertwined, symbiotically referencing each other. A 2003 Heineken ad shows a close-up of two twenty-four-ounce "keg cans" of Heineken beer, side by side. The text above the two cans reads, "They're big. And yeah, they're real." As if the reference to swimsuit models' breast size (and questions about whether some of the models have breast implants) were perhaps too subtle, *Sports Illustrated* juxtaposed the ad with a photo of a swimsuit model, wearing a suit that liberally exposed her breasts.

For the advertisers and for *Sports Illustrated*, the payoff for this kind of intertextual coordination is probably large: for the reader, the text of the swimsuit issue becomes increasingly seamless, as ads and swimsuit text melt into each other, playfully, humorously, and erotically referencing each other. As with the Super Bowl ads, the *Sports Illustrated* swimsuit issue ads become something that viewers learn not to ignore or skip over; instead, the ads become another part of the pleasure of consuming and imagining.

In 2003, Miller Brewing Company and *Sports Illustrated* further developed the symbiotic marketing strategy that they had introduced in 2002. The 2003 swimsuit issue featured a huge Miller Lite ad that included the equivalent of fourteen full pages of ad text. Twelve of these pages were a large, pull-out poster, one side of which was a single photo of "Sophia," a young model wearing a bikini with the Miller Lite logo on the right breast cup. On the opposite side of the poster were four one-page photos and one two-page photo of Sophia posing in various bikinis, with Miller Lite bottles and/or logos visible in each picture. As it did in the 2002 ad, Miller invites viewers to enter a contest to win a trip to the next *Sports Illustrated* swimsuit issue photo shoot. The site of the photo shoot fuses the text-based space of the magazine with the real space of the working models in exotic, erotic landscapes of desire that highlight the sexuality of late capitalist colonialism (Davis 1997). The accompanying text invites the reader to "visit http://www.cnnsi.com" to "check out a 360 degree view of the *Sports Illustrated* swimsuit photo shoot." And the text accompanying most of the photos of Sophia and bottles of Miller Lite teasingly encourages the reader to exercise his consumer power: "So if you had to make a choice, which one would it be?."

This expansive ad evidences a multilevel symbiosis between *Sports Illustrated* and Miller Brewing Company. The playful tease to "choose your favorite" (model, swimsuit, and/or beer) invites the reader to enter another medium—the *Sports Illustrated* swimsuit Web site, which includes access to a *Sports Illustrated* swimsuit photo shoot video sponsored by Miller. The result is a multifaceted media text that stands out as something other than mere advertisement and other than business-as-usual *Sports Illustrated* text. It has an erotic and commercial charge to it that simultaneously teases the reader as a sexual voyeur and hails him as an empowered consumer who can freely choose his own beer and whichever sexy woman he decides is his "favorite."

"LIFE IS HARSH": MALE LOSERS AND ALCOHOLIC ACCOMMODATION

In recent years, the tendency in the *Sports Illustrated* swimsuit issue to position male readers as empowered individuals who can "win" or freely choose the sexy fantasy object of their dreams has begun to shift in other directions. To put it simply, many male readers of the swimsuit issue may find the text erotically charged, but most know that these are two-dimensional images of sexy women who in real life are unavailable to them. In recent years, some swimsuit issue ads have delivered this message directly. In 1997, a two-page ad for Tequila Sauza depicted six women in short red skirts, posing flirtatiously, some of them lifting their blouses provocatively to reveal bare midriffs, or opening their blouses to reveal parts of their breasts. In small letters, across the six women's waists, stretching all the way across the two pages, the text reads, "We can say with 99.9% accuracy that there is no possible way whatsoever in this lifetime that you will ever get a date with one of these women." Then, to the side of the ad is written "LIFE IS HARSH. Your tequila shouldn't be." A similar message appears in other ads. For instance, in the 1999 swimsuit issue, a full-page photo of a Heineken bottle included the written text "The only heiny in this magazine you could actually get your hands on."

These ads play directly to the male reader as loser and invite him to accommodate to his loser status, to recognize that these sexy fantasy women, though "real," are unavailable to him, and to settle for what he can have: a good bottle of Tequila Sauza or a cold (rather than a hot) "Heiny." The Bud Lite Super Bowl commercials strike a similar chord. Many Bud Lite ads either titillate the viewer with sexy fantasy women, point to the ways that relationships with real women are to be avoided, or do both simultaneously. The break that appears near the end of each Bud Lite ad contrasts sharply with the often negative depiction of men's relations with real women in the ad's story line. The viewer sees a close-up of a bottle of Bud Lite. The bottle's cap explodes off, and beer ejaculates out, as a male voice-over proclaims what a man truly can rely on in life: "For the great taste that won't fill you up, and never lets you down . . . make it a Bud Lite."

REVENGE OF THE LOSERS

The accommodation theme in these ads may succeed, momentarily, in encouraging a man to shift his feelings of being a sexual loser toward manly feelings of empowerment through the consumption of brand-name beers and liquor. If the women in the ads are responsible for heightening tensions that result in some men's sense of themselves as losers, one possible outcome beyond simply drinking a large amount of alcohol (or one that accompanies the consumption of alcohol) is to express anger toward women and even to take revenge against them. This is precisely a direction that some of the recent ads have taken.

A full-page ad in the 2002 swimsuit issue showed a large photo of a bottle of Maker's Mark Whiskey. The bottle's reflection on the shiny table on which it sits is distorted in a way that suggests an hourglass-shaped female torso. The text next to the bottle reads, "'Your bourbon has a great body and fine character. I WISH the same could be said for my girlfriend.' D. T., Birmingham, AL." This one-page ad is juxtaposed with a full-page photo of a *Sports Illustrated* model, provocatively using her thumb to begin to pull down the right side of her bikini bottom.

Together, the ad text and *Sports Illustrated* text angrily express the bitch-whore dichotomy that we discussed above. D. T.'s girlfriend is not pictured, but the description of her clearly indicates that not only does she lack a beautiful body; worse, she's a bitch. While D. T.'s girlfriend symbolizes the real woman whom each guy tolerates, and to whom he avoids committing, the juxtaposed *Sports Illustrated* model is the beautiful and sexy fantasy woman. She is unavailable to the male reader in real life; her presence as fantasy image highlights that the reader, like D. T., is stuck, apparently, with his bitchy girlfriend. But at least he can enjoy a moment of pseudo-empowerment by consuming a Maker's Mark whiskey and by insulting his girlfriend's body and character. Together, the Maker's Mark ad and the juxtaposed *Sports Illustrated* model provide a context for the reader to feel hostility toward the real women in his life.

This kind of symbolic male revenge toward women is expressed in a different way in a four-page Captain Morgan rum ad that appeared in the 2003 *Sports Illustrated* swimsuit issue. On the first page, we see only the hands of the cartoon character "Captain Morgan" holding a fire hose spraying water into the air over what appears to be a tropical beach. When one turns the page, a three-page foldout ad reveals that "the Captain" is spraying what appears to be a *Sports Illustrated* swimsuit issue photo shoot. Six young women in tiny bikinis are laughing, perhaps screaming, and running for cover (five of them are huddled under an umbrella with a grinning male character who looks suspiciously like Captain Morgan). The spray from the fire hose causes the women's bathing suits to melt right off their bodies. The readers do not know if the swimsuits are painted on or are made of meltable candy or if perhaps Captain Morgan's ejaculate is just that powerfully corrosive. One way or the other, the image suggests that Captain Morgan is doing a service to the millions of boys and men who read this magazine. Written across a fleeing woman's thigh, below her melting bikini bottom, the text reads "Can you say birthday suit issue?."

Two men—apparently photographers—stand to the right of the photo, arms raised to the heavens (with their clothing fully intact). The men in the picture seem ecstatic with religious fervor. The male reader is perhaps invited to identify with these regular guys: like them, he is always good enough to look at these beautiful women in their swimsuits but never good enough to get them to take it off for him. But here, "the Captain" was clever enough to strip the women naked so that he and all of his male buddies could enjoy a vengeful moment of voyeurism. The relational gender and sexual dynamics of this ad—presented here without overt anger and with cartoonish humor—allegorize the common dynamics of group sexual assaults (Beneke 1982). These sexy women have teased men enough, the ad suggests. First they arouse men, and then they inevitably make them feel like losers. They deserve to be stripped naked against their will. As in many male rape fantasies, the ad suggests that women ultimately find that they like it. And all of this action is facilitated by a bottle of rum, the Captain's magical essence.

TENSION, STABILIZATION, AND MASCULINE CONSUMPTION

We argued in our introduction that contemporary social changes have destabilized hegemonic masculinity. Examining beer and liquor ads in mega sports media events gives us a window into the ways that commercial forces have seized on these destabilizing tendencies, constructing pedagogical fantasy narratives that aim to appeal to a very large group—eighteen- to thirty-four-year-old men. They do so by appealing to a broad zeitgeist among young (especially white, heterosexual) men that is grounded in widespread tensions in the contemporary gender order.[6] The sexual and gender themes of the beer and liquor ads that we examine in this article do not stand alone; rather they reflect, and in turn contribute to, broader trends in popular culture and marketing to young white males. Television shows like *The Man Show*, new soft-core porn magazines like *Maxim* and *FHM*, and radio talk shows like the syndicated *Tom Leykus Show* share similar themes and are targeted to similar audiences of young males. Indeed, radio talk show hosts like Leykus didactically instruct young men to avoid "girlie" things, to eschew emotional commitment, and to think of women primarily as sexual partners (Messner 2002, 107–8). The chronotope of these magazines and television and radio shows constructs young male lifestyles saturated with sexy images of nearly naked, surgically enhanced women; unabashed and unapologetic sexual voyeurism shared by groups of laughing men; and explicit talk of sexual exploits with "hotties" or "juggies." A range of consumer products that includes—often centrally, as in *The Man Show*—consumption of beer as part of the young male lifestyle stitches together this erotic bonding among men. Meanwhile, real women are either absent from these media or they are disparaged as gold diggers (yes, this term has been resuscitated) who use sex to get men to spend money on them and trick them into marriage. The domesticated man is viewed as a wimpy victim who has subordinated his own pleasures (and surrendered his paychecks) to a woman. Within this framework, a young man should have sex with as many women as he can while avoiding (or at least delaying) emotional commitments to any one woman. Freedom from emotional commitment grants 100 percent control over disposable income for monadic consumption and care of self. And that is ultimately what these shows are about: constructing a young male consumer characterized by personal and emotional freedom who can attain a hip lifestyle by purchasing an ever-expanding range of automobile-related products, snack foods, clothes, toiletries, and, of course, beer and liquor.

At first glance, these new media aimed at young men seem to resuscitate a 1950s "*Playboy* philosophy" of men's consumption, sexuality, and gender relations (Ehrenreich 1983). Indeed, these new media strongly reiterate the dichotomous bitch-whore view of women that was such a lynchpin of Hugh Hefner's "philosophy." But today's tropes of masculinity do not simply reiterate the past; rather, they give a postfeminist twist to the *Playboy* philosophy. A half-century ago,

---

[6]These same beer companies target different ads to other groups of men. Suzanne Danuta Walters (2001) analyzes Budweiser ads, e.g., that are aimed overtly at gay men.

Hefner's pitch to men to recapture the indoors by creating (purchasing) one's own erotic "bachelor pad" in which to have sex with women (and then send them home) read as a straightforwardly masculine project. By contrast, today's sexual and gender pitch to young men is delivered with an ironic, self-mocking wink that operates, we think, on two levels. First, it appears to acknowledge that most young men are neither the heroes of the indoors (as Hefner would have it) nor of the outdoors (as the 1970s and 1980s beer ads suggested). Instead, the ads seem to recognize that young white men's unstable status leaves them always on the verge of being revealed as losers. The ads plant seeds of insecurity on this fertile landscape, with the goal of creating a white guy who is a consistent and enthusiastic consumer of alcoholic beverages. The irony works on a second level as well: the throwback sexual and gender imagery—especially the bitch-whore dichotomization of women—is clearly a defensively misogynistic backlash against feminism and women's increasing autonomy and social power. The wink and self-mocking irony allow men to have it both ways: they can engage in humorous misogynist banter and claim simultaneously that it is all in play. They do not take themselves seriously, so anyone who takes their misogyny as anything but boys having good fun just has no sense of humor. The humorous irony works, then, to deflect charges of sexism away from white males, allowing them to define themselves as victims, as members of an endangered species. We suspect, too, that this is a key part of the process that constructs the whiteness in current reconstructions of hegemonic masculinity. As we have suggested, humorous "boys-will-be-boys" misogyny is unlikely to be taken ironically and lightly when delivered by men of color.

The white-guy-as-loser trope, though fairly new to beer and liquor ads, is certainly not new to U.S. media. Part of the irony of this character is not that he is a loser in every sense; rather he signifies the typical everyman who is only a loser in comparison to versions of masculinity more typical to beer and liquor ads past—that is, the rugged guys who regularly get the model-beautiful women. Caught between the excesses of a hypermasculinity that is often discredited and caricatured in popular culture and the increasing empowerment of women, people of color, and homosexuals, while simultaneously being undercut by the postindustrial economy, the "Average Joe" is positioned as the ironic, vulnerable but lovable hero of beer and liquor ads. It is striking that the loser is not, or is rarely, your "José Mediano," especially if we understand the construction as a way to unite diverse eighteen- to thirty-four-year-old men. This is to say that the loser motif constructs the universal subject as implicitly white, and as a reaction against challenges to hegemonic masculinity it represents an ongoing possessive investment in whiteness (Lipsitz 1998).

Our analysis suggests that the fact that male viewers today are being hailed as losers and are being asked to identify with—even revel in—their loser status has its limits. The beer and liquor industry dangles images of sexy women in front of men's noses. Indeed, the ads imply that men will go out of their way to put themselves in position to be voyeurs, be it with a TV remote control, at a yoga class, in a bar, or on the *Sports Illustrated*/Miller Beer swimsuit photo shoot Web site. But ultimately, men know (and are increasingly being told in the advertisements themselves) that these sexy women are not available to them. Worse, if men get too close to these women, these women will most likely humiliate them. By contrast, real women—women who are not model-beautiful fantasy objects—are likely to attempt to ensnare men into a commitment, push them to have or express feelings that make them uncomfortable, and limit their freedom to have fun watching sports or playing cards or pool with their friends. So, in the end, men have only the safe haven of their male friends and the bottle.

This individual sense of victimization may feed young men's insecurities while giving them convenient scapegoats on which to project anger at their victim status. The cultural construction of white males as losers, then, is tethered to men's anger at and desire for revenge against women. Indeed, we have observed that revenge-against-women themes are evident in some of the most recent beer and liquor ads. And it is here that our analysis comes full circle. For, as we suggested in the introduction, the cultural imagery in ads aimed at young men does not simply come from images "out there." Instead, this imagery is linked to the ways that real people live their lives. It is the task of future research—including audience research—to investigate and flesh out the specific links between young men's consumption of commercial images, their consumption of beer and liquor, their attitudes toward and relationships with women, and their tendencies to drink and engage in violence against women.

APPENDIX

Commercials and Advertisements in the Sample

2002 Super Bowl:
- Michelob Lite, "Free to Be"
- Budweiser, "Robobash"
- Budweiser, "Pick-Up Lines"
- Bud Lite, "Hawk"
- Budweiser, "Clydesdales"
- Bud Lite, "Greeting Cards"
- Budweiser, "How Ya Doin'?"
- Bud Lite, "Black Teddy"
- Budweiser, "Meet the Parents"
- Budweiser, "History of Budweiser"
- Budweiser, "Designated Driver"
- Smirnoff Ice

2002 *Sports Illustrated* swimsuit issue (no. of pages):
- Miller Lite (2)
- Jim Beam (1)
- Miller Genuine Draft (2, plus card insert)
- Heineken (1)
- Budweiser (1)
- Captain Morgan Rum (1)
- Martell (1)
- Sam Adams Utopia (1)
- Maker's Mark Whiskey (1)
- Bicardi Rum (1.25)
- José Cuervo Tequila (1)
- Crown Royal (1)
- Chivas (1)

2003 Super Bowl:
- Budweiser, "Zebras"
- Bud Lite, "Refrigerator"
- Bud Lite, "Clown"
- Bud Lite, "Rasta Dog"
- Bud Lite, "Conch"
- Bud Lite, "Date Us Both"
- Smirnoff Lite, "Blind Date"
- Bud Lite, "Sarah's Mom"
- Bud Lite, "Three Arms"
- Coors, "Twins"
- Budweiser, "Good Listener"
- Budweiser, "'How Ya Doin'?' Redux"
- Michelob Ultra, "Low-Carb Bodies"
- Bud Lite, "Yoga Voyeurs"

2003 *Sports Illustrated* swimsuit issue (no. of pages):
- Budweiser (1)
- José Cuervo Tequila (1)
- Smirnoff Vodka (1)
- Captain Morgan Rum (4)
- Seagrams (1)
- Miller Lite (11, including poster pullout)
- Crown Royal (1)
- Heineken (1)
- Skyy Vodka (1)
- Knob Whiskey (1)
- Chivas (1)

REFERENCES

Bakhtin, Mikhail. 1981. "Forms of Time and the Chronotope in the Novel." In *The Dialogic Imagination: Four Essays*, trans. Caryl Emerson and Michael Holmquist, 84–258. Austin: University of Texas Press.

Beneke, Timothy. 1982. *Men on Rape*. New York: St. Martin's.

Collins, Tony, and Wray Vamplew. 2002. *Mud, Sweat, and Beers: A Cultural History of Sport and Alcohol*. New York: Berg.

Connell, R. W. 1995. *Masculinities*. Berkeley: University of California Press.

Curry, Timothy. 2000. "Booze and Bar Fights: A Journey to the Dark Side of College Athletics." In *Masculinities, Gender Relations, and Sport*, ed. Jim McKay, Donald F. Sabo, and Michael A. Messner, 162–75. Thousand Oaks, CA: Sage.

Davis, Laurel L. 1997. *The Swimsuit Issue and Sport: Hegemonic Masculinity in* Sports Illustrated. Albany, NY: SUNY Press.

Dayan, Daniel, and Elihu Katz. 1988. "Articulating Consensus: The Ritual and Rhetoric of Media Events." In *Durkheimian Sociology: Cultural Studies*, ed. Jeffrey C. Alexander, 161–86. Cambridge: Cambridge University Press.

Ehrenreich, Barbara. 1983. *The Hearts of Men: American Dreams and the Flight from Commitment*. New York: Anchor Doubleday.

Ferguson, Ann Arnett. 2000. *Bad Boys: Public Schools in the Making of Black Masculinity*. Ann Arbor: University of Michigan Press.

Goldman, Robert, and Stephen Papson. 1996. *Sign Wars: The Cluttered Landscape of Advertising*. New York: Guilford.

_____. 1998. *Nike Culture: The Sign of the Swoosh*. Thousand Oaks, CA: Sage.

Kimmel, Michael S. 1987. "Men's Responses to Feminism at the Turn of the Century." *Gender and Society* 1(3):261–83.

Koss, Mary, and John A. Gaines. 1993. "The Prediction of Sexual Aggression by Alcohol Use, Athletic Participation, and Fraternity Affiliation." *Journal of Interpersonal Violence* 8(1):94–108.

Leichliter, Jami S., Philip W. Meilman, Cheryl A. Presley, and Jeffrey R. Cashin. 1998. "Alcohol Use and Related Consequences among Students with Varying Levels of Involvement in College Athletics." *Journal of American College Health* 46(6):257–62.

Lipsitz, George. 1981. *Class and Culture in Cold War America: "A Rainbow at Midnight."* New York: Praeger.

_____. 1998. *The Possessive Investment in Whiteness: How White People Profit from Identity Politics*. Philadelphia: Temple University Press.

Martin, Christopher R., and Jimmie L. Reeves. 2001. "The Whole World Isn't Watching (but We Thought They Were): The Super Bowl and U.S. Solipsism." *Culture, Sport, and Society* 4(2):213–54.

May, Elaine Tyler. 1988. *Homeward Bound: American Families in the Cold War Era*. New York: Basic Books.

Messner, Michael A. 2002. *Taking the Field: Women, Men, and Sports*. Minneapolis: University of Minnesota Press.

O'Donohoe, Stephanie. 1997. "Leaky Boundaries: Intertextuality and Young Adult Experiences of Advertising." In *Buy This Book: Studies in Advertising and Consumption*, ed. Mica Nava, Andrew Blake, Ian McRury, and Barry Richards, 257–75. London: Routledge.

Postman, Neil, Christine Nystrom, Lance Strate, and Charlie Weingartner. 1987. *Myths, Men, and Beer: An Analysis of Beer Commercials on Broadcast Television, 1987*. Washington, DC: AAA Foundation for Traffic Safety.

Sabo, Don, Phil Gray, and Linda Moore. 2000. "Domestic Violence and Televised Athletic Events: 'It's a man thing.'" In *Masculinities, Gender Relations, and Sport*, ed. Jim McKay, Don Sabo, and Michael A. Messner, 127–46. Thousand Oaks, CA: Sage.

Sperber, Murray. 2000. *Beer and Circus: How Big-Time College Sports Is Crippling Undergraduate Education*. New York: Henry Holt.

Spigel, Lynn. 1992. *Make Room for TV: Television and the Family Ideal in Postwar America*. Chicago: University of Chicago Press.

Strate, Lance. 1992. "Beer Commercials: A Manual on Masculinity." In *Men, Masculinity, and the Media*, ed. Steve Craig, 78–92. Newbury Park, CA: Sage.

Walters, Suzanna Danuta. 1999. "Sex, Text, and Context: (In) Between Feminism and Cultural Studies." In *Revisioning Gender*, ed. Myra Marx Ferree, Judith Lorber, and Beth B. Hess, 222–57. Thousand Oaks, CA: Sage.

_____. 2001. *All the Rage: The Story of Gay Visibility in America*. Chicago: University of Chicago Press.

Wenner, Lawrence A. 1991. "One Part Alcohol, One Part Sport, One Part Dirt, Stir Gently: Beer Commercials and Television Sports." In *Television Criticism: Approaches and Applications*, ed. Leah R. Vende Berg and Lawrence A. Wenner, 388–407. New York: Longman.

_____. 1998. "In Search of the Sports Bar: Masculinity, Alcohol, Sports, and the Mediation of Public Space." In *Sport and Postmodern Times*, ed. Genevieve Rail, 303–32. Albany, NY: SUNY Press.

Zimbalist, Andrew. 1999. *Unpaid Professionals: Commercialism and Conflict in Big-Time College Sports*. Princeton, NJ: Princeton University Press.

SECTION III

Explanations of Gender

Key Concepts for Section III: Explanations of Gender

Androgyny
Androgens
Berdache
Biological Determinism
Bisexual/Bisexuality
Cognitive Development Theory
Corpus Callosum
Determinants of Women's Status
Developmental Systems Theory (DST)
Differential Socialization
Dimorphism
Division of Labor
Dowry Death
Egalitarian
Endocrinology
Essentialism
Estrogen
Ethnocentrism
Evolutionary Psychology
Exchange Value
Female Genital Cutting
Femicide
Gender Difference
Gender Socialization
Gender Variants
Hermaphrodite
Homosocial Status Systems
Honor Killing
Human Rights
International Bill of Gender Rights (1995)
ISNA (Intersex Society of North America)
"Just-So" Story
Kinsey Scale
Klein's Sexual Orientation Grid (KSOG)
Marxist Theories
Matriarchy
Maximizing Fitness
Medicalization
Parental Investment Theory
Path of Least Resistance
Permissive Effect (of Testosterone)
Rape
Rape Supportive Culture
Rape-Prone Culture
Reproductive Choice

Resource Based Mating System
Separate Spheres (public and private)
Secondary Sexual Characteristics
Sex Roles
Social Learning Theory
Sociobiology
Sociology
Son Preference
Symbolic Violence
Testosterone
Trafficking
Transgenderism
Two Spirit
Use Value

Concepts to Review

Androcentrism
Dichotomy/Dichotomous
Doing Gender
Dominance/Domination
Double Standards
Femininity/Femininities
Gender
Heterosexism
Hierarchy
Homophobia
Homosexuality
Internalized Oppression
Intersectionality
Intersex
Marginalization
Masculinity/Masculinities
Misogyny
Mythical Norm
Oppression
Patriarchy
Power
Privilege
Racism
Sex
Sex-Gender System
Sexism
Socialization
Subordinance/Subordination
Tokenism
Transgender

The Five Sexes, Revisited

Anne Fausto-Sterling

Anne Fausto-Sterling is Professor of Biology and Gender Studies at Brown University. Her influential work in biology and gender has long challenged ideas about sex and gender. In her newest work she uses Dynamic Systems Theory to study and explain how cultural differences impact and contribute to bodily differences, most specifically in bone development. Her books include Sexing the Body: Gender Politics and the Construction of Sexuality *(2000) and* Myths of Gender: Biological Theories About Men and Women *(1985, 1992). This essay appeared in* The Sciences *in 2000.*

The emerging recognition that people come in bewildering sexual varieties is testing medical values and social norms

As Cheryl Chase stepped to the front of the packed meeting room in the Sheraton Boston Hotel, nervous coughs made the tension audible. Chase, an activist for intersexual rights, had been invited to address the May 2000 meeting of the Lawson Wilkins Pediatric Endocrine Society (LWPES), the largest organization in the United States for specialists in children's hormones. Her talk would be the grand finale to a four-hour symposium on the treatment of genital ambiguity in newborns, infants born with a mixture of both male and female anatomy, or genitals that appear to differ from their chromosomal sex. The topic was hardly a novel one to the assembled physicians.

Yet Chase's appearance before the group was remarkable. Three and a half years earlier, the American Academy of Pediatrics had refused her request for a chance to present the patients' viewpoint on the treatment of genital ambiguity, dismissing Chase and her supporters as "zealots." About two dozen intersex people had responded by throwing up a picket line. The Intersex Society of North America (ISNA) even issued a press release: "Hermaphrodites Target Kiddie Docs."

It had done my 1960s street-activist heart good. In the short run, I said to Chase at the time, the picketing would make people angry. But eventually, I assured her, the doors then closed would open. Now, as Chase began to address the physicians at their own convention, that prediction was coming true. Her talk, titled "Sexual Ambiguity: The Patient-Centered Approach," was a measured critique of the near-universal practice of performing immediate, "corrective" surgery on thousands of infants born each year with ambiguous genitalia. Chase herself lives with the consequences of such surgery. Yet her audience, the very endocrinologists and surgeons Chase was accusing of reacting with "surgery and shame," received her with respect. Even more remarkably, many of the speakers who preceded her at the session had already spoken of the need to scrap current practices in favor of treatments more centered on psychological counseling.

What led to such a dramatic reversal of fortune? Certainly, Chase's talk at the LWPES symposium was a vindication of her persistence in seeking attention for her cause. But her invitation to speak was also a watershed in the evolving discussion about how to treat children with ambiguous genitalia. And that discussion, in turn, is the tip of a biocultural iceberg—the gender iceberg—that continues to rock both medicine and our culture at large.

Chase made her first national appearance in 1993, in these very pages, announcing the formation of ISNA in a letter responding to an essay I had written for *The Sciences*, titled "The Five Sexes" [March/April 1993]. In that article I argued that the two-sex system embedded in our society is not adequate to encompass the full spectrum of human sexuality. In its place, I suggested a five-sex system. In addition to males and females, I included "herms" (named after true hermaphrodites, people born with both a testis and an ovary); "merms" (male pseudohermaphrodites, who are born with testes and some aspect of female genitalia); and "ferms" (female pseudohermaphrodites, who have ovaries combined with some aspect of male genitalia).

> Much has changed since 1993. Intersexuals have materialized before our very eyes.

I had intended to be provocative, but I had also written with tongue firmly in cheek. So I was surprised by the extent of the controversy the article unleashed. Right-wing Christians were outraged, and connected my idea of five sexes with the United Nations–sponsored Fourth World Conference on Women, held in Beijing in September 1995. At the same time, the article delighted others who felt constrained by the current sex and gender system.

Clearly, I had struck a nerve. The fact that so many people could get riled up by my proposal to revamp our sex and gender system suggested that change—as well as resistance to it—might be in the offing. Indeed, a lot has changed since 1993, and I like to think that my article was an important stimulus. As if from nowhere, intersexuals are materializing before our very eyes. Like Chase, many have become political organizers, who lobby physicians and politicians to change current treatment practices. But more generally, though perhaps no less provocatively, the boundaries separating masculine and feminine seem harder than ever to define.

Some find the changes under way deeply disturbing. Others find them liberating.

Who is an intersexual—and how many intersexuals are there? The concept of intersexuality is rooted in the very ideas of male and female. In the idealized, Platonic, biological world, human beings are divided into two kinds: a perfectly dimorphic species. Males have an X and a Y chromosome, testes, a penis and all of the appropriate internal plumbing for delivering urine and semen to the outside world. They also have well-known secondary sexual characteristics, including a muscular build and facial hair. Women have two X chromosomes, ovaries, all of the internal plumbing to transport urine and ova to the outside world, a system to support pregnancy and fetal development, as well as a variety of recognizable secondary sexual characteristics.

That idealized story papers over many obvious caveats: some women have facial hair, some men have none; some women speak with deep voices, some men veritably squeak. Less well known is the fact that, on close inspection, absolute dimorphism disintegrates even at the level of basic biology. Chromosomes, hormones, the internal sex structures, the gonads and the external genitalia all vary more than most people realize. Those born outside of the Platonic dimorphic mold are called intersexuals.

In "The Five Sexes" I reported an estimate by a psychologist expert in the treatment of intersexuals, suggesting that some 4 percent of all live births are intersexual. Then, together with a group of Brown University undergraduates, I set out to conduct the first systematic assessment of the available data on intersexual birthrates. We scoured the medical literature for estimates of the frequency of various categories of intersexuality, from additional chromosomes to mixed gonads, hormones and genitalia. For some conditions we could find only anecdotal evidence; for most, however, numbers exist. On the basis of that evidence, we calculated that for every 1,000 children born, seventeen are intersexual in some form. That number—1.7 percent—is a ballpark estimate, not a precise count, though we believe it is more accurate than the 4 percent I reported.

Our figure represents all chromosomal, anatomical and hormonal exceptions to the dimorphic ideal; the number of intersexuals who might, potentially, be subject to surgery as infants is smaller—probably between one in 1,000 and one in 2,000 live births. Furthermore, because some populations possess the relevant genes at high frequency, the intersexual birthrate is not uniform throughout the world.

Consider, for instance, the gene for congenital adrenal hyperplasia (CAH). When the CAH gene is inherited from both parents, it leads to a baby with masculinized external genitalia who possesses two X chromosomes and the internal reproductive organs of a potentially fertile woman. The frequency of the gene varies widely around the world: in New Zealand it occurs in only forty-three children per million; among the Yupik Eskimo of southwestern Alaska, its frequency is 3,500 per million.

Intersexuality has always been to some extent a matter of definition. And in the past century physicians have been the ones who defined children as intersexual—and provided the remedies. When only the chromosomes are unusual, but the external genitalia and gonads clearly indicate either a male or a female, physicians do not advocate intervention. Indeed, it is not clear what kind of intervention could be advocated in such cases. But the story is quite different when infants are born with mixed genitalia, or with external genitals that seem at odds with the baby's gonads.

Most clinics now specializing in the treatment of intersex babies rely on case-management principles developed in the 1950s by the psychologist John Money and the psychiatrists Joan G. Hampson and John L. Hampson, all of Johns Hopkins University in Baltimore, Maryland. Money believed that gender identity is completely malleable for about eighteen months after birth. Thus, he argued, when a treatment team is presented with an infant who has ambiguous genitalia, the team could make a gender assignment solely on the basis of what made the best surgical sense. The physicians could then simply encourage the parents to raise the child according to the surgically assigned gender. Following that course, most physicians maintained, would eliminate psychological distress for both the patient and the parents. Indeed, treatment teams were never to use such words as "intersex" or "hermaphrodite"; instead, they were to tell parents that nature intended the baby to be the boy or the girl that the physicians had determined it was. Through surgery, the physicians were merely completing nature's intention.

Although Money and the Hampsons published detailed case studies of intersex children who they said had adjusted well to their gender assignments, Money thought one case in particular proved his theory. It was a dramatic example, in as much as it did not involve intersexuality at all: one of a pair of identical twin boys lost his penis as a result of a circumcision accident. Money recommended that "John" (as he came to be known in a later case study) be surgically turned into "Joan" and raised as a girl. In time, Joan grew to love wearing dresses and having her hair done. Money proudly proclaimed the sex reassignment a success.

But as recently chronicled by John Colapinto, in his book *As Nature Made Him*, Joan—now known to be an adult male named David Reimer—eventually rejected his female assignment. Even without a functioning penis and testes (which had been removed as part of the reassignment)

John/Joan sought masculinizing medication, and married a woman with children (whom he adopted).

Since the full conclusion to the John/Joan story came to light, other individuals who were reassigned as males or females shortly after birth but who later rejected their early assignments have come forward. So, too, have cases in which the reassignment has worked—at least into the subject's mid-twenties. But even then the aftermath of the surgery can be problematic. Genital surgery often leaves scars that reduce sexual sensitivity. Chase herself had a complete clitoridectomy, a procedure that is less frequently performed on intersexuals today. But the newer surgeries, which reduce the size of the clitoral shaft, still greatly reduce sensitivity.

The revelation of cases of failed reassignments and the emergence of intersex activism have led an increasing number of pediatric endocrinologists, urologists and psychologists to reexamine the wisdom of early genital surgery. For example, in a talk that preceded Chase's at the LWPES meeting, the medical ethicist Laurence B. McCullough of the Center for Medical Ethics and Health Policy at Baylor College of Medicine in Houston, Texas, introduced an ethical framework for the treatment of children with ambiguous genitalia. Because sex phenotype (the manifestation of genetically and embryologically determined sexual characteristics) and gender presentation (the sex role projected by the individual in society) are highly variable, McCullough argues, the various forms of intersexuality should be defined as normal. All of them fall within the statistically expected variability of sex and gender. Furthermore, though certain disease states may accompany some forms of intersexuality, and may require medical intervention, intersexual conditions are not themselves diseases.

McCullough also contends that in the process of assigning gender, physicians should minimize what he calls irreversible assignments: taking steps such as the surgical removal or modification of gonads or genitalia that the patient may one day want to have reversed. Finally, McCullough urges physicians to abandon their practice of treating the birth of a child with genital ambiguity as a medical or social emergency. Instead, they should take the time to perform a thorough medical workup and should disclose everything to the parents, including the uncertainties about the final outcome. The treatment mantra, in other words, should be therapy, not surgery.

I believe a new treatment protocol for intersex infants, similar to the one outlined by McCullough, is close at hand. Treatment should combine some basic medical and ethical principles with a practical but less drastic approach to the birth of a mixed-sex child. As a first step, surgery on infants should be performed only to save the child's life or to substantially improve the child's physical well-being. Physicians may assign a sex—male or female—to an intersex infant on the basis of the probability that the child's particular condition will lead to the formation of a particular gender identity. At the same time, though, practitioners ought to be humble enough to recognize that as the child grows, he or she may reject the assignment—and they should be wise enough to listen to what the child has to say. Most important, parents should have access to the full range of information and options available to them.

Sex assignments made shortly after birth are only the beginning of a long journey. Consider, for instance, the life of Max Beck: Born intersexual, Max was surgically assigned as a female and consistently raised as such. Had her medical team followed her into her early twenties, they would have deemed her assignment a success because she was married to a man. (It should be noted that success in gender assignment has traditionally been defined as living in that gender as a heterosexual.) Within a few years, however, Beck had come out as a butch lesbian; now in her mid-thirties, Beck has become a man and married his lesbian partner, who (through the miracles of modern reproductive technology) recently gave birth to a girl.

Transsexuals, people who have an emotional gender at odds with their physical sex, once described themselves in terms of dimorphic absolutes—males trapped in female bodies, or vice versa. As such, they sought psychological relief through surgery. Although many still do, some so-called transgendered people today are content to inhabit a more ambiguous zone. A male-to-female transsexual, for instance, may come out as a lesbian. Jane, born a physiological male, is now in her late thirties and living with her wife, whom she married when her name was still John. Jane takes hormones to feminize herself, but they have not yet interfered with her ability to engage in intercourse as a man. In her mind Jane has a lesbian relationship with her wife, though she views their intimate moments as a cross between lesbian and heterosexual sex.

> A person who projects a social gender at odds with his or her genitals may die for the transgression.

It might seem natural to regard intersexuals and transgendered people as living midway between the poles of male and female. But male and female, masculine and feminine, cannot be parsed as some kind of continuum. Rather, sex and gender are best conceptualized as points in a multidimensional space. For some time, experts on gender development have distinguished between sex at the genetic level and at the cellular level (sex-specific gene expression, X and Y chromosomes); at the hormonal level (in the fetus, during childhood and after puberty); and at the anatomical level (genitals and secondary sexual characteristics). Gender identity presumably emerges from all of those corporeal aspects via some poorly understood interaction with environment and experience. What has become increasingly clear is that one can find levels of masculinity and femininity in almost every possible permutation. A chromosomal, hormonal and genital male (or female) may emerge with a female (or male) gender identity. Or a chromosomal female with male fetal hormones and masculinized genitalia—but with female pubertal hormones—may develop a female gender identity.

The medical and scientific communities have yet to adopt a language that is capable of describing such diversity. In her book *Hermaphrodites and the Medical Invention of Sex*, the historian and medical ethicist Alice Domurat Dreger of Michigan State University in East Lansing documents the emergence of current medical systems for classifying gender ambiguity. The current usage remains rooted in the Victorian approach to sex. The logical structure of the commonly used terms "true hermaphrodite," "male pseudohermaphrodite" and "female pseudohermaphrodite" indicates that only the so-called true hermaphrodite is a genuine mix of male and female. The others, no matter how confusing their body parts, are really hidden males or females. Because true hermaphrodites are rare—possibly only one in 100,000—such a classification system supports the idea that human beings are an absolutely dimorphic species.

At the dawn of the twenty-first century, when the variability of gender seems so visible, such a position is hard to maintain. And here, too, the old medical consensus has begun to crumble. Last fall the pediatric urologist Ian A. Aaronson of the Medical University of South Carolina in Charleston organized the North American Task Force on Intersexuality (NATFI) to review the clinical responses to genital ambiguity in infants. Key medical associations, such as the American Academy or Pediatrics, have endorsed NATFI. Specialists in surgery, endocrinology, psychology, ethics, psychiatry, genetics and public health, as well as intersex patient-advocate groups, have joined its ranks.

One of the goals of NATFI is to establish a new sex nomenclature. One proposal under consideration replaces the current system with emotionally neutral terminology that emphasizes developmental processes rather than preconceived gender categories. For example, Type I intersexes develop out of anomalous virilizing influences; Type II result from some interruption of virilization; and in Type III intersexes the gonads themselves may not have developed in the expected fashion.

What is clear is that since 1993, modern society has moved beyond five sexes to a recognition that gender variation is normal and, for some people, an arena for playful exploration. Discussing my "five sexes" proposal in her book *Lessons from the Intersexed*, the psychologist Suzanne J. Kessler of the State University of New York at Purchase drives this point home with great effect:

> The limitation with Fausto-Sterling's proposal is that . . . [it] still gives genitals . . . primary signifying status and ignores the fact that in the everyday world gender attributions are made without access to genital inspection. . . . What has primacy in everyday life is the gender that is performed, regardless of the flesh's configuration under the clothes.

I now agree with Kessler's assessment. It would be better for intersexuals and their supporters to turn everyone's focus away from genitals. Instead, as she suggests, one should acknowledge that people come in an even wider assortment of sexual identities and characteristics than mere genitals can distinguish. Some women may have "large clitorises or fused labia," whereas some men may have "small penises or misshapen scrota," as Kessler puts it, "phenotypes with no particular clinical or identity meaning."

As clearheaded as Kessler's program is—and despite the progress made in the 1990s—our society is still far from that ideal. The intersexual or transgendered person who projects a social gender—what Kessler calls "cultural genitals"—that conflicts with his or her physical genitals still may die for the transgression. Hence legal protection for people whose cultural and physical genitals do not match is needed during the current transition to a more gender-diverse world. One easy step would be to eliminate the category of "gender" from official documents, such as driver's licenses and passports. Surely attributes both more visible (such as height, build and eye color) and less visible (fingerprints and genetic profiles) would be more expedient.

A more far-ranging agenda is presented in the International Bill of Gender Rights, adopted in 1995 at the fourth annual International Conference on Transgender Law and Employment Policy in Houston, Texas. It lists ten "gender rights," including the right to define one's own gender, the right to change one's physical gender if one so chooses and the right to marry whomever one wishes. The legal bases for such rights are being hammered out in the courts as I write and, most recently, through the establishment, in the state of Vermont, of legal same-sex domestic partnerships.

No one could have foreseen such changes in 1993. And the idea that I played some role, however small, in reducing the pressure—from the medical community as well as from society at large—to flatten the diversity of human sexes into two diametrically opposed camps gives me pleasure.

Sometimes people suggest to me, with not a little horror, that I am arguing for a pastel world in which androgyny reigns and men and women are boringly the same. In my vision, however, strong colors coexist with pastels. There are and will continue to be highly masculine people out there; it's just that some of them are women. And some of the most feminine people I know happen to be men.

Boygasms and Girlgasms
A Frank Discussion About Hormones and Gender Differences

Julia Serano

Julia Serano earned a PhD in Biochemistry and Molecular Biophysics from Columbia University. She is a researcher in Evolutionary and Developmental Biology at University of California, Berkeley. This essay comes from Whipping Girl: A Transsexual Woman on Sexism and the Scapegoating of Femininity (2007). In addition to her work as a biologist, she is a writer, spoken word performer, and trans activist. Her work has appeared in BITCHfest: Ten Years of Cultural Criticism from the Pages of Bitch Magazine and Word Warriors: 30 Leaders in the Women's Spoken Word Movement.

Though I am often reluctant to indulge people's fascination with the details of my physical transition from male to female, I will often make an exception regarding the psychological changes I experienced due to hormones. The reason for this is quite simple: Sex hormones have become horribly politicized in our culture, evident in the way that people blatantly blame testosterone for nearly all instances of male aggression and violence, or the way that women who become legitimately angry or upset often have their opinions dismissed as mere symptoms of their body chemistry. Such hormonal folklore has strongly influenced medicine, as evidenced by the countless shoddy, pseudoscientific studies claiming to verify popular assumptions about testosterone and estrogen. Of course, such overt politicization has created a significant backlash of people who now play down the role of hormones in human behavior, who argue that most of their presumed effects (making men overly aggressive and women overly emotional) are better explained by socialization—after all, young boys are encouraged to be aggressive and discouraged from showing emotions, and vice versa for girls.

Having experienced both female and male hormones firsthand, I feel it's my duty to spoil this nature-versus-nurture debate by offering the following description and interpretation of my personal experiences "transitioning" from testosterone to estrogen and progesterone. But before I begin, there are two important points that must be made prior to any discussion regarding hormones. First, contrary to popular belief, hormones do not simply act like unilateral on/off switches controlling female/feminine or male/masculine development. All people have both androgens (which include testosterone) and estrogens in their systems, although the balance is tipped more toward the former in men and the latter in women. Not only are there different types of androgens and estrogens, but these hormones require different steroid receptors to function, are metabolized by numerous enzymes that can shift the balance by converting one hormone to another, and function by regulating the levels of scores of "downstream genes," which are more directly responsible for producing specific hormonal effects. Because of all these variables, there's an extensive amount of natural variation built into the way individual people experience and process specific hormones.

The second issue to keep in mind is the difficulty in distinguishing "real" hormone effects from their perceived or presumed effects. For example, shortly after I began hormone therapy, I had a strong craving for eggs. I immediately attributed this to the hormones until other trans women told me that they never had similar cravings. So perhaps that was an effect of the hormones only I had. Or maybe I was going through an "egg phase" that just so happened to coincide with the start of my hormone therapy. Hence, the problem: Not only can hormones affect individuals differently, but we sometimes attribute coincidences to them and project our own expectations onto them.

For these reasons, I will limit my discussion here to those hormonal changes I have experienced that have been corroborated by other trans women I have spoken with. Also, rather than get into the more physical effects of hormones (i.e., muscle/fat distribution, hair growth, etc.) which are not in dispute, I will focus primarily on the "psychological" changes—in my emotions, senses, and sexuality—that I experienced early on when I began taking estrogen along with an anti-androgen, which suppresses endogenous testosterone levels, to shift my hormonal balance into the range that most adult women experience.

People often say that female hormones make women "more emotional" than men, but in my view such claims are an oversimplification. How would I describe the changes I went through, then? In retrospect, when testosterone was the predominant sex hormone in my body, it was as though a thick curtain were draped over my emotions. It deadened their intensity, made all of my feelings pale and vague as if they were ghosts that would haunt me. But on estrogen, I find that I have all of the same emotions that I did back then, only now they come in crystal clear. In other words, it is not the actual emotions, but rather their intensity that has changed—the highs are way higher and the lows are way lower. Another way of saying it is that I feel my emotions more now; they are in the foreground rather than the background of my mind.

The anecdote that perhaps best captures this change occurred about two months after I started hormone therapy. My wife, Dani, and I had an argument and at one point I started to cry—something that was not all that uncommon for me when I was hormonally male. What was different was that after about a minute or so, I began to laugh while simultaneously continuing to cry. When Dani asked me why I was laughing, I replied, "I can't turn it off." Back when I was hormonally male, I felt as though I was always capable of stopping the cry, of holding it all in, if I really wanted to. Now, I find it nearly impossible to hold back the tears once I start crying. I've learned instead to just go with it, to let myself experience the cry, and it feels a lot more cathartic as a result.

In general, even though my emotions are much more intense these days, I certainly do not feel as though they get in the way of my logic or reasoning, or that they single-handedly control my every thought or decision. I remain perfectly capable of acting on rational thought rather than following my feelings. However, what I can no longer do (at least to the extent that I used to) is completely ignore my emotions, repress them, or entirely shut them out of my mind.

The change in the intensity of my emotions is paralleled in my sense of touch as well. I cannot say for sure that my sense of touch has improved—that I am able to feel things that I couldn't before—but it surely plays a greater role in how I experience the world. Whenever I am interested in something, whether it's a book, a piece of artwork, an article of clothing, or an object or material of any kind, I feel compelled to touch it, to handle it, as though my understanding of it would be incomplete without the tactile knowledge of how it physically feels to me. In contrast, when hormonally male, I generally felt satisfied with simply seeing an object of interest.

Unlike my emotions and sense of touch, which seem to have primarily increased in *intensity*, my sense of smell has definitely increased in *sensitivity*. That is to say, I now can smell things that I was previously unable to detect. Though it sounds like a cliché, during the first spring after my transition I was blown away by how flowers smelled to me. While I'd always found them very fragrant, I suddenly smelled all of these subtle notes and perfumes that I had never been aware of before. I also had similar experiences with the aroma of certain foods. Perhaps the most interesting facet of this change for me has been sensing new smells in people. I find that men now sometimes have a really strong, somewhat sweet smell to them that I had never been privy to before. But it is not simply that I have gained the ability to pick up on male odors or "pheromones," because I also now detect new smells with women. During my transition, I noticed that when I would kiss Dani or nuzzle my nose into her neck, it felt as though fireworks were going off in my brain. I was barraged with amazingly sweet, soothing, and sensual smells that not only sexually stimulated me, but also made me feel closer to her, as if I were connected to her in a way that I hadn't been before. Indeed, the increase in my senses of smell and touch, and the way I feel more "in touch" with my emotions, has led me to feel more in tune with the world, and with other people.

Without a doubt, the most profound change that has come with my hormonal transition has been in my sexuality. In fact, the very first change that I noticed—which came during my first few weeks on estrogen/anti-androgens—was a sharp decrease in my sex drive. I noticed this for the first time at the end of a really busy week, after working many hours and being out late most nights. It suddenly occurred to me, only after the fact, that I had neither had sex nor masturbated during the entire week. While this may not seem impressive to some readers, for me, at the time, it was completely unheard-of. I could barely go a day, let alone two days, without some form of release (in fact, for much of my adult male life, masturbating was an activity that I typically indulged in one to three times a day). While my sex drive may have decreased, this surely does not mean that I have lost interest in sex entirely. I still intensely enjoy masturbation and sex, it's just that I crave it about three to four times a week rather than one to three times a day.

While the quantity of my sexual experiences has decreased significantly, the quality of those experiences has increased exponentially. Indeed, I called this chapter "Boygasms and Girlgasms" because, for me, the differences in how my body responds to sexual stimuli—how I "get off," if you will—has been the most dramatic (and in many ways most enjoyable) hormonal change that I've experienced. I began to notice these changes within the first few weeks of starting hormone therapy. Even before I lost the ability to maintain erections, I found that what used to excite me—that back-and-forth stroking action that males typically prefer— really wasn't doing the trick anymore. I just felt like I needed something more. So I started experimenting with Dani's vibrators. When I had tried them in the past, they always felt like too much stimulation, but now they suddenly felt absolutely incredible. And back when I was hormonally male, sexual stimulation would cause me to climb rather rapidly toward the peak of orgasm; if I wanted the experience to last longer, I had to keep pulling back just before I hit that precipice. But now I found that I could go way beyond what used to be the point of orgasm, writhing for fifteen minutes in a sexual state that was far more intense than I had ever experienced before. Now, my orgasms are way more in the female rather than male range: They typically take longer to achieve (but are well worth the wait), each one has a different flavor and intensity, they are less centralized and more diffuse throughout my body, and they are often multiple.

Not surprisingly, changes in my senses have also greatly influenced my sexuality. Not only am I more sexually excited by the scent of my partner, but the increase in my tactile senses make my whole body feel alive—electric—during sex. Nowhere is this more obvious than in my nipples, which seem to have a direct connection to my groin. It also has become apparent to me that I am less visual with regard to my sexuality. I don't think that I recognized this at first, probably because it is harder to notice the gradual loss of a sensation than the appearance of a new one. I only realized it about a year later, when I began taking progesterone for ten days out of the month to simulate the endogenous expression of progesterone in most women. The first thing I noticed upon taking progesterone is that my sex drive, particularly in response to visual input, sharply increased. In fact, the visual effects of progesterone very much reminded me of how I responded to visual stimuli when I was hormonally male.

Upon hearing my experience, I am sure that some people—particularly those who favor social, rather than biological, explanations of gender difference—will be somewhat disappointed at the predictable nature of my transformation. Some may even assume that I am buying into female stereotypes when I describe myself becoming a more weepy, touchy-feely, flower-adoring, less sexually aggressive person. Not only are similar experiences regularly described by other trans women, but trans men typically give reciprocal accounts: They almost universally describe an increase in their sex drives (which become more responsive to visual inputs), male-type orgasms (more centralized, quicker to achieve), a decrease in their sense of smell, and more difficulty crying and discerning their emotions.[1]

On the other hand, those who are eager to have popular presumptions about hormones confirmed will probably be just as disappointed to hear what has *not* noticeably changed during my hormonal transition: my sexual orientation; the "types" of women I am attracted to; my tastes in music, movies, or hobbies; my politics; my sense of humor; my levels of aggression, competitiveness, nurturing, creativity, intelligence; and my ability to read maps or do math. While it would be irresponsible for me to say that these human traits are entirely hormone-independent (as it is possible that fetal hormones potentially play some role in predisposing us to such traits), they clearly are not controlled by adult hormone levels to the extent that many people argue or assume.

While transsexual accounts of hormones are largely in agreement with one another, I also find it illuminating to examine the more subtle differences between our individual experiences. For example, I have heard several trans men describe how they started to consume porn voraciously upon taking testosterone. While my sexuality was definitely more visual when I was hormonally male, and I certainly enjoyed looking at porn on occasion, I still always preferred erotic stories and fantasies to pictures of naked bodies. Similarly, I have heard some trans men say that they almost never cry since taking testosterone, whereas I used to cry somewhat often (although not nearly as often as I do now) when I was hormonally male. Some trans men have also described becoming more aggressive or competitive since taking testosterone (although many others describe themselves as becoming more calm).[2] However, when I was hormonally male, I typically found myself to be the least aggressive or competitive guy in any room that I entered.

---

[1]For trans male accounts of hormones, see Patrick Califia, *Speaking Sex to Power: The Politics of Queer Sex* (San Francisco: Cleis Press, 2002), 393-401; Jamison Green, *Becoming a Visible Man* (Nashville: Vanderbilt University Press, 2004), 98-102, 151-152; Henry Rubin, *Self-Made Men: Identity and Embodiment Among Transsexual Men* (Nashville Vanderbilt Unisversity Press, 2003), 152-163; and Max Wolf Valerio, *The Testosterone Files: My Hormonal and Social Transformation from Female to Male* (Emeryville, CA: Seal Press, 2006).

[2]Summarized in Joan Roughgarden, *Evolution's Rainbow: Diversity, Gender, and Sexuality in Nature and People* (Berkeley: University of California Press, 2004), 220-221; see also sources cited in the previous note.

This is not to say that I was passive, as I have always been motivated and eager to succeed at any task I have taken on. Rather, I have never really felt any desire to have my success come at the expense of others.

Thus, it is clear that typical male levels of testosterone, in and of itself, are insufficient to produce many of these stereotypically male behaviors, most likely because of the variability that exists from person to person in the way this hormone is processed and experienced. While a part of me is tempted to attribute my apparent imperviousness to testosterone to the fact that I am trans—that on some level, I was never fully or completely male—I also realize that many cissexual people are exceptions in this regard as well. I know plenty of non-trans men who are not particularly into porn, who are not very aggressive, and/or who often cry. I have also met women who have high sex drives, who enjoy porn, and/or who are just as aggressive and competitive as the average alpha male. Thus, there seems to be more variation among women and among men than there is between the averages of these two groups.

Acknowledging this variation is absolutely crucial in order for us to finally move beyond overly simplistic (and binary) biology-versus-socialization debates regarding gender. After all, there are very real *biological* differences between hormones: Testosterone will probably make any given person cry less frequently and have a higher sex drive than estrogen will. However, if one were to argue that this biological difference represents an *essential* gender difference—one that holds true for all women and all men—they would be incorrect. After all, there are some men who cry more than certain women, and some women who have higher sex drives than certain men. Perhaps what is most telling is that, as a society, we regulate these hormonally influenced behaviors in a way that seems to exaggerate their natural effects. We actively discourage boys from crying, even though testosterone itself should reduce the chance of this happening. And we encourage men to act on their sex drives (by praising them as "studs") while discouraging women from doing the same (by dismissing them "sluts"), despite the fact that most women will end up having a lower sex drive than most men anyway.

While many gender theorists have focused their efforts on attempting to demonstrate that this sort of socialization *produces* gender differences, it seems to me more accurate to say that in many cases socialization acts to exaggerate biological gender differences that already exist. In other words, it coaxes those of us who are exceptional (e.g., men who cry often or women with high sex drives) to hide or curb those tendencies, rather than simply falling where we may on the spectrum of gender diversity. By attempting to play down or erase the existence of such exceptions, socialization distorts biological gender difference to create the impression that essential differences exist between women and men. Thus, the primary role of socialization is not to produce gender difference de novo, but to create the illusion that female and male are mutually exclusive, "opposite" sexes.

Recognizing the distinction between biological and essential gender differences has enormous ramifications for the future of gender activism. Since there is natural variation in our drives and the way we experience the world, attempts to minimize gender differences (i.e., insisting that people strive to be unisex or androgynous) are rather pointless; we should instead learn to embrace all forms of gender diversity, whether typical (feminine women and masculine men) or exceptional (masculine women and feminine men). Further, since some attributes that are considered feminine (e.g., being more in tune with one's emotions) or masculine (e.g., being preoccupied with sex) are clearly affected by our hormones, attempts by some gender theorists to frame femininity and masculinity as being entirely artificial or performative seem misplaced. Rather than focus on how femininity and masculinity are produced (an issue that has unfortunately dominated the field of gender studies of late), we should instead turn our attention to the ways these gender traits are interpreted.

The issue of interpretation becomes obvious when considering transsexuals. For example, one cannot help but notice how much more empowering trans male descriptions of hormonal transition tend to sound compared to those of trans women. Trans men experience an increase in their sex drive, become less emotional, and their bodies become harder and stronger—all of these changes having positive connotations in our society. In contrast, I have experienced a decrease in my sex drive and become more emotional, softer, and weaker—all traits that are viewed negatively. The reason for these differing connotations is obvious: In our culture, femininity and femaleness are not appreciated nor valued to the extent that masculinity and maleness are. And while embracing my own femaleness and femininity during my transition was personally empowering and rewarding, I nevertheless felt overwhelmed by all of the negative connotations and inferior meanings that other people began to project onto me. These meanings were not only projected onto my female body, but onto the hormones themselves: from the warning label on my progesterone prescription that read, "May cause drowsiness or dizziness" and "Avoid operating heavy machinery," to the men who have hinted that my female hormones were responsible for the fact that I disagreed with their opinion, and the women who sneered, "Why would you ever want to do that?" upon finding out that I have chosen to cycle my hormones.

Once we start thinking about gender as being socially exaggerated (rather than socially constructed), we can finally tackle the issue of sexism in our society without having to dismiss or undermine biological sex in the process. While biological gender differences are very real, most of the connotations, values, and assumptions we associate with female and male biology are not.

"It's Only a Penis"
Rape, Feminism, and Difference

Christine Helliwell

Christine Helliwell is in the Anthropology Department at the Australian National University. Her work focuses on the Borneo Dayak people of Indonesia, most specifically the Gerai. This essay first appeared in Signs: Journal of Women in Culture and Society *in 2000.*

In 1985 and 1986 I carried out anthropological fieldwork in the Dayak community of Gerai in Indonesian Borneo. One night in September 1985, a man of the village climbed through a window into the freestanding house where a widow lived with her elderly mother, younger (unmarried) sister, and young children. The widow awoke, in darkness, to feel the man inside her mosquito net, gripping her shoulder while he climbed under the blanket that covered her and her youngest child as they slept (her older children slept on mattresses nearby). He was whispering, "be quiet, be quiet!" She responded by sitting up in bed and pushing him violently, so that he stumbled backward, became entangled with her mosquito net, and then, finally free, moved across the floor toward the window. In the meantime, the woman climbed from her bed and pursued him, shouting his name several times as she did so. His hurried exit through the window, with his clothes now in considerable disarray, was accompanied by a stream of abuse from the woman and by excited interrogations from wakened neighbors in adjoining houses.

I awoke the following morning to raucous laughter on the longhouse verandah outside my apartment where a group of elderly women gathered regularly to thresh, winnow, and pound rice. They were recounting this tale loudly, and with enormous enjoyment, to all in the immediate vicinity. As I came out of my door, one was engaged in mimicking the man climbing out the window, sarong falling down, genitals askew. Those others working or lounging near her on the verandah—both men and women—shrieked with laughter.

When told the story, I was shocked and appalled. An unknown man had tried to climb into the bed of a woman in the dead, dark of night? I knew what this was called: attempted rape. The woman had seen the man and recognized him (so had others in the village, wakened by her shouting). I knew what he deserved: the full weight of the law. My own fears about being a single woman alone in a strange place, sleeping in a dwelling that could not be secured at night, bubbled to the surface. My feminist sentiments poured out. "How can you laugh?" I asked my women friends; "this is a very bad thing that he has tried to do." But my outrage simply served to fuel the hilarity. "No, not bad," said one of the old women (a particular friend of mine), "simply stupid."

I felt vindicated in my response when, two hours later, the woman herself came onto the verandah to share betel nut and tobacco and to broadcast the story. Her anger was palpable, and she shouted for all to hear her determination to exact a compensation payment from the man. Thinking to obtain information about local women's responses to rape, I began to question her. Had she been frightened? I asked. Of course she had—Wouldn't I feel frightened if I awoke in the dark to find an unknown person inside my mosquito net? Wouldn't I be angry? Why then, I asked, hadn't she taken the opportunity, while he was entangled in her mosquito net, to kick him hard or to hit him with one of the many wooden implements near at hand? She looked shocked. Why would she do that? she asked—after all, he hadn't hurt her. No, but he had wanted to, I replied. She looked at me with puzzlement. Not able to find a local word for *rape* in my vocabulary, I scrabbled to explain myself: "He was trying to have sex with you," I said, "although you didn't want to. He was trying to hurt you." She looked at me, more with pity than with puzzlement now, although both were mixed in her expression. "Tin [Christine], it's only a penis," she said. "How can a penis hurt anyone?"

RAPE, FEMINISM, AND DIFFERENCE

A central feature of many feminist writings about rape in the past twenty years is their concern to eschew the view of rape as a natural function of male biology and to stress instead its bases in society and culture. It is curious, then, that so much of this work talks of rape in terms that suggest—either implicitly or explicitly—that it is a universal practice. To take only several examples: Pauline Bart and Patricia O'Brien tell us that "every female from nine months to ninety years is at risk" (1985, 1); Anna Clark argues that "all women know the paralyzing fear of walking down a dark street at night. . . . It seems to be a fact of life that the fear of rape imposes a curfew on our movements" (1987, 1); Catharine MacKinnon claims that "sexuality is central to women's definition and forced sex is central to sexuality," so "rape is indigenous, not exceptional, to women's social condition" (1989b, 172) and "all women live all the time under the shadow of the threat of sexual abuse" (1989a, 340); Lee Madigan and Nancy Gamble write of "the global terrorism of rape" (1991, 21–22); and Susan Brison asserts that "the fact that all women's lives are restricted by sexual violence is indisputable" (1993, 17). The potted "world histories" of rape—which attempt to trace the practice in a range of different societies against a single historical/evolutionary timeline—found in a number of feminist writings on the topic, further illustrate this universalizing tendency.[1] Just as I, an anthropologist trained to be particularly sensitive to the impact of cultural difference, nevertheless took for granted the occurrence of rape in a social and cultural context that I knew to be profoundly different from my own, so most other feminists also unwittingly assume that the practice occurs in all human societies.[2] This is particularly puzzling given that Peggy Reeves Sanday, for one, long ago demonstrated that while rape occurs widely throughout the world, it is by no means a human universal: some societies can indeed be classified as rape free (1981).

There are two general reasons for this universalization of rape among Western feminists. The first of these has to do with the understanding of the practice as horrific by most women in Western societies. In these settings, rape is seen as "a fate worse than, or tantamount to, death"

---

[1]For recent examples of such histories, see Madigan and Gamble 1991, 11ff.; McColgan 1996, 12–27.

[2]There are some exceptions to this. For example, Peggy Sanday's work on rape among the Minangkabau (1986) and within U.S. college fraternities (1990b) emphasizes very much its contextualized character. In fact, Sanday is one of the few feminists who has attempted to formulate a more general theory concerning the conditions under which rape occurs and under which it does not occur (1981; 1986; 1990b, 8).

(S. Marcus 1992, 387): a shattering of identity that, for instance, left one North American survivor feeling "not quite sure whether I had died and the world went on without me, or whether I was alive in a totally alien world" (Brison 1993, 10). While any form of violent attack may have severe emotional consequences for its victims, the *sexualization* of violence in rape greatly intensifies those consequences for women in Western societies: "To show power and anger through rape—as opposed to mugging or assault—men are calling on lessons women learn from society, from history and religion, to defile, degrade and shame in addition to inflicting physical pain. Rapists have learned, *as have their victims*, that to rape is to do something worse than to assault" (Gordon and Riger 1989, 45; see also Koss and Harvey 1991). Clearly, the intermeshing of sexuality and personal identity in contemporary Western societies—such that Michel Foucault refers to sex as "that secret which seems to underlie all that we are" (1978, 155)—imbues the practice of rape with particular horror for most victims from those societies, since there it involves a violation of personhood itself.[3]

Significantly, almost one-third of the respondents in Bart and O'Brien's sample of U.S. women subject to rape attempts were more afraid of being raped by their attackers than they were of being murdered and/or mutilated by them (1985, 52–53)—an extraordinarily large number given that American women are reported to fear murder more than any other crime (Gordon and Riger 1989, 2).[4] Rape is the second most feared crime among women in America, a situation that is no doubt exacerbated by the frequency with which it occurs there.[5] Margaret Gordon and Stephanie Riger (1989) have documented at length the way fear of rape—"the female fear" or "this special fear," as they call it—pervades the lives and shapes the actions of American women. So deep is this fear for many Western women that they anticipate the possibility of rape everywhere: rape comes to be understood simply as part of the "natural" human condition. Susan Griffin puts it eloquently: "I have never been free of the fear of rape. From a very early age I, like most women, have thought of rape as part of my natural environment—something to be feared and prayed against like fire and lightning. I never asked why men raped; I simply thought it one of the many mysteries of human nature" (1986, 3). Since feminists are, undoubtedly, as subject to this fear as any other Western women, our tendency to universalize rape is almost overwhelming.

---

[3]It is clear from the ethnographic record that while for women in many non-Western societies the experience of rape is similar to that of most Western women, this is not the case in all societies. Material from, e.g., Mehinaku (Gregor 1990) and some Papua New Guinea societies suggests that rape takes on rather different meanings and significances in these settings and, in particular, that rape is not everywhere experienced by women victims in the deeply traumatic terms taken for granted by most Western feminist writers on the topic. Indeed, there is evidence to suggest that, even within specific Western contexts, rape can mean rather different things to different people: Bourque 1989, for instance, has shown that within a single community in southern California, definitions of rape vary enormously, both between men and women and between different women. It is important to point out in this context that to acknowledge the social and cultural variability of the meaning of rape is not to deny its horror or invalidate its trauma for most women victims in the West. The work of such disparate thinkers as Maurice Merleau-Ponty, Foucault, and Pierre Bourdie has demonstrated that bodily (including emotional) responses are largely socially constituted; the fact that they are therefore not universally shared renders them no less real for those who experience them. Iris Marion Young's classic account (1990) of how Western women's oppression is lived in their bodily experience, for instance, makes very clear the connection between social institutions and practices and the bodily/emotional responses of individuals.

[4]Twenty-nine women out of ninety-two were more afraid of being raped by their attackers than of being murdered and/or mutilated by them. Forty-seven women were more afraid of being murdered and/or mutilated, and sixteen were unclear on this point (Bart and O'Brien 1985, 53). Bart and O'Brien suggest that women who are more afraid of being raped than of being murdered and/or mutilated are more likely to avoid rape when attacked by a potential rapist.

[5]Madigan and Gamble state that an estimated 15 to 40 percent of women (presumably of American women) are "victims of attempted or completed rapes during their lifetimes" (1991, 4; see also Russell 1984; Bart and O'Brien 1985, 129–30; Kilpatrick et al. 1987; Koss and Harvey 1991, 22–29). Koss and Harvey cite a study showing that one in 3.6 American college women has been subject to rape or attempted rape in her lifetime (1991, 24). While the frequency rates are lower in most other Western countries, they are nonetheless high; McColgan, e.g., refers to a 1982 study in London that found that one woman in every six had been raped and a further one in five had been subject to attempted rape (1996, 94).

In addition, because within Western feminist discourse rape is depicted as a shockingly bar-baric practice—"illuminat[ing] gendered relations of power in their rawest, most brutal forms" (Dubinsky 1993, 8)—there is a tendency to view it as atavistic. Because the practice is widespread in "civilized" Western countries, it is assumed to pervade all other societies as well, since these latter are understood as located closer to the savagery end of the evolutionary ladder. This relates very closely to what Chandra Mohanty has described as "the third world difference": "that stable ahistorical something" that, in many feminist accounts, oppresses the women of Third World countries in addition to their oppression by men (1991, 53). Under this logic, practices deemed oppressive to women that are not commonly found in the West, such as clitoridectomy and *sati*, are explained as resulting from the barbarism of Third World peoples, while oppressive practices that are common in the West, such as rape, are explained in universalistic terms.[6] The related ten-dency within Western iconography to sexualize black female bodies (see Gilman 1985) means that rape is readily assumed to be a characteristic of "other"—especially black—societies. In fact, the link between this racist iconography and the frequency with which white men rape black women in countries like the United States should lead us to be extremely wary of this kind of assumption. Feminists cannot sidestep this problem by claiming that apparently universalizing statements about rape are meant to refer to Western societies only, since the assumption that unmarked state-ments should automatically be read in this way is itself suggestive of a form of racism. This is a point to which Western feminists, of all people, should be particularly sensitive, having ourselves been engaged in a protracted battle to fracture universalizing masculinist discourses.

A second, equally deep-seated reason for the feminist tendency to universalize rape stems from Western feminism's emphasis on difference between men and women and from its conse-quent linking of rape and difference. Two types of difference are involved here. The first of these is difference in social status and power; thus rape is linked quite explicitly, in contemporary feminist accounts, to patriarchal social forms. Indeed, this focus on rape as stemming from difference in social position is what distinguishes feminist from other kinds of accounts of rape (see Ellis 1989, 10). In this view, inequality between men and women is linked to men's desire to possess, subjugate, and control women, with rape constituting a central means by which the freedom of women is limited and their continued submission to men ensured. For this reason, rape has assumed a significant role within many feminist narratives, with Carole Pateman's account of the social contract as based on an originary rape of a woman by a man providing per-haps the best-known example (1988). Since many feminists continue to believe that patriarchy is universal—or, at the very least, to feel deeply ambivalent on this point—there is a tendency among us to believe that rape, too, is universal.[7]

However, the view of women as everywhere oppressed by men has been extensively critiqued within the anthropological literature. A number of anthropologists have argued that in some so-cieties, while men and women may perform different roles and occupy different spaces, they are

---

[6]Kathleen Barry's recent book on prostitution provides a good example of this kind of approach. Without providing any historical or ethnographic evidence whatsoever, she claims that in "pre-industrial and feudal societies" (the first of four progressive historical "stages of sexual exploitation"), "women's reduction to sex is a fact of their status as the property of their husbands. Under such conditions women are governed by marital relations of power through the exploitation of their unpaid labor in the home, their reproduction, and their sexuality. . . . Men may sexually exploit their wives, take concubines, and buy prostitutes with impunity as the privilege of male domination that services their promiscuity. By contrast, as women are sexual property of men, any sexual act outside of their marriage, including rape and forced prostitution, is usually considered infidelity and the victims are severely punished" (Barry 1995, 51).

[7]Among "radical" feminists such as Andrea Dworkin and Catharine MacKinnon this belief reaches its most extreme version, in which all sexual intercourse between a man and a woman is viewed as akin to rape (Dworkin 1987; MacKinnon 1989a, 1989b).

nevertheless equal in value, status, and power.[8] In addition, Marilyn Strathern, for one, has pointed out that notions such as "inequality" and "domination" cannot necessarily be applied in societies with very different conceptions of agency and personhood: "To argue that what happens to women qua women is a function of what happens to men qua men is not to postulate that women's concerns are relative to or subsumed by those of men but that neither can be understood without comprehending the relationship between them" (1988, 34; see also Strathern 1987). As Strathern sees it, the Western tendency to distinguish between subject and object makes it impossible for Westerners to recognize that in some societies (in this case, Melanesian ones) a person (whether male or female) is, at the same time, both subject and object. Feminist distinctions between male subjects and female objects—and corresponding notions of asymmetry—thus do not make sense in these contexts (Strathern 1988). Viewed in this light, feminist claims concerning the universality of rape begin to look even more problematic.[9]

But there is a second type of difference between men and women that also, albeit largely implicitly, underlies the assumption that rape is universal, and it is the linkage between this type of difference and the treatment of rape in feminist accounts with which I am largely concerned in this article. I refer to the assumption by most Western feminists writing on rape that men and women have different bodies and, more specifically, different genitalia: that they are, in other words, differently sexed. Furthermore, it is taken for granted in most feminist accounts that these differences render the former biologically, or "naturally," capable of penetrating and therefore brutalizing the latter and render the latter "naturally" able to be brutalized. While this assumption was quite explicit in earlier feminist accounts of rape—in particular, in Susan Brownmiller's (1975) argument that men rape primarily because they are biologically equipped with the "tools" (penises) to do so—it is largely implicit in more recent feminist work, where the concern is to eschew biological explanations and to stress instead the social bases of rape.[10] Rape of women by men is thus assumed to be universal because the same "biological" bodily differences between men and women are believed to exist everywhere.

Unfortunately, the assumption that preexisting bodily difference between men and women underlies rape has blinded feminists writing on the subject to the ways the practice of rape itself creates and inscribes such difference. This seems particularly true in contemporary Western societies where the relationship between rape and bodily/genital dimorphism appears to be an extremely intimate one. Judith Butler (1990, 1993) has argued (following Foucault 1978) that the Western emphasis on sexual difference is a product of the heterosexualization of desire within Western societies over the past few centuries, which "requires and institutes the production of discrete and asymmetrical oppositions between 'feminine' and 'masculine,' where these are understood as expressive attributes of 'male' and 'female'" (1990, 17).[11] The practice of rape in

---

[8]Leacock 1978 and Bell 1983 are well-known examples. Sanday 1990a and Marcus 1992 are more recent examples, on Minangkabau and Turkish society, respectively.

[9]MacKinnon suggests, for instance, that Khalka Mongol men's assertion (as quoted by Sanday) that "our women never resist" evokes a society in which sex can be equated with rape (1989a, 322). This suggestion clearly assumes that the individuated "subject" of Western experience is found also among the Khalka Mongol, such that the observer can separate out the "autonomous" interests of husband and wife and thus describe sexual relations between them in the familiar Western terms of "consent" and "resistance." While any categorization of Khalka Mongol society as "rape free" cannot be based simply on male claims of this type, categorization of it as "rape prone" purely on this basis is equally absurd, since it assumes that these kinds of male claims serve the same function here as they often do in the United States: namely, to legitimate male objectification of women. Work such as Strathern's throws into question precisely this kind of assumption.

[10]Some contemporary feminist accounts, however, are more explicit in their adoption of this kind of position. Aileen McColgan, e.g., states that most rapists "are not armed with . . . anything other than their fists, their penises and their superior strength" (1996, 9).

[11]See Laqueur 1990 for a historical account of this process.

Western contexts can only properly be understood with reference to this heterosexual matrix, to the division of humankind into two distinct—and in many respects opposed—types of body (and hence types of person).[12] While it is certainly the case that rape is linked in contemporary Western societies to disparities of power and status between men and women, it is the particular discursive form that those disparities take—their elaboration in terms of the discourse of sex—that gives rape its particular meaning and power in these contexts.

Sharon Marcus has already argued convincingly that the act of rape "feminizes" women in Western settings, so that "the entire female body comes to be symbolized by the vagina, itself conceived of as a delicate, perhaps inevitably damaged and pained inner space" (1992, 398). I would argue further that the *practice* of rape in these settings—both its possibility and its actualization—not only feminizes women but masculinizes men as well.[13] This masculinizing character of rape is very clear in, for instance, Sanday's ethnography of fraternity gang rape in North American universities (1990b) and, in particular, in material on rape among male prison inmates. In the eyes of these rapists the act of rape marks them as "real men" and marks their victims as not men, that is, as feminine.[14] In this iconography, the "masculine" body (along with the "masculine" psyche), is viewed as hard, penetrative, and aggressive, in contrast to the soft, vulnerable, and violable "feminine" sexuality and psyche. Rape both reproduces and marks the pronounced sexual polarity found in these societies.

Western understandings of gender difference have almost invariably started from the presumption of a presocial bodily difference between men and women ("male" and "female") that is then somehow acted on by society to produce gender. In particular, the possession of either male genitals or female genitals is understood by most Westerners to be not only the primary marker of gender identity but, indeed, the underlying cause of that identity. Most feminist models of gender, while wishing to draw attention to the socially constructed character of difference, have nevertheless assumed—however reluctantly—that gender ultimately relates "back" to sex, that is, to the differences between "male" and "female" bodies. Yet this assumption is problematic in light of both feminist challenges to the notion that "sex" is given (and therefore universal) (Butler 1990, 1993) and historical research suggesting that dimorphic "sexing" of bodies is a relatively recent phenomenon in West European history (Trumbach 1989, 1993; Laqueur 1990; van der Meer 1993). This kind of model is especially problematic for using with cross-cultural material, such as that described below.[15]

I seek to do two things in this article. First, in providing an account of a community in which rape does not occur, I aim to give the lie to the widespread assumption that rape is universal and

---

[12]On the equation of body and person within Western (especially feminist) thought, see Moore 1994.

[13]See Plaza 1980: "[Rape] is very sexual in the sense that [it] is frequently a sexual activity, but especially in the sense that it opposes men and women: it is *social sexing* which is latent in rape. . . . Rape is sexual essentially because it rests on the very social difference between the sexes" (31).

[14]The material on male prison inmates is particularly revealing in this respect. As an article by Stephen Donaldson, a former prisoner and the president of the U.S. advocacy group Stop Prisoner Rape, makes clear, "hooking up" with another prisoner is the best way for a prisoner to avoid sexual assaults, particularly gang rapes. Hooking up involves entering a sexual liaison with a senior partner ("jocker," "man," "pitcher," "daddy") in exchange for protection. In this arrangement, the rules are clear: the junior partner gives up his autonomy and comes under the authority of the senior partner; he is often expected by the senior partner "to be as feminine in appearance and behaviour as possible," including shaving his legs, growing long hair, using a feminine nickname, and performing work perceived as feminine (laundry, cell cleaning, giving backrubs, etc.) (Donaldson 1996, 17, 20). See also the extract from Jack Abbott's prison letters in Halperin 1993 (424–25).

[15]Henrietta Moore has pointed out some of the problems with the conventional sex/gender model. These include its assumption that difference lies between bodies (whereas in many societies gender differences are understood to reside within individual bodies) and its stress on the body as the ultimate repository of identity, which relates to the Western belief in the unified, continuous person located in an individual body (a belief that is by no means universal) (Moore 1994, chaps. 1 and 2).

thus to invite Western feminists to interrogate the basis of our own tendency to take its universality for granted.[16] The fundamental question is this: Why does a woman of Gerai see a penis as lacking the power to harm her, while I, a white Australian/New Zealand woman, am so ready to see it as having the capacity to defile, to humiliate, to subjugate and, ultimately, to destroy me?

Second, by exploring understandings of sex and gender in a community that stresses identity, rather than difference, between men and women (including men's and women's bodies), I aim to demonstrate that Western beliefs in the "sexed" character of bodies are not "natural" in basis but, rather, are a component of specifically Western gendering and sexual regimes. And since the practice of rape in Western societies is profoundly linked to these beliefs, I will suggest that it is an inseparable part of such regimes. This is not to say that the practice of rape is always linked to the kind of heterosexual regime found in the West; even the most cursory glance at any list of societies in which the practice occurs indicates that this is not so.[17] But it is to point out that we will be able to understand rape only ever in a purely localized sense, in the context of the local discourses and practices that are both constitutive of and constituted by it. In drawing out the implications of the Gerai stress on identity between men and women for Gerai gender and sexual relations, I hope to point out some of the possible implications of the Western emphasis on gender difference for Western gender and sexual relations—including the practice of rape.

GENDER, SEX, AND PROCREATION IN GERAI

Gerai is a Dayak community of some seven hundred people in the Indonesian province of Kalimantan Barat (West Borneo).[18] In the twenty months I spent in the community, I heard of no cases of either sexual assault or attempted sexual assault (and since this is a community in which privacy as we understand it in the West is almost nonexistent—in which surveillance by neighbors is at a very high level [see Helliwell 1996]—I would certainly have heard of any such cases had they occurred). In addition, when I questioned men and women about sexual assault, responses ranged from puzzlement to outright incredulity to horror.

While relations between men and women in Gerai can be classified as relatively egalitarian in many respects, both men and women nevertheless say that men are "higher" than women (Helliwell 1995, 364). This is especially the case in the context of formal community-wide functions such as village meetings and moots to settle legal disputes. While women are not required to remain silent on such occasions, their voices carry less authority than those of men, and, indeed, legal experts in the community (all men) told me that a woman's evidence in a moot is worth seven-tenths of a man's (see also Tsing 1990). In addition, a husband is granted a degree of formal authority over his wife that she does not have over him; thus a wife's disobedience of her husband is theoretically a punishable offense under *adat*, or local law. I have noted elsewhere that Gerai people stress the ideal of *diri*, literally meaning "standing" or "to stand," according to

---

[16]While I am primarily concerned here with the feminist literature (believing that it contains by far the most useful and insightful work on rape), it needs to be noted that many other (nonfeminist) writers also believe rape to be universal. See, e.g., Ellis 1989; Palmer 1989.

[17]For listings of "rape-prone" societies, see Minturn, Grosse, and Haider 1969; Sanday 1981.

[18]I carried out anthropological fieldwork in Gerai from March 1985 to February 1986 and from June 1986 to January 1987. The fieldwork was funded by an Australian National University Ph.D. scholarship and carried out under the sponsorship of Lembaga Ilmu Pengetahuan Indonesia. At the time that I was conducting my research a number of phenomena were beginning to have an impact on the community— these had the potential to effect massive changes in the areas of life discussed in this article. These phenomena included the arrival of a Malaysian timber company in the Gerai region and the increasing frequency of visits by Malay, Bugis, Chinese, and Batak timber workers to the community; the arrival of two American fundamentalist Protestant missionary families to live and proselytize in the community; and the establishment of a Catholic primary school in Gerai, resulting in a growing tendency among parents to send their children (both male and female) to attend Catholic secondary school in a large coastal town several days' journey away.

which each rice group should take primary responsibility for itself in all spheres of life and make its own decisions on matters concerning its members (Helliwell 1995). It is on the basis of their capacity to stand that rice groups within the community are ranked against one another. The capacity to stand is predicated primarily on the ability to produce rice surpluses: yet, significantly, although men and women work equally at rice-field work, it is only men who occasionally are individually described as standing. As in some other societies in the same region (Ilongot, Wana), Gerai people link men's higher status to their greater bravery.[19] This greater bravery is demonstrated, they say, by the fact that it is men who *pat* (cut down the large trees to make a rice field), who burn off the rice field to prepare for planting, and who enter deep primary jungle in search of game and jungle products such as aloe wood—all notoriously dangerous forms of work.

This greater status and authority does not, however, find expression in the practice of rape, as many feminist writings on the subject seem to suggest that it should. This is because the Gerai view of men as "higher" than women, although equated with certain kinds of increased potency vis-à-vis the world at large, does not translate into a conception of that potency as attached to and manifest through the penis—of men's genitals as able to brutalize women's genitals.

Shelly Errington has pointed out that a feature of many of the societies of insular Southeast Asia is a stress on sameness, even identity, between men and women (1990, 35, 39), in contrast to the Western stress on difference between the passive "feminine" object and the active, aggressive "masculine" subject.[20] Gerai understandings of gender fit Errington's model very well. In Gerai, men and women are not understood as fundamentally different types of persons: there is no sense of a dichotomized masculinity and femininity. Rather, men and women are seen to have the same kinds of capacities and proclivities, but with respect to some, men are seen as "more so" and with respect to others, women are seen as "more so." Men are said to be braver and more knowledgeable about local law (*adat*), while women are said to be more persistent and more enduring. All of these qualities are valued. Crucially, in terms of the central quality of nurturance (perhaps the most valued quality in Gerai), which is very strongly marked as feminine among Westerners, Gerai people see no difference between men and women. As one (female) member of the community put it to me: "We all must nurture because we all need."[21] The capacity both to nurture and to need, particularly as expressed through the cultivation of rice as a member of a rice group, is central to Gerai conceptions of personhood: rice is the source of life, and its (shared) production humanizes and socializes individuals (Helliwell, forthcoming). Women and men have identical claims to personhood based on their equal contributions to rice production (there is no notion that women are somehow diminished as persons even though they may be seen as less "high"). As in Strathern's account of Hagen (1988), the perceived mutuality of rice-field work in Gerai renders inoperable any notion of either men or women as autonomous individual subjects.

It is also important to note that while men's bravery is linked to a notion of their greater physical strength, it is not equated with aggression—aggression is not valued in most Gerai

---

[19]On the Ilongot, see Rosaldo 1980a; on the Wana, see Atkinson 1990.

[20]The Wana, as described by Jane Atkinson (1990), provide an excellent example of a society that emphasizes sameness. Emily Martin points out that the explicit Western opposition between the "natures" of men and women is assumed to occur even at the level of the cell, with biologists commonly speaking of the egg as passive and immobile and the sperm as active and aggressive even though recent research indicates that these descriptions are erroneous and that they have led biologists to misunderstand the fertilization process (1991). See also Lloyd 1984 for an excellent account of how (often latent) conceptions of men and women as having opposed characteristics are entrenched in the history of Western philosophical thought.

[21]The nurture-need dynamic (that I elsewhere refer to as the "need-share dynamic") is central to Gerai sociality. Need for others is expressed through nurturing them; such expression is the primary mark of a "good" as opposed to a "bad" person. See Helliwell (forthcoming) for a detailed discussion.

contexts.[22] As a Gerai man put it to me, the wise man is the one "who fights when he has to, and runs away when he can"; such avoidance of violence does not mark a man as lacking in bravery. This does not mean that in certain contexts male warriorship—the ability to fight and even to take heads—is not valorized; on the contrary, the most popular myths in Gerai are those that tell of the legendary warrior hero (and headhunter without peer) Koling. However, Gerai people make a clear distinction between the fantastic world of the heroes of the past and the mundane world in which the present man of Gerai must make his way.[23] While it is recognized that a man will sometimes need to fight—and skill and courage in fighting are valued—aggression and hot-headedness are ridiculed as the hallmarks of a lazy and incompetent man. In fact, physical violence between adults is uncommon in Gerai, and all of the cases that I did witness or hear about were extremely mild.[24] Doubtless the absence of rape in the community is linked to this devaluing of aggression in general. However, unlike a range of other forms of violence (slapping, beating with a fist, beating with an implement, knifing, premeditated killing, etc.), rape is not named as an offense and accorded a set punishment under traditional Gerai law. In addition, unlike these other forms of violence, rape is something that people in the community find almost impossible to comprehend ("How would he be able to do such a thing?" one woman asked when I struggled to explain the concept of a man attempting to put his penis into her against her will). Clearly, then, more is involved in the absence of rape in Gerai than a simple absence of violence in general.

Central to all of the narratives that Gerai people tell about themselves and their community is the notion of a "comfortable life": the achievement of this kind of life marks the person and the household as being of value and constitutes the norm to which all Gerai people aspire. Significantly, the content of such a life is seen as identical for both men and women: it is marked by the production of bountiful rice harvests each year and the successful raising of a number of healthy children to maturity. The core values and aspirations of men and women are thus identical; of the many life histories that I collected while in the community—all of which are organized around this central image—it is virtually impossible to tell those of men from those of women. Two points are significant in this respect. First, a "comfortable life" is predicated on the notion of a partnership between a man and a woman (a conjugal pair). This is because while men and women are seen to have the same basic skills and capacities, men are seen to be "better" at certain kinds of work and women to be "better" at other kinds. Second, and closely related to this, the Gerai notion of men's and women's work does not constitute a rigid division of labor: both men and women say that theoretically women can perform all of the work routinely carried out by men, and men can perform all of the work routinely carried out by women. However, men

---

[22]In this respect, Gerai is very different from, e.g., Australia or the United States, where, as Michelle Rosaldo has pointed out, aggression is linked to success, and women's constitution as lacking aggression is thus an important element of their subordination (1980b, 416; see also Myers 1988, 600).

[23]The practice of headhunting—seeking out enemies in order to sever their heads, which were then brought back to one's own village and treated with ritual reverence—was, in the past, widely found among Borneo Dayak groups. Gerai people claim that their not-too-distant ancestors practiced headhunting, but my own sense is that they are more likely to have been the hunted than the hunters. While in many respects Gerai resembles some of the "nonviolent" societies found throughout the region—including the Semai (Dentan 1968, 1978) and Chewong (Howell 1989) of Peninsular Malaysia and the Buid (Gibson 1986) of Mindoro in the Philippines—its celebration of violence in certain specified contexts marks it as rather different from many of them. Howell, for instance, claims that none of the indigenous peoples of Peninsular Malaysia "has any history of warfare, either recorded by the outside world or represented in myths and legends" (1989, 35), while Gibson notes that the Buid language "lacks words expressing a positive evaluation of courage or the reciprocation of violence" (1986, 107–8). Gerai people are, in fact, very similar in this respect to another Borneo Dayak people, the Bidayuh, who also valorize male violence in myth but tend to devalue and avoid it in everyday life and who also have a tradition of headhunting but are likely to have been hunted rather than hunters (Geddes 1957).

[24]See Helliwell 1996, 142–43, for an example of a "violent" altercation between husband and wife.

are much better at men's work, and women are much better at women's work. Again, what we have here is a stress on *identity* between men and women at the expense of radical difference.

This stress on identity extends into Gerai bodily and sexual discourses. A number of people (both men and women) assured me that men sometimes menstruate; in addition, menstrual blood is not understood to be polluting, in contrast to how it is seen in many societies that stress more strongly the difference between men and women. While pregnancy and childbirth are spoken of as "women's work," many Gerai people claim that under certain circumstances men are also able to carry out this work—but, they say, women are "better" at it and so normally undertake it. In line with this claim, I collected a Gerai myth concerning a lazy woman who was reluctant to take on the work of pregnancy and childbirth. Her husband instead made for himself a lidded container out of bark, wood, and rattan ("like a betel nut container"), which he attached around his waist beneath his loincloth and in which he carried the growing fetus until it was ready to be born. On one occasion when I was watching a group of Gerai men cut up a boar, one, remembering an earlier conversation about the capacity of men to give birth, pointed to a growth in the boar's body cavity and said with much disapproving shaking of the head: "Look at this. He wants to carry his child. He's stupid." In addition, several times I saw fathers push their nipples into the mouths of young children to quieten them; while none of these fathers claimed to be able to produce milk, people nevertheless claimed that some men in the community were able to lactate, a phenomenon also attested to in myth. Men and women are thought to produce the same genital fluid, and this is linked in complex ways to the capacity of both to menstruate. All of these examples demonstrate the community's stress on bodily identity between men and women.

Furthermore, in Gerai, men's and women's sexual organs are explicitly conceptualized as the same. This sexual identity became particularly clear when I asked several people who had been to school (and hence were used to putting pencil to paper) to draw men's and women's respective organs for me: in all cases, the basic structure and form of each were the same. One informant, endeavoring to convince me of this sameness, likened both to wooden and bark containers for holding valuables (these vary in size but have the same basic conical shape, narrower at the base and wider at the top). In all of these discussions, it was reiterated that the major difference between men's and women's organs is their location: inside the body (women) and outside the body (men).[25] In fact, when I pressed people on this point, they invariably explained that it makes no sense to distinguish between men's and women's genitalia themselves; rather, it is location that distinguishes between penis and vulva.[26]

Heterosexuality constitutes the normative sexual activity in the community and, indeed, I was unable to obtain any information about homosexual practices during my time there. In line with the stress on sameness, sexual intercourse between a man and a woman in Gerai is understood as an equal coming together of fluids, pleasures, and life forces. The same stress also underlies beliefs about conception. Gerai people believe that repeated acts of intercourse between the same two people are necessary for conception, since this "prepares" the womb for pregnancy. The fetus is deemed to be created through the mingling of equal quantities of fluids

---

[25]I have noted elsewhere that the inside-outside distinction is a central one within this culture (Helliwell 1996).

[26]While the Gerai stress on the sameness of men's and women's sexual organs seems, on the face of it, to be very similar to the situation in Renaissance Europe as described by Laqueur 1990, it is profoundly different in at least one respect: in Gerai, women's organs are not seen as emasculated versions of men's—"female penises"—as they were in Renaissance Europe. This is clearly linked to the fact that, in Gerai, as we have already seen, *people* is not synonymous with *men*, and women are not relegated to positions of emasculation or abjection, as was the case in Renaissance Europe.

and forces from both partners. Again, what is seen as important here is not the fusion of two different types of bodies (male and female) as in Western understandings; rather, Gerai people say, it is the similarity of the two bodies that allows procreation to occur. As someone put it to me bluntly: "If they were not the same, how could the fluids blend? It's like coconut oil and water: they can't mix!"

What needs to be stressed here is that both sexual intercourse and conception are viewed as involving a mingling of similar bodily fluids, forces, and so on, rather than as the penetration of one body by another with a parallel propulsion of substances from one (male) body only into the other, very different (female) one. Nor is there anything in Gerai understandings that equates with the Western notion of conception as involving an aggressive active male cell (the sperm) seeking out and penetrating a passive, immobile female cell (the egg) (Martin 1991). What Gerai accounts of both sexual intercourse and conception stress are tropes of identity, mingling, balance, and reciprocity. In this context it is worth noting that many Gerai people were puzzled by the idea of gender-specific "medicine" to prevent contraception—such as the injectable or oral contraceptives promoted by state-run health clinics in the area. Many believed that, because both partners play the same role in conception, it should not matter whether husband or wife received such medicine (and indeed, I knew of cases where husbands had taken oral contraceptives meant for their wives). This suggests that such contraceptive regimes also serve (like the practice of rape) to reinscribe sex difference between men and women (see also Tsing 1993, 104–20).

When I asked why, if conception is predicated on the mingling of two similar bodies, two men or two women could not also come together to create a child, the response was that a man and a woman "fit" with one another (sedang). But while there is some sense of physical compatibility being suggested here, Gerai people were adamant that what is more important in constituting "fit" is the role of each individual's "life force" (semongan') and its intimate connection to particular forms of work. The semongan' is the spiritual essence or force that animates the person, that gives the person his or her individual life. Without his or her semongan', a human being cannot live (this is true of all other elements in the universe as well), and thus when a person dies, the semongan' is understood to have left the body and journeyed away. In turn, an individual's semongan' is centrally linked to the kind of work he or she routinely performs—particularly during the rice-cultivation cycle, which is understood as the source of life itself in Gerai.

While Gerai people stress sameness over difference between men and women, they do, nevertheless, see them as being different in one important respect: their life forces are, they say, oriented differently ("they face different ways," it was explained to me). This different orientation means that women are "better" at certain kinds of work and men are "better" at other kinds of work—particularly with respect to rice-field work. Gerai people conceive of the work of clearing large trees for a new rice field as the definitive man's work and regard the work of selecting and storing the rice seed for the following year's planting—which is correlated in fundamental ways with the process of giving birth—as the definitive woman's work. Because women are perceived to lack appropriate skills with respect to the first, and men are perceived to lack appropriate skills with respect to the second, Gerai people say that to be viable a household must contain both adult males and adult females. And since a "comfortable life" is marked by success in production not only of rice but also of children, the truly viable household must contain at least one conjugal pair. The work of both husband and wife is seen as necessary for the adequate nurturance of the child and successful rearing to adulthood (both of which depend on the successful cultivation of rice). Two women or two men would not be able to provide adequately for a child since they would not be able to produce consistently successful rice harvests; while such a household might be able to select seed, clear a rice field, and so grow rice in some rudimentary fashion, its lack of expertise at one of these tasks would render it perennially poor and its children perennially unhealthy, Gerai people say. For this reason, households with adults of only one gender are greatly pitied by Gerai people, and single parents seek to marry or remarry as quickly as they can. It is the mingling of the respective life forces of a man and a woman, then—linked, as they are, to the work skills of each—that primarily enables conception. It is this, Gerai people say, that allows the child's *semongan'* to come into being. Mingling of the parental bodily fluids, in turn, creates the child's bodily substance, but this substance must be animated in some prior sense by a life force, or the child will die.

Gender difference in Gerai, then, is not predicated on the character of one's body, and especially of one's genitalia, as in many Western contexts. Rather, it is understood as constituted in the differential capacity to perform certain kinds of work, a capacity assigned long before one's bodily being takes shape.[27] In this respect it is important to note that Gerai ontology rests on a belief in predestination, in things being as they should (see Helliwell 1995). In this understanding, any individual's *semongan'* is linked in multifarious and unknowable ways to the cosmic order, to the "life" of the universe as a whole. Thus the new fetus is predestined to become someone "fitted" to carry out either men's work or women's work as part of the maintenance of a universal balance. Bodies with the appropriate characteristics—internal or external genitalia, presence or absence of breasts, and so on—then develop in line with this prior destiny. At first sight this may not seem enormously different from Western conceptions of gender, but the difference is in fact profound. While, for Westerners, genitalia, as significant of one's role in the procreative process, are absolutely fundamental in determining one's identity, in Gerai the work that one performs is seen as fundamental, and genitalia, along with other bodily characteristics, are relegated to a kind of secondary, derivative function.

Gerai understandings of gender were made quite clear through circumstances surrounding my own gender classification while in the community. Gerai people remained very uncertain about my gender for some time after I arrived in the community because (as they later told me) "I did not . . . walk like a woman, with arms held out from the body and hips slightly swaying; I was "brave," trekking from village to village through the jungle on my own; I had bony kneecaps; I did not know how to tic a sarong in the appropriate way for women; I could not distinguish different varieties of rice from one another; I did not wear earrings; I had short hair; I was tall" (Helliwell 1993, 260). This was despite the fact that people in the community knew from my first few days with them both that I had breasts (this was obvious when the sarong that I wore clung to my body while I bathed in the river) and that I had a vulva rather than a penis and testicles (this was obvious from my trips to defecate or urinate in the small stream used for that purpose, when literally dozens of people would line the banks to observe whether I performed these functions differently from them). As someone said to me at a later point, "Yes, I saw that you had a vulva, but I thought that Western men might be different."

My eventual, more definitive classification as a woman occurred largely fortuitously. My initial research proposal focused on the creation of subjectivity and sociality through work and, accordingly, as soon as I arrived in the community, I began accompanying people to work in the rice fields. Once I had negotiated a longhouse apartment of my own in which to live (several weeks after arrival), I also found myself, in concert with all other households in the community,

---

[27]In this respect Gerai is similar to a number of other peoples in this region (e.g., Wana, Ilongot), for whom difference between men and women is also seen as primarily a matter of the different kinds of work that each performs.

preparing and cooking rice at least twice daily. These activities rapidly led to a quest for information concerning rice itself, particularly concerning the different strains, how they are cultivated, and what they are used for. As I learned to distinguish types of rice and their uses, I became more and more of a woman (as I realized later), since this knowledge—including the magic that goes with it—is understood by Gerai people as foundational to femininity. However, while people eventually took to referring to me as a woman, for many in the community my gender identity remained deeply ambiguous, partly because so many of my characteristics and behaviors were more like those of a man than a woman, but also, and more importantly, because I never achieved anything approaching the level of knowledge concerning rice-seed selection held by even a girl child in Gerai.

In fact, Gerai people talk of two kinds of work as defining a woman: the selection and storage of rice seed and the bearing of children.[28] But the first of these is viewed as prior, logically as well as chronologically. People are quite clear that in the womb either "someone who can cut down the large trees for a ricefield is made, or someone who can select and store rice." When I asked if it was not more important whether or not someone could bear a child, it was pointed out to me that many women do not bear children (there is a high rate of infertility in the community), but all women have the knowledge to select and store rice seed. In fact, at the level of the rice group the two activities of "growing" rice and "growing" children are inseparable: a rice group produces rice in order to raise healthy children, and it produces children so that they can in turn produce the rice that will sustain the group once their parents are old and frail (Helliwell, forthcoming). For this reason, any Gerai couple unable to give birth to a child of their own will adopt one, usually from a group related by kinship. The two activities of growing rice and growing children are constantly talked about together, and the same imagery is used to describe the development of a woman's pregnancy and the development of rice grains on the plant. Indeed, the process of pregnancy and birth is seen as intimately connected to the process of rice selection and storage. As one woman explained to me, "It is because we know how to hold the seed in the storage baskets that we are able to hold it in our wombs." But just as the cultivation of rice is seen as in some sense prior to the cultivation of children, so it is said that "knowledge about childbirth comes from knowledge about rice seed."

Gerai, then, lacks the stress on bodily—and especially genital—dimorphism that most feminist accounts of rape assume. Indeed, the reproductive organs themselves are not seen as "sexed." In a sense it is problematic even to use the English categories *woman* and *man* when writing of this community, since these terms are saturated with assumptions concerning the priority of biological (read, bodily) difference. In the Gerai context, it would be more accurate to deal with the categories of, on the one hand, "those responsible for rice selection and storage" and, on the other, "those responsible for cutting down the large trees to make a ricefield." There is no discursive space in Gerai for the distinction between an active, aggressive, penetrating male sexual organ (and sexuality) and a passive, vulnerable, female one. Indeed, sexual intercourse in Gerai is understood by both men and women to stem from mutual "need" on the part of the two partners; without such need, people say, sexual intercourse cannot occur, because the requisite balance is lacking. Since, as I have described at length elsewhere (Helliwell, forthcoming), a relationship of "needing" is always reciprocal (it is almost inconceivable, in Gerai terms, to need someone who does not need you in return, and the consequences of unreciprocated needing are

---

[28]In Gerai, pregnancy and birth are seen not as semimystical "natural" processes, as they are for many Westerners, but simply as forms of work, linked very closely to the work of rice production.

dire for both individual and rice group), the sexual act is understood as preeminently mutual in its character, including in its initiation. The idea of having sex with someone who does not need you to have sex with them—and so the idea of coercing someone into sex—is thus almost unthinkable to Gerai people. In addition, informants asserted that any such action would destroy the individual's spiritual balance and that of his or her rice group and bring calamity to the group as a whole.[29]

In this context, a Gerai man's astonished and horrified question "How can a penis be taken into a vagina if a woman doesn't want it?" has a meaning very different from that of the same statement uttered by a man in the West. In the West, notions of radical difference between men and women—incorporating representations of normative male sexuality as active and aggressive, normative female sexuality as passive and vulnerable, and human relationships (including acts of sexual intercourse) as occurring between independent, potentially hostile, agents—would render such a statement at best naive, at worst misogynist. In Gerai, however, the stress on identity between men and women and on the sexual act as predicated on mutuality validates such a statement as one of straightforward incomprehension (and it should be noted that I heard similar statements from women). In the Gerai context, the penis, or male genitalia in general, is not admired, feared, or envied, nor is the phallus a central signifier in the way postulated by Lacanians. In fact, Gerai people see men's sexual organs as more vulnerable than women's for the simple reason that they are outside the body, while women's are inside. This reflects Gerai understandings of "inside" as representing safety and belonging, while "outside" is a place of strangers and danger, and it is linked to the notion of men as braver than women.[30] In addition, Gerai people say, because the penis is "taken into" another body, it is theoretically at greater risk during the sexual act than the vagina. This contrasts, again, quite markedly with Western understandings, where women's sexual organs are constantly depicted as more vulnerable during the sexual act— as liable to be hurt, despoiled, and so on (some men's anxieties about *vagina dentata* not withstanding). In Gerai a penis is "only a penis": neither a marker of dimorphism between men and women in general nor, in its essence, any different from a vagina.

CONCLUSIONS

The Gerai case suggests that, in some contexts at least, the practice of rape is linked to sexual dimorphism and, indeed, that in these contexts discourses of rape (including the act of rape itself) reinscribe such dimorphism. While the normative sexual practice in Gerai is heterosexual (between men and women), it is not accompanied by a heterosexual regulatory regime in the sense meant by Foucault (1978) in his discussion of the creation of sex as part of the heterosexualization of desire in the West, nor is it part of what Butler terms "the heterosexual matrix" (Butler 1990, 1993). The notion of "heterosexualization" as used by these thinkers refers to far more than the simple establishment of sexual relations between men and women as the normative ideal; it denotes the entire governmental regime that accompanies this normative ideal in Western contexts. Gerai stresses sameness between men and women more than difference, and such difference as occurs is based on the kinds of work people perform. Although this process certainly naturalizes a division between certain kinds of tasks—and the capacity to perform those tasks effectively—clearly, it does not involve sex or sexed bodies in the way Westerners normally

---

[29]Sanday 1986 makes a similar point about the absence of rape among the Minangkabau. See Helliwell (forthcoming) for a discussion of the different kinds of bad fate that can afflict a group through the actions of its individual members.
[30]In Gerai, as in nearby Minangkabau (Sanday 1986), vulnerability is respected and valued rather than despised.

understand those terms—as a naturalized difference between bodies (located primarily in the genitals) that translates into two profoundly different types of person. In this context, sexual assault by a man on a woman is almost unthinkable (both by women and by men).

With this background, I return now to the case with which I began this article—and, particularly, to the great differences between my response to this case and that of the Gerai woman concerned. On the basis of my own cultural assumptions concerning the differences—and particularly the different sexual characters—of men and women, I am inclined (as this case showed me) to read any attempt by a man to climb into a woman's bed in the night without her explicit consent as necessarily carrying the threat of sexual coercion and brutalization. This constant threat has been inscribed onto my body as part of the Western cultural process whereby I was "girled" (to use Butler's felicitous term [1993, 7]), or created as a gendered being in a context where male and female sexualities are perceived as penetrative and aggressive and as vulnerable and self-protective, respectively. The Gerai woman, in contrast, has no fear of coerced sexual intercourse when awakened in the dark by a man. She has no such fear because in the Gerai context "girling" involves the inscription of sexual sameness, of a belief that women's sexuality and bodies are no less aggressive and no more vulnerable than men's.

In fact, in the case in question, the intruding man did expect to have intercourse with the woman.[31] He claimed that the woman had already agreed to this through her acceptance of his initiatory gifts of soap.[32] The woman, however, while privately agreeing that she had accepted such gifts, claimed that no formal agreement had yet been reached. Her anger, then, did not stem from any belief that the man had attempted to sexually coerce her ("How would he be able to do such a thing?"). Because the term "to be quiet" is often used as a euphemism for sexual intercourse in Gerai, she saw the man's exhortation that she "be quiet" as simply an invitation to engage in sex with him, rather than the implicit threat that I read it to be.[33] Instead, her anger stemmed from her conviction that the correct protocols had not been followed, that the man ought to have spoken with her rather than taking her acceptance of the soap as an unequivocal expression of assent. She was, as she put it, letting him know that "you have sexual relations together when you talk together. Sexual relations cannot be quiet."[34]

---

[31]The man left the community on the night that this event occurred and went to stay for several months at a nearby timber camp. Community consensus—including the view of the woman concerned—was that he left because he was ashamed and distressed, not only as a result of having been sexually rejected by someone with whom he thought he had established a relationship but also because his adulterous behavior had become public, and he wished to avoid an airing of the details in a community moot. Consequently, I was unable to speak to him about the case. However, I did speak to several of his close male kin (including his married son), who put his point of view to me.

[32]The woman in this particular case was considerably younger than the man (in fact, a member of the next generation). In such cases of considerable age disparity between sexual partners, the older partner (whether male or female) is expected to pay a fine in the form of small gifts to the younger partner, both to initiate the liaison and to enable its continuance. Such a fine rectifies any spiritual imbalance that may result from the age imbalance and hence makes it safe for the relationship to proceed. Contrary to standard Western assumptions, older women appear to pay such fines to younger men as often as older men pay them to younger women (although it was very difficult to obtain reliable data on this question, since most such liaisons are adulterous and therefore highly secretive). While not significant in terms of value (women usually receive such things as soap and shampoo, while men receive tobacco or cigarettes), these gifts are crucial in their role of "rebalancing" the relationship. It would be entirely erroneous to subsume this practice under the rubric of "prostitution."

[33]Because Gerai adults usually sleep surrounded by their children, and with other adults less than a meter or two away (although the latter are usually inside different mosquito nets), sexual intercourse is almost always carried out very quietly.

[34]In claiming that "sexual relations cannot be quiet," the woman was playing on the expression "be quiet" (meaning to have sexual intercourse) to make the point that while adulterous sex may need to be even "quieter" than legitimate sex, it should not be so "quiet" as to preclude dialogue between the two partners. Implicit here is the notion that in the absence of such dialogue, sex will lack the requisite mutuality.

Yet, this should not be taken to mean that the practice of rape is simply a product of discourse: that brutality toward women is restricted to societies containing particular, dimorphic representations of male and female sexuality and that we simply need to change the discourse in order to eradicate such practices.[35] Nor is it to suggest that a society in which rape is unthinkable is for that reason to be preferred to Western societies. To adopt such a position would be still to view the entire world through a sexualized Western lens. There are, in fact, horrific things that may be done to women in places such as Gerai—things that are no less appalling in their implications for the fact that they do not involve the sexualized brutality of rape. In Gerai, for instance, while a woman does not fear rape, she does fear an enemy's bewitchment of her rice seed (the core of her gendered identity in this context) and the subsequent failure of the seed to sprout, resulting in hunger and illness for herself and her rice group. In extreme cases, bewitchment of rice seed can lead to malignancy of the growing fetus inside the woman; her subsequent death in childbirth, killed by her own "seed"; and her resultant transformation into a particularly vile kind of demon. Gerai women live constantly with the fear of this bewitchment (much as Western women live with the fear of rape), and even talking of it (always in whispers) reduces them to a state of terror.[36] The fact that this kind of attack can be carried out on a woman by either a woman or a man, and that it strikes not at her alone but at her rice group as a whole, marks it as belonging to a very different gendering regime from that which operates in the West. But it is no less horrific in its implications for that.

In order to understand the practice of rape in countries like Australia and the United States, then—and so to work effectively for its eradication there—feminists in these countries must begin to relinquish some of our most ingrained presumptions concerning difference between men and women and, particularly, concerning men's genitalia and sexuality as inherently brutalizing and penetrative and women's genitalia and sexuality as inherently vulnerable and subject to brutalization. Instead, we must begin to explore the ways rape itself *produces* such experiences of masculinity and femininity and so inscribes sexual difference onto our bodies. In a recent article, Moira Gatens asks of other feminists, "Why concede to the penis the power to push us around, destroy our integrity, 'scribble on us,' invade our borders and boundaries, and . . . occupy us in our (always already) conquered 'privacy'?" (1996, 43). This article echoes her lament. The tendency among many Western feminists writing on rape to accept as a seeming fact of nature the normative Western iconography of sexual difference leads them to reproduce (albeit unwittingly) the very discursive framework of Western rapists themselves, with their talk of "tools" and "holes," the very discursive framework in which rape is possible and which it reinscribes. For rape imposes difference as much as it is produced by difference. In fact, the highly racialized character of rape in many Western contexts suggests that the practice serves to police not simply sexual boundaries but racial ones as well. This is hardly surprising, given the history of the present "heterosexual matrix" in the West: as Stoler (1989, 1995) has demonstrated, the process of heterosexualization went hand-in-hand with that of colonialism. As a result, in contemporary Western settings sexual othering is inextricably entangled with racial othering. Unfortunately, in universalizing rape, many Western feminists risk naturalizing these othering processes and so contributing to a perpetuation of the very practices they seek to eradicate.

---

[35] Foucualt, e.g., once suggested (in a debate in French reprinted in *La Folie Encerclee* [see Plaza 1980]) that an effective way to deal with rape would be to decriminalize it in order to "desexualize" it. For feminist critiques of his suggestion, see Plaza 1980; de Lauretis 1987; Woodhull 1988.

[36] Men fear a parallel form of bewitchment that causes death while engaged in the definitive "men's work" of cutting down large trees to make a rice field. Like women's death in childbirth, this is referred to as an "evil death" (*mati jat*) and is believed to involve the transformation of the man into an evil spirit.

REFERENCES

Atkinson, Jane Monnig. 1990. "How Gender Makes a Difference in Wana Society." In *Power and Difference: Gender in Island Southeast Asia*, ed. Jane Monnig Atkinson and Shelly Errington, 59–93. Stanford, Calif.: Stanford University Press.

Barry, Kathleen. 1995. *The Prostitution of Sexuality*. New York and London: New York University Press.

Bart, Pauline B., and Patricia H. O'Brien. 1985. *Stopping Rape: Successful Survival Strategies*. New York: Pergamon.

Bell, Diane. 1983. *Daughters of the Dreaming*. Melbourne: McPhee Gribble.

Bourque, Linda B. 1989. *Defining Rape*. Durham, N.C., and London: Duke University Press.

Brison, Susan J. 1993. "Surviving Sexual Violence: A Philosophical Perspective." *Journal of Social Philosophy* 24(1):5–22.

Brownmiller, Susan. 1975. *Against Our Will: Men, Women, and Rape*. New York: Simon & Schuster.

Butler, Judith. 1990. *Gender Trouble: Feminism and the Subversion of Identity*. New York and London: Routledge.

_____. 1993. *Bodies That Matter: On the Discursive Limits of "Sex."* New York and London: Routledge.

Clark, Anna. 1987. *Women's Silence, Men's Violence: Sexual Assault in England, 1770–1845*. London and New York: Pandora.

de Lauretis, Teresa. 1987. "The Violence of Rhetoric: Considerations on Representation and Gender." In her *Technologies of Gender: Essays on Theory, Film and Fiction*, 31–50. Bloomington and Indianapolis: Indiana University Press.

Dentan, Robert Knox. 1968. *The Semai: A Nonviolent People of Malaya*. New York: Holt, Rinehart & Winston.

_____. 1978. "Notes on Childhood in a Nonviolent Context: The Semai Case (Malaysia)." In *Learning Non-Aggression: The Experience of Non-Literate Societies*, ed. Ashley Montagu, 94–143. New York: Oxford University Press.

Donaldson, Stephen. 1996. "The Deal behind Bars." *Harper's* (August): 17–20.

Dubinsky, Karen. 1993. *Improper Advances: Rape and Heterosexual Conflict in Ontario, 1880–1929*. Chicago and London: University of Chicago Press.

Dworkin, Andrea. 1987. *Intercourse*. London: Secker & Warburg.

Ellis, Lee. 1989. *Theories of Rape: Inquiries into the Causes of Sexual Aggression*. New York: Hemisphere.

Errington, Shelly. 1990. "Recasting Sex, Gender, and Power: A Theoretical and Regional Overview." In *Power and Difference: Gender in Island Southeast Asia*, ed. Jane Monnig Atkinson and Shelly Errington, 1–58. Stanford, Calif.: Stanford University Press.

Foucault, Michel. 1978. *The History of Sexuality*. Vol. 1, *An Introduction*. Harmondsworth: Penguin.

Gatens, Moira. 1996. "Sex, Contract, and Genealogy." *Journal of Political Philosophy* 4(1):29–44.

Geddes, W. R. 1957. *Nine Dayak Nights*. Melbourne and New York: Oxford University Press.

Gibson, Thomas. 1986. *Sacrifice and Sharing in the Philippine Highlands: Religion and Society among the Buid of Mindoro*. London and Dover: Athlone.

Gilman, Sander L. 1985. "Black Bodies, White Bodies: Toward an Iconography of Female Sexuality in Late Nineteenth-Century Art, Medicine, and Literature." In *"Race," Writing, and Difference*, ed. Henry Louis Gates, Jr., 223–40. Chicago and London: University of Chicago Press.

Gordon, Margaret T., and Stephanie Riger. 1989. *The Female Fear*. New York: Free Press.

Gregor, Thomas. 1990. "Male Dominance and Sexual Coercion." In *Cultural Psychology: Essays on Comparative Human Development*, ed. James W. Stigler, Richard A. Shweder, and Gilbert Herdt, 477–95. Cambridge: Cambridge University Press.

Griffin, Susan. 1986. *Rape: The Politics of Consciousness*. San Francisco: Harper & Row.

Halperin, David M. 1993. "Is There a History of Sexuality?" In *The Lesbian and Gay Studies Reader*, ed. Henry Abelove, Michele Barale, and David M. Halperin, 416–31. New York and London: Routledge.

Helliwell, Christine 1993. "Women in Asia: Anthropology and the Study of Women." In *Asia's Culture Mosaic*, ed. Grant Evans, 260–86. Singapore: Prentice Hall.

_____. 1995. "Autonomy as Natural Equality: Inequality in 'Egalitarian' Societies." *Journal of the Royal Anthropological Institute* 1(2):359–75.

_____. 1996. "Space and Sociality in a Dayak Longhouse." In *Things as They Are: New Directions in Phenomenological Anthropology*, ed. Michael Jackson, 128–48. Bloomington and Indianapolis: Indiana University Press.

_____. Forthcoming. *"Never Stand Alone": A Study of Borneo Sociality*. Williamsburg: Borneo Research Council.

Howell, Signe. 1989. *Society and Cosmos: Chewong of Peninsular Malaysia*. Chicago and London: University of Chicago Press.

Kilpatrick, Dean G., Benjamin E. Saunders, Lois J. Veronen, Connie L. Best, and Judith M. Von. 1987. "Criminal Victimization: Lifetime Prevalence, Reporting to Police, and Psychological Impact." *Crime and Delinquency* 33(4):479–89.

Koss, Mary P., and Mary R. Harvey. 1991. *The Rape Victim: Clinical and Community Interventions*. 2d ed. Newbury Park, Calif.: Sage.

Laqueur, Thomas. 1990. *Making Sex: Body and Gender from the Greeks to Freud*. Cambridge, Mass., and London: Harvard University Press.

Leacock, Eleanor. 1978. "Women's Status in Egalitarian Society: Implications for Social Evolution." *Current Anthropology* 19(2):247–75.

Lloyd, Genevieve. 1984. *The Man of Reason: "Male" and "Female" in Western Philosophy*. London: Methuen.

MacKinnon, Catharine A. 1989a. "Sexuality, Pornography, and Method: 'Pleasure under Patriarchy.'" *Ethics* 99:314–46.

_____. 1989b. *Toward a Feminist Theory of the State*. Cambridge, Mass., and London: Harvard University Press.

Madigan, Lee, and Nancy C. Gamble. 1991. *The Second Rape: Society's Continued Betrayal of the Victim*. New York: Lexington.

Marcus, Julie. 1992. *A World of Difference: Islam and Gender Hierarchy in Turkey*. Sydney: Allen & Unwin.

Marcus, Sharon. 1992. "Fighting Bodies, Fighting Words: A Theory and Politics of Rape Prevention." In *Feminists Theorize the Political*, ed. Judith Butler and Joan W. Scott, 385–403. New York and London: Routledge.

Martin, Emily 1991. "The Egg and the Sperm: How Science Has Constructed a Romance Based on Stereotypical Male-Female Roles." *Signs: Journal of Women in Culture and Society* 16(3):485–501.

McColgan, Aileen. 1996. *The Case for Taking the Date Out of Rape*. London: Pandora.

Minturn, Leigh, Martin Grosse, and Santoah Haider. 1969. "Cultural Patterning of Sexual Beliefs and Behaviour." *Ethnology* 8(3):301–18.

Mohanty, Chandra Talpade. 1991. "Under Western Eyes: Feminist Scholarship and Colonial Discourses." In *Third World Women and the Politics of Feminism*, ed. Chandra Talpade Mohanty, Ann Russo, and Lourdes Torres, 51–80. Bloomington and Indianapolis: Indiana University Press.

Moore, Henrietta L. 1994. *A Passion for Difference: Essays in Anthropology and Gender*. Cambridge and Oxford: Polity.

Myers, Fred R. 1988. "The Logic and Meaning of Anger among Pintupi Aborigines." *Man* 23(4):589–610.

Palmer, Craig. 1989. "Is Rape a Cultural Universal? A Re-Examination of the Ethnographic Data." *Ethnology* 28(1):1–16.

Pateman, Carole. 1988. *The Sexual Contract*. Cambridge: Polity.

Plaza, Monique. 1980. "Our Costs and Their Benefits." *m/f* 4:28–39.

Rosaldo, Michelle Z. 1980a. *Knowledge and Passion: Ilongot Notions of Self and Social Life*. Cambridge: Cambridge University Press.

_____. 1980b. "The Use and Abuse of Anthropology: Reflections on Feminism and Cross-cultural Understanding." *Signs* 5(3):389–417.

Russell, Diana E. H. 1984. *Sexual Exploitation: Rape, Child Abuse, and Workplace Harassment*. Beverly Hills, Calif.: Sage.

Sanday, Peggy Reeves. 1981. "The Socio-Cultural Context of Rape: A Cross-Cultural Study." *Journal of Social Issues* 37(4):5–27.

_____. 1986. "Rape and the Silencing of the Feminine." In *Rape*, ed. Sylvana Tomaselli and Roy Porter, 84–101. Oxford: Blackwell.

_____. 1990a. "Androcentric and Matrifocal Gender Representations in Minangkabau Ideology." In *Beyond the Second Sex: New Directions in the Anthropology of Gender*, ed. Peggy Reeves Sanday and Ruth Gallagher Goodenough, 141–68. Philadelphia: University of Pennsylvania Press.

_____. 1990b. *Fraternity Gang Rape: Sex, Brotherhood, and Privilege on Campus*. New York and London: New York University Press.

Stoler, Ann Laura. 1989. "Carnal Knowledge and Imperial Power: Gender, Race, and Morality in Colonial Asia." In *Gender at the Crossroads of Knowledge: Feminist Anthropology in the Postmodern Era*, ed. Micaela di Leonardo, 51–101. Berkeley and Los Angeles: University of California Press.

_____. 1995. *Race and the Education of Desire: Foucault's* History of Sexuality *and the Colonial Order of Things*. Durham, N.C., and London: Duke University Press.

Strathern, Marilyn 1987. "Conclusion." In *Dealing with Inequality: Analysing Gender Relations in Melanesia and Beyond*, ed. Marilyn Strathern, 278–302. Cambridge: Cambridge University Press.

_____. 1988. *The Gender of the Gift: Problems with Women and Problems with Society in Melanesia*. Berkeley and Los Angeles: University of California Press.

Trumbach, Randolph. 1989. "Gender and the Homosexual Role in Modern Western Culture: The Eighteenth and Nineteenth Centuries Compared." In *Homosexuality, Which Homosexuality?* ed. Dennis Altman, 149–69. Amsterdam: An Dekker/Schorer; London: GMP.

_____. 1993. "London's Sapphists: From Three Sexes to Four Genders in the Making of Modern Culture." In *Third Sex, Third Gender: Beyond Sexual Dimorphism in Culture and History*, ed. Gilbert Herdt, 111–36. New York: Zone.

Tsing, Anna Lowenhaupt. 1990. "Gender and Performance in Meratus Dispute Settlement." In *Power and Difference: Gender in Island Southeast Asia*, ed. Jane Monnig Atkinson and Shelly Errington, 95–125. Stanford, Calif.: Stanford University Press.

_____. 1993. *In the Realm of the Diamond Queen: Marginality in an Out-of-the-Way Place*. Princeton, N.J.: Princeton University Press.

van der Meer, Theo. 1993. "Sodomy and the Pursuit of a Third Sex in the Early Modern Period." In *Third Sex, Third Gender: Beyond Sexual Dimorphism in Culture and History*, ed. Gilbert Herdt, 137–212. New York: Zone.

Woodhull, Winifred. 1988. "Sexuality, Power, and the Question of Rape." In *Feminism and Foucault: Reflections on Resistance*, ed. Irene Diamond and Lee Quinby, 167–76. Boston: Northeastern University Press.

Young, Iris Marion. 1990. "Throwing like a Girl: A Phenomenology of Feminine Body Comportment, Motility, and Spatiality." In her *Throwing like a Girl and Other Essays in Feminist Philosophy and Social Theory*, 141–59. Bloomington and Indianapolis: Indiana University Press.

Size 6
The Western Woman's Harem

Fatema Mernissi

Fatima Mernissi is a Moroccan feminist scholar and writer of essays and memoir. She is a sociologist at University Mohammed V in Morocco. She is well known for her work about Islam and women, including The Veil and the Male Elite *and* Beyond the Veil: Male-Female Dynamics in Modern Muslim Society (1975, 1987) *as well as her work* Islam and Democracy: Fear of the Modern World (1992, 2002). *In her memoir,* Dreams of Trespass: Tales of a Harem Girlhood (1994), *she address growing up feminist in the changing dynamics and landscape of the harem in twentieth century Morocco. This essay comes from her book* Schehrezade Goes West (2002).

It was during my unsuccessful attempt to buy a cotton skirt in an American department store that I was told my hips were too large to fit into a size 6. That distressing experience made me realize how the image of beauty in the West can hurt and humiliate a woman as much as the veil does when enforced by the state police in extremist nations such as Iran, Afghanistan, or Saudi Arabia. Yes, that day I stumbled onto one of the keys to the enigma of passive beauty in Western harem fantasies. The elegant sales lady in the American store looked at me without moving from her desk and said that she had no skirt my size. "In this whole big store, there is no skirt for me?" I said. "You are joking." I felt very suspicious and thought that she just might be too tired to help me. I could understand that. But then the saleswoman added a condescending judgment, which sounded to me like an Imam's *fatwa*. It left no room for discussion:

"You are too big!" she said.

"I am too big compared to what?" I asked, looking at her intently, because I realized that I was facing a critical cultural gap here.

"Compared to a size 6," came the saleslady's reply.

Her voice had a clear-cut edge to it that is typical of those who enforce religious laws. "Size 4 and 6 are the norm," she went on, encouraged by my bewildered look. "Deviant sizes such as the one you need can be bought in special stores."

That was the first time that I had ever heard such nonsense about my size. In the Moroccan streets, men's flattering comments regarding my particularly generous hips have for decades led me to believe that the entire planet shared their convictions. It is true that with advancing age, I have been hearing fewer and fewer flattering comments when walking in the medina, and sometimes the silence around me in the bazaars is deafening. But since my face has never met with the local beauty standards, and I have often had to defend myself against remarks such as *zirafa* (giraffe), because of my long neck, I learned long ago not to rely too much on the outside world for my sense of self-worth. In fact, paradoxically, as I discovered when I went to Rabat as a student, it was the self-reliance that I had developed to protect myself against "beauty blackmail" that made me attractive to others. My male fellow students could not believe that I did not give a damn about what they thought about my body. "You know, my dear," I would say in response to one of them, "all I need to survive is bread, olives, and sardines. That you think my neck is too long is your problem, not mine."

In any case, when it comes to beauty and compliments, nothing is too serious or definite in the medina, where everything can be negotiated. But things seemed to be different in that American department store. In fact, I have to confess that I lost my usual self-confidence in that New York environment. Not that I am always sure of myself, but I don't walk around the Moroccan streets or down the university corridors wondering what people are thinking about me. Of course, when I hear a compliment, my ego expands like a cheese soufflé, but on the whole, I don't expect to hear much from others. Some mornings, I feel ugly because I am sick or tired; others, I feel wonderful because it is sunny out or I have written a good paragraph. But suddenly, in that peaceful American store that I had entered so triumphantly, as a sovereign consumer ready to spend money, I felt savagely attacked. My hips, until then the sign of a relaxed and uninhibited maturity, were suddenly being condemned as a deformity.

"And who decides the norm?" I asked the saleslady, in an attempt to regain some self-confidence by challenging the established rules. I never let others evaluate me, if only because I remember my childhood too well. In ancient Fez, which valued round-faced plump adolescents, I was repeatedly told that I was too tall, too skinny, my cheekbones were too high, my eyes were too slanted. My mother often complained that I would never find a husband and urged me to study and learn all that I could, from story-telling to embroidery, in order to survive. But I often retorted that since "Allah had created me the way I am, how could he be so wrong, Mother?" That would silence the poor woman for a while, because if she contradicted me, she would be attacking God himself. And this tactic of glorifying my strange looks as a divine gift not only helped me to survive in my stuffy city, but also caused me to start believing the story myself. I became almost self-confident. I say almost, because I realized early on that self-confidence is not a tangible and stable thing like a silver bracelet that never changes over the years. Self-confidence is like a tiny fragile light, which goes off and on. You have to replenish it constantly.

"And who says that everyone must be a size 6?" I joked to the saleslady that day, deliberately neglecting to mention size 4, which is the size of my skinny twelve-year-old niece.

At that point, the saleslady suddenly gave me an anxious look. "The norm is everywhere, my dear," she said. "It's all over, in the magazines, on television, in the ads. You can't escape it. There is Calvin Klein, Ralph Lauren, Gianni Versace, Giorgio Armani, Mario Valentino, Salvatore Ferragamo, Christian Dior, Yves Saint-Laurent, Christian Lacroix, and Jean-Paul Gaultier. Big department stores go by the norm." She paused and then concluded, "If they sold size 14 or 16, which is probably what you need, they would go bankrupt."

She stopped for a minute and then stared at me, intrigued. "Where on earth do you come from? I am sorry I can't help you. Really, I am." And she looked it too. She seemed, all of a sudden, interested, and brushed off another woman who was seeking her attention with a cutting, "Get someone else to help you, I'm busy." Only then did I notice that she was probably my age, in her late fifties. But unlike me, she had the thin body of an adolescent girl. Her knee length, navy blue, Chanel dress had a white silk collar reminiscent of the subdued elegance of aristocratic French Catholic schoolgirls at the turn of the century. A pearl-studded belt emphasized the slimness of her waist. With her meticulously styled short hair and sophisticated makeup, she looked half my age at first glance.

"I come from a country where there is no size for women's clothes," I told her. "I buy my own material and the neighborhood seamstress or craftsman makes me the silk or leather skirt I want. They just take my measurements each time I see them. Neither the seamstress nor I know exactly what size my new skirt is. We discover it together in the making. No one cares about my size in Morocco as long as I pay taxes on time. Actually, I don't know what my size is, to tell you the truth."

The saleswoman laughed merrily and said that I should advertise my country as a paradise for stressed working women. "You mean you don't watch your weight?" she inquired, with a tinge of disbelief in her voice. And then, after a brief moment of silence, she added in a lower register, as if talking to herself: "Many women working in highly paid fashion-related jobs could lose their positions if they didn't keep to a strict diet."

Her words sounded so simple, but the threat they implied was so cruel that I realized for the first time that maybe "size 6" is a more violent restriction imposed on women than is the Muslim veil. Quickly I said good-bye so as not to make any more demands on the saleslady's time or involve her in any more unwelcome, confidential exchanges about age-discriminating salary cuts. A surveillance camera was probably watching us both.

Yes, I thought as I wandered off, I have finally found the answer to my harem enigma. Unlike the Muslim man, who uses space to establish male domination by excluding women from the public arena, the Western man manipulates time and light. He declares that in order to be beautiful, a woman must look fourteen years old. If she dares to look fifty, or worse, sixty, she is beyond the pale. By putting the spotlight on the female child and framing her as the ideal of beauty, he condemns the mature woman to invisibility. In fact, the modern Western man enforces Immanuel Kant's nineteenth-century theories: To be beautiful, women have to appear childish and brainless. When a woman looks mature and self-assertive, or allows her hips to expand, she is condemned as ugly. Thus, the wars of the European harem separate youthful beauty from ugly maturity.

These Western attitudes, I thought, are even more dangerous and cunning than the Muslim ones because the weapon used against women is time. Time is less visible, more fluid than space. The Western man uses images and spotlights to freeze female beauty within an idealized childhood, and forces women to perceive aging—that normal unfolding of the years—as a shameful devaluation. "Here I am, transformed into a dinosaur," I caught myself saying aloud as I went up and down the rows of skirts in the store, hoping to prove the saleslady wrong—to no avail. This Western time-defined veil is even crazier than the space-defined one enforced by the Ayatollahs.

The violence embodied in the Western harem is less visible than in the Eastern harem because aging is not attacked directly, but rather masked as an aesthetic choice. Yes, I suddenly felt not only very ugly but also quite useless in that store, where, if you had big hips, you were simply out of the picture. You drifted into the fringes of nothingness. By putting the spotlight on the pre-pubescent female, the Western man veils the older, more mature woman, wrapping her in shrouds of ugliness. This idea gives me the chills because it tattoos the invisible harem directly onto a woman's skin. Chinese foot-binding worked the same way: Men declared beautiful only those women who had small, childlike feet. Chinese men did not force women to bandage their feet to keep them from developing normally—all they did was to define the beauty ideal. In feudal China, a beautiful woman was the one who voluntarily sacrificed her right to unhindered physical movement by mutilating her own feet, and thereby proving that her main goal in life was to please men. Similarly, in the Western world, I was expected to shrink my hips into a size 6 if I wanted to find a decent skirt tailored for a beautiful woman. We Muslim women have only one month of fasting, Ramadan, but the poor Western woman who diets has to fast twelve months out of the year. *"Quelle horreur,"* I kept repeating to myself, while looking around at the American women shopping. All those my age looked like youthful teenagers.

According to the writer Naomi Wolf, the ideal size for American models decreased sharply in the 1990s. "A generation ago, the average model weighed 8 percent less than the average American woman, whereas today she weighs 23 percent less. . . . The weight of Miss America plummeted, and the average weight of Playboy Playmates dropped from 11 percent below the national average in 1970 to 17 percent below it in eight years." The shrinking of the ideal size, according to Wolf, is one of the primary reasons for anorexia and other health-related problems: "Eating disorders rose exponentially, and a mass of neurosis was promoted that used food and weight to strip women of . . . a sense of control."

Now, at last, the, mystery of my Western harem made sense. Framing youth as beauty and condemning maturity is the weapon used against women in the West just as limiting access to public space is the weapon used in the East. The objective remains identical in both cultures: to make women feel unwelcome, inadequate, and ugly.

The power of the Western man resides in dictating what women should wear and how they should look. He controls the whole fashion industry, from cosmetics to underwear. The West, I realized, was the only part of the world where women's fashion is a mans business. In places like Morocco, where you design your own clothes and discuss them with craftsmen and -women, fashion is your own business. Not so in the West. As Naomi Wolf explains in *The Beauty Myth*, men have engineered a prodigious amount of fetish-like, fashion-related paraphernalia: "Powerful industries—the $33-billion-a-year diet industry, the $20-billion cosmetic industry, the $300-million cosmetic surgery industry, and the $7-billion pornography industry—have arisen from the capital made out of unconscious anxieties, and are in turn able, through their influence on mass culture, to use, stimulate, and reinforce the hallucination in a rising economic spiral."

But how does the system function? I wondered. Why do women accept it?

Of all the possible explanations, I like that of the French sociologist, Pierre Bourdieu, the best. In his latest book, *La Domination Masculine*, he proposes something he calls *"la violence symbolique"*: "Symbolic violence is a form of power which is hammered directly on the body, and as if by magic, without any apparent physical constraint. But this magic operates only because it activates the codes pounded in the deepest layers of the body." Reading Bourdieu, I had the impression that I finally understood Western man's psyche better. The cosmetic and fashion industries are only the tip of the iceberg, he states, which is why women are so ready to adhere to their dictates. Something else is going on on a far deeper level. Otherwise, why would women belittle themselves spontaneously? Why, argues Bourdieu, would women make their lives more difficult, for example, by preferring men who are taller or older than they are? "The majority of French women wish to have a husband who is older and also, which seems consistent, bigger as far as size is concerned," writes Bourdieu. Caught in the enchanted submission characteristic of the symbolic violence inscribed in the mysterious layers of the flesh, women relinquish what he calls "les signes ordinaires de la hiérarchie sexuelle," the ordinary signs of sexual hierarchy, such as old age and a larger body. By so doing, explains Bourdieu, women spontaneously accept the subservient position. It is this spontaneity Bourdieu describes as magic enchantment.

Once I understood how this magic submission worked, I became very happy that the conservative Ayatollahs do not know about it yet. If they did, they would readily switch to its sophisticated methods, because they are so much more effective. To deprive me of food is definitely the best way to paralyze my thinking capabilities.

Both Naomi Wolf and Pierre Bourdieu come to the conclusion that insidious "body codes" paralyze Western women's abilities to compete for power, even though access to education and professional opportunities seem wide open, because the rules of the game are so different according to gender. Women enter the power game with so much of their energy deflected to their physical appearance that one hesitates to say the playing field is level. "A cultural fixation on female thinness is not an obsession about female beauty," explains Wolf. It is "an obsession about female obedience. Dieting is the most potent political sedative in women's history; a quietly mad population is a tractable one." Research, she contends, "confirmed what most women know too well—that concern with weight leads to a 'virtual collapse of self-esteem and sense of effectiveness' and that . . .' prolonged and periodic caloric restriction' resulted in a distinctive personality whose traits are passivity, anxiety, and emotionality." Similarly, Bourdieu, who focuses more on how this myth hammers its inscriptions onto the flesh itself, recognizes that constantly reminding women of their physical appearance destabilizes them emotionally because it reduces them to exhibited objects. "By confining women to the status of symbolical objects to be seen and perceived by the other, masculine domination . . . puts women in a state of constant physical insecurity. . . . They have to strive ceaselessly to be engaging, attractive, and available." Being frozen into the passive position of an object whose very existence depends on the eye of its beholder turns the educated modern Western woman into a harem slave.

"I thank you, Allah, for sparing me the tyranny of the 'size 6 harem,'" I repeatedly said to myself while seated on the Paris-Casablanca flight, on my way back home at last. "I am so happy that the conservative male elite does not know about it. Imagine the fundamentalists switching from the veil to forcing women to fit size 6."

How can you stage a credible political demonstration and shout in the streets that your human rights have been violated when you cannot find the right skirt?

Bisexuality and the Case against Dualism

Stephanie Fairyington

Stephanie Fairyington is a journalist who has contributed essays on gender, sexuality and bisexuality for publications including the Advocate, OUT and the Gay and Lesbian Review Worldwide, in which this essay was first published in 2005.

It was seeing the movie Kinsey that triggered a heated discussion about bisexuality between me and my girlfriend Meg, whom I had "accused" of being bisexual in light of her history of dating men several years earlier. She vehemently denied that this earlier life made her bisexual, giving rise to that age-old discussion of just what makes a person "bi": Does it involve love or is it only about sex? Do serial partners of both sexes count, or do they have to be simultaneous? Are fantasies about sexual relations with both men and women sufficient, or does one have to act on both impulses? All the theories and stereotypes also came out in the course of our discussion: that bisexuals are sex fiends who'll sleep with anything that moves; that they're unable to commit to a sexual identity; that bisexuality doesn't really exist but serves as a hedge for semi-closeted gay men and sexually adventuresome straight women. That last one reminded us of an old joke: "Bisexual men and bisexual women have one thing in common. They'll both be having sex with men five years from now."

Why is it so hard for us to wrap our minds around bisexuality? Our cultural struggle to conceptualize bisexuality stems in part from the freighted history of the term. When it first appeared in a dictionary in 1824, "bisexual" referred to people possessing the characteristics of both sexes, now referred to as "intersexuals" (or, popularly, as "hermaphrodites"). In the mid-1860's, Karl Heinrich Ulrich postulated that men who have same-sex desires have female souls trapped inside male bodies. Subsequent sex researchers argued that people who desire their own sex have an inverted gender identity. From this sort of logic it was deduced that bisexuals are "psycho-sexual hermaphrodites."

Freud upended the conversation on bisexuality beginning in the early 20th century when he used the term in the modern sense and hypothesized that all people are initially bisexual before a fixed, usually hetero-, sexual identity takes hold. Basing his theories upon contemporary ideas, later discredited, as to the biological bisexuality of the fetus, Freud hypothesized that everyone had a primary and innate bisexual disposition with respect to sex-object choice. But instead of arguing that bisexuality might be a normal manifestation of this inherent predisposition, Freud went on to spin an account of normal human development whereby same-sex desires are repressed or sublimated and heterosexual ones allowed to arise, relegating homosexuality and bisexuality to exceptional states that develop as the result of a series of psychological malfunctions.

Interestingly, one of Freud's associates, Wilhelm Stekel, challenged Freud's hypothesis while using his terminology, pointing out that if bisexuality is the original state and the creation of homosexuality and heterosexuality relies on sublimation and repression, then logically the latter two sexual orientations are the troubled psychosexual states, not bisexuality. Not surprisingly, this theory didn't gain much traction at the time.

A dualistic paradigm of sexuality stayed firmly in place until the groundbreaking and binary-breaking work of Alfred C. Kinsey and his team. What would come to be known as the "Kinsey Scale" posited that sexual orientations form a continuum from 0 to 6, with 0 representing a totally heterosexual person and 6 a totally homosexual one, with many degrees of bisexuality in between. Despite some flaws in Kinsey's research methods, such as the use of snowball sampling, his work exposed a radical disjunction between the sexual mores of post-war America and the reality of people's sex lives. Perhaps most astonishing was his finding that 46 percent of the male population had engaged in both hetero- and homosexual activities in their adult (i.e., sexually mature) lives.

The Kinsey Scale's assault on the hetero-homo divide was nothing short of breathtaking for its time, exposing the complexity of human sexuality while hinting subversively that the heterosexual you know may not be as hetero as you think. As a practical matter, the wall between gay and straight didn't exactly come tumbling down in the wake of Kinsey's research, which did, however, pave the way for more sophisticated models for measuring sexuality, such as Fritz Klein's Sexual Orientation Grid (KSOG), introduced in his 1978 classic, The Bisexual Option.

Klein's grid dramatically improved upon Kinsey's scale, combining five discrete dimensions: sexual attraction, behavior, fantasies, emotional preference, and social preference (lifestyle and self-identification). Assessing a person's past and present behavior along with ideal sexual situations, the KSOG rates desire on a seven-point scale similar to Kinsey's but with simple verbal descriptors (1 = other sex only, 2 = other sex mostly, 3 = other sex somewhat more, 4 = both sexes, 5 = same sex somewhat more, 6 = same sex mostly, 7 = same sex only). Despite these long strides forward, the hetero-homo dichotomy has proved a hard nut to crack. From Kinsey's time to the present, sex research almost always aggregates bisexual and homosexual activities or identities into one category, thereby erasing the concept of bisexuality altogether. (For example, Simon LeVay's famous study of male brains, which found a difference between the brains of gay and straight men, clumped bisexuals with gay men.)

While there are respectable studies that offer reliable statistics on the prevalence of bisexuality, the details about this group are often missing. As researcher Paula C. Rust has observed, only "by triangulating the many studies that have been done to date can we achieve an overall picture of sexuality in the United States. Taken together, these studies provide us with a rough estimate of the prevalence of bisexual behaviors, feelings, and identities in the United States." Keeping Rust's caveat in mind, it is staggering to note that every study I've reviewed reflects a greater amount of bisexual than exclusively homosexual activity and desire, yet popular wisdom has it that there are far fewer bisexuals than homosexuals. Starting with Kinsey's astronomically high estimate—that 46 percent of adult males registering as bi, which is now considered overblown—subsequent research has produced more modest findings but repeatedly confirms that the proportion of people with a bisexual orientation—able to relate to both sexes sexually and emotionally—is greater than the proportion of exclusive homosexuals.

Despite these findings, barriers to the study of bisexuality remain in place, and it is thus an under-researched phenomenon. Let me focus on some of these barriers and consider possible remedies.

The first hurdle is the lack of a clear definition for the term. Who is bisexual? Is a male hustler who markets himself to men by night, but maintains exclusively romantic relations with women by day, bisexual? Are men who engage in same-sex relations in prison but resume exclusive heterosexuality upon release to be classified as "bi"? What about my girlfriend Meg, who had fulfilling romantic relationships with men up until six years ago but now dates only women? What if you have same-and-opposite sex sexual fantasies and desires but never act on half of them? These disparate cases, all of them quite prevalent in the real world, raise the question whether we can even speak of "bisexuality" as a single phenomenon.

A second problem is that many people who are bisexual in a behavioral sense do not self-identify as bi. There are myriad reasons why this may be the case. For one, bisexuals experience disapproval not only from the dominant society but from the gay and lesbian community, as well. Many gay people are reluctant to date someone who's bi because they feel there's an ever-present temptation hovering over every bisexual in a same-sex relationship to "go straight." Because heterosexuality and homosexuality create the fence that bisexuality is forced to sit on, bisexuals have a harder time finding a grounded community to come out to. Brett Beemyn, coauthor of Bisexuality in the Lives of Men (2000), argues that in coming out, "bisexuals rarely can count on finding places where they will be embraced by others like themselves. With only a few exceptions, we don't have bisexual-specific bars, community centers, political organizations, softball teams, and circuit parties."

Because many people refuse to self-identify as bisexual for whatever reason, it might make sense to drop the identity categories altogether and go back to Kinsey's purely behavioral approach whereby research subjects are asked about their activities and fantasies but not about the labels they use. Brett Beemyn endorses this approach: "Most studies are formulated using standard sexual orientation labels: lesbian, gay, bisexual, and heterosexual. To develop a better understanding of human sexuality, researchers need to ask about sexual attraction and behavior, rather than how people label their sexuality." Loraine Hutchins espouses a similar view, arguing that in terms of researching bisexuality "it's much better to talk about exactly what kind of sex and what kind of relationship, as those involved define it, exists." But Rust, arguably the foremost expert on bisexuality, argues for the continued use of the term so longs as its meaning is clearly defined in a given research context.

Once the definition of the term is nailed down, assuming that's possible, the next obstacle is finding a representative sample. Rust, author of the compendious Bisexuality in the United States (Columbia, 1999), describes the difficulty of finding such a sample. "A lot of research is done by convenience samples. For instance, if I go to a gay coffee house and 25 percent of the people are bi, I can't use data extracted from that population in any other context or draw any conclusions from such a sample about the general population." Another essay in Rust's compilation, "Behavior Patterns and Sexual Identity of Bisexual Males," explains that "like virtually all available data on human sexuality, studies have relied on nonprobability 'convenience' samples, including patients of STD clinics, members of accessible organizations, persons who frequent public places for sexual contact, and volunteer respondents to magazine and other publicly-announced surveys," skewing the data in unknown ways. Research on the Internet is another way of obtaining a sample of the general population, but here the problem is one of self-selection. What's more, observes Rust: "People present personas other than their own. Though it's easy to get a large quantity of data on the Internet, it's not representative of the larger population." Some avenues to obtaining more representative samples are electoral registers, postcode files, and telephone numbers; however, these forms of random sampling under-represent certain groups whose lifestyles and behaviors differ from the general population.

Yet another barrier to researching bisexuality has been the sheer lack of funding for this endeavor. Psychologist Lisa Diamond explains: "I know only a few serious scientists who are looking at bisexuality specifically. Major sex research centers are under attack and under-funded." Loraine Hutchins emphasized that only by sheer persistence have most been able to pursue sex research over many years with no funding, citing her friend and colleague Ron Fox for his tenacious commitment to the topic. (Fox is the editor of a recent collection of works studying bisexuality through the lens of psychology and sociology entitled Current Research on Bisexuality. Haworth, 2004). Hutchins echoes Diamond's point, bemoaning the lack of sponsorship: "No one has done the kind of comprehensive survey that Kinsey did; no one will fund it. We live in such an uptight climate." These are indeed conservative times. In 2003, Rep. Patrick Toomey (R-Pa.) proposed to de-fund four NIH grants for research on human sexuality; it didn't pass, but only by a meager two votes. Soon thereafter, the National Institute of Mental Health, which had funded Boston University's Sexuality and Research Treatment Program for twenty years, withdrew its funds, shutting down the operation completely. In recent years, many sex researchers have been forced to seek sponsorship from pharmaceutical companies, constraining the type of research they can pursue. The questions have been reduced to the mechanical, rather than the psychological aspects of sex—a mere clip of the bigger picture.

But the biggest problem researchers have in conceptualizing bisexuality has to do with the unfortunate fact that, in Rust's words, "Westerners think in neat, discrete categories." We are not accustomed to thinking in the space between any two polarized extremes. Martin Weinberg, co-author of Dual Attraction (Oxford University Press, 1994), a study of members of the San Francisco Bisexual Center during the pre-antiretroviral AIDS crisis, has encountered the same problem, concluding that: "People have a difficult time thinking analytically or in anything but the most simplistic (binary) way." Almost every bisexual activist and scholar I spoke with expressed the same viewpoint: "The dichotomy thing, which we also often call binary thinking or either/or thinking, has been our nemesis forever," gripes Hutchins.

Bisexuality erodes the border between homo- and heterosexuality, but it's a boundary that our society is heavily invested in maintaining. Doubtless the reason bisexuality is not adequately researched or understood is because it poses a threat to straight people, first and foremost, who feel secure behind an impenetrable wall of heterosexuality. This is bisexuality's subversive power. The promise of increased research on bisexuality is that just getting people to recognize its prevalence could help chip away at the hetero-versus-homo monolith and facilitate a dissolution of oppressive, traditional notions of what it means to be a man and a woman.

On an even broader scale, the lesson that bisexuality bares is a good one for the 21st century. We live in a world whose reality is more complicated than the simplified binaries of our language and understanding. Learning to reason in the middle of two polarized extremes might dissolve the us-them dichotomy that has spurred an ideological and political civil war in this country. Bisexuality as the synthesis, the middle ground between seemingly irreconcilable differences, is a form of thinking that has boundless possibilities for social progress—but first we have to acknowledge its existence and its prevalence in society.

Masculinity as Homophobia

Michael S. Kimmel

Michael S. Kimmel is Professor of Sociology at SUNY Stonybrook. He earned his PhD at UC Berkeley. His most recent book is Guyland: The Perilous World Where Boys Become Men (2008). He has also written and co-edited more than twenty volumes including, Manhood in America: A Cultural History (1996), Changing Men: New Directions in Research on Men and Masculinity (1987), Men Confront Pornography (1990), The Politics of Manhood (1996), The Gender of Desire (2005) and The History of Men (2005). This essay originally appeared in Theorizing Masculinity (1994).

Even if we do not subscribe to Freudian psychoanalytic ideas, we can still observe how, in less sexualized terms, the father is the first man who evaluates the boy's masculine performance, the first pair of male eyes before whom he tries to prove himself. Those eyes will follow him for the rest of his life. Other men's eyes will join them—the eyes of role models such as teachers, coaches, bosses, or media heroes; the eyes of his peers, his friends, his workmates; and the eyes of millions of other men, living and dead, from whose constant scrutiny of his performance he will never be free. "The tradition of all the dead generations weighs like a nightmare on the brain of the living," was how Karl Marx put it over a century ago (1848/1964, p. 11). "The birthright of every American male is a chronic sense of personal inadequacy," is how two psychologists describe it today (Woolfolk & Richardson, 1978, p. 57).

That nightmare from which we never seem to awaken is that those other men will see that sense of inadequacy, they will see that in our own eyes we are not who we are pretending to be. What we call masculinity is often a hedge against being revealed as a fraud, an exaggerated set of activities that keep others from seeing through us, and a frenzied effort to keep at bay those fears within ourselves. Our real fear, "is not fear of women but of being ashamed or humiliated in front of other men, or being dominated by stronger men" (Leverenz, 1986, p. 451).

This, then, is the great secret of American manhood: *We are afraid of other men.* Homophobia is a central organizing principle of our cultural definition of manhood. Homophobia is more than the irrational fear of gay men, more than the fear that we might be perceived as gay. "The word 'faggot' has nothing to do with homosexual experience or even with fears of homosexuals," writes David Leverenz (1986). "It comes out of the depths of manhood: a label of ultimate contempt for anyone who seems sissy, untough, uncool" (p. 455). Homophobia is the fear that other men will unmask us, emasculate us, reveal to us and the world that we do not measure up, that we are not real men. We are afraid to let other men see that fear. Fear makes us ashamed, because the recognition of fear in ourselves is proof to ourselves that we are not as manly as we pretend, that we are, like the young man in a poem by Yeats, "one that ruffles in a manly pose for all his timid heart." Our fear is the fear of humiliation. We are ashamed to be afraid.

Shame leads to silence—the silences that keep other people believing that we actually approve of the things that are done to women, to minorities, to gays and lesbians in our culture. The frightened silence as we scurry past a woman being hassled by men on the street. That furtive silence when men make sexist or racist jokes in a bar. That clammy-handed silence when guys in the office make gay-bashing jokes. Our fears are the sources of our silences, and men's silence is what keeps the system running. This might help to explain why women often complain that their male friends or partners are often so understanding when they are alone and yet laugh at sexist jokes or even make those jokes themselves when they are out with a group.

The fear of being seen as a sissy dominates the cultural definitions of manhood. It starts so early. "Boys among boys are ashamed to be unmanly," wrote one educator in 1871 (cited in Rotundo, 1993, p. 264). I have a standing bet with a friend that I can walk onto any playground in America where 6-year-old boys are happily playing and by asking one question, I can provoke a fight. That question is simple: "Who's a sissy around here?" Once posed, the challenge is made. One of two things is likely to happen. One boy will accuse another of being a sissy, to which that boy will respond that he is not a sissy, that the first boy is. They may have to fight it out to see who's lying. Or a whole group of boys will surround one boy and all shout "He is! He is!" That boy will either burst into tears and run home crying, disgraced, or he will have to take on several boys at once, to prove that he's not a sissy. (And what will his father or older brothers tell him if he chooses to run home crying?) It will be some time before he regains any sense of self-respect.

Violence is often the single most evident marker of manhood. Rather it is the willingness to fight, the desire to fight. The origin of our expression that one has a chip on one's shoulder lies in the practice of an adolescent boy in the country or small town at the turn of the century, who would literally walk around with a chip of wood balanced on his shoulder—a signal of his readiness to fight with anyone who would take the initiative of knocking the chip off (see Gorer, 1964, p. 38; Mead, 1965).

As adolescents, we learn that our peers are a kind of gender police, constantly threatening to unmask us as feminine, as sissies. One of the favorite tricks when I was an adolescent was to ask a boy to look at his fingernails. If he held his palm toward his face and curled his fingers back to see them, he passed the test. He'd looked at his nails "like a man." But if he held the back of his hand away from his face, and looked at his fingernails with arm outstretched, he was immediately ridiculed as a sissy.

As young men we are constantly riding those gender boundaries, checking the fences we have constructed on the perimeter, making sure that nothing even remotely feminine might show through. The possibilities of being unmasked are everywhere. Even the most seemingly insignificant thing can pose a threat or activate that haunting terror. On the day the students in my course "Sociology of Men and Masculinities" were scheduled to discuss homophobia and male-male friendships, one student provided a touching illustration. Noting that it was a beautiful day, the first day of spring after a brutal northeast winter, he decided to wear shorts to class. "I had this really nice pair of new Madras shorts," he commented. "But then I thought to myself, these shorts have lavender and pink in them. Today's class topic is homophobia. Maybe today is not the best day to wear these shorts."

Our efforts to maintain a manly front cover everything we do. What we wear. How we talk. How we walk. What we eat. Every mannerism, every movement contains a coded gender language. Think, for example, of how you would answer the question: How do you "know" if a man is homosexual? When I ask this question in classes or workshops, respondents invariably provide a pretty standard list of stereotypically effeminate behaviors. He walks a certain way, talks a certain way, acts a certain way. He's very emotional; he shows his feelings. One woman commented that she "knows" a man is gay if he really cares about her; another said she knows he's gay if he shows no interest in her, if he leaves her alone.

Now alter the question and imagine what heterosexual men do to make sure no one could possibly get the "wrong idea" about them. Responses typically refer to the original stereotypes, this time as a set of negative rules about behavior. Never dress that way. Never talk or walk that way. Never show your feelings or get emotional. Always be prepared to demonstrate sexual interest in women that you meet, so it is impossible for any woman to get the wrong idea about you. In this sense, homophobia, the fear of being perceived as gay, as not a real man, keeps men exaggerating all the traditional rules of masculinity, including sexual predation with women. Homophobia and sexism go hand in hand.

The stakes of perceived sissydom are enormous—sometimes matters of life and death. We take enormous risks to prove our manhood, exposing ourselves disproportionately to health risks, workplace hazards, and stress-related illnesses. Men commit suicide three times as often as women. Psychiatrist Willard Gaylin (1992) explains that it is "invariably because of perceived social humiliation," most often tied to failure in business:

> Men become depressed because of loss of status and power in the world of men. It is not the loss of money, or the material advantages that money could buy, which produces the despair that leads to self-destruction. It is the "shame," the "humiliation," the sense of personal "failure." . . . A man despairs when he has ceased being a man among men. (p. 32)

In one survey, women and men were asked what they were most afraid of. Women responded that they were most afraid of being raped and murdered. Men responded that they were most afraid of being laughed at (Noble, 1992, pp. 105–106).

POWER AND POWERLESSNESS IN THE LIVES OF MEN

I have argued that homophobia, men's fear of other men, is the animating condition of the dominant definition of masculinity in America, that the reigning definition of masculinity is a defensive effort to prevent being emasculated. In our efforts to suppress or overcome those fears, the dominant culture exacts a tremendous price from those deemed less than fully manly: women, gay men, nonnative-born men, men of color. This perspective may help clarify a paradox in men's lives, a paradox in which men have virtually all the power and yet do not feel powerful (see Kaufman, 1993).

Manhood is equated with power—over women, over other men. Everywhere we look, we see the institutional expression of that power—in state and national legislatures, on the boards of directors of every major U.S. corporation or law firm, and in every school and hospital administration. Women have long understood this, and feminist women have spent the past three decades challenging both the public and the private expressions of men's power and acknowledging their fear of men. Feminism as a set of theories both explains women's fear of men and empowers women to confront it both publicly and privately. Feminist women have theorized that masculinity is about the drive for domination, the drive for power, for conquest.

This feminist definition of masculinity as the drive for power is theorized from women's point of view. It is how women experience masculinity. But it assumes a symmetry between the public and the private that does not conform to men's experiences. Feminists observe that women, as a group, do not hold power in our society. They also observe that individually, they, as women, do not feel powerful. They feel afraid, vulnerable. Their observation of the social reality and their individual experiences are therefore symmetrical. Feminism also observes that men, as a group, are in power. Thus, with the same symmetry, feminism has tended to assume that individually men must feel powerful.

This is why the feminist critique of masculinity often falls on deaf ears with men. When confronted with the analysis that men have all the power, many men react incredulously. "What do you mean, men have all the power?" they ask. "What are you talking about? My wife bosses me around. My kids boss me around. My boss bosses me around. I have no power at all! I'm completely powerless!"

Men's feelings are not the feelings of the powerful, but of those who see themselves as powerless. These are the feelings that come inevitably from the discontinuity between the social and the psychological, between the aggregate analysis that reveals how men are in power as a group and the psychological fact that they do not feel powerful as individuals. They are the feelings of men who were raised to believe themselves entitled to feel that power, but do not feel it. No wonder many men are frustrated and angry.

This may explain the recent popularity of those workshops and retreats designed to help men to claim their "inner" power, their "deep manhood," or their "warrior within." Authors such as Bly (1990), Moore and Gillette (1991, 1992, 1993a, 1993b), Farrell (1986, 1993), and Keen (1991) honor and respect men's feelings of powerlessness and acknowledge those feelings to be both true and real. "They gave white men the semblance of power," notes John Lee, one of the leaders of these retreats (quoted in Ferguson, 1992, p. 28). "We'll let you run the country, but in the meantime, stop feeling, stop talking, and continue swallowing your pain and your hurt." (We are not told who "they" are.)

Often the purveyors of the mythopoetic men's movement, that broad umbrella that encompasses all the groups helping men to retrieve this mythic deep manhood, use the image of the chauffeur to described modern man's position. The chauffeur appears to have the power—he's wearing the uniform, he's in the driver's seat, and he knows where he's going. So, to the observer, the chauffeur looks as though he is in command. But to the chauffeur himself, they note, he is merely taking orders. He is not at all in charge.[1]

Despite the reality that everyone knows chauffeurs do not have the power, this image remains appealing to the men who hear it at these weekend workshops. But there is a missing piece to the image, a piece concealed by the framing of the image in terms of the individual man's experience. That missing piece is that the person who is giving the orders is also a man. Now we have a relationship *between* men—between men giving orders and other men taking those orders. The man who identifies with the chauffeur is entitled to be the man giving the orders, but he is not. ("They," it turns out, are other men.)

The dimension of power is now reinserted into men's experience not only as the product of individual experience but also as the product of relations with other men. In this sense, men's experience of powerlessness is *real*—the men actually feel it and certainly act on it— but it is not *true*, that is, it does not accurately describe their condition. In contrast to women's lives, men's lives are structured around relationships of power and men's differential access to power, as well as the differential access to that power of men as a group. Our imperfect analysis of our own situation leads us to believe that we men need more power, rather than leading us to support feminists' efforts to rearrange power relationships along more equitable lines.

Philosopher Hannah Arendt (1970) fully understood this contradictory experience of social and individual power:

> Power corresponds to the human ability not just to act but to act in concert. Power is never the property of an individual; it belongs to a group and remains in existence only so long as the group keeps together. When we say of somebody that he is "in power" we actually refer to his being empowered by a certain number of people to act in their name. The moment the group, from which the power originated to begin with . . . disappears, his "power" also vanishes. (p. 44)

Why, then, do American men feel so powerless? Part of the answer is because we've constructed the rules of manhood so that only the tiniest fraction of men come to believe that they are the biggest of wheels, the sturdiest of oaks, the most virulent repudiators of femininity, the most daring and aggressive. We've managed to disempower the overwhelming majority of American men by other means—such as discriminating on the basis of race, class, ethnicity, age, or sexual preference.

Masculinist retreats to retrieve deep, wounded masculinity are but one of the ways in which American men currently struggle with their fears and their shame. Unfortunately, at the very moment that they work to break down the isolation that governs men's lives, as they enable men to express those fears and that shame, they ignore the social power that men continue to exert over women and the privileges from which they (as the middle-aged, middle-class white men who largely make up these retreats) continue to benefit—regardless of their experiences as wounded victims of oppressive male socialization.

Others still rehearse the politics of exclusion, as if by clearing away the playing field of secure gender identity of any that we deem less than manly—women, gay men, nonnative-born men, men of color—middle-class, straight, white men can reground their sense of themselves without those haunting fears and that deep shame that they are unmanly and will be exposed by other men. This is the manhood of racism, of sexism, of homophobia. It is the manhood that is so chronically insecure that it trembles at the idea of lifting the ban on gays in the military, that is so threatened by women in the workplace that women become the targets of sexual harassment, that is so deeply frightened of equality that it must ensure that the playing field of male competition remains stacked against all newcomers to the game.

Exclusion and escape have been the dominant methods American men have used to keep their fears of humiliation at bay. The fear of emasculation by other men, of being humiliated, of being seen as a sissy, is the leitmotif in my reading of the history of American manhood. Masculinity has become a relentless test by which we prove to other men, to women, and ultimately to ourselves, that we have successfully mastered the part. The restlessness that men feel today is nothing new in American history; we have been anxious and restless for almost two centuries. Neither exclusion nor escape has ever brought us the relief we've sought, and there is no reason to think that either will solve our problems now. Peace of mind, relief from gender struggle, will come only from a politics of inclusion, not exclusion, from standing up for equality and justice, and not by running away.

REFERENCES

Arendt, H. (1970). *On revolution*. New York: Viking.

Bly, R. (1990). *Iron John: A book about men*. Reading, MA: Addison-Wesley.

Farrell, W. (1986). *Why men are the way they are*. New York: McGraw-Hill.

Farrell, W. (1993). *The myth of male power: Why men are the disposable sex*. New York: Simon & Schuster.

Ferguson, A. (1992, January). America's new men. *American Spectator*, 25 (1).

Gaylin, W. (1992). *The male ego*. New York: Viking.

Gorer, G. (1964). *The American people: A study in national character*. New York: Norton.

Kaufman, M. (1993). *Cracking the armour: Power and pain in the lives of men*. Toronto: Viking Canada.

Keen, S. (1991). *Fire in the belly*. New York: Bantam.

Leverenz, D. (1986, Fall). Manhood, humiliation and public life: Some stories. *Southwest Review*, 71.

Marx, K., & Engels, F. (1848/1964). The communist manifesto. In R. Tucker (Ed.), *The Marx-Engels reader*. New York: Norton.

Mead, M. (1965). *And keep your powder dry*. New York: William Morrow.

Moore, R., & Gillette, D. (1991). *King, warrior, magician lover*. New York: Harper Collins.

Moore, R., & Gillette, D. (1992). *The king within: Accessing the king in the male psyche*. New York: William Morrow.

Moore, R., & Gillette, D. (1993a). *The warrior within: Accessing the warrior in the male psyche*. New York: William Morrow.

Moore, R., & Gillette, D. (1993b). *The magician within: Accessing the magician in the male psyche*. New York: William Morrow.

Noble, V. (1992). A helping hand from the guys. In K. L. Hagan (Ed.), *Women respond to the men's movement*. San Francisco: HarperCollins.

Rotundo, E. A. (1993). *American manhood: Transformations in masculinity from the revolution to the modern era*. New York: Basic Books.

Woolfolk, R. L., & Richardson, F. (1978). *Sanity, stress and survival*. New York: Signet.

The Problem with Sex/Gender and Nature/Nurture

Anne Fausto-Sterling

Anne Fausto-Sterling *is Professor of Biology and Gender Studies at Brown University. Her influential work in biology and gender has long challenged ideas about sex and gender. In her new work she uses Dynamic Systems Theory to study and explain how cultural differences impact and contribute to bodily differences, most specifically in bone development. Her books include* Sexing the Body: Gender Politics and the Construction of Sexuality *(2000) and* Myths of Gender: Biological Theories About Men and Women *(1985, 1992). This essay appeared in* Debating Biology: Sociological Reflections on Health, Medicine and Society *(2003) edited by Simon J. Williams, Lynda Birke and Gillian Bendelow.*

For a good century and a half, scientists, social scientists and politicians have appealed to biological difference to explain social inequality between men and women, people of African descent and Caucasians, members of different economic classes and people of different religions. In turn, a wide variety of scholars writing over a long period of time have critiqued these scientific claims (Russett 1989; Fausto-Sterling 2000). In the mid-1980s, I drew a composite picture gleaned from the writings of contemporary biological and social scientists: these writers claimed that women are naturally better mothers, while men are genetically predisposed to be aggressive, hasty and fickle. They may rape to pass on their genes. Women's lack of aggressive drive and native ability ensures that they will always earn less, thus guaranteeing equal pay discriminates against men (Fausto-Sterling 1992).

At the time, I critically examined the underlying scientific evidence, demonstrating its procedural and interpretive weaknesses. I also suggested that instead of setting nature against nurture we reject the search for root causes and substitute a more complex analysis in which an individual's capacities emerge from a web of mutual interactions between the biological being and the social environment. Although I had the right idea, the moment was not right to express it in terms that might unify biological scientists, sociologists, developmental psychologists, and feminists. I believe that now that moment of unification is upon us.

In the 1970s, feminist social scientists proposed a theory that created two categories: *sex*, the supposed biological essence that underlay gender and *gender* the social overlay that produced two different categories of being–men and women, through an ill-defined process of socialization. This theoretical approach had many virtues. It permitted the examination of differential treatment of boys and girls in school and men and women in the workplace. It opened the door to a virtual growth industry of cultural analysis examining the construction of gender ideology in the media and on the streets. But it also had a big drawback. Leaving 'sex' in the realm of scientifically verifiable fact left feminism vulnerable to a new tide of biological difference. Indeed, that new tide is very much with us (see for example: Udry 2000; Wizemann and Pardue 2001).

For some, sex encroaches deep into the territory of social difference, while for others it is a minimal entity. If there is something that we could call 'naked sex' (Kraus 2000) – that which is left when all gender is stripped away – we have to argue about for how much of gender difference it can account. If we leave naked sex to biologists and biologically oriented social scientists, we will find that the territory allotted to it is growing apace while the explanatory power of socially produced gender shrinks in proportion. In the sex versus gender model, biological sex is opposed to social sex. Nature is opposed to culture, the body becomes the recipient of culture, and gender becomes the content of culture. Worst of all, for those interested in social change, naked sex is often – albeit incorrectly – seen as immutable, while gender, is often, albeit incorrectly, seen as malleable. To the extent that the sex/gender analysis of social difference reinforces our view of the material body as a natural given, our feminist debate influences the structure of other struggles. Indeed, the biological debates about race and about sex have intersected and mutually constructed one another for a good two centuries (Russett 1989).

In *Sexing the Body: Gender Politics and the Construction of Sexuality* (Fausto-Sterling 2000), I detail several examples of how the biology – culture debate about the body plays out. Let me briefly pick one of these – an alleged sex difference in the structure of a part of the brain called the corpus callosum. Scientists have argued about whether or not there is a sex difference in the corpus callosum for a more than 100 years. Some think that the (real) difference might explain sex/gender variation in verbal and spatial ability and that the knowledge of such difference should be used to shape educational policy. Others believe there is no difference. I use this scientific debate to think about how social arguments sustain scientific disputes, concluding that we will not resolve the *science* at issue until we have reached some form of consensus over the *social policy* at hand.

While the above insight is important, however, I want here to emphasize a different aspect of the problem. Suppose, hypothetically, someone proved beyond a doubt that a sex difference in the corpus callosum was clearly linked to verbal and spatial abilities. Would that mean that feminists adhering to the sex/gender distinction would have to agree that educators need to treat boys and girls differently when they teach maths and English? Would that force us to accept the argument that we cannot expect there to be more women engineers than the 9.2 per cent employed in the US workforce in 1997? At its worst, too strict an adherence to the sex/gender dualism puts us in just such a position. At its best, it leaves feminists in a position of constant defensiveness, with all of our energy focused on refuting or mitigating the latest findings of sex differences produced by biomedical researchers. Psychologist Susan Oyama refers to this as hauling 'phenomena back and forth across the biological border' (Oyama 2000: 190). I, for one, am tired of being in this position, and this weariness has pushed me – and other theorists – to think differently about biology, culture, sex, and gender (see, for example, the chapters by Birke and Annandale, this volume). In making new theory, we reclaim a defining position in the social debate about gender and we can direct our creativity towards breaking new pathways rather than fighting off the dogs that nip constantly at our heels.

I find especially helpful a set of approaches that I have gathered under the flag of Developmental Systems Theory, or DST for short. From the point of view of DST, neither naked sex nor naked culture exist. Findings of so-called biological difference do not imply a claim of immutability or inevitability. Consider once again the corpus callosum. Some scientists believe that this brain structure differs in men and women; others that it differs in left- and right-handers and yet others believe that it differs in gay and straight men (where it is really a stand-in for a gendered account of homosexuality). Elsewhere I write about the uncertain nature of these conclusions (Fausto-Sterling 1992; Fausto-Sterling 2000), but here I want to think about what it might mean if these claims were scientifically uncontestable. In bringing a DST approach to the claim of brain differences in adult men and women, the assertion of difference becomes a starting point. The interesting question is how the differences developed in the first place. For example, this possible difference in the adult corpus callosum is not present in the brains of small children. A DST researcher will want to design experiments to test hypotheses about how different experience leads to a divergence in brain development. Instead of asking how anatomy limits function, one asks how function shapes anatomy. To claim a biological difference is not to claim immutability.

New research questions become apparent when we turn matters around in this way. What childhood experiences and behaviours contribute to the developing anatomy of the brain? Are there particular developmental periods when a child's brain is more or less responsive to functional stimuli? How do nerve cells translate externally generated information into specific growth patterns and neural circuits? Answering these latter questions will require the skills of molecular biologists and cell biologists as well as psychologists, sociologists and cultural theorists. DST will not put basic biologists out of business, but will set their research in a different intellectual framework.

Just as a claim of biological difference does not imply immutability, a claim of socially induced difference does not necessarily imply malleability. For example, if differential social experience produces differences in brain anatomy and thus in brain function, later experiences would then be interpreted and integrated by a differently functioning brain. Change to a pre-differentiated state would be improbable. Many people consider it extremely difficult to change from being hetero- to homosexual or vice versa. But the fact that a particular form of sexual desire is hard to change does not mean that it hasn't been socially caused.

How, more specifically, can DST help to form a new research agenda which depends upon the mutual construction of sex and gender? Psychologists Esther Thelen and Linda Smith list some of the basic goals of developmental systems theory (Thelen and Smith 1994). The first is to understand the origins of novelty. Thelen and Smith discuss behavioural novelty–starting to crawl and then to walk for example, but I would like to use DST to elucidate the emergence by the age of two-and-a-half of gender differences in play and the ability to categorize self and others by gender. Infants are not born with these behaviours. Rather, the behaviours emerge during the first two to three years of life. We have a sketchy idea of the timing of such emergence but little in the way of coherent theory to explain our observations (Ruble and Martin 1998).

A second goal of DST is to reconcile global regularities with local variability. In the case of gender, this means understanding the emergence of general features recognizable as something we call gender, while at the same time incorporating into our story the enormous within-group variability.

A third goal of systems theory is to integrate developmental data at many levels of explanation. Consider Judith Butler's controversial and frequently misunderstood assertion that 'gender ought not to be construed as a stable identity . . . rather, gender is an identity tenuously constituted in time, instituted in an exterior space through a *stylized repetition of acts*' (Butler 1990: 140; emphasis in the original). Butler was not thinking specifically about physiological mechanisms by which the body might materially incorporate gender. Nevertheless, a systems approach to the body insists that relatively stable states of being emerge from a process of repetitive trial and error. Thus Butler's notion of repeated performance, designed to describe gender development at the psychoanalytic level, could become a starting point to design studies aimed at understanding the material basis of gender. 'Material basis' is here understood as a set of physiological and social expressions which emerge as individuals learn about social gender, practice it, and make it their own. That brain anatomy might itself develop in particular ways in response to such practice and repetition seems likely to me, but is a hypothesis that requires specification and testing.

Such an application of DST to Butler's ideas of performance also provide an answer to Pheng Cheah's critique of Butler (Cheah 1996). Cheah argues that Butler's account of gender development is philosophically wanting because it only applies to humans, a fact that leaves human gender critically unconnected to the rest of biology. Most biologists, however (myself included) view human biology – including sex/gender development – as falling along a continuum. DST can provide accounts of how gender materializes in the body that will work for all animals, not just humans. Granted there are some big discussions about consciousness and intentionality in non-human primates that must be held along the way. But stretching claims such as Butler's about repetitive performance to develop a systems account of the biological materialization of gender in humans, will open the door to understanding biological development more broadly, and confront untenable claims that human materiality differs fundamentally from that of other animals.

A fourth goal of developmental systems theory is to provide a biologically plausible yet non-determinist account of the development of behaviour. As Thelen and Smith write, 'the boundaries between what is innate and what is acquired become so blurred as to be at the very least uninteresting compared to the powerful questions of developmental process' (Thelen and Smith 1994). A fifth goal is to understand how local processes, that is, what happens in a particular family or to a particular child or a particular random experience, can lead to global outcomes. For example, most children learn to walk. But the individual paths they take to that accomplishment can vary quite a lot.

A final goal for DST is to establish a theoretical basis for generating and interpreting empirical research that breaks out of the idea of adding up so much nature and so much nurture to create a final outcome. This means learning how to apply statistical systems that do not partition variance. (For critiques of the Analysis of Variance approach to the study of human difference see: Wahlsten 1990.)

Psychologists have most successfully applied DST to phenomena that have little to do with gender. Studying such applications, however, can help us to construct a research agenda aimed at explicating the emergence of gender in early childhood and its subsequent development throughout the life cycle. Consider how Thelen and her colleagues investigate the question of how we learn to walk. In the 1940s and 1950s, psychologists described the stages of learning to walk – up on all fours, crawling, standing, walking holding on, etc. They reasoned that each new stage directly reflected changes in the brain. But how can the millions of neurons, the wide variety of muscle contraction patterns, and the complex patterns of neuronal activity, ever result in a highly specific movement such as putting one leg in front of another? During development, individuals go through periods of instability as they incorporate new tasks – be they motor, cognitive or emotional. In an infant, seemingly random motor activity, for instance, eventually emerges into new and fairly stable forms of movement, first crawling, then walking.

A recent example illustrates why developmental systems theory has begun to replace more rigid accounts of stages of neuromuscular development. In 1992 pediatricians recommended that to minimize the danger of sudden infant death, infants be place on their back (supine) or side to sleep rather than on their bellies (prone). Since the recommendation and a public education campaign, the percentage of US infants sleeping in the prone position has decreased from

70 percent to 27 per cent. With that change has come another – a dramatic shift in the age at which infants reach motor milestones such as pulling to stand up, crawling, creeping and rolling from a prone to supine position (Davis *et al.* 1998). The observation that sleep position affects the timing of motor development makes perfect sense to a systems theorist, since neuromuscular development is an *effect* of use and experience. That both supine and prone sleepers learn to walk at about the same time may reflect the fact that by one year of age they have all developed the strength needed to sustain independent walking. But supine and prone sleepers don't attain that strength in exactly the same way or according to the same time schedule.

As long as the basic conditions – the force of gravity, the firmness of the ground, neuromuscular responses (indeed these are all part of the system of walking), remain stable, the ability to walk remains stable as well. But the stability is what DST theorists call 'softly assembled'. Walking, for example, is a flexible ability. We don't use exactly the same neuromuscular responses when walking on different substrates, yet we walk. Walking can take on different strides – ambling, strolling, fast-walking. It can adjust to an injury in a knee joint, etc. Softly assembled states can dissolve into new periods of instability and new types of stability can emerge from these seemingly chaotic events – learning to walk again following muscle atrophy or traumatic injury would be one such example.

Consider as another example, the development of the retina and the ability to see. The axons of nerve cells from the retina of each eye connect to a part of the brain known as the lateral geniculate nucleus. Some of the retinal axons from the right eye connect to the lateral geniculate nucleus of the left hemisphere while others connect to the right hemisphere, while the opposite is true for axons from the left eye. Within the lateral geniculate nucleus, axons from the two eyes terminate in separate alternating layers. There is also an additional level of organization in these projections called ocular dominance columns. Initially, neither the layering of these lateral geniculate nucleus axons from left to right nor the dominance columns are present, but via an active process of axon retraction and elaboration, eventually the adult connections emerge.

These events do not occur seamlessly in response to some internal logic of genes acting spontaneously inside cells. Rather, visual experience plays a key role. The firing of certain neurons strengthens their connections. Neuroscientists say 'cells that fire together wire together, those that don't won't.' The fact that light, entering the eye after birth is necessary for a completely functional set of eye-brain connections explains why it is so important to remove congenital cataracts no later than six months after birth (Le Grand *et al.* 2001).

In the development of vision, key features of developmental systems theory emerge. First, specific connections are not *programmed* by some genetic blueprint. Genetic activity, rather, guides development by responding to external signals reaching specific cells at specific times. Early in development these signals come from other cells while at a later time signals include spontaneous electrical activity generated by developing nervous tissue and, still later, light entering through the newborn and infant eye. A functional system emerges from a context-bound system in which seemingly random activity – that is spontaneous nerve firings and visual input – evolve into more highly structured form and function. Often these connections must happen during a critical window of development. One general point to be made is that different kinds of connections have different degrees of plasticity. Some critical windows reside only in one stage of the life cycle because that is the only time when (so far as we currently know) the entire system is constructed in a particular way. In some cases an end state can be produced by more than one initial starting point while in others only one initial starting point can produce an end state. Other systems, though, may be open to change more than once in a life cycle or may even be continuously modifiable during the life cycle. Thus a key notion of developmental systems theory is that there are periods of relative stability and other moments of great instability. During unstable moments important changes can occur which in turn resolve into new and stable form and function. An important future task for biologists and social scientists, working together, is to apply these concepts to gender formation during the life cycle.

How might DST apply to the analysis of sex and gender? Consider the uproar over biologist Simon LeVay's 1991 article reporting differences in the microanatomy of both male and female brains and in the brains of gay and straight men (LeVay 1991). The initial response from many of us was to point out the technical shortcomings of the study, but in a recent study some of these have been overcome. Neuroanatomist William Byne could not replicate the gay/straight differences that LeVay reported. But as had LeVay, Byne found measurable differences between men's and women's hypothalamuses (Byne *et al.* 2001). Given that his is the third independent report of this anatomical brain difference, I think we would be hard-pressed to deny the finding. But accepting the difference need not push us into a bio-determinist corner. Instead, we need to insist that scientists ask developmental and functional questions about the difference. Most importantly, we need to hammer home the point that differences found in adults arise during development.

This insistence opens the door for a theory and practice of what contemporary theorists call embodiment. Recall the DST concept of softly-assembled states. Although relatively stable, such states can dissolve into chaotic periods out of which new types of stability can emerge. Consider the conflict between the idea that homosexuality is inborn versus the thought that it is somehow learned after birth. Sometimes this argument resolves into a debate about whether the trait is unchangeable or whether it can be altered by force of will. There is bad thinking on both sides of this argument. For many homosexuals, same-sex attraction is a stable state of desire. If we think of that stability as being softly assembled, however, it becomes less surprising that it can sometimes become destabilized and after a period of disarray, some new quasi-stable form of desire can emerge.

Recent work on the nature of memory in rats can help us conceptualize my argument. Consider rats that have been fear-conditioned to associate a tone with an electric shock. At first, the conditioned response is unstable. It requires about six hours and some protein synthesis to consolidate. The memory associating a tone with shock, however, can be pushed out of what I will call its softly assembled state by preventing more protein synthesis at the time that memory is again evoked by playing the tone (Nader 2000). The conclusion from this experiment is that when a memory is drawn upon and then stored again, new memory proteins are made. In these experiments, memories become destabilized and open to revision for a brief period before a new period of stability begins.

The concept that memory can be revised during episodes of retrieval can be useful in thinking about homosexuality. Consider the statement by a gay person that they always remember being different. Perhaps they remember liking dolls instead of trucks (or for lesbians, liking trucks instead of dolls). If, during the evocation of memory, it is possible to edit and incorporate contemporary information, then memory itself becomes part of a system that produces the sexual preference or gender identity. The memories are perfectly real, but they become progressively adjusted, presumably throughout childhood and into adulthood, to take into account new experiences and newly available information. Surely it is possible for social and neuroscientists to collaborate in applying the study of memory processing and revision to the acquisition of gender identity and sexual orientation. Such applications have the potential to provide a dynamic account of embodiment rather than the less plausible view that some people are born with a homosexual homunculus which merely unfolds over a lifetime.

In light of my discussion of DST I propose a new research agenda for the study of sex and gender differences. First, we need to think more about individual differences than group averages. This means studying individual development and accepting the idea that there are many different individual paths to a global outcome. Feminist social theory contains rich work on the emergence of sex and gender differences, much of which examines mid- and late child development or adulthood. But we know little about the early emergence of difference. And it's the early emergence of difference that is often used as evidence for a biological cause for difference.

We can, however, say a few things about early development. At seven months, on average, infants respond differently to male and female voices. By nine months, they can tell the sexes apart largely on the basis of hair length. But other contributions to an infant's ability to discriminate sexes such as height and smell have not been well studied. Children can differentially label the sexes by about thirty months but they are better at labelling adults than they are at labelling other children. Children take quite a while before they use genitalia as clues to sex and before they are able to do this they rely heavily on hair cues. In the United States small children believe that figures with blond curly hair are female. Adolescents, but not younger children, use dynamic clues, such as running or sitting to identify gender (Ruble and Martin 1998).

The racial specificity of such findings make future, culturally specific studies imperative. Most studies of early development of gender perception have been done on white middle-class children in America and the entire question of constructing culturally neutral accounts of gender difference continues to vex feminist theory. Indeed, a central component of a feminist social science research agenda must be to examine the early development of gender constructs and behaviours in different cultures and in different socio-economic groups and within different ethnic and racially-defined communities (see also part II, this volume). If we develop process-based theories of human development rather than relying on averages and statistical norms, we will have fewer problems including human variation in our accounts of gender development.

After children learn to identify gender they then develop a separate concept – that gender is constant and stable. At first children don't necessarily believe that 'once a girl always a girl'. It takes a while for young children to develop the notion that, first, genitalia provide a reliable way of distinguishing between boys and girls and second that one of the implications of knowing about genital difference is that gender is fixed. The ages at which these two ideas develop – although certainly older than three years – have yet to be clearly resolved.

By about two-and-a-half years of age (white, middle-class American) children begin to show knowledge of gender stereotypes, about objects (dresses versus trousers, trucks versus flowers) and activities (active playing, passive playing, playing in the home-making corner, throwing a ball, playing with trucks). Although they know about these gendered stereotypes, social scientists have yet to assess which ones children learn first. I offer the above, abbreviated description of the development of gender awareness in children not as an account of how gender emerges, but rather as an invitation. I ask developmental systems theorists who have produced fascinating but non-gendered accounts of motor and cognitive development to use DST to think about gender. Similarly, I request social scientists who study gender to break away from the traditional biological, psychoanalytic, cognitive social learning or gender schema approaches. Instead, I encourage them to look at the trajectory that I've sketched above, fill in important gaps, and begin to use developmental systems theory to understand the process by which gender emerges at very young ages. How does it stabilize? What might contribute to its destabilization, and how does it restabilize and change during the process of an entire life cycle?

At the same time I invite feminist theorists in the humanities to revisit the social sciences with a new developmental systems theory vision. This is the impulse of the current vogue of the term embodiment among feminist theorists. Embodiment suggests a process by which we *acquire* a body rather than a passive unfolding of some preformed blueprint. Beginning to understand that the world works via systems will enable us to specify more clearly the links between culture and the body and to understand how nature and nurture, sex and gender are indivisible concepts. Finally, the political fallout from these ideas remains to be addressed. We – and here I mean feminist political theorists – need to think harder about how engaging with the world of sex and gender from a DST point of view will affect our strategies for social change.

REFERENCES

Butler, J. (1990) *Gender Trouble: Feminism and the Subversion of Identity*, New York: Routledge.

Byne, W., Tobet, S. and Mattiace, Linda, A. *et al.* (2001) 'The interstitial nuclei of the human anterior hypothalamus: an investigation of variation with sex, sexual orientation and HIV status', *Hormones and Behavior*, **40**: 86–92.

Cheah, P. (1996) 'Mattering', *Diacritics*, **26**, 1: 108–39.

Davis, B.E., Moon, R.Y., Sachs, H.C. and Ottolini, M.C. (1998) 'Effects of sleep position on infant motor development', *Pediatrics*, **102**, 5: 1135–40.

Fausto-Sterling, A. (1992) *Myths of Gender: Biological Theories about Women and Men*, New York: Basic Books.

Fausto-Sterling, A. (2000) *Sexing the Body: Gender Politics and the Construction of Sexuality*, New York: Basic Books.

Kraus, C. (2000) 'Naked sex in exile: on the paradox of the "sex question" in feminism and science', *National Women's Studies Association Journal*, **12**, 3: 151–77.

Le Grand, R., Mondloch, C.J., Maurer, D. and Brent, H.P. (2001) 'Early visual experience and face processing', *Nature*, **410**: 890.

LeVay, S. (1991) 'A difference in hypothalamic structure between heterosexual and homosexual men', *Science*, **253**: 1034–7.

Nader, K., Schafe, G.E. and Le Doux, J. E. (2000). 'Fear memories require protein synthesis in the amygdala for reconsolidation after retrieval', *Nature*, **406**: 722–6.

Oyama, S. (2000) *Evolution's Eye: A System's View of the Biology-Culture Divide*, Durham: Duke University Press.

Ruble, D. and Martin, C.L. (1998) 'Gender development', in N. Eisenberg (ed.) *Social, Emotional and Personality Development*, New York: Wiley, pp. 933–1016.

Russett, C.E. (1989) *Sexual Science: The Victorian Construction of Womanhood*, Cambridge: Harvard University Press.

Thelen, E. and Smith, L.B. (1994) *A Dynamic Systems Approach to the Development of Cognition and Action*, Cambridge: MIT Press.

Udry, J.R. (2000) 'Biological limits of gender construction', *American Sociological Review*, **65**, 3: 443–57.

Wahlsten, D. (1990) 'Insensitivity of the analysis of variance to heredity-environment interaction', *Behavior and Brain Sciences*, **13**: 109–61.

Wizemann, T.M. and Pardue, M.-L. (eds) (2001) *Exploring the Biological Contributions to Human Health: Does Sex Matter?* Washington, DC: National Academy Press.

SECTION IV

Gender in Education

Key Concepts for Section IV: Gender in Education

Achievement Gap	**Concepts to Review**
Active Learning	Androcentrism
Backlash	Biological Determinism
Biosocial Framework	Dichotomy/Dichotomous
Borderwork	Differential Socialization
Boy Crisis	Doing Gender
Bullying	Dominance/Domination
Chilly Climate	Double Standards
Civil Rights Restoration Act of 1987	Femininity/Femininities
Claiming an Education	Gender
Cross-Sex Interactions	Gender Studies
Educator-Based Model	Hierarchy
Feminist Pedagogy	Internalized Oppression
Feminization of Education	Marginalization
Formal Curriculum	Masculinity/Masculinities
Hidden Curriculum	Men's Studies
Homophobic Harassment	Myth of Meritocracy
Individual or Student-Based Model	Mythical Norm
Internalized Stereotypes	Oppression
Microinequity	Patriarchy
Parallel Curriculum	Reproductive Choice
Sexual Harassment	Sex
Sex Segregation	Sex Roles
Title VI of the Civil Rights Act	Sex-Gender System
Title VII of the Civil Rights Act	Socialization
Title IX of Education Amendments of 1972	Women's Studies
Two Worlds Model	

The Chilly Climate
Subtle Ways in Which Women Are Often Treated Differently at Work and in Classrooms

Bernice R. Sandler

Bernice Sandler earned a Doctorate in Education in Counseling and Personnel Services form the University of Maryland. She is a Senior Scholar at the Women's Research and Education Institute in Washington DC. She focuses on making both education and the workplace more equitable for women. She is considered "The Godmother of Title IX". "The Chilly Climate" first appeared in the newsletter About Women on Campus in 1999. The material was drawn from The Chilly Classroom Climate: A Guide to Improve the Education of Women (1996) by Bernice R. Sandler, Lisa A Silverberg and Roberta M. Hall, published by the National Association for Women in Education, Washington, D.C.

The word "women" as used here includes all women. However, for women of color, disabled women, lesbians and older women these behaviors may be exacerbated and these women may experience other forms of differential behavior as well. Additionally, other "outsiders" such as men of color, persons for whom English is a second language, and those from working class backgrounds often experience many of the same behaviors described here.

Most of the behaviors are what has been described as "microinequities," a term coined by Mary Rowe of Massachusetts Institute of Technology. They describe the small everyday inequities through which individuals are often treated differently because of their gender, race, age, or other "outsider" status. Taken by itself, a microinequity may have a minuscule effect, if it has any at all, and is typically not noticed by the person it happens to or by the person who asserts it. Yet when these behaviors occur again and again, and especially if they are not noticed or understood, they often have a damaging cumulative effect, creating an environment that is indeed chilly—an environment that dampens women's self-esteem, confidence, aspirations and their participation.

Because overt behaviors are more easily recognized, they have generally been omitted from this article. Those that are included here are the types of behaviors that are typically minimized by the person engaging in the behavior. Some of the behaviors below may fit in more than one category.

This article appeared in the Summer 1999 issue *About Women on Campus, Vol. 8, Number 3* published by the Association of American Colleges and Universities. Virtually all of the material was drawn from *The Chilly Classroom Climate: A Guide to Improve the Education of Women*, by Bernice R. Sandler, Lisa A Silverberg and Roberta M. Hall, published by the now defunct National Association for Women in Education, Washington, D.C. in 1996. The book is no longer in print. Sandler is a Senior Scholar at the Women's Research and Education Institute; the article also appears on her web site, www.bernicesandler.com.

BEHAVIORS THAT COMMUNICATE LOWER EXPECTATIONS FOR WOMEN

Asking women easier, more factual questions, men the harder, open-ended ones that require critical thinking.

Grouping women in ways which indicate they have less status or are less capable.

Doubting women's work and accomplishments: "Did you really do that without any help from someone else?"

Expecting less of women in the future.

Calling males "men" and women "girls" or "gals" which implies that women are not as serious or as capable as men.

YIELDING TO THE INFLUENCE OF INTERNALIZED STEREOTYPES

Using examples that reflect stereotypes.

Addressing women in ways that reinforce stereotypes and social roles rather than intellectual ones, for instance, calling women "honey."

Focusing on a woman's appearance, personal qualities and relationships rather than on her accomplishments: "I'd like you to meet our new charming colleague" rather than "I'd like you to meet the new hot-shot we just hired."

Judging women by their physical appearance and downgrading those who are not "attractive."

Describing women by their physical characteristics, such as a "blonde."

Using a different vocabulary to describe similar behavior or accomplishments, such as "angry man" but "bitchy woman."

Expressing stereotypes that discourage women from pursuing professional careers, such as "Women are naturally more caring and men are naturally more aggressive."

Assigning classroom tasks according to stereotyped roles. Women are assigned to be the note-takers.

Falling back on disparaging stereotyped words when angry or annoyed with females: "Look here, sweetie," and "Don't talk back to me, little girl."

EXCLUDING WOMEN FROM PARTICIPATION IN MEETINGS AND CONVERSATIONS

Ignoring women while recognizing men, even when women clearly volunteer to participate by raising their hands.

Addressing a group as if there were no women present: "When you were a boy . . ."

Interrupting women more than men or allowing their peers to interrupt them.

Women may be more vulnerable when interrupted—they may not participate again for the rest of a meeting.

TREATING MEN AND WOMEN DIFFERENTLY WHEN THEIR BEHAVIOR OR ACHIEVEMENTS ARE THE SAME

Treating women who ask extensive questions as trouble-makers and men as interested and bright.

Believing that women who ask for information don't know the materials, but that men who ask are smart, inquisitive and involved.

Viewing marriage and parental status differently for men and women—as disadvantages for women and advantages for men.

Attributing women's achievements to something other than their abilities, such as good luck, affirmative action, beauty, or having "slept their way to the top."

Frowning when women speak (male and female students may also do this). Men and women alike may be less reinforcing when women speak.

Judging women who speak tentatively as being less competent or knowledgeable.

GIVING WOMEN LESS ATTENTION AND INTELLECTUAL ENCOURAGEMENT

Making less eye contact with women.

Nodding and gesturing more and paying more attention in general to men than to women when they speak.

Responding more to men's comments by making additional comments, coaching, and asking questions, and responding more often to women with "uh-huh."

Calling on males more frequently in meetings and in conversations.

Calling males by name more frequently.

Coaching men but not women: "Tell me more about that."

Waiting longer for a man to respond to a question than a woman, before going on to another person.

Crediting men's comments to their owner or "author" ("As Bill said . . .") but not giving authorship or ownership to women. Sometimes a comment made by a woman is later credited to a male.

Giving men more detailed instructions for a task.

Giving women less feedback—less criticism, less help and less praise. (This is one of the critical ways in which women and men are treated differently.)

Being more concerned about men's behavior than that of women's, such as worrying about a male who doesn't participate but not being concerned about women who do not.

Giving women less encouragement to take on harder tasks.

Engaging in more informal conversation with men than with women.

DISCOURAGING WOMEN THROUGH POLITENESS

Using some forms of politeness that shift the focus from intellectual activities to social behavior: "I like to see the girls' smiling faces."

Males may perform hands-on tasks for women (as when helping them with a computer task) under the guise of being helpful, thereby depriving women of the experience and communicating lower expectations for them.

Faculty members may be excessively kind and paternalistic or maternalistic in trying to be helpful and hold women to a lower standard.

Men may tell a group that they are refraining from telling certain jokes or using certain words because there are "ladies" present.

(True courtesy and respect does not patronize, trivialize or depersonalize another person's abilities and talents, nor do they disappear when a woman acts in a way that deviates from gender stereotypes.)

SINGLING OUT WOMEN

Singling out women and other groups such as people of color: "What do you women think about this?"

Males are more likely to touch women than other men. If touch is being used to reassure or indicate friendliness, males are being excluded. Touch is often associated with power; frequently the message transmitted by a touch conveys a "power play."

DEFINING WOMEN BY THEIR SEXUALITY

Relating to women in a sexual manner—sexual comments about or toward specific women or women in general, such as discussing appearance or physical attributes or using sexual humor.

Valuing and praising women for their physical appearance, not for their intellectual ability.

Devaluing or ignoring comments made by women perceived as "unfeminine" or believed to be lesbian or bisexual.

Using the words "lesbian" and "bisexual" as pejorative terms, especially when women raise women's issues.

Engaging in sexually harassing behaviors or allowing others to do so.

OVERT HOSTILE BEHAVIOR TOWARD WOMEN

Ridiculing or making denigrating remarks about women's issues, or making light of issues such as sexual harassment and sexual assault.

Discouraging women from conducting research on women's issues.

Calling women names if they are interested in women's issues or protest sexism.

Making sexist remarks about women in general or about specific women.

USING HUMOR IN A HOSTILE MANNER

Engaging in negative body language or behavior (for example, men rolling their eyeballs) when women speak.

Hissing or ridiculing women who raise women's issues.

Denigrating or ridiculing women or engaging in other rude behaviors that express hostility to women.

Telling sexist or sexual jokes which denigrate women.

Not taking women's comments or their work seriously.

DEVALUATION

Devaluation is often used as a partial explanation or rationale for differential treatment.

Gender affects our view of someone's competence. What is viewed as male is usually seen as more important than that associated with women.

Perceptual bias is not uncommon. For instance, a woman's success, such as getting into a prestigious program, is said to result from "luck" or "affirmative action" while a man's similar success will be attributed to talent.

Women's issues may be devalued, as well as women's ways of speaking.

DEVALUATION AND POWER

It is the power difference between men and women that gives value to or devalues whatever differences exist.

Stereotypes which reinforce differences are maintained precisely because they reinforce power and privilege. Behaviors which are valued such as competitive, status-seeking behavior, are behaviors that reinforce privilege. Males may assert power and expect to be treated more favorably than females.

Why Jimmy Isn't Failing
The Myth of the Boy Crisis

Cara Okopny

Cara Okopny earned her BA in Liberal Studies at Grand Valley State University and an MA in Women's Studies from the University of South Florida. After teaching mass media, diversity and Gender Studies as a Visiting Assistant Professor at GVSU, she began pursuing a PhD at the University of Maryland Baltimore County in Language, Literacy and Culture. This essay was published in Feminist Teacher *in 2008.*

Jimmy is a good student, but he is bored and struggles in English class. He is uninterested in class readings, and his teachers fail to find humor in his rambunctious behavior. Jimmy's parents argue that his needs and the needs of other boys like him are ignored in the U.S. education system. They argue that Jimmy's brain works differently from those of his female classmates, and because his classes have become "feminized," Jimmy is falling behind his female classmates and facing an educational crisis. But Jimmy's problems are not due to any pervasive "boy crisis." Instead, Jimmy's advocates have imagined a crisis, creating a contentious classroom climate for feminist teachers. I contend that this perceived crisis is increasingly leading to a divisive learning environment for teachers and students.

A recent flurry of reporting in mainstream media argues that boys are drowning in a female-centered U.S. education system. According to proponents of the boy crisis argument, boys are just biologically and developmentally different from girls, and it is educators' responsibility to teach to this perceived difference. The U.S. education system, they contend, is failing boys by failing to recognize innate differences in the way boys and girls learn. Boy crisis advocates argue for the adoption of boy-friendly strategies that promote "boys' ways of learning," and propose single-sex education as a potential remedy.

Herein, I present two analytical constructs that may serve to assist feminist teachers in the deconstruction of the boy crisis argument. Using these constructs, I explain that boy crisis ideology may influence the decisions of policymakers and parents, altering the ability of teachers to create an equitable classroom climate. In the *Individual or Student-Based Model*, I deconstruct the argument that boys are struggling academically because their brains are biologically different from those of girls—resulting in poor grades and low male college enrollment. Using an *Educator-Based Model*, I counter the argument that boys are struggling academically because schools have become overly feminized. Finally, I address *Policy Changes*, outlining potentially misinformed and simplistic policy formulations which may result from public advocacy of a boy crisis. I address the suggestion that single-sex education is the best way to ameliorate a boy crisis. In rebuking the major boy crisis arguments, I hope to provide feminist teachers with the tools necessary to combat these arguments from colleagues, parents, and administrators, and encourage the power of daily feminist activism.

I. INDIVIDUAL PERSPECTIVE: BIOLOGICAL DETERMINANTS

Boy Crisis Claims:

- Boys' brains are biologically different from girls' brains.
- Boys are struggling academically because of biological aptitudes.
- Male college enrollment numbers are down, which implies the failure of primary and secondary education to adequately prepare male students.
- Males dominate scientific fields due to genetic predispositions.

A main contention of boy crisis advocates is that boys' brains are biologically different from girls' brains. Dan Kindlon and Michael Thompson claim that, "there are *two clear biological differences* [emphasis added] between boys and girls. Girls' verbal abilities, on average, mature faster than boys': they talk earlier and more fluently. The second difference is that boys tend to be more physically active than girls, moving faster and staying in motion longer" (12). Kindlon and Thompson argue that these factors prevent boys from doing well in the standard American educational model, which encourages dialogue, reflection, and compliance. According to boy crisis theorists, this educational model tends to favor girls' biological aptitudes.

But are there *clear biological differences*? Many boy crisis advocates posit scientific theories as absolute fact and deny the notion that scientists may construct their theories to confirm their own observations. For example, the corpus callosum (CC)—a bundle of nerve cells linking the left and right brain hemispheres—is often used to explain biological differences between women and men. Some scientists point to the size of the CC to explain why women do not pursue higher levels of math and physics, or why women's intuition may be more developed than men's, while others point to the thickness of the CC to explain other gendered traits (Fausto-Sterling, *Sexing the Body* 118). Feminist biologist Anne Fausto-Sterling examines the complex relationship between gender socialization and biology and contends that scientists cannot "produce accurate measurements of a structure as complex and irregularly shaped as the corpus callosum" (*Sexing the Body* 119). She adds that in order to study the CC, scientists must separate it from the rest of the brain, "fundamentally altering the object of study"—examining it out of context (*Sexing the Body* 121). Scientists' methodology may be inherently flawed in the way that research is conducted and answers are sought. Boy crisis advocates fail to acknowledge such partiality, and may use misconstructed research to buttress their arguments.

Even if researchers are correct in concluding that differences in the CC explain differing aptitudes and behaviors in men and women, developmental differences in the male and female CC's must be acknowledged. Fausto-Sterling argues that differences in the adult CC are not present within the CC's of small children. "Instead of asking how anatomy limits function" she observes, "one asks how function shapes anatomy" ("Problem" 125). The CC is not an immutable object; therefore, data regarding the CC cannot be held as irrefutable by boy crisis advocates.

Many boy crisis advocates also base their claims on biological theories that fail to acknowledge the dynamic relationship between gender and sex. Fausto-Sterling writes, "In most public and most scientific discussions, sex and nature are thought to be real, while gender and culture are seen as constructed. But these are false dichotomies" (*Sexing the Body* 27). In order to confront the biological determinism argumentation of the boy crisis, feminist teachers and mainstream feminist authors are often forced to take up a social constructionist argument, potentially forcing feminists to defend gender and gender socialization blindly without recognition of how sex and biology intermingle with gender. In order to reframe the boy crisis "debate" and transcend dimorphic argumentation, feminists must acknowledge the fluid relationship between gender and sex.

Fausto-Sterling points to her study on human bones to illustrate the relationship between sex and gender. She contends that the characteristics of male and female bones cannot be inextricably linked to gender because bones tend to respond to environmental activities in density and development. In societies where women are responsible for traditional gendered labor (e.g., gathering), for instance, their bones have adjusted to such labor, just as they would have if women performed more laborious (i.e., "male") work. Fausto-Sterling writes: "A hyperflexed and damaged big toe, a bony growth on the femur, the knee, or the vertebrae, for example, tell bioarchaeologist Theya Molleson that women in a Near Eastern agricultural community routinely ground grain on all fours, grasping a stone grinder with their hands and pushing back and forth on a saddle-shaped stone. The bones of these neolithic people bear evidence of a gendered division of labor, culture, and biology intertwined" ("Bare Bones" 1499). The body cannot be viewed as immutable in the context of this debate, because it is molded through socialization. Nor can we continue to employ strict dichotomies when sex and gender share a complicated, nuanced relationship. We must instead realize that brains, just like bones and genders, are malleable. Fausto-Sterling continues, "As we grow and develop we literally, not just 'discursively' (that is, through language and cultural practices), construct our bodies, incorporating experience into our very flesh" (*Sexing the Body* 20). If we continue to train children according to a conception of their biological sex, then we may in turn be training their brains to respond according to prescribed gender norms. It is feminists' responsibility to challenge boy crisis advocates' over-reliance on biological determinism and science as absolute truth in order to refute boy crisis argumentation and propose a more nuanced view of the relationship between gender, biology, and socialization.

Much of the boy crisis argumentation also relies on the idea that boys are not doing well in school because schools encourage collaborative work and oral and written competence in a controlled learning environment. Boy crisis proponents fail to point out, however, that during the nineteenth century, privileged boys who did not have trade apprenticeships studied Latin, English, writing, and math, all of which formed the basis for critical thinking, dialogue, and writing—in a controlled classroom environment. Boy crisis advocates imply that today's classroom represents a new educational model shaped by feminist ideology and Title IX. They rely on an anti-feminist mainstream culture, promulgating the idea that our educational model favors girls, and girls' ways of learning, while ignoring the biological needs of boys. Their arguments fail to recognize that the U.S. educational model and pedagogy are historically situated, and not intrinsically gender-preferential. Why is it that no one started worrying about a boy crisis in the nineteenth century?

Girls do tend to have higher grades than boys in U.S. schools (Sadker, "Report Card"), but this may be in part due to time spent studying. According to a 2004 study by the University of Michigan, American girls ages six to seventeen spent nearly an hour more a week studying than their male counterparts (Swanbrow). And despite girls' higher overall GPAs, female ACT and SAT scores continue to lag behind those of male students. In 2003, the average SAT score for boys was 1,049, while the average score for girls was 1,006 (Carpenter). Girls scored an average of thirty-four points lower than boys in the math section and nine points lower in the verbal section of the test, despite the perception of an educational gender gap favoring girls (Carpenter).

According to Sadker, girls' test scores have increased dramatically in recent years, "Yet they lag behind males on a number of important tests, scoring lower on both the verbal and mathematics sections of the SAT, the Advanced Placement exams, and the Graduate Record Exam ("Educator's Primer" 238). Due to success in standardized testing, boys are also more likely than girls to receive scholarships and be accepted into better schools. Sadker et al. report that higher test scores "unlock scholarship money at 85 percent of private colleges and 90 percent of the public ones" ("Gender Equity" 73).

Boy crisis advocates tend to link the decline in male college enrollment to male's biological aptitudes. Crisis theorists use college enrollment statistics to claim that boys are now in the minority in college, and they imply that secondary schools are under-preparing or failing boys. Melana Zyla Vickers asserts that the number of boys in college is decreasing dramatically and cites a study indicating that once girls get to college, "one in four of them will be mathematically unable to find a male peer to go out with."

But Vickers and her colleagues rely on faulty information to advance their claims. According to a National Education Association (NEA) report cited by Caryl Rivers and Rosalind Chait Barnett, the overall gender gap in colleges and universities is relatively small. The NEA study shows that the overall gender composition in institutions of higher learning is 51 percent female to 49 percent male. The report also reveals that men outnumber women in Ivy League schools. David Sadker notes that according to a 2000 report by the U.S. Department of Education, "white males and females attend college in fairly equal proportions" ("Report Card"). Department of Education research indicates that while gender representation may not be 50/50, the discrepancies are far from dramatic, as boy crisis advocates would have us believe.

Jay Mathews of the *Washington Post* writes, "Using data compiled from the National Assessment of Educational Progress, a federally funded accounting of student achievement since 1971, the Washington-based think tank 'Education Sector' found that, over the past three decades, boys' test scores are mostly up, more boys are going to college and more are getting bachelor's degrees." Mathews goes on to posit that some in the media have interpreted girls' educational success as boys' failure. He rightly notes that this is a critical fallacy, and highlights a crucial issue in this debate—we need to shift the paradigm from thinking that girls and boys are necessarily in an academic competition with one another and that one gender's successes equal another's failure. In examining this debate, it is important to develop a holistic way of looking at girls' and boys' academic successes. We need to transcend gender categorization and evaluate students individually—focusing instead on socio-economic backgrounds and academic abilities.

In February 2005 former Harvard President Lawrence Summers made controversial remarks regarding women and science, inflaming an already divisive biological determinism debate. During a closed-door conference, Summers noted three reasons why women are not highly represented within tenured math and science positions. Katha Pollitt summarized his words, "One, women choose family commitments over the necessary eighty-hour weeks . . . those fields require; two, fewer women than men have the necessary genetic gifts; and three, women are discriminated against."

Boy crisis advocate John Leo supports Summers's claims, concluding that we cannot have a 50/50 representation of females and males in education or careers because males and females are drawn to different fields due to genetic aptitudes. He cites numerous professions that are split along gender lines, for instance, science-related fields with "low social components" such as engineering or entomology. These careers tend to be dominated by males while careers with "higher social components," such as sociology or child psychology, tend to be female-dominated (Leo).

Leo later writes, "I suggest we open all the doors, forget about the numbers, and just let students choose their paths freely." Crisis advocates like Leo assume that people are always free to choose their vocation. But discrimination and pressure to conform to one's gender role often create circumstances in which men and women are faced with limited choices. Vocational choices are limited by the over-whelming pressure to stay within traditional gender norms as well as demands from teachers, parents, friends, and patriarchal social norms.

It is important that students and young people of all genders feel free to pursue the fields or subjects they find interesting, and not be constrained by "gender specific" pursuits. False "conventional wisdom" is compounded by the statements of public figures like Summers who continue to promote genetics as the primary reason for female career choices or a male inability to sit still in class. This argumentation helps create diverging, largely predetermined sets of career paths for boys and girls.

Like many other boy crisis proponents, Leo ignores the relationship between gender and sex. Social psychologist Alice Eagly argues that a "biosocial" framework provides a more nuanced lens to examine gender and sex, blending the biological and social constructionist theories. She posits that, "sex differences derive from the interaction between the physical specialization of the sexes, especially female reproduction capacity, and the economic and social structural aspects of societies" (Eagly and Wood 699). Women may be more drawn to careers with high social components not because of their social component level, but rather because these jobs are more flexible for women who want to have children. For example, many female K-12 teachers are able to take advantage of a schedule that enables them to have summers off and routinely come home earlier than they would in lower social component careers. Family needs, not social component levels, shape women's career choices in ways that they never would for men.

Women who pick flexible careers such as teaching can work Summers's "necessary eighty-hour weeks," while still leaving time for family. Comments like those by Summers tend to echo what many in the public already intuit about boys and what is promoted in popular media. These types of statements also make it socially acceptable not to promote girls' education within "non-traditionally female" fields such as science and math, because females are supposed to already lack a "genetic gift." Public figures and the popular media are able to mold public opinion, making it more difficult for feminist teachers to create an equitable learning environment for both girls and boys while dealing with concerned (if misinformed) parents.

Why encourage a girl to pursue math or science if she is bound to face discrimination, is unable or unwilling to work eighty hours a week, or is just biologically unable to compete with the boys? This type of argument is not unlike those made during the nineteenth century when conventional wisdom dictated that women's blood would rush from their ovaries to their brains if they entered higher education. Boy crisis argumentation is slightly less simplistic, but it continues to create two disparate yet binding paths specific to a person's gender.

II. EDUCATIONAL SYSTEM: FEMINIZATION OF EDUCATION

Boy Crisis Claims:

- Teachers provide preferential treatment to girls and are tougher on boys because "boys will be boys."
- Boys are struggling academically because of a feminization of educational materials.

Boy crisis advocates also claim that U.S. schools have become too "feminized." They argue that teachers provide preferential treatment to girls and are tougher on boys. This logic is linked with the conventional wisdom that "boys will be boys." Cathy Young writes, "In numerous surveys, both boys and girls agree that teachers generally favor girls over boys." Michael Gurian and Kathy Stevens argue that because of biological gender differences, teachers are acting out of necessity when they amend their teaching styles to accommodate boys.

A study by Deborah Garrahy, however, contradicts these claims. In one instance cited in Garrahy's work, a third-grade teacher named Brenda defended the actions of a boy, Mike, toward another student, Kallie. Kallie complained to her teacher that Mike was teasing her in a sexual way. Brenda divulged that Kallie had been sexually abused and that Mike had a condition called neurofibromatosis, which impaired his speech and motor abilities (Garrahy 89). Brenda attributed Mike's harmful words to his physical condition, dismissing Kallie's concerns. Brenda also believed Mike was just trying to fit in with other boys, so even though his actions were offensive, Brenda could justify his actions to herself and the students. Garrahy expounds: "she [Kallie] heard from her teacher that boys' vulgarity is to be expected and that her teacher would not prevent it. Although Brenda saw this as an example of how girls and boys differ in their humor, she did not see that this incident demonstrated a stereotypical pattern of female oppression. Many adults attribute such behaviors to the 'boys will be boys' mentality and downplay them so that girls are often left victimized" (90).

Baltimore middle school teacher Deborah Roffman contends that a "boys will be boys" attitude presents conflicting rules for boys—granting boys permission to misbehave while also creating lower expectations for boys than girls. "Many boys I've talked with," Roffman writes, "are pretty savvy about the permission-giving that 'boys will be bad' affords, and use it to their advantage in their relationships with adults. 'Well, they really don't expect as much from us as they do from girls,' said one 10th-grade boy. 'It makes it easier to get away with a lot of stuff.'" "Boys will be boys" attitudes often serve to enable poor performances in school, academically and behaviorally.

Garrahy's study also contradicts boy crisis proponents' claims of a chilly educational climate for boys. She finds that female teachers actually tend to favor boys and reinscribe traditional gender norms. In another of Garrahy's examples, a teacher named Mary solicited vacation stories from her students. Mary expected her third-grade students to raise their hands in order to respond to questions, but in this episode, Mary did not enforce her own rule. Garrahy explains: "Jake called out and mentioned that he had gone hiking with his father at a state park. After Jake finished his comments, Mary thanked him and said 'Who's next?' Immediately after hearing Jake's story, Elizabeth started to describe her vacation but did so without raising her hand. Mary interrupted and said, 'Elizabeth what is our rule?' At that point Elizabeth was not permitted to continue her story. (86) Garrahy's episode demonstrates how teachers may shift lessons, teaching styles, and rules to fit boys.

Another component of the perceived "feminization of education" is an alleged feminization of materials. Many boy crisis proponents argue that boys are not performing well in school because they are forced to read female-centered texts that do not appeal to them. Gurian and Stevens advise teachers to use boy-friendly texts, arguing that "boys will in general read what is interesting to them—what fits their hormonal, neurological, and psychological base. They will reject what is boring, what does not fit" (138). Journalist Peg Tyre recounts the story of Nikolas, a 15-year-old boy who, according to his mother, had "always been an advanced reader, but his grades [were] erratic," and who received a D in his high school English class after reading two "girls' favorites": *Memoirs of a Geisha* and *The Secret Life of Bees*. Vickers asserts that, "boys get worse grades in the touchy-feely stuff."

These claims lead us to believe that boys and girls have vastly different interests and that educators must appeal to "boy interests" in order to get boys to learn. They also assume that

Nikolas and other boys should not be expected to take an interest in readings with a female protagonist. Boys' struggles, though, may be largely due to socialized ideas of masculinity and not a feminized classroom (Kimmel 367). It is less socially acceptable for boys to do well in "female" subjects like English, so their lack of enthusiasm for these subjects, particularly when readings involve female protagonists, is grounded in the socially-reinforced notion that they are not supposed to be engaged. Socialization promotes boys as primary agents, and they may become frustrated and bored when they are not depicted as such in classroom materials.

It is just as important for boys to read books with girls as protagonists as it is for girls to read boy-centered books. Reading and learning about one another is crucial to understanding each other. We do not live in a social vacuum, and it is crucial that both boys and girls cultivate their language and critical thinking skills, even if, as some argue, boys have a harder time doing so. Blaming "feminized" materials or classrooms distracts us from inequities in standardized tests scores, pre-ordained career paths, and socially constructed gender roles.

III. POLICY CHANGES: RE-EXAMINING EDUCATION

How do we prevent a movement toward gender-specific schooling? Schools for girls might focus excessively on language development and schools for boys might lean more toward science and math programs. Many single-sex education advocates assume that boys and girls learn in different ways according to their sex. What do we do with students who do not fit with socially proscribed gender norms?

Venerable organizations like the American Association of University Women (AAUW) and the American Federation of Teachers (AFT) do not support single-sex education. Elayne Clift writes, "AAUW strongly supports the development of 'strong, fair, public schools' since '90 per cent of elementary and secondary students attend public schools.'" The AFT advocates for smaller class sizes as a more effective way to reach students, instead of single-sex education, in which results tend to be more mixed (Price). Many boy crisis proponents argue that because boys' needs are not adequately addressed in the classroom, boys' and girls' needs must be met separately. Clift writes, "Conservative organizations like the American Enterprise Institute [AEI] and the National Association for Single-Sex Public Education (NASSPE) argue that single-sex school settings are better because brain development is different, and more advanced in girls than it is in boys, and because girls and boys have different learning styles." When these groups advocate single-sex education based purely on biological differences, they essentialize the argument over co-education, reducing it to an unsophisticated either/or dialectic. These types of proscriptions may lead to increasingly limited opportunities for women and men in education and careers.

Dr. Judith Shapiro, the out-going president of Barnard College, offers a more nuanced view of the role of single-sex education and cautions against the rationale that groups like the AEI use to support their advocacy of single-sex classrooms. Shapiro believes that single-sex education provides a "liberated zone for women" to excel (Clift). Other noteworthy feminists such as Senator Hillary Clinton and Senator Barbara Milkulski also support single-sex education for many of the same reasons as Shapiro. Clift explains, "They [Clinton and Milkulski] see it as a way to ensure that girls derive the psychological, social and educational benefits of an all-female environment during important stages of female development." In the framework proposed by Shapiro, Clinton, and Milkulski, advocacy of single-sex education is premised upon the understanding that we live in a patriarchal society where education is often affected by long-standing social constraints; boy crisis alarmists tend to support single-sex education based solely on a belief in a biological divide between females and males.

A second suggestion of boy crisis proponents is that educators use special tactics to address poor performance among male students. These strategies, however, tend to create further differentiation between male and female students and color the way teachers perceive their students. Kathy Stevens, for instance, suggests including "brain breaks," making homework more "meaningful," and placing stress balls in the classroom to relieve tension (cited in Viadero). Debra Viadero quotes Stevens as saying, "'The worst thing you can do for little boys is make them sit down and be quiet.'"

The implementation of learning strategies based upon narrowly focused notions of gender will hinder our ability to create effective learning strategies beneficial to both genders. The assumption that only boys would benefit from "brain breaks" or stress balls is simplistic. Stevens's suggestions illustrate how boy crisis advocates continue to compartmentalize boys and girls, rather than acknowledge the overlap of gender, sex, and individual ability.

IV: RE-CONCEPTUALIZING THE BOY CRISIS

A closer examination of boy crisis argumentation demonstrates that many of the boy crisis claims are myopic. Instead of encouraging a more nuanced look at the educational issues facing American boys, boy crisis proponents tend to essentialize the vast experiences of boys to further their socio-political agenda. It is irresponsible for boy crisis proponents to categorize *all* boys as a monolithic group. Instead of recognizing the fluidity of gender and sex, boy crisis proponents would have schools conform to a false conception of the way that *all* boys learn. Revamping schools to suit boys' "needs" may result in girls getting less access to educational and vocational opportunities because of falsely perceived gender aptitudes and gender roles.

Proponents of the boy crisis tend to cover up the *real* educational crisis—that low-income boys of color are struggling when compared to non-minority, middle-class boys. According to Rivers and Barnett, who cite an Urban Institute study, "76 percent of students who live in middle- to higher-income areas are likely to graduate from high school, while only 56 percent of students who live in lower-income areas are likely to do so." Proponents of a boy crisis rarely highlight such variance in boys' experiences. Michael Kimmel notes, "Differences among boys—by race, or class, for example—do not typically fall within the radar of the cultural critics who would rescue boys" (365). In order to promulgate their positions, boy crisis advocates ignore economic and racial inequalities in American society. High school graduation rates for African American men are particularly distressing. According to a 2004 report by the Schott Educational Inequity Index: "In 2001/2002 59 percent of African-American males did not receive diplomas with their cohort[s]. Two states—South Dakota and Maine—graduated less than 30 percent of their small number of Black male students on schedule. Thirteen others—Wisconsin, South Carolina, New York, Nebraska, Montana, Ohio, Illinois, Michigan, Indiana, Georgia, Florida, North Carolina and Hawaii—graduated only between 30 percent and 40 percent with their peer group" (Holzman). Unfortunately, the educational problems that low-income boys of color generally face are continually ignored in the media and even more so by those who promote themselves as champions for *all* boys.

It is imperative that feminist teachers not ignore the arguments presented here because boy crisis advocates continue to author popular books, appear on television, and publish in mainstream magazines and newspapers—disseminating their misleading proscriptions throughout popular culture and attempting to shape conventional wisdom. Boy crisis alarmists have assumed the power to persuade Americans and may eventually misdirect U.S. educational policies. Their ideas have already started to permeate the discussions of parents and administrators who worry that their school-age boys are not being treated fairly. Feminists have historically fought to strengthen the position of women and girls in education, and yet boy crisis advocates seek to undo the progress we have made in order to further their position. Feminists must prevent boy crisis proponents from stripping away female students' opportunities in the name of "saving boys." If we fail to act, we risk losing the momentum gained during the second and third waves of feminism.

The feminist movement has historically brought about significant and important changes in the culture of education and within individual lives. In his article, "Feminism Brings Benefits to All—Men Included," Neil Chethik reminds us of feminism's role in education. He writes of growing up in the 1950s and '60s and feeling the pressure to be the sole bread-winner: "Feminism freed me from the expectation that I would be the primary wage-earner in my family." Realizing that he was not bound to a perceived gender role enabled Chethik to pursue a passion for writing. Chethik moved beyond what boy crisis proponents argue is a boy's "natural" biological aptitude, transcending a perceived gender norm in order to explore his individual interests.

Feminist principles can help engender a more harmonious society, where women and men are not bound solely by their biological sex and rather have the opportunity to explore what makes them happy as individuals. We need to remain continuously conscious of the positive power of feminism to combat popular fiction like the boy crisis. It is our responsibility as educators to deconstruct the boy crisis's faulty arguments and ensure that all children receive a fair education and are free to pursue their individual interests and career goals.

RESOURCES FOR FEMINIST TEACHERS

I. Individual Perspective: Biological Determinants

Boy Crisis Claims:

- Boys' brains are biologically different from girls' brains.
- Boys are struggling academically because of genetic aptitudes.
- Male college enrollment numbers are down, which implies the failure of primary and secondary education to adequately prepare male students.
- Males dominate scientific fields due to genetic predispositions.

Sources Refuting these Claims:

- Carpenter, Mackenzie. "Why Girls Score Low on SATs Baffling." *Pittsburgh Post-Gazette*. 27 August 2003. 11 April 2006 <http://www.postgazette.com/pg/03239/215443.stm>.
- Eagly, Alice, and Wendy Wood. "A Cross-Cultural Analysis of the Behavior of Women and Men: Implications for the Origins of Sex Differences." *Psychological Bulletin* 128 (2002): 699–726. *FirstSearch*. OCLC. 8 March 2007 <http://www.firstsearch.org>.
- Fausto-Sterling, Anne. "The Bare Bones of Sex: Part I—Sex and Gender." *Signs* 30 (2005): 1491–1527. 8 March 2007 <http://bms.brown.edu/faculty/f/afs/afs_publications_articles.htm>.
- _____. "The Problem with Sex/Gender and Nature/Nurture." *Debating Biology: Sociological Reflections on Health, Medicine and Society*. Ed. Simon J. Williams, Lynda Birke, and Gillian A. Bendelow. New York: Routledge, 2003. 123–32.
- _____. *Sexing the Body: Gender Politics and the Construction of Sexuality*. New York: Basic Books, 2000.

- Mathews, Jay. "Study Casts Doubt on the 'Boy Crisis': Improving Test Scores Cut Into Girls' Lead." *The Washington Post* 26 June 2006. 6 March 2007 <http://www.washingtonpost.com/wp-dyn/content/article/2006/06/25/AR2006062501047.html>.
- Pollitt, Katha. "Summers of Our Discontent." *The Nation* 21 February 2005. 6 March 2007 <http://www.thenation.com/doc/20050221/pollitt>.
- Rivers, Caryl, and Rosalind Chait Barnett. "The Myth of 'The Boy Crisis.'" *Washington Post* 9 April 2006. 1 March 2006 <http://www.washingtonpost.com/wp-dyn/content/article/2006/04/07/AR2006040702025.html>.
- Sadker, David. "An Educator's Primer on the Gender War." *Phi Delta Kappan* 84.3 (Nov. 2002): 235–40.
- _____. "Report Card: The Costs of Gender Bias." 2000. 22 May 2006 <http://www.american.edu/sadker/thereportcard.htm>.
- Sadker, David, Myra Sadker, Lynn Fox, and Melinda Salata. "Gender Equity in the Classroom: The Unfinished Agenda." *Women: Images and Realities, A Multicultural Anthology*. Ed. Amy Kessleman, Lily D. McNair, and Nancy Schniedewind. New York: McGraw-Hill, 2003. 73–76.
- Swanbrow, Diane. "U.S. Children and Teens Spend More Time on Academics." *The University Record Online* 6 December 2004. 15 March 2006 <http://www.umich.edu/~urecord/0405/Dec06_04/20.shtml>.

II. Educational System: Feminization of Education

Boy Crisis Claims:

- Teachers provide preferential treatment to girls and are tougher on boys because "boys will be boys."
- Boys are struggling academically because of a feminization of educational materials.

Sources Refuting these Claims:

- Garrahy, Deborah A. "Three Third-Grade Teachers' Gender-Related Beliefs and Behavior." *The Elementary School Journal* 102 (2001): 81–94. *JSTOR*. 30 January 2006 <http://www.jstor.org/>.
- Kimmel, Michael. "What About the Boys?" *Reconstructing Gender: A Multicultural Anthology*. Ed. Estelle Disch. New York: McGraw-Hill, 2006. 361–73.
- Roffman, Deborah. "What Does 'Boys Will Be Boys' Really Mean?" *The Washington Post* 5 Febuary 2006. 15 March 2006. <http://www.washingtonpost.com/wp-dyn/content/article/2006/02/04/AR2006020400220.html>.

REFERENCES

Carpenter, Mackenzie. "Why Girls Score Low on SATs Baffling." *Pittsburgh Post-Gazette*. 27 August 2003. 11 April 2006 <http://www.postgazette.com/pg/03239/215443.stm>.

Chethik, Neil. "Feminism Brings Benefits to All—Men Included." *AlterNet* 22 January 2007. 11 February 2007. <http://www.alternet.org/story/47080/>.

Clift, Elayne. "To Be or Not to Be Co-Ed." *Women's Feature Service* 6 October 2003. *ProQuest*. 8 March 2007 <http://www.proquest.com>.

Eagly, Alice, and Wendy Wood. "A Cross-Cultural Analysis of the Behavior of Women and Men: Implications for the Origins of Sex Differences." *Psychological Bulletin* 128 (2002): 699–726. *FirstSearch*. OCLC. 8 March 2007 <http://www.firstsearch.org>.

Fausto-Sterling, Anne. "The Bare Bones of Sex: Part I—Sex and Gender." *Signs* 30 (2005): 1491–1527. 8 March 2007 <http://bms.brown.edu/faculty/f/afs/afs_publications_ articles.htm>.

_____. "The Problem with Sex/Gender and Nature/Nurture." *Debating Biology: Sociological Reflections on Health, Medicine and Society*. Ed. Simon J. Williams, Lynda Birke, and Gillian A. Bendelow. New York: Routledge, 2003. 123–32.

_____. *Sexing the Body: Gender Politics and the Construction of Sexuality*. New York: Basic Books, 2000.

Garrahy, Deborah A. "Three Third-Grade Teachers' Gender-Related Beliefs and Behavior." *The Elementary School Journal* 102 (2001): 81–94. *JSTOR*. 30 January 2006 <http://www .jstor.org/>.

Gurian, Michael, and Kathy Stevens. *The Minds of Boys: Saving Our Sons from Falling Behind in School and Life*. San Francisco: Jossey-Bass, 2005.

Holzman, Michael. "Public Education and Black Male Students: A State Report Card. Schott Educational Inequity Index." In *The Schott Foundation for Public Education*. Cambridge, Mass.: The Schott Foundation for Public Education, 2004. 12 May 2006 <www.schottfoundation .org/publications/Public_Education_and_Black_Male_Students.pdf>.

Kimmel, Michael. "What About the Boys?" *Reconstructing Gender: A Multicultural Anthology*. Ed. Estelle Disch. New York: McGraw-Hill, 2006. 361–73.

Kindlon, Dan, and Michael Thompson. *Raising Cain: Protecting the Emotional Life of Boys*. New York: Ballantine, 2000.

Leo, John. "What Larry Meant to Say." *U.S. News and World Report* 6 February 2005. 6 March 2007 <http://www.usnews.com/usnews/opinion/articles/050214/14john.htm>.

Mathews, Jay. "Study Casts Doubt on the 'Boy Crisis': Improving Test Scores Cut Into Girls' Lead." *The Washington Post* 26 June 2006. 6 March 2007 <http://www.washingtonpost.com/ wpdyn/content/article/2006/06/25/AR2006062501047.html>.

Pollitt, Katha. "Summers of Our Discontent." *The Nation* 21 February 2005. 6 March 2007 <http://www.thenation.com/doc/20050221/pollitt>.

Price, Joyce Howard. "Academic Underachievers." *The Washington Times* 30 January–6 February 2006. 6 March 2007 <www.americasnewspaper.com>.

Rivers, Caryl, and Rosalind Chait Barnett. "The Myth of 'The Boy Crisis.'" *Washington Post* 9 April 2006. 1 March 2006 <http://www.washingtonpost.com/wpdyn/content/article/2006/04/07/ AR2006040702025.html>.

Roffman, Deborah. "What Does 'Boys Will Be Boys' Really Mean?" *The Washington Post* 5 Febuary 2006. 15 March 2006. <http://www.washingtonpost.com/wpdyn/content/ article/2006/02/04/AR2006020400220.html>.

Sadker, David. "An Educator's Primer on the Gender War." *Phi Delta Kappan* 84.3 (Nov. 2002): 235–40.

_____. "Report Card: The Costs of Gender Bias." 2000. 22 May 2006 <http://www.american .edu/sadker/thereportcard.htm>.

Sadker, David, Myra Sadker, Lynn Fox, and Melinda Salata. "Gender Equity in the Classroom: The Unfinished Agenda." *Women: Images and Realities, A Multicultural Anthology*. Ed. Amy Kessleman, Lily D. McNair, and Nancy Schniedewind. New York: McGraw-Hill, 2003. 73–76.

Swanbrow, Diane. "U.S. Children and Teens Spend More Time on Academics." *The University Record Online* 6 December 2004. 15 March 2006 <http://www.umich.edu/~urecord/0405/Dec06_04/20.shtml>.

Tolley, Kim. "Science for Ladies, Classics for Gentleman: A Comparative Analysis of Scientific Subjects in the Curricula of Boys' and Girls' Secondary Schools in the United States." *History of Education Quarterly* 36.2 (1996): 129–53. *JSTOR*. 8 March 2007 <www.jstor.org>.

Tyre, Peg. "The Trouble with Boys." *Newsweek* 30 January 2006. 24 January 2006 <http://www.newsweek.com/id/47522>.

Viadero, Debra. "Concern over Gaps Shifting to Boys." *Education Week* 25.27 (15 March 2006). *ProQuest*. 12 May 2006 <http://www.proquest.com>.

Vickers, Melana Zyla. "Where the Boys Aren't." *The Weekly Standard* 2 January 2006. 9 June 2006 <http://www.weeklystandard.com/Content/Public/Articles/000/000/006/531ffoaa.asp>.

Young, Cathy. "The Lost Boys." *The Boston Globe* 6 February 2006. 6 June 2006 <http://www.boston.com/news/globe/editorial_opinion/oped/articles/2006/02/06/the_lost_boys/>.

Claiming an Education

Adrienne Rich

Adrienne Rich's most recent books of poetry are Telephone Ringing in the Labyrinth: Poems 2004–2006 *and* The School Among the Ruins: 200–2004. *A selection of her essays* Arts of the Possible: Essays and Conversations, *appeared in 2003. She edited Muriel Rukeyser's* Selected Poems *for the Library of America.* A Human Eye: Essays on Art in Society, *appeared in April 2009. She is a recipient of the National Book Foundation's 2006 Medal for Distinguished Contribution to American Letters, among other honors. She lives in California.*

For this convocation, I planned to separate my remarks into two parts: some thoughts about you, the women students here, and some thoughts about us who teach in a women's college. But ultimately, those two parts are indivisible. If university education means anything beyond the processing of human beings into expected roles, through credit hours, tests, and grades (and I believe that in a women's college especially it *might* mean much more), it implies an ethical and intellectual contract between teacher and student. This contract must remain intuitive, dynamic, unwritten; but we must turn to it again and again if learning is to be reclaimed from the depersonalizing and cheapening pressures of the present-day academic scene.

The first thing I want to say to you who are students, is that you cannot afford to think of being here to *receive* an education; you will do much better to think of yourselves as being here to *claim* one. One of the dictionary definitions of the verb "to claim" is: *to take as the rightful owner; to assert in the face of possible contradiction.* "To receive" is *to come into possession of; to act as receptacle or container for; to accept as authoritative or true.* The difference is that between acting and being acted-upon, and for women it can literally mean the difference between life and death.

One of the devastating weaknesses of university learning, of the store of knowledge and opinion that has been handed down through academic training, has been its almost total erasure of women's experience and thought from the curriculum, and its exclusion of women as members of the academic community. Today, with increasing numbers of women students in nearly every branch of higher learning, we still see very few women in the upper levels of faculty and administration in most institutions. Douglass College itself is a women's college in a university administered overwhelmingly by men, who in turn are answerable to the state legislature, again composed predominantly of men. But the most significant fact for you is that what you learn here, the very texts you read, the lectures you hear, the way your studies are divided into categories and fragmented one from the other—all this reflects, to a very large degree, neither objective reality, nor an accurate picture of the past, nor a group of rigorously tested observations about human behavior. What you can learn here (and I mean not only at Douglass but any college in any university) is how *men* have perceived and organized their experience, their history, their ideas of social relationships, good and evil, sickness and health, etc. When you read or hear about "great issues," "major texts," "the mainstream of Western thought," you are hearing about what men, above all white men, in their male subjectivity, have decided is important.

Black and other minority peoples have for some time recognized that their racial and ethnic experience was not accounted for in the studies broadly labeled human; and that even the sciences can be racist. For many reasons, it has been more difficult for women to comprehend our exclusion, and to realize that even the sciences can be sexist. For one thing, it is only within the last hundred years that higher education has grudgingly been opened up to women at all, even to white, middle-class women. And many of us have found ourselves poring eagerly over books with titles like: *The Descent of Man; Man and His Symbols; Irrational Man; The Phenomenon of Man; The Future of Man; Man and the Machine; From Man to Man; May Man Prevail?; Man, Science and Society;* or *One-Dimensional Man*—books pretending to describe a "human" reality that does not include over one-half the human species.

Less than a decade ago, with the rebirth of a feminist movement in this country, women students and teachers in a number of universities began to demand and set up women's studies courses—to *claim* a woman-directed education. And, despite the inevitable accusations of "unscholarly," "group therapy," "faddism," etc., despite backlash and budget cuts, women's studies are still growing, offering to more and more women a new intellectual grasp on their lives, new understanding of our history, a fresh vision of the human experience, and also a critical basis for evaluating what they hear and read in other courses, and in the society at large.

But my talk is not really about women's studies, much as I believe in their scholarly, scientific, and human necessity. While I think that any Douglass student has everything to gain by investigating and enrolling in women's studies courses, I want to suggest that there is a more essential experience that you owe yourselves, one which courses in women's studies can greatly enrich, but which finally depends on you, in all your interactions with yourself and your world. This is the experience of *taking responsibility toward yourselves*. Our upbringing as women has so often told us that this should come second to our relationships and responsibilities to other people. We have been offered ethical models of the self-denying wife and mother; intellectual models of the brilliant but slapdash dilettante who never commits herself to anything the whole way, or the intelligent woman who denies her intelligence in order to seem more "feminine," or who sits in passive silence even when she disagrees inwardly with everything that is being said around her.

Responsibility to yourself means refusing to let others do your thinking, talking, and naming for you; it means learning to respect and use your own brains and instincts; hence, grappling with hard work. It means that you do not treat your body as a commodity with which to purchase superficial intimacy or economic security; for our bodies and minds are inseparable in this life, and when we allow our bodies to be treated as objects, our minds are in mortal danger. It means insisting that those to whom you give your friendship and love are able to respect your mind. It means being able to say, with Charlotte Brontë's *Jane Eyre:* "I have an inward treasure born with me, which can keep me alive if all the extraneous delights should be withheld or offered only at a price I cannot afford to give."

Responsibility to yourself means that you don't fall for shallow and easy solutions—predigested books and ideas, weekend encounters guaranteed to change your life, taking "gut" courses instead of ones you know will challenge you, bluffing at school and life instead of doing solid work, marrying early as an escape from real decisions, getting pregnant as an evasion of already existing problems. It means that you refuse to sell your talents and aspirations short, simply to avoid conflict and confrontation. And this, in turn, means resisting the forces in society which say that women should be nice, play safe, have low professional expectations, drown in love and forget about work, live through others, and stay in the places assigned to us. It means that we insist on a life of meaningful work, insist that work be as meaningful as love and friendship in our lives. It means, therefore, the courage to be "different"; not to be continuously available to others when we need time for ourselves and our work; to be able to demand of others—parents, friends, roommates, teachers, lovers, husbands, children—that they respect our sense of purpose and our integrity as persons. Women everywhere are finding the courage to do this, more and more, and we are finding that courage both in our study of women in the past who possessed it, and in each other as we look to other women for comradeship, community, and challenge. The difference between a life lived actively, and a life of passive drifting and dispersal of energies, is an immense difference. Once we begin to feel committed to our lives, responsible to ourselves, we can never again be satisfied with the old, passive way.

Now comes the second part of the contract. I believe that in a women's college you have the right to expect your faculty to take you seriously. The education of women has been a matter of debate for centuries, and old, negative attitudes about women's role, women's ability to think and take leadership, are still rife both in and outside the university. Many male professors (and I don't mean only at Douglass) still feel that teaching in a women's college is a second-rate career. Many tend to eroticize their women students—to treat them as sexual objects—instead of demanding the best of their minds. (At Yale a legal suit [*Alexander* v. *Yale*] has been brought against the university by a group of women students demanding a stated policy against sexual advances toward female students by male professors.) Many teachers, both men and women, trained in the male-centered tradition, are still handing the ideas and texts of that tradition on to students without teaching them to criticize its antiwoman attitudes, its omission of women as part of the species. Too often, all of us fail to teach the most important thing, which is that clear thinking, active discussion, and excellent writing are all necessary for intellectual freedom, and that these require *hard work*. Sometimes, perhaps in discouragement with a culture which is both antiintellectual and antiwoman, we may resign ourselves to low expectations for our students before we have given them half a chance to become more thoughtful, expressive human beings. We need to take to heart the words of Elizabeth Barrett Browning, a poet, a thinking woman, and a feminist, who wrote in 1845 of her impatience with studies which cultivate a "passive recipiency" in the mind, and asserted that "women want to be made to *think actively:* their apprehension is quicker than that of men, but their defect lies for the most part in the logical faculty and in the higher mental activities." Note that she implies a defect which can be remedied by intellectual training; *not* an inborn lack of ability.

I have said that the contract on the student's part involves that you demand to be taken seriously so that you can also go on taking yourself seriously. This means seeking out criticism, recognizing that the most affirming thing anyone can do for you is demand that you push yourself further, show you the range of what you *can* do. It means rejecting attitudes of "take-it-easy," "why-be-so-serious," "why-worry-you'll-probably-get-married-anyway." It means assuming your share of responsibility for what happens in the classroom, because that affects the quality of your daily life here. It means that the student sees herself engaged *with* her teachers in an active, ongoing struggle for a real education. But for her to do this, her teachers must be committed to the belief that women's minds and experience are intrinsically valuable and indispensable to any civilization worthy the name; that there is no more exhilarating and intellectually fertile place in the academic world today than a women's college—*if* both students and teachers in large enough numbers are trying to fulfill this contract. The contract is really a pledge of mutual seriousness about women, about language, ideas, methods, and values. It is our shared commitment toward a world in which the inborn potentialities of so many women's minds will no longer be wasted, raveled-away, paralyzed, or denied.

Hostile Hallways
Bullying, Teasing, and Sexual Harassment in School

AAUW Educational Foundation

*The **AAUW** (American Association of University Women) is an organization that has worked to promote educational equity for women and girls since its inception in 1881 through public policy and legal advocacy, education and support of research on issues related to equity in education.*

EXECUTIVE SUMMARY AND MAJOR FINDINGS

Eight years ago, the AAUW Educational Foundation commissioned Louis Harris & Associates (now Harris Interactive) to conduct the first nationally representative survey on sexual harassment in public school. The original *Hostile Hallways: The AAUW Survey on Sexual Harassment in America's Schools* (1993) revealed the widespread occurrence of sexual harassment and the accompanying bullying and teasing in students' school lives and explored the impact that the harassment had on the educational environment and learning experience. This current survey, also by Harris, revisits these issues:

- Do students view sexual harassment as a large problem in their school?
- Are students aware that their schools have a policy or distribute literature on sexual harassment?
- How often do students experience sexual harassment in their school lives?
- How do boys and girls differ in their experience of school sexual harassment?
- What role does the type or frequency of sexual harassment have on students' experiences?
- What are the emotional and behavioral consequences of sexual harassment?
- What changes concerning these issues have occurred since 1993?

Students' answers were analyzed, where possible, to identify any difference by gender, race/ethnicity (white, black, or Hispanic), grade level (eighth and ninth or 10th and 11th), and area of school (urban or suburban/rural).

Harassment in Schools

As in 1993, today nearly all students say they know what sexual harassment is. When asked to provide their own definitions, students mention physical and nonphysical behaviors: touch, words, looks, and gestures.

For the purposes of this survey, students were given the following definition of sexual harassment:

> Sexual harassment is **unwanted** and **unwelcome** sexual behavior that interferes with your life. Sexual harassment is **not** behaviors that you **like** or **want** (for example **wanted** kissing, touching, or flirting).

Examples of Harassment

- Made sexual comments, jokes, gestures, or looks
- Showed, gave, or left you sexual pictures, photographs, illustrations, messages, or notes
- Wrote sexual messages/graffiti about you on bathroom walls, in locker rooms, etc.
- Spread sexual rumors about you
- Said you were gay or lesbian
- Spied on you as you dressed or showered at school
- Flashed or "mooned" you
- Touched, grabbed, or pinched you in a sexual way
- Intentionally brushed up against you in a sexual way
- Pulled at your clothing in a sexual way
- Pulled off or down your clothing
- Blocked your way or cornered you in a sexual way
- Forced you to kiss him/her
- Forced you to do something sexual other than kissing

Students were also given 14 examples of harassment. Half the examples involve physical contact, while half do not.

One way to categorize these examples is on a continuum, from nonphysical to physical. Students say the most upsetting acts, however, span the nonphysical and physical. About equal numbers of students—three-quarters of those surveyed—say they would be very upset if someone spread sexual rumors about them, if someone pulled off or down their clothing, or if someone called them gay or lesbian. Thus, the survey shows, some forms of speech are as upsetting as actions.

Greater Awareness of School Policies and Materials

Two findings stand out dramatically from 1993: Students today are much more likely to say their schools have a sexual harassment policy or their schools distribute literature on sexual harassment. Seven in 10 students say yes, their schools have a policy on sexual harassment, while more than one-third say yes, their schools distribute literature about this issue. Both findings represent substantial increases over 1993, when the plurality of students answered the same question with either no or I'm not sure.

Personal Experiences of School Sexual Harassment

How common is school sexual harassment? As in 1993, eight in 10 students experience some form of sexual harassment at some time during their school lives. One striking change since 1993 is the increase in the number of boys who often experience school sexual harassment.

As mentioned previously, sexual harassment encompasses a range of behaviors, both those that involve physical contact as well as those that do not. In addition, the frequency of occurrence ranges from ever experiencing to often experiencing. Is school sexual harassment as prevalent a problem when viewed by these differing definitions?

In terms of type of harassment, nonphysical is the most prevalent. Three-quarters of students ever experience this type of harassment, with more than half experiencing it often or occasionally. Physical harassment lags not far behind. The majority of students experience physical harassment at some point during their school lives, with one in three experiencing it often or occasionally. In terms of frequency, six in 10 students experience some form of sexual harassment often or occasionally, with fully one-quarter experiencing it often.

Although most students experience some form of sexual harassment during their school lives, all students' experiences are not equivalent. Girls are more likely than boys to experience nonphysical or physical harassment, and they are more likely than boys to experience it more frequently. These differing experiences may explain girls' and boys' differing views on their school environment as a whole. Girls are more likely than boys to say that they know someone who has experienced sexual harassment at school and that there is a lot of or some sexual harassment in their school.

Given the prevalence of harassment at school, how do these experiences affect students and learning? In addition to feeling upset, students report other consequences more directly tied to education. One-quarter of the students who experience harassment say they do not talk as much in class or do not want to go to school, and two in 10 found it hard to pay attention. The type of harassment plays a role in the impact. Students who experience physical harassment are more likely than those who experience nonphysical to report such behavioral and educational consequences.

Conclusions

When the original *Hostile Hallways* survey was conducted in 1993, a large majority of students had experienced sexual harassment at some point in their school lives. And for many students, this experience reverberated throughout their educational and emotional lives. Eight years later, this picture looks the same in key aspects. But students today are more likely to say their schools have a policy or distribute literature on sexual harassment.

Because of the widespread nature of sexual harassment in school life, some students report that it's not a big deal and many accept it as part of everyday life. The results of this current survey reaffirm that despite students' seemingly offhanded acceptance, experiencing sexual harassment in school life has broad consequences, both subtle and direct, on girls' and boys' education.

Major Findings

Significant numbers of students are afraid of being hurt or bothered in their school lives.

- Two in 10 students (18 percent) fear that someone will hurt or bother them at school.
- Girls and boys are almost equally likely to feel this way, and these levels do not differ substantially between urban and suburban/rural schools.

Sexual harassment is widespread in school life. While boys today are even more likely than boys in 1993 to experience sexual harassment, they are still less likely than girls to have this experience.

- Eight in 10 students (81 percent) experience some form of sexual harassment during their school lives: six in 10 (59 percent) often or occasionally and one-quarter (27 percent) often. These levels have not changed since 1993.
- Girls are more likely than boys to experience sexual harassment ever (83 percent vs. 79 percent) or often (30 percent vs. 24 percent).
- Boys today are more likely than those in 1993 to experience sexual harassment often or occasionally (56 percent vs. 49 percent) or often (24 percent vs. 18 percent).
- Three-quarters of students (76 percent) experience nonphysical sexual harassment at some point in their school lives, more than half (54 percent) often or occasionally.
- Six in 10 students (58 percent) experience physical sexual harassment at some point in their school lives, one-third (32 percent) often or occasionally.
- One-third (32 percent) of students are afraid of being sexually harassed. Girls are more than twice as likely as boys to feel this way (44 percent vs. 20 percent).

School sexual harassment has a negative impact on students' emotional and educational lives.

- Nearly half (47 percent) of all students who experience sexual harassment feel very or somewhat upset right afterward.
- Students who experience physical harassment are more likely than those who experience nonphysical harassment to feel very or somewhat upset (56 percent vs. 26 percent).
- Students who experience sexual harassment are most likely to react by avoiding the person who bothered or harassed them (40 percent), talking less in class (24 percent), not wanting to go to school (22 percent), changing their seat in class to get farther away from someone (21 percent), and finding it hard to pay attention in school (20 percent).

Students today are much more likely than those in 1993 to say their schools have a policy or distribute literature on sexual harassment.

- Seven in 10 students (69 percent), compared to just 26 percent in 1993, say their schools have a policy on sexual harassment to deal with sexual harassment issues and complaints.
- More than one-third (36 percent) of students, compared to 13 percent in 1993, say their schools distribute booklets, handouts, and other literature and materials about sexual harassment.

Nearly all students surveyed know what sexual harassment is.

- Ninety-six percent of students say they know what sexual harassment is.
- This percentage is higher for students who say their schools both have a policy and distribute materials on sexual harassment than for those who say their schools do neither (98 percent vs. 91 percent).

The most upsetting examples of sexual harassment in school life involve speech as well as actions. Students are most likely to be very upset if someone did the following:

- Spread sexual rumors about them (75 percent)
- Pulled off or down their clothing (74 percent)
- Said they were gay or lesbian (73 percent)
- Forced them to do something sexual other than kissing (72 percent)
- Spied on them as they dressed or showered (69 percent)
- Wrote sexual messages or graffiti about them on bathroom walls, in locker rooms, etc. (63 percent)

A sizeable minority of students reports high levels of sexual harassment in school.

- Fourteen percent of students say there is a lot of sexual harassment in school.
- This level has not substantially changed since 1993 (14 percent today; 15 percent in 1993).

Most experiences involve students harassing other students, although many experiences involve school adults harassing students.

- As in 1993, nearly nine in 10 students (85 percent) report that students sexually harass other students at their schools.
- A large number of students report that teachers and other school employees sexually harass students, although this number has declined since 1993 (38 percent today vs. 44 percent in 1993).

Slightly more than half (54 percent) of students say they have sexually harassed someone during their school lives.

- This represents a decline from 1993, when six in 10 students (59 percent) said they sexually harassed someone.
- In particular, boys today are less likely to report being a perpetrator (57 percent today vs. 66 percent in 1993).

The Little Law That Could

Denise Kiernan

Denise Kiernan *is a writer and producer. She has contributed to* The New York Times, The Wall Street Journal, The Village Voice, *and* Ms. *magazine, in which this essay was first published in 2001.*

Angela was home for the summer and wanted to play a little pick-up hockey at her local rink. "No women," said the woman guarding the entrance.

"I can really play," she said, assuming the attendant was concerned for her safety on the ice. "No women."

The place: Saint Clair Shores, Michigan.

The year: 1999.

The player: Angela Ruggiero, 1998 Olympic hockey gold medalist.

Ruggiero is one of thousands of women athletes who benefited from Title IX of the Education Amendments of 1972, the federal law that prohibits discrimination in federally funded educational programs. That Ruggiero played on an Olympic ice hockey team is evidence of how far women have come since Title IX. That she was turned away from her hometown rink is a sign of how far we still have to go—not just in the courts but in a culture that still resists women's evolving roles.

Perhaps no other legislative act has had a greater impact on the lives of girls and women in the United States, yet remains so misunderstood. Its original purpose has been clouded by media squabbles and misinformation campaigns and has been overshadowed by highly publicized events that have lulled us into a false sense of security.

Although Title IX is now synonymous with equality in women's sports, it originally had nothing to do with athletics. In order to look at where the legislation is headed, it's helpful to glance back at where it started—not with soccer and basketball players but with Ivy League students and college professors.

As a schoolgirl in the 1930s and '40s, Bernice Sandler wanted to do three things: change the inkwells, operate the slide projectors, and be a school crossing guard. But girls weren't allowed to do any of these things, and at that time, there was no word to explain this inequity.

By 1969, when Sandler was turned down three times for three different jobs as a professor, the word "sexism" was still only rarely used. "Too strong for a woman" was part of the justification for one of the rejections. The assumption that she would miss work if her children were sick was another.

Now 72, Sandler says that she knew what happened to her was immoral and suspected it could be illegal. She was right about the former but wrong about the latter. While there were laws against various types of discrimination, there were loopholes that failed to protect women at educational institutions.

- Title VII of the Civil Rights Act prohibited discrimination in employment on the basis of race, color, religion, national origin, and sex but excluded educational institutions.
- Title VI of the Civil Rights Act prohibited discrimination in federally assisted programs—which could include educational institutions—but only on the basis of race, color, and national origin, not sex.
- The Equal Pay Act prohibited salary discrimination on the basis of sex, but not for professional and administrative employees, which included professors.

Sandler was curious about what African Americans had done in terms of desegregation in education. Her curiosity led her to a report by the U.S. Commission on Civil Rights, which mentioned Executive Order 11246, prohibiting federal contractors from discrimination in employment based on race, color, religion, and national origin. But there was a footnote: President Lyndon Johnson had amended this executive order to include discrimination based on sex. Sandler reasoned that the amendment gave women who were fighting discrimination at educational institutions that received federal funds a legal leg to stand on.

To confirm her suspicion, she called the Department of Labor's Office of Federal Contract Compliance and met with a higher-up, who assured her she was right but asked her not to disclose his name. Though he couldn't publicly support her, he helped her file a complaint, and a secret alliance was forged.

"He was essentially telling me how to put pressure on his office," Sandler says. "I knew very little about legislation and lobbying, and he taught me."

Sandler found an ad in the newspaper that put her in touch with the Women's Equity Action League (WEAL) and together they filed a class-action complaint against all colleges and universities with federal contracts and then launched a nationwide campaign inviting women to share their stories. Since Sandler alone was named in the subsequent complaints, women could gather evidence about discrimination and file charges without being named.

Sandler sent copies of all complaints that WEAL received to Representative Edith Green (D.-Oreg.), chair of the special subcommittee on education and a WEAL advisory board member. For seven days during the summer of 1970. Green held the first ever congressional hearing on women's education and employment. The bill that would become Title IX was born. It reads: "No person in the United States shall, on the basis of sex, be excluded from participation in, be denied the benefits of, or be subjected to discrimination under any educational program or activity receiving federal financial assistance."

The testimones heard by Congress—or "horror stories," as Sandler describes them—focused on higher education. One woman professor said she taught at a university for free because the school told her that her husband worked there and they could afford to pay only one of them. More than one woman was told that she would not get tenure because, well, she was a woman.

There were complaints that many want ads were still segregated according to sex and that there were strict quotas limiting the number of women students allowed into universities in general—and medical and law programs in particular. Women said they were often required to have higher test scores than men. And it was reported that over one three-year period in the

1960s, the state of Virginia refused 21,000 women admission to state institutions. During the same period, Sandler says, "not one male student was rejected."

Green dissuaded Sandler and others from lobbying prior to the final passage of the House bill, reasoning that the less attention drawn to it the better. She was right. Indiana's Democratic Senator Birch Bayh ushered the bill through the Senate—where athletics were mentioned for the first time. The concern was that under the bill, women would be allowed to play football, and so a colloquy was added stating that they would not. (Green also snuck in an amendment to the Equal Pay Act to include administrators and executives, which helped professors.) Congress passed Title IX on June 23, 1972, and on July 1, President Richard Nixon signed it into law. "He's not thinking Title IX is a big deal," Sandler says. "It's just a little thing that's in there."

Sexual harassment was not originally discussed during the drafting of the legislation. The phrase "sexual harassment" didn't even exist until around 1975. But in 1976, a federal case held that sexual harassment was a form of sexual discrimination in the workplace, and in 1977, the first sexual harassment charges against an educational institution (Yale) were filed under Title IX. The case was lost, but, the judge made clear that sexual harassment was a form of discrimination. And in 1992, the Supreme Court ruled that monetary damages can be awarded under Title IX.

During the same year, ten-year-old LaShonda Davis told her mother, Aurelia, about the fifth-grade boy who kept rubbing against her and telling her that he wanted to have sex with her. Five months of repeated complaints to all the right authorities had little result. LaShonda's grades dropped, and she eventually wrote a suicide note. A criminal complaint was filed, and the boy pled guilty to sexual battery. Aurelia Davis then sued the Monroe County school board under Title IX. In June of 1999, the Supreme Court ruled in favor of the Davies. Verna Williams, lead counsel on the case, says the decision "is making schools reevaluate how they deal with sexual harassment."

> **FACT**
>
> Although 33% of K-12 students in U.S. public schools are children of color, an overwhelming 90% of teachers are white, and 42% of public schools have no teachers of color at all.

And they'd better. Statistics gathered by the American Association of University Women show that 81 percent of students surveyed (85 percent of girls, 76 percent of boys) have experienced sexual harassment. Williams says the Davis case also offsets some of the backlash caused by highly publicized incidents that portray sexual harassment cases as political correctness run amok, like the boy who made the papers after kissing a fellow pupil. "It makes sexual harassment appear to be a joke," says Williams. "That the gender police are out to get boys." Compare that to a call Williams got about second-grade boys pretending to rape a girl. "That kind of stuff doesn't get attention," she says.

But one of Title IX's most significant developments came about two years after its passage when the National Collegiate Athletic Association (NCAA) inquired whether this new law applied to athletics.

"Slowly but surely the implications became apparent," says Donna Lopiano, now executive director of the Women's Sports Foundation, and a former championship softball player. This aspect of education suddenly presented very quantifiable inequities.

"All hell broke loose," says Lopiano.

Growing up in the 1950s and '60s, Lopiano, like Sandler, wanted to be on safety patrol. She also wanted to take wood shop, be an altar girl—and play in Little League.

Lopiano was so good that at ten, when she tried out for Little League, she was drafted first. She was waiting for her uniform when a father walked up to her with the Little League rule book that clearly stated girls were not allowed to play. She went home and cried. Girls wouldn't be allowed to play in Little League until around the same time that a grown-up Lopiano and the Association for Intercollegiate Athletics for Women sat across the table from representatives of the NCAA—which at that time did not govern women's sports—and the American Football Coaches Association to iron out the regulations for Title IX.

The women said to "'split the pie down the middle,' and the guys fell off their chairs," Lopiano laughs. What the football coaches and NCAA came back with was the now highly contested three-pronged test. Only one prong must be met for an institution to be in compliance: 1. "Substantial proportionality"—the percentage of female undergrads must be roughly equal to the percentage of female athletes; 2. Proof of "fully and effectively accommodating the interests and abilities of women"; 3. "A history and continuing practice of adding teams."

Lopiano believed the three-pronged test was a way for the football folks to maintain the status quo, and a glance at 1973 stats supports that. With 60 percent of college students male, men would have the financial upper hand in proportionality. There was an assumption that women weren't interested in sports, so item 2 wasn't a problem. And item 3 looked like it gave colleges a never-ending period to achieve compliance.

The football coaches and NCAA walked away with what they considered to be a win over the women, and at that time no one had any idea what an impact Title IX would have on athletics. The issue of sports was so important, says Lopiano, because "it was a highly visible cultural institution that was previously all male. It's sex-separate, in-your-face discrimination. And it played into the press coverage beautifully."

Nearly 30 years after it was devised, the three-pronged test remains controversial. And, with women making up more than 50 percent of college enrollment and women's sports more popular than ever, Title IX itself has come under fire from school administrators who don't want to pay for women's teams.

In 1984, a court decision known as *Grove City* v. *Bell* limited the jurisdiction of Title IX to specific *programs* that received federal funding, such as financial aid, rather than to *institutions* that received federal funds. This decision exempted almost all athletic programs from Title IX compliance from 1984 to 1988.

But the most visible legal decision regarding athletics and Title IX came in 1996—*Cohen* v. *Brown University*—in which a federal appeals court upheld a 1993 district court ruling that Brown illegally discriminated against its female athletes. (*Ms.*, January/February 1998) Brown gymnast Amy Cohen, in response to her squad being cut from the varsity program, hoped that the threat of a lawsuit would get the school to comply. Instead, the school retaliated, curtailing the women's use of the locker rooms and failing to provide them with athletic trainers. In the end, Brown's legal fees far surpassed the $64,000 that would have been required to keep both the women's gymnastics and volleyball teams on the varsity roster.

Cohen, meanwhile, had become a poster girl for Title IX, riding a wave of media attention paid to women athletes. The late 1990s was a watershed: U.S. women competed for the first time in Olympic soccer and won the gold; ditto for the first U.S. women's Olympic ice hockey team. There was the birth of the Women's National Basketball Association (WNBA). The 1999 Women's World Cup soccer competition proved that not only could women play sports, but hundreds of thousands of people would pay to watch them do it. With all this, it's easy to overlook the onset of backlash. As Lopiano says, "A singular event gives the impression that the problem is over with."

And with the backlash centering around the *Q* word—quotas—Title IX has come full circle. In 1972, *proponents* of Title IX wanted to eliminate quotas since they were being used to limit the number of women allowed into colleges. Now it's the *opponents* of Title IX who want to eliminate what they consider a gender quota—the proportionality aspect of Title IX compliance in athletics.

College wrestling, more than any other college sport, has undergone a decline in recent years, and Title IX apparently presented a convenient scapegoat when wrestling coaches started looking for a reason for the decline. Anti–Title IX groups like Americans Against Quotas and the Independent Women's Forum point to a high number of cancelled wrestling programs— evidence, they say, that opportunities are being wrenched from boys and foisted on girls who are not even interested. Indeed, when money is tight, school administrators often *do* cut minor men's teams, such as wrestling, in order to add women's teams and thus comply with Title IX. This gives athletic directors an opportunity to say that Title IX is the reason they don't have money for minor mens' sports instead of looking at funding for major sports, like football or basketball. Speaker of the House and former wrestling coach Dennis Hastert has backed efforts to change Title IX enforcement.

Says Lopiano: "People don't realize that the regs the wrestling coaches are now trying to change—proportionality and the rest—was the position of the NCAA and the American Football Coaches Association—not the women."

But Title IX is an easy target compared to the behemoth budgets of football and basketball, which take up 69 percent of the men's athletic operating budgets of Division I-A schools. In 1997, the average Division I school spent $576,000 on men's football compared with the $478,000 it spent on *all* its women's sports programs. "The football coaches are keeping their mouths shut, trying to let the wrestling coaches fight their battle for them," says Lopiano. "The wrestling coaches are being duped."

In fact, if the coaches look at the numbers, they'd see that most schools have a long way to go before women's sports outspend men's. Women receive only 38 percent of all athletic scholarship money, 27 percent of recruiting money, and 23 percent of overall athletic budgets. Between 1992 and 1997, men's athletic operating budgets increased 139 percent, women's increased 89 percent. For every new dollar spent on women, three were spent on men.

And while many wrestling advocates point to Title IX as the reason for the sport's decline, it was during the four years that *Grove City* was in effect (1984–88) and Title IX was benched that wrestling experienced a decline of 18.3 percent. That's greater than the 15.6 percent decline it experienced in the ten years after Title IX's jurisdiction over athletics was reinstated.

While sports gets the lion's share of Title IX play, with sexual harassment a close second, the issue looming on the horizon is one that hearkens back to inequities commonplace in Title IX's infancy: career and vocational education.

Carpentry, auto mechanics. It's déjà vu all over again in middle and high schools where girls tend not to get the kind of training that translates into high pay. Thirty years ago girls weren't even allowed in most wood shop or auto mechanics classes. Now, there are other concerns, such as counselors who hand out pamphlets about careers in construction to males but not to females and teachers who pay less attention to girls in their shop classes.

In 1997, when the National Coalition for Women and Girls in Education published its report card on gender equity for Title IX's twenty-fifth anniversary, the organization gave career education a C, noting that "sex segregation persists in vocational education—men are clustered in high-skill, high-wage job tracks, women in the low-wage, traditionally female tracks." The report further noted that the new programs that came out of Congress's School-to-Work Opportunities Act of 1994 "are also segregated by sex."

Vocational education "is going to be an emerging issue," says Verna Williams. "These are avenues that girls typically don't go into, or if they do, they're finding it really hard to stick it out."

While no cases are currently being argued, Williams has received anecdotal evidence of problems. "So, for example," Williams says, "a female student in a carpentry class is assigned to sweeping up after the boys while the boys are learning how to make cabinets."

The potential damage is even greater in areas where technology is making vocational education a lucrative option. Auto mechanics, in particular, focuses on technological advances that provide students with training that enables them to earn as much as $80,000 a year, right out of high school. "This will be an avenue for kids who may not go to college," says Williams. "It's like a digital divide issue, with a gender spin."

So, where does that leave Title IX? Although women's sports may seem to draw too much attention from Title IX's other aspects, sports remains an appropriate arena in which to fight the gender equity battle. Last year was the first year women competed in Olympic pole vaulting. A new professional women's soccer league is set to launch. The Little League reject who made a gas mask instead of an Easter bonnet in art class because she wasn't allowed to take shop, sat at her brother's wedding and laughed to herself at the sight of an altar girl whose Adidas peeked out from under her robe. Lopiano described it as "the perfect snapshot of change."

So after 28 years, it's part celebration, part wake-up call. The Independent Women's Forum wants to dismantle Title IX, while athletic girls and their families fight to preserve it. And no sane politician wants to ostracize the female voter in what's odiously come to be known as the era of the "soccer mom."

But a gold medal still doesn't get a gal on the ice at her hometown rink. "People recognize we're not just talking about jobs," Sandler says. "It's about changing the world, and that makes people very scared."

The Triumphs of Title IX
Women's educational equity turns 35, and there's plenty to celebrate

Ms. Magazine first appeared in 1971 as an insert in the New York Magazine. Since its first regular issue appeared in July 1972, it has continued to provide a source of U.S. and international news, fiction, poetry with a feminist perspective.

Patsy Mink dreamed of becoming a doctor, but none of the 20 medical schools she applied to accepted women. Edith Green wanted to become an electrical engineer, but her family told her "not to be silly." Bernice Sandler, teaching part time at a university after earning her doctorate, learned that her department would not consider her for a full time position because she "[came] on too strong for a woman."

These three women, carrying with them personal experiences of discrimination, came together in the early 1970s to help create and defend the first legislation specifically prohibiting sex discrimination in education: Title IX of the Education Amendments of 1972. It reads:

No person in the United States shall, on the basis of sex, be excluded from participation in, be denied the benefits of, or be subjected to discrimination under any education program or activity receiving federal financial assistance.

Sandler, who became a specialist with the Special Subcommittee on Education in the U.S. House of Representatives, filed discrimination complaints against 250 colleges and universities—with the support of many women academics and feminist organizations—which convinced Rep. Edith Green (D-Ore.) to hold the first congressional hearings on sex discrimination in education. Green, with the cosponsorship of Rep. Patsy Mink (D-Hawaii) and others, introduced Title IX, which was passed by Congress two years later with little attention and was signed into law by President Richard Nixon.

Though the word "sports" did not appear in the original Title IX, the law has become synonymous with increased opportunities for girls in athletics. But this is only a small part of the story. As the following two reports show, Title IX also played the pivotal role in opening doors to educational opportunities for girls and women in all areas of education, from kindergarten through graduate school.

"It all grew from the power of an idea," said David Sadker, a renowned expert in gender equity in education who has been studying the issue for close to 40 years. "You did have a law supporting it, but really it was the idea more than the penalty. . . . This was an idea revolution."

Unfortunately, soon after it was written into law, Title IX was subjected to relentless attack—and Mink became the law's greatest defender. In 1984, the Supreme Court during the Reagan administration succeeded in virtually overturning the law for four years—until feminists and civil rights leaders fought back with the Civil Rights Restoration Act of 1987. Most recently, the Bush administration weakened Title IX with new rules allowing public, sex-segregated classes and schools—which critics say almost always disadvantage girls—for purposes other than to remedy discrimination.

"I was extraordinarily naive," Sandler has confessed. "I believed that if we passed Title IX, it would only take a year or two for all the inequities based on sex to be eliminated."

Much remains to be done. But while staying vigilant about its survival and enforcement, we shouldn't forget to celebrate Title IX. After all, American women and girl students of every age and interest—kindergartners and doctoral candidates, athletes and bookworms, aspiring auto mechanics and physicists—can thank the law, and its advocates, for opportunities they might never have received without it.

Girls and Boys Together . . . But Mostly Apart
Gender Arrangements in Elementary Schools

Barrie Thorne

Barrie Thorne is Professor of Sociology and Women's Studies at UC Berkeley. She previously taught at Michigan State University. She is the U.S. Editor of Childhood: A Global Journal of Child Research. *She is the author of* Gender Play: Girls and Boys in School *(1993) and co-editor of* Feminist Sociology: Life Histories of a Movement *(1997), and* Rethinking the Family: Some Feminist Questions *(1992). This essay was published in* Relationships and Development *(1986) edited by Willard W. Hartup and Zick Rubin.*

Throughout the years of elementary school, children's friendships and casual encounters are strongly separated by sex. Sex segregation among children, which starts in preschool and is well established by middle childhood, has been amply documented in studies of children's groups and friendships (e.g., Eder & Hallinan, 1978; Schofield, 1981) and is immediately visible in elementary school settings. When children choose seats in classrooms or the cafeteria, or get into line, they frequently arrange themselves in same-sex clusters. At lunchtime, they talk matter-of-factly about "girls' tables" and "boys' tables." Playgrounds have gendered turfs, with some areas and activities, such as large playing fields and basketball courts, controlled mainly by boys, and others—smaller enclaves like jungle-gym areas and concrete spaces for hopscotch or jumprope—more often controlled by girls. Sex segregation is so common in elementary schools that it is meaningful to speak of separate girls' and boys' worlds.

Studies of gender and children's social relations have mostly followed this "two worlds" model, separately describing and comparing the subcultures of girls and of boys (e.g., Lever, 1976; Maltz & Borker, 1983). In brief summary: Boys tend to interact in larger, more age-heterogeneous groups (Lever, 1976; Waldrop & Halverson, 1975; Eder & Hallinan, 1978). They engage in more rough and tumble play and physical fighting (Maccoby & Jacklin, 1974). Organized sports are both a central activity and a major metaphor in boys' subcultures; they use the language of "teams" even when not engaged in sports, and they often construct interaction in the form of contests. The shifting hierarchies of boys' groups (Savin-Williams, 1976) are evident in their more frequent use of direct commands, insults, and challenges (Goodwin, 1980).

Fewer studies have been done of girls' groups (Foot, Chapman, & Smith, 1980: McRobbie & Garber, 1975), and—perhaps because categories for description and analysis have come more from male than female experience—researchers have had difficulty seeing and analyzing girls' social relations. Recent work has begun to correct this skew. In middle childhood, girls' worlds are less public than those of boys; girls more often interact in private places and in smaller groups or friendship pairs (Eder & Hallinan, 1978; Waldrop & Halverson, 1975). Their play is more cooperative and turn-taking (Lever, 1976). Girls have more intense and exclusive friendships, which take shape around keeping and telling secrets, shifting alliances, and indirect ways of expressing disagreement (Goodwin, 1980: Lever, 1976; Maltz & Borker, 1983). Instead of direct commands, girls more often use directives which merge speaker and hearer, e.g., "let's" or "we gotta" (Goodwin, 1980).

Although much can be learned by comparing the social organization and subcultures of boys' and of girls' groups, the separate worlds approach has eclipsed full, contextual understanding of gender and social relations among children. The separate worlds model essentially involves a search for group sex differences, and shares the limitations of individual sex difference research. Differences tend to be exaggerated and similarities ignored, with little theoretical attention to the integration of similarity and difference (Unger, 1979). Statistical findings of difference are often portrayed as dichotomous, neglecting the considerable individual variation that exists; for example, not all boys fight, and some have intense and exclusive friendships. The sex difference approach tends to abstract gender from its social context, to assume that males and females are qualitatively and permanently different (with differences perhaps unfolding through separate developmental lines). These assumptions mask the possibility that gender arrangements and patterns of similarity and difference may vary by situation, race, social class, region, or subculture.

Sex segregation is far from total, and is a more complex and dynamic process than the portrayal of separate worlds reveals. Erving Goffman (1977) has observed that sex segregation has a "with-then-apart" structure; the sexes segregate periodically, with separate spaces, rituals, groups, but they also come together and are, in crucial ways, part of the same world. This is certainly true in the social environment of elementary schools. Although girls and boys do interact as boundaried collectivities—an image suggested by the separate worlds approach—there are other occasions when they work or play in relaxed and integrated ways. Gender is less central to the organization and meaning of some situations than others. In short, sex segregation is not static, but is a variable and complicated process.

To gain an understanding of gender which can encompass both the "with" and the "apart" of sex segregation, analysis should start not with the individual, nor with a search for sex differences, but with social relationships. *Gender should be conceptualized as a system of relationships rather than as an immutable and dichotomous given.* Taking this approach, I have organized my research on gender and children's social relations around questions like the following: How and when does gender enter into group formation? In a given situation, how is gender made more or less salient or infused with particular meanings? By what rituals, processes, and forms of social organization and conflict do "with-then-apart" rhythms get enacted? How are these processes affected by the organization of institutions (e.g., different types of schools, neighborhoods, or summer camps), varied settings (e.g., the constraints and possibilities governing interaction on playgrounds vs. classrooms), and particular encounters?

METHODS AND SOURCES OF DATA

This study is based on two periods of participant observation. In 1976–1977 I observed for 8 months in a largely working-class elementary school in California, a school with 8% Black and 12% Chicana/o students. In 1980 I did fieldwork for 3 months in a Michigan elementary school of similar size (around 400 students), social class, and racial composition. I observed in several classrooms—a kindergarten, a second grade, and a combined fourth-fifth grade—and in school hallways, cafeterias, and playgrounds. I set out to follow the round of the school day as children experience it, recording their interactions with one another, and with adults, in varied settings.

Participant observation involves gaining access to everyday, "naturalistic" settings and taking systematic notes over an extended period of time. Rather than starting with preset categories for recording, or with fixed hypotheses for testing, participant-observers record detail in ways which maximize opportunities for discovery. Through continuous interaction between observation and analysis, "grounded theory" is developed (Glaser & Strauss, 1967).

The distinctive logic and discipline of this mode of inquiry emerges from: (1) theoretical sampling—being relatively systematic in the choice of where and whom to observe in order to maximize knowledge relevant to categories and analysis which are being developed; and (2) comparing all relevant data on a given point in order to modify emerging propositions to take account of discrepant cases (Katz, 1983). Participant observation is a flexible, open-ended and inductive method, designed to understand behavior within, rather than stripped from, social context. It provides richly detailed information which is anchored in everyday meanings and experience.

DAILY PROCESSES OF SEX SEGREGATION

Sex segregation should be understood not as a given, but as the result of deliberate activity. The outcome is dramatically visible when there are separate girls' and boys' tables in school lunchrooms, or sex-separated groups on playgrounds. But in the same lunchroom one can also find tables where girls and boys eat and talk together, and in some playground activities the sexes mix. By what processes do girls and boys separate into gender-defined and relatively boundaried collectivities? And in what contexts, and through what processes, do boys and girls interact in less gender-divided ways?

In the school settings I observed much segregation happened with no mention of gender. Gender was implicit in the contours of friendship, shared interest, and perceived risk which came into play when children chose companions—in their prior planning, invitations, seeking-of-access, saving-of-places, denials of entry, and allowing or protesting of "cuts" by those who violated the rules for lining up. Sometimes children formed mixed-sex groups for play, eating, talking, working on a classroom project, or moving through space. When adults or children explicitly invoked gender—and this was nearly always in ways which separated girls and boys—boundaries were heightened and mixed-sex interaction became an explicit arena of risk.

In the schools I studied, the physical space and curricula were not formally divided by sex, as they have been in the history of elementary schooling (a history evident in separate entrances to old school buildings, where the words "Boys" and "Girls" are permanently etched in concrete). Nevertheless, gender was a visible marker in the adult-organized school day. In both schools, when the public address system sounded, the principal inevitably opened with: "Boys and girls . . ." and in addressing clusters of children, teachers and aides regularly used gender terms ("Heads down, girls"; "The girls are ready and the boys aren't"). These forms of address made gender visible and salient, conveying an assumption that the sexes are separate social groups.

Teachers and aides sometimes drew upon gender as a basis for sorting children and organizing activities. Gender is an embodied and visual social category which roughly divides the population in half, and the separation of girls and boys permeates the history and lore of schools and playgrounds. In both schools—although through awareness of Title IX, many teachers had changed this practice—one could see separate girls' and boys' lines moving, like caterpillars, through the school halls. In the 4th–5th grade classroom the teacher frequently pitted girls against boys for spelling and math contests. On the playground in the Michigan school, aides regarded the space close to the building as girls' territory, and the playing fields "out there" as boys' territory. They sometimes school children of the other sex away from those spaces, especially boys who ventured near the girls' area and seemed to have teasing in mind.

In organizing their activities, both within and apart from the surveillance of adults, children also explicitly invoked gender. During my fieldwork in the Michigan school, I kept daily records of who sat where in the lunchroom. The amount of sex segregation varied: It was least at the first grade tables and almost total among sixth graders. There was also variation from classroom to classroom within a given age, and from day to day. Actions like the following heightened the gender divide:

> In the lunchroom, when the two second grade tables were filling, a high-status boy walked by the inside table, which had a scattering of both boys and girls, and said loudly, "Oooo, too many girls," as he headed for a seat at the far table. The boys at the inside table picked up their trays and moved, and no other boys sat at the inside table, which the pronouncement had effectively made taboo.

In the end, that day (which was not the case every day), girls and boys ate at separate tables.

Eating and walking are not sex-typed activities, yet in forming groups in lunchrooms and hallways children often separated by sex. Sex segregation assumed added dimensions on the playground, where spaces, equipment, and activities were infused with gender meanings. My inventories of activities and groupings on the playground showed similar patterns in both schools: Boys controlled the large fixed spaces designated for team sports (baseball diamonds, grassy fields used for football or soccer); girls more often played closer to the building, doing tricks on the monkey bars (which, for 6th graders, became an area for sitting and talking) and using cement areas for jumprope, hopscotch, and group games like four-square. (Lever, 1976, provides a good analysis of sex-divided play.) Girls and boys most often played together in kickball, and in group (rather than team) games like four-square, dodgeball, and handball. When children used gender to exclude others from play, they often drew upon beliefs connecting boys to some activities and girls to others:

> A first grade boy avidly watched an all-female game of jump rope. When the girls began to shift positions, he recognized a means of access to the play and he offered, "I'll swing it." A girl responded, "No way, you don't know how to do it, to swing it. You gotta be a girl." He left without protest.

Although children sometimes ignored pronouncements about what each sex could or could not do, I never heard them directly challenge such claims.

When children had explicitly defined an activity or a group as gendered, those who crossed the boundary—especially boys who moved into female-marked space—risked being teased. ("Look! Mike's in the girls' line!"; "'That's a girl over there,' a girl said loudly, pointing to a boy sitting at an otherwise all-female table in the lunchroom.") Children, and occasionally adults, used teasing—especially the tease of "liking" someone of the other sex, or of "being" that sex by virtue of being in their midst—to police gender boundaries. Much of the teasing drew upon heterosexual romantic definitions, making cross-sex interaction risky, and increasing social distance between boys and girls.

RELATIONSHIPS BETWEEN THE SEXES

Because I have emphasized the "apart" and ignored the occasions of "with," this analysis of sex segregation falsely implies that there is little contact between girls and boys in daily school life.

In fact, relationships between girls and boys—which should be studied as fully as, and in connection with, same-sex relationships—are of several kinds:

1. "Borderwork," or forms of cross-sex interaction which are based upon and reaffirm boundaries and asymmetries between girls' and boys' groups;
2. Interactions which are infused with heterosexual meanings;
3. Occasions where individuals cross gender boundaries to participate in the world of the other sex; and
4. Situations where gender is muted in salience, with girls and boys interacting in more relaxed ways.

Borderwork

In elementary school settings boys' and girls' groups are sometimes spatially set apart. Same-sex groups sometimes claim fixed territories such as the basketball court, the bars, or specific lunchroom tables. However, in the crowded, multi-focused, and adult-controlled environment of the school, groups form and disperse at a rapid rate and can never stay totally apart. Contact between girls and boys sometimes lessens sex segregation, but gender-defined groups also come together in ways which emphasize their boundaries.

"Borderwork" refers to interaction across, yet based upon and even strengthening gender boundaries. I have drawn this notion from Fredrik Barth's (1969) analysis of social relations which are maintained across ethnic boundaries without diminishing dichotomized ethnic status.[1] His focus is on more macro, ecological arrangements: mine is on face-to-face behavior. But the insight is similar: Groups may interact in ways which strengthen their borders, and the maintenance of ethnic (or gender) groups can best be understood by examining the boundary that defines the group, "not the cultural stuff that it encloses" (Barth, 1969, p. 15). In elementary schools there are several types of borderwork: contests or games where gender-defined teams compete; cross-sex rituals of chasing and pollution; and group invasions. These interactions are asymmetrical, challenging the separate-but-parallel model of "two worlds."

Contests

Boys and girls are sometimes pitted against each other in classroom competitions and playground games. The 4th–5th grade classroom had a boys' side and a girls' side, an arrangement that re-emerged each time the teacher asked children to choose their own desks. Although there was some within-sex shuffling, the result was always a spatial moiety system—boys on the left, girls on the right—with the exception of one girl (the "tomboy" whom I'll describe later), who twice chose a desk with the boys and once with the girls. Drawing upon and reinforcing the children's self-segregation, the teacher often pitted the boys against the girls in spelling and math competitions, events marked by cross-sex antagonism and within-sex solidarity:

> The teacher introduced a math game; she would write addition and subtraction problems on the board, and a member of each team would race to be the first to write the correct answer. She wrote two score-keeping columns on the board: 'Beastly Boys' ... 'Gossipy Girls.' The boys yelled out, as several girls laughed, 'Noisy girls! Gruesome girls!' The girls sat in a row on top of their desks: sometimes they moved collectively, pushing their hips or whispering 'pass it on.' The boys stood along the wall, some reclining against desks. When members of either group came back victorious from the front of the room, they would do the 'giving five' hand-slapping ritual with their team members.

On the playground a team of girls occasionally played against a team of boys, usually in kickball or team two-square. Sometimes these games proceeded matter-of-factly, but if gender became the explicit basis of team solidarity, the interaction changed, becoming more antagonistic and unstable:

> Two fifth-grade girls played against two fifth-grade boys in a team game of two-square. The game proceeded at an even pace until an argument ensued about whether the ball was out or on the line. Karen, who had hit the ball, became annoyed, flashed her middle finger at the other team, and called to a passing girl to join their side. The boys then called, out to other boys, and cheered as several arrived to play. 'We got five and you got three!' Jack yelled. The game continued, with the girls yelling, 'Bratty boys! Sissy boys!' and the boys making noises—'weee haw' 'ha-ha-ha'—as they played.

Chasing

Cross-sex chasing dramatically affirms boundaries between girls and boys. The basic elements of chase and elude, capture and rescue (Sutton-Smith, 1971) are found in various kinds of tag with formal rules, and in informal episodes of chasing which punctuate life on playgrounds. These episodes begin with a provocation (taunts like "You can't get me!" or "Slobber monster!"; bodily pokes or the grabbing of possessions). A provocation may be ignored, or responded to by chasing. Chaser and chased may then alternate roles. In an ethnographic study of chase sequences on a school playground, Christine Finnan (1982) observes that chases vary in number of chasers to chased (e.g., one chasing one, or five chasing two); form of provocation (a taunt or a poke); outcome (an episode may end when the chased outdistances the chaser, or with a brief touch, being wrestled to the ground, or the recapturing of a hat or a ball); and in use of space (there may or may not be safety zones).

Like Finnan (1982), and Sluckin (1981), who studied a playground in England, I found that chasing has a gendered structure. Boys frequently chase one another, an activity which often ends in wrestling and mock fights. When girls chase girls, they are usually less physically aggressive; they less often, for example, wrestle one another to the ground.

Cross-sex chasing is set apart by special names—"girls chase the boys"; "boys chase the girls"; "the chase"; "chasers"; "chase and kiss"; "kiss chase"; "kissers and chasers"; "kiss or kill"—and by children's animated talk about the activity. The names vary by region and school, but contain both gender and sexual meanings (this form of play is mentioned, but only briefly analzyed, in Finnan, 1981; Sluckin, 1981; Parrott, 1972; and Borman, 1979).

In "boys chase the girls" and "girls chase the boys" (the names most frequently used in both the California and Michigan schools) boys and girls become, by definition, separate teams. Gender terms override individual identities, especially for the other team ("Help, a girl's chasin' me!"; "C'mon Sarah, let's get that boy"; "Tony, help save me from the girls"). Individuals may call for help from, or offer help to others of their sex. They may also grab someone of their sex and turn them over to the opposing team: "Ryan grabbed Billy from behind, wrestling him to the ground. 'Hey girls, get 'im,' Ryan called."

Boys more often mix episodes of cross-sex with same-sex chasing. Girls more often have safety zones, places like the girls' restroom or an area by the school wall, where they retreat to rest and talk (sometimes in animated postmortems) before new episodes of cross-sex chasing begin.

Early in the fall in the Michigan school, where chasing was especially prevalent, I watched a second grade boy teach a kindergarten girl how to chase. He slowly ran backwards, beckoning her to pursue him, as he called, "Help, a girl's after me." In the early grades chasing mixes with fantasy play, e.g., a first-grade boy who played "sea monster," his arms outflung and his voice growling, as he chased a group of girls. By third grade, stylized gestures—exaggerated stalking motions, screams (which only girls do), and karate kicks—accompany scenes of chasing.

Names like "chase and kiss" mark the sexual meanings of cross-sex chasing, a theme I return to later. The threat of kissing—most often girls threatening to kiss boys—is a ritualized form of provocation. Cross-sex chasing among sixth graders involves elaborate patterns of touch and touch avoidance, which adults see as sexual. The principal told the sixth graders in the Michigan school that they were not to play "pom-pom," a complicated chasing game, because it entailed "inappropriate touch."

Rituals of Pollution

Cross-sex chasing is sometimes entwined with rituals of pollution, as in "cooties," where specific individuals or groups are treated as contaminating or carrying "germs." Children have rituals for transferring cooties (usually touching someone else and shouting "You've got cooties!"), for immunization (e.g., writing "CV" for "cootie vaccination" on their arms), and for eliminating cooties (e.g., saying "no gives" or using "cootie catchers" made of folded paper) (described in Knapp & Knapp, 1976). While girls may give cooties to girls, boys do not generally give cooties to one another (Samuelson, 1980).

In cross-sex play, either girls or boys may be defined as having cooties, which they transfer through chasing and touching. Girls give cooties to boys more often than vice versa. In Michigan, one version of cooties is called "girl stain"; the fourth-graders whom Karkau, 1973, describes, used the phrase "girl touch." "Cootie queens," or "cootie girls" (there are no "kings" or "boys") are female pariahs, the ultimate school untouchables, seen as contaminating not only by virtue of gender, but also through some added stigma such as being overweight or poor.[2] That girls are seen as more polluting than boys is a significant asymmetry, which echoes cross-cultural patterns, although in other cultures female pollution is generally connected to menstruation, and not applied to prepubertal girls.

Invasions

Playground invasions are another asymmetric form of borderwork. On a few occasions I saw girls invade and disrupt an all-male game, most memorably a group of tall sixth-grade girls who ran onto the playing field and grabbed a football which was in play. The boys were surprised and frustrated, and, unusual for boys this old, finally tattled to the aide. But in the majority of cases, boys disrupt girls' activities rather than vice versa. Boys grab the ball from girls playing four-square, stick feet into a jumprope and stop an ongoing game, and dash through the area of the bars, where girls are taking turns performing, sending the rings flying. Sometimes boys ask to join a girls' game and then, after a short period of seemingly earnest play, disrupt the game:

> Two second-grade boys begged to "twirl" the jumprope for a group of second-grade girls who had been jumping for some time. The girls agreed, and the boys began to twirl. Soon, without announcement, the boys changed from "seashells, cockle bells" to "hot peppers" (spinning the rope very fast), and tangled the jumper in the rope. The boys ran away laughing.

Boys disrupt girls' play so often that girls have developed almost ritualized responses: They guard their ongoing play, chase boys away, and tattle to the aides. In a playground cycle which enhances sex segregation, aides who try to spot potential trouble before it occurs sometimes shoo boys away from areas where girls are playing. Aides do not anticipate trouble from girls who seek to join groups of boys, with the exception of girls intent on provoking a chase sequence. And indeed, if they seek access to a boys' game, girls usually play with boys in earnest rather than breaking up the game.

A close look at the organization of borderwork—or boundaried interactions between the sexes—shows that the worlds of boys and girls may be separate, but they are not parallel, nor are they equal. The worlds of girls and boys articulate in several asymmetric ways:

1. On the playground, boys control as much as ten times more space than girls, when one adds up the area of large playing fields and compares it with the much smaller areas where girls predominate. Girls, who play closer to the building, are more often watched over and protected by the adult aides.
2. Boys invade all-female games and scenes of play much more than girls invade boys. This, and boys' greater control of space, correspond with other findings about the organization of gender, and inequality, in our society: compared with men and boys, women and girls take up less space, and their space, and talk, are more often violated and interrupted (Greif, 1982; Henley, 1977; West & Zimmerman, 1983).
3. Although individual boys are occasionally treated as contaminating (e.g., a third grade boy who both boys and girls said was "stinky" and "smelled like pee"), girls are more often defined as polluting. This pattern ties to themes that I discuss later: It is more taboo for a boy to play with (as opposed to invade) girls, and girls are more sexually defined than boys.

A look at the boundaries between the separated worlds of girls and boys illuminates within-sex hierarchies of status and control. For example, in the sex-divided seating in the 4th-5th grade classroom, several boys recurringly sat near "female space": their desks were at the gender divide in the classroom, and they were more likely than other boys to sit at a predominantly female table in the lunchroom. These boys—two nonbilingual Chicanos and an overweight "loner" boy who was afraid of sports—were at the bottom of the male hierarchy. Gender is sometimes used as a metaphor for male hierarchies; the inferior status of boys at the bottom is conveyed by calling them "girls":

> Seven boys and one girl were playing basketball. Two younger boys came over and asked to play. While the girl silently stood, fully accepted in the company of players, one of the older boys disparagingly said to the younger boys, 'You girls can't play.'[3]

In contrast, the girls who more often travel in the boys' world, sitting with groups of boys in the lunchroom or playing basketball, soccer, and baseball with them, are not stigmatized. Some have fairly high status with other girls. The worlds of girls and boys are assymetrically arranged, and spatial patterns map out interacting forms of inequality.

Heterosexual Meanings

The organization and meanings of gender (the social categories "woman/man," "girl/boy") and of sexuality vary cross-culturally (Ortner & Whitehead, 1981)—and, in our society, across the life course. Harriet Whitehead (1981) observed that in our (Western) gender system, and that of many traditional North American Indian cultures, one's choice of a sexual object, occupation, and one's dress and demeanor are closely associated with gender. However, the "center of gravity" differs in the two gender systems. For Indians, occupational pursuits provide the primary imagery of gender; dress and demeanor are secondary, and sexuality is least important. In our system, at least for adults, the order is reversed: heterosexuality is central to our definitions of "man" and "woman" ("masculinity"/"femininity"), and the relationships that obtain between them, whereas occupation and dress/demeanor are secondary.

Whereas erotic orientation and gender are closely linked in our definitions of adults, we define children as relatively asexual. Activities and dress/demeanor are more important than sexuality in the cultural meanings of "girl" and "boy." Children are less heterosexually defined than adults, and we have nonsexual imagery for relations between girls and boys. However, both children and adults sometimes use heterosexual language—"crushes," "like," "goin' with," "girlfriends," and "boyfriends"—to define cross-sex relationships. This language increases through the years of elementary school; the shift to adolescence consolidates a gender system organized around the institution of heterosexuality. In everyday life in the schools, heterosexual and romantic meanings infuse some ritualized forms of interaction between groups of boys and girls (e.g., "chase and kiss") and help maintain sex segregation. "Jimmy likes Beth" or "Beth likes Jimmy" is a major form of teasing, which a child risks in choosing to sit by or walk with some-one of the other sex. The structure of teasing, and children's sparse vocabulary for relationships between girls and boys, are evident in the following conversation which I had with a group of third-grade girls in the lunchroom:

> Susan asked me what I was doing, and I said I was observing the things children do and play. Nicole volunteered, 'I like running, boys chase all the girls. See Tim over there? Judy chases him all around the school. She likes him.' Judy, sitting across the table, quickly responded, 'I hate him. I like him for a friend.' 'Tim loves Judy.' Nicole said in a loud, sing-song voice.

In the younger grades, the culture and lore of girls contains more heterosexual romantic themes than that of boys. In Michigan, the first-grade girls often jumped rope to a rhyme which began: "Down in the valley where the green grass grows, there sat Cindy (name of jumper), as sweet as a rose. She sat, she sat, she sat so sweet. Along came Jason, and kissed her on the cheek . . . first comes love, then comes marriage, then along comes Cindy with a baby carriage. . . ." Before a girl took her turn at jumping, the chanters asked her "Who do you want to be your boyfriend?" The jumper always proferred a name, which was accepted matter-of-factly. In chasing, a girl's kiss carried greater threat than a boy's kiss; "girl touch," when defined as contaminating, had sexual connotations. In short, starting at an early age, girls are more sexually defined than boys.

Through the years of elementary school, and increasing with age, the idiom of heterosexuality helps maintain the gender divide. Cross-sex interactions, especially when children initiate them, are fraught with the risk of being teased about "liking" someone of the other sex. I learned of several close cross-sex friendships, formed and maintained in neighborhoods and church, which went underground during the school day.

By the fifth grade a few children began to affirm, rather than avoid, the charge of having a girlfriend or a boyfriend; they introduced the heterosexual courtship rituals of adolescence:

> In the lunchroom in the Michigan school, as the tables were forming, a high-status fifth-grade boy called out from his seat at the table: 'I want Trish to sit by me.' Trish came over, and almost like a king and queen, they sat at the gender divide—a row of girls down the table on her side, a row of boys on his.

In this situation, which inverted earlier forms, it was not a loss, but a gain in status to publically choose a companion of the other sex. By affirming his choice, the boy became unteasable (note the familiar asymmetry of heterosexual courtship rituals: the male initiated). This incident signals a temporal shift in arrangements of sex and gender.

Traveling in the World of the Other Sex

Contests, invasions, chasing, and heterosexually-defined encounters are based upon and reaffirm boundaries between girls and boys. In another type of cross-sex interaction, individuals (or sometimes pairs) cross gender boundaries, seeking acceptance in a group of the other sex. Nearly all the cases I saw of this were tomboys—girls who played organized sports and frequently sat with boys in the cafeteria or classroom. If these girls were skilled at activities central in the boys' world, especially games like soccer, baseball, and basketball, they were pretty much accepted as participants.

Being a tomboy is a matter of degree. Some girls seek access to boys' groups but are excluded; other girls limit their "crossing" to specific sports. Only a few—such as the tomboy I mentioned earlier, who chose a seat with the boys in the sex-divided fourth-fifth grade—participate fully in the boys' world. That particular girl was skilled at the various organized sports which boys played in different seasons of the year. She was also adept at physical fighting and at using the forms of arguing, insult, teasing, naming, and sports-talk of the boys' subculture. She was the only Black child in her classroom, in a school with only 8% Black students; overall that token status, along with unusual athletic and verbal skills, may have contributed to her ability to move back and forth across the gender divide. Her unique position in the children's world was widely recognized in the school. Several times, the teacher said to me, "She thinks she's a boy."

I observed only one boy in the upper grades (a fourth grader) who regularly played with all-female groups, as opposed to "playing at" girls' games and seeking to disrupt them. He frequently played jumprope and took turns with girls doing tricks on the bars, using the small gestures—for example, a helpful push on the heel of a girl who needed momentum to turn her body around the bar—which mark skillful and earnest participation. Although I never saw him play in other than an earnest spirit, the girls often chased him away from their games, and both girls and boys teased him. The fact that girls seek, and have more access to boys' worlds than vice versa, and the fact that girls who travel with the other sex are less stigmatized for it, are obvious asymmetries, tied to the asymmetries previously discussed.

Relaxed Cross-Sex Interactions

Relationships between boys and girls are not always marked by strong boundaries, heterosexual definitions, or by interacting on the terms and turfs of the other sex. On some occasions girls and boys interact in relatively comfortable ways. Gender is not strongly salient nor explicitly invoked, and girls and boys are not organized into boundaried collectivities. These "with" occasions have been neglected by those studying gender and children's relationships, who have emphasized either the model of separate worlds (with little attention to their articulation) or heterosexual forms of contact.

Occasions where boys and girls interact without strain, where gender wanes, rather than waxes in importance, frequently have one or more of the following characteristics:

1. The situations are organized around an absorbing task, such as a group art project or creating a radio show, which encourages cooperation and lessens attention to gender. This pattern accords with other studies finding that cooperative activities reduce group antagonism (e.g., Sherif & Sherif, 1953, who studied divisions between boys in a summer camp; and Aronson et al., 1978, who used cooperative activities to lessen racial divisions in a classroom).
2. Gender is less prominent when children are not responsible for the formation of the group. Mixed-sex play is less frequent in games like football, which require the choosing of teams,

and more frequent in games like handball or dodgeball which individuals can join simply by getting into a line or a circle. When adults organize mixed-sex encounters—which they frequently do in the classroom and in physical education periods on the playground—they legitimize cross-sex contact. This removes the risk of being teased for choosing to be with the other sex.

3. There is more extensive and relaxed cross-sex interaction when principles of grouping other than gender are explicitly invoked—for example, counting off to form teams for spelling or kickball, dividing lines by hot lunch or cold lunch, or organizing a work group on the basis of interests or reading ability.

4. Girls and boys may interact more readily in less public and crowded settings. Neighborhood play, depending on demography, is more often sex and age integrated than play at school, partly because with fewer numbers, one may have to resort to an array of social categories to find play partners or to constitute a game. And in less crowded environments there are fewer potential witnesses to "make something of it" if girls and boys play together.

Relaxed interactions between girls and boys often depend on adults to set up and legitimize the contact.[4] Perhaps because of this contingency—and the other, distancing patterns which permeate relations between girls and boys—the easeful moments of interaction rarely build to close friendship. Schofield (1981) makes a similar observation about gender and racial barriers to friendship in a junior high school.

IMPLICATIONS FOR DEVELOPMENT

I have located social relations within an essentially spatial framework, emphasizing the organization of children's play, work, and other activities within specific settings, and in one type of institution, the school. In contrast, frameworks of child development rely upon temporal metaphors, using images of growth and transformation over time. Taken alone, both spatial and temporal frameworks have shortcomings; fitted together, they may be mutually correcting.

Those interested in gender and development have relied upon conceptualizations of "sex role socialization" and "sex differences." Sexuality and gender, I have argued, are more situated and fluid than these individualist and intrinsic models imply. Sex and gender are differently organized and defined across situations, even within the same institution. This situational variation (e.g., in the extent to which an encounter heightens or lessens gender boundaries, or is infused with sexual meanings) shapes and constrains individual behavior. Features which a developmental perspective might attribute to individuals, and understand as relatively internal attributes unfolding over time, may, in fact, be highly dependent on context. For example, children's avoidance of cross-sex friendship may be attributed to individual gender development in middle-childhood. But attention to varied situations may show that this avoidance is contingent on group size, activity, adult behavior, collective meanings, and the risk of being teased.

A focus on social organization and situation draws attention to children's experiences in the present. This helps correct a model like "sex role socialization" which casts the present under the shadow of the future, or presumed "endpoints" (Speier, 1976). A situated analysis of arrangements of sex and gender among those of different ages may point to crucial disjunctions in the life course. In the fourth and fifth grades, culturally defined heterosexual rituals ("goin' with") begin to suppress the presence and visibility of other types of interaction between girls and boys, such as nonsexualized and comfortable interaction, and traveling in the world of the other sex. As "boyfriend/girlfriend" definitions spread, the fifth grade tomboy I described had to work to sustain "buddy" relationships with boys. Adult women who were tomboys often speak of early adolescence as a painful time when they were pushed away from participation in boys' activities. Other adult women speak of the loss of intense, even erotic ties with other girls when they entered puberty and the rituals of dating, that is, when they became absorbed into the institution of hetero-sexuality (Rich, 1980). When Lever (1976) describes best-friend relationships among fifth-grade girls as preparation for dating, she imposes heterosexual ideologies onto a present which should be understood on its own terms.

As heterosexual encounters assume more importance, they may alter relations in same-sex groups. For example, Schofield (1981) reports that for sixth- and seventh-grade children in a middle school, the popularity of girls with other girls was affected by their popularity with boys, while boys' status with other boys did not depend on their relations with girls. This is an asymmetry familiar from the adult world; men's relationships with one another are defined through varied activities (occupations, sports), while relationships among women—and their public status—are more influenced by their connections to individual men.

A full understanding of gender and social relations should encompass cross-sex as well as within-sex interactions. "Borderwork" helps maintain separate, gender-linked subcultures, which, as those interested in development have begun to suggest, may result in different milieux for learning. Daniel Maltz and Ruth Borker (1983) for example, argue that because of different interactions within girls' and boys' groups, the sexes learn different rules for creating and interpreting friendly conversation, rules which carry into adulthood and help account for miscommunication between men and women. Carol Gilligan (1982) fits research on the different worlds of girls and boys into a theory of sex differences in moral development. Girls develop a style of reasoning, she argues, which is more personal and relational; boys develop a style which is more positional, based on separateness. Eleanor Maccoby (1982), also following the insight that because of sex segregation, girls and boys grow up in different environments, suggests implications for gender differentiated prosocial and antisocial behavior.

This separate worlds approach, as I have illustrated, also has limitations. The occasions when the sexes are together should also be studied, and understood as contexts for experience and learning. For example, assymetries in cross-sex relationships convey a series of messages: that boys are more entitled to space and to the nonreciprocal right of interrupting or invading the activities of the other sex; that girls are more in need of adult protection, and are lower in status, more defined by sexuality, and may even be polluting. Different types of cross-sex interaction-relaxed, boundaried, sexualized, or taking place on the terms of the other sex-provide different contexts for development.

By mapping the array of relationships between and within the sexes, one adds complexity to the overly static and dichotomous imagery of separate worlds. Individual experiences vary, with implications for development. Some children prefer same-sex groupings; some are more likely to cross the gender boundary and participate in the world of the other sex; some children (e.g., girls and boys who frequently play "chase and kiss") invoke heterosexual meanings, while others avoid them.

Finally, after charting the terrain of relationships, one can trace their development over time. For example, age variation in the content and form of borderwork, or of cross and same-sex touch, may be related to differing cognitive, social, emotional, or physical capacities, as well as to age-associated cultural forms. I earlier mentioned temporal shifts in the organization of cross-sex chasing, from mixing with fantasy play in the early grades to more elaborately ritualized and sexualized forms by the sixth grade. There also appear to be temporal changes in same and cross-sex touch. In kindergarten, girls and boys touch one another more freely than in fourth grade, when children avoid relaxed cross-sex touch and instead use pokes, pushes, and other forms of mock violence, even when the touch clearly couches affection. This touch taboo is obviously related to the risk of seeming to *like* someone of the other sex. In fourth grade, same-sex touch begins to signal sexual meanings among boys, as well as between boys and girls. Younger boys touch one another freely in cuddling (arm around shoulder) as well as mock violence ways. By fourth grade, when homophobic taunts like "fag" become more common among boys, cuddling touch begins to disappear for boys, but less so for girls.

   Overall, I am calling for more complexity in our conceptualizations of gender and of children's social relationships. Our challenge is to retain the temporal sweep, looking at individual and group lives as they unfold over time, while also attending to social structure and context, and to the full variety of experiences in the present.

REFERENCES

Aronson, E. et al. (1978). *The jigsaw classroom.* Beverly Hills, CA: Sage.

Barth, F. (Ed.). (1969). *Elliptic groups and boundaries.* Boston: Little, Brown.

Borman, K. M. (1979). Children's interactions in playgrounds. *Theory into Practice,* 18, 251–257.

Eder, D., & Hallinan, M. T. (1978). Sex differences in children's friendships. *American Sociological Review,* 43, 237–250.

Finnan, C. R. (1982). The ethnography of children's spontaneous play. In G. Spindler (Ed.). *Doing the ethnography of schooling* (pp. 358–380). New York: Holt, Rinehart & Winston.

Foot, H. C., Chapman, A. L., & Smith. J. R. (1980). Introduction. *Friendship and social relations in children* (pp. 1–14). New York: Wiley.

Gilligan, C. (1982). *In a different voice: Psychological theory and women's development.* Cambridge, MA: Harvard University Press.

Glaser, B. G., & Strauss, A. L. (1967). *The discovery of grounded theory.* Chicago: Aldine.

Goffman, F. (1977). The arrangement between the sexes. *Theory and Society,* 4, 301–336.

Goodwin, M. H. (1980). Directive-response speech sequences in girls' and boys' task activities. In S. McConnell-Ginet, R. Borker, & N. Furman (Eds.), *Women and language in literature and society,* (pp. 157–173). New York: Praeger.

Greif, E. B. (1980). Sex differences in parent-child conversations. Women's *Studies International Quarterly,* 3, 253–258.

Henley, N. (1977). *Body politics: Power, sex, and nonverbal communication.* Englewood Cliffs, NJ: Prentice-Hall.

Karkau, K. (1973). *Sexism in the fourth grade.* Pittsburgh: KNOW, Inc. (pamphlet)

Katz, J. (1983). A theory of qualitative methodology: The social system of analytic fieldwork. In R. M. Emerson (Ed.), *Contemporary field research* (pp. 127–148). Boston: Little, Brown.

Knapp, M., & Knapp, H. (1976). *One potato, two potato: The secret education of American children.* New York: W. W. Norton.

Lever, J. (1976). Sex differences in the games children play. *Social problems,* 23, 478–487.

Maccoby, E. (1982). *Social groupings in childhood: Their relationship to prosocial and antisocial behavior in boys and girls.* Paper presented at conference on The Development of Prosocial and Antisocial Behavior. Voss, Norway.

Maccoby, E., & Jacklin, C. (1974). *The psychology of sex differences.* CA: Stanford University Press.

Maltz, D. N., & Borker, R. A. (1983). A cultural approach to male-female miscommunication. In J. J. Gumperz (Ed.), *Language and social identity* (pp. 195–216). New York: Cambridge University Press.

McRobbie, A., & Garber, J. (1975). Girls and subcultures. In S. Hall and T. Jefferson (Eds.), *Resistance through rituals* (pp. 209–223). London: Hutchinson.

Ortner, S. B., & Whitehead, H. (1981). *Social meanings.* New York: Cambridge University Press.

Parrott, S. (1972). Games children play: Ethnography of a second-grade recess. In J. P. Spradley & D. W. McCurdy (Eds.), *The cultural experience* (pp. 206–219). Chicago: Science Research Associates.

Rich, A. (1980). Compulsory heterosexuality and lesbian existence. *Signs*, 5, 631–660.

Samuelson, S. (1980). The cooties complex. *Western Folklore*, 39, 198–210.

Savin-Williams, R. C. (1976). An ethological study of dominance formation and maintenance in a group of human adolescents. *Child Development*, 47, 972–979.

Schofield, J. W. (1981). Complementary and conflicting identities: Images and interaction in an interracial school. In S. R. Asher & J. M. Gottman (Eds.), *The development of children's friendships* (pp. 53–90). New York: Cambridge University Press.

Sherif, M., & Sherif, C. (1953). *Groups in harmony and tension.* New York: Harper.

Sluckin, A. (1981). *Growing up in the plavground,* London: Roudedge & Kegan Paul.

Speier, M. (1976). The adult ideological viewpoint in studies of childhood. In A. Skolnick (Ed.), *Rethinking childhood* (pp. 168–186). Boston: Little. Brown.

Sutton-Smith, B. (1971). A syntax for play and games. In R. E. Herron and B. Sutton-Smith (Eds.), *Child's Play* (pp. 298–307). New York: Wiley.

Unger, R. K. (1979). Toward a redefinition of sex and gender. *American Psychologist*, 34, 10851–094.

Waldrop, M. F., & Halverson, C. F. (1975). Intensive and extensive peer behavior: Longitudinal and cross-sectional analysis. *Child Development*, 46, 19–26.

West, C, & Zimmerman, D. H. (1983). Small insults: A study of interruptions in cross-sex conversations between unacquainted persons. In B. Thorne, C. Kramarae, & N. Henley (Eds.), *Language, gender and society.* Rowley. MA: Newbury House.

Whitehead, H. (1981). The how and the burden strap: A new look at institutionalized homosexuality in Native America. In S. B. Ortner & H. Whitehead (Eds.), *Sexual meanings* (pp. 80–115). New York: Cambridge University Press.

SECTION V

Reworking Labor and Families

Key Concepts for Section V: Reworking Labor and Families

Aid to Families with Dependent Children
    (AFDC)
Breadwinner
Civil Marriage
Civil Union
Comparable Worth
Equal Employment Opportunity Commission
Equal Pay Day
Equal Pay Act
Export Processing Zones
Fair Pay Act
Family Friendly Work Policies
Family Medical Leave Act of 1993
Fatherhood Wage Premium
Feminization of Poverty
Food Security
Glass Ceiling
Homosocial Reproduction
Hostile Work Environment Sexual Harassment
Human Capital Approach
Lily Ledbetter Act of 2009
Low Wage Labor Market
Mommy Track
Motherhood Wage Penalty
Nuclear Family
Pay Equity Act of 1963
"the Personal is Political"
Personal Responsibility and Work
    Opportunity Reconciliation Act
    (PRWORA) of 1996
Pregnancy Discrimination Act 1978
Promotion Gap
Quid Pro Quo Sexual Harassment
Radical Heterosexuality
Reasonable Person Standard
Same-Sex Marriage
Second Shift
Sexual Harassment
Social Security Act of 1935
Sticky Floor
Temporary Assistance to Needy Families
    (TANF)
Title VII of the 1964 Civil Rights Act

Unpaid Labor
Wage gap (gender pay gap)
Welfare-to-Work

Concepts to Review

Androcentrism
Backlash
Chilly Climate
Civil Rights Restoration Act of 1987
Determinants of Women's Status
Dichotomy/Dichotomous
Differential Socialization
Division of Labor
Doing Gender
Dominance/Domination
Double Standards
Egalitarian
Exchange Value
Femininity/Femininities
Gender
Heterosexism
Hierarchy
Homophobia
Homosexuality
Marxist Theories
Masculinity/Masculinities
Microinequity
Misogyny
Myth of meritocracy
Racism
Separate Spheres (public and private)
Sex
Sex Roles
Sex Segregation
Sex-Gender System
Sexism
Sexual Harassment
Subordinance/Subordination
Title IX of Education Amendments of 1972
Title VI of the Civil Rights Act
Title VII of the Civil Rights Act
Tokenism
Use value

Radical Heterosexuality . . . Or How to Love a Man and Save Your Feminist Soul

Naomi Wolf

Naomi Wolf is the author of several books including the bestseller The Beauty Myth *(1991),* Promiscuities: The Secret Struggle for Womanhood *(1997)* The End of America: Letter of Warning to a Young Patriot *(2007), and* Give Me Liberty: A Handbook for American Revolutionaries *(2008). She has contributed essays to* The New Republic, Wall Street Journal, Glamour, Ms. *and the* New York Times. *She is the cofounder of the Woodhull Institute for Ethical Leadership. This essay first appeared in* Ms. *magazine in 1992.*

All over the country, millions of feminists have a secret indulgence. By day they fight gender injustice; by night they sleep with men. Is this a dual life? A core contradiction? Is sleeping with a man "sleeping with the enemy"? And is razor burn from kissing inherently oppressive?

It's time to say you can hate sexism and love men. As the feminist movement grows more mature and our understanding of our enemies more nuanced, three terms assumed to be in contradiction—radical feminist heterosexuality—can and must be brought together.

RULES OF THE RELATIONSHIP

But how? Andrea Dworkin and Catharine MacKinnon have pointed out that sexism limits women to such a degree that it's questionable whether the decision to live with a man can ever truly be free. If you want to use their sound, if depressing, reasoning to a brighter end, turn the thesis around: radical heterosexuality demands substituting choice for dependency.

Radical heterosexuality requires that the woman be able to support herself. This is not to belittle women who must depend financially on men; it is to recognize that when our daughters are raised with the skills that would let them leave abusers, they need not call financial dependence love.

Radical heterosexuality needs alternative institutions. As the child of a good lifetime union, I believe in them. But when I think of pledging my heart and body to a man—even the best and kindest man—within the existing institution of marriage, I feel faint. The more you learn about its legal structure, the less likely you are to call the caterers.

In the nineteenth century, when a judge ruled that a husband could not imprison and rape his wife, the London Times bemoaned, "One fine morning last month, marriage in England was suddenly abolished." The phrase "rule of thumb" descends from English common law that said a man could legally beat his wife with a switch "no thicker than his thumb."

If these nightmarish echoes were confined to history, I might feel more nuptial; but look at our own time. Do I want the blessing of an institution that doesn't provide adequate protection from marital rape? That gives a woman less protection from assault by her husband than by a stranger? That assigns men 70 percent of contested child custodies?

Of course I do not fear any such brutality from the man I want to marry (no bride does). But marriage means that his respectful treatment of me and our children becomes, despite our intentions, a kindness rather than a legally grounded right.

We need a heterosexual version of the marriages that gay and lesbian activists are seeking: a commitment untainted by centuries of inequality; a ritual that invites the community to rejoice in the making of a new freely chosen family.

The radical heterosexual man must yield the automatic benefits conferred by gender. I had a lover once who did not want to give up playing sports in a club that had a separate door for women. It must be tempting to imagine you can have both—great squash courts and the bed of a liberated woman—but in the mess hall of gender relations, there is no such thing as a free lunch.

Radical heterosexual women too must give up gender benefits (such as they are). I know scores of women—independent, autonomous—who avoid assuming any of the risk for a romantic or sexual approach.

I have watched myself stand complacently by while my partner wrestles with a stuck window, an intractable computer printer, maps, or locks. Sisters, I am not proud of this, and I'm working on it. But people are lazy—or at least I am—and it's easy to rationalize that the person with the penis is the one who should get out of a warm bed to fix the snow on the TV screen. After all, it's the very least owed to me personally in compensation for centuries of virtual enslavement.

Radical heterosexuals must try to stay conscious—at all times, I'm afraid—of their gender imprinting, and how it plays out in their erotic melodramas. My own psyche is a flagrant son et lumiere of political incorrectness. Three of my boyfriends had motorcycles; I am easy pickings for the silent and dysfunctional. My roving eye is so taken by the oil-stained persona of the labor organizer that myopic intellectuals have gained access to my favors merely by sporting a Trotsky button.

We feminists are hard on each other for admitting to weakness. Gloria Steinem caught flak from her left-wing sisters for acknowledging in Revolution from Within that she was drawn to a man because he could do the things with money and power that we are taught men must do. And some were appalled when Simone de Beauvoir's letters revealed how she coddled Sartre.

But the antifeminist erotic template is in us. We would not be citizens of this culture if swooning damsels and abandoned vixens had not been beamed at us from our first solid food to our first vote. We can't fight it until we admit to it. And we can't identify it until we drag it, its taffeta billowing and its bosom heaving, into the light of day.

I have done embarrassing, reactionary, abject deeds out of love and sexual passion. So, no doubt, has Norman Schwarzkopf. Only when we reveal our conditioning can we tell how much of our self-abasement is neurotic femininity, and how much is the flawed but impressive human apparatus of love.

IN THE BEDROOM

Those are the conditions for the radical heterosexual couple. What might this new creation look like in bed? It will look like something we have no words or images for—the eroticization of consent, the equal primacy of female and male desire.

We will need to tell some secrets—to map our desire for the male body and admit to our fascination with the rhythms and forces of male arousal, its uncanny counterintuitive spell.

We will also need to face our creature qualities. Animality has for so long been used against us—bitch, fox, Penthouse pet—that we struggle for the merit badges of higher rationality, ambivalent about our animal nature.

The truth is that heterosexual women believe that men, on some level, are animals; as they believe that we are animals. But what does "animal" mean?

Racism and sexism have long used animal metaphors to distance and degrade the Other. Let us redefine "animal" to make room for that otherness between the genders, an otherness fierce and worthy of respect. Let us define animal as an inchoate kinship, a comradeship, that finds a language beyond our species.

I want the love of two unlikes: the look of astonishment a woman has at the sight of a male back bending. These manifestations of difference confirm in heterosexuals the beauty that similarity confirms in the lesbian or gay imagination. Difference and animality do not have to mean hierarchy.

MEN WE LOVE

What must the men be like? Obviously, they're not going to be just anyone. Esquire runs infantile disquisitions on "Women We Love" (suggesting, Lucky Girls!). Well, I think that the men who are loved by feminists are lucky. Here's how they qualify to join this fortunate club.

Men We Love understand that, no matter how similar our backgrounds, we are engaged in a cross-cultural (if not practically biracial) relationship. They know that we know much about their world and they but little of ours. They accept what white people must accept in relationships with people of other ethnicities: to know that they do not know.

Men We Love don't hold a baby as if it is a still-squirming, unidentifiable catch from the sea.

Men We Love don't tell women what to feel about sexism. (There's a postcard that shows a dashing young fellow, drawn Love-comix-style, saying to a woman, "Let me explicate to you the nature of your oppression.") They do not presume that there is a line in the sand called "enlightened male," and that all they need is a paperback copy of Djuna Barnes and good digital technique. They understand that unlearning gender oppressiveness means untying the very core of how we become female and male. They know this pursuit takes a lifetime at the minimum.

Sadly, men in our lives sometimes come through on personal feminism but balk at it intellectually. A year ago, I had a bruising debate with my father and brother about the patriarchal nature of traditional religious and literary canons. I almost seized them by their collars, howling "Read Mary Daly! Read Toni Morrison! Take Feminism 101. No, I can't explain it to you between the entree and dessert!"

By spring, my dad, bless his heart, had asked for a bibliography, and last week my brother sent me Standing Again at Sinai, a Jewish-feminist classic. Men We Love are willing, sooner or later, to read the Books We Love.

Men We Love accept that successful training in manhood makes them blind to phenomena that are fact to women. Recently, I walked down a New York City avenue with a woman friend, X, and a man friend, Y. I pointed out to Y the leers, hisses, and invitations to sit on faces. Each woman saw clearly what the other woman saw, but Y was baffled. Sexual harassers have superb timing. A passerby makes kissy-noises with his tongue while Y is scrutinizing the menu of the nearest bistro. "There, there! Look! Listen!" we cried. "What? Where? Who?" wailed poor Y, valiantly, uselessly spinning.

What if, hard as they try to see, they cannot hear? Once I was at lunch with a renowned male crusader for the First Amendment. Another Alpha male was present, and the venue was the

Supreme Court lunchroom—two power factors that automatically press the "mute" button on the male ability to detect a female voice on the audioscope. The two men began to rev their motors; soon they were off and racing in a policy-wonk grand prix. I tried, once or twice, to ask questions. But the free-speech champions couldn't hear me over the testosterone roar.

Men We Love undertake half the care and cost of contraception. They realize that it's not fair to wallow in the fun without sharing the responsibility. When stocking up for long weekends, they brave the amused glances when they ask, "Do you have this in unscented?"

Men We Love know that just because we can be irrational doesn't mean we're insane. When we burst into premenstrual tears—having just realized the cosmic fragility of creation—they comfort us. Not until we feel better do they dare remind us gently that we had this same revelation exactly 28 days ago.

Men We Love must make a leap of imagination to believe in the female experience. They do not call women nags or paranoid when we embark on the arduous, often boring, nonnegotiable daily chore of drawing attention to sexism. They treat it like adults taking driving lessons: if irked in the short term at being treated like babies, they're grateful in the long term that someone is willing to teach them patiently how to move through the world without harming the pedestrians. Men We Love don't drive without their gender glasses on.

A PLACE FOR THEM

It's not simple gender that pits Us against Them. In the fight against sexism, it's those who are for us versus those who are against us—of either gender.

When I was 16, my boyfriend came with me to hear Andrea Dworkin speak. While hearing great feminist oratory in a sea of furious women changed my life, it nearly ended my boyfriend's: he barely escaped being drawn and quartered.

It is time to direct our anger more acutely at the Men We Hate—like George Bush—and give the Men We Love something useful to do. Not to take over meetings, or to set agendas; not to whine, "Why can't feminists teach us how to be free?" but to add their bodies, their hearts, and their numbers, to support us.

I meet many young men who are brought to feminism by love for a woman who has been raped, or by watching their single mothers struggle against great odds, or by simple common sense. Their most frequent question is, "What can I do to help?"

Imagine a rear battalion of committed "Men Against Violence Against Women" (or Men for Choice, or what have you)—of all races, ages, and classes. Wouldn't that be a fine sight to fix in the eyes of a five-year-old boy?

Finally, the place to make room for radical feminist heterosexuality is within our heads. If the movement that I dearly love has a flaw, it is a tendency toward orthodoxies about other women's pleasures and needs. This impulse is historically understandable: in the past, we needed to define ourselves against men if we were to define ourselves at all. But today, the most revolutionary choice we can make is to affirm other women's choices, whether lesbian or straight, bisexual or celibate.

NOW President Patricia Ireland speaks for me even though our sexual lives are not identical. Simone de Beauvoir speaks for me even though our sexual lives are not identical. Audre Lorde speaks for me even though our sexual lives are not identical. Is it the chromosomes of your lovers that establish you as a feminist? Or is it the life you make out of the love you make?

"It's Almost Like I Have a Job, but I Don't Get Paid"
Fathers at Home Reconfiguring Work, Care, and Masculinity

Andrea Doucet

Andrea Doucet *earned a PhD in Social & Political Sciences at Cambridge University. She is an Associate Professor in the Department of Sociology and Anthropology at Carleton University in Canada. In addition to her research and teaching on gender and the impact of fathering, mothering, and work, she also worked for several years as a gender and development consultant in Central and South America and the Caribbean. Her most recent book,* Gender Relations: Intersectionality and Beyond *(2008) was co-written with Janet Siltanen. This essay appeared in* Fathering, *a journal of the* Men's Studies Press, *in 2004.*

It's funny. There were lots of pros and cons about being home. . . . One of the things I missed was that you lose a sense of stature, a sense of common ground between myself and other men, a sense of being able to say—"Hey, I'm a man too." I think a lot of that revolved around not having employment. Not working and being at home. For me not working was the bigger issue than being at home. . . . I liked the domestic stuff, cooking and all that. I like that stuff a lot. But I missed work. . . . As a man you have no status at all if you don't work (Adam).

Adam, a 42-year-old man living in rural Ontario, was a stay-at-home father of three children for a decade. He is one of 70 fathers in the study, as well as part of a larger study of Canadian fathers who self-define as primary caregivers of their children. Adam's children are older now (17, 15, and 11), and he works full-time as an economist for the government, yet he still remembers the difficulties he faced when he was not employed outside of the home. He began his interview by saying that although he "liked the domestic stuff, cooking and all that," it was "not working" that posed such difficulties for him "as a man." In speaking about his typical weekly and daily routine when his first two children, Jeffrey and Bryn, were pre-kindergarten age, he immediately let me know that he also fixed cars while he cared for his young son and daughter:

Jeffrey and I, those first two years, were joined at the hip. And then Bryn and I were joined at the hip for the next while. We did a lot of stuff whereby they would come along with me to do things. Jeffrey would hang around when I was doing things. Like we had a series of old cars. He would hang around while I fixed the cars.

While Adam made a link between caring and repairing cars, all of the fathers' narratives were peppered with references to varied configurations of paid and unpaid work. It was clear that while fathers were at home, they were also carving out complex sets of relations between home, paid and unpaid work, community work, and their own sense of masculinity. In seeking to explore the ways that work and family interact for stay-at-home fathers, this paper argues that they reconstruct the meanings of both, while also demonstrating complex intersections between work, home, community, and masculinity.

The paper makes three key arguments, all of which pull together these intricate connections. First, fathers retain very close links to paid work even when they have temporarily or permanently left a career to care for children. While there are three dominant patterns that characterize fathers' home-work balances, all of the fathers fall under the weight of community scrutiny for being primary caregivers and not primary breadwinners, thus confirming research that has argued that mothers' and fathers' "moral" responsibilities as carers and earners remain differently framed and experienced (Berk, 1985; Finch & Mason, 1993; McMahon, 1995). Second, where fathers have given up a formal investment in the full-time labor force, many replace employment with "self-provisioning" work (Gershuny & Pahl, 1979; Pahl, 1984; Wallace, 2002; Wallace & Pahl, 1985) that allows them to contribute economically to the household economy as well as to display masculine practices, both to themselves and their wider community. That is, although stay-at-home fathers "trade cash for care" (Hobson & Morgan, 2002, p. 1), they also remain connected to traditionally masculine sources of identity such as paid work as well as self-provisioning at home and in the community as public displays of masculinity. Their narratives speak volumes about the ways in which the long shadow of hegemonic masculinity hangs over them. Third and finally, this paper argues that stay-at-home fathers' narratives of emergent and generative practices of caring represent a slow process of critical resistance as they begin to critique concepts of "male time" (Daly, 1996; Davies, 1990, 1994) and market capitalism approaches to work and care (Crittenden, 2001; Folbre, 2001; Williams, 2000).

The paper concludes by suggesting that fathers neither reproduce nor challenge hegemonic masculinity, as has been argued recently by some authors (Brandth & Kvande, 1998; Dryden, 1999; but see Plantin, Sven-Axel, & Kearney, 2003). Rather, stay-at-home fathers create new forms of masculinity that, while enacted against a weighty backdrop of hegemonic masculinity, nevertheless incorporate varied aspects of femininities. This paper hints at the need for discussions on men and masculinities to move into new theoretical ground that can assist us in making sense of fathers' living and working in traditional female dominated or symbolically feminine domains. These arguments and findings are based on a qualitative research project with and on Canadian fathers, which will be described below, following a brief outline of the theoretical perspectives informing this work.

THEORETICAL FRAMEWORKS

My study on fathering is framed by a layered process of investigating and understanding the social worlds inhabited—and co-constructed—by fathers and others. Several overlapping bodies of theory underpin this research, including structuration theory (Bourdieu & Wacquant, 1992; Connell, 1987; Giddens, 1984), a focus on gender relations and gender regimes (Connell, 1987, 1995, 2000; Smith, 1987, 1996), and a critical realist position (Code, 1993; Sayer, 1999). This work is further framed by symbolic interactionism, studies on fatherhood, and feminist and profeminist work on masculinities and femininities. Only the latter three theoretical approaches will be discussed here since they are most relevant to the findings presented in this paper.

Symbolic Interactionism and Family Life

The study that informs this paper is rooted in principles of symbolic interactionism and by a rich tradition of family research that employs such principles (Barker, 1994; Daly, 1996, 2002; Finch & Mason, 1993; McMahon, 1995). Particular emphasis is placed on attempts to gain people's accounts of their own understandings and actions as well as how they, in turn, interpret these understandings and actions in light of the observations and judgments of other people. A central concept within my work has been that of moral dimensions of fathering and mothering, as well detailed in Janet Finch and Jennifer Mason's work (1993) on negotiating eldercare responsibilities, particularly in their discussion of the interwoven material and moral dimensions of family responsibilities. Drawing on symbolic interactionist ideas, they argue that it is "through human interaction that people develop a common understanding of what a particular course of action will *mean*: for example, if I offer financial help to my mother in her old age, will it seem generous, or demeaning, or whatever?" (Finch & Mason, 1993, p. 61). These ideas are applicable to our understandings of mothering and fathering and are intricately connected to "people's identities as moral beings" that "are being constructed, confirmed and reconstructed—identities as a reliable son, a generous mother, a caring sister or whatever it might be" (Finch & Mason, 1993, p. 170). To add a moral dimension is to incorporate an understanding of the critical role of social networks, how fathers and mothers feel they should act, and how they think others within their community networks will view these actions (Mauthner, 2002; McMahon, 1995).

Studies on Fatherhood and Gender Divisions of Domestic Labour

My study is also rooted in a burgeoning and excellent body of scholarship on fatherhood and gender divisions of domestic labor. This literature has drawn attention to the continued salience of key obstacles to greater fatherhood involvement including, for example, the role of work in fathers' lives (Deutsch, 1999; Dowd, 2000; Pleck, 1985), parental modeling after one's own father (Coltrane, 1996; Cowan & Cowan, 1987, Daly, 1993; Pleck, 1985; Snarey, 1993), maternal gatekeeping from wives or female partners (Allen & Hawkins, 1999; Parke, 1996; Pleck, 1985), co-constructed processes of "doing gender" by both mothers and fathers (Berk, 1985; Coltrane, 1989, 1996; Risman, 1998; West & Zimmerman, 1987), gender identities and ideologies (Deutsch, 1999; Hochschild, 1989), and discourses of fatherhood (Dienhart, 1998; Lupton & Barclay, 1997; Mandell, 2002). My work recognizes the validity of all of these facilitating and constraining factors in fathers' involvement but also gives greater emphasis to the role of social networks and the community as well as to the moral assumptions about what it means to be a "good mother" or a "good father," which are held and reinforced within particular communities.

Men and Masculinities

In addition to symbolic interactionist studies on families and research on gender divisions of labour, my work on fathering is also heavily influenced by theoretical literature on men and masculinities. Five points, gleaned from the literature on masculinities, underpin this paper. First, while there has been much debate on the usefulness of the concept "masculinities" (Clatterbaugh, 1998; Hearn, 1996), I hold with Connell that "we need some way of talking about men and women's involvement in the domain of gender "and that masculinities and femininities remain theoretically useful concepts to assist us with making sense of understanding gender relations as well as "gender ambiguity" (Connell, 2000, pp. 16-17). Second, there are a plurality of masculinities (Brittan, 1989; Hearn & Morgan, 1990); the meanings of masculinities differ across and within settings, and there are, at the level of practice, varied kinds of relations between different kinds of masculinities (Connell, 2000). Third, masculinities are not essences but occur in social relations where issues of power and difference are at play and where masculinities exist at both the level of agency and structure. As detailed by Connell, "The patterns of conduct our society defines as masculine may be seen in the lives of individuals, but they also have an existence beyond the individual. Masculinities are defined in culture and sustained in institutions" (Connell, 2000, p. 11). A fourth point is that there is a distinction between men and masculinities in that "sometimes masculine conduct or masculine identity goes together with a female body" and, similarly, it is also "very common for a (biological) man to have elements of feminine identity, desire and patterns of conduct" (Connell, 2000, p. 16). These observations are particularly astute when studying men who are engaging in female-dominated or feminine-identified work such as caregiving.

A fifth critical point about masculinity relates to the much discussed concept of "hegemonic masculinity" (Coltrane, 1994; Connell, 1987, 1995, 2000; Kimmel, 1994; Messner, 1997). Traditionally it has been defined as "the most honored or desired" form of masculinity (Connell 2000, p. 10), one that usually aligns itself with traditional masculine qualities of "being strong, successful, capable, reliable, in control. That is (t)he hegemonic definition of manhood is a man *in* power, a man *with* power, and a man *of* power" (Kimmel, 1994, p. 125). Further, as Connell points out, hegemonic masculinity is perhaps most strongly identified "as the opposite of femininity" (Connell, 2000, p. 31). Other forms of masculinity, then, have come to be viewed as *subordinated* (especially gay masculinities), *marginalized* (exploited or oppressed groups such as ethnic minorities), and *complicit* masculinities (those organized around the complicit acceptance of what has come to be termed a "patriarchal dividend" (Connell, 1995, 2000).

While initial discussions of hegemonic masculinity were largely embraced within the community of scholars working on masculinity, the gaps between varied masculinities and between theory and practice have recently begun to emerge. Increased empirical and ethnographic studies of men's lives have shed light on the diverse ways that hegemonic, subordinated, and complicit masculinities can play out in the same setting. In particular, the issue of where caring and fathering fits into this spectrum is one that requires greater attention. Some authors have argued that fathers' caring practices are "adopted by the hegemonic form of masculinity" so that, rather than challenge hegemonic masculinity, caring becomes incorporated into it (Brandth & Kvande, 1998; Dryden, 1999). Others have recently argued that fathering and caring can be seen as *complicit* in that fathers can express support for equal parenting while also maintaining more traditional patterns of gender divisions of labor (see Plantin, Sven-Axel, & Kearney, 2003). Whatever the configuration of diverse masculinities, it is clear that "the interplay between hegemonic and subordinate masculinities suggests the experience of masculinity is far from uniform and that new ways of theorizing these differences need to be developed" (Hearn & Morgan, 1990, p. 11). Moreover, as indicated by Connell, research on these varied combinations of masculinities "is surely an empirical question, not one to be settled in advance by theory" (Connell, 2000, p. 23).

A key question, then, in empirical studies of fathers' lives is how their everyday caring practices confirm or challenge current theoretical understandings of masculinities. Given the continuing salience of the concept of hegemonic masculinity, it is thus worth asking whether or not fathers as carers exhibit subordinated, complicit or hegemonic masculinity. Furthermore, given that hegemonic masculinity is largely associated with the devaluation of the feminine while caring is often equated with feminine practice, what is the relationship between hegemonic masculinity and care? Does fathers' caregiving disrupt the smooth surfaces of hegemonic masculinity? In examining stay-at-home fathers' home-work balances, this question will be explored in this paper.

METHOD

The arguments developed in this paper draw from a four-year qualitative research study on changing fatherhood. The study's location is Canada where, as in many other industrialized nations, demographic and social factors have translated into the need to redistribute the caring work traditionally assumed by women. My central interest in undertaking this study was to gain a sense of how fathering and mothering were changing against shifting social and economic landscapes. More specifically, I was interested in understanding men's lives and masculinities in the midst of dramatic changes in family life and to engage with David Morgan's compelling claim that "one strategy of studying men and masculinities would be to study those situations where masculinity is, as it were, on the line" (Morgan, 1992, p. 99). My research thus adopted a central case study of men who self-define as primary caregivers (stay-at-home fathers and single fathers) since practices, identities, and discourses of caring remain strongly linked with femininity and women's social lives (Finch & Mason, 1993; Fox, 2001; Graham, 1983; McMahon, 1995).

Sample

The larger study on primary caregiving fathers that underpins this paper includes an extensive range of caregiving experiences: 40 single fathers (28 sole custody, nine joint custody, and three widowers); 58 stay-at-home fathers (at home for at least one year, including two fathers on paid and unpaid parental leave for one year); and 12 fathers who are single and are/were stay-at-home. In the later stages of the study, I broadened my categories to include 10 shared caregiving fathers—in an effort to include participants who did not necessarily fit into the categories of stay-at-home fathers or single fathers. I was thus able to include gay fathers who did not have legal custody but were active caregivers in their children's lives and several immigrant fathers for whom stay-at-home fathering was not readily compatible with their cultural traditions.

This particular paper focuses on the narratives of 70 fathers who have had the experience of being at home with their children for at least a year. The overwhelming majority of stay-at-home fathers had partners living with them while they were at home (64/70). For the six fathers who were both single *and* at home, only one father was raising his child without any participation of the child's mother. The broad majority of these fathers (53/70 or 76%) are currently at home with their children whereas 13/70 fathers reflected back to when they were stay-at-home fathers; this latter group of fathers were included in the study so as to gain a sense of the differing experiences and social supports over time for stay-at-home fathers. The fathers who participated in the study saw themselves as primary or shared primary caregivers of children, and 70 fathers were identified as stay-at-home fathers on the basis of their leaving full-time work for a period of a year or more or through arranging their part-time or flexible working around their childcare responsibilities.

The study employed a wide sampling strategy; fathers were recruited through schools and varied community centers (i.e., health-related, community, and ethnic minority groups), in parks and playgrounds, and through placing ads in mainstream Canadian newspapers and in many small community papers. Finally, several fathers were found through snowball sampling whereby one father would provide me with the name of an acquaintance (Miles & Huberman, 1994). For the 70 stay-at-home fathers whose narratives inform this paper, geographical location is as follows: 46 fathers from Ottawa, the capital city of Canada, a further 12 from other parts of Ontario (two from Ontario cities and 10 from small towns and rural communities), and 12 fathers from six other Canadian provinces. The sample of 70 stay-at-home fathers was very diverse in terms of occupations, social class, and education levels. The sample also includes participation from 10 fathers from visible ethnic minorities, two First Nation fathers, and two gay fathers.

Interviewing and Analysis

The interviewing of the 70 stay-at-home fathers occurred between 2000 and 2003 in the following ways: 48 in person (46 face-to-face interviews and two fathers through focus groups), 12 by telephone, and 10 by Web correspondence. Web correspondence was used in order to attract a larger number of fathers to the study as well as to include fathers who might prefer a more limited involvement in the project. In the end, one-third of the Web-based surveys with stay-at-home fathers (i.e., 5/15) were followed up with face-to-face or telephone interviews. The Web-based data were viewed as a supplement to the main data set of in-depth interviews. While approximately one-fourth of the accounts were retrospective, in my analysis I did not treat these accounts differently from the more current ones except to place them in differing social contexts from which these stories are produced.

Fourteen heterosexual couples (with a stay-at-home father and with some diversity along the lines of income, social class, and ethnicity) were interviewed in order to include some mothers' (and couples') views in the study. As the project's lead researcher with a strong belief in the epistemological significance and importance of data collection sites and interactions, I personally interviewed all of the fathers except for one (i.e., 45 of the 46 individual interviews and all of the telephone interviews, focus groups, and couple interviews).

Analysis of the data consisted of several components. First, research assistants carried out in-depth readings of verbatim interview transcripts on their own and then in conjunction with me, utilizing the "Listening Guide" (Brown & Gilligan, 1992; Mauthner & Doucet, 1998, 2003). My layered theoretical approach, moving heuristically from individuals to social relationships to wider social structures, was reflected in the multiple readings employed within this analytic strategy. Group discussions of common themes and issues were then conducted, thus producing divergent or shared interpretations of particular transcripts and the subsequent development of 25 case studies. A final stage of analysis entailed a lengthy process of coding (conducted mainly by myself) using the data analysis computer program, ATLAS.ti data analysis brought forth many interesting findings about fathers' experiences of caregiving and their home-work balances; these findings will be illustrated through brief snapshots from the fathers' narratives.

Paid Work and Home

For the 70 stay-at-home fathers, three sets of patterns, with varying degrees of overlap, characterized their home-work balances. First, there were 12 fathers who had achieved financial and professional success and wanted to take a break from working and/or were seeking to move into another line of work once their children were in school. The overarching commonality with this group of fathers was that they seemed to have achieved their career goals and were looking for other forms of fulfillment, one of which was caring for their children as well as alternative work or leisure interests (e.g., travel, sports, writing). Second, 28 fathers were taking a break from working (as was the case with the two fathers on extended parental leave), were in a clear transition between jobs, were planning to go back to college or university for further education or training, or were currently taking evening courses along this path. Third, 30 fathers were working part-time, flexibly from a home office, or as an employee in their wife/partner's business; of these 30 fathers, 10 (one-third) were both working part-time *and* in transition between jobs. For all of these stay-at-home fathers, the decision to relinquish full-time employment was a result of a complex mix of factors that included variations of the following themes: their wife/partner having the higher income with employment benefits and a stronger career interest (at this stage of their lives); strong views on the importance of home care; the view that there was a paucity of good childcare facilities in Canada; the cost of childcare; and, in some cases, a child with particular developmental, physical or health needs. Each of the three patterns of home-work balances will be illustrated through a brief case study.

Fathers with Work Success: "It's Not Like I'm Saying 'This Kid is Holding Me Back'"

The first pathway to staying at home is well represented in the case study of Rory, a 53-year-old stay-at-home father living in Calgary, Alberta, who gave up his consulting business as quality-control expert on gas pipelines to stay at home with Tristan, who is now seven years old. His wife is a high-level civil servant with the provincial government. At home for four years, he has been president of the school's parent council, takes language courses to assist with French immersion schooling, and cooks a daily special diet for his son, who has debilitating food allergies. He also renovates the home and takes on community work that relates to his son's interests. In his words, "The way I see it, if my son is really interested in something, I am really interested in it. If not, I don't have the time." Rory describes the reasoning behind his decision to leave work:

> He had been having problems with a stutter and he had been in a home daycare. We were both working. The kids in the daycare all had colds, so I kept him home. Things were pretty slow at work that week. So we decided I would stay home with him that week. His stutter started to get better. The next week he stayed home because he had the cold. Then his stutter got even better. And so I said to my wife, "If this is what it is going to take to get him better, then this is what I will do."

Unlike many of the stay-at-home fathers, Rory seems to have a particular sense of ease about his time at home. At the end of the interview, he adds that they have no debt, the house has been paid off, his wife is younger than he is, it was her turn for her career to take off, and his age is definitely a factor in his sense of ease:

> If I had been 20 years old with a son with a stutter and food allergies, I would have responded completely differently. How I would have, I don't know, but I would have responded differently. . . . I mean, I have traveled; I have worked in many different places. It's not like I'm saying that this kid is holding me back.

Two other fathers can be briefly mentioned here as good illustrations of this pattern of fathers who had achieved work success. Martin, a 42-year-old father of a preschool boy and a second generation Czech Canadian who worked as an insurance adjuster for 20 years, says:

> I don't have a huge stigma about not being out there earning the money. Again, it's probably because Denise and I just worked it out in a way . . . like, I worked the first 20 years. We joke about it once in a while. Well, I just worked the first 20 years, and I worked to help pay off her student loans and get those paid off, and that was all on my back. I worked since I was 17.

Richard, a French Canadian stay-at-home father of three who was a car mechanic for many years, is quite blunt about his aspirations for a career: "I've done it. I did it before. I made money. I went to work. I used to have expectations and dreams. And I don't want to work anymore."

Fathers like Rory, Martin, and Richard who identified themselves as having met their own standards of employment success were a small part of the study. It was more likely that most of the fathers, as described in the next two sections, were in transition between jobs and/or working part-time.

Fathers in Transition: "This is Not the Kind of Thing I Want to Do for the Rest of My Life"

Approximately 37% of the stay-at-home fathers (28 fathers) were in transition between jobs or careers. Craig, a 40-year old stay-at-home father to triplets, four-year old Michael and Zachary, and Jonathon who had recently died, typifies the "in transition" father. Although identifying himself as a musician, his *paid* job for many years was in auto parts as a mechanic. Craig now works at a home hardware store for two evenings a week and Saturdays; his plans are that he is eventually "going back to school in computers." When I ask him how he came to be at home with his sons, he responds:

> When my wife became pregnant—my wife is a psychiatric nurse, she has a career. . . . I am a musician from a long time ago, and that's what I like to do primarily. My job was just that, it was not a career, so it was a very easy choice. We looked at it, and I was working in auto parts, mostly car dealerships, and before that I was in forklifts and things like that, parts for these machines. But we looked at it, and when we found out that it was going to be triplets and without even thinking that there would be anything other than three happy normal bouncing kids running around, my salary would have been eaten up by daycare, and I figured well, what the heck, we're going to be in the same boat financially, so I'll stay home until they go to school. That's how we came to the decision; it took us like not even a minute to come to that decision.

A similar story is provided by Andrew, a water supply engineer whose wife has a demanding job that involves international travel. He says: "I was also thinking about getting out of the business anyway. This is not the kind of thing I want to do for the rest of my life. We thought two years. Ideally three." In the end, Andrew stayed home for two years and then went back to a teachers' college when his children were both in school.

Within this group of in-transition fathers, some had lost their jobs, others went through a serious illness that forced them to re-think their career paths at the same time as they were juggling expensive childcare arrangements, and still others found that their jobs were "dead-end" ones that did not justify two stressful jobs and the high cost of childcare. While some men took a break altogether in order to concentrate on the demands of childcare while simultaneously preparing for a new career, others, as described in the next section, took on part-time work or moved their jobs into a more home-based setting.

Fathers Juggling Paid Work and Caring: "My Shop Is in the Garage"

Of the 70 stay-at-home fathers in the study, 30 fathers were employed in part-time jobs or were working flexible hours from a home-based workplace. Within this group, one-third of the fathers were also in transition between careers but were working part-time to supplement the family income. Shahin, a 43-year-old Iranian Canadian, provides a good example of the home-working father. Shahin began staying at home with his son, now six years old, when his wife, a French-Canadian lawyer, went back to work after a four-month maternity leave. A self-employed cabinetmaker, he has a workshop in his garage. In reflecting upon how he and his wife came to the decision that he stay at home, he says:

> Well, the decision was, I think, rather simple because my wife makes more money than I do, and I did not want my son to be raised without at least one parent at home . . . So the decision was made on that basis, based on economical feasibility. It just seemed more logical for me to stay home, especially since I have my own business. I could do at least part-time work.

In his long descriptions about his routine when his son was an infant, he frequently invoked the way in which he juggled work at home and childcare:

> My shop is in my garage. It's rather practical. So I had the monitor in the shop. . . . He had this rocking chair . . . you know, you put the baby in there, and it goes back and forth. He loved to sleep in it and it was 45 minutes, I think, the cycle. So I used to run every half an hour and crank it up.

Shahin and 29 other fathers kept their hand in paid work through part-time or home-based working. The range of occupations and creative flexibility within this group was astounding. Of the 30 stay-at-home fathers who work part-time, several diverse examples can be highlighted. Sam is a driving instructor two evenings a week and Saturdays. Jamal, a Somali immigrant father, takes care of his two sons during the day while his wife studies English, and he works nights conducting surveys by phone. Brandon, a sole-custody father, has balanced the raising of his three sons with running his organic farm. Jerome, at home for the past 11 years, works about eight hours a week as office manager in his wife's pediatrician practice in a small Nova Scotia town. Cameron has taken in a foster son, which "allows me to stay at home and look after the kids. Otherwise, we couldn't survive on the one salary." Finally, Harry at home for the past nine years in rural Ontario has taken on many different jobs: "I've helped the neighbors with the hay and, well, . . . I do cleaning for two hours a week at the church in Griffith . . . I have my chickens and the garden. . . . And last year I looked after a couple of other kids in the morning—well, I got paid for putting them all on the bus."

The patterns described above could be viewed as somewhat similar to those taken by mothers as they seek to find creative ways of combining working and caring. Anita Garey (1999), for example, in her work on women "weaving work and motherhood," details a wide array of patterning for working mothers, including varied kinds of "sequencing" and the "midlife switch" (pp. 165-190). Her work has some parallels with the narratives of the fathers in this study. One large difference, however, is that the majority of fathers in my study felt compelled to talk about paid work in relation to caring, whereas mothers, as described by Garey, were more likely to focus on how their caring responsibilities were not hindered by working. There is thus a slight shift in the balance of emphasis with fathers feeling the weight and pull of moral responsibilities as earners whereas mothers feel pulled by a moral responsibility to care. This is explored more fully in the section that follows.

The Weight of Social Scrutiny and Gendered Moral Responsibilities: "I Felt I Wasn't Being a Good Man"

Each and every father interviewed referred in some way to the weight of community scrutiny and how he felt social pressure to be earning. Some fathers claimed that they were unaffected by this pressure, but nevertheless they all felt this societal gaze upon them. Peter, a stay-at-home father of two young sons for the past five years, describes this quite well. His former job in desktop publishing was gradually phased out, but he was able to maintain his connection with his former employer and take on contract work for about 12 hours a week from a home office. His wife is a high school teacher. He very much identifies with the "stay-at-home father" label and has done some media appearances on this. Nevertheless, he says:

> Despite that fact, I've always—in social occasions, dinner parties, talking with other people, or whatever—other men, I guess, especially—just being able to talk about something I do in the *"real world"* was kind of important socially—that didn't make me sound limited, or stuck . . . to show that I am able to work, although I have chosen to do this.

Marc, a father who began staying at home 15 years ago with his two young sons, also talks about how important it was to be able to say that he was working and that "it was hard at times, and quite honestly I am not sure that I would have done it full time for as long as I did if I had not been working part-time, if I didn't have some sense of worth." He further points to how different moral expectations weigh on women and men and that both he and his wife felt the pressure to fulfill their traditional gendered roles with him "providing more money for the family" and his wife "filling her traditional role." He says:

> Back then, I think there were times when I felt I wasn't being a good man, by not providing more money for the family. And that I wasn't doing something more masculine. And there were times when my wife felt that she wasn't filling her traditional role as a wife and a mother.

While Marc mentions how he felt judged for not "being a good man," Archie goes further to suggest that communities cast a suspicious eye toward men at home. Archie, who used to work as a gas service technician and has been home for seven years, says: "For the most part, there is a sense that if a man stays home there is something wrong with him, he's lost his job, or he's a little off kilter. It's not their job. They shouldn't be there."

A final example of the expression of this negative social gaze on fathers who relinquish a primary identity as breadwinner is given by Jesse, a freelance artist and stay-at-home father, for two years, of a now three-year-old daughter. He pulls together the ways in which these perceptions are "so engrained" through men's upbringing, how it "can weigh on you" and the particularly gendered quality of this ("*It's a guy thing*"):

> These things are so ingrained in us. . . . It can weigh on you, those kinds of things. Sometimes I do wonder if people have that sort of perception of me as a stay-at-home father. I am still not sure if there is a widespread acceptance of it. I think some people still wonder, "Why is the father at home? Like he can't earn as much as his partner or something?" I struggle with that, because it is also my own internalized kind of condition, too, that I have this struggle. You know, my background, working class, a strong work ethic. And it's a guy thing.

In referring to "a guy thing," these fathers are implicitly referring to the connections between dominant or hegemonic masculinity and paid work and the associated sense of vertigo that men feel when they relinquish earning as a primary part of their identity (LaBier, 1986; Pahl, 1995; Waddington, Chritcher, & Dicks, 1998). Fathers remained connected with paid work partly to maintain a link with masculine conceptions of identity and to respond to deeply felt moral precepts that, as one father put it, "There's a certain male imperative to be bringing in money, to feel like you are actually caring for your family, a sense of providing." One of the ways that men deal with these losses is to take on unpaid work that has masculine qualities.

UNPAID WORK AND HOME

Whatever the status of their relationship with paid work, the overwhelming majority of fathers made it a point to let me know that they were taking on self-provisioning work, mainly "working on the house," and/or doing community work. These two strands of unpaid work will be examined here.

Self-Provisioning: "We Get Together and Talk Tools"

Most of the stay-at-home fathers spoke about work they were doing on the house, landscaping, carpentry, woodworking or repairing cars. Richard, for example, a 39-year-old French Canadian father, draws attention to this issue without even being asked about it. He left his work as an electronic technician two years ago to be at home with his children, now aged seven and two, plus a two-month-old infant. In his joint interview with his wife, Richard takes out a photo album and shows me before-and-after pictures of his household renovation, saying, "Now you can see how much I've done." He enjoys the domestic routine and has excelled at making award-winning birthday cakes for the kids (and proudly shows photos of his creations); he also makes homemade baby food and does a batch of jams and jellies every fall. When I ask him about the long-term plans, he says, "I am not going back to work," but rather, as he says:

I'll be doing work on the house. Renovations. Cooking, cleaning. They're only gone for six hours. I'll probably be more involved in the school. I'll do these things I've been wanting to do for years. Simple things like organizing my recipes. Organizing my tapes and music. . . . I have a lot of projects that I want to do in woodworking, but I don't have the time.

Like Richard, many of the stay-at-home fathers in this study reconstruct the meanings of work and home to include unpaid self-provisioning work (Pahl, 1984; Wallace & Pahl, 1985), specifically "male self-provisioning activities" (Mingione, 1988, p. 560) that include "building, renovation . . . carpentry, electrical repairs and plumbing, furniture making, decorating, constructing doors and window frames, agricultural cultivation for own use, repairing vehicles" (see Mingione, 1988, pp. 560-561). While some of these can be viewed as masculine hobbies, which these men would have likely picked up from their fathers or male peers, these are also activities that display or justify men's masculinity and seem to alleviate some of the discomfort men feel with giving up breadwinning.

Fathers' narratives are replete with references to masculine self-provisioning activities. For example, Howard, a stay-at-home father for five years of two school-aged children, highlights how he likes the renovation but not cleaning: "I do a lot of work around the house. I do the renovation, the house repairs, and a lot of construction. . . . I don't like cleaning. I like renovations and home repair work." Meanwhile, Luke, who works with mentally challenged adults and has been a stay-at-home parent for 12 years while working nights at a group home, says: "I'm always building something. I'm a renovator. I've renovated the whole house, all on my own." Martin, who often takes his four-year-old son to Home Depot, describes his typical day with Ethan and then notes how the day comes to an end: "And then as soon as Denise gets in, I'm gone! I go down to the basement and work on renovations for an hour, an hour and a half." Tom, a stay-at-home father of three children in rural Quebec, shows me his woodworking shed at the end of our interview. In talking about his typical week, he also adds that in addition to caring for the kids: "I'll call my neighbors whom I do woodworking with, and we'll talk woodworking. . . . That's a guy thing. . . . We get together and talk tools, and that is great."

These accounts add to the evidence detailed by family scholars on the intricate intersections between the theoretical concepts and physical sites of home and work. Feminist scholars, for example, have long pointed to how women have often found ways to add to the family economy through household provisioning work (Bradbury, 1984; Folbre, 1991; Land, 1980; Mackintosh, 1988). Moreover, while most studies on divisions of household labor have focused on a range of domestically based tasks such as cooking, cleaning, shopping for groceries, shopping for children's clothes, and laundry (i.e., Risman, 1998, p. 59; Brannen & Moss, 1994; Duetcher, 1999; Hochschild, 1989), my amendment to these studies would be to argue for greater inclusion of nonroutine domestic tasks such as household repair and maintenance.

A further line of argument that bolsters this claim for a wider conception of the domestic is that developed decades ago by Gershuny and Pahl wherein they maintained that households devise complex sets of "household work strategies" based on differing ways of working between the household, the community, and the formal economy (Gershuny & Pahl, 1979). More recent thinking on "household work strategies" and "self-provisioning" has highlighted how the decision about which work to do oneself and which work to contract out is partly based on "material necessities and preferences," but it is also based on "cultural norms and values as to what one should do oneself and what can be contracted out" (Wallace, 2002, p. 284). For many men in my study, the impulse to take on self-provisioning was partly financial, but it was also part of an effort to justify their being at home through emphasizing more masculine work and hobbies that involve traditional male qualities, such as building, construction, and physical strength. This very much carried over into the community work that men took on, where the emphasis was often on sports and occasionally on traditional masculine roles of physical labor and leadership/management.

Community Work: "They Call Me 'Bob the Builder'"

In addition to unpaid self-provisioning work, men also take on unpaid community work, particularly involvement in school and extracurricular activities. This is well illustrated by Bob, a former sign-maker who lives in rural Quebec. A stay-at-home father for three years of two sons (aged 6 and 4), he left work because of a back injury that affected his ability to keep running his own company. He speaks about having done a lot of "hard physical labor and often outside" for the past 25 years. While at home, he is slowly building up a workshop in the garage and is starting to do renovation jobs for himself and his neighbors. He also has a particular involvement at his son's school:

> I'm head of maintenance at my son's kindergarten. . . . They call me "Bob the Builder"—"fix this, fix that."
> Every time I go in, they are always asking me to do things. . . . It takes up my morning so I can't get back to
> do my own renovation work.

The unpaid community work done by fathers often has gender-neutral tones such as volunteering in the classroom or on school trips, but fathers also emphasize work that has masculine qualities. Building on traditional male interests such as sports (Messner, 1987, 1990) and physical labor, men translated these skills into assets in their caregiving and became involved in recreational sports as organizers and coaches and took on tasks involving physical labor in the classroom. Some fathers also took on leadership positions in school councils and community organizations. Archie, for example, highlights how his position as president of the parent-teacher council became "a full time job."

It is also important to emphasize that this community work constitutes *a part of domestic labor* in that it builds bridges between parents, between households, and between households and other social institutions (schools, health settings, community centers). This widening of the domestic is well captured in varied guises and with differing names in feminist work on families and households. Concepts such as "kin work" (Di Leonardo, 1987; Stack, 1974), "servicing work" (Balbo, 1987) and "household service work" (Sharma, 1986) describe the domestic work that goes on beyond the more commonly identified spheres of housework and childcare. This recognition of community work as part of domestic labour is a further insight that this research adds to work on fathering and divisions of domestic labour (see also Doucet, 2000, 2001; Morris, 1995, Hessing, 1993).

It is important to point out that the majority of unpaid work in communities remains in the hands of women. A extensive body of research evidence suggests that women typically do a varied range of work that links the household to the school and to the wider community (Balbo, 1987; Crittenden, 2001; Di Leonardo, 1987; Doucet, 2000, 2001; Stueve & Pleck, 2003). While Anita Garey has pointed out that "homework, volunteer work and extracurricular activities are ways in which mothers link their children to the public world—and are symbolic arenas in their strategies of being mothers" (Garey, 1999, p. 40), fathers also play a role in children's extracurricular activities such as sporting as well as in community work which emphasizes leadership, sports, construction, and building. In this regard, one area largely overlooked by researchers is the rapidly growing involvement of children in recreation and competitive sports and the very large role that fathers play in this (Doucet, 2004b; Plantin et al., 2003). Many stay-at-home fathers view coaching and assisting in children's sports at school and in the community as a venue that makes their fathering more enjoyable for themselves while also easing community scrutiny of their decision to give up work. Moreover, fathers' involvement in children's lives in a manner that builds on traditional male interests also provides for the possibility of building their own community networks on the basis of traditional areas of male connection such as sports (Messner, 1987, 1990). As argued below, this involvement reflects the way in which fathers seek to distinguish their caring from mothering and to reconstruct particular kinds of "masculine care" (Brandth & Kvande, 1998).

RECONSTRUCTING CARING, FATHERING, AND MASCULINITIES

While taking on masculine self-provisioning and/or community work that sometimes involved masculine qualities, what seemed very clear in most fathers' narratives was that they were quite adamant, from within their practices and identities of caring, to distinguish themselves *as men*, as heterosexual (with the exception of gay fathers), as masculine, and as fathers, *not* as mothers. In my first focus group with fathers, Sam, stay-at-home father of two for five years, interjected several times, half jokingly: "Well we're still *men*, aren't we?" Another father, Mitchell, stay-at-home father of three for seven years, made several pointed references in his interview to how he often worked out at a gym and enjoyed "seeing the women in lycra." These men's words add further support to what theorists of work have underlined about men working in nontraditional or female dominated occupations (such as nursing or elementary school teaching) and how they must actively work to expel the idea that they might be gay, unmasculine, or not men (Fisher & Connell, 2002; Sargent, 2000; Williams, 1992). This leads to men finding ways of reinforcing their masculinity—such as engaging in sports or physical labor so as to maintain masculine affiliations and to exhibit public displays of masculinity (see Bird, 1996). Additionally, the men in my study are attempting to carve out their own paternal and masculine identities within spaces traditionally considered maternal and feminine. These processes of masculine identification and distancing from the feminine occurred in at least three ways.

First, the overwhelming majority of fathers spoke about their efforts to impart a more "masculine quality" to their family care through promoting their children's physical and outdoor activities, independence, risk taking, and the fun and playful aspects of care (see Brandth & Kvande, 1998; Doucet, 2004a). Second, given that domestic space, the *home*, is metaphorically configured as a maternal space with feminine connotations of comfort and care (Grosz, 1995; Walker, 2002) many fathers, as described above, more readily identified with the *house* as something to build and rebuild. Finally, many men also made it a point of saying how they had to "hang out with the guys"—playing traditionally male sports such as hockey or baseball or working with men on activities involving physical labor—so as to balance out the time that they were home caring. Owen, a stay-at-home father of two children for seven years, says: "At the same time *I was still needing the men thing*. I needed a break from the kids. . . . I would build sets for the theater. I would hang out with the guys."

A set of theoretical assumptions that can initially assist us in making sense of these processes are feminist theoretical discussions on how men distance themselves from and devalue the feminine (Bird, 1996; Chodorow, 1978; Connell, 1987, 1995, 2000; Johnson, 1988; Thorne, 1993) as well as the concept of hegemonic masculinity. While there have been varied discussions of the meanings and relevance of hegemonic masculinity, most recently the author who penned it, Connell, has boiled it down to being defined partly "as the opposite of femininity"

(Connell, 2000, p. 31). These fathers' narratives, as touched upon in this paper, are filled with visible and inchoate contradictions that tell about how fathers are both determined to distance themselves from the feminine, but are also, in practice, radically revisioning masculine care to include some aspects of femininities. In effect their narratives move us beyond the issue of whether they reproduce or challenge hegemonic masculinity (see also Plantin et al., 2003) and, rather, speak to the ways in which they are creating new kinds of masculinities that join together varied configurations of masculinities and femininities.

Audible effects of this revisioning of masculinity can be picked up in these fathers' narratives because they are spoken partly from the borders of the most traditional arena of men's dominance within the "gender order," that of paid work. When men—like the stay-at-home fathers described in this paper—relinquish their identities and practices as full time workers and primary breadwinners, it is inevitable that processes of personal and social readjustment will occur. Perhaps most notable is that fathers' relation to paid work begins to shift, their meanings of work are dramatically altered, and men begin, at least partially, to take on perspectives that are more aligned with women's social positioning (Gilligan, 1982, 1993) and ultimately feminine (Noddings, 2003) or feminist (Friedman, 1993, 2000; Stoljar, 2000; Tronto, 1989) vantage points. There are many instances demonstrating the ways in which these movements occur, three of which will be briefly mentioned here.

First, fathers noted ensuing personal and "generative" (Hawkins, Christiansen, Sargent, & Hill, 1993; Hawkins & Dollahite, 1996) changes as they make the shift from worker to carer. Aaron, for example, who used to be a lawyer in a "cutthroat" environment "where you have to be strong," says that "my hard edges have softened" and how he had a steep learning curve "about sharing, feelings, and spending time with them, sort of mellowing out a little." In a similar way, many fathers also find that their time at home gives them the opportunity to reflect on what it is they actually want to do once they return to the work force. Frank, who has been at home with two children for four years, reflects on how this time has been "a real personal growth experience for me" and how he would not have realized that his strengths and interests are in social work and not in accounting where he had previously worked. In his words: "When you're wrapped up in everyday work, you don't reflect on where you are and where you're going."

Second, most fathers mentioned how parenting is the "hardest" or "most difficult" job they have ever done. In the words of Archie, at home for seven years "it's the hardest work I ever done in my whole life," and "its like I have a full-time job, but I don't get paid." From this place where they see that it is "hard"—and yet some of them admit they have "softened"—men also come to appreciate how vitally important caring work is and yet also socially devalued. They thus add their voices to a large chorus of generations of women who have argued for the valuing of unpaid work (Crittenden, 2001; Luxton, 1997; Luxton & Vosko, 1998; Waring, 1998). As Joe, a Cree stay-at-home father of two, says: "This Mr. Mom business—here I am complaining about it, and women have been putting up with for a hundred years now." Rory sees caring for his son Tristan as a "job," and more specifically *his* job: "I know what my job is here. . . . *I will make sure that everything is going right in Tristan's life, because that is my job.*"

A third way that stay-at-home fathers' relation to paid work changes is that they are adamant that they will remain very involved with their children if and when they go back to full-time employment. While issues of home-work balance have been configured largely as women's issues for decades, with women being the ones who make adjustments in work schedules to accommodate children (Brannen & Moss, 1991; Hochschild, 1989), fathers at home come to join their female partners in recognizing the need for what researchers have recently termed greater "work-life integration" (Johnson, Lero, & Rooney, 2001). In two-parent families, many men commented on how their ideal home-work arrangement was that both parents worked part-time or that one parent worked from home. Sam, who has been at home for five years thinks that his wife, a lawyer, should also have the opportunity to stay home for a while. He speaks from the recognition of the benefits of close and sustained connection with his children and the "loss" that occurs if parents do not take this "chance in your life to do that":

> If we had another child, I would want to go back to work and have my wife stay at home. Because it is a chance in your life to do that. . . . If you don't have a chance to raise them yourself, that is a great loss."

CONCLUSIONS

Just as Adam, mentioned at the beginning of this paper, let me know how he repaired cars while his children toddled around him, most of the 70 stay-at-home fathers within my larger study on Canadian fathers as primary caregivers, viewed staying at home as a way of combining part-time paid work, "working on the house," caring, and housework. Sometimes these skills extended into the community as fathers often volunteered to coach sports, a venue that allowed them to be involved in their children's lives while also building on a traditional area of male interests. Most of the fathers maintained a connection with paid work, through working part-time, studying part-time for a new career, or taking a break from work in order to carve out a new line of work. The narratives of these fathers and their activities represent the complex intersections between the sites and theoretical concepts of home, work, community and masculinity. Moreover, at a practical level, it could be reasonably argued that the term "stay-at-home" father may be a slight misnomer since most fathers bring together varied configurations of home, paid and unpaid work, and community work. Just as Anita Garey (1999) uses the metaphor of "weaving" to discuss the ways in which mothers weave together complex patterns of employment and motherhood, stay-at-home fathers are in the process of "building" new models of varied employment patterns and fatherhood that represent not only changes in the institution of fatherhood but also suggest potential shifts in social relations between women and men in the social institution of work.

This study contributes to the growing body of excellent work on fatherhood and gender divisions of labor by emphasizing three points. First, this study gives considerable emphasis to the role of social networks and to the community in imparting a "social gaze" on men who stay at home to care for children (see also Doucet, 2000, 2001; Radin, 1982, 1988; Russell, 1983, 1987). The decision to even partially "trade cash for care" (Hobson & Morgan, 2002, p. 1) places these fathers in a position whereby they are often forced to justify this decision to their peers, kin, work colleagues, and community onlookers, who cast a critical lens on this disruption to the smooth functioning of contemporary gender regimes. This social gaze is rooted in and reinforces moral assumptions that link being a good mother to caring and being a good father to earning (see also Coltrane 1996; Finch & Mason, 1993; McMahon, 1995). This research also highlights the need for a wider conception of domestic labor to include nonroutine maintenance work and community work. In the case of the former, these are areas where men *do* make strong contributions both to domestic labor and to the domestic economy. This is not to underplay arguments that there needs to be greater symmetry between women and men's divisions of domestic labor, still largely weighted on the side of women, but it allows for greater visibility and recognition of what men actually *do*. In the case of community labor such as involvement in school, community councils, and children's sports, fathers may find a comfortable fit between their gendered upbringing, their sense of masculinity, and their fathering.

This study on stay-at-home fathers also lends itself to several theoretical and political implications about the meanings of work and masculinities. First, I would maintain that these men's stories do not represent any of the key masculinities (complicit, subordinate, or hegemonic) detailed by Connell (1987, 1995) but rather, as his recent work highlights, processes "of internal complexity and contradiction" as well as the "dynamics" of changing and evolving masculinities (Connell, 2000, p. 13). In this vein, Connell further writes that "masculinities are not fixed" and are not "homogenous, simple states of being," but rather are "often in tension, within and without" and that "such tensions are important sources of change" (p. 13). Living and working for sustained periods as primary carers while maintaining only a tenuous relation with bread-winning, stay-at-home fathers are in a unique position to create new forms of masculinity. They do so through delicate balancing acts of simultaneously embracing and rejecting both femininity and hegemonic masculinity. They provide "abundant evidence that masculinities do change. Masculinities are created in specific historical circumstances and, as those circumstances change, the gender practices can be contested and reconstructed" (Connell, 2000, pp. 13-14).

Furthermore, fathers' grappling with how to be "a good man" while also recognizing the "softening" that occurs while intimately involved in caregiving, points to the need to move beyond current theorizations around masculinities and to draw on other theoretical tools and approaches. Jeff Hearn and David Morgan (199) underline that "the experience of masculinity is far from uniform and that *new ways of theorizing these differences need to be developed*" (p. 11; emphasis added). Our understandings of men's lives and their subjective conceptions of masculinities could, for example, benefit from longstanding feminist debates on the intricate linkages between theoretical and empirical concepts of justice and care, autonomy and connection, and individual rights and relational responsibilities (Benhabib, 1992; Doucet, 1995; Gilligan, 1988; Kittay, 1999; Minow & Shanley, 1996; Sevenhuijsen, 1998, 2000; Tronto, 1993, 1995). That is, men's practices and identities of caregiving go beyond current conceptions of masculinities and femininities and may reflect philosophical and political concepts of self, identity, and subjectivity that embrace varied degrees of dependence, independence, and interdependence as well as varied versions of "relational autonomy" (Friedman, 1993, 2000). This study hints at the need for greater exploration of this line of theoretical inquiry.

A final concluding point refers to the political implications that can be drawn from this work and to the potential role that men could play in the social recognition and valuing of unpaid work (Armstrong & Armstrong, 1993; Doucet, 2004a; Luxton, 1980, 1997; Luxton & Vosko, 1998). Freed somewhat from the breadwinner imperative that is the norm for most men in most societies, the stay-at-home fathers in this study can be viewed as representing some of what Karin Davies refers to in her Swedish study of women, work and time. Davies argues that decisions to work part-time or to take time off from work constitute "breaking the pattern" (p. 217) out of "wage labor as the over-riding structure and an unconditional adherence to male time" (Davies, 1990, p. 208). She maintains that "by limiting the time spent in wage labor, a soil is provided whereby visions of what is important to fight and strive for can find space" (p. 208). While writing about women two decades ago, the views of Davies as applied to men have a particularly powerful effect because the "the overriding structure" and "male time" she refers to have strong connections with masculinity, especially hegemonic masculinity. It is men's overall privileged access to the rewards of paid employment and their concurrent lesser role in the care of dependent others that partly account for the overall dominance and associated "patriarchal dividend" (Connell, 1995) from which men benefit. The slow process of critical resistance documented here by fathers as they critique concepts of "male time" constitutes some unraveling of their relation to the structural effects of hegemonic masculinity.

Nevertheless, these stories are marginal ones; they sit quietly on the borders of most men's lives in most contemporary societies. Connell poignantly cautions that "the gender order does not blow away at a breath" and "the historical process around masculinity is a process of struggle in which, ultimately, large resources are at stake" (2000, p. 14). We are reminded of the need to move beyond these vignettes of everyday caring and the generative changes that ensue to focus on wider social relations and the need for greater structural changes and policy measures to assist both women and men in achieving work-life integration (Folbre, 1994, 2001; Fraser, 1997; Hobson, 2002; Plantin et al., 2003). While Davies' work highlights how "it is up to women to exert influence" in this vein since they are more likely to have "experience of rejecting male time" and thus "concrete knowledge and understanding of how we can produce and reproduce new forms of daily life . . . which are not so oppressive" (1990, p. 247), this study suggests that stay-at-home fathers are also lodged in this distinctive position as well. Indeed, adding father's voices to these issues can also "exert influence" very loudly indeed, both theoretically and politically.

REFERENCES

Allen, S. M., & Hawkins, A. J. (1999). Maternal gatekeeping: Mothers' beliefs and behaviors that inhibit greater father involvement in family work. *Journal of Marriage and the Family, 61,* 199–212.

Armstrong, P., & Armstrong, H. (1993). *The double ghetto* (3rd ed.). Toronto: McClelland and Stewart.

Balbo, L. (1987). Crazy quilts: Rethinking the welfare state debate from a woman's point of view. In A.S. Sassoon (Ed.), *Women and the State* (pp. 45-71). London: Unwin Hyman.

Barker, R.W. (1994). *Lone fathers and masculinities.* Avebury, UK: Aldershot.

Benhabib, S. (1992). *Situating the self.* Cambridge: Polity Press.

Berk, S.F. (1985). *The gender factory: The apportionment of work in American households.* New York: Plenum.

Bird, S.R. (1996). Welcome to the men's club: Homosociality and the maintenance of hegemonic masculinity. *Gender & Society, 19(2),* 120–132.

Bourdieu, P., & Wacquant, L. (1992). *An invitation to a reflexive sociology.* Chicago: University of Chicago Press.

Bradbury, B. (1984). Pigs, cows and boarders: Non-wage forms of survival among Montreal families, 1861–1881. *Labour/Le Travail, 14,* 9–46.

Brandth, B., & Kvande, E. (1998). Masculinity and child care: The reconstruction of fathering. *The Sociological Review, 46(2),* 293-313.

Brannen, J., & Moss, P. (1991). *Managing mothers: Dual earner households after maternity leave.* London: Unwin Hyman.

Brittan, A. (1989). *Masculinity and power.* Oxford: Basil Blackwell.

Brown, L.M., & Gilligan, C. (1992). *Meeting at the crossroads: Women's psychology and girls' development.* Cambridge, MA: Harvard University Press.

Chodorow, N. (1978). *The reproduction of mothering.* Berkeley and Los Angeles: University of California Press.

Clatterbaugh, K. (1998). What is problematic about masculinities? *Men and Masculinities, 1(1),* 24–45.

Code, L. (1993). Taking subjectivity into account. In L. Alcoff & E. Potter (Eds.), *Feminist epistemologies* (pp. 15-48). New York and London: Routledge.

Coltrane, S. (1989). Household labor and the routine production of gender. *Social Problems, 36(5),* 473–490.

Coltrane, S. (1994). Theorizing masculinities in contemporary social science. In H. Brod & M. Kaufman (Eds.), *Theorizing masculinities* (pp. 39-60). Thousand Oaks: Sage Publications.

Coltrane, S. (1996). *Family man: fatherhood, housework, and gender equity.* Oxford: Oxford University Press.

Connell, R.W. (1987). *Gender and power.* Cambridge, UK: Polity Press.

Connell, R.W. (1995). *Masculinities.* London: Polity Press.

Connell, R.W. (2000). *The men and the boys.* Berkeley: University of California Press.

Cowan, C.P., & Cowan, P.A. (Eds.). (1987). *Men's involvement in parenthood: Identifying the antecedents and understanding the barriers.* Hillsdale, NJ: Erlbaum.

Crittenden, A. (2001). *The price of motherhood: Why the most important job in the world is still the least valued.* New York: Henry Holt and Company.

Daly, K. (1993). Reshaping fatherhood: Finding the models. *Journal of Family Issues, 14,* 510–530.

Daly, K. (1996). *Families and time: Keeping pace in a hurried culture.* Thousand Oaks, CA: Sage Publications.

Daly, K. (2002). Time, gender, and the negotiation of family schedules. *Symbolic Interaction, 25*(3), 323–342.

Davies, K. (1990). *Women, time and weaving the strands of everyday life.* Avebury, UK: Gower Publishing Company.

Davies, K. (1994). The tension between process time and clock time in care work: The example of day nurseries. *Time and Society, 3,* 276–303.

Deutsch, F.M. (1999). *Halving it all: How equally shared parenting works.* Cambridge, MA: Harvard University Press.

Di Leonardo, M. (1987). The female world of cards and holidays: Women, families and the world of kinship. *Signs, 12*(3), 440–453.

Dienhart, A. (1998). *Reshaping fatherhood: The social construction of shared parenting.* London: Sage Publications.

Doucet, A. (1995). Gender equality and gender differences in household work and parenting. *Women's Studies International Forum, 18*(3), 271–284.

Doucet, A. (2000). "There's a huge difference between me as a male carer and women": Gender, domestic responsibility, and the community as an institutional arena. *Community Work and Family, 3*(2), 163–184.

Doucet, A. (2001). "You see the need perhaps more clearly than I have": Exploring gendered processes of domestic responsibility. *Journal of Family Issues, 22,* 328–357.

Doucet, A. (2004a). Fathers and the responsibility for children: A puzzle and a tension. *Atlantis: A Women's Studies Journal, 28*(2), 103–114.

Doucet, A. (2004b). *Do men mother?* Manuscript submitted for publication.

Dowd, N.E. (2000). *Redefining fatherhood.* New York: New York University Press.

Finch, J., & Mason, J. (1993). *Negotiating family responsibilities.* London: Routledge.

Fisher, M., & Connell, R.W. (2002). *Masculinities and men in nursing.* Paper presented at the 3rd College of Health Sciences Research Conference "From Cell to Society", Leura, Australia.

Folbre, N. (1991). The unproductive housewife: Her evolution in nineteenth century thought. *Signs, 16*(3), 463–484.

Folbre, N. (1994). *Who pays for the kids? Gender and the structures of constraint.* London: Routledge, Chapman and Hall.

Folbre, N. (2001). *The invisible heart: Economics and family values.* New York: The New Press.

Fox, B. (2001). The formative years: How parenthood creates gender. *Canadian Review of Sociology and Anthropology, 38*(4), 373–390.

Fraser, N. (1997). After the family wage: A postindustrialist thought experiment. In N. Fraser (Ed.), *Justice interruptus: Critical reflections of the "postsocialist condition"* (pp. 41–66). New York: Routledge.

Friedman, M. (1993). Beyond caring: The demoralization of gender. In M.J. Larrabee (Ed.), *An ethic of care: Feminist and interdisciplinary perspectives* (pp. 258-274). London: Routledge.

Friedman, M. (2000). Autonomy, social disruption and women. In C. Mackenzie & N. Stoljar (Eds.), *Relational autonomy: Feminist perspectives on autonomy, agency, and the social self* (pp. 35–51). Oxford: Oxford University Press.

Garey, A.I. (1999). *Weaving work and motherhood.* Philadelphia: Temple University Press.

Gershuny, J.I., & Pahl, R.E. (1979). Work outside employment: Some preliminary speculations. *New Universities Quarterly, 34,* 120–135.

Giddens, A. (1984). *The constitution of society: Outline of the theory of structuration.* Cambridge, UK: Polity Press.

Gilligan, C. (1982). *In a different voice: Psychological theory and women's development.* Cambridge, MA: Harvard University Press.

Gilligan, C. (1988). Remapping the moral domain: New images of the self in relationship. In C. Gilligan, J.V. Ward, J.M. Taylor, & B. Bardige (Eds.), *Mapping the moral domain: A contribution of women's thinking to psychological theory and education* (pp. 3–19). Cambridge, MA: Harvard University Press.

Gilligan, C. (1993). Reply to critics. In M.J. Larrabee (Ed.), *An ethic of care: Feminist and interdisciplinary perspectives* (pp. 207–214). New York: Routledge.

Graham, H. (1983). Caring: A labor of love. In J. Finch & D.A. Groves (Eds.), *A labor of love: Women, work and caring* (pp. 13-30). London: Routledge and Kegan Paul.

Grosz, E. (1995). *Space, time and perversion.* London: Routledge and Kegan Paul.

Hawkins, A.J., Christiansen, S.L., Sargent, K.P., & Hill, E.J. (1993). Rethinking fathers' involvement in child care: A developmental perspective. *Journal of Family Issues, 14,* 531–549.

Hawkins, A.J., & Dollahite, D.C. (1996). *Generative fathering: Beyond deficit perspectives.* Thousand Oaks, CA: Sage Publications.

Hearn, J. (1996). Is masculinity dead? A critique of the concept of masculinity/masculinities. In M. Mac an Ghaill (Ed.), *Understanding masculinities* (pp. 202–217). Buckingham, UK: Open University Press.

Hearn, J., & Morgan, D.H.J. (1990). Men, masculinities and social theory. In D.H.J. Morgan (Ed.), *Men, masculinities and social* theory (pp. 1-17). London: Unwin Hyman.

Hobson, B. (Ed.). (2002). *Men, masculinities and the social politics of fatherhood.* Cambridge, UK: Cambridge University Press.

Hobson, B., & Morgan, D.H.J. (2002). Introduction: Making men into fathers. In B. Hobson (Ed.), *Men, masculinities and the social politics of fatherhood.* (pp. 1-21). Cambridge, UK: Cambridge University Press.

Hochschild, A.R. (1989). *The second shift.* New York: Avon Books.

Johnson, K.L., Lero, D.S., & Rooney, J.A. (2001). *Work-life compendium 2001: 150 Canadian statistics on work, family and well-being.* Guelph, Ontario: Centre for Families, Work and Well-Being, University of Guelph.

Johnson, M.M. (1988). *Strong mothers, weak wives: The search for gender equality.* Berkeley: University of California Press.

Kimmel, M.S. (1994). Masculinity as homophobia: Fear, shame and silence in the construction of gender identity. In H. Brod & M. Kaufman (Eds.), *Theorizing masculinities* (pp. 119–141). Thousand Oaks, CA: Sage Publications.

Kittay, E.F. (1999). *Love's labor: Essays on women, equality and dependency.* Oxford: Oxford University Press.

LaBier, D. (1986). *Modern madness: The hidden link between work and emotional conflict.* New York: Simon and Schuster.

Land, H. (1980). The family wage. *Feminist Review, 6,* 55–77.

Lupton, D., & Barclay, L. (1997). *Constructing fatherhood: Discourses and experiences.* London: Sage Publications.

Luxton, M. (1980). *More than a labor of love: Three generations of women's work in the home.* Toronto: Women's Press.

Luxton, M. (Ed.). (1997). *Feminism and families: Critical policies and changing practices.* Halifax: Fernwood Publishing.

Luxton, M., & Vosko, L. (1998). The Census and women's work. *Studies in Political Economy, 56,* 49–82.

Mackintosh, M.M. (1988). Domestic labour and the household. In R.E. Pahl (Ed.), *On work: Historical, comparative and theoretical approaches* (pp. 392-406). Oxford: Basil Blackwell.

Mandell, D. (2002). *Deadbeat dads: Subjectivity and social construction.* Toronto: University of Toronto Press.

Mauthner, N.S. (2002). *The darkest days of my life: Stories of postpartum depression.* Cambridge, MA: Harvard University Press.

Mauthner, N.S., & Doucet, A. (1998). Reflections on a voice centred relational method of data analysis: Analysing maternal and domestic voices. In J. Ribbens & R. Edwards (Eds.), *Feminist dilemmas in qualitative research: Private lives and public texts* (pp. 119–144). London: Sage Publications.

Mauthner, N.S., & Doucet, A. (2003). Reflexive accounts and accounts of reflexivity in qualitative data analysis. *Sociology, 37*(3), 413–431.

McMahon, M. (1995). *Engendering motherhood: Identity and self-transformation in women's lives.* New York: The Guilford Press.

Messner, M.A. (1987). The meaning of success: The athletic experience and the development of male identity. In H. Brod (Ed.), *The making of masculinities: The new men's studies* (pp. 193–209). Boston: Allen and Unwin.

Messner, M.A. (1990). Boyhood, organized sports, and the construction of masculinities. *Journal of Contemporary Ethnography, 18*(4), 416–444.

Messner, M.A. (1997). *Politics of masculinities: Men in movements.* Thousand Oaks, CA: Sage Publications.

Miles, M.B., & Huberman, M.A. (1994). *Qualitative data analysis: An expanded sourcebook.* London: Sage Publications.

Mingione, E. (1988). Work and informal activities in urban southern Italy. In R.E. Pahl (Ed.), *On work: Historical, comparative and theoretical approaches* (pp. 548-578). Oxford: Basil Blackwell.

Minow, M., & Shanley, M.L. (1996). Relational rights and responsibilities: Revisioning the family in liberal political theory and law. *Hypatia, 11*(1), 4-29.

Morgan, D.H.J. (1992). *Discovering men.* London: Routledge.

Noddings, N. (2003). *Caring: A feminine approach to ethics and moral education* (2nd ed.). Berkeley: University of California Press.

Pahl, R.E. (1984). *Divisions of labour.* Oxford: Basil Blackwell.

Pahl, R.E. (1995). *After success:* Fin-de-siecle *anxiety and identity.* Cambridge, UK: Polity.

Parke, R.D. (1996). *Fatherhood.* Cambridge, Massachusetts: Harvard University Press.

Plantin, L., Sven-Axel, M., & Kearney, J. (2003). Talking and doing fatherhood: On fatherhood and masculinity in Sweden and England. *Fathering, 1*(1), 3–26.

Pleck, J.H. (1985). *Working wives, working husbands.* London: Sage.

Radin, N. (1982). Primary caregiving and role sharing fathers. In M.E. Lamb (Ed.), *Non-traditional families: Parenting and child development* (pp. 173–204). Hillsdale, NJ: Erlbaum.

Radin, N. (1988). Primary caregiving fathers of long duration. In P. Bronstein & C. P. Cowan (Eds.), *Fatherhood today: Men's changing roles in the family* (pp. 127–143). New York: John Wiley and Sons.

Risman, B.J. (1998). *Gender vertigo: American families in transition.* New Haven: Yale University Press.

Russell, G. (1983). *The changing role of fathers.* St. Lucia, Australia: University of Queensland Press.

Russell, G. (1987). Problems in role reversed families. In C. Lewis & M. O'Brien (Eds.), *Reassessing fatherhood: New observations on fathers and the modern family* (pp. 161-182). London: Sage Publications.

Sargent, P. (2000). Real men or real teachers? Contradictions in the lives of men elementary teachers. *Men and Masculinities, 2*(4), 410-433.

Sayer, A. (1999). *Realism and social science.* London: Sage Publications.

Sevenhuijsen, S. (1998). *Citizenship and the ethics of care: Feminist considerations on justice, morality and politics.* London: Routledge.

Sevenhuijsen, S. (2000). Caring in the third way: The relation between obligation, responsibility and care in Third Way discourse. *Critical Social Policy: A Journal of Theory and Practice in Social Welfare, 25*(1), 5–38.

Smith, D. (1987). *The everyday world as problematic: A feminist sociology.* Milton Keynes, UK: Open University Press.

Smith, D. (1996). Telling the truth after postmodernism. *Studies in Symbolic Interaction, 19*(3), 171–202.

Snarey, J. (1993). *How fathers care for the next generation.* Cambridge, Massachusetts: Harvard University Press.

Stoljar, N. (2000). Autonomy and feminist intuition. In C. Mackenzie & N. Stoljar (Eds.), *Relational autonomy: Feminist perspectives on autonomy, agency, and the social self* (pp. 94–111). New York and Oxford: Oxford University Press.

Stueve, J.L., & Pleck, J.H. (2003). Fathers' narratives of arranging and planning: Implications for understanding parental responsibility. *Fathering, 1*(1), 51–70.

Thorne, B. (1993). *Gender play: Girls and boys in school.* Buckingham, UK: Open University Press.

Tronto, J. (1989). Women and caring: What can feminists learn about morality from caring? In A. M. Jaggar & S. Bordo (Eds.), *Gender/body/knowledge: Feminist reconstructions of being and knowing* (pp. 172–187). New Brunswick, NJ: Rutgers University Press.

Tronto, J. (1993). *Moral boundaries: A political argument for an ethic of care.* New York: Routledge.

Tronto, J. (1995). Care as a basis for radical political judgements (Symposium on Care and Justice). *Hypatia, 10*(2), 141–149.

Waddington, D., Chritcher, C., & Dicks, B. (1998). "All jumbled up": Employed women with unemployed husbands. In J. Popay, J. Hearn, & J. Edwards (Eds.), *Men, gender divisions and welfare* (pp. 231-258). New York: Routledge.

Walker, L. (2002). Home making: An architectural perspective. *Signs: Journal of Women in Culture and Society, 27*(3), 823–836.

Wallace, C.D. (2002). Household strategies: Their conceptual relevance and analytical scope in social research. *Sociology, 36*(2), 275–292.

Wallace, C.D., & Pahl, R.E. (1985). Household work strategies in an economic recession. In N. Redclift & E. Mingione (Eds.), *Beyond employment* (pp. 189–227). Oxford: Basil Blackwell.

Waring, M. (1998). *If women counted.* San Francisco: Harper and Row.

West, C., & Zimmerman, R. (1987). Doing gender. *Gender & Society, 1*, 30–37.

Williams, C.L. (1992). The glass escalator: Hidden advantage for men in the "female" professions. *Social Problems, 39*(3), 253–267.

Williams, J. (2000). *Unbending gender: Why family and work conflict and what to do about it.* Oxford: Oxford University Press.

Too Many Eggs in the Wrong Basket
A Queer Critique of the
Same-Sex Marriage Movement

Michael C. LaSala

Michael C. LaSala is an Associate Professor of Social Work at the Rutgers University School of Social Work. He earned his PhD at School of Social Welfare at SUNY Albany. In addition to his teaching and research, he works with gay and lesbian clients at the Institute for Personal Growth in Highland Park, New Jersey. This essay appeared in Social Work *in 2007.*

The fight for legally recognized same-sex marriage dominates the contemporary gay rights movement and has ignited national debate. However, missing from the current discourse is a critical view of the privileges of marriage. Arguments for legal, same-sex marriage center on the many rights and benefits married heterosexual couples enjoy but from which same-sex couples are excluded. However, lesbian and gay activists and social workers are notably silent on whether it is fair that marriage bestows such privileges. Following is a critique of the privilege of marriage from a queer theory perspective and its implications for social action and future directions of the lesbian and gay rights movement.

MARRIAGE PRIVILEGES

In U.S. culture, marriage is indeed privileged. Among the many benefits available to married people are coverage under a spouse's insurance and the ability to inherit his or her Social Security benefits, pension, and personal assets without excessive taxation (Chauncey, 2004). Married people are virtually always able to visit spouses in the hospital and can make health care decisions when their spouses are rendered incapable. Husbands and wives cannot be forced to testify against each other in court and may pursue litigation in their wrongful deaths. In addition, there are many social benefits attached to marriage. Being married is seen by society as healthy and normal, and the mental health and maturity of those who remain single is considered suspect (Warner, 1999). As the fight to legalize same-sex marriage proceeds, it is important to question why such privileges are bestowed on marriage and why social work, with its commitment to social justice, has not challenged this privileging.

WHY PRIVILEGE MARRIAGE?

Since the 1960s, the proportion of people in the United States who marry each year has decreased by 50 percent, and the proportion of marriages ending in divorce has increased to 50 percent (Whitehead & Popenoe, 2004). The decline of marriage is a likely result of the growing financial independence of women, the increased effectiveness and acceptability of contraception, and the historical transformation of Western culture, which up to 150 years ago emphasized obedience to authority and now prizes personal freedom, pleasure, and individual choice (Graff, 2004). Conservatives concerned about this trend believe marriage must be privileged to stem its waning importance (Haskins, McLanahan, & Donahue, 2005). They argue that heterosexual marriage is healthy for men and women, provides the optimum environment for children, and is therefore worthy of advantages and status (Santorum, 2003; Spalding, 2004).

To bolster their arguments, conservatives selectively cite findings to declare that compared with singles, married people are better off physically and psychologically and that children living with married rather than single or divorced parents fare better physically and emotionally. These conclusions, however, do not stand up to more comprehensive, critical reviews of the available research (Manning & Lichter, 1996; McClanahan & Sandefur, 1994; Waldron, Hughes, & Brooks, 1996). For example, it is unclear whether marriage actually makes people better off, or that wealthier, healthier people are more likely to marry. Furthermore, for children in single and divorced families, it is difficult to untangle the effects of parental status from the higher rates of poverty, parental stress, and discord these families also experience (Graff; Lamb, 1997).

Conservatives also argue that marriage tames sexuality, and this taming is necessary to ensure the survival of civilization. To make the limiting of one's sexuality to marriage more palatable, society must provide rewards and reinforcements as well as punishments for noncompliance (Warner, 1999). Conservative Christianity in tandem with the U.S. government has historically attempted to limit nonprocreative sexuality not only outside but also **within** marriage (Graff, 2004). Until *Griswold v. Connecticut* in 1965, the state could prevent a married couple from using birth control (Graff), and some conservative Christians still condemn not only birth control but **all** nonprocreative sex, even within marriage (Shorto, 2006). Legalizing same-sex marriage would sanction nonprocreative sex, and therefore, according to conservatives, must be opposed.

Like conservatives, same-sex marriage advocates view marriage as the building block of society and stress its potential physical and psychological benefits to gay men and lesbians (Rauch, 2004; Sullivan, 2004). However, the most repeated argument for same-sex marriage is that gay men and lesbians deserve access to the same rights and privileges afforded heterosexuals. What is troubling is that same-sex marriage advocates are silent on whether this privileging is fair or legitimate. Early gay activists challenged the restrictive sexual norms of marriage (Jagose, 1996; Katz, 1976; Warner, 1999), but these challenges are rarely heard now. This silence should concern all who care about social justice and personal freedom.

QUESTIONING THE PRIVILEGING OF MARRIAGE

According to queer theorists, leaders in politics, religion, and medicine sustain social control by imposing the norm of heterosexual monogamous marriage and condemning people when they fail to adhere to it (Warner, 1999). Rather than preserving families or benefiting children, as conservatives claim, marriage privileges are meant to reward and legitimize certain relationships and sexual behaviors and in so doing stigmatize and marginalize others. Limiting access to rights such as affordable health care to those who are married, and simultaneously penalizing those who do not restrict their sexuality in this way (for example, gay men, lesbians, and single heterosexuals) is a form of oppressive social control (Ettelbrick, 2004; Warner).

Are those who cannot find a partner or choose not to limit their sexual behavior or relationships to marriage less worthy of affordable health care than those who are married? One could argue that there is currently a caste system of married people and unmarried people in our culture wherein unmarried people must, for example, buy their own health insurance if not covered at the workplace and suffer marginalization and stigma in our traditional family-oriented culture. Should efforts to perpetuate and replicate these inequities among gay men and lesbians be supported?

For gay and lesbian activists and social workers, the answer to this question must be no. Rather than assimilating to society's narrow sexual and relationship norms by seeking to uncritically adopt the institution of marriage, gay men and lesbians must illuminate the irrelevance and unfairness of the privileges attached to it. Social workers ethically bound to support social justice and self-determination must join them. Sexuality and relationships can be expressed in many forms, and it is unjust to privilege only a portion of them. Fighting to legitimize not only same-sex, long-term dyadic unions but also other alternatives such as polyamorous relationships is a worthy cause that will shed light on the unrealistic and unnatural limits our culture places on sexuality and relating.

THE PRIVILEGING OF MARRIAGE AND SOCIAL ACTION

As Warner (1999) stated, the argument for gay marriage is appealing because legal same-sex marriage would provide gay men and lesbians a shortcut to acquiring the legal and social benefits of marriage. Nevertheless, benefits such as affordable health care and the right to leave assets to whomever one chooses should not be linked to one's willingness or ability to commit to a long-term, legally sanctioned relationship. Anyone who wants to marry should be able to marry. However, a large portion of the energy activists expend to fight for same-sex marriage should be invested, for example, in the quest for affordable, accessible health care for everyone, no matter what a person's sexual orientation or marital status. Patients, not the state, should decide who should make health care decisions for them and who should be able to visit them in the hospital. Instead of putting so many eggs into the same-sex marriage basket, social workers and gay and lesbian activists must advocate for freedom of sexual expression as well as economic and legal equity for all, regardless of marital status, relationship style, or sexual orientation.

REFERENCES

Chauncey, G. (2004). *Why marriage? The history shaping today's debate over gay equality.* Cambridge, MA: Basic Books.

Ettelbrick, P. (2004). *Since when is marriage a path to liberation?* In A. Sullivan (Ed.), *Same-sex marriage: Pro and con. A reader* (pp. 122–128). New York: Vintage Books.

Graff, E. J. (2004). *What is marriage for? The strange social history of our most intimate institution.* Boston: Beacon Press.

Griswold v. Connecticut, 381 U.S. 479 (1965).

Haskins, R., McLanahan, S., & Donahue, E. (2005). The decline of marriage: What to do [Policy Brief]. *Future of Children, 15*, 1–8.

Jagose, A. (1996). *Queer theory: An introduction.* New York: New York University Press.

Katz, J. (1976). *Gay American history: Lesbians and gay men in the U.S.A.* New York: Thomas Cromwell.

Lamb, M. E. (1997). *The role of the father in child development* (3rd ed.). New York: Wiley.

Manning, W.D., & Lichter, D.T. (1996). Parental cohabitation and children's economic well-being. *Journal of Marriage and the Family, 58*, 998–1010.

McLanahan, S., & Sandefur, G. (1994). *Growing up with a single parent: What hurts, what helps.* Boston: Harvard University Press.

Rauch, J. (2004). *Gay marriage: Why it is good for gays, good for straights, and good for America.* New York: Owl Books.

Santorum, R. (2003, October 23). *The necessity of marriage* [Heritage Lectures # 804]. Washington, DC: Heritage Foundation.

Shorto, R. (2006, May 7). Contra-contraception: Is this the beginning of the next culture war? *New York Times Magazine*, pp. 48–55, 68, 83.

Spalding, M. (2004). *A defining moment: Marriage, the courts, and the Constitution* [Backgrounder 1759]. Washington, DC: Heritage Foundation. Retrieved May 15, 2006, from http:/www.heritage.org/Research/legalIssues/bg1759.cfm

Sullivan, A. (Ed.). (2004). *Same-sex marriage: Pro and con. A reader.* New York: Vintage Books.

Waldron, I., Hughes, M. E., & Brooks, T. L. (1996). Marriage protection and marriage selection—Prospective evidence for reciprocal effects of marital status and health. *Social Science & Medicine, 43*, 113–123.

Warner, M. (1999). *The trouble with normal: Sex, politics, and the ethics of queer life.* New York: Free Press.

Whitehead, B. D., & Popenoe, D. (2004). *The marrying kind: Which men marry and why.* Piscataway, NJ: Rutgers University, National Marriage Project. Retrieved May 15, 2006, from http://marriage.rutgers.edu/Publications/SOOU/TEXTSOOU2004.htm#Marriage

Welfare-to-Work, Farewell to Families? US Welfare Reform and Work/Family Debates

Randy Albelda

Randy Albelda is a Professor of Economics and Senior Research Fellow at the Center for Social Policy at University of Massachusetts Boston. Her published work includes Lost Ground: Poverty, Welfare Reform, and Beyond *(2002).* She co-authored Glass Ceilings and Bottomless Pits: Women's Work, Women's Poverty *(1999),* The War on the Poor: A Defense Manual *(1996) and* Unlevel Playing Fields: Understanding Wage Inequality and Discrimination *(2004). This essay appeared in* Feminist Economics *in 2001.*

INTRODUCTION

If asked what image exemplifies the work/family dilemma in the US, many might conjure up a mental picture of a "soccer mom." We might see her riding in her SUV, cell phone cradled to her ear, as she arranges dinner plans, the next drop-off, a doctor's appointment, or finishes up that last bit of work while frantically driving to the soccer game in time to see her child play. She is a hassled, middle-class, white, suburban, working mom struggling to juggle the demands of her job along with the everyday needs of her family. Most people find this a sympathetic image, even though some conservatives would paint her as a woman who selfishly "wants it all."

If asked what image exemplifies the work/family dilemma in the US of a woman on welfare, many respondents would alter their picture to that of a black mother with far too many children, watching television and being slovenly. Some believe she has far too much family and not nearly enough work. This is not a very flattering or sympathetic picture.

The divergent imagery illustrates an economic, policy, and intellectual gap between how US society and academics treat or think about the work/family binds of poor parents—especially single-mothers—and how they perceive and address the comparable problems of middle class, married, and professional parents. This paper argues that US welfare reform has thrown new light on the work and family bind. It has done so by imposing "self-sufficiency" on poor families through work requirements for the women who head those families. Women who move between welfare and employment—the vast majority of poor mothers—usually participate in the low-wage labor market and find themselves back on welfare precisely because they can not be the family breadwinner without public assistance or a deep kinship network. The nature of the low-wage labor market, the family demands of single parents, and policies toward mothers are ill suited for welfare reform's purposes. Indeed, these policies impose the supreme squeeze that work/family researchers highlight. The parameters of welfare reform, however, provide a unique opportunity to close some of the gaps. The work/family dilemmas faced by the soccer mom and by women on or leaving welfare are not all that different—except that the welfare (or, more likely, former-welfare) mother doesn't have the soccer mom's resources for juggling work and family, and probably has a lot less flexibility at work as well.

WELCOME TO THE GAP

The work/family bind is by no means new. During the 1960s and 1970s, feminist literature referred to it as the "double day" and applied it mainly to women who needed employment to help support their families, mostly working-class white women and women of color. While working mothers were more common at the turn of the 20th century than during the 1950s, many, if not most, mothers have always held jobs or engaged in income-generating activities. Historically, there was only a short period of time following WWII when most men earned a "family wage" sufficient to assure that their wives did not have to be employed, largely as a result of industrial unionization in the 1930s and 1940s. In part because of the women's movement, an increased demand for low-wage work in the US, and the fall in men's wages, more and more mothers and wives are employed. As this phenomenon has become more widespread amongst white, middle-class women the problem has a new name as well as more recognition amongst scholars, the media, and even politicians.

Ironically, just as more and more middle-class white women are feeling the very real crunch of trying to earn income and raise families, the US has passed legislation that makes that task mandatory and substantially more difficult for poor mothers. Along with the passage of the Family and Medical Leave Act of 1993, which allows eligible employees a 12-week, job-protected unpaid leave from work for family or medical reasons, welfare reform can be thought of as the most significant piece of work/family legislation in the 1990s, one which demands paid work from some women, regardless of the expense to their families. The US lags far behind internationally on both the welfare and work/family score. The US has amongst the most shallow benefits and harshest set of rules applied to lone mother families who receive assistance. In addition, the US is one of the few countries without mandatory vacation or paid maternity leave.

* * *

The policies toward poor women are now and historically have been remarkably intrusive and judgmental of women's marital choices and sexual activities (Theresa Funiciello 1993; Linda Gordon 1994). Women who receive welfare–the program intended to allow women to raise families when they do not have secure or steady family income support–are subjected to intense scrutiny and often disdain. Welfare mothers are the only mothers in the US who must disclose the paternity of their children to be eligible for government income assistance. They are also the only mothers forced to leave their children in the care of others in order to take employment (Gwendolyn Mink 1998). Caseworkers are required to obtain and certify not only employment histories and general personal information, but also intimate family details (like sexual partners) before women can receive their meager welfare checks. It is a humiliating process. By contrast, unemployment insurance or social security applications can now be processed with a phone call.

Both family structures and the types of work men and women do have changed radically since the 1930s when these policies were constructed. It is not surprising that the policies are no longer adequate. While all industrialized nations are facing similar problems with their social welfare systems, the solutions in the US have been considerably different. In the US, replacing these social welfare benefits are much contested and for now seem to be a particularly bad blend of leaving unchallenged women's unpaid care responsibilities characteristic of traditional families

Families with children (by type of family) in top and bottom 20 percentile of family income distribution, 1999

	Percent of all families with children	Of all families with children, percent in:	
		Bottom 20 percentile of family income	Top 20 percentile of family income
Single-mother families	23%	59%	4%
Married-couple families	70%	32%	94%

Source: Calculation by author using March 2000 Current Population Survey.

and embodying the more modern expectation of women's–especially mothers'–employment. This is no clearer than in recent welfare changes. The message is: welfare is altogether bad, while marriage and work are good. Federal legislation (the Personal Responsibility and Work Opportunity Reconciliation Act–H.R. 3734) in 1996 repealed AFDC and established Temporary Assistance for Needy Families (TANF). The fond hopes of the framers of the legislation that women should be married are embodied in the findings section (101) of the bill–which leads with: "(1) Marriage is the foundation of a successful society; and (2) Marriage is an essential institution of a successful society which promotes the interests of children" (Public Law: 104–93). However, the most widely wielded stick in welfare reform is the work requirements, backed by time limits. Welfare is no longer an entitlement. Single mothers are no longer supposed to raise their children with public support alone; instead rules require mothers to be employed and fathers to play a financial role. These polices were passed and are popular, despite indisputable evidence that women receiving welfare have always worked and have often lived with the fathers of their children (e.g. Roberta Spalter-Roth, Beverly Burr, Heidi Hartmann and Lois Shaw 1995; Kathryn Edin and Laura Lein 1997; Lisa Dodson 1998). Research on poor women's employment and living patterns clearly indicates the problem is not finding men or work, the problem is finding men and/or jobs that are good for families in terms of income and emotional support and stability.

There is also an important economic gap between poor single-mother families and middle-income, married mothers. Growing income and wealth inequality in the US is well documented (Lawrence Mishel, Jared Bernstein and John Schmitt 1999; Edward Wolff 2000). Also, while part of that gap stems from the declining fortunes of men with low educational attainment as well as from economic conditions that benefit wealth holders, much of the gap derives from the fact that high-income families have two earners, rather than one (John Donahue 1999). Women with high educational attainment have higher labor-force participation rates than other women and are most likely to be married to men with similar educational backgrounds, facilitating the trend. In 1999, more than half (56 percent) of all single-mother families resided in the lowest 20th percentile of the family income distribution, compared to 10 percent of married couples with children.[1] Table 1 depicts the percentages of single-mother families and married-couples with children of all families with children that have incomes in the bottom and top 20th percentiles of all families (households with two or more persons). Single-mother families make up about one-quarter of all families with children, yet they comprise 59 percent of all families with children with incomes in the bottom 20th percentile of the family income distribution and only 4 percent of

[1]Calculations by author using the Current Population Survey's Annual Demographic Survey (CPS March 2000 Supplement) via the Census Bureau's on-line "Ferret" program.

all families with children in the top 20th percentile. Married-couples with children make up 70 percent of all families with children, but such families are only one-third of the families with children whose incomes fall in the bottom 20th percentile; they are virtually all of the families with children in the top 20th percentile of family income.

* * *

WELFARE REFORM AND THE WORK BIND

Welfare reform swept the US in the 1990s, culminating in the repeal of Aid to Families with Dependent Children (AFDC) in the federal Personal Responsibility and Work Opportunity Reconciliation Act of 1996. This act codified the US' growing emphasis on retracting public assistance as an entitlement to all those who qualified by creating block grants, establishing time limits, and allowing states to define who is "needy." Despite the framers' desires for promoting marriage as a substitute for welfare, most supporters seem to believe that, like other mothers, welfare mothers should be employed. The often-used phrase "welfare-to-work" embodies much of what welfare reform has come to mean.

Welfare-to-work includes a wide range of methods for promoting paid work. It spans the punitive "work-first" policies pursued by over half the states, to the more liberal strategies that include a generous package of training and education options, financial incentives, day care, transportation, and health care. And, despite its current popularity, the notion of putting welfare mothers to work is hardly new. Gwendolyn Mink (1998) traces the history of work requirements in AFDC since the legislation's inception and argues that, by the late 1960s, work requirements were seen as an important way to get women, particularly black women, off the welfare rolls. It is, however, only in the early 1990s that paid work has been viewed as the main alternative in light of time-limited benefits.

Most researchers, politicians, agency heads, and advocates assume "work" is good and that people on public assistance, if physically possible, *should* be working. It is easy to see why. Conservatives argue that employment breaks welfare recipients' presumed (although not empirically validated) "cycle of dependency." For liberals, when adult recipients "work," even if they receive hefty supplements, they are not perceived as receiving handouts and become deserving. Feminists, too, have traditionally applauded women's employment, as it serves to provide a basis for financial independence from individual men and the state, promoting women's economic equality.

How is welfare-to-work working? There are scores of studies, mostly conducted at the state level, of women leaving welfare. They are referred to as "leaver" studies. What is astonishing about the results from the leaver studies is how similar they are, despite the supposed diversity of programs adopted by the states. When interviewed after leaving welfare, of those who did not return (about 20 percent), between two-thirds and three-quarters of adults are employed, most often for about 35 hours a week, earning an average hourly wage of around $7.50. As often as not, these jobs do not have health care benefits, rarely provide sick days, and give little or no vacation time.[2] Evidence is mounting that many leavers do not stay employed for very long, reproducing a pattern well established before welfare reform of cycling in and out of the labor market (Spalter-Roth *et al.* 1995). However, now some are not able to cycle back onto welfare because of time limits.

Consider the employment outcomes for one state's welfare leavers. Welfare administrators in Massachusetts received federal funding to study welfare leavers and released their findings in

---

[2]There are many "leaver" studies, too many to mention. A catalog of them can be found at http://www.researchforum.org/. For an excellent list of studies, go to http://www.welfareinfo.org/trackingstudies.htm. In addition, Appendix L to the 2000 Congressional "Green Book" includes findings from leaver studies (US House of Representatives 2000).

December 2000 (Massachusetts Department of Transitional Assistance 2000). Massachusetts' situation allows for a close examination of those facing time limits, since the state has relatively short time limits for receiving benefits (24 months out of any 60-month period), which were implemented on December 1, 1996. Two distinct samples were interviewed: 210 adults who had left welfare but who were not yet subject to time limits, and 440 adults who had reached the state's time limit for welfare receipt. Employment rates for both groups were high: 70 percent for non-time limit adults and 73 percent for those who had hit the time limit. However, a closer look at that employment reveals it is almost uniformly low-wage work, has very limited benefits attached, and is not stable. The average time from when respondents initially left welfare to when they were interviewed was 10 months. In that brief span, 55 percent of all leavers not subject to time limits were no longer in the first job they had held once leaving welfare, and 18 percent had returned to the rolls. Two out of every five adults who had hit their time limits were in a different job and 8 percent were back on welfare (by receiving an extension or exemption). Of those who had hit their time limits, 17 percent held jobs as retail clerks, 10 percent were in cleaning jobs, 10 percent in food service, 10 percent in child care, and 15 percent in clerical work. All of these are female-dominated occupations, and all are relatively low paying. Three out of every five (61 percent) employed persons hitting time limits are in jobs with no paid sick days, and 51 percent say their jobs do not offer vacation time. And, while well over 90 percent of all the adults surveyed currently have health coverage for themselves and their children, 55 percent of those hitting their time limits said that their employers do not offer health care coverage.[3]

* * *

Studies of the families leaving welfare indicate the majority of families are still at or near poverty levels (Wendell Primus, Lynette Rawlings, Kathy Larin and Kathryn Porter 1999; Gregory Acs and Pamela Loprest 2000). And, whilst families have more income from earnings than when they were on welfare, they receive less public assistance, because they have lost welfare and food stamps (and in some cases WIC and Medicaid). The loss of public assistance often swamps increases in earnings and tax credits, leaving the average "leaver" families with about the same income that they had when receiving welfare. These not-so-spectacular results have occurred during the best economic expansion in 40 years and prior to when most states time limits on welfare receipt take effect. In short, these are the best results we can expect from the current system of welfare reform. Nothing is reported (because it is impossible to track this information) on those who are not turning to welfare, even though they need it. While few talk about this group, they are no doubt a substantial reason why caseloads have fallen so dramatically.

State and federal politicians are thrilled with the results. Almost universally they tout declines in caseloads as evidence of the resounding success of welfare reform. The other source of success cited is the leaver studies themselves, indicating most of those who were once on welfare are currently employed (Sanford Schram and Joe Soss forthcoming). Some researchers are also touting the success of welfare reform. For example, the introduction of a recent edited volume on employment and welfare reform by the highly respected and liberal US labor economists Rebecca Blank and David Card (2000: 17–18) concludes, "So far, the evidence suggests that welfare reform is proceeding as well as or better than most analysts had expected. In terms of declining caseloads and increasing work effort among single mothers, welfare reform has been an astonishing success . . . The research in this book suggest we are on the right track with many policy efforts."

---

[3]All data on Massachusetts leavers come from Massachusetts Department of Transitional Assistance (2000) and author's calculation using the field report from University of Massachusetts Boston's Center for Survey Research, who conducted the survey for the state.

WORK/FAMILY ISSUES IN THE WELFARE-TO-WORK DEBATES

It is remarkably easy to make the case that the work/family research agenda can help uncover some of the complex effects of welfare-to-work policies. A recent article surveying work and family literature in the 1990s highlights several important themes (Maureen Perry-Jenkins, Rena Repetti and Ann Crouter 2000). These are maternal employment and its impact on children, workplace conditions and their impact on family life, and the ways in which parents manage multiple roles of workers and caregivers. Applying these themes to welfare-to-work outcomes, one may arrive at very different conclusions about the efficacy of welfare reform efforts than are currently being portrayed. Considering that TANF comes up for Congressional reauthorization in 2002, the perceptions of both the public and policy makers of how welfare reform is working is vitally important.

Maternal Employment and its Impact on Children

It is hard to find anyone arguing that poor single mothers have a "right" to welfare assistance without any work obligation. The policy of promoting employment is being touted in other industrialized countries as well. And, while there are clearly important and laudable reasons to want to see low-income mothers employed, there should also be considerable unease with current efforts to put US welfare mothers to work. Welfare policies have insisted that the primary adult in the family responsible for generating stable income and taking care of children be employed full-time. But, is this possible, desirable, or even realistic?

A recent article by Philip Cohen and Suzanne Bianchi (1999) specifically calls attention to the often neglected observation that married women with young children are increasingly employed, but not full-time. This underscores the unrealistic expectations policy makers have of women leaving welfare. They found that, in 1998, 34.7 percent of all married women with children under the age of 6 were employed year-round, full-time. They concluded, "Rather than being in step with levels of employment of married mothers, current reforms require paid-work efforts on the part of single mothers that put them substantially ahead of the curve" (Philip Cohen and Suzanne Bianchi 1999:30).

What is happening to children in single-parent families with a good deal of paid work, but not much income, is a bit harder to assess. In the Massachusetts study of welfare leavers, about 60 percent of children of 12 years and younger were in non-parental care. Of those children, about 60 percent were cared for by relatives at little or no expense. Few have examined the quality of care that children of "leavers" are receiving. However, other research on low-quality or no care finds that it results in a range of undesirable individual and societal results, such as poorer school performance and behavior problems (Maureen Perry-Jenkins, Rena Repetti and Ann Crouter 2000).

Workplace Conditions and Their Impact on Family Life

Whilst receiving welfare without work requirements, mothers not only have time to prepare low-cost meals and care for children, making sure they get to school and back home safely, but they have the time to secure the services and programs available to the poor that are so often necessary for survival on very low incomes (such programs require visiting food pantries and going to requisite appointments at welfare and food stamps' offices). Off welfare and employed, or on welfare but fulfilling work requirements, mothers have much less time for everything, especially taking care of family members and participating in community life.

Even though families may earn more income at times than when on welfare, there are much higher expenses associated with employment, and income may not be as stable. The leaver studies confirm this. Most studies find that food insecurity is worse while off welfare than when receiving it. Utilities are more likely to be turned off, and families are much more likely to go through periods with no income. For example, in Massachusetts, 20 percent of the leaver sample had no job, were not receiving welfare, and were not living with any other adult who had income. Administrative annual or quarterly earnings data (unemployment insurance records which provide quarterly wage information) show that many, if not most, families are still in poverty. The administrative data, unlike the leaver surveys, examine earnings over a period of time. Median earnings, reported from administrative data that include total earnings for a quarter or year, are not much higher than the very low levels of income received when on welfare. This information, coupled with the employment rates reported in survey data, suggest women are cycling in and out of the labor market. It is hard to imagine that the income and employment instability welfare leaver families are facing does not place enormous stress on family life.

Then, of course, there is the issue of work hours and family life. Single-mother families find themselves in a Catch 22. In order to make enough to support a family, a single female wage earner with low-educational attainment will have to work long hours. However, long hours mean high child-care costs and little time with children. Working more "family-friendly" hours leaves time for children, but not enough income to house, feed, and clothe them.

Multiple Roles of Worker and Caregiver

US labor markets and social welfare policies are built on a family model in which there is one breadwinner and one caretaker–and these are not the same people. The breadwinner establishes the family's employment-based rights (health benefits, pensions, social security, and unemployment insurance) through continuous employment, and earns enough to support a family precisely because he (or she) can work long hours uninterrupted by the demands of doing the care work families need. The caretaker provides the necessary care for families to support a breadwinner to go to work. Welfare was established in recognition that there was no breadwinner in single-mother families.

This model has been breaking down for all families. For poor single mothers, however, there is nothing left in its wake; the working adult is now neither a full-time caregiver nor a successful family breadwinner, but she is no longer eligible for public assistance (at least for very long) and has few employment-based benefits. What welfare policies have done is to establish that there is no longer a "right" to receive income for taking care of your children. Unless women can move into a disability category that makes them eligible for SSI (Social Supplemental Income) or SSDI (Social Supplemental Disability Income), low-income mothers must rely on employment, employment-based benefits, family members and fathers of their children, or nothing. Child support has improved over the years, but it is still relatively low and often sporadic. Tapping other family members may work for a while, but it is uncertain and deletes the economic resources of family members. This leaves the tenuous and non-sustaining world of low-wage work.

The type of work that low-income mothers find often excludes them from the employment-based benefits that are part and parcel of the breadwinner/caregiver model. In this sense, the policy of requiring employment for single mothers in the US has very different consequences than it might in other industrialized countries. Unlike in other countries, the cost of child rearing in the US is mostly privatized; health benefits, private pensions and paid leave from work (for vacation, illness, or caring for newborns) are not guaranteed, and the low-wage labor market is large. Employment-based benefits are tied to long-term employment and often based on wage levels. As reported earlier, the majority of welfare leavers are in jobs that do not offer health insurance or even paid sick days or vacation time, let alone pensions. Previous research indicates that many poor mothers used welfare as a form of unemployment insurance, for which they were often not eligible because their wages were too low or job tenure too tenuous (Roberta Spalter-Roth *et al.* 1995). A national survey of employees and their use of family and medical leave found that more than 20 percent of women who did not receive paid leave turned to welfare when they had a child (Randy Albelda and Tiffany Manuel 2000).

These findings mean that every welfare mother faces the ultimate work/family dilemma, but with much more limited resources than her middle-class counterpart. Without sustained wage supplements, even full-time employment will usually not generate enough to support a family. While part-time work is often manageable and "family-friendly" in terms of hours at work, it does not pay nearly enough and rarely offers benefits.

* * *

CLOSING THE GAPS

The recurring themes of the work/family literature are to uncover how family demands affect one's ability to do paid work, to document how employment infringes on family life, and to promote workplace and public policies that can improve both work and family life. These are precisely the most important issues that need to be publicly discussed regarding welfare reform. There are material reasons and conditions to argue that the research, ideological, and economic gaps can and should be closed. Low-income single mothers actually have a good deal in common with married and middle (or higher) class women. Probably because of welfare reform, the labor-force participation rates of single mothers with children in the US, which since 1970 had been lower than those of married women, just surpassed them again (Philip Cohen and Suzanne Bianchi 1999). Low-income mothers have a long history of coping with work/family binds and have much to teach us.

Further, it is in the low-wage labor market that the corresponding lack of family-sustaining policies for everyone becomes glaringly obvious. The absence of required health coverage and paid leave policies (including mandatory paid sick days and vacation time), unaffordable or unsafe child-care, a narrowing unemployment insurance net, and inadequate wages and job supports for the lowest 20 percent of all workers severely hinder low-income families whose breadwinner(s) often moves into and out of employment. Importantly, these same conditions lower the wage and benefits floor for many workers.

Whilst the family constraints that low-income working families face are similar to those of other families, often the workplaces and job conditions are not. This means that much of the work/family research that focuses on what managers and professionals want or what works for them may not be applicable to low-wage workers. The focus on employer-based changes, whilst an important area of study, may not be appropriate or at least not adequate for low-wage workers. If left to individual employers or even to individual unions, as is the case now, work/family policies will remain highly stratified, benefiting only a privileged portion of the employed population. Expanding the view of employment and government policy solutions may be necessary. A set of policies that helped low-income single mothers deal with the demands of care giving and paid employment would aid all parents facing this dilemma, provided the programs and policies are made available to more than just the very poorest. This means spending significantly more than we do now and will likely require a substantial rethinking of public policy and employment relations.

There is an opportunity to close some gaps. Even though the category of "welfare" poor disappears with declining caseloads, it has not meant poverty has been eliminated or even reduced. Increasingly, the poor are spending more time in the labor force (Marlene Kim 2000), which might help close the ideological gap between the "deserving" and "undeserving" poor. That is, employment may make poor, single-mother families more deserving in the eyes of policy makers and the public. Directing policies toward alleviating the work/family bind in low-income families may also reduce the income gap, as it is possible that this would shift resources from the top to the middle and the bottom–depending on how these policies are crafted. Finally, paying attention to the work/family literature may make some welfare and poverty researchers less wedded to the national obsession of making mothers "job ready" and more willing to think about whether jobs are "mother ready." If work/family researchers took a closer look at the problems facing poor mothers, their notions of what work/family policies should be might substantially expand to include health care and wage reform. Good policies can trickle up, but they require a good view from the bottom.

REFERENCES

Abramovitz, Miriam. 1996. *Under Attack, Fighting Back: Women and Welfare in the United States.* New York: Cornerstone Books, Monthly Review Press.

Acs, Gregory and Pamela Loprest. 2000. "Synthesis of ASPE Funded Leaver Studies." Mimeo, Urban Institute.

Albelda, Randy and Tiffany Manuel. 2000. *Filling the Work and Family Gap: Paid Parental Leave in Massachusetts.* Boston, MA: Labor Resource Center, University of Massachusetts Boston.

Bacon, Jean and Laura Henze Russell with Diana Pearce. 2000. *The Self-Sufficiency Standard: Where Massachusetts Families Stand.* Boston, MA: Women's Educational and Industrial Union.

Blank, Rebecca and David Card. 2000. "Introduction: The Labor Market and Welfare Reform," in Rebecca Blank and David Card (eds.) *Finding Jobs: Work and Welfare Reform*, pp. 1–19. New York: Russell Sage Foundation.

Cohen, Philip N. and Suzanne M. Bianchi. 1999. "Marriage, children and women's employment: What do we know?" *Monthly Labor Review* 122(12): 22–31.

Dodson, Lisa. 1998. *Don't Call Us Out of Name: The Untold Lives of Women and Girls in Poor America.* Boston: Beacon Press.

Donahue, John D. 1999. *Hazardous Crosscurrents: Confronting Inequality in an Era of Devolution.* New York: Century Foundation.

Edin, Kathryn and Laura Lein. 1997. *Making Ends Meet: How Single Mothers Survive Welfare and Low-wage Work.* New York: Russell Sage Foundation.

Funiciello, Theresa. 1993. *The Tyranny of Kindness: Dismantling the Welfare System to End Poverty in America.* New York: Atlantic Monthly Press.

Gordon, Linda. 1994. *Pitied But Not Entitled: Single Mothers and the History of Welfare.* New York: Free Press.

Kim, Marlene. 2000. "Problems Facing the Working Poor," in Eileen Appelbaum (ed.) *Balancing Acts: Easing the Burdens and Improving the Options for Working Families*, pp. 49–57. Washington DC: Economic Policy Institute.

Lambert, Susan J. 1999. "Lower-Wage Workers and the New Realitites of Work and Family." *The Annals of the American Academy of Political and Social Sciences* 562(March): 174–90.

Massachusetts Department of Transitional Assistance. 2000. *After Time Limits: A study of Households Leaving Welfare Between December 1998 and April 1999*. Boston, MA: Department of Transitional Assistance.

Mink, Gwendolyn. 1998. *Welfare's End*. Ithaca, NY: Cornell University Press.

Mishel, Lawrence, Jared Bernstein, and John Schmitt. 1999. *The State of Working America, 1998–99*. Ithaca, NY: Cornell University Press.

Newman, Katherine S. 2000. "On the High Wire: How the Working Poor Juggle Job and Family Responsibilities," in Eileen Appelbaum (ed.) *Balancing Acts: Easing the Burdens and Improving the Options for Working Families*, pp. 85–94. Washington DC: Economic Policy Institute.

Perry-Jenkins, Maureen, Rena L. Repetti, and Ann C. Crouter. 2000. "Work and Family in the 1990s." *Journal of Marriage and the Family* 62(November): 981–98.

Primus, Wendell, Lynette Rawlings, Kathy Larin, and Kathryn Porter. 1999. *The Initial Impact of Welfare Reform on the Incomes of Single-Mother Families*. Washington DC: Center on Budget and Policy Priorities.

Sanford, Schram and Joe Soss. Forthcoming. "Success Stories: Welfare Reform, Policy Discourse, and the Politics of Research." *The Annals of the American Academy of Political and Social Sciences*. November 2001.

Spalter-Roth, Roberta, Beverly Burr, Heidi Hartmann, and Lois Shaw. 1995. *Welfare That Works: The Working Lives of AFDC Recipients*. Washington DC: Institute for Women's Policy Research.

US Census Bureau. 2000. *Statistical Abstract of the United States, 1999*. Washington DC: Government Printing Office.

US House of Representatives, Committee on Ways and Means. 2000. *2000 Green Book: Background Material and Data on Programs Within the Jurisdiction of the Committee on Ways and Means*. Washington DC: Government Printing Office.

Wolff, Edward N. 2000. *Recent Trends in Wealth Ownership, 1983–1998*. Working Paper No. 300. Annadale, NY: Jerome Levy Economics Institute.

Race and Gender in Families and at Work
The Fatherhood Wage Premium

Rebecca Glauber

Rebecca Glauber is an Assistant Professor in the Department of Sociology at the University of New Hampshire and a Faculty Fellow at the Carsey Institute. This essay appeared in the journal Gender & Society in 2008.

Black men are often publicly portrayed as irresponsible or peripheral fathers (Hamer 2001; Smith et al. 2005). Although the rate of non-marital births has disproportionately increased during the past five decades in the United States for Black women, the popular image of absent Black fathers conceals a range of men's experiences in families. More than one-third of Black children have a married mother and father (U.S. Census Bureau 2005). Politicians and social scientists have focused considerable attention on unmarried Black fathers, leaving important questions on married Black fathers' work and family experiences, gender, and racial inequality unanswered. Do all married men, Blacks, whites, and Latinos, benefit from fatherhood in the same way?

The current study presents answers to this question by exploring the intersections of gender and race on married white, Black, and Latino fathers' labor market outcomes. Numerous studies have shown that women pay a wage penalty for motherhood (Avellar and Smock 2003; Budig and England 2001; Glauber 2007; Waldfogel 1997), and a few recent studies have shown that married men earn a wage premium for fatherhood (Lundberg and Rose 2000, 2002). Other studies have found that compared to childless men, fathers spend more time at work (Knoester and Eggebeen 2006) and are viewed as more capable in their jobs and more deserving of promotions (Correll, Benard, and Paik 2007).

Although the mechanisms of the fatherhood wage premium remain somewhat elusive, most gender scholars argue that the premium—and its corollary, the motherhood wage penalty—reflect institutionalized gender inequalities and essentialist cultural conceptions of motherhood and fatherhood (Ridgeway and Correll 2004a, 2004b). Most likely, men experience an increase in their earnings on the birth of a child because (1) the gender division of household and paid labor becomes less equal and frees or motivates men to become more productive in their paid work and (2) hegemonic cultural constructions of masculinity, fatherhood, and bread-winning (Coltrane 1997; Connell 1987, 1995) lead employers to favor fathers over childless men.

Despite ample evidence that work and family experiences are both gendered and racialized (e.g., Browne and Misra 2003; Glenn 2002; Kennelly 1999), few studies have analyzed racial differences in married fathers' labor market outcomes. The current study draws on longitudinal data and explores the associations among fatherhood and adult white, Black, and Latino men's annual earnings, annual time spent at work, and hourly wages. In short, I argue that the fatherhood wage premium is one mechanism of gender inequality. The organization of families and work around gender is associated with an increase in men's and particularly fathers' economic independence and occupational prospects at the same time as it is associated with a decrease in women's and mothers' economic independence and occupational prospects (Sorensen and McLanahan 1987). The fatherhood wage premium, along with the motherhood wage penalty, widens the gender gap in earnings over women's and men's life courses. Furthermore, the current analysis shows that gender stratification systems in families and work are racialized and that inequality is more pronounced in married white and Latino families than in married Black families. In terms of their own earnings, married Black fathers benefit—albeit less than do white and Latino fathers—from gendered family and work experiences.

THEORIES OF FATHERS' LABOR MARKET ADVANTAGES

Gender scholars have long argued that family and work are connected, but most studies have explored these connections by focusing on women and on the dilemmas that mothers face in negotiating demands of work and families (Gerson 1985; Hays 1996; Hochschild 1989). In an analysis of men's family and work arrangements, Gerson (1993) argued that men have entered a territory of "no man's land" where the cultural constructions of masculinity and fatherhood are open ended. Others have also noted that men have lost their hold on primary breadwinning status, and they now face new and conflicting conceptions of breadwinning and involved fatherhood (Griswold 1993).

Despite the contemporary open-ended meaning of fatherhood, the birth of a child continues to be associated with an increase in men's time spent at work and an increase in men's hourly wages. Drawing on longitudinal data from the Panel Study of Income Dynamics, Lundberg and Rose (2002) found that the birth of a first child is associated with a 4 percent increase in men's hourly wages and that the birth of a second child is associated with a 7 percent increase in men's hourly wages. The authors also found that men work about 82 more hours per year after the birth of their first child and another 26 more hours per year after the birth of their second child. Other studies have found that fatherhood is positively correlated with men's work hours (Knoester and Eggebeen 2006; Sanchez and Thompson 1997). However, Kaufman and Uhlenberg (2000) found that fatherhood is positively correlated with men's work hours only for those who express a traditional set of gender beliefs. For men who express an egalitarian set of gender beliefs, fatherhood is negatively correlated with work hours.

Gendered Employment Experiences

One explanation for the fatherhood premium proposes that gender and cultural conceptions of motherhood and fatherhood structure employment relations. As Ridgeway and Correll (2004b), Lorber (1994), and Risman (1998, 2004) argued, gender refers to an institutionalized system of organizing social relations and constituting differences between two categories of individuals. Gender is a process rather than an outcome, and conceptions of essential differences between men and women structure modern organizational rewards and relations (Acker 1990; Connell

1987). Theoretically, ideal workers are fully committed because they are free from external family obligations (Williams 2000). Ridgeway and Correll (2004a, 2004b) proposed that widely held beliefs of men as instrumental providers and of women as expressive caretakers structure employer–worker interactions and reproduce gender inequalities. Fatherhood signals conformity to hegemonic masculinity, and, as Coltrane (2004, 215) argued, "When men become husbands and fathers, coworkers and superiors perceive them as being more serious and more deserving of career advancement than their single or childless counterparts."

Many studies have shown that mothers are discriminated against in the labor market. Women are viewed as primarily committed to their families and only secondarily committed to their jobs (Hays 1996). Fewer studies have analyzed how employers perceive of and respond to fathers. In one recent exception, Correll, Benard, and Paik (2007) analyzed experimental and audit data and found that motherhood is viewed as a devalued status characteristic, which results in biased evaluations of competency and commitment. In contrast, fatherhood signals greater competency, ability, and commitment. They also found that compared to equally qualified childless men, fathers received a significantly higher average recommended starting salary.

Gendered Family Experiences

An alternative (although not mutually exclusive) explanation for the fatherhood wage premium centers on the gender division of household and paid labor. The birth of a child increases the amount of time that women spend in housework and decreases the amount of time that they spend in paid work (Sanchez and Thompson 1997). These changes may free men or motivate them to become more productive in their paid jobs. Many studies have shown that marriage increases men's work productivity and hourly wages (Cohen 2002; Gray 1997; Korenman and Neumark 1991; Loh 1996), most likely by increasing the amount of time that women spend in household labor (Bianchi et al. 2000) and by decreasing the amount of time that men spend in household labor (Gupta 1999). Wives provide care that directly contributes to men's well-being.

Decisions surrounding the division of labor reflect cultural conceptions of gender and economic and power differences between men and women. Studies have found that as the gaps in husbands' and wives' earnings and work hours converge, the gap in their household labor also converges. At the point at which wives earn more than their husbands, however, husbands reduce the amount of time that they spend in household labor to compensate for their diminished breadwinning status (Bittman et al. 2003; Brines 1994; Tichenor 2005). These findings imply that structural gender inequalities and cultural conceptions of differences between women and men shape family experiences. The same processes that underlie the marriage wage premium may also lead to an additional fatherhood wage premium for married men. That is, men may first earn a premium for marriage and then may again earn a premium for fatherhood within marriage.

Racial Inequality and Men's Experiences in Families and Work

Despite evidence that family and work experiences are both gendered and racialized, previous research on fatherhood and men's earnings has not explored racial variation among men. There are at least two aspects of racial inequality that affect married Black men's experiences as fathers. First, there is a large literature that shows that employers discriminate against Black workers in favor of white workers. Employers view Black men as lacking soft skills (Moss and Tilly 1996; Wilson 1996), and employers discriminate against Black individuals in hiring practices (Pager 2003) and in ratings of job performance. Employers also hold racialized and gendered conceptions of workers' family statuses. Kennelly (1999) found that not only do employers perceive all working women as mothers and as less capable in their jobs, but they also perceive all Black women as single mothers. Race and gender intersect to create unique disadvantages for Black women. Similarly, race and gender may intersect to create unique advantages for working white and Latino men. Although Kennelly's research did not address the issue, employers likely hold racialized conceptions of fatherhood. White and Latino fathers tend to be perceived as breadwinning providers and committed workers, whereas Black fathers tend to be perceived as irresponsible providers and uncommitted workers (Hamer 2001). These perceptions may affect hiring and promotion decisions.

Racial inequality also affects men's experiences within their families. Black men suffer from job instability (Wilson 1996), network disadvantages (Royster 2007), and earnings and wealth inequalities (Conley 1999). Latinos also suffer from racial discrimination and inequality (McCall 2001), but as with white men, they have a relatively higher earnings advantage over their wives than Black men. Black women have historically maintained higher levels of employment and economic independence than white women and Latinas (Landry 2000; Sorensen and McLanahan 1987; Winkler, McBride, and Andrews 2005; Winslow-Bowe 2006), although among younger cohorts, Black women are slightly less likely than white women to be employed (Browne and Askew 2005; England, Garcia-Beaulieu, and Ross 2004; Reid 2002).

Married Black couples tend to divide housework and paid work somewhat more equally than do married white and Latino couples (Gupta 2006; John and Shelton 1997; Orbuch and Eyster 1997; Shelton and John 1993). This may explain why Black men earn a slightly smaller wage premium for marriage than do white men (Cohen 2002). It may also lead to a smaller fatherhood wage premium for Blacks than for whites and Latinos. Historically, marriage has offered less protection against Black women's economic vulnerability (Hirschl, Altobelli, and Rank 2003; Smock, Manning, and Gupta 1999; Wilson 2003), and Black women have tended to experience motherhood and employment as complementary rather than as competing (Collins 1991). Many groups of Latinas have also experienced motherhood and employment as complementary and have faced multiple intersecting disadvantages because of their race, class, and gender. For example, Segura (1989) highlighted the intersections of a race- and gender-segmented labor market on immigrant and nonimmigrant Mexican women's experiences of occupational mobility. Hondagneu-Sotelo's (2001) study showed that paid Latina domestic workers in Los Angeles tend to work very long hours, even when they are mothers. In general, however, studies have shown that Latino couples divide housework somewhat less equally than do Black couples.

Expectations

When viewed together, research on the fatherhood wage premium and on racial inequality in men's experiences in families and work should lead us to expect that Black men experience a smaller wage premium for fatherhood than do white men and Latinos. This expectation follows from two premises. First, employers discriminate against Black men and tend to perceive them as less skilled and committed than white men. Constructions of masculinity, fatherhood, and breadwinning are also racialized, and Black men may be perceived of as absent or irresponsible fathers. Employers may prefer white and Latino fathers over white and Latino childless men, but they may not prefer Black fathers over Black childless men. Second, institutionalized racial inequality has led to (1) diminished job stability and earnings for Black men relative to white men and (2) a smaller relative earnings and employment advantage over their wives and a more equal gender division of paid and unpaid labor for Black men as compared to white men and Latinos. Therefore, compared to white men and Latinos, Black men may not experience as much of an increase in their wages, annual earnings, and annual work hours following the birth of a child. Black men's wages and work hours may also be less sensitive to their wives' work hours.

*   *   *

CONCLUSION

Many studies on gender inequality in families and work have focused on women. Fewer studies have focused on men's family and work experiences, and even fewer studies have asked how gender and race intersect to shape men's experiences. The current analysis extends existing research by providing a descriptive account of differences in fathers' labor market outcomes among whites, Blacks, and Latinos. I report two new sets of findings. First, there are some similarities among fathers. For all men, the fatherhood wage premium is tied to marriage. Men experience an increase in their wages first when they marry and then again when they have children within marriages. Unmarried men do not experience an increase in their hourly wages on the birth of a child. Unmarried men may not appear to conform to cultural ideals of normative, breadwinning fatherhood, and employers may not extend preferential treatment to unmarried fathers. It is also possible that unmarried fathers do not benefit as much as married fathers from a gender division of household labor, or that unmarried fathers do not experience as much of an increase in their commitment to breadwinning status because their children tend to not live with them.

Second, there are three important differences among married fathers. Compared to white men and Latinos, (1) Black men experience a smaller premium for fatherhood in terms of both hourly wages and annual earnings, (2) Black men do not experience an increase in their annual time spent at work, whereas white men and Latinos do, and (3) Black men do not earn any more or work any more when their wives work less, whereas white men experience an increase in their earnings and time spent at work and Latinos experience an increase in their earnings when their wives work less.

These findings are consistent with the expectations described in the beginning of this study. Masculinity, fatherhood, and men's work experiences are racialized. Employers may be less likely to view Black fathers as committed breadwinners, and Black men may experience less of a labor market bonus for fatherhood. Latino men also suffer from racial discrimination and labor market inequalities, but stereotypes about Latinos do not generally include notions of irresponsible fatherhood. Moreover, because of institutionalized racial inequalities, the gender division of paid and unpaid labor is somewhat more equal in Black families, and Black men may not experience as much of an increase in their work productivity and annual work hours following the birth of a child. Again, although Latinos also suffer from systematic racial inequality, they tend to divide paid labor and housework with their wives somewhat less equally than do Black men. These mechanisms may lead to greater discrepancies among white and Latino mothers and fathers than among Black mothers and fathers. Studies on racial differences in household labor have found similar results. Namely, although gender differences within married couples are more pronounced than racial differences between married couples, gender inequality is more pronounced in white marriages than in Black marriages (John and Shelton 1997; Orbuch and Eyster 1997; Shelton and John 1993).

REFERENCES

Acker, Joan. 1990. Hierarchies, jobs, bodies: A theory of gendered organizations. *Gender & Society* 4 (2): 139–58.

Avellar, Sarah, and Pamela Smock. 2003. Has the price of motherhood declined over time? A cross-cohort comparison of the motherhood wage penalty. *Journal of Marriage and Family* 65 (3): 597–607.

Baca Zinn, Maxine, and Bonnie Thornton Dill. 1996. Theorizing difference from multiracial feminism. *Feminist Studies* 22 (2): 321–31.

Bianchi, Suzanne M., Melissa A. Milkie, Liana C. Sayer, and John P. Robinson. 2000. Is anyone doing the housework? Trends in the gender division of household labor. *Social Forces* 79 (1): 191–228.

Bittman, Michael, Paula England, Liana Sayer, Nancy Folbre, and George Matheson. 2003. When does gender trump money? Bargaining and time in household work. *American Journal of Sociology* 109 (1): 186–214.

Brines, Julie. 1994. Economic dependency, gender, and the division of labor at home. *American Journal of Sociology* 100 (3): 652–88.

Browne, Irene, and Rachel Askew. 2005. Race, ethnicity, and wage inequality among women: What happened in the 1990s and early 21st century? *American Behavioral Scientist* 48 (9): 1275–92.

Browne, Irene, and Joya Misra. 2003. The intersection of gender and race in the labor market. *Annual Review of Sociology* 29:487–513.

Budig, Michelle J., and Paula England. 2001. The wage penalty for motherhood. *American Sociological Review* 66 (2): 204–25.

Cohen, Philip N. 2002. Cohabitation and the declining marriage premium for men. *Work and Occupations* 29 (3): 346–63.

Collins, Patricia Hill. 1991. *Black feminist thought: Knowledge, consciousness, and the politics of empowerment.* New York: Routledge.

Coltrane, Scott. 1997. *Family man: Fatherhood, housework, and gender equity.* New York: Oxford University Press.

———. 2004. Elite careers and family commitment: It's (still) about gender. *ANNALS of the American Academy of Political and Social Science* 596 (1): 214–20.

Conley, Dalton. 1999. *Being Black, living in the red: Race, wealth, and social policy in America.* Berkeley: University of California Press.

Connell, R. W. 1987. *Gender and power: Society, the person, and sexual politics.* Stanford, CA: Stanford University Press.

———. 1995. *Masculinities.* Berkeley: University of California Press.

Correll, Shelley J., Stephen Benard, and In Paik. 2007. Getting a job: Is there a motherhood penalty? *American Journal of Sociology* 112 (5): 1297–1338.

England, Paula, Carmen Garcia-Beaulieu, and Mary Ross. 2004. Women's employment among Blacks, whites, and three groups of Latinas: Do more privileged women have higher employment? *Gender & Society* 18 (4): 494–509.

Gerson, Kathleen. 1985. *Hard choices: How women decide about work, career, and motherhood.* Berkeley: University of California Press.

———. 1993. *No man's land: Men's changing commitments to family and work.* New York: Basic Books.

Glauber, Rebecca. 2007. Marriage and the motherhood wage penalty among African Americans, Hispanics, and whites. *Journal of Marriage and Family* 69 (4): 951–61.

Glenn, Evelyn Nakano. 2002. *Unequal freedom: How race and gender shaped American citizenship and labor.* Cambridge, MA: Harvard University Press.

Gray, Jeffrey S. 1997. The fall in men's return to marriage: Declining productivity effects or changing selection? *Journal of Human Resources* 32 (3): 481–504.

Griswold, Robert L. 1993. *Fatherhood in America: A history.* New York: Basic Books.

Gupta, Sanjiv. 1999. The effects of transitions in marital status on men's performance of housework. *Journal of Marriage and Family* 61 (3): 700–711.

———. 2006. The consequences of maternal employment during men's childhood for their adult housework performance. *Gender & Society* 20 (1): 60–86.

Hamer, Jennifer. 2001. *What it means to be daddy: Fatherhood for Black men living away from their children.* New York: Columbia University Press.

Hays, Sharon. 1996. *The cultural contradictions of motherhood.* New Haven, CT: Yale University Press.

Hirschl, Thomas A., Joyce Altobelli, and Mark R. Rank. 2003. Does marriage increase the odds of affluence? Exploring the life course probabilities. *Journal of Marriage and Family* 65 (4): 927–38.

Hochschild, Arlie Russell. 1989. *The second shift: Working parents and the revolution at home.* New York: Viking.

Hondagneu-Sotelo, Pierrette. 2001. *Doméstica: Immigrant workers cleaning and caring in the shadows of affluence.* Berkeley: University of California Press.

John, Daphne, and Beth Anne Shelton. 1997. The production of gender among Black and white women and men: The case of household labor. *Sex Roles: A Journal of Research* 36 (3–4): 171–93.

Kaufman, Gayle, and Peter Uhlenberg. 2000. The influence of parenthood on the work effort of married men and women. *Social Forces* 78 (3): 931–47.

Kennelly, Ivy. 1999. "That single-mother element": How employers typify Black women. *Gender & Society* 13 (2): 168–92.

Knoester, Chris, and David J. Eggebeen. 2006. The effects of the transition to parenthood and subsequent children on men's well-being and social participation. *Journal of Family Issues* 27 (11): 1532–60.

Korenman, Sanders, and David Neumark. 1991. Does marriage really make men more productive? *Journal of Human Resources* 26 (2): 282–307.

Landry, Bart. 2000. *Black working wives: Pioneers of the American family revolution.* Berkeley: University of California Press.

Loh, Eng Seng. 1996. Productivity differences and the marriage wage premium for white males. *Journal of Human Resources* 31 (3): 566–59.

Lorber, Judith. 1994. *Paradoxes of gender.* New Haven, CT: Yale University Press.

Lundberg, Shelly, and Elaina Rose. 2000. Parenthood and the earnings of married men and women. *Labour Economics* 7 (6): 689–710.

———. 2002. The effects of sons and daughters on men's labor supply and wages. *Review of Economics and Statistics* 84 (2): 251–68.

McCall, Leslie. 2001. *Complex inequality: Gender, class, and race in the new economy.* New York: Routledge.

———. 2005. The complexity of intersectionality. *Signs: Journal of Women in Culture and Society* 30 (3): 1771–1800.

Moss, Philip, and Chris Tilly. 1996. "Soft" skills and race: An investigation of Black men's employment problems. *Work and Occupations* 23 (3): 252–76.

Orbuch, Terri L., and Sandra L. Eyster. 1997. Division of household labor among Black couples and white couples. *Social Forces* 76 (1): 301–32.

Pager, Devah. 2003. The mark of a criminal record. *American Journal of Sociology* 108 (5): 937–75.

Reid, Lori L. 2002. Occupational segregation, human capital, and motherhood: Black women's higher exit rates from full-time employment. *Gender & Society* 16 (5): 728–47.

Ridgeway, Cecilia L., and Shelley J. Correll. 2004b. Motherhood as a status characteristic. *Journal of Social Issues* 60 (4): 683–700.

———. 2004b. Unpacking the gender system: A theoretical perspective on gender beliefs and social relations. *Gender & Society* 18 (4): 510–31.

Risman, Barbara J. 1998. *Gender vertigo: American families in transition.* New Haven, CT: Yale University Press.

———. 2004. Gender as a social structure: Theory wrestling with activism. *Gender & Society* 18 (4): 429–50.

Royster, Deirdre A. 2007. What happens to potential discouraged? Masculinity norms and the contrasting institutional and labor market experiences of less affluent Black and white men. *ANNALS of the American Academy of Political and Social Science* 609 (1): 153–80.

Sanchez, Laura, and Elizabeth Thomson. 1997. Becoming mothers and fathers: Parenthood, gender, and the division of labor. *Gender & Society* 11 (6): 747–72.

Segura, Denise A. 1989. Chicana and Mexican immigrant women at work: The impact of class, race, and gender on occupational mobility. *Gender & Society* 2 (1): 37–52.

Shelton, Beth Anne, and Daphne John. 1993. Race, ethnicity and difference: A comparison of white, Black and Hispanic men's household labor time. In *Men, work and family*, edited by Jane Hood. Beverly Hills, CA: Sage.

Smith, Carolyn A., Marvin D. Krohn, Rebekah Chu, and Oscar Best. 2005. African American fathers: Myths and realities about their involvement with their firstborn children. *Journal of Family Issues* 26 (7): 975–1001.

Smock, Pamela J., Wendy D. Manning, and Sanjiv Gupta. 1999. The effect of marriage and divorce on women's economic well-being. *American Sociological Review* 64 (6): 794–812.

Sorensen, Annemette, and Sara McLanahan. 1987. Married women's economic dependency, 1940–1980. *American Journal of Sociology* 93 (3): 659–87.

Tichenor, Veronica Jaris. 2005. *Earning more and getting less: Why successful wives can't buy equality.* Rutgers, NJ: Rutgers University Press.

U.S. Census Bureau. 2005. *America's families and living arrangements.* Washington, DC: U.S. Census Bureau.

Waldfogel, Jane. 1997. The effect of children on women's wages. *American Sociological Review* 62 (2): 209–17.

Williams, Joan. 2000. *Unbending gender: Why family and work conflict and what to do about it.* Oxford, UK: Oxford University Press.

Wilson, Andrea E. 2003. Race and women's income trajectories: Employment, marriage, and income security over the life course. *Social Problems* 50 (1): 87–110.

Wilson, William J. 1996. *When work disappears: The world of the new urban poor.* New York: Knopf.

Winkler, Anne E., Timothy D. McBride, and Courtney Andrews. 2005. Wives who outearn their husbands: A transitory or persistent phenomenon for couples? *Demography* 42 (3): 523–35.

Winslow-Bowe, Sarah. 2006. The persistence of wives' income advantage. *Journal of Marriage and Family* 68 (4): 824–42.

SECTION VI

Gendered Bodies

Key Concepts for Section VI: Gendered Bodies

Abstinence-Only Sex Education
Abstinence-Plus Sex Education
Action Beauty
Adolescent Family Life Act (AFLA) of 1981
Adonis Complex
Anorexia Nervosa
Backlash Beauty
Beauty Ideal
Beauty Myth
Body Dysmorphia
Body Image
Bulimia Nervosa
Comprehensive Sex Education
Culture of Thinness
Disordered Eating
Eating Disorders
Fat Oppression
The Erotic
Gender Actualizing
Gendered Sexual Socialization
Maternal and Child Health (MCH) Bureau
Pornography
Section 510(b) of the Social Security Act
Sexual Double Standard
Sexual Gender Gap
Sexually Transmitted Infections
Sickbed Aesthetic
Special Programs of Regional and National
    Significance-Community Based Abstinence
    Education Grants
Standards of Beauty

Concepts to Review
Backlash
Dehumanization
Discourse
Doing Gender
Double Standards
Dreamworld
Emphasized Femininity
Female Genital Cutting
Femininity/Femininities
Filmic techniques from *Dreamworlds*

Gaze
Gender
Hegemonic Masculinity
Ideology
Infantilization
Internalized Oppression
Intersectionality
Intersex
Male Gaze
Masculinity/Masculinities
Meaning
Media Activism
Media Literacy
Medicalization
Metaphor
Misogyny
Motif
Mythical Norm
Objectification
Personal Responsibility and Work
    Opportunity Reconciliation Act
    (PRWORA) of 1996
Pink Think
Popular Culture
Pornographic Imagination
Problem with No Name
Rape
Rape Supportive Culture
Rape-Prone Culture
Rhetorical Triangle
Sex
Sex Roles
Sex-Gender System
Sexism
Sexual Object
Sexual Subject
Socialization
Sticky Floor
Symbol
Theme
Tough Guise
Tropes
Voyeurism

Beauty and the Backlash

Susan Faludi

Susan Faludi This selection is from Susan Faludi's book Backlash: The Undeclared War Against American Women *(1991), which won the National Book Critics Circle Award for Nonfiction. Her most recent book is* The Terror Dream: Fear and Fantasy in Post-9/11 America *(2008). She has written articles for* The New Yorker, The Wall Street Journal, The New York Times, the Los Angeles Times, *and* The Nation.

With the aid of a metal rod, the first woman of "the New Generation" stands in Robert Filoso's Los Angeles workshop, her feet dangling a few inches off the floor. Her clay arms are bandaged in gauze strips and her face hooded in a plastic bag, knotted at the neck to keep out dust motes. A single speck could cause a blemish.

"There are no imperfections in my models," the thirty-eight-year-old mannequin sculptor explains. "They all have to be taken out." The dank environment inside the bag, however, has bred its own facial flaws. Between the woman's parted lips, a green mold is growing.

On this April morning in 1988, Filoso is at work on the model that will set the standard for the following year. Ever since he brought "the new realism" to female mannequins—chiseling detailed vertebrae, toes, and nipples—Filoso has led the $1.2 billion dummy industry, serving all the better retailers. This year, he is making some major changes. His New Generation woman has shrunk in height, gained almost three inches on her breasts, shed an inch from her waist, and developed three sets of eyelashes. The new vital statistics, 34-23-36, are voluptuous by mannequin standards, but the Lacroix era of strapless gowns and bone-tight bodices requires bigger busts and wasp waists. "Fashion," Filoso says, "determines the shape of my girls."

The sculptor gingerly unwinds the cloth strips and hands them to his assistant and model, Laurie Rothey. "It seems like so many of the girls are getting breast implants," Rothey is saying as they work, and she isn't referring to the mannequins. "It's the only way you can get jobs because big breasts are all the [modeling] agencies are hiring now. . . ."

Filoso interrupts her with a curse. The clay hasn't dried yet and the mannequin's arm has flopped off its metal bone. The sculptor tries to reattach the limb but now one arm is shorter than the other. "Look at her now, she's a disaster," Filoso cries, throwing his towel on the floor and departing in a huff.

Later that day, his composure regained, Filoso describes his vision for the New Generation. He pictures an in-shape upscale Marilyn Monroe, a "curvy but thin" society lady who can "afford to go to Bergdorf Goodman's and buy anything." Their poses, too, he says, will be "more feminine, more contained. . . . In the 1970s, mannequins were always out there, reaching for something. Now they are pulling into themselves." That's the way it is for real women in the '80s, too, he says: "Now you can be yourself, you can be a lady. You don't have to be a powerhouse."

In Filoso's opinion, these developments are a big improvement over the '70s, when women "didn't care" about their appearance. "The stores didn't want beautiful mannequins, because they were afraid women customers would look at them and say, 'God, I could never look like that in a million years.'" That era, Filoso is happy to report, has passed. "Now, mannequins are really coming to life. They are going to start getting prettier again—more like the fashion photography you'd see in old magazines from the 1950s." And what of female customers who might say, as he put it, "God, I could never look like that in a million years"? But that's the good news, Filoso says. "Today, women can look at a beautiful mannequin in a store and say, 'I want to look like her,' and they actually can! They can go to their doctor and say, 'Doc, I want these cheekbones.' 'Doc, I want these breasts.'"

He sighs. "If I were smart, I would have become a plastic surgeon."

*   *   *

During the '80s, mannequins set the beauty trends—and real women were expected to follow. The dummies were "coming to life," while the ladies were breathing anesthesia and going under the knife. The beauty industry promoted a "return to femininity" as if it were a revival of natural womanhood—a flowering of all those innate female qualities supposedly suppressed in the feminist '70s. Yet the "feminine" traits the industry celebrated most were grossly unnatural—and achieved with increasingly harsh, unhealthy, and punitive measures.

The beauty industry, of course, has never been an advocate of feminist aspirations. This is not to say that its promoters have a conscious political program against women's rights, just a commercial mandate to improve on the bottom line. And the formula the industry has counted on for many years—aggravating women's low self-esteem and high anxiety about a "feminine" appearance—has always served them well. (American women, according to surveys by the Kinsey Institute, have more negative feelings about their bodies than women in any other culture studied.) The beauty makers' motives aren't particularly thought out or deep. Their overwrought and incessant instructions to women are more mindless than programmatic; their frenetic noise generators create more static than substance. But even so, in the '80s the beauty industry belonged to the cultural loop that produced backlash feedback. Inevitably, publicists for the beauty companies would pick up on the warning signals circulating about the toll of women's equality, too—and amplify them for their own purposes.

"Is your face paying the price of success?" worried a 1988 Nivea skin cream ad, in which a business-suited woman with a briefcase rushes a child to day care—and catches a glimpse of her career-pitted skin in a store window. If only she were less successful, her visage would be more radiant. "The impact of work stress . . . can play havoc with your complexion," *Mademoiselle* warned; it can cause "a bad case of dandruff," "an eventual loss of hair" and, worst of all, weight gain. Most at risk, the magazine claimed, are "high-achieving women," whose comely appearance can be ravaged by "executive stress." In ad after ad, the beauty industry hammered home its version of the backlash thesis: women's professional progress had downgraded their looks; equality had created worry lines and cellulite. This message was barely updated from a century earlier, when the late Victorian beauty press had warned women that their quest for higher education and employment was causing "a general lapse of attractiveness" and "spoiling complexions."

The beauty merchants incited fear about the cost of women's occupational success largely because they feared, rightly, that that success had cost *them*—in profits. Since the rise of the women's movement in the '70s, cosmetics and fragrance companies had suffered a decade of flat-to-declining sales, hair-product merchandisers had fallen into a prolonged slump, and hair-dressers had watched helplessly as masses of female customers who were opting for simple low-cost cuts defected to discount unisex salons. In 1981, Revlon's earnings fell for the first time since 1968; by the following year, the company's profits had plunged a record 40 percent. The industry aimed to restore its own economic health by persuading women that *they* were the ailing patients—and professionalism their ailment. Beauty became medicalized as its lab-coated army of promoters, and real doctors, prescribed physician-endorsed potions, injections for the skin, chemical "treatments" for the hair, plastic surgery for virtually every inch of the torso. (One doctor even promised to reduce women's height by sawing their leg bones.) Physicians and hospital administrators, struggling with their own financial difficulties, joined the industry in this campaign. Dermatologists faced with a shrinking teen market switched from treating adolescent pimples to "curing" adult female wrinkles. Gynecologists and obstetricians frustrated with a sluggish birthrate and skyrocketing malpractice premiums traded their forceps for liposuction scrapers. Hospitals facing revenue shortfalls opened cosmetic-surgery divisions and sponsored extreme and costly liquid-protein diet programs.

The beauty industry may seem the most superficial of the cultural institutions participating in the backlash, but its impact on women was, in many respects, the most intimately destructive—to both female bodies and minds. Following the orders of the '80s beauty doctors made many women literally ill. Antiwrinkle treatments exposed them to carcinogens. Acid face peels burned their skin. Silicone injections left painful deformities. "Cosmetic" liposuction caused severe complications, infections, and even death. Internalized, the decade's beauty dictates played a role in exacerbating an epidemic of eating disorders. And the beauty industry helped to deepen the psychic isolation that so many women felt in the '80s, by reinforcing the representation of women's problems as purely personal ills, unrelated to social pressures and curable only to the degree that the individual woman succeeded in fitting the universal standard—by physically changing herself.

The emblems of pulchritude marketed in the '80s—frailty, pallor, puerility—were all beauty marks handed down by previous backlash eras. Historically, the backlash Venus has been an enervated invalid recovering on the chaise longue, an ornamental and genteel lady sipping tea in the drawing room, a child bride shielded from the sun. During the late Victorian era, the beauty industry glorified a cult of invalidism—and profited from it by promoting near-toxic potions that induced a chalky visage. The wasting-away look helped in part to unleash the nation's first dieting mania and the emergence of anorexia in young women. In times of backlash, the beauty standard converges with the social campaign against wayward women, allying itself with "traditional" morality; a porcelain and unblemished exterior becomes proof of a woman's internal purity, obedience, and restraint. The beautiful backlash woman is controlled in both senses of the word. Her physique has been domesticated, her appearance tamed and manicured as the grounds of a gentleman's estate.

By contrast, athleticism, health, and vivid color are the defining properties of female beauty during periods when the culture is more receptive to women's quest for independence. In the late 1910s and early 1920s, female athletes began to eclipse movie stars as the nation's beauty archetypes; Coco Chanel's tan launched a nationwide vogue in ruddy outdoor looks; and Helena Rubinstein's brightly tinted cosmetics made loud and flamboyant colors acceptable. By the late 1920s and '30s, however, the beauty press denounced women who tanned their faces and companies fired women who showed up at work sporting flashy makeup colors. Again, during World War II, invigorated and sun-tanned beauties received all the praise. *Harper's Bazaar* described "the New American Look of 1943" this way: "Her face is out in the open and so is she. Her figure is lithe and strong. Its lines are lines of action. The glamour girl is no more." With the war over, however, the beauty industry restored that girl—encouraged by a new breed of motivational research consultants who advised cosmetics companies to paint more passive images of femininity. Beauty publicists instructed women to inflate their breasts with padding or silicone, to frost their hair with carcinogenic dyes, to make themselves look paler by whitening their face and lips with titanium—to emulate, in short, that most bleached and medicalized glamour girl of them all, Marilyn Monroe.

Under the '80s backlash, the pattern would repeat, as "Action Beauty," as it was so labeled and exalted in '70s women's magazines, gave way to a sickbed aesthetic. It was a comprehensive transformation carried out at every level of the beauty culture—from the most superficially applied scent to the most invasive and dangerous operations.

Letting Ourselves Go
Making Room for the Fat Body in Feminist Scholarship

Cecilia Hartley

Cecilia Hartley earned a B.A. in English from the University of Louisville. She is co-author with S. Morgan Gresham of "The Use of Electronic Communication in Facilitating Feminist Modes of Discourse: An Irigaraian Heuristic" in Feminist Cyberscapes: Essays on Gender in Electronic Spaces *(2000). This essay appeared in* Bodies Out of Bounds: Fatness and Transgression *(2001).*

There is something wrong with the female body. Women learn early—increasingly, as early as five or six years old—that their bodies are fundamentally flawed. The restructuring process begins often as soon as a child is able to understand that there is a difference between the sexes. When that awareness reveals a female body, the realization soon follows that that body must be changed, molded, reconfigured into an ideal that will never be reached by "letting nature take its course."

Not surprisingly, self-hatred often becomes a part of a woman's body image. By the onset of puberty, a sense of body deficiency is very firmly in place, and that sense of deficiency is exacerbated as the body matures. According to one study, 53 percent of thirteen-year-old girls are dissatisfied with their bodies, and that number increases to 78 percent when the girls reach eighteen. Seventy-five percent of those over eighteen believe they are overweight, including 45 percent who are technically *underweight*.[1]

This "tyranny of slenderness" has created a culture in which as many as 60 percent of women experience some type of difficulty in eating and one in five teenage girls will develop an eating disorder such as anorexia or bulimia.[2] Feminist scholars such as Sandra Bartky,[3] Susan Bordo, Naomi Wolf, and others have rightly identified this epidemic as a feminist issue and have sought theoretical explanations for women's desire to starve themselves. The fact remains, however, that pacing the exponential rise in eating disorders in the last two decades has been the increase in

---

[1]Susan Bordo, *Unbearable Weight: Feminism, Western Culture, and the Body* (Berkeley: University of California Press, 1993), 185.

[2]See Marcia Millman, *Such a Pretty Face: Being Fat in America* (New York: Norton, 1980); Susie Orbach, *Fat Is a Feminist Issue: The Anti-Diet Guide to Permanent Weight Loss* (1978; reprint, New York: Berkley, 1994); and Naomi Wolf, *The Beauty Myth: How Images of Beauty Are Used against Women* (New York: Anchor Books/Doubleday, 1992). On the "tyranny of slenderness," see Kim Chernin, *The Obsession: Reflections on the Tyranny of Slenderness* (New York: Harper and Row, 1981); the figure of 60 percent comes from Wolf, 183.

[3]Sandra Lee Bartky, *Femininity and Domination: Studies in the Phenomenology of Oppression* (New York: Routledge, 1990).

the numbers of women who are, by modern standards, fat.[4] Susie Orbach reports that approximately 50 percent of American women are overweight by cultural standards; both Marcia Millman and Laura Brown put the figure at 25 percent.[5] Despite the prevalence of women who resist (or fail to resist) the tyranny of slenderness, the fat body has largely been ignored in feminist studies that attempt to theorize the female body.

How should these women be theorized? Are there similarities between what drives the starvation impulse and the feeding impulse? Is there a place in feminist scholarship for the fat body? I examine these questions in terms of the culture's production of docile female bodies, through which the ideal female form is constructed in some cases and rejected in others. I scrutinize the culture's embrace of those who achieve the ideal form (even when those bodies are literally starving) and its brutal rejection of those who do not, or cannot, meet that ideal. Finally, I identify the sexism inherent in sizism (which produces both the slender and the fat body) and look at the ways in which rejecting fat oppression can lead to a heightened feminist awareness.

THE FEMININE IDEAL AND THE PRODUCTION OF "DOCILE BODIES"

Modern American standards require that the ideal feminine body be small. A woman is taught early to contain herself, to keep arms and legs close to her body and take up as little space as possible. This model of femininity suggests that real women are thin, nearly invisible. The women idealized as perfect are these days little more than waifs. The average fashion model today weighs 23 percent less than the average woman; a generation ago the gap was only 8 percent.[6] Not surprisingly, those women who claim more than their share of territory are regarded with suspicion. Brown notes that "Fat oppression carries the less-than-subtle message that women are forbidden to take up space (by being large of body) or resources (by eating food ad libitum)."[7] In recent years, of course, there has been an increasing move toward fitness and bodybuilding for women, and some hope that a different ideal female body may be developing. There is reason to regard such a shift with suspicion, however. This new ideal still requires a complete restructuring of the female body, a removal of softness, and a rejection of any indication of fat tissue. It is still based on the notion that the large female body is inherently wrong. In addition, the most successful female bodybuilders, those who become large through muscle mass, are often seen as taking on masculine characteristics. A quick flip through *Vogue* demonstrates that the waif model still persists as feminine.

Men are under no such size restrictions and are allowed—often encouraged—to take up as much space as they can get away with. But when a woman's stature or girth approaches or exceeds that of a man's, she becomes something freakish. By becoming large, whether with fat tissue or muscle mass, she implicitly violates the sexual roles that place her in physical subordination to the man. As Naomi Wolf points out in *The Beauty Myth*, the focus on the smallness of the

---

[4]Millman (*Such a Pretty Face*) and Laura S. Brown ("Fat-Oppressive Attitudes and the Feminist Therapist: Directions for Change," in *Fat Oppression and Psychotherapy: A Feminist Perspective*, ed. Brown and Esther D. Rothblum [New York: Haworth Press, 1989], 19–30) have explained why the term *fat* is preferable to terms such as *overweight* or *obese*. While *fat* is merely a descriptive term, *overweight* implies an ideal weight based upon weight tables, many of which have been proven obsolete, and *obese* is a clinical medical term based on similar principles. Both scholars argue that the word *fat* should be reclaimed until pejorative connotations have been removed and the word no longer has wince-value.

[5]Orbach, *Fat Is a Feminist Issue*, 3; Laura S. Brown, "Women, Weight, and Power: Feminist Theoretical and Therapeutic Issues," *Women and Therapy* 4, no. 1 (1985): 61–71.

[6]Wolf, *The Beauty Myth*, 183.

[7]Brown, "Fat-Oppressive Attitudes," 20.

woman's body has increased in the United States at the same time that women have begun to gain a real measure of power. The male need to establish superiority, undermined by the relative success of the feminist movement, has reasserted itself by inscribing inferiority onto the female body. She declares, "A cultural fixation on female thinness is not an obsession about female beauty but an obsession about female obedience."[8]

Bartky agrees that cultural expectations have progressively shifted away from what a woman is allowed to *do* onto what a woman is allowed to *look like:* "Normative femininity is coming more and more to be centered on woman's body—not its duties and obligations or even its capacity to bear children, but its sexuality, more precisely, its presumed heterosexuality and appearance."[9] As women have claimed intellectual and economic power for themselves, culture has simply found new ways for them to be inferior. Brown calls the ideal feminine body a "manifestation of misogynist norms flowing from a culture where women are devalued and disempowered."[10] That is, because women themselves are seen as somehow less than men, their bodies must demonstrate that inferiority.

These "misogynist norms" are not simply inflicted on women from the outside. Such overt oppression would be relatively easy for women to identify and resist. As Michel Foucault notes, however, the success of a society's imposition of discipline upon bodies depends on those bodies learning *to regulate themselves.*[11] That is, women feel the need to construct female bodies that are demonstrably smaller and weaker than men's bodies in part because they have, in Brown's words, "internalized fat oppressive notions."[12] Because the male gaze is always present, even when it is physically absent, women must continually produce bodies that are acceptable to that gaze. Thus a woman's own gaze becomes a substitute for a man's gaze, and she evaluates her own body as ruthlessly as she expects it to be evaluated by him.

Bartky discusses this "state of conscious and permanent visibility" while examining the ways in which women participate in the construction of their own bodies as inferior. Referring to Foucault's account of how docile bodies are produced by internalizing society's codes and expectations, she asks an important question: "Where is the account of the disciplinary practices that engender the 'docile bodies' of women, bodies more docile than the bodies of men?"[13] But given the number of female bodies that have not proved their docility by producing smaller, quieter, more ornamental versions of male bodies, I suggest that there must also be a follow-up question: Where is the account of the ways self-regulation *fails to* engender the "docile bodies" of women? That is, how and why are unruly (ungovernable?) bodies of fat women constructed?

Bartky further identifies three categories of disciplinary practices that produce the recognizably feminine body:

- those that aim to produce a body of a certain size and general configuration
- those that bring forth from this body a specific repertoire of gestures, postures, and movements
- those directed toward the display of this body as an ornamental surface[14]

She does not, however, suggest what might happen when those disciplinary practices are not successfully instilled in women, implicitly raising another question: What processes go into

---

[8]Wolf, *The Beauty Myth*, 187.
[9]Bartky, *Femininity and Domination*, 80.
[10]Brown, "Women, Weight, and Power," 63.
[11]For complete discussion of the role of self-regulation in producing docile bodies, see Michel Foucault's *Discipline and Punish: The Birth of the Prison*, trans. Alan Sheridan (New York: Vintage, 1979), 135–228.
[12]Brown, "Women, Weight, and Power," 68.
[13]Bartky, *Femininity and Domination*, 65.
[14]Ibid.

constructing the body that is *not* recognizably feminine? The construction of the body is undoubtedly a social act insofar as gender (that is, the construction of a body that is recognizably masculine or feminine) is performed for the satisfaction of both performer and audience.[15] In characterizing femininity as "spectacle," something performed for a watcher, Bartky admits that "under the current 'tyranny of slenderness' women are forbidden to become large or massive. . . . The very contours a woman's body takes on as she matures—the fuller breasts and rounded hips— have become distasteful."[16] Yet she fails to link our culture's attempt to construct the small female body with its distaste for the bodies that refuse to be constructed to those ideals. Since women *do* become large, what can we say about culture's rejection of them?

Women who do not maintain rigid control over the boundaries of their bodies, allowing them to grow, to become large and "unfeminine," are treated with derision in our society, and that derision is tied inextricably to the personal freedom of women. Women who are fat are said to have "let themselves go." The very phrase connotes a loosening of restraints. Women in our society are bound. In generations past, the constriction was accomplished by corsets and girdles that cut into the skin and left welts, marks of discipline. The girdles are now, for the most part, gone, but they have been replaced by bindings even more rigid. Women today are bound by fears, by oppression, and by stereotypes that depict large women as ungainly, unfeminine, and unworthy of appreciation. Large chunks of time and energy that could be channeled into making real, substantive changes in society are being spent pursuing the ideal body image: weighing, measuring, preparing and portioning food, weighing and measuring the body, jogging, stair-stepping, crunching away any softness of belly, taking pills, seeing specialists, finding clothes that hide figure flaws. Women in particular are literally terrified of getting fat. In survey after survey, being fat is listed as a primary fear.[17]

The fear of missing the mark of ideal beauty has generated, or been generated by, solid economic realities. The $33 billion a year diet industry and $300 million cosmetic surgery industry[18] are founded on women's fears and attempts at bodily constraint. Mounting evidence shows the ineffectiveness of low-calorie diets and the dangers of cosmetic surgeries that have set women up for repeated personal failures in attempting to attain an ever-elusive ideal, but the oppressive social control made possible by fat-phobia grips women as tightly as ever. Above all, women must control themselves, must be careful, for to relax their vigilance might lead to the worst possible consequence: being fat.

FAT OPPRESSION AND AMERICAN CULTURE

In modern American culture, women are expected to be beautiful, and beautiful equals thin. Whether we are given waifs or athletes to view, we are constantly bombarded by media images of women with little or no breast tissue and slim, boyish hips. The almost impossible ideal is set before women as the mold in which to construct their bodies, molds which the vast majority of bodies simply will not fit. Virtually every woman learns to hate her body, regardless of her size, and so she learns to participate in her own oppression. As Brown notes, "data suggests that North American women of most cultures, and all body sizes and eating styles tend to have fat-oppressive and fat-negative attitudes towards their own bodies and, by inference, those of other women."[19]

---

[15]For a discussion of the ways in which gender can be read as a performative act, see Judith Butler's *Bodies That Matter: On the Discursive Limits of "Sex"* (New York: Routledge, 1993).

[16]Bartky, *Femininity and Domination*, 73.

[17]Millman, *Such a Pretty Face*, and Wolf, *The Beauty Myth*.

[18]Wolf, *The Beauty Myth*, 17.

[19]Brown, "Fat-Oppressive Attitudes," 20.

The fat woman, Millman observes, is "stereotypically viewed as unfeminine, in flight from sexuality, antisocial, out of control, hostile, aggressive."[20] Because they do not construct bodies that conform to the feminine ideal, fat women are perceived as violating socially prescribed sexual roles, and that violation is a threat to existing power structures. Women may have made gains in intellectual and economic power, but there is a price to be paid. At all costs, a woman must not be allowed to maintain (or win) physical power as well. If she does, she is in rebellion, not only against male power structures but against all that is feminine.

It is no wonder that such fat-oppressive attitudes have been internalized. Fat women in American society are perpetually victimized by public ridicule. They are "weighed down . . . by the force of hatred, contempt and pity, amusement and revulsion. Fat bodies are invaded by comments, measured with hatred, pathologized by fear and diagnosed by ignorance."[21] Fat-phobia is one of the few acceptable forms of prejudice left in a society that at times goes to extremes to prove itself politically correct. One study indicates that fat girls have only one-third the chance of being admitted to prestigious colleges as slim girls with similar school records.[22] Fat jokes still abound. Women who get fat publicly (Elizabeth Taylor, Oprah Winfrey, Sarah Ferguson) are openly censured and scorned as if their bodies were public property. And when they lose weight, as all three of these women have, they are met with an approval that again marks their bodies as public property.

Of course, a woman does not have to be a public figure for her body to receive similar treatment. Fat has become a moral issue unlike any other type of deviation from what society considers normal. The fat woman is often dismissed as sloppy, careless, lazy, and self-indulgent. Large women know all too well that strangers often feel no compunction about stepping forward to criticize a woman's size with statements such as "Should you really be eating that?"; "I know a good doctor who could help you"; "You have such a pretty face, if you'd just lose some weight. . . ."

Why does American society have such a visceral reaction to fat? Some, like Brown, agree that "a fat woman by her presence violates primal norms of misogynist society that deny nurturance, space, power and visibility to women."[23] But Wolf and others have drawn an analogy between the view of fat in modern culture and the view of sex in Victorian times: "What hysteria was to the nineteenth-century fetish of the asexual woman locked in the home, anorexia is to the late-twentieth-century fetish of the hungry woman."[24] For the Victorian woman, sex was forbidden, dirty, and shameful, and her repression of her desires led to hysteria. For the modern woman, "fat" is forbidden, dirty, and shameful, and her strict control over and repression of her bodily needs are manifested once again in the body, not in hysteria but in eating disorders. Although many studies refute a simple correlation between weight gain and overeating, Susan Bordo notes that American culture still sees fat only in terms of self-indulgence: "Anorexia could thus be seen as an extreme development of the capacity for self-denial and repression of desire . . . ; obesity, as an extreme capacity to capitulate to desire."[25]

In "capitulating to desire," fat women are seen as standing in rebellion against the strictures of society. They are breaking the rules, and culture's immediate reaction is to punish them. Bordo sees this ostensible rebellion as the source of society's hostility toward fat women: "the

[20]Millman, *Such a Pretty Face*, xi.
[21]R. Bull, quoted in Susan Tenzer, "Fat Acceptance Therapy (F.A.T.): A Non-Dieting Group Approach to Physical Wellness, Insight, and Acceptance," in Brown and Rothblum, *Fat Oppression and Psychotherapy*, 47.
[22]Millman, *Such a Pretty Face*, 90.
[23]Brown, "Fat-Oppressive Attitudes," 26.
[24]Wolf, *The Beauty Myth*, 198.
[25]Bordo, *Unbearable Weight*, 201.

obese—particularly those who claim to be happy although overweight—are perceived as not playing by the rules at all. If the rest of us are struggling to be acceptable and 'normal,' we cannot allow them to get away with it; they must be put in their place, be humiliated and defeated."[26]

The same society that valorizes the female body, making it a cultural icon for beauty, subtly undermines any sense of self-love a woman might have for her body—even those bodies that meet the ideal. The body is suspect, needy, always in danger of erupting into something that will grasp more than is allowed. The end result is that women, fat or thin, often develop an antagonistic relationship with their bodies. The size and shape those bodies take on become directly connected to a woman's self-esteem. As Bartky notes, "Overtly, the fashion-beauty complex seeks to glorify the female body and to provide opportunities for narcissistic indulgence. More important than this is its *covert* aim, which is to depreciate woman's body and deal a blow to her narcissism."[27] The fat body, then, comes to represent all that must be avoided and all that is denied to women in American society. Because it must be avoided so strenuously, those who do not, or cannot, avoid fatness are a source of public discomfort, outrage, or both. The fat body, Brown tells us, is a reminder of all that a woman cannot and should not be:

> Fat women are ugly, bad, and not valuable because they are in violation of so many of the rules. A fat woman is visible, and takes up space. A fat woman stands out. She occupies personal territory in ways that violate the rules for the sexual politics of body movement.
>
> . . . A fat woman has strong muscles from moving her weight around in the world. She clearly has fed herself. . . . Thus, for women to not break the rules, and for women to not be ugly, bad, and invaluable, women must fear fat, and hate it in themselves.[28]

The fat woman demonstrates by her very presence that she has not submitted to the rules that society has established for feminine behavior. Overtly, her body shape *may* be a result of a conscious rejection of societal and cultural norms. More insidiously, however, that body also may be a result of years of dieting and refeeding in attempts to achieve the ideal form. Her own body's rejection of starvation and its subsequent padding of itself in protection against future periods of deprivation serve as a subtle indictment of patriarchy's requirement that she be unnaturally thin.

The link to patriarchy here might well be questioned. My study has focused on the fat *female* body even though a large percentage of the fat population is male. As has been noted, however, it is only the female body that has been rigidly inscribed as *necessarily* thin, that thinness rendering a woman visibly smaller and weaker than the average male. The male gaze, characterized by Brown as a "patriarchal psychic tapeworm,"[29] serves as a continual reminder that the female body must be smaller than man's to be acceptable. Bartky notes that "insofar as the disciplinary practices of femininity produce 'subjected and practiced,' an inferiorized body, they must be understood as aspects of a far larger discipline, an oppressive and inegalitarian system of sexual subordination."[30] I would suggest that the emaciated female body stands as a symbol of woman's sexual subordination.

---

[26]Ibid., 203.
[27]Bartky, *Femininity and Domination*, 39–40.
[28]Brown, "Women, Weight, and Power," 65.
[29]Ibid., 63.
[30]Bartky, *Femininity and Domination*, 75.

THE MALE GAZE AND THE SEXISM OF SIZISM

Biologically, women have more fat than men, 10 to 15 percent more body fat until the onset of puberty. At puberty, as evidence of maturity and fertility, women's fat-to-muscle ratio increases as the male's decreases, widening the gap even more.[31] Ironically, however, it is that fat, crucial to a woman's reproductive health, that renders her undesirable in a heterosexual relationship. Culturally, women face far stricter limits than men on what amount of body fat is acceptable. The intensity of public scorn of the fat female body drives many women to take extreme measures in order to meet those guidelines. There is evidence, however, that the male sexual gaze indicates the attitude toward corpulence more accurately than does the sex of the body being constructed. It is not only women who must conform to the male ideal of beauty. Recent research has shown that internalized fat-oppressive attitudes are more often present in persons of *either sex* who want to be found attractive by men and that they are less common in persons of either sex who wish to be found attractive by women.[32] Still, while men are at much higher risk from illness due to obesity, 80 to 90 percent of all weight loss surgery is performed on women, despite the grave risks and complications that have been linked to the procedures.[33] Between 90 to 95 percent of anorectics and bulimics are women.[34]

As Wolf reminds us, "the demonic characterizations of a simple body substance do not arise from its physical properties but from old-fashioned misogyny, for above all, fat is female."[35] That which distinguishes women outwardly from men—the curves of breast and hip—are primarily accumulations of adipose tissue, the same adipose tissue that is attacked with such ferocity and treated as the enemy of women. Brown adds, "Most of the ways in which women feel physically 'wrong' e.g., having womanly hips, bellies, breasts, and thighs, are manifestations of how their body is not that of a man."[36]

It is here that the construction of the sexual female body takes a curious turn. The states of anorexia and obesity, both extreme reactions to the sexism/sizism of American culture,[37] situate women as simultaneously asexual and hypersexual. In the anorexic state, the body is stripped of all excess fat tissue, feminine curves disappear, and the female body is rendered nearly prepubescent in form. The anorexic body changes internally as well. When body fat drops below a certain percentage, ovulation and menstruation cease. "Infertility and hormone imbalance are common among women whose fat-to-lean ratio falls below 22 percent," Wolf points out.[38] In essence, femaleness is rejected in favor of a state of asexuality. One woman refers to her bout with anorexia as "killing off the woman in me."[39]

While anorexia is in very physical and chemical ways an "absolute negation of the female state,"[40] it is the anorexic and nearly anorexic body that is glamorized on runways, on magazine covers, and in television shows and movies. In its asexuality, the thin female body becomes, ironically, hypersexualized, culturally "feminine" and admired, accepted in its very rejection of excess

---

[31]Wolf, *The Beauty Myth*, 192.

[32]Brown, "Fat-Oppressive Attitudes," 25; Millman, *Such a Pretty Face*, 245.

[33]Jaclyn Packer, "The Role of Stigmatization in Fat People's Avoidance of Physical Exercise," in Brown and Rothblum, *Fat Oppression and Psychotherapy*, 52.

[34]Wolf, *The Beauty Myth*, 181.

[35]Ibid., 92.

[36]Brown, "Women, Weight, and Power," 85.

[37]Studies indicate that dieting itself may cause both eating disorders and obesity; see Wolf, *The Beauty Myth*; Brown, "Fat-Oppressive Attitudes"; and Millman, *Such a Pretty Face*.

[38]Wolf, *The Beauty Myth*, 192.

[39]Millman, *Such a Pretty Face*, 125.

[40]Wolf, *The Beauty Myth*, 184.

flesh. Anorexia in many ways reflects an ambivalence about femininity, a rebellion against feminization that manifests itself by means of the disease as both a rejection and an exaggeration of the feminine ideal.

The fat body also exists in a state of simultaneous asexuality and hypersexuality. Increased stores of fat exaggerate the outward sexuality of the female body; breasts and hips become fuller and more prominent. A fat woman's body is unmistakably, maturely female. Internally, the body experiences heightened sexuality as well. Fat cells store estrogen, and increases in fat increase levels of that hormone in the body. In addition, some studies suggest that fat women desire sex more often than do thin.[41] Yet even as the thin female body is perceived as hypersexual by culture, the fat female body is perceived as asexual. "In our society," Millman points out, "fat women are viewed as unfeminine, unattractive, masculine, out of the running. In a word, they are desexualized."[42]

In many ways, both of these groups of women are attempting to remove themselves from their bodies, to live from the neck up. Anorexia can be read as an attempt to deny physiology, to make the body itself disappear. While obesity may be characterized as the reverse, as celebrating or reveling in the body, the issue is more complex. Certainly many fat women have made a conscious decision to allow their bodies free rein. Many other women, however, perhaps the majority, become fat because they are disconnected from their bodies and have trouble learning to use and move them in productive ways. Millman links this inability to use the body in physical ways to the male gaze and cultural expectations of femininity: "Women are prone to disembodiment not only because they are constantly exposed to intrusive judgments about their bodies but also because they are taught to regard their bodies as passive objects others should admire. Unlike men who are raised to *express themselves* unself-consciously through physical activity and sports, women's bodies are employed to be looked at."[43] Either extreme, being fat or being anorexic, can therefore be seen as a rejection of the body as object of the male gaze. Thus a first step in reclaiming the female body might well be a loosening of the cultural restraints on it—an acknowledgment that the female body naturally contains more fat cells than a man's and a commitment to living *inside* the body. But such a step on the part of women is sure to be perceived as a threat as great as the suffrage movement of the nineteenth century or the women's liberation movement of the twentieth.

THE THREAT OF FEMALE FLESH

Women are still raised in our society to be nurturers. They are taught to tend first to the needs of others and only then to themselves. Nowhere is this more evident than in feeding patterns. Men are expected at every turn to eat more. The perception is that they are larger, that their bodies need more fuel, and that women are generally dieting anyway. This notion persists despite evidence that a woman's daily caloric needs are only 250 calories less than a man's.[44] The idea that a woman's body needs less fuel than a man's is evidently held to apply from birth. Orbach cites one study of mother-child interaction in which 99 percent of baby boys were breastfed, while only 66 percent of the girls were. In addition, the girls were weaned significantly earlier than the boys and spent 50 percent less time feeding.[45] This study suggests that females

---

[41]Ibid., 192.
[42]Millman, *Such a Pretty Face*, 98.
[43]Ibid., 202.
[44]Wolf, *The Beauty Myth*, 192.
[45]Orbach, *Fat Is a Feminist Issue*, 18.

may be undernourished and undernurtured from the outset,[46] a pattern of undernourishment that may well be the root cause of both obesity and bulimia. Binge eating is more accurately classified by many eating disorder specialists as "refeeding," a term connoting that binge eating is a physical reaction to prolonged periods of nutritional deprivation.

Women's self-feeding represents a type of deviant behavior: it sets itself in opposition to what has been prescribed as "normal," and at the same time it promotes the construction of a body that is not culturally recognized as small and therefore feminine. Self-feeding in women is thus viewed with suspicion, seen perhaps rightly as a rejection of cultural codes that require women to remain quiescent and needy. Millman notes that "eating is sometimes used [by women] in the spirit of *asserting oneself* against an outside force or power (and therefore, asserting personal control)."[47] Orbach argues even more strongly that "[g]etting fat can . . . be understood as a definite and purposeful act; it is a directed, conscious or unconscious, challenge to sex-role stereotyping and culturally defined experience of womanhood."[48]

Once the fat woman has rejected those roles, she often finds unexpected benefits to refusing to construct the acceptably feminine body. Orbach declares: "For many women, compulsive eating and being fat have become one way to avoid being marketed or seen as the ideal woman: 'My fat says "screw you" to all who want me to be the perfect mom, sweetheart, maid and whore. Take me for who *I* am, not for who I'm supposed to be. If you are really interested in *me*, you can wade through the layers and find out who I am.' In this way, fat expresses a rebellion against the powerlessness of the woman."[49] As Brown notes, being fat is "is an ultimate form of female covert power."[50] It allows a woman to nurture herself, to reject sexually stereotyped roles, to deny society's demand that she be the perfect woman, and to stake a claim on the world, taking up space without having to demand it.

The fat body speaks its construction just as the thin body does. As Orbach reminds us, the mouth has two functions, to speak and to eat.[51] When the mouth is silent, whether it is closed against food or filled with food, the body speaks its needs to the world. The fat body is not merely lazy or self-indulgent: it is inscribed by culture, and it is a reflection of oppression as surely as is the body of the rail-thin anorectic. Just as we have come to realize that the thin ideal is not an innocent construction, so we can no longer afford to dismiss the fat body as making no particular response to the society that would construct it otherwise. We now recognize that the idealized female body has been culturally encoded to mark a woman as physically passive, taking up little space, and non-self-nurturing. To the extent that the fat body has been vilified as marking a woman who refuses to accept that prescribed construction, a place must be made in feminist scholarship for theorizing the fat body in ways that acknowledge the power of her refusal.

REFERENCES

Bartky, Sandra Lee. *Femininity and Domination: Studies in the Phenomenology of Oppression.* New York: Routledge, 1990.

Bordo, Susan. *Unbearable Weight: Feminism, Western Culture, and the Body.* Berkeley: University of California Press, 1993.

---

[46]See Millman, *Such a Pretty Face.*
[47]Ibid., 43.
[48]Orbach, *Fat Is a Feminist Issue,* 6.
[49]Ibid., 9.
[50]Brown, "Women, Weight, and Power," 66.
[51]Orbach, *Fat Is a Feminist Issue,* 76.

Brown, Laura S. "Fat-Oppressive Attitudes and the Feminist Therapist: Directions for Change." In *Fat Oppression and Psychotherapy: A Feminist Perspective*, edited by Brown and Esther D. Rothblum, 19–30. New York: Haworth Press, 1989.

_____. "Women, Weight, and Power: Feminist Theoretical and Therapeutic Issues." *Women and Therapy* 4, no. 1 (1985); 61–71.

Butler, Judith. *Bodies That Matter: On the Discursive Limits of "Sex."* New York: Routledge, 1993.

Chernin, Kim. *The Obsession: Reflections on the Tyranny of Slenderness.* New York: Harper and Row, 1981.

Foucault, Michel. *Discipline and Punish: The Birth of the Prison.* Translated by Alan Sheridan. New York: Vintage, 1979.

Lyons, Pat. "Fitness, Feminism and the Health of Fat Women." In *Fat Oppression and Psychotherapy: A Feminist Perspective*, edited by Laura S. Brown and Esther D. Rothblum, 65–77. New York: Haworth Press, 1989.

Millman, Marcia. *Such a Pretty Face: Being Fat in America.* New York: Norton, 1980.

Orbach, Susie. *Fat Is a Feminist Issue: The Anti-Diet Guide to Permanent Weight Loss.* 1978. Reprint, New York: Berkley, 1994.

Packer, Jaclyn. "The Role of Stigmatization in Fat People's Avoidance of Physical Exercise." In *Fat Oppression and Psychotherapy: A Feminist Perspective*, edited by Laura S. Brown and Esther D. Rothblum, 49–63. New York: Haworth Press, 1989.

Tenzer, Susan. "Fat Acceptance Therapy (F.A.T.): A Non-Dieting Group Approach to Physical Wellness, Insight and Acceptance." In *Fat Oppression and Psychotherapy: A Feminist Perspective*, edited by Laura S. Brown and Esther D. Rothblum, 39–47. New York: Haworth Press, 1989.

Wolf, Naomi. *The Beauty Myth: How Images of Beauty Are Used against Women.* New York: Anchor Books/Doubleday, 1992.

The Black Beauty Myth

Sirena J. Riley

Sirena Riley earned a degree in Women's Studies from the University of Maryland-College Park. She has worked as a campus organizer for the Feminist Majority Foundation and co-directed the Campus Leadership Program. She is also a jazz singer; her debut album, The Lunatic The Lover and the Poet, was released in 2008. This essay appeared in Colonize This! Young Women of Color on Today's Feminism *(2002).*

For those of you well versed in the study of body image, I don't need to tell you that negative body image is an all too common phenomenon. The issue of young women's and girls' dissatisfaction with their bodies in the United States has slowly garnered national attention and has made its way into the public discourse. Unfortunately, the most visible discussions surrounding body image have focused on white women. As a result, we presume that women of color don't have any issues when it comes to weight and move on. As a black woman, I would love to believe that as a whole we are completely secure with our bodies. But that would completely miss the racism, sexism and classism that affect the specific ways in which black women's beauty ideals and experiences of body dissatisfaction are often different from those of white women.

To our credit, black women have often been praised for our positive relationships with our bodies. As a teenager, I remember watching a newsmagazine piece on a survey comparing black and white women's body satisfaction. When asked to describe the "perfect woman," white women said she'd be about five foot ten, less than 120 pounds, blond and so on. Black women described this ideal woman as intelligent, independent and self-confident, never mentioning her looks. After the survey results were revealed to the group of both black and white twentysomethings, the white women stood, embarrassed and humiliated that they could be so petty and shallow. They told stories of starving themselves before dates and even before sex. The black women were aghast! What the hell were these white women talking about?!

I was so proud. I went around telling everyone about the survey results. I couldn't believe it. Black women being praised on national television! There they were telling the whole country that their black men loved the "extra meat on their bones." Unfortunately, my pride also had a twinge of envy. In my own experience, I couldn't quite identify with either the black women or the white women.

In my black middle-class suburban family, we were definitely expected to be smart. My family didn't work so hard so that we could be cute and dumb. I'd expressed interest in medical school and I got nothing but support in my academics. Raised by a single mother, independence was basically in my blood. But in a neighborhood of successful, often bourgeois black families, it was obvious that the "perfect woman" was smart, pretty and certainly not overweight. As a child, no one loved the "extra meat" on my bones. I was eight years old when I first started exercising to Jane Fonda and the cadre of other leotard-clad fitness gurus. I knew how to grapevine and box step as well as I knew my multiplication tables. I now have a sister around that age, and when I look at her and realize how young that is, it breaks my heart that I was so concerned about weight back then.

Still, I consider myself lucky. I had an even temper. That made me no fun to tease, since I wouldn't give the perpetrator any satisfaction by reacting. Plus, I had good friends who would be there to have my back. But despite this support, I was a very self-conscious middle-school girl. And that's where I gained the most weight, sixty pounds in the course of three years. Because hindsight is twenty-twenty, it is easy to understand why I put on so much weight then. My mom got married when I was ten years old. The next year she had my first little sister, and then another sister was added when I turned fourteen. I love them, but that's a lot of stress for a little kid. My single-parent, only-child home had turned into a pseudo-nuclear family almost overnight. My grades started slipping and the scale started climbing.

Enter my first year of high school. Being an overweight teenager, I don't need to describe the hell that was gym class. To my relief, I only had to take one year of gym and then never had to do it again. Plus, in high school I had options. In addition to regular gym, there was an aerobic dance class and something called "physical training." Now, considering that Jane Fonda and I were well acquainted, I wanted to take the aerobics class. But when I went to register, the class was full. I guess I wasn't the only one who'd had it with the kickball scene. I was left with either regular gym or this physical training class. I decided that I'd played my last game of flag football and opted for the latter.

Physical training turned out to be running and lifting weights. And when I say weights, I mean *real* weights. None of those wimpy three-pound dumbbells. We were lifting heavy weights and learning professional weight-lifting moves. Well, it worked. By sophomore year I'd lost over forty pounds. The thing is, I didn't even know it. Remember, I had only enrolled in the class to get out of regular gym. I'd thought it might have been nice to lose some weight, but that wasn't what I was concentrating on. After all, I'd been doing exercise videos since I was a kid and I'd only managed to gain weight.

How did I not notice that I'd lost weight? Well, I was completely out of touch with my body. I didn't want to live there. I don't even think I really considered it a part of *me*. No one ever said anything good about it, so I just pretended it didn't exist. I basically swept my body under the rug. All I was wearing back then were big baggy jeans and sweatshirts, so most of my clothes still fit despite the weight loss. People had been asking me for several months if I'd lost weight before I noticed. They were also asking me how I did it, as if I knew. While back-to-school shopping before my sophomore year, I decided to just see if I could fit into size 10 jeans. Not only did those fit me, I could even squeeze into a size 8.

Ironically, it wasn't being overweight that really screwed up my body image and self-esteem, it was *losing* weight. All of a sudden I was pretty. No one had ever really told me that I was pretty before. So if I was pretty now, then I must have been ugly then. My perception of myself before my weight loss was forever warped. I ripped up pictures of myself from middle school. I never wanted to be fat again! Boys had never really been interested in me before, but now guys were coming out of the woodwork. Family I hadn't seen in years just couldn't believe it was *me*. Some even told me that they always knew I'd grow out of my "baby fat" to become a beautiful woman. At fifteen, this was my introduction to womanhood. I had dates now. I could go shopping and actually fit into cool clothes. I was planning for college and looking forward to my new life as a pretty, smart, successful, independent black superwoman.

For a few years I actually did eat and exercise at what I'd consider a comfortable rate. But after that year of intense exercising, it was impossible to completely maintain my significant weight loss. I just didn't have the time, since it wasn't built into my schedule anymore. I settled in at around a size 12, although at the time I still wanted to be a "perfect" size 8. This actually was the most confusing time for me. I kept telling everyone that I still wanted to lose twenty pounds. Even my family was divided on this one. My grandmother told me that I was fine the way I was now, that I shouldn't gain any weight, but I didn't need to lose any more. She didn't want me to be fat but thought it was good that I was curvy. Meanwhile, my grandfather told me that if I lost twenty more pounds, he'd give me one thousand dollars to go shopping for new clothes. And my mom thought that my skirts were too short and my tops too low cut, even though as a child she prompted me to lose weight by saying that if I stayed fat, I wouldn't be able to wear pretty clothes when I grew up. What the hell did these people want from me?

I wasn't overeating and my self-esteem had improved but for all of the wrong reasons. I thought I was happier because I was thinner. In reality, I still hadn't made peace with myself or my body. Over the years I gained the weight back, but not before dabbling in some well-known eating disorders. I had a stint with bulimia during my second semester of my first year away at college. But I never got to the clinical stage. I pretty much only did it when something bad happened, not on a daily basis. I didn't binge on huge amounts of food. I'd eat two bowls of Lucky Charms and the next thing you know, I'd be sticking the spoon down my throat. This was not at all like the bulimics I saw on those after-school specials. They were eating sheets of cake, loaves of bread, sticks of butter, anything and everything they could get their hands on. That wasn't me.

Then I started compulsively exercising. I mean I couldn't think straight if I hadn't been to the gym that morning. And even after I went to the gym, all I could think about was how great it was going to be to work out tomorrow. I was also planning my whole day around my food. It wasn't necessarily that I was dieting, but I was always aware of when I was going to eat, how much and how long it would be until I ate again. I was completely obsessed.

Around my junior year in college, I finally realized that something was wrong. I just couldn't take it anymore, so I started seeing a counselor on campus. At first I didn't tell her about my encounters with bulimia, but any trained therapist could see right through me. One day she asked me point blank if I'd ever had an eating disorder, so I told her everything. I realized then that what I had been doing was considered disordered eating. I also realized that inherently I knew it wasn't right, since this was the first time I had breathed a word about it to anyone. I had never even tried to articulate it. I decided not to exercise or worry about what I ate until I got through therapy.

Throughout my course of therapy, I was in three body image and eating disorder therapy groups with other young women on my campus. I was always the only black woman. The memory of that television news survey I had seen as a teen comparing body image issues for black and white women stayed with me over the years. Looking at the other women in my therapy groups, I had to wonder if I was an anomaly. I had read one or two stories in black women's magazines about black women with eating disorders, but it was still treated like a phenomenon that was only newsworthy because of its rarity.

As a women's studies major in college, body image was something we discussed almost ad nauseam. It was really cathartic because we embraced the personal as political and felt safe telling our stories to our sister feminists. Whenever body image was researched and discussed as a project, however, black women were barely a footnote. Again, many white feminists had failed to step out of their reality and see beyond their own experiences to understand the different ways in which women of color experience sexism and the unattainable beauty ideals that society sets for women.

Discussions of body image that bother to include black women recognize that there are different cultural aesthetics for black and white women. Black women scholars and activists have attacked the dominance of whiteness in the media and illuminated black women's tumultuous history with hair and skin color. The ascension of black folks into the middle class has positioned them in a unique and often difficult position, trying to hold onto cultural ties while also trying to be a part of what the white bourgeois has created as the American Dream. This not only permeates into capitalist material goals, but body image as well, creating a distinctive increase in black women's body dissatisfaction.

White women may dominate pop culture images of women, but black women aren't completely absent. While self-deprecating racism is still a factor in the way black women view themselves, white women give themselves too much credit when they assume that black women still want to look like them. Unfortunately, black women have their own beauty ideals to perpetually fall short of. The representation of black women in Hollywood is sparse, but among the most famous loom such beauties as Halle Berry, Jada Pinkett Smith, Nia Long, Iman and Angela Bassett. In the music scene there are the young women of Destiny's Child, Lauryn Hill and Janet Jackson. Then, of course, there is model Naomi Campbell and everyone's favorite cover girl, Tyra Banks. Granted, these women don't necessarily represent the waif look or heroin chic that plagues the pages of predominately white fashion and entertainment magazines, but come on. They are still a hard act to follow.

In addition to the pressure of unrealistic body images in the media, another force on women's body image can be men's perspectives. In this category black men's affinity for big butts always comes up. Now, I'm not saying that this is a completely false idea—just about every black guy I know has a thing for the ass. I've heard both black guys and white guys say, "Damn, she's got a big ass"—the former with gleeful anticipation and the latter with loathsome disgust. Of course, dwelling on what men find attractive begs the question, why the hell do we care so much what they think anyway, especially when not all women are romantically involved with men?

Indeed, many songs have been written paying homage, however objectifying, to the black behind. "Baby Got Back," "Da Butt" and "Rumpshaker" are by now old standards. There's a whole new crop of ass songs like "Shake Ya Ass," "Wobble Wobble" and everyone's favorite, "The Thong Song." But did anyone actually notice what the girls in the accompanying videos look like? Most of those women are models, dancers and aspiring actresses whose full-time job it is to make sure they look unattainably beautiful. So what if they're slightly curvier?

Now that rap music is all over MTV, the rock videos of the eighties and early nineties featuring white women in leather and lace have been replaced with black and Latino models in haute couture and designer thongs. Rappers of the "ghetto-fabulous" genre are selling platinum several times over. Everyday, their videos are requested on MTV's teen-driven Total Request Live (TRL) by mostly white, suburban kids—the largest group of consumers of hip-hop culture. It is the latest mainstream forum for objectifying women of color, because almost all of the ghetto-fabulous black male rappers have the obligatory video girls parading around everywhere from luxury liner cruise ships to mansions in the Hamptons. If this doesn't speak to the distinctive race/class twist that these images add to the body image discussion, I don't know what does.

The old mantra "You can never be too rich, or too thin" may have been associated with the excessive eighties, but some of that ideal still holds true today. Obesity is associated with poverty and in our society, poverty is not pretty. Being ghetto-fabulous is all about going from rags to riches. It includes having the money, house(s), car(s), clothes and throngs of high-maintenance women at your disposal. An ironic twist to the American Dream, considering many of these rappers claim to have attained their wealth not with a Puritan work ethic but through illegal activity.

Overweight women of color aren't included in these videos because they aren't seen as ghetto-fabulous, just ghetto (Not that I'm waiting for the day when *all* women can wash rappers' cars in cutoffs with twelve of their girlfriends, but you get the picture). Talented comedienne Mo'nique, star of UPN's *The Parkers*, is representative of this idea. She is a full-figured woman whose character, Nikki, has a crush on a black, upwardly mobile college professor who lives in her apartment building. Through his eyes she's seen as uncouth and out of control. For the audience her sexual advances are funny because she's loud, overweight and can't take a hint. He squirms away from her at every turn and into the arms of some slim model-type.

The professor in *The Parkers* views Nikki the same way that many middle-class people view overweight people, greedy and out of control. Instead, we get to see it through a black lens—ghetto women with no class, talking loud, wearing bright colors and tight clothes. I'm sure in true sitcom fashion, the professor and Nikki will eventually get together, but well after we've had our fun at Nikki's expense.

For the past few years a popular black R&B radio station in Washington, D.C., has a contest where they give away free plastic surgery every summer. You know, to get ready for thong season. Needless to say, the average contestant is a woman. At first it was just breast implants and reductions, but now they've expanded to liposuction and even pectoral implants for the men. That hasn't had much impact on the demographics of the participants. Despite the expanded offerings, the contestant pool remains overwhelmingly female. In order to win the "prize" you have to send in a letter, basically pouring out all of your insecurities to get the DJs to see why you need the surgery more than the other contestants do. Sick, isn't it? Anyone who thinks that black women are oblivious to body insecurities needs to listen to some of these letters, which by the way pour in by the thousands. The one thing they have in common is that all the women really want to "feel better about themselves." Even in this black middle-class metropolis, somewhere these women got the idea that plastic surgery is the way to go. Clearly, it is not just white America telling them this.

Sexism has played a starring role in every facet of popular culture, with men by and large determining what shows up on TV and in the movies, and the fact is that they've fallen for it, too. I have male friends and relatives who buy into these unrealistic beauty ideals and feel no shame in letting me know where they think I stack up, so to speak. Just yesterday, for example, my grandfather decided to make it his business to know how much weight I had gained in the past few months. Now I'm old enough and secure enough to know that his and other men's comments have nothing to do with me, with who I am. But growing up, these comments shaped the way I saw myself.

I've consciously decided to treat my body better by not being obsessed with diet and exercise and not comparing myself to anyone (including my former self). When I'm eating well and exercising regularly, I'm usually in the size 12 to 14 range. This is OK with me, but I know for a fact that this is another place where many white women and I don't connect. As much as we get praised for loving our full bodies, many young white women would rather be dead than wear a size 14. They nod their heads and say how great it is that we black women can embrace our curves, but they don't want to look like us. They don't adopt our presumably more generous beauty ideals. White women have even told me how lucky black women are that our men love and accept our bodies the way they are. I've never heard a white woman say that she's going to take her cue from black women and gain a few pounds, however. In a way it is patronizing, because they're basically saying, "It's OK for you to be fat, but not me. You're black. You're different."

In this society we have completely demonized fat. How many times have you had to tell a friend of yours that she isn't fat? How many times has she had to tell you the same thing? Obviously, when people have unrealistic perceptions of themselves it should not go unnoticed, but in this act, while we are reassuring our friends, we put down every woman who is overweight. The demonization of fat and the ease of associating black women with fat exposes yet another opportunity for racism.

If we really want to start talking more honestly about all women's relationships with our bodies, we need to start asking the right questions. Just because women of color aren't expressing their body dissatisfaction in the same way as heterosexual, middle-class white women, it doesn't mean that everything is hunky-dory and we should just move on. If we are so sure that images of rail-thin fashion models, actresses and video chicks have contributed to white girls' poor body image, why aren't we addressing the half-naked black female bodies that have replaced the half-naked white female bodies on MTV? Even though young black women slip through the cracks from time to time, I still believe that feminism is about understanding the intersections of all forms of oppression. It only works when we all speak up and make sure that our voices are heard. I don't plan to wait any longer to include young women of color in a larger discussion of body image.

Uses of the Erotic
The Erotic as Power

Audre Lorde

Audre Lorde was a black lesbian feminist activist, poet and essayist. She is famous for her poetry, essays and her memoirs including The Cancer Journals *and* Zami: a New Spelling of My Name *(1983. This piece comes from her collected essays,* Sister Outsider *(1984). Her life and struggle with breast cancer are documented in the film* A Litany for Survival: The Life and Work of Audre Lorde *(1995). Lorde succumbed to breast cancer in 1992.*

There are many kinds of power, used and unused, acknowledged or otherwise. The erotic is a resource within each of us that lies in a deeply female and spiritual plane, firmly rooted in the power of our unexpressed or unrecognized feeling. In order to perpetuate itself, every oppression must corrupt or distort those various sources of power within the culture of the oppressed that can provide energy for change. For women, this has meant a suppression of the erotic as a considered source of power and information within our lives.

We have been taught to suspect this resource, vilified, abused, and devalued within western society. On the one hand, the superficially erotic has been encouraged as a sign of female inferiority; on the other hand, women have been made to suffer and to feel both contemptible and suspect by virtue of its existence.

It is a short step from there to the false belief that only by the suppression of the erotic within our lives and consciousness can women be truly strong. But that strength is illusory, for it is fashioned within the context of male models of power.

As women, we have come to distrust that power which rises from our deepest and nonrational knowledge. We have been warned against it all our lives by the male world, which values this depth of feeling enough to keep women around in order to exercise it in the service of men, but which fears this same depth too much to examine the possibilities of it within themselves. So women are maintained at a distant/inferior position to be psychically milked, much the same way ants maintain colonies of aphids to provide a life-giving substance for their masters.

But the erotic offers a well of replenishing and provocative force to the woman who does not fear its revelation, nor succumb to the belief that sensation is enough.

The erotic has often been misnamed by men and used against women. It has been made into the confused, the trivial, the psychotic, the plasticized sensation. For this reason, we have often turned away from the exploration and consideration of the erotic as a source of power and information, confusing it with its opposite, the pornographic. But pornography is a direct denial of the power of the erotic, for it represents the suppression of true feeling. Pornography emphasizes sensation without feeling.

The erotic is a measure between the beginnings of our sense of self and the chaos of our strongest feelings. It is an internal sense of satisfaction to which, once we have experienced it, we know we can aspire. For having experienced the fullness of this depth of feeling and recognizing its power, in honor and self-respect we can require no less of ourselves.

It is never easy to demand the most from ourselves, from our lives, from our work. To encourage excellence is to go beyond the encouraged mediocrity of our society is to encourage excellence. But giving in to the fear of feeling and working to capacity is a luxury only the unintentional can afford, and the unintentional are those who do not wish to guide their own destinies.

This internal requirement toward excellence which we learn from the erotic must not be misconstrued as demanding the impossible from ourselves nor from others. Such a demand incapacitates everyone in the process. For the erotic is not a question only of what we do; it is a question of how acutely and fully we can feel in the doing. Once we know the extent to which we are capable of feeling that sense of satisfaction and completion, we can then observe which of our various life endeavors bring us closest to that fullness.

The aim of each thing which we do is to make our lives and the lives of our children richer and more possible. Within the celebration of the erotic in all our endeavors, my work becomes a conscious decision—a longed-for bed which I enter gratefully and from which I rise up empowered.

Of course, women so empowered are dangerous. So we are taught to separate the erotic demand from most vital areas of our lives other than sex. And the lack of concern for the erotic root and satisfactions of our work is felt in our disaffection from so much of what we do. For instance, how often do we truly love our work even at its most difficult?

The principal horror of any system which defines the good in terms of profit rather than in terms of human need, or which defines human need to the exclusion of the psychic and emotional components of that need—the principal horror of such a system is that it robs our work of its erotic value, its erotic power and life appeal and fulfillment. Such a system reduces work to a travesty of necessities, a duty by which we earn bread or oblivion for ourselves and those we love. But this is tantamount to blinding a painter and then telling her to improve her work, and to enjoy the act of painting. It is not only next to impossible, it is also profoundly cruel.

As women, we need to examine the ways in which our world can be truly different. I am speaking here of the necessity for reassessing the quality of all the aspects of our lives and of our work, and of how we move toward and through them.

The very word *erotic* comes from the Greek word *eros*, the personification of love in all its aspects—born of Chaos, and personifying creative power and harmony. When I speak of the erotic, then, I speak of it as an assertion of the lifeforce of women; of that creative energy empowered, the knowledge and use of which we are now reclaiming in our language, our history, our dancing, our loving, our work, our lives.

There are frequent attempts to equate pornography and eroticism, two diametrically opposed uses of the sexual. Because of these attempts, it has become fashionable to separate the spiritual (psychic and emotional) from the political, to see them as contradictory or antithetical. "What do you mean, a poetic revolutionary, a meditating gunrunner?" In the same way, we have attempted to separate the spiritual and the erotic, thereby reducing the spiritual to a world of flattened affect, a world of the ascetic who aspires to feel nothing. But nothing is farther from the truth. For the ascetic position is one of the highest fear, the gravest immobility. The severe abstinence of the ascetic becomes the ruling obsession. And it is one not of self-discipline but of self-abnegation.

The dichotomy between the spiritual and the political is also false, resulting from an incomplete attention to our erotic knowledge. For the bridge which connects them is formed by the erotic—the sensual—those physical, emotional, and psychic expressions of what is deepest and strongest and richest within each of us, being shared: the passions of love, in its deepest meanings.

Beyond the superficial, the considered phrase, "It feels right to me," acknowledges the strength of the erotic into a true knowledge, for what that means is the first and most powerful guiding light toward any understanding. And understanding is a handmaiden which can only wait upon, or clarify, that knowledge, deeply born. The erotic is the nurturer or nursemaid of all our deepest knowledge.

The erotic functions for me in several ways, and the first is in providing the power which comes from sharing deeply any pursuit with another person. The sharing of joy, whether physical, emotional, psychic, or intellectual, forms a bridge between the sharers which can be the basis for understanding much of what is not shared between them, and lessens the threat of their difference.

Another important way in which the erotic connection functions is the open and fearless underlining of my capacity for joy. In the way my body stretches to music and opens into response, hearkening to its deepest rhythms, so every level upon which I sense also opens to the erotically satisfying experience, whether it is dancing, building a bookcase, writing a poem, examining an idea.

That self-connection shared is a measure of the joy which I know myself to be capable of feeling, a reminder of my capacity for feeling. And that deep and irreplaceable knowledge of my capacity for joy comes to demand from all of my life that it be lived within the knowledge that such satisfaction is possible, and does not have to be called *marriage*, nor *god*, nor *an afterlife*.

This is one reason why the erotic is so feared, and so often relegated to the bedroom alone, when it is recognized at all. For once we begin to feel deeply all the aspects of our lives, we begin to demand from ourselves and from our life-pursuits that they feel in accordance with that joy which we know ourselves to be capable of. Our erotic knowledge empowers us, becomes a lens through which we scrutinize all aspects of our existence, forcing us to evaluate those aspects honestly in terms of their relative meaning within our lives. And this is a grave responsibility, projected from within each of us, not to settle for the convenient, the shoddy, the conventionally expected, nor the merely safe.

During World War II, we bought sealed plastic packets of white, uncolored margarine, with a tiny, intense pellet of yellow coloring perched like a topaz just inside the clear skin of the bag. We would leave the margarine out for a while to soften, and then we would pinch the little pellet to break it inside the bag, releasing the rich yellowness into the soft pale mass of margarine. Then taking it carefully between our fingers, we would knead it gently back and forth, over and over, until the color had spread throughout the whole pound bag of margarine, thoroughly coloring it.

I find the erotic such a kernel within myself. When released from its intense and constrained pellet, it flows through and colors my life with a kind of energy that heightens and sensitizes and strengthens all my experience.

We have been raised to fear the *yes* within ourselves, our deepest cravings. But, once recognized, those which do not enhance our future lose their power and can be altered. The fear of our desires keeps them suspect and indiscriminately powerful, for to suppress any truth is to give it strength beyond endurance. The fear that we cannot grow beyond whatever distortions we may find within ourselves keeps us docile and loyal and obedient, externally defined, and leads us to accept many facets of our oppression as women.

When we live outside ourselves, and by that I mean on external directives only rather than from our internal knowledge and needs, when we live away from those erotic guides from within ourselves, then our lives are limited by external and alien forms, and we conform to the needs of a structure that is not based on human need, let alone an individual's. But when we begin to live from within outward, in touch with the power of the erotic within ourselves, and allowing that power to inform and illuminate our actions upon the world around us, then we begin to be responsible to ourselves in the deepest sense. For as we begin to recognize our deepest feelings, we begin to give up, of necessity, being satisfied with suffering and self-negation, and with the numbness which so often seems like their only alternative in our society. Our acts against oppression become integral with self, motivated and empowered from within.

In touch with the erotic, I become less willing to accept powerlessness, or those other supplied states of being which are not native to me, such as resignation, despair, self-effacement, depression, self-denial.

And yes, there is a hierarchy. There is a difference between painting a back fence and writing a poem, but only one of quantity. And there is, for me, no difference between writing a good poem and moving into sunlight against the body of a woman I love.

This brings me to the last consideration of the erotic. To share the power of each other's feelings is different from using another's feelings as we would use a kleenex. When we look the other way from our experience, erotic or otherwise, we use rather than share the feelings of those others who participate in the experience with us. And use without consent of the used is abuse.

In order to be utilized, our erotic feelings must be recognized. The need for sharing deep feeling is a human need. But within the european-american tradition, this need is satisfied by certain proscribed erotic comings-together. These occasions are almost always characterized by a simultaneous looking away, a pretense of calling them something else, whether a religion, a fit, mob violence, or even playing doctor. And this misnaming of the need and the deed give rise to that distortion which results in pornography and obscenity – the abuse of feeling.

When we look away from the importance of the erotic in the development and sustenance of our power, or when we look away from ourselves as we satisfy our erotic needs in concert with others, we use each other as objects of satisfaction rather than share our joy in the satisfying, rather than make connection with our similarities and our differences. To refuse to be conscious of what we are feeling at any time, however comfortable that might seem, is to deny a large part of the experience, and to allow ourselves to be reduced to the pornographic, the abused, and the absurd.

The erotic cannot be felt secondhand. As a Black lesbian feminist, I have a particular feeling, knowledge, and understanding for those sisters with whom I have danced hard, played, or even fought. This deep participation has often been the forerunner for joint concerted actions not possible before.

But this erotic charge is not easily shared by women who continue to operate under an exclusively european-american male tradition. I know it was not available to me when I was trying to adapt my consciousness to this mode of living and sensation.

Only now, I find more and more women-identified women brave enough to risk sharing the erotic's electrical charge without having to look away, and without distorting the enormously powerful and creative nature of that exchange. Recognizing the power of the erotic within our lives can give us the energy to pursue genuine change within our world, rather than merely settling for a shift of characters in the same weary drama.

For not only do we touch our most profoundly creative source, but we do that which is female and self-affirming in the face of a racist, patriarchal, and anti-erotic society.

Sex(less) Education
The Politics of Abstinence-only Programs in the United States

Stephanie Block

Stephanie Block developed this article, which appeared in Women's Health Journal of the Latin American and Caribbean Women's Health Network in 2005, from a report she prepared when she worked as an intern with CELADE, the Latin American and Caribbean Demographic Center, affiliated with the United Nations Population Fund. CELADE developed the first population survey in Latin America and has served as a leader in researching population issues for over 50 years.

INTRODUCTION

The United States has the highest rate of teen pregnancy and sexually transmitted infections (STIs) in the industrialized world. Each year, one out of three teenage girls becomes pregnant.[1] Although teen pregnancy rates have dropped from 61.8 births per 1,000 in 1991 to 41.7 births per 1,000 in 2003, pregnancy rates in the U.S. still are declining at slower rates than those in other developed nations.[2]

These sobering statistics are the basis of an ongoing battle: the fight for abstinence-only versus comprehensive sex education. Although proponents of both types of sex education aim to reduce teenage pregnancy and STIs, their approaches vary greatly. Abstinence-only advocates believe that sex before marriage is immoral and harmful; they promote abstinence as the sole option to help young people avoid STIs and teen pregnancy, mentioning condoms and contraceptives only in terms of their failure rates.[3] Abstinence advocates feel that "Americans are not suffering from a lack of knowledge about sex but an absence of values."[4]

In contrast, proponents of comprehensive sex education and abstinence-plus-education promote abstinence as a good method for avoiding pregnancy and STIs but also teach students the benefits of condoms and different contraceptive methods.

---

[1]International Planned Parenthood Federation, "Country Profiles: The United States," http://www.ippfnet.ippf.org/pub/IPPF_Regions/IPPF_CountryProfile.asp.

[2]Albert R. Hunt, "Beware the Moral Cops," *The Wall Street Journal*, December 2, 2004.

[3]Planned Parenthood of New York City, "Issues and Trends in Reproductive Health: Federal Sex Education Policy," http://www.ppnyc.org/facts/facts/federal_policy.html.

[4]Concerned Women for America, "Abstinence: Why Sex is Worth the Wait," September 2002, http://www.cwfa.org/articledisplay.asp?id=1195&department=CWA&categoryid=family.

Although comprehensive sex education programs have greater recorded success in delaying the age of sexual initiation and in reducing teenage pregnancy, abstinence-only programs have gained increasing political support and federal funding over the past twenty years. This article explores the roots of the abstinence-only movement and its newfound popularity.

A BRIEF HISTORY OF SEX EDUCATION IN THE U.S.

According to a poll by the Alan Guttmacher Institute, 75 percent of parents in the U.S. want their children to receive a variety of information on subjects including contraception and condom use, STIs, sexual orientation and safer sex practices.[5] Given the choice, only one to five percent of parents remove their children from comprehensive sex education programs. Nevertheless, abstinence-only programs continue to gain federal support, despite the absence of evidence proving their effectiveness.

The issue of sex education first arose in the United States in 1912 when the National Education Association called for teacher-training programs on sexuality education. The issue resurfaced in 1940 when the U.S. Public Health Service strongly advocated sexuality education in the schools, calling it an "urgent need." By 1953, the American School Health Association launched a nationwide program in "family life education." Two years later, the American Medical Association and the National Education Association worked together to publish pamphlets for schools commonly referred to as "the sex education series."[6]

By the 1960s, all leading public health organizations were calling for sex education in America's schools, and by the 1970s, sex education's most vocal opponents had united: the political and the Christian Right. Alarmed by growing sexual promiscuity and the breakdown of what is considered 'traditional' values, the Christian Crusade, an early expression of right-wing Christianity, aimed to bar sex education from schools, calling it "smut" and "raw sex." The John Birch Society, political allies of the Christian Right, called the effort to teach sexuality "a filthy Communist plot," and Phyllis Schlafly, the leader of the far-right Eagle Forum, argued that sex education increased sexual activity among teens.[7]

The war over sexual education had begun, and for many years, social conservatives lost. Evidence showing that sex education programs delay sexual activity and decrease teen pregnancy helped such initiatives gain widespread support. By 1983, sexuality education was being taught within the context of more comprehensive family life education programs. Courses emphasizing not only reproduction but also the importance of self-esteem, responsibility and decision-making spread across the nation.

However, the arrival of the HIV/AIDS epidemic in the 1980s forever changed the sex education debate. In 1986, U.S. Surgeon General C. Everett Koop issued a report calling for comprehensive HIV/AIDS and sexuality education in public schools beginning as early as the third grade. "There is now no doubt that we need sex education in schools . . . The need is critical, and the price of neglect is high," he said. Even social conservatives could no longer deny the need to educate U.S. teens. Accordingly, the Christian Right changed its strategy from denouncing "sex ed" altogether to advocating *abstinence-only education*.[8]

---

[5]Planned Parenthood Federation of America, "Abstinence Only 'Sex' Education," http://www.plannedparenthood.org/pp2/portal/files/portal/medicalinfo/teensexualhealth/factabstinence-education.xml.

[6]Priscilla Pardini, "The History of Sexuality Education." *Rethinking Schools Online* (Summer 1998), http://www.rethinkingschools.org/archive/12_04/sexhisto.shtml.

[7]Ibid.

[8]Priscilla Pardini, "Abstinence-Only Education Continues to Flourish," *Rethinking Schools Online* (Summer 1998), http://www.rethinkingschools.org/archive/12_04/sexhisto1.shtml.

The Christian Right—an umbrella group of conservative Christians that unites behind shared causes—includes evangelicals, Pentecostals and other conservative Protestants and conservative Roman Catholics. The focus of their campaign—the "values clarification movement"—can be defined broadly as defending "traditional Christian values such as the authority of the Bible in all areas of life."[9] This position includes banning or heavily restricting abortion; banning stem cell research with human embryos; fighting the gay-rights movement; supporting the presence of Christianity in the public sphere (i.e., prayer in schools and the teaching of creationism); ending government funding restrictions against religious charities and schools; opposing U.S. court decisions on the separation of Church and State; and censoring books, music, television programs and films that they view as "indecent."[10]

> Abstinence-only advocates believe that sex before marriage is immoral and harmful; they promote abstinence as the sole option to help young people avoid STIs and teen pregnancy, mentioning condoms and contraceptives only in terms of their failure rates.

Through grassroots organizing the Christian Right has become a powerful political force and an important base of support for the Republican Party.[11] According to a study in the Washington magazine *Campaigns and Elections*, Christian conservatives now exercise either "strong" or "moderate" influence in 44 Republican state committees, as compared with 31 committees in 1994. Their control is "weak" only in six states, all in the north-east of the country. Ralph Reed, the Christian Coalition leader until 1997, now runs the Georgia Republican party.[12] Before the 2004, presidential elections, Reverend Jerry Falwell, one of the Christian Coalition's principal leaders, stated that "the Republican Party does not have the head count to elect a president without the support of religious conservatives." Evangelical Christians are now by far the largest constituency within the Republican Party, Falwell continued, and "if the candidate running for president is not pro-life, pro-family . . . [he's] not going to win."[13]

In fact, a Republican did win: President George W. Bush, an evangelical Christian, fully committed to his socially conservative constituency. Since 2000, Bush has appointed at least five abstinence-only proponents to key government posts, including Dr. Joe McIlhaney to the Advisory Committee of the Center for Disease Control (CDC). In the 1990s, the Texas Commission of Health questioned McIlhaney's accountability, finding that his presentations on STIs were misleading. Bush also has pressured the CDC into supporting an abstinence-only stance even though every public agency responsible for disseminating health and sexuality education information recommends comprehensive education. In 2002, a list of sexuality education "Programs that Work" disappeared from the CDC's website because they were not abstinence-only.[14] Increasingly, public health organizations that support comprehensive sex education have become subject to government harassment—both SIECUS and Advocates for Youth have been audited with unusual frequency over the past years.[15]

---

[9]Grant Walker, "The Christian Right" (Duke University Divinity School National Humanities Center), http://www.nhc.rtp.nc.us/tserve/twenty/tkeyinfo/chr_rght.htm.

[10]Wikipedia, "The Christian Right," http://en.wikipedia.org/wiki/Christian_right.

[11]Planned Parenthood Federation of America, op. cit.

[12]"A Conservative President Has More Problems with One Section of his Party's Right-Wing Base Than You May Think," *The Economist*, May 2003, http://www.economist.com/world/na/printerfriendly.cfm?story_ID=1781279.

[13]Scott Shepard, "Falwell Says Evangelical Christians Now in Control of Republican Party," *Cox News Service*, September 2004, http://www.signonsandiego.com/uniontrib/20040925/news_1n25christ.html.

[14]Kate Petre, "The Sexual Miseducation of the American Teen," *Los Angeles City Beat*, January 2005, http://www.lacitybeat.com/article.php?id=1541&IssueNum=84.

[15]Ibid.

Alarmed by the government's growing financial support for untested abstinence-only programs, Democratic Representative Henry A. Waxman ordered a minority staff report entitled *The Content of Federally Funded Abstinence-Only Education Programs* in December 2004. The report found that abstinence-only programs contained false information about the effectiveness of contraceptives and the risks of abortion; that they blurred religion and science and included scientific errors; and that they treated stereotypes about girls and boys as scientific fact.[16] Worse still, abstinence programs ignored the reality that more than 80 percent of all people in the U.S. have intercourse before marriage and that more than half of all U.S. adolescents are sexually active by the age of 18.[17]

There is no evidence that young people who participate in abstinence-only programs delay sexual intercourse longer than others. However, when they do become sexually active, adolescents who have received abstinence-only education often fail to use condoms or other contraceptives. In fact, 88 percent of students who pledged virginity in middle and high school still engage in premarital sex. Students who break this pledge are less likely to use contraception at first intercourse, and they have similar rates of STIs as non-pledgers. Meanwhile, students in comprehensive sexuality education courses do not engage in sexual activity more often or earlier, but they do use contraception and practice safer sex more consistently once they are sexually active.[18]

FEDERAL SUPPORT FOR ABSTINENCE-ONLY EDUCATION

Since the 1960s, social conservatives have united with the Republican Party to push an abstinence-only agenda. By steadily increasing federal funding, Republicans aim to implement abstinence-only education on a national scale. Both health organizations and policy-makers opposed to abstinence-only education are working together to overcome growing government support for abstinence-only education, but the future of sexuality education in the U.S. is uncertain. It seems that as long as the Christian Right continues to wield great influence over the Republican policy, federal funding for abstinence-only education will flow.

A Republican government first invested in abstinence-only education in 1981, when the U.S. Office of Population Affairs began administering the Adolescent Family Life Act (AFLA), known as the "Chastity Act." Designed to promote "self-discipline and other prudent approaches to the problem of adolescent premarital sexual relations," it allocated US$11 million in grants to public and nonprofit organizations promoting chastity and providing care to pregnant adolescents and teen parents.

Soon after the initiation of the program, the national debate over the legality of abstinence-only programs began. Because AFLA often promoted specific religious values, the American Civil Liberties Union filed suit in 1983, charging that AFLA violated the separation of Church and State.[19] In 1985, a U.S. district judge found AFLA unconstitutional, but on appeal in 1988, the U.S. Supreme Court reversed the decision and remanded the case to a lower court. In 1993, an out-of-court settlement stipulated that AFLA could continue functioning so long as its sexuality education programs: 1) did not include religious references; 2) were medically accurate; 3) respected the "principle of self-determination" regarding contraceptive referral for teenagers;

---

[16]Henry A. Waxman, *The Content of Federally Funded Abstinence-Only Education Programs* (United States House of Representatives Committee on Government Reform—Minority Staff Special Investigations Division, December 2004), http://www.democrats.reform. house.gov.

[17]Petre, op. cit.

[18]Planned Parenthood Federation of America, op. cit.

[19]Advocates For Youth, "Abstinence-Only-Until-Marriage Programs: History of Government Funding," http://www.advocatesformyouth.org/rrr/history.htm.

and 4) did not allow grantees to use church premises for their programs or to give presentations in parochial schools during school hours. Within these limitations, AFLA continues to finance abstinence-only education. In 2000, it disbursed US$19 million in federal funds.[20]

> Nevertheless, abstinence-only programs continue to gain federal support, despite the absence of evidence proving their effectiveness.

Fifteen years later in 1996, a new abstinence-only program was passed surreptitiously as part of welfare reform. During the final version of the Welfare Reform Act, when only small corrections and technical revisions normally are made, conservative members of Congress quietly inserted a provision for abstinence-only education into the sweeping bill. The authors of the provision aimed to "put Congress on the side of social tradition—never mind that some observers now think the tradition outdated—that sex should be confined to married couples. That both the practices and standards in many communities across the country clash with the standard required by the law is precisely the point."[21]

Never openly discussed by the public nor in Congress, Section 510(b) of the Social Security Act was approved as part of the expansive Personal Responsibility and Work Opportunity Reconciliation Act (PRWORA) and signed into law by President Clinton. The provision guaranteed US$50 million in annual funding for abstinence-only education grants to the states over five years (1998–2002) although funding has been extended every year since the date of expiration. Funds under this program are awarded through the Maternal and Child Health (MCH) Bureau and allocated to states based on a federal formula related to the number of low-income children in each state. States must contribute three dollars for every four dollars of federal money.[22]

"Just Say No!"

EXAMPLES OF ABSTINENCE-ONLY EDUCATION IN THE UNITED STATES

- **Public funds go to religious institutions for anti-sexuality education.** In Montana, the Catholic diocese of Helena received US$14,000 from the state's Department of Health & Human Services for classes in the "Assets for Abstinence." In Louisiana, a network of pastors is bringing the abstinence-only message to religious congregations with public funds, and the Governor's Program on Abstinence appointed regional coordinators and other staff members from such religious organizations as the Baptist Collegiate Ministries, Rapides Station Community Ministries, Diocese of Lafayette, Revolution Ministries, Caring to Love Ministries, All Saints Crusade Foundation, Concerned Christian Women of Livingston, Catholic Charities, Christian Counseling Center and Community Christian Concern.
- **Public schools host "chastity" events.** In California, Pennsylvania, Alabama and many other states, schools regularly host chastity pledges and rallies on school premises during school hours. During these rituals, students often pledge "to God" that they will remain abstinent until they marry.

---

[20]Ibid.

[21]SIECUS, Sexuality Information and Education Council of the United States, "Exclusive Purpose: Abstinence-Only Proponents Create Federal Entitlement in Welfare Reform," *SIECUS Report* 24: 4. Available online at http://www.siecus.org/policy/sreport/srep0001.html.

[22]Ibid., 2.

- **Textbooks are censored.** The Texas State Board of Education approved the purchase of new health textbooks that exclusively promote abstinence. As Texas is the second largest buyer of textbooks in the United States, it is likely that these same books will appear in classrooms throughout the nation. The school board in Franklin County, North Carolina, ordered three chapters literally sliced out of a ninth-grade health textbook because the material did not adhere to state law mandating abstinence-only education. The chapters covered AIDS and other sexually transmitted infections, marriage and partnering, and contraception. In Lynchburg, Virginia, school board members refused to approve a high school science textbook unless an illustration of a vagina was covered or cut out.

- **Crucial health programs are canceled.** A petition from 28 parents resulted in the cancellation of a highly regarded, comprehensive AIDS-prevention presentation for high-school students in the Syracuse, New York, area given by the local AIDS Task Force. In Illinois, critics blasted a U.S. Centers for Disease Control and Prevention program called "Reducing the Risk," because they claim it was inconsistent with an abstinence-only message.

- **Sexuality education teachers are disciplined for doing their jobs.** In Belton, Missouri, a seventh-grade health teacher was suspended when a parent complained that she had discussed "inappropriate" sexual matters in class. The teacher had answered a student's query about oral sex. In Orlando, Florida, a teacher was suspended when he showed a student-made videotape called *Condom Man and his K-Y Commandos* about preventing AIDS transmission.

- **Teachers are threatened with lawsuits; student journalists intimidated.** In Granite Bay, California, an article in the student paper prompted charges that a sexuality education teacher engaged in "sexual misconduct" and threats of a lawsuit against the teacher and the paper's faculty adviser. The article took the position that newly mandated abstinence-only education was doing nothing to stop either sexual activity or widespread sexual ignorance among students. In Santa Clarita, California, a high-school principal censored from the student paper an article entitled "Sex: Raw and Uncensored." The article was actually about the benefits of abstinence and methods of safer sex.

- **Students suffer from ignorance.** Comprehensive, medically accurate sexuality education is becoming the exception rather than the rule. As a result, more students lack basic information. In Granite Bay, one student asked where his cervix was, and another inquired if she could become pregnant from oral sex. Students in New York City protested that the increased focus on abstinence-only has curtailed access to education about HIV/AIDS. The Colorado Council of Black Nurses decided to return $16,000 in abstinence-only funding because the program "was just too restrictive. It did not teach responsible sexual behavior."

*From the website of the Planned Parenthood Federation of America, http://www.plannedparenthood.org

For the purposes of the legislation, the term "abstinence education" means an educational or motivational program that:

A) has the exclusive purpose of teaching the social, physiological and health gains to be realized by abstaining from sexual activity;

B) teaches abstinence from sexual activity outside marriage as the expected standard for all school-age children;

C) teaches that abstinence from sexual activity is the only certain way to avoid out-of-wedlock pregnancy, sexually transmitted diseases and other associated health problems;

D) teaches that a mutually faithful, monogamous relationship in the context of marriage is the expected standard of human sexual activity;

E) teaches that sexual activity outside of the context of marriage is likely to have harmful psychological and physical effects;

F) teaches that bearing children out-of-wedlock is likely to have harmful consequences for the child, the child's parents and society;

> There is no evidence that young people who participate in abstinence-only programs delay sexual intercourse longer than others. However, when they do become sexually active, adolescents who have received abstinence-only education often fail to use condoms or other contraceptives.

G) teaches young people how to reject sexual advances and how alcohol and drug use increases vulnerability to sexual advances; and

H) teaches the importance of attaining self-sufficiency before engaging in sexual activity.[23]

While grant recipients of Section 510(b) are not required to emphasize equally all eight points listed above, the information they provide cannot be inconsistent with any of them. Because the first element requires that programs have the "exclusive purpose" of promoting abstinence outside of marriage, programs may not in any way advocate contraceptive use or discuss contraceptive methods except to emphasize their failure rates.[24]

Nevertheless, it is up to each state to decide whether to implement abstinence education in the way that the federal government intends it to be used. States may either administer the programs themselves directly, or they can award grants to nonprofit, private, faith-based or public organizations. While some states narrowly interpret the definition of abstinence-only education, others have been more flexible, circumventing an exclusive focus on abstinence education by funding programs that include tutoring, career counseling and community service.[25]

Displeased by individual states' loose interpretation of abstinence education, Congress passed new—and far more restrictive—legislation under President Bush in 2000. The Special Programs of Regional and National Significance-Community Based Abstinence Education grants (SPRANS-CBAE) are awarded directly by the federal government to community-based organizations that teach abstinence only to youth, completely avoiding state intervention.[26] Programs awarded SPRANS funds must adhere to a far stricter definition of abstinence education. While programs receiving Section 510(b) funds only must be *consistent* with the eight-point definition of abstinence-only education, SPRANS recipients must be *responsive* to them, directly addressing each of the points.

Since its inception, SPRANS has become the largest and fastest growing source of abstinence-only education. The program awards two types of grants: one-year planning grants that range from US$50,000 to 75,000 and three-year implementation grants that range from US$250,000 to 1 million.[27] In its first year of funding (Fiscal Year 2001), SPRANS received

---

[23]Cynthia Dailard, "Abstinence Promotion and Teen Family Planning: The Misguided Drive for Equal Funding," *The Guttmacher Report on Public Policy* 5:1 (February 2002): 2, http://www.guttmacher.org/pubs/tgr/05/1/gr050101.html.

[24]Ibid.

[25]Planned Parenthood of New York City, op. cit.

[26]Ibid.

[27]Chris Collins, Priya Alagiri and Todd Summers, *Abstinence Only vs. Comprehensive Sex Education* (Policy Monograph Series, San Francisco: AIDS Policy Research Center & Center for AIDS Prevention Studies, 2002) 6.

US$20 million for grants to 33 organizations. A year later, the amount doubled to US$40 million. By 2004, the program had over 100 grantees and a budget of US$75 million. The current funding for SPRANS is US$104 million, a 30% increase since last year, although President Bush originally asked for US$186 million for the program.[28]

There is no sign that support for abstinence-only education will taper off any time soon; federal funding for abstinence education in FY 2005 reached US$167 million—more than twice its original funding in 1996 but far less than the US$270 million proposed by President Bush. Although there is no proof that abstinence education has any effect on reducing rates of teenage pregnancy or sexually transmitted infections, abstinence-only programs continue to obtain federal funding.[29]

The Education of Shelby Knox

In "The Education of Shelby Knox," a new film by Marion Lipschutz and Rose Rosenblatt, 15-year-old Knox pledges to abstain from sexual relations until marriage. She celebrates her decision with her parents, pastor and peers in a ceremony at her Baptist church in Lubbock, Texas. But Knox's life takes an unexpected turn when she discovers that the rates of teen pregnancy and sexually transmitted diseases in her county are among the highest in the state.

Convinced that her high school's abstinence-only policy is keeping teens in the dark, Knox becomes an advocate for comprehensive sex education. The filmmakers follow Knox as she persuades her city-sponsored youth group to take up the cause and as she weathers the resulting media storm with aplomb.

In heart-to-hearth talks with her evangelical pastor, Knox struggles to convey that she has not abandoned her faith. Rather, she has embraces the Christian values of compassion and respect for difference. But the film's moist poignant moments are Knox's searching discussions with her parents who gently point out the ramifications of her decisions but never withdraw their support, even when they disagree.

*From: Elizabeth Coleman, "Unlikely Advocate," Ford Foundation Report, Spring/Summer 2005. For more information, visit http//www.pbs.org/pov/pov2005/shelbyknox.

CONCLUSION

The debate over sexuality education represents democracy at work with all of its virtues and flaws. Abstinence-only education is not popular among the majority of Americans. No scientific evidence has shown its effectiveness; if anything, abstinence education is probably harmful, causing a decrease in condom and contraceptive use once teens do initiate sexual activity. Nevertheless, because it is a pet cause of an important Republican Party constituency, it enjoys widespread political support. The only way to win the war of abstinence versus comprehensive sex education is through politics. Those who oppose abstinence-only education must make their voices as loud and as demanding as the voices of those of who support it.

---

[28]Waxman, op. cit., 2.
[29]Ibid.

SECTION VII

Gender, Violence and Anti-Violence Activism

Key Concepts for Section VII: Gender, Violence, and Anti-Violence Activism

Antioch "Sexual Offense" Policy of 1992
Conflict Tactics Scale (CTS)
Dating Violence
Domestic Violence
Family Violence
Frustration-Aggression Hypothesis
Hate Crimes
Homophobic Bullying
Homosocial Competition
National Coalition Against Domestic
   Violence (NCADV)
Rape
Rape Free Culture
Sexual Assault
Sexual Bellicosity
Stalking
Stealing Beauty
Vagina Monologues
Violence Against Women Act

Concepts to Review
Androcentrism
Dehumanization
Determinants of Women's Status
Dichotomy/Dichotomous
Doing Gender
Dominance/Domination
Double Standards
Dreamworld

Emphasized Femininity
Femicide
Femininity/Femininities
Gender
Gender Actualizing
Gender Difference
Gender Socialization
Gendered Sexual Socialization
Heterosexism
Homophobia
Masculinity/Masculinities
Misogyny
Objectification
Patriarchy
"the Personal is Political"
Pornography
Power
Rape Supportive Culture
Rape-Prone Culture
Sex
Sex Roles
Sex-Gender System
Sexism
Sexual Harassment
Sexual Object
Sexual Subject
Socialization
Subordinance/Subordination

Asking for Consent is Sexy

Andrew Abrams

Andrew Abrams earned a degree in Anthropology from Antioch College. His essay about his involvement in creating the Antioch Sexual Offense Policy was published in Just Sex: Students Rewrite the Rules on Sex, Violence, Activism, and Equality *(2000) edited by Jodi Gold and Susan Villari.*

In June 1992—the spring term of my junior year—the board at Antioch College passed an amendment to the school's sexual offense policy: a new clause about sexual consent. Basically, the consent clause says that if two people are going to have sex, then whoever initiates the sex needs to ask the other person if it's okay and the other person needs to say yes or no. That way, you'll know that you're not raping or sexually harassing someone; it's not enough to assume that you can tell nonverbally. Ideally, the policy kicks in when you first begin to touch.

Everyone outside the college always wants to know if I follow the policy step by step. They think that it's crazy because they've never tried it.

It makes sense. On TV and in the mass media, all you ever see is people who know each other for five minutes, look in each other's eyes, and then get it on. But the fact is that sex is just better when you talk.

Before the consent policy, I was infatuated with an artist named Leah. She lived downstairs in the dorm and was friends with my roommate. We started hanging out together in the second quarter. I sat down in her room one night and said, "I just want you to know—you probably know this already—but I am attracted to you." She didn't say a word. She wouldn't look at me, wouldn't respond to what I said. Somehow during my second year we became friends. She was very uncomfortable with sex, and so we would lie in bed and I'd ask her: "Is it all right if I kiss you?" "Can I put my hand on your stomach?" The progression was very slow. I asked her permission basically every step of the way. It seems like a lot of work, but it's sexy to ask permission to kiss a woman, and it's exciting to hear her say yes.

People say that Antioch is topsy-turvy: The men are beaten down and the women are on top. But I'm not submissive, I don't feel beaten down, and I've never felt like my life at Antioch was controlled by the agenda of women. The policy isn't asking me to do anything that I don't think I should be doing anyway.

The fall term of my second year was the quarter from hell. A student had died in a van accident, and in a community this small, when one person dies, it's traumatic. The next quarter a woman died of a brain aneurysm during a meeting in front of fifty people, and a friend of mine was killed in a car accident. There were also two student rapes reported on campus. That fall was easily the worst quarter I had as a student at Antioch.

Antioch has a tradition of holding community meetings to discuss campus issues. Around this time a new group, the Womyn of Antioch, showed up at one unannounced. About seventy-five people were there, sitting in a lecture-class auditorium. The Womyn walked in dressed in black, filing down the stairs to the front of the room. They had pieces of tape with the word "RAPED" written on them, and every three minutes they would put one on another woman's back. They explained that every three minutes a woman is raped, and they demanded a policy to deal with sexual offenses on campus. Soon after that they drafted a sexual offense policy and brought it to the administrative council at a hearing packed with student supporters. It became official in 1991. The thing to remember is that the SOP was brought about by students, and that a majority of students still support it.

At the cafeteria, in my friends' rooms, the question I kept on hearing from men was, "What if someone is unfairly accused?" Lots of men see it as a threat even to this day. But why would someone lie about being raped? I can't imagine that anyone would put themselves through all the emotional stress of the hearing process just to attack someone. Basically, you have nothing to worry about as long as you ask.

I think it's important to ask and to be asked in sexual situations, in order to feel comfortable with the person you are with, and to deal with issues about safer sex. Asking a woman if you can kiss her makes it easier to ask whether she has had high-risk partners, to talk about what being safe means to each other. It seems crazy to risk your life just because you're not comfortable talking about condoms. Also, men tend to be more assertive in sexual situations, and I think that the policy balances that out.

I never stayed in one relationship for a long time: That isn't unusual at Antioch. But after a series of sexual experiences—some of them very good ones—I started looking at that as a real problem. About a year ago a woman invited me back to her room. We were fooling around, and at what you might call the height of passion I realized this wasn't what I wanted. I said, "I'm sorry, this isn't comfortable for me." As a man, I'd been brought up to believe that I should be capable, ready, willing all of the time. But the policy made me realize that I had sexual choices—that it was okay sometimes to say, "Time out."

I've been in a relationship with a woman now for close to five months. I met Lorien playing volleyball: She's tall and she's a good athlete. We took Human Sexuality together, but we stayed friends for a year before we started going out. The first time Lorien and I kissed, we talked about the idea of becoming physically intimate for an hour beforehand. Finally she said, "So are we going to kiss or what?" I said, "I think you should kiss me." So she kissed my hand. Then I kissed her hand. She kissed my cheek and I kissed hers. . . .

That doesn't mean that every time we kiss each other we have a ten-minute discussion. You don't always stop when you're falling asleep together to ask, "May I kiss you good night?" But if we're having sex, we talk about what we want and what feels good. I don't like rough sex and I hate hickeys; I like to be touched softly. But nobody's going to know that automatically. If you don't talk, then all you've got is guesswork. Go home and try it, see what happens. I bet you'll end up thanking me.

Demands from the Women of Antioch

Kristine Herman

Kristine Herman graduated from Antioch College in 1994 and went on to earn an M.A. in Social Work from Tulane University and then a law degree from Northeastern University. Her essay documenting the development of the Antioch Sexual Offense Policy was published in Just Sex: Students Rewrite the Rules on Sex, Violence, Activism, and Equality *(2000) edited by Jodi Gold and Susan Villari.*

The women of Antioch, in response to the recent rapes on campus, demand that the following become Antioch College policy:

1. That a community member who is accused of rape shall immediately (within twenty-four hours of the report of rape) be removed from campus until guilt is assessed; and that if this person is determined to be guilty, that s/he shall be immediately and permanently removed from the Antioch community (a student must be expelled, an employee must be fired);
2. That the Dean of Students and/or the Advocate shall immediately inform the community that a rape has occurred; and that the rape survivor shall determine whether the name of the rapist and/or the name of the survivor shall be publicized;
3. That the rape survivor be informed of her/his rights; and informed of, supported with, her/his rights to prosecute;
4. That a support network be established for rape survivors that includes a new position, a woman Advocate who could act as the rape survivor's representative, and who would ensure that disciplinary measures against the rapist be carried out. This Advocate shall be given the power to enact the above disciplinary measures against said rapist;
5. That a one-credit PE self-defense course shall be offered each quarter;
6. That orientation shall incorporate rape education, rape awareness, and consent workshops for men and women;
7. That a permanent support group for survivors of rape and sexual assault be established in the counseling center.

If these demands are not met by November 13, 1990, we, the women of Antioch, will (1) inform the Antioch community of this lack of support for rape survivors; (2) distribute a (national) press release detailing Antioch College's lack of support for rape survivors and discussing the recent rapes on campus and the lack of effective disciplinary measures taken; and (3) hold a Day of Action wherein radical physical measures will be taken.

—Created 5 November 1990.

THE DEVELOPMENT OF THE ANTIOCH COLLEGE SEXUAL OFFENSE POLICY

This list of demands was formulated by women in the Antioch community after being outraged at administrative handling of two reported rapes on campus. There would be a policy and protocol established specific to sexual offense, even if it meant that some women would sacrifice credits, sleep, sanity, and their degrees.

It took enormous efforts on the part of many women at Antioch to get the Antioch Sexual Offense Policy implemented at last, a policy known nationally as radical, innovative, and, to some, extreme. The policy has been viewed as both paternalistic—for coddling women and treating them as inherent victims—and empowering for both men and women—because of its reliance on verbal consent. But only those of us who were there, saw it come together, understand its history, and lived under it truly know how important and monumental the policy is in the movement to prevent and fight sexual violence.

I entered Antioch College, a small liberal arts college located in Yellow Springs, Ohio, in 1990 at the age of seventeen. Antioch is known for its commitment to social justice and political activism. I began confronting my experience as a rape survivor in the context of the two reported rapes on campus and the early formulations of the Sexual Offense Policy. I nervously attended meetings and participated in the larger protests, but my attitude about the policy was that it was too harsh.

I arrived at college believing that rape was wrong . . . but if a woman was drinking, well, then things became a little ambiguous. After I was raped at the age of thirteen, I internalized the messages that tell us we are responsible and that you can't blame a guy for taking advantage of a situation if, after all, you asked for it. Instead of feeling angry, I felt guilt and embarrassment.

That fall of 1990 there were two reported rapes of students by students. In each incident the woman knew her perpetrator and reported the rape to the dean. At that time there existed only an ambiguous written policy addressing sexual harassment. The dean of students spoke with the perpetrators and made her decision as to what disciplinary measures would be taken if any.

One woman's perpetrator was removed from campus but remained enrolled. The other woman's perpetrator was not removed from campus. This lax administrative response to these rapes enraged the women at Antioch and led to the list of demands that ended in the student-initiated Sexual Offense Policy. Emergency meetings at the Women's Center drew nightly crowds of over fifty women to discuss and strategize a response to the inadequate administrative response to rape. The meetings were emotional and volatile, as we found divisions among the women's community at Antioch. Some women thought that we should allow input from the men at Antioch; other women felt strongly that we had waited long enough and that support from men was welcomed but their input was not. In the end, men were not involved in the drafting of the original policy.

Over the course of a few crucial days political actions were staged to get the need for a Sexual Offense Policy on the college's official agenda. Over thirty women stood silently along the walls during a meeting of the Advisory Committee to the President: dressed in black, rape whistles hanging symbolically from their necks. This action successfully pressured the committee into putting The List on the committee agenda. Another action, intended to demonstrate the prevalence of rape and enlist the support of other students, took place at one of our weekly campus community meetings. Every six minutes a woman broke out crying as a piece of duct tape was slapped on her back with the word "RAPED" written across it, reflecting that every six minutes a woman is raped in the United States.

A group of fifteen third- and fourth-year women students, many of them friends of the survivors of the two on-campus rapes, wrote the first draft of the Antioch Sexual Offense Policy. Some were so dedicated that they sacrificed graduation because so much time and energy went into developing the policy.

The policy was intended to outline the protocol for addressing incidents of sexual offense on our campus, but it was obvious that to do so required defining what was and was not a sexual offense. The Antioch Sexual Offense Policy outlined six forms of sexual offense: rape (any nonconsensual penetration of the vagina or anus, nonconsensual fellatio or cunnilingus); sexual assault (nonconsensual sexual conduct exclusive of that included in the definition of rape, but including attempted penetrations, attempted fellatio, or attempted cunnilingus); sexual imposition (nonconsensual sexual contact that includes the touching of thighs, genitals, buttocks, the pubic region, or the breast/chest area); insistent/persistent sexual harassment (insistent/persistent emotional, mental, or verbal intimidation or abuse found to be sexually threatening or offensive); nondisclosure of a known positive HIV status or other known sexually transmitted disease. The Sexual Offense Policy requires that all sexual conduct and contact with an Antioch community member must be consensual.

The policy defines consent as "the act of willingly and verbally agreeing to engage in specific sexual act of conduct." It requires consent by all parties in a sexual encounter and states that "obtaining consent is an ongoing process in any sexual interaction. Verbal consent should be given with each new level of physical and/or sexual contact in any given interaction." The media latched on to this controversial element. Camille Paglia found the policy absurd "as if sex occurs on the verbal realm," a belief that is dangerously reminiscent of outdated notions of what sex should be like in an age that sees AIDS as the number-one killer of people between the ages of twenty-three to forty-four years of age, and when one in four college women are victims of rape or attempted rape.

The bulk of the policy is devoted to the procedures available when a sexual offense has occurred. A gradated list of remedies is included in the policy; for instance, an individual found to have committed rape according to the policy's definition is to be expelled immediately, whereas someone found to have been in violation of the policy's definition of sexual imposition may receive suspension or be required to undergo some sort of educational/counseling program.

Equally important in the policy is the element of antirape education, including mandatory sexual consent workshops for all students, and self-defense courses. The Sexual Offense Prevention and Survivors' Advocacy Program features year-round antirape education, residence advisor training, and group and individual counseling services for survivors of rape and sexual abuse.

The Sexual Offense Prevention and Survivors' Advocacy Program was beginning to develop by my second year at college. I came to know other survivors, hear their stories, and I grew angry. I was seeing patterns of violence, not the sporadic, unrelated occurrences of rape by a stranger in the bushes at knife point. My involvement as an advocate for survivors of rape began and grew; I became a residence advisor for a dorm of first-year women and became active in community politics. My opinion about the policy changed drastically, and my job as a residence advisor convinced me that anything short of verbal and willing consent could result in a harmful "sexual experience." In this role I witnessed several first-year students, many of them seventeen years old, assaulted and raped, often under the influence of alcohol. These women came to me, slept in my room because of nightmares or fear of being alone, and asked for support. They needed to be told of their right not to be victimized, regardless of how much they had to drink or whether or not they were flirting, brought someone back to their room, or made the first move to kiss.

In light of these experiences I became convinced that the important work had to begin with prevention—not the standard "teaching women how not to fall prey to sexual victimization," as if the responsibility once again lies with the victim, but addressing the potential perpetrators and circumstances that lend themselves to sexual violence. The emphasis on consent in the policy attempts to do just that, by requiring people to obtain verbal consent for every level of a sexual interaction, and by trying to eliminate the gray areas that exist when people make silent assumptions about what their partner wants, then act without consulting their partner.

Undoubtedly the Antioch Sexual Offense Policy validated all women's and men's rights not to be sexually victimized. By requiring all persons to seek verbal consent, permission, for each new level of a sexual interaction, responsibility is shifted to the initiator of sexual contact. I felt tremendously empowered living on a campus where I was supposed to be asked before being touched, where my voice was required to be heard. Silence does not equal consent. As a survivor struggling to regain a healthy sense of sexuality, it was much easier for me to say no once I was asked than for me to stop nonconsensual advances once someone has already violated my boundaries. For many survivors it is extremely difficult to voice an objection when it is apparent that someone is just moving ahead physically. A freezing phenomenon occurs, wherein we shut down and just wait for it to be over because it has proved either futile to protest a sexual offense in our pasts, or too scary a situation. This is particularly true when there is a noticeable difference in size and physical stature between the survivor and the person we are with. Being asked gives us the space as well as the confidence that our opinion will be respected this time, that this person wants to make sure that we want to move forward physically too.

In June of 1992 the final revision of the Antioch Sexual Offense Policy was passed by the Advisory Committee to the President and approved by the University Board of Directors. The next two entering classes attended mandatory workshops designed to educate students about the policy and its definition of "consent," and to address the importance of, and new students' concerns about, living under the policy. As a result of these workshops and ongoing campus dialogue, the idea of verbal consent was no longer so shocking. The controversy around the Sexual Offense Policy had died down.

In late 1993 a reporter for the *San Francisco Examiner* mentioned the Antioch Sexual Offense Policy in a story about a California campus rape. Immediately following the *Examiner* article, Jane Gross of the *New York Times* did an in-depth article about the Antioch policy, which led to the AP newswire running the story worldwide; and so began the media explosion of 1993. During the 1993-94 academic year, Antioch received visits from, and provided interviews for, hundreds of national and international publications and radio and television programs.

By this point I was working in antirape education in several capacities: I facilitated sexual consent workshops; consulted with the police department regarding their sexual assault protocol; served as an advocate for survivors of sexual offense on campus; and worked as liaison to the Sexual Offense Prevention and Survivors' Advocacy Program for the Student Housing Office. As a result I was asked by the college administration to be a media spokesperson. I participated in panels at nearly a dozen universities and appeared on numerous television and radio programs and talk shows.

The policy, as it received global recognition and attention from figures such as Rush Limbaugh, Katie Roiphe, Camille Paglia, and Doctor Ruth, was criticized on a number of levels, many of which were riddled with misinformation about its contents. Instead of the policy's being viewed as an instrument by which we hoped to curtail the incidence of sexual violence on our campus, we were seen as legislating sex.

MEDIA INTERPRETATION AND RESPONSE FROM OUTSIDE

The media, within their own limited scope and understanding of the policy, defined it in terms of its effects on sexual interactions according to gender roles only. This artificial polarization of men's and women's interests was not based in the reality of the Antioch policy but was an over-simplification of the issue of sexual violence on college campuses. Media coverage framed the Antioch policy in a way that divided men and women into groups with conflicting and competing interests, instead of portraying a policy that created a cohesive community devoted to eliminating the frequency with which sexual violence is perpetrated on college campuses.

A widely ignored aspect of the policy was its intentionally non-gender-specific language. The Antioch Policy recognizes, acknowledges, and validates that men and women can be raped, and that both men and women can be perpetrators of sexual violence. The policy strives to be non-heterosexist and is inclusive of all sexual orientations. To describe the policy as "requiring men to ask women at each level of a sexual interaction" excludes a large portion of our campus and society who are gay, lesbian, and bisexual, and does not acknowledge that sexual violence occurs between people of the same sex.

The policy has also been criticized under the notion that it limits the spontaneity of romantic sexual relations and unrealistically burdens students to talk about sex. Anyone who is currently sexually active must be aware of the dangers of STD/HIV/AIDS infection and the necessity to talk about safer sex. This alone makes the idea of nonverbal sex both outdated and dangerous. Communication is a vital component of sexual interaction. When verbal communication is not a central part of a sexual encounter, false assumptions occur that can result in a sexual assault.

The media have contributed to a backlash against women and the antirape movement by misdirecting the issues. Instead of accurately gathering data on the incidence of rape on college campuses, the media have responded with a different slant to the debates about rape, prevention, and sexual relations. An example of the minimization of the problem of rape can be found in Dr. Ruth Westheimer's comments about the Antioch Sexual Offense Policy on *Eye to Eye with Connie Chung*. Dr. Ruth chose to focus not on rape or sexual assault at all, but instead on the way the policy might affect a man's ability to maintain an erection if he is expected to be verbal during a sexual encounter. This clearly demonstrates the priorities of mainstream media when addressing a movement focused on the prevention of sexual violence.

Part of the fascination about the policy was that it actually redefined rape, and in doing so threatened the ways in which we have all been socialized to conceptualize sex. In the context of the Clarence Thomas hearings and the Lorena Bobbitt story, discussions about sexual abuse, harassment, and rape were occurring nationally. The Antioch Sexual Offense Policy contributed to this debate.

The implications of the necessity for verbal consent are vast in that we, culturally, must look at the mechanisms by which people are socialized and the messages that are sent regarding sexual relations. The *Connie Chung* segment showed a clip from the movie classic *Gone with the Wind*, where Rhett Butler whisks Scarlett O'Hara into his arms as she struggles to get away, beating on him as he carries her up the stairs to their bedroom. The next day she is happy and giddy, implying that she really wanted it or at least enjoyed it. We used to view this—the woman saying no when she really means yes—as a romantic scene; many still do. By Antioch definitions, and considering many of the shifting attitudes about rape, this could now be viewed as a rape scene.

The media's focus on the Antioch Sexual Offense Policy diverted a strong movement of anti-rape education toward addressing issues of old-fashioned notions about spontaneity, what it means to be romantic, and how the burden of verbal consent will affect men. This is not surprising, given that acceptance of Antioch's definitions of sexual violence, and the expectation of consent, forces us all to reexamine our own sexual histories. Many of us find that we have ambiguous and uncomfortable pasts—we may have done something that could now be called sexual assault, or we may have experienced a sexual assault but did not call it so at the time.

Challenging "traditional" beliefs about sex has resulted in societal defensiveness and negative reactions to documents such as the Antioch policy, and other instances whereby the status quo is shaken. Another example of this type of response can be seen in the battle against homophobia. Some major corporations are finally beginning to acknowledge domestic partnerships, while some states are responding by passing discriminatory homophobic legislature. The struggles of all women, people of color, and gay, lesbian, and bisexual people overlap in that they threaten to disrupt the dominant paradigm.

Though the general public missed the urgent need for the policy, Antioch College received an incredible response from other universities, with over two hundred requested copies of the policy during the fall of 1993 alone.

POSTGRADUATION IMPACT

In my own life, as a second-year law student with a master's in social work, my work in the anti-rape movement continues. The Antioch Sexual Offense Policy affected my views on sex and power dynamics in sexual situations. Women and men are not on completely equal ground sexually; many women have internalized messages that tell us we owe sex if a man has spent a lot of money on us, or if we have allowed a situation to go to a certain point. A first-year man in a sexual consent workshop at Antioch once expressed what many men fear about the policy when he said, "But if I have to ask for what I want, I won't get it."

The Antioch Sexual Offense Policy introduced the importance of consent in sexual interactions. It aims to resocialize students to be verbal with each other in sexual situations in order to eliminate different perceptions of the same experience. The efforts of the original drafters of the policy, as well as all of us who participated, and the resulting document are something to be extremely proud of. For many the Antioch Sexual Offense Policy is the embodiment of the principle that the personal is political.

With the issue of sexual violence introduced into the public arena, we must now look at the directions that need to be explored to further decrease the prevalence of rape and sexual assaults on college campuses. Anthropologists such as Peggy Sanday, and feminist theorists such as bell hooks, have begun writing about a "rape culture." Some people consider this to be the third wave of the antirape movement, one that aggressively addresses rape, domestic violence, and sexual harassment in a new light, armed with social science research, statistics, and personal stories. What we have learned from the Antioch Sexual Offense Policy and from the efforts of students on campuses all over the United States is that we are involved in a process of learning from each other strategies, ideas, and tools to combat sexual violence on an interpersonal, campus, societal, national, and international level.

Swept Awake! Negotiating Passion on Campus

Bonnie Pfister

Bonnie Pfister is a reporter for the Pittsburg Tribune-Review. *She has contributed to* The Nation, The New York Times *and written articles for the Associated Press. Ms. Pfister earned a dual Bachelor of Arts degree in Magazine Journalism and International Relations from Syracuse University. This piece originally appeared in* On the Issues: Progressive Women's Quarterly.

With the introduction of their "Sexual Offense Policy" in 1992, Ohio's Antioch College took a dramatic—and controversial—step to establish firmer rules of sexual conduct on their campus. This policy, requiring ongoing verbal consent throughout every stage of a sexual encounter, is based on the premise that clear communication is necessary for healthy, consensual sex, and a college administration should take active steps to create the safest environment possible. This 1994 essay, from On the Issues: The Progressive Women's Quarterly, *examines Antioch's policy and discusses other activism against sexual violence taking place on college campuses.*

What's an activist to do when everyone from George Will to "Saturday Night Live" satirizes your work and accuses you of infantilizing women and taking the fun out of sex?

"I find it exciting," says Jodi Gold, coordinator of STAAR, Students Together Against Acquaintance Rape at the University of Pennsylvania in Philadelphia. "You don't get a backlash until you've ruffled some feathers. It means we've really pushed the envelope and things are happening."

The backlash has all but obscured the radical importance of student efforts to develop new—fairer—rules for sexual liaisons. The emerging new code includes the apparently controversial idea that potential lovers should *ask* before foisting sexual attention on their partners, and that partners should clearly *answer* "yes" or "no." In other words: people should communicate about their desires before making love, rather than waiting to be "swept away" by overwhelming passion.

While a deadpan legalistic approach to sex is easy to ridicule, Jodi Gold believes that the real reason media coverage of today's campus activism is so highly critical is that Americans are still scared silly by its sexual frankness—a frankness that today's generation of young people desperately needs.

"Sexuality is perhaps the most defining issue for today's students," says Alan Guskin, president of Antioch College in Ohio for nine years, and a supporter of the often-mocked Sexual

Offense Policy, the student-written rules for sexual conduct at the college, which have been in place since fall 1992.

"Men and women students come to the campus with a very different consciousness about sexuality," notes Dr. Guskin. "The women have learned they have a right to determine how their bodies are used, but many of the young men still think the central question is how to get women to do what they want." The best way to deal with the situation, says Guskin, is for women and men to learn to communicate with each other. "The policy gives no specific checklist or statements. But there is a sense of how you should behave."

The Antioch policy says verbal consent is needed before all sexual contact, and that consent is an on-going process that can be withdrawn at any time. Students who are sleeping or unconscious or incapacitated by alcohol or drugs are not considered capable of consent. The policy also defines offenses as unwanted touching, verbal harassment, and non-disclosure of sexually transmitted disease, including HIV, and defines punishments for violations of various parts of the policy. All students are required to attend an educational workshop on consent and sexual offense each academic year.

Guskin notes that the media swarming over the campus for two and a half months reporting on the controversial policy accomplished more student education on the issue than the college's past five years of effort.

The policy emerged when thirty feminists disrupted a campus government meeting in November 1990 demanding institutional rules to deal with rape, says Bethany Saltman, Antioch '93 and member of the original group, the Womyn of Antioch. Even at this tiny (650 students last fall) alternative college, the administration seemed to prefer to keep rape reports under wraps. Faced with vehement, relentless protest and a flurry of local news attention, the administration reluctantly accepted the feminists' demand to remove any accused perpetrator from campus within twenty-four hours of a reported rape. But the rule was adopted on the condition that a committee of concerned staff and students would work to retool the policy while the administration consulted lawyers about its constitutionality. Womyn of Antioch demanded the policy out of strength, not weakness, notes Saltman. "We get to say who touches us, and where."

The policy has been criticized as a return to the 1950s that disempowers women by viewing them as damsels in distress and spells the death of *amour*.

Perhaps the critics are upset because they're embarrassed, says Elizabeth Sullivan, Antioch '93, now of Seattle. "It's still very hard for people to be explicit about sexual intimacy. The policy limits certain options, such as casual, thoughtless sex, while encouraging other options, such as accountability, sexual equality, and living in a community with a reduced fear of harassment or coerced sex."

Sullivan notes that critics act as though, without this policy, there is no social context influencing students' interactions at all. "Most of us acquire a whole set of norms and attitudes before we become sexual with other people. We learn who is an acceptable partner, we learn unspoken codes of how to proceed, and we develop a set of expectations about what sex should be," says Sullivan. In an intentional community like Antioch, people can choose to restructure that context.

Some students from other campuses who have adopted the Antioch rules as their own, don't understand what all the fuss is about. Matthew Mizel, a student at Stanford (CA), likens the current resistance to people's initial embarrassment about asking a partner to use a condom during the early years of the AIDS crisis. "Why do people feel asking is not romantic?" asks Mizel. "All it does is clarify things. For me, it's not a romantic situation until I know the woman is comfortable."

As a letter writer to *The New Yorker* noted, asking permission, as in—"may I kiss the hollow of your neck?"—does not have to be devoid of *amour*.

Students should be relieved to discard the old stereotypes that "masculine sexuality is dangerous, passionate, reckless, and that the woman is passive and just laying back there," according to Mizel.

Callie Cary, an Antioch spokeswoman, herself out of college for less than a decade, scoffs at the idea that the asking-before-you-touch policy infantilizes women. "The assumption that this policy is about women saying no to men is based on the idea that men initiate sex all the time. But I know there are men on this campus who feel the women are very aggressive."

ACTIVISM ON OTHER CAMPUSES

While Antioch's policy contains the most detailed rules for sexual correctness to date, feminist actions on a number of campuses have expanded from helping rape victims *after* the fact to including a preventive approach. These efforts by female—and male—students are cropping up at conservative, co-ed universities like Syracuse (NY) and Vanderbilt (TN), as well as traditionally liberal women's colleges, such as Barnard (NY) and Mount Holyoke (MA). Private schools such as Stanford and Duke (NC) Universities boast dynamic men's groups examining why men rape and striving to prevent it, while students at public Evergreen State (WA) and Rutgers University (NJ) are reaching out to local high school girls with educational programs. On black college campuses the emphasis is on how the negative depiction of women in rap music discourages fair treatment in the sexual arena.

Most student organizers express some reservations over Antioch's policy—some hate it, while others herald it as swinging the pendulum dramatically to the side of open communication about sex—so far, in fact that they might not need to adopt such a radical approach at their own schools (phew!).

"I would love to address the Antioch policy, but from what I can gather from other people on our committee, it would be suicide for us to consider it here," says Melinda Lewis, a sophomore at Vanderbilt University in Nashville and president of Students For Women's Concerns. After speaking in spring 1992 with rape survivors who felt revictimized by the school's judicial system, Lewis returned in the fall to push for a new sexual assault policy. Although she is sensitive to Katie Roiphe-inspired charges of "victim feminism," she counters that the term does not accurately describe the activism—or the problems—she sees around her.

RATS IN THE IVORY TOWERS

At Lehigh University (PA), Jeanne Clery was robbed, sodomized and murdered in her dorm bed by a student she had never met. Jeanne's own actions that night—it is believed that she left her door unlocked for her roommate's convenience—made it clear that students are often shockingly oblivious to the dangers around them. At the time, in 1986, Lehigh students regularly propped open outside doors to allow friends to come and go easily. Lehigh had "studied" the security problem for eleven years but taken no action until after Jeanne's death, according to Lynda Getchis of Security on Campus, a group founded by Clery's parents.

After this incident, then-freshman Congressman Jim Ramstad (R-MN) joined forces with Clery's parents and crafted the Campus Sexual Assault Victims Bill of Rights. Signed into law in 1990, it requires that all post-secondary schools that receive federal funding publish annual reports about crime statistics on campus, institute policies to deal with sexual assault and offer rape awareness educational programs.

For 1991, the first year statistics were collected, 2,300 American campuses reported 30 murders, 1,000 rapes, and more than 1,800 robberies, according to *The Chronicle of Higher Education*. Most campus crime (78%) is student-on-student. While the crime incidence on campus is lower than that of the country as a whole, student and parent perceptions of the campus as a safe haven make the crime levels seem more shocking.

There is much controversy about just how many women experience sexual assault at college—the figures range from a scary 1 in 25 to a horrifying 1 in 4. But even the smallest estimates amount to a large threat to women's safety.

So it's no wonder that student activists are increasingly pressing their colleges to own up to the reality of crime and to codify, in writing, the kind of campus they want. The demands usually include more stringent acquaintance rape policies and mandatory peer education for students of both genders.

In the past five years, student activists have increasingly focused on university policies, notes Claire Kaplan, sexual assault education coordinator at the University of Virginia. "This strategy can be construed as students asking for protection, but it is not a throwback to *in loco parentis*. The institution has a contract with the student—the same kind of contract that could result in a third party suit against employers or landlords who fail to provide adequate protection against crime on their premises."

Today's students are also coming of age in a litigious, capitalist culture and many adopt a consumerist creed: "I pay a lot of money to go to this school, I deserve to be protected from assault and, at the very least, informed of its incidence on campus."

COMING OF AGE IN THE '90S

Today's young activists have a point of view so different from those of the 1960s and '70s, that commentators have had difficulty making the connections. In the '60s it was college men who had their lives on the line with the threat of being drafted to serve in the unpopular war in Vietnam. But today it is the women, and threat of rape, that's the flashpoint.

And unlike the rebels of the '60s and '70s who were trying to tear down repressive rules, institutions and social establishments, the generation growing up in the no-rules '90s is striving to build up a foundation of acceptable personal conduct and institutionalized norms.

At Evergreen State College in Olympia, WA, the administration had spent two years, with no end in sight, developing an anti-rape protocol. In the spring of 1993, rage at slow adjudication of a rape charge boiled over into graffiti hits around campus. The scribblers named names and proclaimed, "Rape Me and I'll Kill You," said Nina Fischer, a member of the Rape Response Coalition. The university protocol went into effect last fall, and students plan to take their rape awareness workshops to local high schools this spring.

Radical approaches are less popular at a school like North Carolina State University in Raleigh, says Brian Ammons, a founder of that school's REAL-Men (Rape Education and Active Leadership). Originally active as the male-involvement voice in crafting a campus sex offense protocol, Ammons formed the group to examine male socialization and responsibility in a rape culture. In fact, at NCSU, it was REAL-Men that organized last fall's Take Back the Night march. The resident women's group, Help, Education and Activism on Rape (HEAR-Women) developed out of that.

"In some ways it was easier for a group of men to come together to offer some legitimacy on the issue," Ammons says. "Women on our campus are afraid to speak up about a lot of things. The fear of being labeled a feminist and being alienated here is very real."

WHITE WOMEN'S FEMINISM?

Melinda Lewis, an African American, is a sophomore at Vanderbilt and president of Students For Women's Concerns, a predominantly white feminist group. "People question my involvement," she says. "The rape issue is perceived as something with which only Anglo, middle-class women are concerned. But that's a misguided notion. Women of color are raped and assaulted much more frequently than Anglo women."

Jennifer Lipton, a Barnard College student involved in rewriting sexual offense policy for the Columbia-Barnard community amidst administrator recalcitrance, agrees that the perception of acquaintance rape as a "white women's issue" flies in the face of reality. At the rape crisis center at St. Luke's-Roosevelt Hospital nearby, where she is a volunteer, most of the survivors she sees are women of color, most very poor, some homeless.

"Their concerns are very different," Lipton says. "If their perpetrator is also black, they wonder if they should report it to the police. They are very aware of the racism of the judicial system, and worried about what it will do to their own community if they turn in this man. They also know that, as poor black women, society doesn't really value what they say."

However at many African American colleges, date rape is a significantly less prominent gender concern than how women are depicted in rap music and advertising, reports Dionne Lyne, a student at the all-women Spelman College in Atlanta and member of the new campus organization SISTERS (Sisters in Solidarity to Eradicate Sexism). There's also anger at the persistent reference to certain Pan-Hellenic parties as "Greek Freaks," because of the use of "freak" as a disparaging term depicting black women as nymphomaniacs.

"There is a silence on the issue, a sense of, 'Yeah, it happens but we really don't want to know about it.' It reinforces the [idea] that these things happen to bad women, and we're just going to assume that we are all striving to be Spelman women, who are finer than that," Lyne says.

Spelman and brother school Morehouse College frequently co-sponsor educational programs about acquaintance rape, but Lyne says many women get the sense that Morehouse men are lecturing them about the issue, as if the men don't have a thing or two of their own to learn about date rape. Morehouse organizations have frequently scheduled their programs on Spelman's campus rather than their own, and fill the room with women and just one or two men.

Thomas Prince, associate director of counseling at Morehouse, counters that there are numerous anti-rape programs on the men's campus for co-ed groups, but his description of them seemed to indicate upon whom the responsibility is placed.

"We cover the FBI statistics, . . . talk about the things that might be contributing to the rise of acquaintance rapes and what to do if it happens to you. [That is] . . . what women can do if they find themselves in that situation," Prince said.

Prince states that there is no student group specifically organizing around this problem at Morehouse, and felt the Antioch policy did not encompass the way African-American men and women communicate about sex. "The language used around African American males is different," Prince said. "They have their own way of communicating verbally."

MEN AGAINST RAPE

Some male activists are just as disturbed as their female counterparts with men's penchants during educational programs, for doggedly questioning the technical definition of rape or assault, rather than focusing on the nature of sexual relationships themselves.

"It's always coming up: 'What if this happens? Is this rape? How about that—is that rape?'" said James Newell, a senior at Syracuse University and president of the five-year-old coed student group SCARED (Students Concerned About Rape Education). "Men feel victimized by groups like ours. But we are not a group that's against sex."

Examining male expectations of sex is one tactic used at Duke University in Durham, NC, by the four-year-old student group Men Acting for Change (MAC). Pornography as sex education for men is a focal point of at least one of the eight-session course on men and gender issues, a topic that precedes the class on rape, says Jason Schultz, a MAC co-founder who graduated in spring 1993.

While most of the women activists interviewed praised the men's organizations that are working against sexual violence, many expressed reservations and some suspicions about token support from other men's groups. One woman who asked not to be named criticized a men's group on her campus whose sole pro-feminist action is an annual day-long wearing of white ribbons to signify opposition to sexual assault. "Frankly I think it's a very shallow and trivial way of responding," she said.

Kelly Wall, a founder of HEAR-Women at North Carolina State, expressed irritation that the most visible anti-rape presence on campus before HEAR was comprised of men.

The REAL-Men group is aware of the apparent irony of the situation. "We're very conscious of what our place is. We don't want to take over the issue," Ammons says. Although his group does deal with "secondary survivors" (men who are grappling with their feelings about the rape of a lover, friend or relative), it is with some hesitation that they discuss the issues of male survivors of sexual offense.

Anti-rape activist Matthew Mizel at Stanford University says he sometimes feels his motivation questioned. Mizel founded Stanford Men's Collective in fall 1992 to discuss where rape comes from and how to stop it by examining men's own behavior. A talkative, outgoing senior easily recognized on campus by his long blond hair, Mizel says the praise he gets from women for his work generates curiosity and the occasional impression that he's doing it to "get laid."

"Men have asked if I'm trying to gain points with women and be some kind of super-heterosexual. . . . And some women have asked if I'm gay—as if there was no chance that I'm just a regular person who cares about this issue," Mizel said.

These young men make it clear that anti-rape work is not just a woman's thing, and that the most progressive voices among college students are determined to rewrite the sexual code to fit the needs of their generation.

And they agree that a rewrite is necessary. At the University of Virginia, Claire Kaplan described a seminar in which several fraternity men asserted: "When you get to a certain point during sex you can't stop," an attitude she thought had long since fallen to the wayside. "That's why the Antioch policy was created," she notes. "There is still the attitude, 'don't talk, just do.'"

Combating Impunity and Femicide in Ciudad Juárez

Lourdes Godínez Leal

Lourdes Godínez Leal is a reporter for the press agency CIMAC (Communication and Information About Women). She has written numerous articles about human rights issues in Central America. This piece comes from the 2008 NACLA Report on the Americas.

Over the past 15 years, some 400 women have been murdered, and hundreds more have disappeared in Ciudad Juárez, the Mexican city that borders El Paso. The victims, most of them teenagers, have typically been abducted, raped, strangled, and left in empty city lots, often on their way home from work. Although the authorities have arrested and convicted a number of perpetrators—by the end of 2006 at least 160 were serving prison sentences—the killings have continued at the same pace.[1] To date, law enforcement has not seriously investigated the serial nature of the killings, and the motivation for them remains a mystery. These crimes, together with official indifference, have given rise to a new term in Mexico: *femicide*, the systematic murder of women.

Neither the end of the PAN's political dominance in the state of Chihuahua in 1998 nor the end of the PRI's decades of autocratic rule at the federal level in 2000 have had any effect on the official indifference to the killings. The impunity for violence against women that has prevailed for so long in Chihuahua has been maintained by officials of various parties. Even though the state attorney general's office recently acknowledged that at least 364 women were murdered in the city between 1993 and 2005—and research has shown that this kind of anti-woman violence occurs elsewhere in the country—the problem of femicide has never taken its rightful place as a national electoral issue.

Throughout the 1990s, Juárez was Mexico's fastest-growing center of industrial production. It expanded explosively over that decade, with no warning and no planning. It generated low-paying and insecure jobs, while its urban services, from road maintenance to primary education, remained nowhere close to adequate for its burgeoning population. Set opposite El Paso on the Texas-Chihuahua border, the city is now home to an estimated 1.5 million people and nearly 300 export-oriented assembly plants, or maquiladoras. More than 225,000 Juárez residents, nearly half the city's labor force, work in the *maquiladoras*, most of them women under the age of 30.

The city attracts impoverished campesinos and unemployed workers from throughout north-central Mexico, as well as transnational factory owners, who appreciate the city's modern

---

[1]Guadalupe Morfín Otero, Commission to Prevent and Eradicate Violence Against the Women of Ciudad Juárez, "Third and Final Report," Mexico City, November 23, 2006.

industrial parks, low-wage workforce, and proximity to the United States. Transnational drug traffickers come to Juárez for the same reasons; they are also attracted by, and make profitable use of, the city's social disorganization.

As the killings and disappearances continue in Juárez and throughout the state of Chihuahua, the police and various attorneys general have been the great missing force in the investigation and resolution of the long wave of violence. In 1996, in the midst of the ongoing serial killings, then governor Francisco Barrio remarked that the killings were within the range of what was to be expected in a city like Juárez. Other state and local officials have justified their lack of investigative fervor by stressing that many of the victims have been prostitutes and involved in the drug trade.

Another theory was proposed a few years ago by Diana Washington Valdez, a reporter for the *El Paso Times*. "The best information we have," she told NPR in 2003, is that "men are committing crimes simply for the sport of it. The authorities know who the killers are, and nothing's being done about it."[2]

In the face of Mexican authorities' neglect and their disregard for the many recommendations offered by national and international human rights organizations, mothers of the victims have formed organizations, embarking on two long missions: recovering the bodies of their daughters and seeking just punishment for those responsible for the murders. Two of those organizations, perhaps the most significant in terms of their continuous work and determination to shed light on the murders, are Justice for Our Daughters and Our Daughters Return Home.

Since 1995, they have demanded federal inquiries, succeeding only in the last four years in pressing the state and federal governments to investigate. During the long absence of official interest, they took on the job themselves, beginning their activism by simply documenting the femicides: For the period 1993–2005, Our Daughters Coming Home, by clipping the articles that appeared almost daily in the local press, documented 430 murders and 600 disappearances. Justice for Our Daughters, using local reports as well as the findings of a team of Argentine forensic anthropologists working in Juárez, documented 433 murders. And Casa Amiga, an umbrella group, has identified 265 of the dead.[3]

In November 2003, the first official investigation into the femicides began, headed by a specially convened federal body known as the Commission to Prevent and Eradicate Violence Against the Women of Ciudad Juárez. The commission, chaired by the former commissioner for human rights of the state of Jalisco, Guadalupe Morfín, addressed femicide not only in the state of Chihuahua, but throughout the country. Indeed, the commission demonstrated that the problem was nationwide, despite the lack of statistics and reliable information. The mothers' organizations have largely supported the commission, because it is the only body that gives them a line of communication to the federal government.

But it never had sufficient personnel or resources to carry out its work. The federal government's lack of interest is so great that since November 2006, when Morfín left her position, the group has yet to name her successor. Thus most of the investigation continues to be undertaken by civil society, reflecting the continuing pattern of official neglect.

The citizen observatory on femicide, formed in August, is the latest civic organization to addresses the crisis. Composed of various groups—Catholics for the Right to Decide, the

---

[2] Diana Washington Valdez, cited in John Burnett, "Explosive Theory on Killings of Juarez Women," NPR, www.npr.org/templates/story/story.php?storyId=1532607.

[3] Deputy Marcela Lagarde, Federal Chamber of Deputies, Report of the LIX Legislature, "Femicide Violence in Chihuahua, Mexico," Mexico City, April 2006.

Mexican Commission to Defend and Promote Human Rights, the Morelos Academy of the Woman, and eight other activist and academic organizations—it monitors femicide on a national level, producing statistics and policy proposals, while formulating national standards to enforce the 2007 General Law of Access of Women to a Life Free of Violence.

International organizations, mainly women's groups and human rights defenders, have been watching the situation closely, frequently criticizing various branches and levels of the Mexican government for its neglect. Even European lawmakers have discussed the question: In October, the European Parliament issued a report in which it concluded that the government of Mexico (along with those of Central America) had not taken sufficient steps "to attack the roots of the femicides." The report emphasized that fighting violence against women requires good law enforcement as well as preventive measures, such as the creation of a legitimate social order as well as education on human rights and gender equality.[4]

Recognizing the prevailing climate of impunity surrounding these cases, the report also recommended a larger budget for investigative organizations, better witness-protection programs, and more support for judicial organisms and general investigators to pursue these cases.

International support has also come in the form of an expert team of forensic anthropologists from Argentina that arrived in Ciudad Juárez in 2004, to help identify human remains. Until then, the Chihuahua attorney generals office had been delivering the corpses of murdered women to the wrong families, or buried them in common graves, as it still does.

According to Mercedes Doretti, one of the forensic anthropologists, the team has identified 27 remains, which have been delivered to the proper families.[5] Nevertheless, this leaves a large number yet to be identified. Doretti confirms the Mexican government's lack of interest, noting that official files on the victims typically include no information on where the recovered bodies, frequently unidentified, are buried. The team began its search in the cemeteries, whose registers proved unreliable because the majority of the women were buried in the area reserved for unidentified indigents.

"We depended to a great extent on the memory of the grave diggers," Doretti says. She adds that although according to official documentation, bodies were sent to common graves until 1997, her team is still finding remains buried as recently as 2005 in the common graves, requiring continued exhumations. In December, after the Chihuahua attorney general's office recommended that the common graves filled between 1993 and 2005 be exhumed, the NGOs of Ciudad Juárez and Chihuahua asked the governor, José Reyes Baeza, to extend the forensic team's contract to conduct the research. Doretti, suggesting that her team had already done all that was humanly possible to find and exhume the remains of missing women, warns that while much work remains to be done at the level of identification, "there is little hope of finding more women's remains."[6]

Femicide is a crime of the state," SAYS MARCELA Lagarde, a feminist federal legislator who presided over a special commission of the Chamber of Deputies established to look into the Juárez killings. A report produced by the commission defines femicide as the combination of

---

[4]Interview with Humberto Guerrero Rosales, director of the Mexican Commission for the Defense and Promotion of Human Rights, CIMACNoticias, October 11, 2007.
[5]Author's interview with Mercedes Doretti, January 29, 2008.
[6]Ibid.

"violent misogynist acts against women" and the institutional violence against women exerted by the authorities who block their access to justice. Femicide, Lagarde continues, furthermore constitutes "the rupture of the state of law, since the state is incapable of guaranteeing the life of women, of acting with legality and enforcing respect, of achieving justice and preventing and eradicating the violence to which it gives rise."[7]

There have been some advances in recent years against gender-based violence in Chihuahua at the legislative level—an increase in penalties for sexual abuse, including sexual harassment, and the classification of rape within marriage as a crime. It also eliminates a requirement that plaintiffs in rape cases were "chaste and honest" when the crime took place.

Nonetheless, official indifference still rules the day in Ciudad Juárez and the state of Chihuahua. After 400 unexplained, apparently senseless murders in 15 years, this indifference itself is femicide.

---

[7] Deputy Marcela Lagarde, Federal Chamber of Deputies, Report of the LIX Legislature, "Femicide Violence in Chihuahua, Mexico," Mexico City, April 2006.

SECTION VIII

Feminism(s) and Gender Justice

Key Concepts for Section VIII: Feminism(s) and Gender Justice

Anti-Sexist
Anti-Feminist
Black Feminism
Compulsory Heterosexuality
Consciousness Raising (CR)
Displaced Homemaker
Equal Rights Amendment
Feminism
Feminist Consciousness
Feminist Majority Foundation
Feminist Movement (Women's Movement)
Feminist Paradigm
First-Wave Feminism
Global Feminism
Hegemonic Feminism
Jane Collective
Liberal Feminism
Men's Liberation Movement
Multiracial Feminism
National Organization for Men
    Against Sexism (NOMAS)
National Organization for Women (NOW)
National Women's Studies Association
    (NWSA)
Nineteenth Amendment
Our Bodies, Ourselves
Paradigm
Praxis
Radical Feminism
Reproductive Freedom
Second-Wave Feminism
Seneca Falls Convention of 1848
Suffragist
Third-Wave Feminism
White Anti-Racist Feminism
Womanist

Concepts to Review

Ageism
Androcentrism

Claiming an Education
Classism
Dichotomy/Dichotomous
Dominance/Domination
Equal Employment Opportunity
    Commission (1968)
Equal Pay Act
Equal Pay Day
Essentialism
Family Friendly Work Policies
Femininity/Femininities
Gender
Gender Neutral Pronouns
Gender Studies
Glass Ceiling
Heterosexism
Hierarchy
Homophobia
Internalized Oppression
Intersectionality
"Just-So" Story
Masculinity/Masculinities
Media Activism
Men's Studies
Misogyny
Oppression
Path of Least Resistance
Patriarchy
"the Personal is Political"
Power
Privilege
Queer Theory
Racism
Radical Heterosexuality
Reproductive Choice
Same-Sex Marriage
Sex
Sex-Gender System
Transphobia
Women's Studies

The Declaration of Sentiments

Elizabeth Cady Stanton

The Declaration of Sentiments and Resolutions was signed by eighty-six women and thirty-two men, all participants at The Seneca Falls Women's Rights Convention of 1848. The convention was planned by Elizabeth Cady Stanton, Lucretia Mott, Martha Wright, Mary Ann M'Clintock and Jane Hunt. The history of the convention and the document, including all of the signers, is chronicled at the U.S. Women's Rights National Historical Park in Seneca Falls, NY.

When, in the course of human events, it becomes necessary for one portion of the family of man to assume among the people of the earth a position different from that which they have hitherto occupied, but one to which the laws of nature and of nature's God entitle them, a decent respect to the opinions of mankind requires that they should declare the causes that impel them to such a course.

We hold these truths to be self-evident: that all men and women are created equal; that they are endowed by their Creator with certain inalienable rights; that among these are life, liberty, and the pursuit of happiness; that to secure these rights governments are instituted, deriving their just powers from the consent of the governed. Whenever any form of government becomes destructive of these ends, it is the right of those who suffer from it to refuse allegiance to it, and to insist upon the institution of a new government, laying its foundation on such principles, and organizing its powers in such form, as to them shall seem most likely to effect their safety and happiness. Prudence, indeed, will dictate that governments long established should not be changed for light and transient causes; and accordingly all experience hath shown that mankind are more disposed to suffer. while evils are sufferable, than to right themselves by abolishing the forms to which they are accustomed. But when a long train of abuses and usurpations, pursuing invariably the same object, evinces a design to reduce them under absolute despotism, it is their duty to throw off such government, and to provide new guards for their future security. Such has been the patient sufferance of the women under this government, and such is now the necessity which constrains them to demand the equal station to which they are entitled. The history of mankind is a history of repeated injuries and usurpations on the part of man toward woman, having in direct object the establishment of an absolute tyranny over her. To prove this, let facts be submitted to a candid world.

The history of mankind is a history of repeated injuries and usurpations on the part of man toward woman, having in direct object the establishment of an absolute tyranny over her. To prove this, let facts be submitted to a candid world.

From Elizabeth Cady Stanton, *A History of Woman Suffrage*, vol. 1 (Rochester, N.Y.: Fowler and Wells, 1889), pages 70–71.

He has never permitted her to exercise her inalienable right to the elective franchise.

He has compelled her to submit to laws, in the formation of which she had no voice.

He has withheld from her rights which are given to the most ignorant and degraded men—both natives and foreigners.

Having deprived her of this first right of a citizen, the elective franchise, thereby leaving her without representation in the halls of legislation, he has oppressed her on all sides.

He has made her, if married, in the eye of the law, civilly dead.

He has taken from her all right in property, even to the wages she earns.

He has made her, morally, an irresponsible being, as she can commit many crimes with impunity, provided they be done in the presence of her husband. In the covenant of marriage, she is compelled to promise obedience to her husband, he becoming, to all intents and purposes, her master—the law giving him power to deprive her of her liberty, and to administer chastisement.

He has so framed the laws of divorce, as to what shall be the proper causes, and in case of separation, to whom the guardianship of the children shall be given, as to be wholly regardles of the happiness of women—the law, in all cases, going upon a flase supposition of the supremacy of man, and giving all power into his hands.

After depriving her of all rights as a married woman, if single, and the owner of property, he has taxed her to support a government which recognizes her only when her property can be made profitable to it.

He has monopolized nearly all the profitable employments, and from those she is permitted to follow, she receives but a scanty remuneration. He closes against her all the avenues to wealth and distinction which he considers most homorable to himself. As a teacher of theoloy, medicine, or law, she is not known.

He has denied her the facilities for obtaining a thorough education, all colleges being closed against her.

He allows her in church, as well as state, but a suborinate position, claiming apostolic authority for her exclusion from the ministry, and, with some exceptions, from any public participation in the affairs of the church.

He has created a false public sentiment by giving to the world a different code of morals for men and women, by which moral delinquencies which exclude women from society, are not only tolerated, but deemed of little account in man.

He has usurped the prerogative of Jehovah himself, claiming it as his right to assign for her a sphere of action, when that belongs to her conscience and to her God.

He has endeavored, in every way that he could, to destroy her conficence in her own powers, to lessen her self-respect, and to make her willing to lead a dependent and abject life.

Now, in view of this entire disfranchisement of one-half the people of this country, their social and religious degradation—in view of the unjust laws above mentioned, and because women do feel themselves aggrieved, oppressed, and fraudulently deprived of their most sacred rights, we insist that they have immediate admission to all the rights and privileges which belong to them as citizens of the United States.

Womanist

Alice Walker

Alice Walker *is best known for her novel* The Color Purple *(1982), which won both a Pulitzer Prize and an American Book Award. She earned a B. A. from Sarah Lawrence. Among her many novels are* The Third Life of Grange Copeland *(1970),* Meridians *(1976),* Possessing the Secret of Joy *(1992). Her poetry collections include* Once, Revolutionary Petunias and Other Poems *(1973) and* Her Blue Body Everything We Know: Earthling Poems 1965–1990 Complete *(1991). This piece is an excerpt from her collection of essays* In Search of Our Mothers' Gardens: Womanist Prose, *which won the Lillian Smith Book Award in 1984.*

Womanist 1. From *womanish*. (Opp. of "girlish," i.e., frivolous, irresponsible, not serious.) A black feminist or feminist of color. From the black folk expression of mothers to female children, "You acting womanish," i.e., like a woman. Usually referring to outrageous, audacious, courageous or *willful* behavior. Wanting to know more and in greater depth than is considered "good" for one. Interested in grown-up doings. Acting grown up. Being grown up. Interchangeable with another black folk expression: "You trying to be grown." Responsible. In charge. *Serious.*

* * *

2. *Also:* A woman who loves other women, sexually and/or nonsexually. Appreciates and prefers women's culture, women's emotional flexibility (values tears as natural counterbalance of laughter), and women's strength. Sometimes loves individual men, sexually and/or nonsexually. Committed to survival and wholeness of entire people, male *and* female. Not a separatist, except periodically, for health. Traditionally universalist, as in: "Mama, why are we brown, pink, and yellow, and our cousins are white, beige, and black?" Ans.: "Well, you know the colored race is just like a flower garden, with every color flower represented." Traditionally capable, as in: "Mama, I'm walking to Canada and I'm taking you and a bunch of other slaves with me." Reply: "It wouldn't be the first time."

* * *

3. Loves music. Loves dance. Loves the moon. *Loves* the Spirit. Loves love and food and roundness. Loves struggle. *Loves* the Folk. Loves herself. *Regardless.*

* * *

4. Womanist is to feminist as purple to lavender.

Excerpt from Manifesta
Young Women, Feminism, and the Future

Amy Richards and Jennifer Baumgardner

Jennifier Baumgardner and *Amy Richards* collaborate and write extensively on Third Wave Feminism. This excerpt is from their work Manifesta: Young Women, Feminism, and the Future (2000). They are also co-founders of the progressive speakers' bureau Soapbox. Richards is a co-founder of the Third Wave Foundation, she writes Ask Amy an online advice column at feminist.com and is the author of Opting In: Having a Child Without Losing Yourself (2008). Baumgardner writes for dozens of magazines, including Glamour, The Nation, Real Simple, and Harper's. She is the author of Look Both Ways: Bisexual Politics (2007) and Abortion and Life (2008).

A DAY WITHOUT FEMINISM

We are both born in 1970, the baptismal moment of a decade that would change dramatically the lives of American women. The two of us grew up thousands of miles apart, in entirely different kinds of families, yet we both came of age with the awareness that certain rights had been won by the women's movement. We've never doubted how important feminism is to people's lives—men's and women's. Both of our mothers went to consciousness-raising-type groups. Amy's mother raised Amy on her own, and Jennifer's mother, questioning the politics of housework, staged laundry strikes.

With the dawn of not just a new century but a new millennium, people are looking back and taking stock of feminism. Do we need new strategies? Is feminism dead? Has society changed so much that the idea of a feminist movement is obsolete? For us, the only way to answer these questions is to imagine what our lives would have been if the women's movement had never happened and the conditions for women had remained as they were in the year of our births. Imagine that for a day it's still 1970, and women have only the rights they had then. Sly and the Family Stone and Dionne Warwick are on the radio, the kitchen appliances are Harvest Gold, and the name of your Whirlpool gas stove is Mrs. America. What is it like to be female?

Babies born on this day are automatically given their father's name. If no father is listed, "illegitimate" is likely to be typed on the birth certificate. There are virtually no child-care centers, so all preschool children are in the hands of their mothers, a baby-sitter, or an expensive nursery school. In elementary school, girls can't play in Little League and almost all of the teachers are female. (The latter is still true.) In a few states, it may be against the law for a male to teach grades lower than the sixth, on the basis that it's unnatural, or that men can't be trusted with young children.

In junior high, girls probably take home ec; boys take shop or small-engine repair. Boys who want to learn how to cook or sew on a button are out of luck, as are girls who want to learn how to fix a car. *Seventeen* magazine doesn't run feminist-influenced current columns like "Sex + Body" and "Traumarama." Instead the magazine encourages girls not to have sex; pleasure isn't part of its vocabulary. Judy Blume's books are just beginning to be published, and *Free to Be . . . You and Me* does not exist. No one reads much about masturbation as a natural activity; nor do they learn that sex is for anything other than procreation. Girls do read mystery stories about Nancy Drew, for whom there is no sex, only her blue roadster and having "luncheon." (The real mystery is how Nancy gets along without a purse and manages to meet only white people.) Boys read about the Hardy Boys, for whom there are no girls.

In high school, the principal is a man. Girls have physical-education class and play half-court basketball, but not soccer, track, or cross country; nor do they have any varsity sports teams. The only prestigious physical activity for girls is cheerleading, or being a drum majorette. Most girls don't take calculus or physics; they plan the dances and decorate the gym. Even when girls get better grades than their male counterparts, they are half as likely to qualify for a National Merit Scholarship because many of the test questions favor boys. Standardized tests refer to males and male experiences much more than to females and their experiences.[1] If a girl "gets herself pregnant," she could lose her membership in her local chapter of the National Honor Society.[2]

Girls and young women might have sex while they're unmarried, but they may be ruining their chances of landing a guy full-time, and they're probably getting a bad reputation. If a pregnancy happens, an enterprising gal can get a legal abortion only if she lives in New York or is rich enough to fly there, or to Cuba, London, or Scandinavia. There's also the Chicago-based Jane Collective, an underground abortion-referral service, which can hook you up with an illegal or legal termination. (Any of these options are going to cost you. Illegal abortions average $300 to $500, sometimes as much as $2,000.) To prevent pregnancy, a sexually active woman might go to a doctor to be fitted for a diaphragm, or take the high-dose birth-control pill, but her doctor isn't likely to inform her of the possibility of deadly blood clots. Those who do take the Pill also may have to endure this contraceptive's crappy side effects: migraine headaches, severe weight gain, irregular bleeding, and hair loss (or gain), plus the possibility of an increased risk of breast cancer in the long run. It is unlikely that women or their male partners know much about the clitoris and its role in orgasm unless someone happens to fumble upon it. Instead, the myth that vaginal orgasms from penile penetration are the only "mature" (according to Freud) climaxes prevails.

Lesbians are rarely "out," except in certain bars owned by organized crime (the only businessmen who recognize this untapped market), and if lesbians don't know about the bars, they're less likely to know whether there are any other women like them. Radclyffe Hall's depressing early-twentieth-century novel *The Well of Loneliness* pretty much indicates their fate.

---

[1] Phyllis Rosser pioneered the research that named the gender gap in SAT and PSAT scores. She wrote to us as we were finishing the book that in the past couple of years "the gender gap on the PSAT has narrowed from 45 to 20 points (in SAT terms). This means that women will receive about $1,500,000 more in scholarship money in 2000 than in previous years." See Rosser's book, *The SAT Gender Gap: Identifying the Causes*, published by the Center for Women's Policy Studies (1989) for more information.

[2] In 1999, the Women's Rights Project of the American Civil Liberties Union (ACLU) settled a landmark Title IX case. Two high-school girls from Covington, Kentucky, brought suit against the Grant County School District Chapter of the National Honor Society for ignoring their qualifying GPAs in light of their pregnancy and parental status. The school district argued that the girls weren't denied admission because of their parental status (and implicitly acknowledged that such a practice would be unlawful) but because "they engaged in premarital sex." The school relied solely on pregnancy as proof of sexual activity, though, a determining factor that can apply only to women. (No males had ever been excluded from the school's chapter of the National Honor Society on grounds of having had sex—Title IX prevailed!)

The Miss America Pageant is the biggest source of scholarship money for women.[3] Women can't be students at Dartmouth, Columbia, Harvard, West Point, Boston College, or the Citadel, among other all-male institutions. Women's colleges are referred to as "girls' schools." There are no Take Back the Night marches to protest women's lack of safety after dark, but that's okay because college girls aren't allowed out much after dark anyway. Curfew is likely to be midnight on Saturday and 9 or 10 p.m. the rest of the week. Guys get to stay out as late as they want. Women tend to major in teaching, home economics, English, or maybe a language—a good skill for translating someone else's words.[4] The women's studies major does not exist, although you can take a women's studies course at six universities, including Cornell and San Diego State College.[5] The absence of women's history, black history, Chicano studies, Asian-American history, queer studies, and Native American history from college curricula implies that they are not worth studying. A student is lucky if he or she learns that women were "given" the vote in 1920, just as Columbus "discovered" America in 1492. They might also learn that Sojourner Truth, Mary Church Terrell, and Fannie Lou Hamer were black abolitionists or civil-rights leaders, but not that they were feminists. There are practically no tenured female professors at any school, and campuses are not racially diverse. Women of color are either not there or they're lonely as hell. There is no nationally recognized Women's History Month or Black History Month. Only 14 percent of doctorates are awarded to women. Only 3.5 percent of MBAs are female.

Only 2 percent of everybody in the military is female, and these women are mostly nurses. There are no female generals in the U.S. Air Force, no female naval pilots, and no Marine brigadier generals. On the religious front, there are no female cantors or rabbis, Episcopal canons, or Catholic priests. (This is still true of Catholic priests.)

Only 44 percent of women are employed outside the home. And those women make, on average, fifty-two cents to the dollar earned by males. Want ads are segregated into "Help Wanted Male" and "Help Wanted Female." The female side is preponderantly for secretaries, domestic workers, and other low-wage service jobs, so if you're a female lawyer you must look under "Help Wanted Male." There are female doctors, but twenty states have only five female gynecologists or fewer. Women workers can be fired or demoted for being pregnant, especially if they are teachers, since the kids they teach aren't supposed to think that women have sex. If a boss demands sex, refers to his female employee exclusively as "Baby," or says he won't pay her unless she gives him a blow job, she either has to quit or succumb—no pun intended. Women can't be airline pilots. Flight attendants are "stewardesses"—waitresses in the sky— and necessarily female. Sex appeal is a job requirement, wearing makeup is a rule, and women are fired if they exceed the age or weight deemed sexy. Stewardesses can get married without getting canned, but this is a new development. (In 1968 the Equal Employment Opportunity Commission—EEOC—made it illegal to forcibly retire stewardesses for getting hitched.) Less than 2 percent of dentists are women; 100 percent of dental assistants are women. The "glass ceiling" that keeps women from moving naturally up the ranks, as well as the sticky floor that keeps them unnaturally down in low-wage work, has not been named, much less challenged.

---

[3]Beauty contests are still the largest source of college scholarships for women. For example, the Miss America winner receives upward of $50,000, and the Miss America Organization has given more than $100 million in grants since 1945, when it began awarding scholarships. It remains the largest "scholarship organization" in the world.

[4]Anonymous was a woman, as were the translators of most "great" works. For instance, the first English translation of *The Communist Manifesto* was done by a woman, Helen McFarlane. We intend to have any translations of *Manifesta* done by a man.

[5]Before 1969, there were no women's studies departments, and very few individual courses. As of 2000, the National Women's Studies Association counted 728 women's studies courses in their database in the United States alone.

When a woman gets married, she vows to love, honor, and obey her husband, though he gets off doing just the first two to uphold his end of the bargain. A married woman can't obtain credit without her husband's signature. She doesn't have her own credit rating, legal domicile, or even her own name unless she goes to court to get it back. If she gets a loan with her husband—and she has a job—she may have to sign a "baby letter" swearing that she won't have one and have to leave her job.

Women have been voting for up to fifty years, but their turnout rate is lower than that for men, and they tend to vote right along with their husbands, not with their own interests in mind.[6] The divorce rate is about the same as it is in 2000, contrary to popular fiction's blaming the women's movement for divorce. However, divorce required that one person be at fault, therefore if you just want out of your marriage, you have to lie or blame your spouse. Property division and settlements, too, are based on fault. (And at a time when domestic violence isn't a term, much less a crime, women are legally encouraged to remain in abusive marriages.) If fathers ask for custody of the children, they get it in 60 to 80 percent of the cases. (This is still true.) If a husband or a lover hits his partner, she has no shelter to go to unless she happens to live near the one in northern California or the other in upper Michigan. If a woman is downsized from her role as a housewife (a.k.a. left by her husband), there is no word for being a displaced homemaker. As a divorcée, she may be regarded as a family disgrace or as easy sexual prey. After all, she had sex with one guy, so why not *all* guys?

If a woman is not a Mrs., she's a Miss. A woman without makeup and a hairdo is as suspect as a man with them. Without a male escort she may be refused service in a restaurant or a bar, and a woman alone is hard-pressed to find a landlord who will rent her an apartment. After all, she'll probably be leaving to get married soon, and, if she isn't, the landlord doesn't want to deal with a potential brothel.

Except among the very poor or in very rural areas, babies are born in hospitals. There are no certified midwives, and women are knocked out during birth. Most likely, they are also strapped down and lying down, made to have the baby against gravity for the doctor's convenience. If he has a schedule to keep, the likelihood of a cesarean is also very high. *Our Bodies, Ourselves* doesn't exist, nor does the women's health movement. Women aren't taught how to look at their cervixes, and their bodies are nothing to worry their pretty little heads about; however, they are supposed to worry about keeping their little heads pretty. If a woman goes under the knife to see if she has breast cancer, the surgeon won't wake her up to consult about her options before performing a Halsted mastectomy (a disfiguring radical procedure, in which the breast, the muscle wall, and the nodes under the arm, right down to the bone, are removed). She'll just wake up and find that the choice has been made for her.

Husbands are likely to die eight years earlier than their same-age wives due to the stress of having to support a family and repress an emotional life, and a lot earlier than that if women have followed the custom of marrying older, authoritative, paternal men. The stress of raising kids, managing a household, and being undervalued by society doesn't seem to kill off women at the same rate. Upon a man's death, his beloved gets a portion of his Social Security. Even if she has worked outside the home for her entire adult life, she is probably better off with that portion

---

[6]The McGovern-Nixon election of 1972 marked the emergence of a "gender gap," the first election in which there was a clear difference between men's and women's voting patterns. During the 1980 Carter-Reagan election, the gap had become wide enough for politicians to worry about getting the women's vote. (Only 46 percent of women voted for Reagan, according to the Gallup poll, but 54 percent of men did.)

than with hers in its entirety, because she has earned less and is likely to have taken time out for such unproductive acts as having kids.[7]

Has feminism changed our lives? Was it necessary? After thirty years of feminism, the world we inhabit barely resembles the world we were born into. And there's still a lot left to do.

* * *

WHAT IS FEMINISM?

In the most basic sense, feminism is exactly what the dictionary says it is: the movement for social, political, and economic equality of men and women. Public-opinion polls confirm that when women are given this definition, 71 percent say they agree with feminism, along with 61 percent of men. We prefer to add to that seemingly uncontroversial statement the following: Feminism means that women have the right to enough information to make informed choices about their lives. And because *women* is an all-encompassing term that includes middle-class white women, rich black lesbians, and working-class straight Asian women, an organic intertwining with movements for racial and economic equality, as well as gay rights, is inherent in the feminist mandate. Some sort of allegiance between women and men is also an important component of equality. After all, equality is a balance between the male and the female with the intention of liberating the individual.

Breaking down that one very basic definition, feminism has three components. It is a *movement*, meaning a group working to accomplish specific goals. Those goals are *social* and *political change*—implying that one must be engaged with the government and laws, as well as with social practices and beliefs. And implicit in these goals is *access* to sufficient information to enable women to make responsible choices.

The goals of feminism are carried out by everyday women themselves, a point that is often lost on the media. Maybe you aren't sure you need feminism, or you're not sure it needs you. You're sexy, a wallflower, you shop at Calvin Klein, you are a stay-at-home mom, a big Hollywood producer, a beautiful bride all in white, an ex-wife raising three kids, or you shave, pluck, *and* wax. In reality, feminism wants you to be whoever you are—but with a political consciousness. And vice versa: you want to be a feminist because you want to be exactly who you are. That may be someone patriarchal society doesn't value or allow—from a female cadet at the Citadel to a lesbian mother. Maybe you feel aligned with the self-determination and human rights implicit in feminism, but you also organize your life around race, religion, or class, rather than solely around gender. For instance, in *The Reader's Companion to U.S. Women's History*, the editors list seventeen prominent kinds of feminism based on identity, including American Indian, Arab-American, Asian-American, Jewish, Latina, lesbian, Marxist, Puerto Rican, and working-class. There are also womanists, which, as coined and defined by novelist and poet Alice Walker, designates a black feminist (womanists are rarely men) without having to "add a color to become visible." Womanism, as distinct from feminism's often white-centered history, is an alternative casting of the same basic beliefs about equality and freedom, and few womanists would deny the link to feminism. While each of these groups is magnetized by political equality, some additional aspect of their personhood needs to be emphasized because it affects their struggle for equality.

---

[7]Statistics and facts from "A Day without Feminism" come from a few sources: *The American Woman 1994–95: Where We Stand, Women and Health*, edited by Cynthia Costello and Anne J. Stone for the Women's Research and Education Institute (New York: W. W. Norton, 1994); *The Book of Women's Firsts*, by Phyllis J. Read and Bernard L. Witlieb (New York: Random House, 1992); *Mothers on Trial: The Battle for Children and Custody*, by Phyllis Chesler; *The Reader's Companion to U.S. Women's History*; and the U.S. Bureau of Labor Statistics. (For full citations of all other books mentioned, see the Bibliography.)

Using a qualifier in order to further define identity is very different from forgoing the feminist label altogether. For instance, women within other social-justice movements—environmental, peace, human rights, and hip-hop, for example—often opt for the term *humanist*. Although humanism includes men (and especially those who aren't white or otherwise privileged), in reality it is a retreat from feminism. Using *humanism* as a replacement for *feminism* is also a misuse of the term; theologically, humanism is a rejection of supernaturalism, not an embrace of equality between men and women. Feminism seeks to include *women* in human rights. Internationally, nearly twice as many women as men are illiterate, and it was only in 1998 that an international court denounced rape as a form of torture in prison, and as a war crime when conducted systematically by the military. Along those lines, gender-based persecution isn't recognized as grounds for asylum in the United States, which means that women who are likely to be killed by their husbands or sure to be genitally mutilated if they return to their countries are usually put on the next plane back, regardless of this potential danger. (Or, like Adelaide Abankwah and Fauziya Kassindja, they are imprisoned for years, and granted permanent residency, and later asylum, only after long campaigns conducted on their behalf by U.S. feminists.)

Most women come to feminism through personal experience, as we noted in "The Dinner Party," which is one of the reasons the core identity of feminism has to be so elastic. The term represents an incredible diversity of individual lives. Often, a woman who otherwise wouldn't align herself with feminism seeks it out when she is confronted with an abusive relationship, or if her boss is paying her less than her male counterparts are paid, or, on a positive note, if she needs credit to start her own beauty salon. Historically, who else besides feminists have been there to help women, whether they be Calvin Klein devotees or vegan Earth Mothers? Many women tap into or create feminist resources while not even knowing they are on a feminist path. On the work front, secretaries founded 9 to 5—a union for (mainly) pink-collar women workers—and feminists supported the National Committee on Pay Equity as well as microlending and the Equal Credit Opportunity Act, because no one else was interested in the problems of working women. Kris, a stylist who wrote in to Ask Amy, turned to feminist resources when she wanted to open her own salon. She didn't appeal to the Small Business Administration (SBA) because its process is complicated and full of red tape, when all she needed was a little money to tide her over as she built up her client base. Amy sent her to New York City's Women's Venture Fund, which makes microloans. Women even turn to feminism when they want to learn how to masturbate—vulvas were mapped out in Betty Dodson's video *Sex for One*, and orgasms expanded on in Susie Bright's 1990 *Susie Sexpert's Lesbian Sex World*. Most safe-sex shops were founded by feminists, from Eve's Garden in New York City, opened by Dell Williams in 1974, and Good Vibrations, founded by sex therapist Joani Blank in San Francisco in 1977, to newer sex shops like Toys in Babeland in New York City and Seattle.

Clearly, the only people who are actively paving the paths to women's equality are feminists. Eventually, most women seeking to expand or change their lives find feminism. This makes it sound as if the movement is a huge force of conscious feminists constantly fortified by new recruits. Actually, though, diminishing "enrollment" is a problem in the movement, largely due to political co-optation. The moment a concern pioneered and promoted by feminists—such as domestic violence, microenterprise, the fight for affordable health care, and day care—becomes mainstream or at all successful, it is no longer seen as a women's issue but simply as a newsworthy issue. It becomes depoliticized, taken out of the hands of the grass roots, and divorced from the very process that was necessary to its success.

The most recognizable example of feminist issues being co-opted is the movement against domestic violence. Before feminism, there was no word for battered women or domestic violence, no legal argument of self-defense for women who killed their abusers, and no shelter system. In the seventies and eighties, shelters, funded by grassroots feminist groups and fledgling foundations (like the early Ms. Foundation for Women), proliferated, but the government, the police, and the media outlets still paid very little attention to violence inside the home. For example, the first shelter for women in the United States was started in California in 1964. (This was out of pure need, not because feminists were franchising.) Now, there is an organized battered women's movement of shelters, awareness campaigns, reformed laws and police practices, and legislative strategies. October is Domestic Violence Awareness month, and 1994 saw the passage of the Violence Against Women Act, which set the precedent for prosecuting abusers who cross state lines, and a mandate for nationwide enforcement of protection orders. Nonetheless, in 1994, when Nicole Brown Simpson was murdered and her hulking football-hero ex-husband was accused of the crime, domestic violence was launched into the mainstream—"professionalized," according to one young activist—and divorced by the media from the grassroots organizations that had named its reality and pioneered its treatment. What this means is that a woman like GE executive Sam Allison can now be on the board of the Women's Center in Milwaukee and claim that she's not a feminist but simply an "advocate to end violence against women."

Similarly, in 1991 entrepreneur Melissa Bradley broke ground in the field of women's economic development without connecting it to the feminist legacy of this work—for example, the pioneering work done by Connie Evans, who started the Women's Self-Employment Project a dozen years earlier. By 1998, Evans had dispensed more than $1.3 million in six hundred short-term microloans, establishing the largest small-business fund for low-income women—all undertaken by her as feminist work. Bradley, who is the founder of the Entrepreneurial Development Institute and worked for the federal government's Office of Thrift and Supervision, where she advised on and critiqued welfare-to-work programs, until recently didn't consider her work to be feminist.

This could be construed as assimilation, and in some ways it is our goal. After all, as long as Women's History and African-American History are independent curricula, history itself will still be a white man's story. In that same way, the women's rights movement will have been successful when we no longer have to advocate separately for half the population's human rights. On the other hand, ideally women's egos would be more invested in their work. You can't continue change if you don't know the process that got you this far. If feminists first exposed domestic violence as a reality in many women's lives, funded the first women's shelters, and drafted and fought for legislation that is now working to end violence against women, then an "advocate to end violence against women" (Sam Allison's term for herself) is just another term for *feminist*. Issues divorced from their feminist roots eventually become depoliticized, and the resulting social programs are reduced to treating the symptoms rather than curing—or preventing—the disease. In order to have a robust movement, domestic violence and economic development need to be reidentified as feminist issues and victories. And people like Allison and Bradley need to be outed as feminists.

* * *

THIRD WAVE MANIFESTA: A THIRTEEN-POINT AGENDA

1. To out unacknowledged feminists, specifically those who are younger, so that Generation X can become a visible movement and, further, a voting block of eighteen- to forty-year-olds.
2. To safeguard a woman's right to bear or not to bear a child, regardless of circumstances, including women who are younger than eighteen or impoverished. To preserve this right throughout her life and support the choice to be childless.

3. To make explicit that the fight for reproductive rights must include birth control; the right for poor women and lesbians to have children; partner adoption for gay couples; subsidized fertility treatments for all women who choose them; and freedom from sterilization abuse. Furthermore, to support the idea that sex can be—and usually is—for pleasure, not procreation.

4. To bring down the double standard in sex and sexual health, and foster male responsibility and assertiveness in the following areas: achieving freedom from STDs; more fairly dividing the burden of family planning as well as responsibilities such as child care; and eliminating violence against women.

5. To tap into and raise awareness of our revolutionary history, and the fact that almost all movements began as youth movements. To have access to our intellectual feminist legacy and women's history; for the classics of radical feminism, womanism, *mujeristas*, women's liberation, and all our roots to remain in print; and to have women's history taught to men as well as women as a part of all curricula.

6. To support and increase the visibility and power of lesbians and bisexual women in the feminist movement, in high schools, colleges, and the workplace. To recognize that queer women have always been at the forefront of the feminist movement, and that there is nothing to be gained—and much to be lost—by downplaying their history, whether inadvertently or actively.

7. To practice "autokeonony" ("self in community"): to see activism not as a choice between self and community but as a link between them that creates balance.

8. To have equal access to health care, regardless of income, which includes coverage equivalent to men's and keeping in mind that women use the system more often than men do because of our reproductive capacity.

9. For women who so desire to participate in all reaches of the military, including combat, and to enjoy all the benefits (loans, health care, pensions) offered to its members for as long as we continue to have an active military. The largest expenditure of our national budget goes toward maintaining this welfare system, and feminists have a duty to make sure women have access to every echelon.

10. To liberate adolescents from slut-bashing, listless educators, sexual harassment, and bullying at school, as well as violence in all walks of life, and the silence that hangs over adolescents' heads, often keeping them isolated, lonely, and indifferent to the world.

11. To make the workplace responsive to an individual's wants, needs, and talents. This includes valuing (monetarily) stay-at-home parents, aiding employees who want to spend more time with family and continue to work, equalizing pay for jobs of comparable worth, enacting a minimum wage that would bring a full-time worker with two-children over the poverty line, and providing employee benefits for freelance and part-time workers.

12. To acknowledge that, although feminists may have disparate values, we share the same goal of equality, and of supporting one another in our efforts to gain the power to make our own choices.

13. To pass the Equal Rights Amendment so that we can have a constitutional foundation of righteousness and equality upon which future women's rights conventions will stand.

Multiracial Feminism
Recasting the Chronology
of Second Wave Feminism

Becky Thompson

Becky Thompson is an Associate Professor of Sociology at Simmons College sociology, African American Studies and Gender and Cultural Studies. She is coeditor (with Sangeeta Tyagi) of Beyond a Dream Deferred: Multicultural Education and the Politics of Excellence. *She is the author of* A Hunger So Wide and So Deep *(1996),* A Promise and a Way of Life: White Antiracist Activism *(2001) and* Mothering without a Compass: White Mother's Love, Black Son's Courage *(2000). This piece was originally published in* Feminist Studies *in 2002.*

In the last several years, a number of histories have been published that chronicle the emergence and contributions of Second Wave feminism.[1] Although initially eager to read and teach from these histories, I have found myself increasingly concerned about the extent to which they provide a version of Second Wave history that Chela Sandoval refers to as "hegemonic feminism."[2] This feminism is white led, marginalizes the activism and world views of women of color, focuses mainly on the United States, and treats sexism as the ultimate oppression. Hegemonic feminism deemphasizes or ignores a class and race analysis, generally sees equality with men as the goal of feminism, and has an individual rights-based, rather than justice-based vision for social change.

Although rarely named as hegemonic feminism, this history typically resorts to an old litany of the women's movement that includes three or four branches of feminism: liberal, socialist, radical, and sometimes cultural feminism.[3] The most significant problem with this litany is that

---

For hegemonic historical periods, see Verta Taylor and Nancy Whittier, "The New Feminist Movement," in *Feminist Frontiers IV,* ed. Richardson et al. (New York: McGraw-Hill, 1997).

[1] For example of histories that focus on white feminism, see Sheila Tobias, *Faces of Feminism: An Activist's Reflections on the Women's Movement* (Boulder: Westview Press, 1997); Barbara Ryan, *Feminism and the Women's Movement: Dynamics of Change in Social Movement Ideology and Activism* (New York: Routledge, 1992); Alice Echols, *Daring to Be Bad: Radical Feminism in America, 1967–1975* (Minneapolis; University of Minnesota Press, 1989).

[2] Chela Sandoval, *Methodology of the Oppressed* (Minneapolis: University of Minnesota Press, 2000), 41–42.

[3] Of these branches of feminism (liberal, socialist, and radical), socialist feminism, which treats sexism and classism as interrelated forms of oppression, may have made the most concerted effort to develop an antiracist agenda in the 1970s. For example, "The Combahee River Collective Statement" was first published in Zillah Eisenstein's *Capitalist Patriarchy and the Case for Socialist Feminism* (New York: Monthly Review Press, 1979), 362–72, before it was published in Barbara Smith's, *Home Girls: A Black Feminist Anthology* (New York: Kitchen Table, Women of Color Press, 1983). *Radical America,* a journal founded in 1967 and whose contributors and editors include many socialist feminists, consistently published articles that examined the relationship between race, class, and gender. The 1970s socialist feminist organization, the Chicago Women's Liberation Union, which considered quality public education, redistribution of wealth, and accessible childcare key to a feminist agenda, also made room for a race analysis by not privileging sexism over other forms of oppression. However, the fact that socialist feminist organizations were typically white dominated and were largely confined to academic and/or middle-class circles, limited their effectiveness and visibility as an antiracist presence in early Second Wave feminism. For early socialist feminist documents, see Rosalyn Baxandall and Linda Gordon, eds., *Dear Sisters: Dispatches from the Women's Liberation Movement* (New York: Basic Books, 2000).

Becky Thompson's "Multiracial Feminism: Recasting the Chronology of Second Wave Feminism," was originally published in *Feminist Studies, Volume 28, Number 2* (Summer 2002): 337–360. Reprinted by permission of the publisher, Feminist Studies, Inc.

it does not recognize the centrality of the feminism of women of color in Second Wave history. Missing too, from normative accounts is the story of white antiracist feminism which, from its emergence, has been intertwined with, and fueled by the development of, feminism among women of color.[4]

Telling the history of Second Wave feminism from the point of view of women of color and white antiracist women illuminates the rise of multiracial feminism—the liberation movement spearheaded by women of color in the United States in the 1970s that was characterized by its international perspective, its attention to interlocking oppressions, and its support of coalition politics.[5] Bernice Johnson Reagon's naming of "coalition politics"; Patricia Hill Collins's understanding of women of color as "outsiders within"; Barbara Smith's concept of "the simultaneity of oppressions"; Cherrie Moraga and Gloria Anzaldúa's "theory in the flesh"; Chandra Talpade Mohanty's critique of "imperialist feminism"; Paula Gunn Allen's "red roots of white feminism"; Adrienne Rich's "politics of location"; and Patricia Williams's analysis of "spirit murder" are all theoretical guideposts for multiracial feminism.[6] Tracing the rise of multiracial feminism raises many questions about common assumptions made in normative versions of Second Wave history. Constructing a multiracial feminist movement time line and juxtaposting it with the normative time line reveals competing visions of what constitutes liberation and illuminates schisms in feminist consciousness that are still with us today.

THE RISE OF MULTIRACIAL FEMINISM

Normative accounts of the Second Wave feminist movement often reach back to the publication of Betty Friedan's *The Feminine Mystique* in 1963, the founding of the National Organization for Women in 1966, and the emergence of women's consciousness-raising (CR) groups in the late 1960s. All signaled a rising number of white, middle-class women unwilling to be treated like second-class citizens in the boardroom, education, or in bed. Many of the early protests waged by this sector of feminist movement picked up on the courage and forthrightness of 1960s' struggles—a willingness to stop traffic, break existing laws to provide safe and accessible abortions, and contradict the older generation. For younger women, the leadership women had demonstrated in 1960s' activism belied the sex roles that had traditionally defined domestic, economic, and political relations and opened new possibilities for action.

This version of the origins of Second Wave history is not sufficient in telling the story of multiracial feminism. Although there were Black women involved with NOW from the outset and Black and Latina women who participated in CR groups, the feminist work of women of color also extended beyond women-only spaces. In fact, during the 1970s, women of color were involved on three fronts—working with white-dominated feminist groups; forming women's

---

[4]For an expanded discussion of the contributions and limitations of white antiracism from the 1950s to the present, see Becky Thompson, *A Promise and a Way of Life: White Antiracist Activism* (Minneapolis: University of Minnesota Press, 2001).

[5]For a discussion of the term "multiracial feminism," see Maxine Baca Zinn and Bonnie Thornton Dill, "Theorizing Difference from Multiracial Feminism," *Feminist Studies* 22 (Summer 1996): 321–31.

[6]Bernice Johnson Reagon, "Coalition Politics: Turning the Century," in *Home Girls*, 356–69; Patricia Hill Collins, *Black Feminist Thought: Knowledge, Consciousness, and the Politics of Empowerment* (Boston: Unwin Hyman, 1990), 11; Barbara Smith, introduction, *Home Girls*, xxxii; Cherrie Moraga and Gloria Anzaldúa, eds., *This Bridge Called My Back: Writings by Radical Women of Color* (New York: Kitchen Table, Women of Color Press, 1981); Chandra Talpade Mohanty, "Under Western Eyes: Feminist Scholarship and Colonial Discourses," in *Third World Women and the Politics of Feminism*, ed. Chandra Talpade Mohanty, Ann Russo, and Lourdes Torres (Bloomington: Indiana University Press, 1991), 51–80; Paula Gunn Allen, "Who Is Your Mother? Red Roots of White Feminism," in her *The Sacred Hoop: Recovering the Feminine in American Indian Traditions* (Boston: Beacon Press, 1986), 209–21; Adrienne Rich, *Blood, Bread, and Poetry* (New York: Norton, 1986), Patricia Williams, *The Alchemy of Race and Rights* (Cambridge: Harvard University Press, 1991).

caucuses in existing mixed-gender organizations; and developing autonomous Black, Latina, Native American and Asian feminist organizations.[7]

This three-pronged approach contrasts sharply with the common notion that women of color feminists emerged in reaction to (and therefore later than) white feminism. In her critique of "model making" in Second Wave historiography, which has "all but ignored the feminist activism of women of color," Benita Roth "challenges the idea that Black feminist organizing was a later variant of so-called mainstream white feminism."[8] Roth's assertion—that the timing of Black feminist organizing is roughly equivalent to the timing of white feminist activism—is true about feminist activism by Latinas, Native Americans, and Asian Americans as well.

One of the earliest feminist organizations of the Second Wave was a Chicana group—Hijas de Cuauhtemoc (1971)—named after a Mexican women's underground newspaper that was published during the 1910 Mexican Revolution. Chicanas who formed this *femenista* group and published a newspaper named after the early-twentieth-century Mexican women's revolutionary group, were initially involved in the United Mexican American Student Organization which was part of the Chicano/a student movement.[9] Many of the founders of Hijas de Cuauhtemoc were later involved in launching the first national Chicana studies journal, *Encuentro Femenil.*

An early Asian American women's group, Asian Sisters, focused on drug abuse intervention for young women in Los Angeles. It emerged in 1971 out of the Asian American Political Alliance, a broad-based, grass-roots organization largely fueled by the consciousness of first-generation Asian American college students. Networking between Asian American and other women during this period also included participation by a contingent of 150 Third World and white women from North America at the historic Vancouver Indochinese Women's Conference (1971) to work with Indochinese women against U.S. imperialism.[10] Asian American women provided services for battered women, worked as advocates for refugees and recent immigrants, produced events spotlighting Asian women's cultural and political diversity, and organized with other women of color.[11]

The best-known Native American women's organization of the 1970s was Women of All Red Nations (WARN). WARN was initiated in 1974 by women, many of whom were also members of the American Indian Movement which was founded in 1968 by Dennis Banks, George Matchell, and Mary Jane Wilson, an Anishinable activist.[12] WARN's activism included fighting

---

[7]Here I am using the term "feminist" to describe collective action designed to confront interlocking race, class, gender, and sexual oppressions (and other systematic discrimination). Although many women in these organizations explicitly referred to themselves as "feminist" from their earliest political work, others have used such terms as "womanist," "radical women of color," "revolutionary," and "social activist." Hesitation among women of color about the use of the term "feminist" often signaled an unwillingness to be associated with white-led feminism, but this wariness did not mean they were not doing gender-conscious, justice work. The tendency not to include gender-conscious activism by women of color in dominant versions of Second Wave history unless the women used the term "feminist" fails to account for the multiple terms women of color have historically used to designate activism that keeps women at the center of analysis and attends to interlocking oppressions. Although the formation of a women's group—an Asian women's friendship group, a Black women's church group or a Native American women's arts council—is not inherently a feminist group, those organizations that confront gender, race, sexual, and class oppression, whether named as "feminist" or not, need to be considered as integral to multiracial feminism.

[8]Benita Roth, "The Making of the Vanguard Center: Black Feminist Emergence in the 1960s and 1970s," in *Still Lifting, Still Climbing: African American Women's Contemporary Activism*, ed. Kimberly Springer (New York: New York University Press, 1999), 71.

[9]Sherna Berger Gluck, "Whose Feminism, Whose History? Reflections on Excavating the History of (the) U.S. Women's Movement(s)," in *Community Activism and Feminist Politics: Organizing across Race, Class, and Gender*, ed. Nancy A. Naples (New York: Routledge, 1998), 38–39.

[10]Miya Iwataki, "The Asian Women's Movement: A Retrospective," *East Wind* (spring/summer 1983): 35–41; Gluck, 39–41.

[11]Sonia Shah, "Presenting the Blue Goddess: Toward a National Pan-Asian Feminist Agenda," in *The State of Asian America: Activism and Resistance in the 1990s*, ed. Karin Aguilar-San Juan (Boston: South End Press, 1994), 147–58.

[12]M. Annette Jaimes with Theresa Halsey, "American Indian Women: At the Center of Indigenous Resistance in Contemporary North America," in *The State of Native America: Genocide, Colonization, and Resistance*, ed. M. Annette Jaimes (Boston: South End Press, 1992), 329.

sterilization in public health service hospitals, suing the U.S. government for attempts to sell Pine Ridge water in South Dakota to corporations and networking with indigenous people in Guatemala and Nicaragua.[13] WARN reflected a whole generation of Native American women activists who had been leaders in the takeover of Wounded Knee in South Dakota in 1973, on the Pine Ridge reservation (1973–76), and elsewhere. WARN, like Asian Sisters and Hijas de Cuauhtemoc, grew out of—and often worked with—mixed-gender nationalist organizations.

The autonomous feminist organizations that Black, Latina, Asian, and Native American women were forming during the early 1970s drew on nationalist traditions through their recognition of the need for people of color-led, independent organizations.[14] At the same time, unlike earlier nationalist organizations that included women and men, these were organizations specifically for women.

Among Black women, one early Black feminist organization was the Third World Women's Alliance which emerged in 1968 out of the Student Nonviolent Coordinating Committee (SNCC) chapters on the East Coast and focused on racism, sexism, and imperialism.[15] The foremost autonomous feminist organization of the early 1970s was the National Black Feminist Organization (NBFO). Founded in 1973 by Florynce Kennedy, Margaret Sloan, and Doris Wright, it included many other well-known Black women including Faith Ringgold, Michelle Wallace, Alice Walker, and Barbara Smith. According to Deborah Gray White, NBFO, "more than any organization in the century . . . launched a frontal assault on sexism and racism."[16] Its first conference in New York was attended by 400 women from a range of class backgrounds.

Although the NBFO was a short-lived organization nationally (1973–75), chapters in major cities remained together for years, including one in Chicago that survived until 1981. The contents of the CR sessions were decidedly Black women's issues—stereotypes of Black women in the media, discrimination in the workplace, myths about Black women as matriarchs, Black women's beauty, and self-esteem.[17] The NBFO also helped to inspire the founding of the Combahee River Collective in 1974, a Boston-based organization named after a river in South Carolina where Harriet Tubman led an insurgent action that freed 750 slaves. The Combahee River Collective not only led the way for crucial antiracist activism in Boston through the decade, but it also provided a blueprint for Black feminism that still stands a quarter of a century later.[18] From Combahee member Barbara Smith came a definition of feminism so expansive that it remains a model today. Smith writes that "feminism is the political theory and practice to free *all* women: women of color, working-class women, poor women, physically challenged women, lesbians, old women, as well as white economically privileged heterosexual women. Anything less than this is not feminism, but merely female self-aggrandizement."[19]

These and other groups in the early and mid-1970s provided the foundation for the most far-reaching and expansive organizing by women of color in U.S. history. These organizations also fueled a veritable explosion of writing by women of color, including Toni Cade's pioneering, *The*

---

[13]Stephanie Autumn, ". . . This Air, This Land, This Water—If We Don't Start Organizing Now, We'll Lose It," *Big Mama Rag* 11 (April 1983): 4–5.

[14]For an insightful analysis of the multidimensionality of Black nationalism of the later 1960s and early 1970s, see Angela Davis, "Black Nationalism: The Sixties and the Nineties," in *The Angela Davis Reader*, ed. Joy James (Maiden, Mass: Blackwell, 1998), 289–96.

[15]Ibid., 15, 314.

[16]Deborah Gay White, *Too Heavy a Load: Black Women in Defense of Themselves* (New York: Norton, 1999) 242.

[17]Ibid., 242–53.

[18]Combahee River Collective, "The Combahee River Collective Statement," in *Home Girls*, 272–82.

[19]See Moraga and Anzaldúa.

Black Woman: An Anthology in 1970, Maxine Hong Kingston's *The Woman Warrior* in 1977, and in 1981 and 1983, respectively, the foundational *This Bridge Called My Back: Writings by Radical Women of Color* and *Home Girls: A Black Feminist Anthology*.[20] While chronicling the dynamism and complexity of a multidimensional vision for women of color, these books also traced for white women what is required to be allies to women of color.

By the late 1970s, the progress made possible by autonomous and independent Asian, Latina, and Black feminist organizations opened a space for women of color to work in coalition across organizations with each other. During this period, two cohorts of white women became involved in multiracial feminism. One group had, in the late 1960s and early 1970s, chosen to work in anti-imperialist, antiracist militant organizations in connection with Black Power groups—the Black Panther Party, the Black Liberation Army—and other solidarity and nationalist organizations associated with the American Indian, Puerto Rican Independence, and Chicano Movements of the late 1960s and early 1970s. These women chose to work with these solidarity organizations rather than work in overwhelmingly white feminist context. None of the white antiracist feminists I interviewed (for a social history of antiracism in the United States) who were politically active during the civil rights and Black Power movements had an interest in organizations that had a single focus on gender or that did not have antiracism at the center of their agendas.

Militant women of color and white women took stands against white supremacy and imperialism (both international and external colonialism); envisioned revolution as a necessary outcome of political struggle; and saw armed propaganda (armed attacks against corporate and military targets along with public education about state crime) as a possible tactic in revolutionary struggle. Although some of these women avoided or rejected the term "feminist" because of its association with hegemonic feminism, these women still confronted sexism both within solidarity and nationalist organizations and within their own communities. In her autobiographical account of her late-1960s politics, Black liberation movement leader Assata Shakur writes: "To me, the revolutionary struggle of Black people had to be against racism, classism, imperialism and sexism for real freedom under a socialist government."[21] During this period, Angela Davis was also linking anti-capitalist struggle with the fight against race and gender oppression.[22] Similarly, white militant activist Marilyn Buck, who was among the first women to confront Students for a Democratic Society (SDS) around issues of sexism, also spoke up for women's rights as an ally of the Black Liberation Army.

Rarely, however, have their stories—and those of other militant antiracist women—been considered part of Second Wave history. In her critique of this dominant narrative, historian Nancy MacLean writes: "Recent accounts of the rise of modern feminism depart little from the story line first advanced two decades ago and since enshrined as orthodoxy. That story stars white middle-class women triangulated between the pulls of liberal, radical/cultural, and socialist feminism. Working-class women and women of color assume walk-on parts late in the plot, after tendencies and allegiances are already in place. The problem with this script is not simply that it has grown stale from repeated retelling. It is not accurate. . . ."[23]

---

[20]Toni Cade, ed., *The Black Woman: An Anthology* (New York: Signet, 1970); Maxine Hong Kingston, *The Woman Warrior* (New York: Vintage Books, 1977); Moraga and Anzaldúa; Smith.

[21]Assata Shakur, *Assata: An Autobiography* (Chicago: Lawrence Hill Books, 1987), 197.

[22]Angela Davis, *Angela Davis: An Autobiography* (New York: Random House, 1974).

[23]Nancy MacLean, "The Hidden History of Affirmative Action: Working Women's Struggles in the 1970s and the Gender of Class," *Feminist Studies* 25 (spring 1999): 47.

The omission of militant white women and women of color from Second Wave history partly reflects a common notion that the women's movement followed and drew upon the early civil rights movement and the New Left, a trajectory that skips entirely the profound impact that the Black Power movement had on many women's activism. Omitting militant women activists from historical reference also reflects a number of ideological assumptions made during the late 1960s and early 1970s—that "real" feminists were those who worked primarily or exclusively with other women; that "women's ways of knowing" were more collaborative, less hierarchical, and more peace loving than men's; and that women's liberation would come from women's deepening understanding that "sisterhood is powerful."

These politics are upheld both by liberal and radical white feminists. These politics did not, however, sit well with many militant women of color and white women who refused to consider sexism the primary, or most destructive, oppression and recognized the limits of gaining equality in a system that, as Malcolm X had explained, was already on fire. The women of color and white militant women who supported a race, class, and gender analysis in the late 1960s and 1970s often found themselves trying to explain their politics in mixed-gender settings (at home, at work, and in their activism), sometimes alienated from the men (and some women) who did not get it, while simultaneously alienated from white feminists whose politics they considered narrow at best and frivolous at worst.

By the late 1970s, the militant women who wanted little to do with white feminism of the late 1960s and 1970s became deeply involved in multiracial feminism. By that point, the decade of organizing among women of color in autonomous Black, Latina, and Asian feminist organizations led militant antiracist white women to immerse themselves in multiracial feminism. Meanwhile, a younger cohort of white women, who were first politicized in the late 1970s, saw feminism from a whole different vantage point than did the older, white, antiracist women. For the younger group, exposure to multiracial feminism led by women of color meant an early lesson that race, class, and gender were inextricably linked. They also gained vital experience in multiple organizations—battered women's shelters, conferences, and health organizations—where women were, with much struggle, attempting to uphold this politic.[24]

From this organizing came the emergence of a small but important group of white women determined to understand how white privilege had historically blocked cross-race alliances among women, and what they, as white women, needed to do to work closely with women of color. Not surprisingly, Jewish women and lesbians often led the way among white women in articulating a politic that accounted for white women's position as both oppressed and oppressor—as both

---

[24]As a woman who was introduced to antiracist work through the feminist movement of the late 1970s—a movement shaped in large part by women of color who called themselves "womanists," "feminists," and "radical women of color"—I came to my interest in recasting the chronology of Second Wave feminism especially hoping to learn how white antiracist women positioned themselves vis-à-vis Second Wave feminism. I wanted to learn how sexism played itself out in the 1960s and how antiracist white women responded to Second Wave feminism. And I wanted to find out whether the antiracist baton carried in the 1960s was passed on or dropped by feminist activists.

One of the most compelling lessons I learned from white women who came of age politically before or during the civil rights and Black Power movements was how difficult it was for many of them to relate to or embrace feminism of the late 1960s and early 1970s. White antiracist women resisted sexism in SDS and in militant organizations. As they talked about the exclusions they faced in the 1960s' organizations and criticized early feminist organizing that considered gender oppression its main target, I realized how much different the feminist movement they saw in the early 1970s. By then, there was a critical mass of seasoned feminists who were keeping race at the center of the agenda. They were teaching younger feminists that race, class, gender, and sexuality are inextricably connected and that it is not possible to call oneself a feminist without dealing with race.

women and white.[25] Both groups knew what it meant to be marginalized from a women's movement that was, nevertheless, still homophobic and Christian biased. Both groups knew that "there is no place like home"—among other Jews and/or lesbians—and the limits of that home if for Jews it was male dominated or if for lesbians it was exclusively white. The paradoxes of "home" for these groups paralleled many of the situations experienced by women of color who, over and over again, found themselves to be the bridges that everyone assumed would be on their backs.

As the straight Black women interacted with the Black lesbians, the first-generation Chinese women talked with the Native American activists, and the Latina women talked with the Black and white women about the walls that go up when people cannot speak Spanish, white women attempting to understand race knew they had a lot of listening to do. They also had a lot of truth telling to reckon with, and a lot of networking to do, among other white women and with women of color as well.

RADICALS, HEYDAYS, AND HOT SPOTS

The story of Second Wave feminism, if told from the vantage point of multiracial feminism, also encourages us to rethink key assumptions about periodization. Among these assumptions is the notion that the 1960s and 1970s were the height of the radical feminist movement. For example, in her foreword to Alice Echol's *Daring to Be Bad: Radical Feminism in America, 1967–1975*, Ellen Willis asserts that by the mid-1970s, the best of feminism had already occurred.[26] In her history of the women's liberation movement, Barbara Ryan writes that the unity among women evident in the early 1970s declined dramatically by the late 1970s as a consequence of divisions within the movement.[27]

Looking at the history of feminism from the point of view of women of color and antiracist white women suggests quite a different picture. The fact that white women connected with the Black Power movement could rarely find workable space in the early feminist movement crystallized for many of them with the 1971 rebellion at Attica Prison in New York State in response to human rights abuses.[28] For antiracist activist Naomi Jaffe, who was a member of SDS, the Weather Underground, and WITCH (Women's International Terrorist Conspiracy from Hell), attempts to be part of both early Second Wave feminism and an antiracist struggle were untenable. The Attica rebellion, which resulted in the massacre by state officials of thirty-one prisoners and nine guards, pushed Jaffe to decide between the two. She vividly remembers white feminists arguing that there was no room for remorse for the "male chauvinists" who had died at Attica. Jaffe disagreed vehemently, arguing that if

---

[25]Several key Jewish feminist texts that addressed how to take racism and anti-Semitism seriously in feminist activism were published during this period and included Evelyn Torton Beck, ed., *Nice Jewish Girls: A Lesbian Anthology* (Trumansburg, N.Y.: Crossing Press, 1982); Melanie Kaye/Kantrowitz and Irena Klepfisz, eds., *The Tribe of Dina: A Jewish Women's Anthology* (Boston: Beacon Press, 1989), first published as a special issue of *Sinister Wisdom*, nos. 29/30 (1986); Melanie Kaye/Kantrowitz, *The Issue Is Power: Essays on Women, Jews, Violence, and Resistance* (San Francisco: Aunt Lute, 1992); Irena Klepfisz, *Periods of Stress* (Brooklyn, N.Y.: Out & Out Books, 1977), and *Keeper of Accounts* (Watertown, Mass.: Persephone Press, 1982).

For key antiracist lesbian texts, see Adrienne Rich, *On Lies, Secrets, and Silence: Selected Prose, 1966–1978* (New York: Norton, 1979); Joan Gibbs and Sara Bennett, *Top Ranking: A Collection of Articles on Racism and Classism in the Lesbian Community* (New York: Come! Unity Press, 1980); Mab Segrest, *My Mama's Dead Squirrel: Lesbian Essays on Southern Culture* (Ithaca, N.Y.: Firebrand Books, 1985); Elly Bulkin, Minnie Bruce Pratt, and Barbara Smith, *Yours in Struggle: Three Feminist Perspectives on Anti-Semitism and Racism* (Brooklyn, N.Y.: Long Haul Press, 1984).

[26]Ellen Willis, foreword to *Daring to Be Bad*, vii.

[27]Barbara Ryan.

[28]Howard Zinn, *A People's History of the United States* (New York: HarperPerennial, 1990), 504–13.

white feminists could not understand Attica as a feminist issue, then she was not a feminist. At the time, Black activist and lawyer Florynce Kennedy had said: "We do not support Attica. We ARE Attica. We are Attica or we are nothing." Jaffe claimed: "That about summed up my feelings on the subject."[29] With this consciousness, and her increasing awareness of the violence of the state against the Black Panthers, antiwar protesters, and liberation struggles around the world, Jaffe continued to work with the Weather Underground. She went underground from 1970–1978.

Naomi Jaffe, like other white women working with the Black Power movement, was turned off by a feminism that they considered both bourgeois and reductionist. They stepped out of what antiracist historian Sherna Berger Gluck has termed "the master historical narrative," and they have been written out of it by historians who have relied upon a telling of Second Wave feminism that focused solely on gender oppression. Although the late 1960s and 1970s might have been the "heyday" for white "radical" feminists in CR groups, from the perspective of white antiracists, the early 1970s were a low point of feminism—a time when many women who were committed to an antiracist analysis had to put their feminism on the back burner in order to work with women and men of color and against racism.

Coinciding with the frequent assumption that 1969 to 1974 was the height of "radical feminism," many feminist historians consider 1972 to 1982 as the period of mass mobilization and 1983 to 1991 as a period of feminist abeyance.[30] Ironically, the years that sociologists Verta Taylor and Nancy Whittier consider the period of mass mobilization for feminists (1972–82) are the years that Chela Sandoval identifies as the period when "ideological differences divided and helped to dissipate the movement from within.[31] For antiracist women (both white and of color), the best days of feminism were yet to come when, as Barbara Smith explains, "Those issues that had divided many of the movement's constituencies—such as racism, anti-Semitism, ableism, and classism—were put out on the table."[32]

Ironically, the very period that white feminist historians typically treat as a period of decline within the movement is the period of mass mobilization among antiracist women—both straight and lesbian. The very year that Taylor and Whittier consider the end of mass mobilization because the ERA failed to be ratified, 1982, is the year that Gluck rightfully cites as the beginning of a feminism far more expansive than had previously existed. She writes: "By 1982, on the heels of difficult political struggle waged by activist scholars of color, ground breaking essays and anthologies by and about women of color opened a new chapter in U.S. feminism. The future of the women's movement in the U.S. was reshaped irrevocably by the introduction of the expansive notion of feminisms."[33] Angela Davis concurs, citing 1981, with the publication of *This Bridge Called My Back*, as the year when women of color had developed as a "new political subject," due to substantial work done in multiple arenas.[34]

---

[29]For a published version of Florynce Kennedy's position on Attica and Naomi Jaffe's perspective, see Barbara Smith, "'Feisty Characters' and 'Other People's Causes,'" in *The Feminist Memoir Project: Voices from Women's Liberation*, ed. Rachel Blau DuPlessis and Ann Snitow (New York: Three Rivers Press), 479–81.

[30]Verta Taylor and Nancy Whittier, "The New Feminist Movement," in *Feminist Frontiers IV*, ed. Laurel Richardson, Verta Taylor, and Nancy Whittier (New York: McGraw-Hill, 1997), 544–45.

[31]Chela Sandoval, "Feminism and Racism: A Report on the 1981 National Women's Studies Association Conference," in *Making Face, Making Soul: Haciendo Caras: Creative and Critical Perspectives by Women of Color*, ed. Gloria Anzaldúa (San Francisco: Aunt Lute, 1990), 55.

[32]Smith, "'Feisty Characters,'" 479–80.

[33]Gluck, 32.

[34]James, 313.

In fact, periodization of the women's movement from the point of view of multiracial feminism would treat the late 1960s and early 1970s as its origin and the mid-1970s, 1980s, and 1990s as a height. A time line of that period shows a flourishing multiracial feminist movement. In 1977, the Combahee River Collective Statement was first published; in 1979, *Conditions: Five*, the Black women's issue, was published, the First National Third World Lesbian Conference was held, and Assata Shakur escaped from prison in New Jersey with the help of prison activists.[35] In 1981, Byllye Avery founded the National Black Women's Health Project in Atlanta; Bernice Johnson Reagon gave her now-classic speech on coalition politics at the West Coast Women's Music Festival in Yosemite; and the National Women's Studies Association held its first conference to deal with racism as a central theme, in Storrs, Connecticut, where there were multiple animated interventions against racism and anti-Semitism in the women's movement and from which emerged Adrienne Rich's exquisite essay, "Disobedience and Women's Studies."[36] Then, 1984 was the year of the New York Women against Rape Conference, a multiracial, multiethnic conference that confronted multiple challenges facing women organizing against violence against women—by partners, police, social service agencies, and poverty. In 1985, the United Nations Decade for Women Conference in Nairobi, Kenya, took place; that same year, Wilma Mankiller was named the first principal chief of the Cherokee Nation. In 1986, the National Women's Studies Association conference was held at Spelman College. The next year, 1987, the Supreme Court ruled that the Immigration and Naturalization Service must interpret the 1980s' Refugee Act more broadly to recognize refugees from Central America, a ruling that reflected the work on the part of thousands of activists, many of whom were feminists, to end U.S. intervention in Central America.

In 1991, Elsa Barkely Brown, Barbara Ransby, and Deborah King launched the campaign called African American Women in Defense of Ourselves, within minutes of Anita Hill's testimony regarding the nomination of Clarence Thomas to the Supreme Court. Their organizing included an advertisement in the *New York Times* and six Black newspapers which included the names of 1,603 Black women. The 1982 defeat of the ERA did not signal a period of abeyance for multiracial feminism. In fact, multiracial feminism flourished in the 1980s, despite the country's turn to the Right.

Understanding Second Wave feminism from the vantage point of the Black Power movement and multiracial feminism also shows the limit of the frequent assignment of the term "radical" only to the white anti-patriarchal feminists of late 1960s and early 1970s. Many feminist historians link the development of radical feminism to the creation of several anti-patriarchy organizations—the Redstockings, Radicalesbians, WITCH, and other CR groups. How the term "radical" is used by feminist historians does not square, however, with how women of color and white antiracists used that term from the 1960s through the 1980s. What does it mean when feminist historians apply the term "radical" to white, anti-patriarchy women but not to antiracist white women and women of color (including Angela Davis, Kathleen Cleaver, Marilyn Buck, Anna Mae Aquash, Susan Saxe, Vicki Gabriner, and Laura Whitehorn) of the same era whose "radicalism" included attention to race, gender, and imperialism and a belief that revolution might require literally laying their lives on the line? These radical women include political prisoners—Black, Puerto Rican, and white—some of whom are still in prison for their antiracist

---

[35]Activists who helped Assata Shakur escape include political prisoners Marilyn Buck, Sylvia Baraldini, Susan Rosenberg, and Black male revolutionaries.

[36]Adrienne Rich, "Disobedience and Women's Studies," *Blood, Bread, and Poetry* (New York: Norton, 1986), 76–84.

activism in the 1960s and 1970s. Many of these women openly identify as feminists and/or lesbians but are rarely included in histories of Second Wave feminism.

What does it mean when the term "radical" is only assigned to white, antipatriarchy women when the subtitle to Cherríe Moraga and Gloria Anzaldúa's foundational book, *This Bridge Called My Back*, was "Writings by *Radical* Women of Color"?[37] To my mind, a nuanced and accurate telling of Second Wave feminism is one that shows why and how the term "radical" was itself contested. Recognizing that there were different groups who used the term "radical" does not mean that we then need an overarching definition of "radical feminism" that includes all these approaches. It does mean understanding that white feminists of the "daring to be bad period" (from 1967 to 1975) do not have exclusive rights to the term.[38] An expansive history would emphasize that Second Wave feminism drew on the civil rights movement, the New left, *and* the Black Power movement which, together, helped to produce three groups of "radical" women.

PRINCIPLES OF A MOVEMENT

Although analysis of the feminist movement that accounts for competing views of what it means to be "radical" is a step forward in developing a complex understanding of Second Wave history, what most interests me about comparing normative feminist history with multiracial feminism are the contestations in philosophy embedded in these coexisting frameworks. Both popular and scholarly interpretations of Second Wave feminism typically link two well-known principles to the movement—"Sisterhood Is Powerful" and the "Personal Is Political." From the point of view of multiracial feminism, both principles are a good start but, in themselves, are not enough.

Conversations and struggles between women of color and white women encouraged white women to think about the limits of the popular feminist slogan "Sisterhood is Power." There were many reasons why the editors of *This Bridge Called My Back* titled one of the sections of the book, "And When You Leave, Take Your Pictures with You: Racism in the Women's Movement." Lorraine Bethel's poem, "What Chou Mean *We* White Girl? Or the Cullud Lesbian Feminist Declaration of Independence" (Dedicated to the proposition that all women are not equal, i.e., identical/ly oppressed), clarifies that a "we" between white and Black is provisional, at best.[39] Anthropologist Wendy Rose's critique of "white shamanism"—white people's attempt to become native in order to grow spiritually—applies as well to white feminists who treat Native American women as innately spiritual, as automatically their spiritual mothers.[40]

Cross-racial struggle made clear the work that white women needed to do in order for cross-racial sisterhood to *really* be powerful. Among the directives were the following: Don't expect women of color to be your educators, to do all the bridge work. White women need to be the bridge—a lot of the time. Do not lump African American, Latina, Asian American, and Native American women into one category. History, culture, imperialism, language, class, region, and sexuality make the concept of a monolithic "women of color" indefensible. Listen to women of color's anger. It is informed by centuries of struggle, erasure, and experience. White women, look to your own history for signs of heresy and rebellion. Do not take on the histories of Black, Latina, or American Indian women as your own. They are not and never were yours.

A second principle associated with liberal and radical feminism is captured in the slogan "The Personal Is Political," first used by civil rights and New Left activists and then articulated with

---

[37]Moraga and Anzaldúa.

[38]I am borrowing that phrase from Alice Echols's chronicling of white radical feminist history.

[39]Lorraine Bethel, "What Chou Mean *We*, White Girl," in *Conditions: Five* (1979): 86.

[40]Wendy Rose, "The Great Pretenders: Further Reflections on Whieshamanism," in *The State of Native America*, 403–23.

more depth and consistency by feminist activists. The idea behind the slogan is that many issues that historically have been deemed "personal"—abortion, battery, unemployment, birth, death, and illness—are actually deeply political issues.

Multiracial feminism requires women to add another level of awareness—to stretch the adage from "The Personal Is Political" to, in the words of antiracist activist Anne Braden, "The Personal Is Political and The Political Is Personal."[41] Many issues that have been relegated to the private sphere are, in fact, deeply political. At the same time, many political issues need to be personally committed to—whether you have been victimized by those issues or not. In other words, you don't have to be part of a subordinated group to know an injustice is wrong and to stand against it. White women need not be victims of racism to recognize it is wrong and stand up against it. Unless that is done, white women will never understand how they support racism. If the only issues that feminists deem political are those they have experienced personally, their frame of reference is destined to be narrowly defined by their own lived experience.

The increasing number of antiracist white women who moved into mixed-gender, multi-issue organizations in the 1980s and 1990s after having helped to build women's cultural institutions in the 1970s and 1980s may be one of the best examples of an attempt to uphold this politic. Mab Segrest, perhaps the most prolific writer among lesbian antiracist organizers, provides the quintessential example of this transition in her move from working on the lesbian feminist journal, *Feminary*, in the late 1970s and early 1980s, to becoming the director of North Carolinians against Racist and Religious Violence in the 1980s. A self-reflective writer, Segrest herself notes this transition in the preface to her first book, *My Mama's Dead Squirrel: Lesbian Essays on Southern Culture*. Segrest writes: "In the first [essay] I wrote, 'I believe that the oppression of women is the first oppression.' Now I am not so sure. Later, I wrote, 'Relationships between women matter to me more than anything else in my life.' Now what matters most is more abstract and totally specific: the closest word to it, justice . . . During the early years the writing comes primarily out of work with other lesbians; later on, from work where I am the only lesbian."[42] The book opens with autobiographical essays about her family and women's writing, but the last essays chronicle the beginning of her organizing against the Klan—essays that became the backdrop to her second book, *Memoir of a Race Traitor*. In Segrest's view, by 1983, her work in building lesbian culture—through editing *Feminary* and her own writing—"no longer seemed enough, it seemed too literary." Segrest found herself both "inspired by and frustrated with the lesbian feminist movement." Segrest recalls that she

> had sat in many rooms and participated in many conversations between lesbians about painful differences in race and class, about anti-Semitism and ageism and ablebodiedism. They had been hard discussions, but they had given me some glimpse of the possibility of spinning a wider lesbian movement, a women's movement that truly incorporates diversity as its strength. But in all those discussions, difficult as they were, we had never been out to kill each other. In the faces of Klan and Nazi men—and women—in North Carolina I saw people who would kill us all. I felt I needed to shift from perfecting consciousness to putting consciousness to the continual test of action. I wanted to answer a question that had resonated through the lesbian writing I had taken most to heart: "What will you undertake?"[43]

This, I believe, remains a dogged and crucial question before us and one that requires us to move beyond litanies ultimately based on only a narrow group's survival.

---

[41]Thompson. See also Anne Braden, *The Wall Between* (Knoxville: University of Tennessee Press, 1999); Anne Braden, "A Second Open Letter to Southern White Women," *Southern Exposure* 6 (winter 1977): 50.

[42]Segrest, *My Mama's Dead Squirrel*, 12.

[43]Mab Segrest, "Fear to Joy: Fighting the Klan," *Sojourner: The Women's Forum* 13 (November 1987): 20.

The tremendous strength of autonomous feminist institutions—the festivals, conferences, bookstores, women's studies departments, women's health centers—were the artistic, political, and social contributions activists helped to generate. All of these cultural institutions required women to ask of themselves and others a pivotal question Audre Lorde had posited: Are you doing your work? And yet, by the mid-1980s, the resurgence of the radical Right in the United States that fueled a monumental backlash against gays and lesbians, people of color, and women across the races led multiracial feminists to ask again: Where and with whom are you doing your work? Many antiracist feminists who had helped to build the largely women-led cultural institutions that left a paper trail of multiracial feminism moved on, into mixed-gender, multiracial grassroots organizations, working against the Klan, in support of affirmative action and immigrant rights, and against police brutality and the prison industry. It is in these institutions that much of the hard work continues—in recognizing that "sisterhood is powerful" only when it is worked for and not assumed and that the "personal is political" only to the extent that one's politics go way beyond the confines of one's own individual experience.

BLUEPRINTS FOR FEMINIST ACTIVISM

There are multiple strategies for social justice embedded in multiracial feminism: a belief in building coalitions that are based on a respect for identity-based groups; attention to both process and product but little tolerance for "all-talk" groups; racial parity at every level of an organization (not added on later but initiated from the start); a recognition that race can not be seen in binary terms; a recognition that racism exists in your backyard as well as in the countries the United States is bombing or inhabiting economically; and a recognition of the limits to pacifism when people in struggles are up against the most powerful state in the world. Multiracial feminism is the heart of an inclusive women's liberation struggle. The race-class-gender-sexuality-nationality framework through which multiracial feminism operates encompasses and goes way beyond liberal, radical, and socialist feminist priorities—and it always has. Teaching Second Wave feminist history requires chronicling how hegemonic feminism came to be written about as "the" feminism and the limits of that model. Teaching Second Wave history by chronicling the rise of multiracial feminism challenges limited categories because it puts social justice and antiracism at the center of attention. This does not mean that the work done within hegemonic feminism did not exist or was not useful. It does mean that it was limited in its goals and effectiveness.

Although the strategies for multiracial feminism were firmly established in the 1970s and 1980s, I contend that these principles remain a blueprint for progressive, feminist, antiracist struggle in this millennium. These are principles we will need in order to build on the momentum begun in Seattle (as activist energy shocked the World Trade Organization out of its complacency) while we refuse to reproduce the overwhelmingly white composition of most of the groups involved in that protest. We will need the principles introduced by multiracial feminism to sustain a critique of the punishment industry that accounts for the increasing number of women caught in the penal system. These are principles we will need to nurture what critical race theorist Mari Matsuda has named a "jurisprudence of anti-subordination." Matsuda writes: "A jurisprudence of anti-subordination is an attempt to bring home the lost ones, to make them part of the center, to end the soul-killing tyranny of inside/outside thinking. Accountability revisited. I want to bring home the women who hate their own bodies so much that they would let a surgeon's hand cut fat from it, or a man's batter and bruise it. I want to bring home the hungry ones eating from the trashbins; the angry ones who call me names; the little ones in foster care."[44] The principles of anti-subordination embedded in multiracial feminism, in antiracism feminism, are a crucial piece of this agenda.

Because written histories of social movements are typically one generation behind the movements themselves, it makes sense that histories of the feminist movement are just now emerging. That timing means that now is the time to interrupt normative accounts before they begin to repeat themselves, each time, sounding more like "the truth" simply because of the repetition of the retelling. This interruption is necessary with regard to Second Wave feminism as well as earlier movements.

In her retrospective account of Black nationalism of the late 1960s and early 1970s, Angela Davis describes how broad-based nationalism has dropped almost completely out of the frame of reference in popular representations of the Black Power movement. This nationalism included alliances between Black and Chicano studies, in which students in San Diego were demanding the creation of a college called Lumumba-Zapata, and Huey Newton was calling for an end to "verbal gay bashing, urging an examination of black male sexuality, and calling for an alliance with the developing gay liberation movement." Davis writes: "I resent that the legacy I consider my own—one, I also helped to construct—has been rendered invisible. Young people with 'nationalist' proclivities ought, at least, to have the opportunity to choose which tradition of nationalism they will embrace. How will they position themselves en masse in defense of women's rights, in defense of gay rights, if they are not aware of the historical precedents for such positionings?"[45]

In a parallel way, I want young women to know the rich, complicated, contentious, and visionary history of multiracial feminism and to know the nuanced controversies within Second Wave feminism. I want them to know that Shirley Chisholm ran for president in 1972; that Celestine Ware wrote a Black radical feminist text in the 1970s which offered an inspiring conception of revolution with a deep sense of humanity; that before Mab Segrest went to work for an organization against the Klan in North Carolina, she and others published an independent lesbian journal in the 1970s that included some of the most important and compelling race-conscious writing by white women and women of color to date.[46] I want people to know that there are antiracist feminist women currently in prison for their antiracist activism in the 1960s and since.[47] Among them is Marilyn Buck, a poet, political prisoner and, in her words, "a feminist with a small 'f,'" who is serving an eighty-year sentence in California.[48] Her poems, including "To the Woman Standing Behind Me in Line Who Asks Me How Long This Black History

[44]Mari Matsuda, "Voices of America: Accent, Antidiscrimination Law, and a Jurisprudence for the Last Reconstruction," *Yale Law Journal* 100 (March 1991): 1405.

[45]Davis, "Black Nationalism," 292.

[46]See *Feminary: A Feminist journal for the South Emphasizing Lesbian Visions.* Schlesinger Library at the Radcliffe Institute for Advanced Study at Harvard University has scattered issues of *Feminary.* Duke University Rare Book, Manuscript, and Special Collection Library has vols. 5–15 from 1974–1985. For analysis of the import of working on this journal on Mab Segrest's consciousness and activism, see Jean Hardisty, "Writer/Activist Mab Segrest Confronts Racism," *Sojourner: The Women's Forum* 19 (August 1994): 1–2; Segrest, *My Mama's Dead Squirrel.*

[47]Marilyn Buck, Linda Evans, Laura Whitehorn, and Kathy Boudin are among the white political prisoners who are either currently in prison or, in the case of Laura Whitehorn and Linda Evans, recently released, serving sentences whose length and severity can only be understood as retaliation for their principled, antiracist politics.

[48]Marilyn Buck is in a federal prison in Dublin, California, for alleged conspiracies to free political prisoners, to protest government policies through the use of violence, and to raise funds for Black liberation organizations.

Month Is Going to Last," eloquently capture why Buck must be included in tellings of multiracial feminism.[49] She writes:

the whole month
even if it is the shortest month
a good time in this prison life

you stare at me
and ask why I think February is so damned fine
I take a breath
prisoners fight for February
African voices cross razor wire
Cut through the flim-flam
of Amerikkan history
call its cruelties out
confirm the genius of survival
creation and
plain ole enduring

a celebration.

*   *   *

The woman drops her gaze
looks away and wishes
she had not asked
confused that white skin did not guarantee
a conversation she wanted to have

she hasn't spoke to me since
I think I'll try to stand
in line with her
again

Marilyn Buck's poems and the work of other multiracial feminist activists help show that the struggle against racism is hardly linear, that the consolidation of white-biased feminism was clearly costly to early Second Wave feminism, and that we must dig deep to represent the feminist movement that does justice to an antiracist vision.

The author would like to thank several people for their generous help on this article, especially Monisha Das Gupta, Diane Harriford, and two *Feminist Studies* anonymous reviewers.

---

[49]Marilyn Buck's poem, "To the Woman Standing Behind Me in Line Who Asks Me How Long This Black History Month Is Going to Last," is reprinted with written permission from the author.

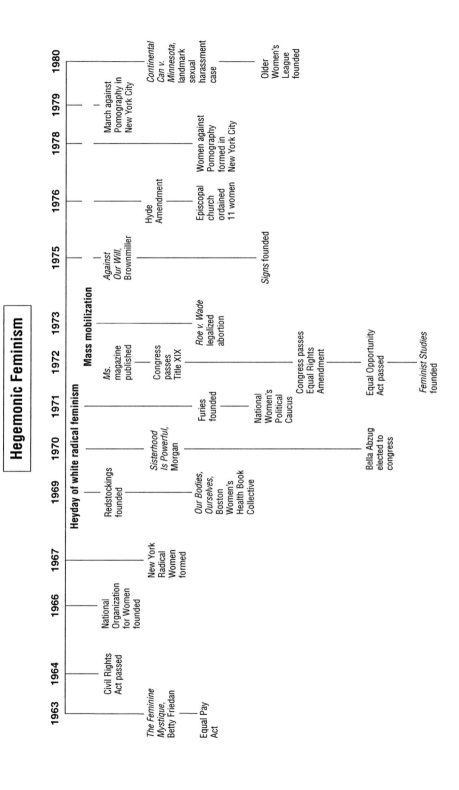

Hegemonic Feminism

| 1963 | 1964 | 1966 | 1967 | 1969 | 1970 | 1971 | 1972 | 1973 | 1975 | 1976 | 1978 | 1979 | 1980 |

Heyday of white radical feminism

Mass mobilization

Civil Rights Act passed

National Organization for Women founded

New York Radical Women formed

Redstockings founded

Sisterhood Is Powerful, Morgan

Ms. magazine published

Congress passes Title XIX

Against Our Will, Brownmiller

March against Pornography in New York City

Continental Can v. Minnesota, landmark sexual harassment case

The Feminine Mystique, Betty Friedan

Equal Pay Act

Our Bodies, Ourselves, Boston Women's Health Book Collective

Furies founded

Roe v. Wade legalized abortion

Hyde Amendment

Women against Pornography formed in New York City

Episcopal church ordained 11 women

National Women's Political Caucus

Congress passes Equal Rights Amendment

Signs founded

Older Women's League founded

Bella Abzug elected to congress

Equal Opportunity Act passed

Feminist Studies founded

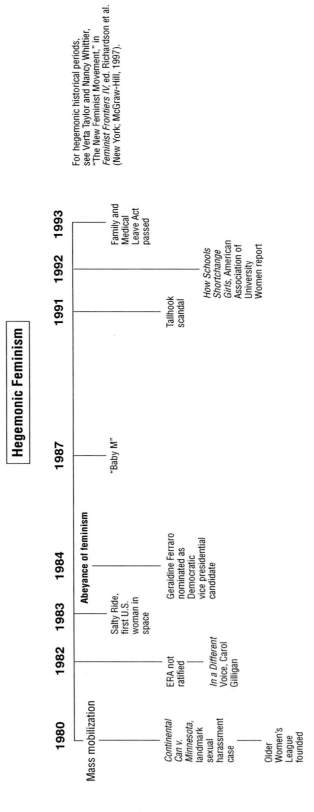

Hegemonic Feminism

1980

Mass mobilization

Continental Can v. Minnesota, landmark sexual harassment case

Older Women's League founded

1982

ERA not ratified

In a Different Voice, Carol Gilligan

1983

Sally Ride, first U.S. woman in space

1984

Abeyance of feminism

Geraldine Ferraro nominated as Democratic vice presidential candidate

1987

"Baby M"

1991

Tailhook scandal

1992

How Schools Shortchange Girls, American Association of University Women report

1993

Family and Medical Leave Act passed

For hegemonic historical periods, see Verta Taylor and Nancy Whittier, "The New Feminist Movement," in *Feminist Frontiers IV,* ed. Richardson et al. (New York: McGraw-Hill, 1997).

Multiracial Feminism

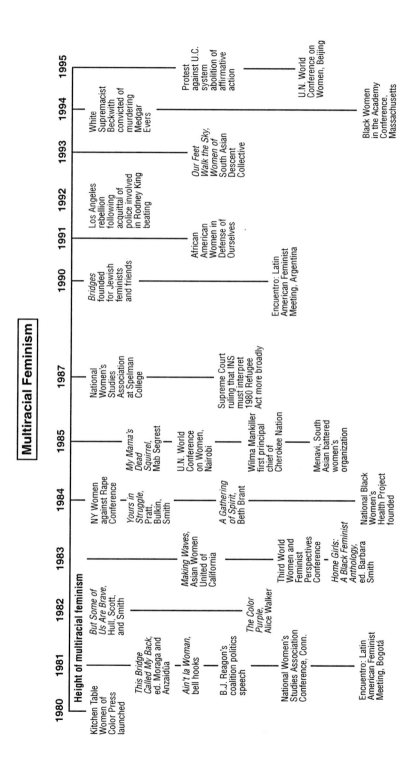

1980 1981 1982 1983 1984 1985 1987 1990 1991 1992 1993 1994 1995

Height of multiracial feminism

Kitchen Table Women of Color Press launched

But Some of Us Are Brave, Hull, Scott, and Smith

NY Women against Rape Conference

National Women's Studies Association at Spelman College

Bridges founded for Jewish feminists and friends

Los Angeles rebellion following acquittal of police involved in Rodney King beating

White Supremacist Beckwith convicted of murdering Medgar Evers

Protest against U.C. system abolition of affirmative action

This Bridge Called My Back, ed. Moraga and Anzaldúa

Yours in Struggle, Pratt, Bulkin, Smith

My Mama's Dead Squirrel, Mab Segrest

Ain't la Woman, bell hooks

Making Waves, Asian Women United of California

U.N. World Conference on Women, Nairobi

African American Women in Defense of Ourselves

Our Feet Walk the Sky, Women of South Asian Descent Collective

U.N. World Conference on Women, Beijing

B.J. Reagon's coalition politics speech

The Color Purple, Alice Walker

A Gathering of Spirit, Beth Brant

Supreme Court ruling that INS must interpret 1980 Refugee Act more broadly

Wilma Mankiller first principal chief of Cherokee Nation

Black Women in the Academy Conference, Massachusetts

National Women's Studies Association Conference, Conn.

Third World Women and Feminist Perspectives Conference

Home Girls: A Black Feminist Anthology, ed. Barbara Smith

Menavi, South Asian battered women's organization

Encuentro: Latin American Feminist Meeting, Argentina

Encuentro: Latin American Feminist Meeting, Bogotá

National Black Women's Health Project founded

335

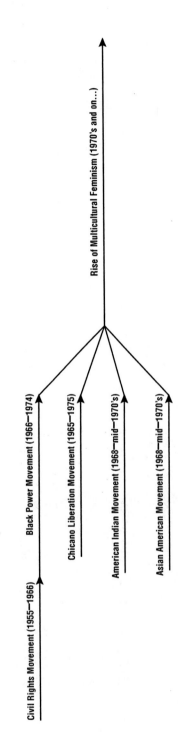

Toward a Comparative Feminist Movement

Civil Rights Movement (1955—1966)

Black Power Movement (1966—1974)

Chicano Liberation Movement (1965—1975)

American Indian Movement (1968—mid—1970's)

Asian American Movement (1968—mid—1970's)

Rise of Multicultural Feminism (1970's and on…)

Except from "Feminism A Movement to End Sexist Oppression"

bell hooks

bell hooks is a renowned writer and activist who has written over 25 books about race, gender, education and community. She earned her B.A. in English from Stanford University in 1973 and her M.A. in English from the University of Wisconsin-Madison in 1976. In 1983, she earned her Doctorate in Literature from the University of California, Santa Cruz. In 2004 hooks joined the faculty at Berea College as a Distinguished Professor-in-Residence. This piece comes from Feminist Theory from Margin to Center *(1984).*

The great majority of women who have benefited in any way from feminist-generated social reforms do not want to be seen as advocates of feminism. Conferences on issues of relevance to women, that would never have been organized or funded had there not been a feminist movement, take place all over the United States and the participants do not want to be seen as advocates of feminism. They are either reluctant to make a public commitment to feminist movement or sneer at the term. Individual African-American, Native American Indian, Asian-American, and Hispanic American women find themselves isolated if they support feminist movement. Even women who may achieve fame and notoriety (as well as increased economic income) in response to attention given their work by large numbers of women who support feminism may deflect attention away from their engagement with feminist movement. They may even go so far as to create other terms that express their concern with women's issues so as to avoid using the term feminist. The creation of new terms that have no relationship to organized political activity tend to provide women who may already be reluctant to explore feminism with ready excuses to explain their reluctance to participate. This illustrates an uncritical acceptance of distorted definitions of feminism rather than a demand for redefinition. They may support specific issues while divorcing themselves from what they assume is feminist movement.

In a recent article in a San Francisco newspaper, "Sisters—Under the Skin," columnist Bob Greene commented on the aversion many women apparently have to the term feminism. Greene finds it curious that many women "who obviously believe in everything that proud feminists believe in dismiss the term "feminist" as something unpleasant; something with which they do not wish to be associated." Even though such women often acknowledge that they have benefited from feminist-generated reform measures which have improved the social status of specific groups of women, they do not wish to be seen as participants in feminist movement:

> There is no getting around it. After all this time, the term "feminist" makes many bright, ambitious, intelligent women embarrassed and uncomfortable. They simply don't want to be associated with it.
>
> It's as if it has an unpleasant connotation that they want no connection with. Chances are if you were to present them with every mainstream feminist belief, they would go along with the beliefs to the letter—and even if they consider themselves feminists, they hasten to say no.

Many women are reluctant to advocate feminism because they are uncertain about the meaning of the term. Other women from exploited and oppressed ethnic groups dismiss the term because they do not wish to be perceived as supporting a racist movement; feminism is often equated with white women's rights effort. Large numbers of women see feminism as synonymous with lesbianism; their homophobia leads them to reject association with any group identified as pro-lesbian. Some women fear the word "feminism" because they shun identification with any political movement, especially one perceived as radical. Of course there are women who do not wish to be associated with women's rights movement in any form so they reject and oppose feminist movement. Most women are more familiar with negative perspectives on "women's lib" than the positive significations of feminism. It is this term's positive political significance and power that we must now struggle to recover and maintain.

Currently feminism seems to be a term without any clear significance. The "anything goes" approach to the definition of the word has rendered it practically meaningless. What is meant by "anything goes" is usually that any woman who wants social equality with men regardless of her political perspective (she can be a conservative right-winger or a nationalist communist) can label herself feminist. Most attempts at defining feminism reflect the class nature of the movement. Definitions are usually liberal in origin and focus on the individual woman's right to freedom and self-determination. In Barbara Berg's *The Remembered Gate: Origins of American Feminism*, she defines feminism as a "broad movement embracing numerous phases of woman's emancipation." However, her emphasis is on women gaining greater individual freedom. Expanding on the above definition, Berg adds:

> It is the freedom to decide her own destiny; freedom from sex-determined role; freedom from society's oppressive restrictions; freedom to express her thoughts fully and to convert them freely into action. Feminism demands the acceptance of woman's right to individual conscience and judgment. It postulates that woman's essential worth stems from her common humanity and does not depend on the other relationships of her life.

This definition of feminism is almost apolitical in tone; yet it is the type of definition many liberal women find appealing. It evokes a very romantic notion of personal freedom which is more acceptable than a definition that emphasizes radical political action.

Many feminist radicals now know that neither a feminism that focuses on woman as an autonomous human being worthy of personal freedom nor one that focuses on the attainment of equality of opportunity with men can rid society of sexism and male domination. Feminism is a struggle to end sexist oppression. Therefore, it is necessarily a struggle to eradicate the ideology of domination that permeates Western culture on various levels as well as a commitment to reorganizing society so that the self-development of people can take precedence over imperialism, economic expansion, and material desires. Defined in this way, it is unlikely that women would join feminist movement simply because we are biologically the same. A commitment to feminism so defined would demand that each individual participant acquire a critical political consciousness based on ideas and beliefs.

All too often the slogan "the personal is political" (which was first used to stress that woman's everyday reality is informed and shaped by politics and is necessarily political) became a means of encouraging women to think that the experience of discrimination, exploitation, or oppression automatically corresponded with an understanding of the ideological and institutional apparatus shaping one's social status. As a consequence, many women who had not fully examined their situation never developed a sophisticated understanding of their political reality and its relationship to that of women as a collective group. They were encouraged to focus on giving voice to personal experience. Like revolutionaries working to change the lot of colonized people globally, it is necessary for feminist activists to stress that the ability to see and describe one's own reality is a significant step in the long process of self-recovery; but it is only a beginning. When women internalized the idea that describing their own woe was synonymous with developing a critical political consciousness, the progress of feminist movement was stalled. Starting from such incomplete perspectives, it is not surprising that theories and strategies were developed that were collectively inadequate and misguided. To correct this inadequacy in past analysis, we must now encourage women to develop a keen, comprehensive understanding of women's political reality. Broader perspectives can only emerge as we examine both the personal that is political, the politics of society as a whole, and global revolutionary politics.

Feminism defined in political terms that stress collective as well as individual experience challenges women to enter a new domain—to leave behind the apolitical stance sexism decrees is our lot and develop political consciousness. Women know from our everyday lives that many of us rarely discuss politics. Even when women talked about sexist politics in the heyday of contemporary feminism, rather than allow this engagement with serious political matters to lead to complex, in-depth analysis of women's social status, we insisted that men were "the enemy," the cause of all our problems. As a consequence, we examined almost exclusively women's relationship to male supremacy and the ideology of sexism. The focus on "man as enemy" created, as Marlene Dixon emphasizes in her essay, "The Rise and Demise of Women's Liberation: A Class Analysis," a "politics of psychological oppression" which evoked world views which "pit individual against individual and mystify the social basis of exploitation."* By repudiating the popular notion that the focus of feminist movement should be social equality of the sexes and emphasizing eradicating the cultural basis of group oppression, our own analysis would require an exploration of all aspects of women's political reality. This would mean that race and class oppression would be recognized as feminist issues with as much relevance as sexism.

When feminism is defined in such a way that it calls attention to the diversity of women's social and political reality, it centralizes the experiences of all women, especially the women whose social conditions have been least written about, studied, or changed by political movements. When we cease to focus on the simplistic stance "men are the enemy," we are compelled to examine systems of domination and our role in their maintenance and perpetuation. Lack of adequate definition made it easy for bourgeois women, whether liberal or radical in perspective, to maintain their dominance over the leadership of the movement and its direction. This hegemony continues to exist in most feminist organizations. Exploited and oppressed groups of women are usually encouraged by those in power to feel that their situation is hopeless, that they can do nothing to break the pattern of domination. Given such socialization, these women have often felt that our only response to white, bourgeois, hegemonic dominance of feminist movement is to trash, reject, or dismiss feminism. This reaction is in no way threatening to the women who wish to maintain control over the direction of feminist theory and praxis. They prefer us to be silent, passively accepting their ideas. They prefer us speaking against "them" rather than developing our own ideas about feminist movement.

Feminism is the struggle to end sexist oppression. Its aim is not to benefit solely any specific group of women, any particular race or class of women. It does not privilege women over men. It has the power to transform in a meaningful way all our lives. Most importantly, feminism is neither a lifestyle nor a ready-made identity or role one can step into. Diverting energy from feminist movement that aims to change society, many women concentrate on the development of a counter-culture, a woman-centered world wherein participants have little contact with men. Such attempts do not indicate a respect or concern for the vast majority of women who are unable to integrate their cultural expressions with the visions offered by alternative woman-centered communities. In *Beyond God the Father*, Mary Daly urged women to give up "the securities offered by the patriarchal system" and create new space that would be woman-centered. Responding to Daly, Jeanne Gross pointed to the contradictions that arise when the focus of feminist movement is on the construction of new space:

> Creating a "counterworld" places an incredible amount of pressure on the women who attempt to embark on such a project. The pressure comes from the belief that the only true resources for such an endeavor are ourselves. The past which is totally patriarchal is viewed as irredeemable . . .
>
> If we go about creating an alternative culture without remaining in dialogue with others (and the historical circumstances that give rise to their identity) we have no reality check for our goals. We run the very real risk that the dominant ideology of the culture is re-duplicated in the feminist movement through cultural imperialism.

Equating feminist struggle with living in a counter-cultural, woman-centered world erected barriers that closed the movement off from most women. Despite sexist discrimination, exploitation, or oppression, many women feel their lives as they live them are important and valuable. Naturally the suggestion that these lives could be simply left or abandoned for an alternative "feminist" lifestyle met with resistance. Feeling their life experiences devalued, deemed solely negative and worthless, many women responded by vehemently attacking feminism. By rejecting the notion of an alternative feminist "lifestyle" that can emerge only when women create a subculture (whether it is living space or even space like women's studies that at many campuses has become exclusive) and insisting that feminist struggle can begin wherever an individual woman is, we create a movement that focuses on our collective experience, a movement that is continually mass-based.

Over the past six years, many separatist-oriented communities have been formed by women so that the focus has shifted from the development of woman-centered space towards an emphasis on identity. Once woman-centered space exists, it can be maintained only if women remain convinced that it is the only place where they can be self-realized and free. After assuming a "feminist" identity, women often seek to live the "feminist" lifestyle. These women do not see that it undermines feminist movement to project the assumption that "feminist" is but another pre-packaged role women can now select as they search for identity. The willingness to see feminism as a lifestyle choice rather than a political commitment reflects the class nature of the movement. It is not surprising that the vast majority of women who equate feminism with alternative lifestyle are from middle class backgrounds, unmarried, college-educated, often students who are without many of the social and economic responsibilities that working class and poor women who are laborers, parents, homemakers, and wives confront daily. Sometimes lesbians have sought to equate feminism with lifestyle but for significantly different reasons. Given the prejudice and discrimination against lesbian women in our society, alternative communities that are woman-centered are one means of creating positive, affirming environments. Despite positive reasons for developing woman-centered space, (which does not need to be equated with a "feminist" lifestyle) like pleasure, support, and resource-sharing, emphasis on creating a counter-culture has alienated women from feminist movement, for such space can be in churches, kitchens, etc.

Longing for community, connection, a sense of shared purpose, many women found support networks in feminist organizations. Satisfied in a personal way by new relationships generated in what was called a "safe," "supportive" context wherein discussion focused on feminist ideology, they did not question whether masses of women shared the same need for community. Certainly many black women as well as women from other ethnic groups do not feel an absence of community among women in their lives despite exploitation and oppression. The focus on feminism as a way to develop shared identity and community has little appeal to women who experience community, who seek ways to end exploitation and oppression in the context of their lives. While they may develop an interest in a feminist politic that works to eradicate sexist oppression, they will probably never feel as intense a need for a "feminist" identity and lifestyle.

Often emphasis on identity and lifestyle is appealing because it creates a false sense that one is engaged in praxis. However, praxis within any political movement that aims to have a radical transformative impact on society cannot be solely focused on creating spaces wherein would-be-radicals experience safety and support. Feminist movement to end sexist oppression actively engages participants in revolutionary struggle. Struggle is rarely safe or pleasurable.

Focusing on feminism as political commitment, we resist the emphasis on individual identity and lifestyle. (This should not be confused with the very real need to unite theory and practice.) Such resistance engages us in revolutionary praxis. The ethics of Western society informed by imperialism and capitalism are personal rather than social. They teach us that the individual good is more important then the collective good and consequently that individual change is of greater significance than collective change. This particular form of cultural imperialism has been reproduced in feminist movement in the form of individual women equating the fact that their lives have been changed in a meaningful way by feminism "as is" with a policy of no change need occur in the theory and praxis even if it has little or no impact on society as a whole, or on masses of women.

To emphasize that engagement with feminist struggle as political commitment we could avoid using the phrase "I am a feminist" (a linguistic structure designed to refer to some personal aspect of identity and self-definition) and could state "I advocate feminism." Because there has been undue emphasis placed on feminism as an identity or lifestyle, people usually resort to stereotyped perspectives on feminism. Deflecting attention away from stereotypes is necessary if we are to revise our strategy and direction. I have found that saying "I am a feminist" usually means I am plugged into preconceived notions of identity, role, or behavior. When I say "I advocate feminism" the response is usually "what is feminism?" A phrase like "I advocate" does not imply the kind of absolutism that is suggested by "I am." It does not engage us in the either/or dualistic thinking that is the central ideological component of all systems of domination in Western society. It implies that a choice has been made, that commitment to feminism is an act of will. It does not suggest that by committing oneself to feminism, the possibility of supporting other political movements is negated.

As a black woman interested in feminist movement, I am often asked whether being black is more important than being a woman; whether feminist struggle to end sexist oppression is more important than the struggle to end racism and vice-versa. All such questions are rooted in competitive either/or thinking, the belief that the self is formed in opposition to an other. Therefore one is a feminist because you are not something else. Most people are socialized to think in terms of opposition rather than compatibility. Rather than see anti-racist work as totally compatible with working to end sexist oppression, they are often seen as two movements competing for first place. When asked "Are you a feminist?" it appears that an affirmative answer is translated to mean that one is concerned with no political issues other than feminism. When one is black, an affirmative response is likely to be heard as a devaluation of struggle to end racism. Given the fear of being misunderstood, it has been difficult for black women and women in exploited and oppressed ethnic groups to give expression to their interest in feminist concerns. They have been wary of saying "I am a feminist." The shift in expression from "I am a feminist" to "I advocate feminism" could serve as a useful strategy for eliminating the focus on identity and lifestyle. It could serve as a way women who are concerned about feminism as well as other political movements could express their support while avoiding linguistic structures that give primacy to one particular group. It would also encourage greater exploration in feminist theory.

The shift in definition away from notions of social equality towards an emphasis on ending sexist oppression leads to a shift in attitudes in regard to the development of theory. Given the class nature of feminist movement so far, as well as racial hierarchies, developing theory (the guiding set of beliefs and principles that become the basis for action) has been a task particularly subject to the hegemonic dominance of white academic women. This has led many women outside the privileged race/class group to see the focus on developing theory, even the very use of the term, as a concern that functions only to reinforce the power of the elite group. Such reactions reinforce the sexist/racist/classist notion that developing theory is the domain of the white intellectual. Privileged white women active in feminist movement, whether liberal or radical in perspective, encourage black women to contribute "experiential" work, personal life stories. Personal experiences are important to feminist movement but they cannot take the place of theory. Charlotte Bunch explains the special significance of theory in her essay, "Feminism and Education: Not By Degrees":

> Theory enables us to see immediate needs in terms of long-range goals and an overall perspective on the world. It thus gives us a framework for evaluating various strategies in both the long and the short run and for seeing the types of changes that they are likely to produce. Theory is not just a body of facts or a set of personal opinions. It involves explanations and hypotheses that are based on available knowledge and experience. It is also dependent on conjecture and insight about how to interpret those facts and experiences and their significance.

Since bourgeois white women had defined feminism in such a way as to make it appear that it had no real significance for black women, they could then conclude that black women need not contribute to developing theory. We were to provide the colorful life stories to document and validate the prevailing set of theoretical assumptions.* Focus on social equality with men as a definition of feminism led to an emphasis on discrimination, male attitudes, and legalistic reforms. Feminism as a movement to end sexist oppression directs our attention to systems of domination and the inter-relatedness of sex, race, and class oppression. Therefore, it compels us to centralize the experiences and the social predicaments of women who bear the brunt of sexist oppression as a way to understand the collective social status of women in the United States. Defining feminism as a movement to end sexist oppression is crucial for the development of theory because it is a starting point indicating the direction of exploration and analysis.

The foundation of future feminist struggle must be solidly based on a recognition of the need to eradicate the underlying cultural basis and causes of sexism and other forms of group oppression. Without challenging and changing these philosophical structures, no feminist reforms will have a long range impact. Consequently, it is now necessary for advocates of feminism to collectively acknowledge that our struggle cannot be defined as a movement to gain social equality with men; that terms like "liberal feminist" and "bourgeois feminist" represent contradictions that must be resolved so that feminism will not be continually co-opted to serve the opportunistic ends of special interest groups.

More Than a Few Good Men

Jackson Katz

Jackson Katz *earned a minor in Women's Studies from the University of Amherst and a M.A. from the Harvard Graduate School of Education. He is earning a PhD in Cultural Studies and Education from UCLA. His research and activism has been on violence and masculinity about which he as created or co-created several educational videos including* Tough Guise *(2000),* Wrestling with Manhood *(2002) and* Spin the Bottle *(2004). He also wrote the book* The Macho Paradox: Why Some Men Hurt Women and How All Men Can Help *(2006) from which this essay comes.*

"As long as we take the view that these are problems for women alone to solve, we cannot expect to reverse the high incidence of rape and child abuse . . . and domestic violence. We do know that many men do not abuse women and children; and that they strive always to live with respect and dignity. But until today the collective voice of these men has never been heard, because the issue has not been regarded as one for the whole nation. From today those who inflict violence on others will know they are being isolated and cannot count on other men to protect them. From now on all men will hear the call to assume their responsibility for solving this problem."—President Nelson Mandela, 1997, National Men's March, Pretoria, South Africa

Since the very beginning of the women-led movements against domestic and sexual violence in the 1970s, there have been men who personally, professionally, and politically supported the work of those women. In addition, over the past several decades there have been repeated attempts by men to create organizations and targeted initiatives to address men's roles in ending men's violence against women. Some of the early efforts were undertaken by groups of concerned men who responded to the challenge from women's organizations to educate, politicize, and organize other men. Some of these men chose to volunteer in supportive roles with local rape crisis centers or battered women's programs. Others contributed to the development of the fledgling batterer intervention movement in the late 1970s and 1980s. Some of the better known programs for batterers were Emerge in Cambridge, Massachusetts; RAVEN (Rape and Violence End Now) in St. Louis, Missouri; and Men Stopping Violence in Atlanta, Georgia. Still other men created political and activist educational organizations, like the National Organization for Men Against Sexism (NOMAS), which has held "Men and Masculinity" conferences annually since 1975; the Oakland Men's Project in the San Francisco Bay Area; Men Stopping Rape in Madison, Wisconsin; DC Men Against Rape; and Real Men, an anti-sexist men's organization I co-founded in Boston in 1988.

The rapidly growing field of "men's work" also produced community centers that combine batterer-intervention and counseling services for men with educational outreach and social activism. One of the groundbreaking programs in this field is the Men's Resource Center of Western Massachusetts, founded in Amherst in 1982. In the 1990s anti-sexist men's initiatives in the U.S. and around the world increased dramatically. One of the most visible has been the White Ribbon Campaign, an activist educational campaign founded by a group of men in Canada in 1991. They started the WRC in response to a horrific incident on December 6, 1989, at the University of Montreal, where an armed twenty-five-year-old man walked into a classroom, separated the women from the men and proceeded to shoot the women. Before he finished his rampage, he had murdered fourteen women in cold blood—and shaken up an entire country. The significance of the white ribbon—which has been adopted on hundreds of college campuses and communities in the U.S. as well as a number of other countries—is that men wear it to make a visible and public pledge "never to commit, condone, nor remain silent about violence against women."

Despite these notable efforts over the past thirty years, the movement of men committed to ending men's violence against women has only recently picked up significant momentum. There are more men doing this work in the United States and around the world than ever before. Halfway through the first decade of the twenty-first century there is reason for optimism, especially about the emergence of a new generation of anti-sexist men. But there are nowhere near enough men yet involved to make a serious dent in this enormous problem. Several key challenges lie ahead:

- How to increase dramatically the number of men who make these issues a priority in their personal and professional lives
- How to expand the existing infrastructure of men's anti-rape and domestic violence prevention groups, and other campus and community-based initiatives
- How to institutionalize gender violence prevention education at every level of the educational system
- How to build multiracial and multiethnic coalitions that unite men across differences around their shared concerns about sexist violence and the sexual exploitation of children
- How to insure that federal, state, and local funding for efforts to reduce gender violence are maintained and expanded in the coming years
- And finally, how to make it socially acceptable—even cool—for men to become vocal and public allies of women in the struggle against all forms of men's violence against women and children

A "BIG TENT" APPROACH

As I have made clear in this book, there is much that we can do to prevent men's violence against women—if we find the collective will in male culture to make it a priority. I am convinced that millions of men in our society are deeply concerned about the abuse, harassment, and violence we see—and fear—in the lives of our daughters, mothers, sisters, and lovers. In fact, a recent poll conducted for Lifetime Television found that 57 percent of men aged sixteen to twenty-four believe gender violence is an "extremely serious" problem. A 2000 poll conducted by the Family Violence Prevention Fund found that one-quarter of men would do more about the issue if they were asked. And some compelling social norms research on college campuses suggests that one of the most significant factors in a man's decision to intervene in an incident is his perception of how other men would act in a similar situation. Clearly, a lot of men are uncomfortable with other men's abusive behaviors, but they have not figured out what to do about it—or have not yet mustered the courage to act on their own. So there is great potential to increase dramatically the number of men who commit personal time, money, and institutional clout to the effort to reduce men's violence against women. But in order to achieve this we need to think outside the box about how to reach into the mainstream of male culture and social power.

One promising approach employs elements of what might be called "big tent" movement building. The big tent concept comes from politics, where it has been used most famously to describe efforts to unite various constituencies and single-issue special-interest groups under the Republican Party label. A number of questions arise when this concept is applied to gender violence prevention: How do we attract individuals and organizations not known for their advocacy of the issues of men's violence? What are some of the necessary compromises required in order to broaden the coalition of participating individuals and groups? What are some of the costs and benefits of engaging new partners, who might not have the depth of experience or the ideological affinities of the majority of women and men currently in the movement?

Growing pains always accompany growth. A bigger movement will inevitably create new conflicts. One way to think about the question of broadening the base of the movement is to consider the concept embodied in the geometric model of the Venn diagram. The Venn diagram captures the idea that coalition building involves identifying shared objectives between groups with different interests, not creating a perfect union between fully compatible partners. The diagram consists of two overlapping circles. In this case we might say that one circle represents the needs and interests of the battered women's and rape crisis movements. The other circle represents any men's organization that has not historically been part of these movements. Clearly, there are large areas where the circles do not overlap. But the big tent approach does not dwell on the areas of disconnection. It focuses on the center area, where there are points of agreement and shared objectives. If individuals and groups of men and women can agree that reducing men's violence against women is an urgent objective, then perhaps they can agree for the moment to table their other differences.

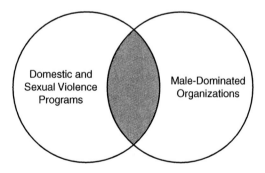

CHALLENGES

There are obvious downsides to incautiously expanding the big tent. Take, for example, the costs and benefits of working with men in the sports culture. Many women in domestic and sexual violence advocacy have long seen the benefit to partnering with athletic teams or utilizing high-profile male athletes in public service campaigns. But some of these same women worry about the potential risks inherent in such collaboration. They fear that a male athlete who speaks out publicly against men's violence could undermine the integrity of the movement if his private behavior does not match his public rhetoric. Happily, in recent years this fear has begun to dissipate as more male athletes speak out, in part because with increased men's participation there is less pressure on any one man to be the "perfect" poster child for anti-violence efforts. We can also never lose sight of the fact that professional sports teams are not social justice organizations. They are businesses that sometimes have huge investments in players. Say a team takes a public stand against men's violence, and then at some point one of its star players is arrested for domestic violence or sexual assault. Is the team likely to respond based on what they think is best for the community, or for their own bottom line?

The participation of faith-based organizations in the big tent presents significant opportunities, but comes with its own unique set of challenges. As the Rev. Dr. Marie Fortune, a pioneer in the movements against domestic and sexual violence and founder of the FaithTrust Institute in Seattle, Washington, points out, "Millions of men participate in faith-based communities whose leaders, often male, typically enjoy significant moral authority and shape in important ways the values and behaviors of men in their congregations." There are male clergy in every denomination who are strong allies of women in the domestic and sexual violence prevention movements. But many clergy and religious leaders have received no training on the issue of men's violence against women. To this day many male clergy are reluctant to take strong public stands on issues of sexual and domestic violence. What further complicates matters is that many religious traditions have "reflected and reinforced," in the words of Rev. Fortune, "patriarchal values that have been at the core of violence against women." But perhaps even more troubling are the clergy sex abuse scandals that have become routine in recent years. It is plain to see that even men with impeccable religious credentials can be private hypocrites.

The participation of faith-based organizations in gender violence prevention also raises the question of how much ideological incompatibility is tolerable in the quest for big tent inclusiveness. Can feminist religious and secular leaders work in coalition with religious leaders who have resisted the advancement of women in the family and the pulpit? Can progressive religious and secular leaders who support full sexual equality work side by side with religious leaders who oppose gay civil rights?

Similar questions arise about an organization like the Boy Scouts. Scouting plays an important role in the lives of millions of boys and adolescent males. Many local Boy Scout chapters have participated in events of domestic violence and sexual assault awareness month. But if the Scouts went a step further and made participation in gender violence prevention a major nationwide organizational goal, they could have a tremendous impact, especially since the Scouts have a presence in many communities where there is currently little male participation in domestic and sexual violence programs. But many progressive organizations refuse to work with the Boy Scouts because their official policy discriminates against openly gay scouts and scoutmasters. Does their anti-gay stance make the Boy Scouts an unacceptable coalition partner in the struggle against teen-relationship abuse and sexual assault?

Until now most men in the movement to end men's violence against women have been profeminist and politically liberal or progressive. But this does not preclude them from framing one aspect of the gender-violence issue in language about crime and punishment that resonates with conservatives. In fact, many politically conservative men have played an important role in this fight—particularly men in law enforcement, the military, and government. After all, domestic and sexual violence are more than social problems; they are crimes. Nonetheless, millions of abusive men continue to receive suspended sentences, probation, and other light penalties, which signals that their crimes are not taken seriously. In order to be effective, decisive action is required by police, prosecutors, and judges. The goal of punishment is to send the message to would-be perps that the price for transgression is steep. Conservative as well as progressive men who take the idea of personal responsibility seriously should support policies that hold law-breakers accountable, and advocacy that strengthens the community's desire to do so. But a criminal justice approach is also fraught with potential problems. For one thing, there are not enough jail cells to house all the men who could be prosecuted for domestic and sexual violence. As I have discussed, class bias and racism are factors in any discussion about the criminal justice system. Efforts to attract conservative men's support by emphasizing a law enforcement approach might exact too high a cost—and jeopardize the increased participation of people of color who are concerned about both gender violence *and* the over-representation of men in color in the "prison industrial complex." In addition, since most gender violence—including the vast majority of rape—is currently not reported, it is questionable how effective a criminal justice approach can be.

MEN AND WOMEN

The special challenge of gender violence prevention politics is that women's trust of men is not a given. Some women are understandably wary of men's motivations and skeptical about their commitment to gender justice. As increasing numbers of men get involved, they worry that men might try to "take over" the movement, or take it in a direction that suits men's needs rather than women's. Women are always eager to see whether men "walk their talk." For example, an administrator in a domestic-violence agency recently told me about a talented young man who had applied for a youth outreach position. He seemed to know the issues really well, she explained, and he grasped some of the subtle racial and ethnic issues involved in this work. He also had an engaging personal style. But he had not yet mastered the "micro-politics" of how to interact with women in positions of leadership. He often cut off women co-presenters, or talked over them in an effort to prove his knowledge. Was it worth the risk of hiring him?

For their part, some men are well-meaning but oblivious to the sensitivities required for effective inter-gender collaboration on an issue where women have historically been the leaders. For example, I have heard stories too many times about earnest young men on college campuses who were inspired to start anti-rape groups, but neglected first to check in with women who were already engaged in rape prevention work, like the director of the campus women's center. These sorts of political missteps can cause unnecessary tension and discord at the earliest stages and can undermine successful coalition-building.

Even so, there are numerous examples across the country of men and women working together to create and sustain sexual and domestic violence prevention initiatives. In fact, many successful college men's anti-violence programs have actually been started by women. Among the more well-known are Men Against Violence at Louisiana State University, begun by Dr. Luoluo Hong, and the Fraternity Anti-Violence Education Project at West Chester University in Pennsylvania, led by Dr. Deborah Mahlstedt.

WHAT CAN MEN DO?

At a small state college in the Northeast, a controversy erupted in early 2005 when the editors of the student newspaper distributed a sex survey across campus that included a question about which professor on campus they would most like to "get it on with." The person chosen was the coordinator of the women's studies program, who responded with a lengthy letter to the editor in which she wrote that it was "offensive and hurtful" to be disrespected by students in this way, and as a professional it undermined her ability to do her job. In her letter she posed a number of questions for an alternative survey, including one to men which asked, "What are you willing to do to help reduce rape and sexual assault among college students?" In response, a male columnist for the student newspaper wrote dismissively: "I will not rape anyone. Is there anything more I should add to this?" The student's response might have been glib and a bit obnoxious, but he spoke for a lot of men. Many of them have never even considered the wide range of choices men have to reduce rape and sexual assault, and every other type of gender violence. What follows is a brief discussion about how men can be effective anti-sexist agents, both as individuals and in their various public and private leadership roles within institutions.

Have the Courage to Look Inward

One of the most important steps any man can take if he wants to be an ally to women in the struggle against gender violence is to be honest with himself. A key requirement for men to become effective anti-sexist agents is their willingness to examine their own attitudes and behaviors about women, sex, and manhood. This is similar to the sort of introspection required of anti-racist whites. It is not an easy process, especially when men start to see that they have inadvertently perpetuated sexism and violence through their personal actions, or their participation in sexist practices in male culture. Because defensiveness is the enemy of introspection, it is vital that men develop ways to transcend their initial defensive reactions about men's mistreatment of women and move toward a place where they are grounded enough to do something about it.

Support Survivors

In a social climate where women who report sexual and domestic violence are often disbelieved and called "accusers," it is crucial that men personally and publicly support survivors—girls and boys, women and men. This can mean the offer of a supportive ear in a conversation, or a shoulder for a friend to cry on. It can also mean challenging others—men and women—who seek to discredit victims' accounts of their victimization. For example, when a girl or woman reports a sexual assault and her alleged attacker is a popular guy with a network of supporters, people often rally around him—even when they have nothing more than his word to go on that she is lying. Sadly, some of them try to smear her character and reputation. It is not fair to assume the man's guilt; he is entitled to a presumption of innocence until proven guilty. But alleged victims are entitled to a presumption as well—the presumption that they are telling the truth about what was done to them. They also have the right to be treated with respect, and to expect the people around them to defend their integrity if it is ever questioned.

Seek Help

Men who are emotionally, physically, or sexually abusive to women and girls need to seek help now. But first they have to acknowledge to themselves that they have a problem. I once gave a speech about men's violence against women at a big state university in the West. After the event was over, a blond-haired college student in jeans and a T-shirt approached me in the main lobby of the student center. His voice quivered as he said, "I just realized that I have done bad things to women." He did not elaborate, nor did I ask him to. But I could tell he had a troubled conscience by the look in his eyes, and because he waited nearly half an hour to talk to me. The question of what to do about men who have been abusive will take on ever greater urgency as more men become involved in the movement against gender violence. Many men who were formerly abusive to women have become effective professionals in batterer intervention programs.

They share their personal stories and serve as models for how men can grow and change. This is crucial because millions of men have committed mild or severe acts of cruelty toward women and children, and whether they were charged with and convicted of a crime or not, we have to figure out ways to integrate most of them back into our families and communities. Of course, sometimes this is easier said than done. For example, in recent years families in communities across the U.S. have faced the challenge of living in neighborhoods alongside convicted child molesters. This raises another set of questions: When do the rights of children and their parents to be free from the threat of sexual abuse and violence out-weigh the rights of men (or women) who have served their sentences and are seeking to rebuild their lives? If a man has committed acts of sexual or domestic violence, should those acts define him for the rest of his life?

Refuse to Condone Sexist and Abusive Behavior by Friends, Peers, and Coworkers

As I have argued in this book, if we want to dramatically increase the number of men who make men's violence against women a priority, it is not useful to engage them as perpetrators or potential perpetrators. Instead, it makes sense to enlist them as empowered bystanders who can do something to confront abusive peers, or who can help to create a climate in male peer culture that discourages some men's sexist attitudes and behaviors. This is often easier said than done, because it can be quite awkward for men to confront each other about how they talk about and treat women. Consider an experience I had when I was in my early thirties at a wedding of an old friend of mine. A few minutes after I was introduced to the best man at a cocktail reception the day before the wedding, he confidently told me and a group of other guys a tasteless joke about battered women. I was not sure how to react. If I said something, I feared that it could create a chill between us, and this was the first day of a long weekend. But if I did not say something, I feared my silence might imply approval of the joke. I felt similar to how I would have felt if a white friend had told a racist joke. There was an added concern: How could I—or anyone else—know the full context of his joke-telling? The guy may have been personally harmless, but at the very least his gender politics were suspect, and at the worst he also may have been a closeted batterer who was subtly seeking public approval for his private behavior. I managed to mutter a feeble objection, something like, "Surely you have other topics to joke about." But I never told the guy how I really felt.

Sometimes men who take a strong stand against gender violence can face serious interpersonal consequences for their efforts. Mike LaRiviere, a police officer who is deeply committed to domestic and sexual violence prevention, trains police across the country in domestic violence policies and procedures. He recounts an incident many years ago when he was relatively new to his small-city New England police force. He and his more senior partner answered a domestic violence call, and when they arrived at the apartment it was obvious that the man had assaulted the woman. Mike thought it was clear they should make an arrest, both for the victim's safety and to hold the man accountable for what he had done. But the senior partner had another idea.

He just wanted to tell the guy to cool down. Mike and he had a hushed but heated conversation in another room about what to do. They finally arrested the man, but for the next five or six months, Mike's partner barely spoke with him. The atmosphere in the squad car was tense and chilly, which in police work can be dangerous as well as unpleasant, because you can never be certain that someone who seethes with resentment will always have your back.

In spite of how difficult it can be for men to challenge each other about sexism, it does happen. In fact, it might happen more often than many people realize. In any case, it is important for men to hear each other's stories about this type of intervention, so they can see that other men feel as they do and so they can get potentially useful ideas. I heard one such story about a bachelor party road trip that Al Emerick, a leader of Men Against Violence Against Women in Jacksonville, Florida, took a couple of years ago with some friends. They were a group of well-off white guys in their thirties who had been playing poker together for nine years. There were four married men in the car along with the groom, and the discussion came up about strip clubs. The best man was ready to drop a pile of one-dollar bills on some "fine ladies' asses." Al said he would not be joining them, and the guys immediately got on him. "Whattya gay?" "What's the big deal, the wife's not here." "Cut loose." Because the guys had known Al for quite some time, they knew he was no prude, nor were his objections based on his religious beliefs. But they did know he had been working with a men's group that was affiliated with the local domestic violence shelter. He told them he did not want to take part because he had a problem with the objectification of women—even when it is voluntary. As he tells it, this group of friends spent two hours in an "intense but wonderful" conversation about sexism, domestic violence, male privilege, power, and control. In the course of the conversation Al fielded a range of predictable challenges like: "I'm not an abuser because I look at chicks." He countered with questions like, "What about men in the audience who might be abusers or rapists? By us being there and supporting the action, aren't we reinforcing their behaviors?" In the end, they never went to the strip clubs. Since that event, they have had further conversations about these issues, and according to Al, one of the guys has even offered to help produce a public service announcement for the anti-sexist men's group.

Make Connections between Men's Violence against Women and Other Issues

Gender violence contributes to a wide range of social problems that include youth violence, homelessness, divorce, alcoholism, and the transmission of HIV/AIDS. Men who care about these problems need to educate themselves about the relationship between gender violence and these issues, and then integrate this understanding in their work and daily life.

Perhaps nowhere are the effects of gender violence more pronounced than with HIV/AIDS, the global pandemic that has already killed twenty million people and infected forty-five million. Across the world, there is an inextricable linkage between men's violence against women and transmission of the virus. Forms of gender violence that are fueling transmission include sexual coercion and rape, men's refusal to wear condoms, and married or monogamous men's solicitation of prostitutes followed by unprotected sex with their wives or partners. Gender violence also takes the form of civil and customary laws that perpetuate male privilege and prerogative and deny women's human rights. This might include civil and customary laws that do not recognize marital rape or the dangers of early marriage, as well as systematic prohibitions against females inheriting wealth and property—a reality that ultimately forces millions of widows and daughters to lives of abject poverty and economic dependence on men. But according to M.I.T. research fellow and United Nations consultant Miriam Zoll, while heterosexual transmission may be the primary route of HIV/AIDS infection today, few HIV-prevention programs actually address the underlying gender, power, and sexual dynamics between men and women that contribute to infection, including violence. In a 2004 report entitled "Closing the HIV/AIDS Prevention Gender Gap?" Zoll surveyed men's and women's attitudes about gender and sexuality on several continents. She found that men and women's cultural definitions and perceptions of masculinity and femininity often reinforced men's power over women in ways that make sexually transmitted infections more likely. In the report, Zoll featured the work of men and women who are implementing promising gender-based prevention strategies. For example, Dean Peacock is a white South African who lived for many years in the U.S., where he worked in San Francisco as a facilitator in a batterer intervention program. Peacock returned to South Africa a couple of years ago to lead HIV prevention work with men in a program called Men As Partners, sponsored by Engender Health and Planned Parenthood of South Africa. As Zoll reports, from his unique vantage point Peacock observed with groups of men in prevention trainings in South Africa many of the same ideas about masculinity that he encountered with batterers in the U.S.: "A real man doesn't negotiate with a woman." "A real man doesn't use condoms." "A real man doesn't worry about his health status." "A real man doesn't get tested." "A real man has sex with multiple partners." Even so, Peacock says that men in South Africa with whom he has worked are very open to gender equitable work. "The paradox of the HIV/AIDS epidemic is that it has opened the door to gender equality. We say to these men, 'If you work with us, your life will become richer.' We appeal to them as moral agents. We ask them, 'What is your responsibility to take this to the community, to challenge other men's behaviors, to confront men who are violent, to confront other men who are placing their partners at risk?'"

Contribute Financial Resources

Men with significant financial resources need to think creatively about what they can do to help support the growing number of domestic and sexual-assault prevention initiatives that target boys and men. This is the cutting edge of prevention work, and the field is new enough that a small number of wealthy men could make an enormous impact. Ted Waitt, founder of the Gateway Computer Company, has been one of the early leaders in this area. Philanthropic individuals and organizations can and should continue to fund services for women and girls who are victims and survivors of men's violence, especially when state and federal funds are being cut; funds that target work with men and boys should never compete with funds for direct services for women and girls. But they should not have to, because the pool of available resources should increase as more influential men get involved and bring new ideas and energy to the task of preventing men's violence against women.

Be Creative and Entrepreneurial

A number of enterprising men have used their imagination and creativity to raise other men's awareness of sexism, and to challenge the sexist attitudes and behaviors of men around them. Any list of these individuals is necessarily subjective and abbreviated, but I would nonetheless people to each other, is a former federal prosecutor with extensive experience prosecuting domestic violence, sexual assault, rape, child abuse, and hate crimes. He formerly served as special counsel to the Violence Against Women Office at the United States Department of Justice and is an expert in the federal civil rights of people with disabilities.

Start Anti-Sexist Men's Groups

The power of individuals to catalyze change increases exponentially when they work together to create new institutions and organizations. A growing number of organizations have made significant contributions in recent years to gender violence prevention efforts with men and boys. Some of these groups have paid staff and operate along the lines of traditional non-profit educational organizations; others are more grass roots and volunteer-oriented. It is not possible to provide anything close to a comprehensive list of these various initiatives, but consider a handful of examples from around the country: The Washington, D.C.-based group Men Can Stop Rape regularly conducts anti-rape trainings with high school, college, and community organizations. Their "strength campaign" posters and other materials have been widely circulated. The Institute on Domestic Violence in the African American Community, headed by Dr. Oliver Williams, regularly brings together scholars and activists to discuss issues of particular interest to men (and women) of color, such as the potential role of the hip-hop generation in preventing men's violence against women. The anti-rape men's group One in Four has chapters on dozens of college campuses. In 1999, a group of men in the famous fishing town of Gloucester, Massachusetts—carpenters and clergy, bartenders and bankers—started Gloucester Men Against Domestic Abuse. They march annually in the town's popular Fourth of July parade and sponsor a billboard that says "Strong Men Don't Bully," a public testimonial of sorts that features the names of five hundred Gloucester men. The Men's Leadership Forum in San Diego, California, is a high-profile annual conference held on Valentine's Day. Since 2001, MLF has brought together a diverse group of men and boys (and women) from across the city to learn how men in business, labor unions, the sports culture, education, the faith community, and the human services can contribute to ending men's violence against women. Some men are politicized about sexism out of concern for their daughters, or as a result of things that have happened to them. One of the most effective organizations that addresses these concerns is Dads and Daughters, a Duluth, Minnesota-based advocacy group led by Joe Kelly. Part of the mission of DADS is to mobilize concerned fathers to challenge companies whose marketing is sexist and exploitative—especially when it involves the sexualization of young girls or adolescents, or treats men's violence against women as a joke.

In addition to some of these now well-established organizations, anti-sexist men on college campuses and in local communities have worked—often in collaboration with women's centers or domestic and sexual violence programs—to educate men and boys about the role men can play in confronting and interrupting other men's abusive behaviors. One venue for this collaboration has been the proliferating number of V-Day events held on college campuses. While V-Day is woman-centered, male students have played all sorts of supportive roles, such as organizing outreach efforts to men and coproducing and promoting performances of the Eve Ensler play *The Vagina Monologues*.

Some anti-sexist men's efforts have been ad hoc and customized to fit the needs and experiences of various communities. For example, in 2003 a group of Asian American men in Seattle organized to support the local chapter of the National Asian Pacific American Women's Forum in their opposition to a restaurant that was promoting "naked sushi" nights, where patrons took sushi off the bodies of semi-nude models wrapped in cellophane. And in the summer of 2004, a group of men (and women) in the "punk, indie, alternative" music scene organized a Different Kind of Dude Fest in Washington, D.C. Along the lines of the Riot Girrls and Girlfest, Hawaii, they sought to use art as an organizing tool. Their goal was to call attention to the ways in which progressive political punk culture, while promising liberation from other forms of social conformity and oppression, nonetheless helped to perpetuate sexism and patriarchal domination. The organizers of the music festival also explicitly affirmed the need for men to be allies of feminists in the fight for gender justice and social equality.

Champion Institutional Reform

Men who hold positions of power in government, non-profit organizations, business, and labor unions can do much to prevent men's violence against women if they take two critical steps: 1.) Recognize domestic and sexual violence prevention as a leadership issue for men, and 2.) Start to think creatively about how they can push their institutions to address it. The problem is that many men in positions of institutional authority do not yet see gender violence prevention in this way. That is why I strongly suggest that public or private institutions who want to begin serious primary prevention initiatives first arrange trainings for men in positions of senior leadership—and the more senior, the better. If done well, gender violence prevention training for men can be transformative. Men often come out of such trainings with an entirely new sensibility about their professional and personal responsibilities to women and children, as well as to other men. This is important because in the long term, dramatic reductions in the incidence of men's violence against women in the U.S. and around the world will only come about when people with power—which often means *men* in power—make gender violence issues a priority. Among other things, this means that male leaders must set and maintain a tone—in educational institutions, corporations, the military—where sexist and abusive behavior is considered unacceptable and unwelcome, not only because women don't like it but because other men will not stand for it. This sounds good, but people often ask me how to get powerful men to take these issues seriously. For example, how do you convince male legislators, educational administrators, business leaders, or military commanders to attend gender violence prevention training? There are a variety of strategies, but the bottom line is that they do not necessarily have to be motivated—at least initially—by altruism or concerns about social justice. They need instead to be persuaded that prevention is a widely shared institutional goal, and that it is their responsibility to be as knowledgeable and proactive about these issues as possible.

Think and Act Locally and Globally

The focus of this book has been mostly on the U.S., but obviously men's violence against women is an issue everywhere in the world. Since 9/11, many Americans have learned what many people around the world have long known—in the modern era, what happens in foreign cultures thousands of miles away can affect people right here at home, sometimes in ways that are impossible to predict. That is the irrevocable reality of the global environment in which we now live. As I have maintained throughout, gender violence is best seen not as aberrational behavior perpetrated by a few bad men but as an expression of much more deeply seated structures of male dominance and gender inequality. This is much easier to see when you are looking at someone else's culture. For example, in radical fundamentalist Islamic countries, women have few rights, and in many instances men's violence against them is legal and even expected—especially when they defy male authority. In other words, men's violence against women functions in some cultures to maintain a highly authoritarian, even fascistic male power structure. In that sense, gender violence is clearly a political crime with potentially far-reaching consequences. As a result, the way that men in distant lands treat women—individually and as a group—cannot be dismissed as a private family or cultural matter. It has too much bearing on political developments that could affect all of us—like the possibility of nuclear war, or the constant threat of terrorist attacks.

At the same time, it is tempting for some Americans to hear and read about the way men mistreat women in foreign cultures and attribute that mistreatment to cultural deficiencies and even barbarism. But it is important to remember that by world standards, the incidence of men's violence against women here in the U.S. is embarrassingly high. No doubt many American men would be offended to hear people in other countries speculating about the shortcomings of American men—and the inferiority of the culture that produced them.

Fortunately, the growing movement of men who are speaking out about men's violence against women is international in scope. There are anti-sexist men's initiatives in scores of countries across the world. In addition, one of the most promising developments in the history of international human rights law is the growing international movement to identify men's violence against women as a human rights issue. A pivotal moment in that movement came in 2001, when the United Nations war crimes tribunal named rape and sexual slavery as war crimes. And today, a number of international organizations—most prominently Amnesty International—have begun to focus on gender violence and link the physical and sexual exploitation of women to a host of other social and political problems. One of the major challenges for American anti-sexist men in the coming years will be to make connections between men's violence against women in the U.S. with violence around the world, and to support efforts everywhere to reduce men's violence and advance gender equality—not only because it is the right thing to do, but also because it is arguably in our national interest.

What's in It for Men?

Men who occupy positions of influence in boys' lives—fathers, grandfathers, older brothers, teachers, coaches, religious leaders—need to teach them that men of integrity value women and do not tolerate other men's sexism or abusive behavior. Obviously they have to lead by example. But that is not enough. In a cultural climate where the objectification of women and girls has accelerated, and boys are exposed to ever more graphic displays of brutality toward women disguised as "entertainment," men need to preemptively provide clear guidelines for boys' behavior. This does not always have to be defined in negative terms, e.g., "Don't hit women." It can be framed as a positive challenge to young men, especially if they aspire to something more special than being "one of the guys" at all costs.

In fact, when I give talks about men's violence against women to groups of parents, I am often asked by parents of sons if there is something positive we can offer young men as a substitute for what we are taking away from them. "We constantly say to our kids, 'Don't do this, don't do that, I wish you wouldn't listen to this music.' We tell them they shouldn't treat girls a certain way, they shouldn't act tough. We spend a lot of time telling our sons what they shouldn't be. It's so negative. Why shouldn't they just tune us out? What's in it for them?"

My answer is really quite simple, and it is as true for the fathers as it is for the sons. When we ask men to reject sexism and the abuse of women, we are not taking something away from them. In fact, we are giving them something very valuable—a vision of manhood that does not depend on putting down others in order to lift itself up. When a man stands up for social justice, non-violence, and basic human rights—for women as much as for men—he is acting in the best traditions of our civilization. That makes him not only a better man, but a better human being.

New Black Man

Mark Anthony Neal

Mark Anthony Neal is a Professor in African and African American Studies at Duke University. His research and teaching is in Black Popular Culture. His books include What the Music Said: Black Popular Music and Black Public Culture *(1998) and* New Black Man: Rethinking Black Masculinity *(2005) from which this essay comes.*

Why write a book like *New Black Man*? What's to be gained by calling forth a generation of pro-feminist, anti-homophobic, nurturing black men? Scholars all have an intellectual project, a basic issue that they seek to address during the course of their careers. My goal has always been to address the concept of black community. Although many have interpreted the fissures and crevices within the so-called black community (particularly in the post-civil-rights era) as evidence of weakness, I believe that a diversity of ideas and identities actually strengthens our communities. I've been committed to doing work that highlights the value of those who have been marginalized in our communities, including but not limited to black youth, black women (and black feminists in particular), and black gays and lesbians.

I've been equally committed to using my work and my civic voice to challenge the real violence—physical, rhetorical, and emotional—that we inflict on those marginalized bodies in our communities. It's not enough to close ranks around those who we marginalize; we need to take aim at the very forms of privilege that allow folks to continue to be marginalized. As a heterosexual black man in my late thirties, I have access to modes of privilege within black communities and the larger society, namely patriarchy and social status. These are privileges that many of those marginalized within our communities simply don't possess. *New Black Man* is my attempt to talk openly and honestly about those privileges, especially black male privilege, and to think out loud about the ways that black men can develop relationships with their mothers, daughters, sisters, friends, and colleagues that are pro-feminist and anti-sexist. There's no doubt in my mind that Black America must address sexism, misogyny, and homophobia at this point in our history. Below are just a few things for us to think about when pursuing the life of a *New Black Man*.

UNDERSTANDING BLACK MALE PRIVILEGE

Too often when I discuss black male privilege with black men, they fall back on defense mechanisms that highlight the effects of racism and unemployment in the lives of black men. There's no question that these issues are real challenges to black men, but just because black men are under siege in White America, it doesn't mean that they don't exhibit behaviors that do real damage to others, particularly within black communities. What many of these young men want to do is excuse the behavior of black men because of the extenuating circumstances under which black manhood is lived in our society. What they are suggesting is that black male behaviors that oppress women, children, and gays and lesbians in our community are understandable given the amount of oppression that some black men face from White America. This is unacceptable because one form of oppression cannot be used to justify another. Furthermore, it neglects the fact that others, some black women, for example, are also oppressed by White America because of their race and gender.

Countless conferences, books, pamphlets, articles, and online discussions are devoted to the crises that black men face, and the violence that is manifested against them, but there is comparatively little discussion of the very violence that black men often wield against black women. In fact, conversations about black male violence against black women and children are often interpreted as being part of the very racism that black men face. Those who speak out about black male violence are seen as traitors. We must get to a point where black male violence against black women, children, gays, and lesbians is openly challenged for what it is—behavior that is deeply harmful to the entire black community—and not just in the cases where the culprit is some young black male of the hip-hop generation. It has been too easy to blame the indiscretions and crimes of hip-hop generation figures like R. Kelly, Mystikal, or Tupac on the moral failings of the hip-hop generation, when we should be owning up to the fact that their behavior might have been influenced by their perceptions of how black male privilege operates in our communities.

BLACK FEMINISM IS NOT THE ENEMY

One of the main attributes of black male privilege is the unwillingness or incapability to fully understand the plight of black women in our communities. Yes, there are acknowledgments of incidents where black women are affected by blatant racism, but fewer when black women are affected because they are *black women* as opposed to being simply black people. Black feminism has sought to address this issue, creating a body of writings and activist events that highlight the conditions of black women globally. For example, it was not surprising that during the vice-presidential debate in October 2004 neither Vice-President Dick Cheney nor Democratic nominee John Edwards were aware that for black women between the ages of twenty-five and thirty-four, HIV disease was the largest cause of death. Tellingly, the debate was hosted by television journalist Gwen Ifill, an African-American woman. Black feminism has sought to make such information available and a topic of conversation, especially among the black political leadership.

Much of the violence against black women happens close to home, so it shouldn't be surprising that black men come under close scrutiny and criticism by black feminism. Yes, some of the criticism is very angry, and admittedly not all of it is constructive (as with criticisms of white racism), but it is absolutely necessary in a society where black women's critical voices are so often silenced. For those black men who don't understand the anger that many black women feel toward them, it might be helpful to think about the amount of anger that many blacks still harbor toward whites, given the history of racism in this country. Indeed, some black men have oppressed black women in ways that closely resemble the historical oppression of blacks by whites in American society.

Very often those black men who are critical of feminism simply have not done their homework. They are responding to hearsay they've heard on call-in talk shows or read online, rather than actually reading any black feminist writings themselves. These men should check them-selves, and check out a book by Audre Lorde, June Jordan, Barbara Christian, Pat Parker, Cheryl Clarke, Barbara Smith, Patricia Hill-Collins, Jewelle Gomez, Beverly Guy-Sheftall, Johnetta Cole, Cathy Cohen, Sharon Patricia Holland, Gwendolyn Pough, Joy James, and Alice Walker, Sonia Sanchez, Nikki Giovanni, and Masani Alexis DeVeaux—just a few of the women who have contributed to the body of literature known as Black Feminist Thought. Black feminism is wide ranging, and is concerned not only with dealing with violence against black women and girls, but also pressing issues of patriarchy, black women's healthcare, sex, and sexuality, black women's education, and racism. We do no justice to the legitimate issues that these women and others have raised if we don't seriously engage their work.

Black men also need to be serious about finding out the issues that affect the black women in their lives. For example, some studies have shown that eighty percent of black women in the United States will suffer from some form of fibroid disease and yet most black men are unaware of the fact, largely because they view it, like menstrual cycles, as simply a "woman's issue." Could we ever imagine a malady that affected eighty percent of all black men in the United States that the majority of black women would be unaware of? Of course not.

REAL BLACK MEN ARE NOT HOMOPHOBES

The prevailing notion on the ground is that real black men ain't "fags." This concept not only goes against any notion of community, it also simply isn't true. Black gay men have been valu-able contributors to all aspects of black life in the United States. The same faulty logic that suggests real black men ain't "fags" also suggests that black women are lesbians because black men have failed to live up to some "Strong Black Man" ideal, as if black lesbians were solely motivated by their displeasure with black men as opposed to their own social, cultural, and sex-ual desires. In either case, the presence of black gays and lesbians is often interpreted as a sign of failed black masculinity.

It's time that we start championing a movement where "real black men are not homophobes," given the damage that homophobia does in our community. Such a movement would encourage black men to forcefully challenge homophobia wherever they encounter it, whether it's expressed as heterosexist jokes on the *Tom Joyner in the Morning Show*, BET's *Comic View*, or in the kinds of homophobic violence, rhetorical and literal, that circulate regularly in our churches, on college campuses, in barbershops, within hip-hop, and other institutions within black com-munities. It's not enough for us to simply eradicate homophobia in our own lives, we need to make the message loud and clear that homophobia is not welcome in our communities. We also need to think differently about black masculinity and understand that black men exhibit a range of attitudes and behaviors that don't always fit neatly into some mythical notion of a "Strong Black Man." We do incredible damage to ourselves and to those around us by submitting to an idea that there is some little box that all black men must fit into. We are bigger than that.

REAL BLACK FATHERS ARE LOVING FATHERS

It has long been believed that the only responsibilities black men have in relation to their fami-lies are to provide financially and to dispense discipline. Although these are important aspects of parenting, this model of fatherhood does not allow black men to be emotionally available to their children and wives as nurturers. The idea that black men can be nurturers is often viewed skep-tically, as evidence of some kind of weakness. Therefore, many black men who are unable to find work often think that they aren't good fathers because the only model of fatherhood they know is one where black men are, above all else, providers. I suspect this thinking can be directly correlated to the number of black men who have chosen to be involved in the illicit underground drug economy.

This narrow view of fatherhood can take men away from their sons and daughters by means of incarceration or worse, death, and it can prompt men to leave their families because they feel unfit as fathers if they fall upon hard times. We need black men to be there for their children, not just financially, but physically and emotionally. So it is crucial that we establish new rules of fatherhood that allow black men to be good fathers regardless of their temporary economic status.

Rethinking black fatherhood goes hand-in-hand with rethinking black masculinity. We need to applaud black fathers who see themselves as partners in the full range of parenting activities, and who take seriously their roles as nurturers. We need to build a model of black feminist fatherhood, one in which black men aren't just the protectors of their daughters, but also seriously consider how black girls and black women live in the world and the challenges and dangers that they are liable to face. In a world where young black girls are so often silenced and invisible, black fathers have a responsibility, along with black mothers, to create the spaces where the plight of black girls is taken seriously. This also requires sensitizing young black boys, both our sons and those that we come in contact with on a regular basis, to the importance of black girls and black women.

HIP-HOP IS NOT THE ENEMY, BUT IT IS A PROBLEM

Like it or not, hip-hop is the soundtrack of black youth. It's been so easy to point to the moral failings of the hip-hop generation, particularly in relation to the sexism, misogyny, and homophobia that circulates in some of the music and videos, but those moral failings are often just a reflection of how the larger society and black communities think about black women, children, gays, and lesbians. Many criticisms of hip-hop simply deflect attention from equally disturbing practices within more traditional and acceptable black institutions. Too often, the criticisms of hip-hop are done without a real understanding of how ideas, knowledge, language, emotions, and relationships are cultivated by the hip-hop generation. It's not as if the hip-hop generation is beyond scrutiny, but if our elders are going to hold us accountable, they should at least make an effort to understand our worldview and the reasons why we make the choices we make. The world that the post–civil–rights generation(s) inhabits is fundamentally different from the one that produced the freedom movement of the 1950s and 1960s, and our elders need to acknowledge that fact. Our demons are not their demons, and our elders do us no good pretending that our current dilemma is somehow the product of our moral failings and our inability to pay homage to the freedom fighters who came before us. That said, the hip-hop generation also needs to appreciate the sacrifices made by our elders and accept that there are worthwhile lessons to be learned from their examples.

Just as hip-hop has been used to help politicize the hip-hop generation, it must also be used to create better gender relationships within the hip-hop generation. We need to make language available to young men in hip-hop that will help them rethink their gender politics. Young men often see hip-hop as a haven to articulate their frustrations with women—girlfriends, mothers, baby-mamas, groupies—but they are rarely capable of turning the critique upon themselves in order to interrogate their own roles in creating and maintaining dysfunctional relationships with women. The dialogue with young men is beginning in the work of black feminists of the hip-hop generation—Gwendolyn Pough and Joan Morgan come immediately to mind—and it is valuable work that I hope will continue to engage hip-hop music and those who listen and produce it, so that an honest conversation takes place, not just scolding and finger-wagging.

Young black women, of course, are also learning about and expressing their gender and sexuality through hip-hop. Talk about women and hip-hop, or hip-hop and gender, is often reduced to issues of misogyny and homophobia. Although these critiques *must* be made, the conversation typically remains focused on how men portray women in their lyrics and music videos. Rarely do we discuss how women use hip-hop to articulate their view of the world, a view that may or may not be predicated on what the men in hip-hop (or their lives) might be doing. For example, many black women hip-hop artists, scholars, and journalists speak about "desire" (sexual and otherwise) and the ways that women artists articulate desire in their art. Unfortunately, these issues are rarely discussed in mainstream discussions about hip-hop. Perhaps some of the critical energy focused so much on what black men in hip-hop are saying about women would be better spent by learning to listen to the voices of black women themselves.

BECOMING A NEW BLACK MAN

I am a man of my times, but the times don't know it yet!

—Erik Todd Dellums as Bayard Rustin in *Boycott*

Finally, it is important the readers remember that I am not *the* New Black Man, but rather that the New Black Man is a metaphor for an imagined life—a way to be "strong" as a black man in new ways: strong commitment to diversity in our communities, strong support for women and feminism, and strong faith in love and the value of listening. I struggle, and often falter, to live up to these ideals every day of my life. It's a challenge, but one I know is well worth facing for myself, for my wife, and for my beautiful daughters. After reading these words, I hope you will join me, men and women, in making the New Black Man the man of our times.

Homophobia
A Weapon of Sexism

Suzanne Pharr

Suzanne Pharr *describes herself as a "Political Handywoman". In her work she focuses on racism, sexism and homophobia and the ways that these forms of oppression and discrimination intersect. Her goal is social and economic justice. Her books include* In the Time of the Right: Reflections on Liberation *(1996) and* Homophobia: A Weapon of Sexism *(1997) from which this excerpt comes. Her books are available to read in their entirety for free on her blog. Her work is guided by the question "How can we make it possible for everyone to live as a whole person, to have self-determination, to be treated with dignity and respect, and to have access to material necessities as well as joy?" (qtd from: www.suzannepharr.org)*

HOMOPHOBIA: A WEAPON OF SEXISM

HOMOPHOBIA—The irrational fear and hatred of those who love and sexually desire those of the same sex. Though I intimately knew its meaning, the word homophobia was unknown to me until the late 1970s, and when I first heard it, I was struck by how difficult it is to say, what an ugly word it is, equally as ugly as its meaning. Like racism and anti-Semitism, it is a word that calls up images of loss of freedom, verbal and physical violence, death.

In my life I have experienced the effects of homophobia through rejection by friends, threats of loss of employment, and threats upon my life; and I have witnessed far worse things happening to other lesbian and gay people: loss of children, beatings, rape, death. Its power is great enough to keep ten to twenty percent of the population living lives of fear (if their sexual identity is hidden) or lives of danger (if their sexual identity is visible) or both. And its power is great enough to keep the remaining eighty to ninety percent of the population trapped in their own fears.

Long before I had a word to describe the behavior, I was engaged in a search to discover the source of its power, the power to damage and destroy lives. The most common explanations were that to love the same sex was either abnormal (sick) or immoral (sinful).

My exploration of the sickness theory led me to understand that homosexuality is simply a matter of sexual identity, which, along with heterosexual identity, is formed in ways that no one conclusively understands. The American Psychological Association has said that it is no more abnormal to be homosexual than to be lefthanded. It is simply that a certain percentage of the population *is*. It is not healthier to be heterosexual or righthanded. What is unhealthy—and sometimes a source of stress and sickness so great it can lead to suicide—is homophobia, that societal disease that places such negative messages, condemnation, arid violence on gay men and lesbians that we have to struggle throughout our lives for self-esteem.

The sin theory is a particularly curious one because it is expressed so often and with such hateful emotion both from the pulpit and from laypeople who rely heavily upon the Bible for evidence. However, there is significant evidence that the approximately eight references to homosexuality in the Bible are frequently read incorrectly, according to Dr. Virginia Ramey Mollenkott in an essay in *Christianity and Crisis*:

> Much of the discrimination against homosexual persons is justified by a common misreading of the Bible. Many English translations of the Bible contain the word homosexual in extremely negative contexts. But the fact is that the word *homosexual* does not occur anywhere in the Bible. No extant text, no manuscript, neither Hebrew nor Greek, Syriac, nor Aramaic, contains the word. The terms *homosexual* and *heterosexual* were not developed in any language until the 1890's, when for the first time the awareness developed that there are people with a lifelong, constitutional orientation toward their own sex. Therefore the use of the word *homosexuality* by certain English Bible translators is an example of the extreme bias that endangers the human and civil rights of homosexual persons. (pp. *383–4, Nov. 9, 1987*)

Dr. Mollenkott goes on to add that two words in I Corinthians 6:9 and one word in Timothy 1:10 have been used as evidence to damn homosexuals but that well into the 20th century the first of these was understood by everyone to mean masturbation, and the second was known to refer to male prostitutes who were available for hire by either women or men. There are six other Biblical references that are thought by some to refer to homosexuals but each of these is disputed by contemporary scholars. For instance, the sin in the Sodom and Gomorrah passage (Genesis 19: 1-10) is less about homosexuality than it is about inhospitality and gang rape. The law of hospitality was universally accepted and Lot was struggling to uphold it against what we assume are heterosexual townsmen threatening gang rape to the two male angels in Lot's home. While people dwell on this passage as a condemnation of homosexuality, they bypass what I believe is the central issue or, if you will, *sin:* Lot's offering his two virgin daughters up to the men to be used as they desired for gang rape. Here is a perfectly clear example of devaluing and dehumanizing and violently brutalizing women.

The eight Biblical references (and not a single one by Jesus) to alleged homosexuality are very small indeed when compared to the several hundred references (and many by Jesus) to money and the necessity for justly distributing wealth. Yet few people go on a rampage about the issue of a just economic system, using the Bible as a base.

Finally, I came to understand that homosexuality, hetero-sexuality, bi-sexuality are *morally neutral*. A particular sexual identity is not an indication of either good or evil. What is important is not the gender of the two people in relationship with each other but the content of that relationship. Does that relationship contain violence, control of one person by the other? Is the relationship a growthful place for the people involved? It is clear that we must hold all relationships, whether opposite sex or same sex, to these standards.

The first workshops that I conducted were an effort to address these two issues, and I assumed that if consciousness could be raised about the invalidity of these two issues then people would stop feeling homophobic and would understand homophobia as a civil rights issue and work against it. The workshops took a high moral road, invoking participants' compassion, understanding, and outrage at injustice.

The eight-hour workshops raised consciousness and increased participants' commitment to work against homophobia as one more oppression in a growing list of recognized oppressions, but I still felt something was missing. I felt there was still too much unaccounted for power in homophobia even after we looked at the sick and sinful theories, at how it feels to be a lesbian in a homophobic world, at why lesbians choose invisibility, at how lesbian existence threatens male dominance. All of the pieces seemed available but we couldn't sew them together into a quilt.

As I conducted more workshops over the years I noticed several important themes that led to the final piecing together:

1) Women began to recognize that economics was a central issue connecting various oppressions;
2) Battered women began talking about how they had been called lesbians by their batterers;
3) Both heterosexual and lesbian women said they valued the workshops because in them they were given the rare opportunity to talk about their own sexuality and also about sexism in general.

Around the same time (1985-86), the National Coalition Against Domestic Violence (NCADV) entered into a traumatic relationship with the U.S. Department of Justice (DOJ), requesting a large two-year grant to provide domestic violence training and information nationally. At the time the grant was to be announced, NCADV was attacked by conservative groups such as the Heritage Foundation as a "pro-lesbian, pro-feminist, anti-family" organization. In response to these attacks, the DOJ decided not to award a grant; instead they formulated a "cooperative agreement" that allowed them to monitor and approve all work, and they assured conservative organizations that the work would not be pro-lesbian and anti-family. The major issue between NCADV and the DOJ became whether NCADV would let an outside agency define and control its work, and finally, during never-ending concern from the DOJ about "radical" and "lesbian" issues, the agreement was terminated by NCADV at the end of the first year. Throughout that year, there were endless statements and innuendoes from the DOJ and some members of NCADV's membership about NCADV's lesbian leadership and its alleged concern for only lesbian issues. Many women were damaged by the crossfire, NCADV's work was stopped for a year, and the organization was split from within. It was lesbian baiting at its worst.

As one of NCADV's lesbian leadership during that onslaught of homophobic attacks, I was still giving homophobia workshops around the country, now able to give even more personal witness to the virulence of the hatred and fear of lesbians and gay men within both institutions and individuals. It was a time of pain and often anger for those of us committed to creating a world free of violence, and it was a time of deep distress for those of us under personal attack. However, my mother, like many mothers, had always said, "All things work for the good" and sure enough, it was out of the accumulation of these experiences that the pieces began coming together to make a quilt of our understanding.

On the day that I stopped reacting to attacks and gave my time instead to visioning, this simple germinal question came forth for the workshops: "What will the world be like without homophobia in it—for everyone, female and male, whatever sexual identity?" Simple though the question is, it was at first shocking because those of us who work in the anti-violence movement spend most of our time working with the damaging, negative results of violence and have little time to vision. It is sometimes difficult to create a vision of a world we have never experienced, but without such a vision, we cannot know clearly what we are working toward in our social change work.

From this question, answer led to answer until a whole appeared of our collective making, from one workshop to another.

Here are some of the answers women have given:

- Kids won't be called tomboys or sissies; they'll just be who they are, able to do what they wish.
- People will be able to love anyone, no matter what sex; the issue will simply be whether or not she/he is a good human being, compatible, and loving.
- Affection will be opened up between women and men, women and women, men and men, and it won't be centered on sex; people won't fear being called names if they show affection to someone who isn't a mate or potential mate.
- If affection is opened up, then isolation will be broken down for all of us, especially for those who generally experience little physical affection, such as unmarried old people.
- Women will be able to work whatever jobs we want without being labeled masculine.
- There will be less violence if men do not feel they have to prove and assert their manhood. Their desire to dominate and control will not spill over from the personal to the level of national and international politics and the use of bigger and better weapons to control other countries.
- People will wear whatever clothes they wish, with the priority being comfort rather than the display of femininity or masculinity.
- There will be no gender roles.

It is at this point in the workshops—having imagined a world without homophobia—that the participants see the analysis begin to fall into place. Someone notes that all the things we have been talking about relate to sexual gender roles. It's rather like the beginning of a course in Sexism 101. The next question is "Imagine the world with no sex roles—sexual identity, which may be in flux, but no sexual gender roles." Further: imagine a world in which opportunity is not determined by gender or race. Just the imagining makes women alive with excitement because it is a vision of freedom, often just glimpsed but always known deep down as truth. Pure joy.

We talk about what it would be like to be born in a world in which there were no expectations or treatment based on gender but instead only the expectation that each child, no matter what race or sex, would be given as many options and possibilities as society could muster. Then we discuss what girls and boys would be like at puberty and beyond if sex role expectations didn't come crashing down on them with girls' achievement levels beginning to decline thereafter; what it would be for women to have the training and options for economic equity with men; what would happen to issues of power and control, and therefore violence, if there were real equality. To have no prescribed sex roles would open the possibility of equality. It is a discussion women find difficult to leave. Freedom calls.

PATRIARCHY—an enforced belief in male dominance and control—is the ideology and sexism the system that holds it in place. The catechism goes like this: Who do gender roles serve? Men and the women who seek power from them. Who suffers from gender roles? Women most completely and men in part. How are gender roles maintained? By the weapons of sexism: economics, violence, homophobia.

Why then don't we ardently pursue ways to eliminate gender roles and therefore sexism? It is my profound belief that all people have a spark in them that yearns for freedom, and the history of the world's atrocities—from the Nazi concentration camps to white dominance in South Africa to the battering of women—is the story of attempts to snuff out that spark. When that spark doesn't move forward to full flame, it is because the weapons designed to control and destroy have wrought such intense damage over time that the spark has been all but extinguished.

Sexism, that system by which women are kept subordinate to men, is kept in place by three powerful weapons designed to cause or threaten women with pain and loss. As stated before, the three are economics, violence, and homophobia. The stories of women battered by men, victims of sexism at its worst, show these three forces converging again and again. When battered women tell why they stayed with a batterer or why they returned to a batterer, over and over they say it was because they could not support themselves and their children financially, they had no skills for jobs, they could not get housing, transportation, medical care for their children. And how were they kept controlled? Through violence and threats of violence, both physical and verbal, so that they feared for their lives and the lives of their children and doubted their own abilities and self-worth. And why were they beaten? Because they were not good enough, were not "real women," were dykes, or because they stood up to him as no "real woman" would. And the male batterer, with societal backing, felt justified, often righteous, in his behavior—for his part in keeping women in their place.

ECONOMICS must be looked at first because many feminists consider it to be the root cause of sexism. Certainly the United Nations study released at the final conference of the International Decade on Women, held in Nairobi, Kenya, in 1985, supports that belief: of the world's population, women do 75% of the work, receive 10% of the pay and own 1% of the property. In the United States it is also supported by the opposition of the government to the idea of comparable worth and pay equity, as expressed by Ronald Reagan who referred to pay equity as "a joke." Obviously, it is considered a dangerous idea. Men profit not only from women's unpaid work in the home but from our underpaid work within horizontal female segregation such as clerical workers or upwardly mobile tokenism in the workplace where a few affirmative action promotions are expected to take care of all women's economic equality needs. Moreover, they profit from women's bodies through pornography, prostitution, and international female sexual slavery. And white men profit from both the labor of women and of men of color. Forced economic dependency puts women under male control and severely limits women's options for self-determination and self-sufficiency.

This truth is borne out by the fact that according to the National Commission on Working Women, on average, women of all races working year round earn only 64 cents to every one dollar a man makes. Also, the U.S. Census Bureau reports that only 9 percent of working women make over $25,000 a year. There is fierce opposition to women gaining employment in the nontraditional job market, that is, those jobs that traditionally employ less than 25 percent women. After a woman has gained one of these higher paying jobs, she is often faced with sexual harassment, lesbian baiting, and violence. It is clear that in the workplace there is an all-out effort to keep women in traditional roles so that the only jobs we are "qualified" for are the low-paid ones.

Actually, we have to look at economics not only as the root cause of sexism but also as the underlying, driving force that keeps all the oppressions in place. In the United States, our economic system is shaped like a pyramid, with a few people at the top, primarily white males, being supported by large numbers of unpaid or low-paid workers at the bottom. When we look at this pyramid, we begin to understand the major connection between sexism and racism because those groups at the bottom of the pyramid are women and people of color. We then begin to understand why there is such a fervent effort to keep those oppressive systems (racism and sexism and all the ways they are manifested) in place to maintain the unpaid and low-paid labor.

Susan DeMarco and Jim Hightower, writing for *Mother Jones*, report that *Forbes* magazine indicated that "the 400 richest families in America last year had an average net worth of

$550 million each. These and less than a million other families—roughly one percent of our population—are at the prosperous tip of our society. In 1976, the wealthiest 1 percent of America's families owned 19.2 percent of the nation's total wealth. (This sum of wealth counts all of America's cash, real estate, stocks, bonds, factories, art, personal property, and anything else of financial value.) By 1983, those at this 1 percent tip of our economy owned 34.3 percent of our wealth. *Today, the top 1 percent of Americans possesses more net wealth than the bottom 90 percent."* (My italics.) *(May, 1988, pp. 32–33)*

In order for this top-heavy system of economic inequity to maintain itself, the 90 percent on the bottom must keep supplying cheap labor. A very complex, intricate system of institutionalized oppressions is necessary to maintain the status quo so that the vast majority will not demand its fair share of wealth and resources and bring the system down. Every institution—schools, banks, churches, government, courts, media, etc—as well as individuals must be enlisted in the campaign to maintain such a system of gross inequity.

What would happen if women gained the earning opportunities and power that men have? What would happen if these opportunities were distributed equitably, no matter what sex one was, no matter what race one was born into, and no matter where one lived? What if educational and training opportunities were equal? Would women spend most of our youth preparing for marriage? Would marriage be based on economic survival for women? What would happen to issues of power and control? Would women stay with our batterers? If a woman had economic independence in a society where women had equal opportunities, would she still be thought of as owned by her father or husband?

Economics is the great controller in both sexism and racism. If a person can't acquire food, shelter, and clothing and provide them for children, then that person can be forced to do many things in order to survive. The major tactic, worldwide, is to provide unrecompensed or inadequately recompensed labor for the benefit of those who control wealth. Hence, we see women performing unpaid labor in the home or filling low-paid jobs, and we see people of color in the lowest-paid jobs available.

The method is complex: limit educational and training opportunities for women and for people of color and then withhold adequate paying jobs with the excuse that people of color and women are incapable of filling them. Blame the economic victim and keep the victim's self-esteem low through invisibility and distortion within the media and education. Allow a few people of color and women to succeed among the profit-makers so that blaming those who don't "make it" can be intensified. Encourage those few who succeed in gaining power now to turn against those who remain behind rather than to use their resources to make change for all. Maintain the myth of scarcity—that there are not enough jobs, resources, etc., to go around—among the middleclass so that they will not unite with laborers, immigrants, and the unemployed. The method keeps in place a system of control and profit by a few and a constant source of cheap labor to maintain it.

If anyone steps out of line, take her/his job away. Let homelessness and hunger do their work. The economic weapon works. And we end up saying, "I would do this or that—be openly who I am, speak out against injustice, work for civil rights, join a labor union, go to a political march, etc.—if I didn't have this job. I can't afford to lose it." We stay in an abusive situation because we see no other way to survive.

In the battered women's movement abusive relationships are said to be about power and control and the way out of them is through looking at the ways power and control work in our lives, developing support, improving self-esteem, and achieving control over our decisions and lives. We have yet to apply these methods successfully to our economic lives. Though requiring massive change, the way there also lies open for equality and wholeness. But the effort will require at least as much individual courage and risk and group support as it does for a battered woman to leave her batterer, and that requirement is very large indeed. Yet battered women find the courage to leave their batterers every day. They walk right into the unknown. To break away from economic domination and control will require a movement made up of individuals who possess this courage and ability to take risks.

VIOLENCE is the second means of keeping women in line, in a narrowly defined place and role. First, there is the physical violence of battering, rape, and incest. Often when battered women come to shelters and talk about their lives, they tell stories of being not only physically beaten but also raped and their children subjected to incest. Work in the women's anti-violence movement during almost two decades has provided significant evidence that each of these acts, including rape and incest, is an attempt to seek power over and control of another person. In each case, the victim is viewed as an object and is used to meet the abuser's needs. The violence is used to wreak punishment and to demand compliance or obedience.

Violence against women is directly related to the condition of women in a society that refuses us equal pay, equal access to resources, and equal status with males. From this condition comes men's confirmation of their sense of ownership of women, power over women, and assumed right to control women for their own means. Men physically and emotionally abuse women because they *can*, because they live in a world that gives them permission. Male violence is fed by their sense of their *right* to dominate and control, and their sense of superiority over a group of people who, because of gender, they consider inferior to them.

It is not just the violence but the threat of violence that controls our lives. Because the burden of responsibility has been placed so often on the potential victim, as women we have curtailed our freedom in order to protect ourselves from violence. Because of the threat of rapists, we stay on alert, being careful not to walk in isolated places, being careful where we park our cars, adding incredible security measures to our homes—massive locks, lights, alarms, if we can afford them—and we avoid places where we will appear vulnerable or unprotected while the abuser walks with freedom. Fear, often now so commonplace that it is unacknowledged, shapes our lives, reducing our freedom.

As Bernice Reagan of the musical group Sweet Honey in the Rock said at the 1982 National Coalition Against Domestic Violence conference, women seem to carry a genetic memory that women were once burned as witches when we stepped out of line. To this day, mothers pass on to their daughters word of the dangers they face and teach them the ways they must limit their lives in order to survive.

Part of the way sexism stays in place is the societal promise of survival, false and unfulfilled as it is, that women will not suffer violence if we attach ourselves to a man to protect us. A woman without a man is told she is vulnerable to external violence and, worse, that there is something wrong with her. When the male abuser calls a woman a lesbian, he is not so much labeling her a woman who loves women as he is warning her that by resisting him, she is choosing to be out-side society's protection from male institutions and therefore from wide-ranging, unspecified, ever-present violence. When she seeks assistance from woman friends or a battered women's shelter, he recognizes the power in woman bonding and fears loss of her servitude and loyalty: the potential loss of his control. The concern is not affectional/sexual identity: the concern is disloyalty and the threat is violence.

The threat of violence against women who step out of line or who are disloyal is made all the more powerful by the fact that women do not have to do anything—they may be paragons of virtue and subservience—to receive violence against our lives: the violence still comes. It comes because of the woman-hating that exists throughout society. Chance plays a larger part than virtue in keeping women safe. Hence, with violence always a threat to us, women can never feel completely secure and confident. Our sense of safety is always fragile and tenuous.

Many women say that verbal violence causes more harm than physical violence because it damages self-esteem so deeply. Women have not wanted to hear battered women say that the verbal abuse was as hurtful as the physical abuse: to acknowledge that truth would be tantamount to acknowledging that *virtually every woman is a battered woman.* It is difficult to keep strong against accusations of being a bitch, stupid, inferior, etc., etc. It is especially difficult when these individual assaults are backed up by a society that shows women in textbooks, advertising, TV programs, movies, etc., as debased, silly, inferior, and sexually objectified, and a society that gives tacit approval to pornography. When we internalize these messages, we call the result "low self-esteem," a therapeutic individualized term. It seems to me we should use the more political expression: when we internalize these messages, we experience *internalized sexism,* and we experience it in common with all women living in a sexist world. The violence against us is supported by a society in which woman-hating is deeply imbedded.

In "Eyes on the Prize," a 1987 Public Television documentary about the Civil Rights Movement, an older white woman says about her youth in the South that it was difficult to be anything different from what was around her when there was no vision for another way to be. Our society presents images of women that say it is appropriate to commit violence against us. Violence is committed against women because we are seen as inferior in status and in worth. It has been the work of the women's movement to present a vision of another way to be.

Every time a woman gains the strength to resist and leave her abuser, we are given a model of the importance of stepping out of line, of moving toward freedom. And we all gain strength when she says to violence, "Never again!" Thousands of women in the last fifteen years have resisted their abusers to come to this country's 1100 battered women's shelters. There they have sat down with other women to share their stories, to discover that their stories again and again are the same, to develop an analysis that shows that violence is a statement about power and control, and to understand how sexism creates the climate for male violence. Those brave women are now a part of a movement that gives hope for another way to live in equality and peace.

HOMOPHOBIA works effectively as a weapon of sexism because it is joined with a powerful arm, heterosexism. Heterosexism creates the climate for homophobia with its assumption that the world is and must be heterosexual and its display of power and privilege as the norm. Heterosexism is the systemic display of homophobia in the institutions of society. Heterosexism and homophobia work together to enforce compulsory heterosexuality and that bastion of patriarchal power, the nuclear family. The central focus of the rightwing attack against women's liberation is that women's equality, women's self-determination, women's control of our own bodies and lives will damage what they see as the crucial societal institution, the nuclear family. The attack has been led by fundamentalist ministers across the country. The two areas they have focused on most consistently are abortion and homosexuality, and their passion has led them to bomb women's clinics and to recommend deprogramming for homosexuals and establishing camps to quarantine people with AIDS. To resist marriage and/or heterosexuality is to risk severe punishment and loss.

It is not by chance that when children approach puberty and increased sexual awareness they begin to taunt each other by calling these names: "queer' "faggot' "pervert?" It is at puberty that the full force of society's pressure to conform to heterosexuality and prepare for marriage is brought to bear. Children know what we have taught them, and we have given clear messages that those who deviate from standard expectations are to be made to get back in line. The best controlling tactic at puberty is to be treated as an outsider, to be ostracized at a time when it feels most vital to be accepted. Those who are different must be made to suffer loss. It is also at puberty that misogyny begins to be more apparent, and girls are pressured to conform to societal norms that do not permit them to realize their full potential. It is at this time that their academic achievements begin to decrease as they are coerced into compulsory heterosexuality and trained for dependency upon a man, that is, for economic survival.

There was a time when the two most condemning accusations against a woman meant to ostracize and disempower her were "whore" and "lesbian?" The sexual revolution and changing attitudes about heterosexual behavior may have led to some lessening of the power of the word *whore*, though it still has strength as a threat to sexual property and prostitutes are stigmatized and abused. However, the word *lesbian* is still fully charged and carries with it the full threat of loss of power and privilege, the threat of being cut asunder, abandoned, and left outside society's protection.

To be a lesbian is to be *perceived* as someone who has stepped out of line, who has moved out of sexual/economic dependence on a male, who is woman-identified. A lesbian is perceived as someone who can live without a man, and who is therefore (however illogically) against men. A lesbian is perceived as being outside the acceptable, routinized order of things. She is seen as someone who has no societal institutions to protect her and who is not privileged to the protection of individual males. Many heterosexual women see her as someone who stands in contradiction to the sacrifices they have made to conform to compulsory heterosexuality. A lesbian is perceived as a threat to the nuclear family, to male dominance and control, to the very heart of sexism.

Gay men are perceived also as a threat to male dominance and control, and the homophobia expressed against them has the same roots in sexism as does homophobia against lesbians. Visible gay men are the objects of extreme hatred and fear by heterosexual men because their breaking ranks with male heterosexual solidarity is seen as a damaging rent in the very fabric of sexism. They are seen as betrayers, as traitors who must be punished and eliminated. In the beating and killing of gay men we see clear evidence of this hatred. When we see the fierce homophobia expressed toward gay men, we can begin to understand the ways sexism also affects males through imposing rigid, dehumanizing gender roles on them. The two circumstances in which it is legitimate for men to be openly physically affectionate with one another are in competitive sports and in the crisis of war. For many men, these two experiences are the highlights of their lives, and they think of them again and again with nostalgia. War and sports offer a cover of all-male safety and dominance to keep away the notion of affectionate openness being identified with homosexuality. When gay men break ranks with male roles through bonding and affection outside the arenas of war and sports, they are perceived as not being "real men," that is, as being identified with women, the weaker sex that must be dominated and that over the centuries has been the object of male hatred and abuse. Misogyny gets transferred to gay men with a vengeance and is increased by the fear that their sexual identity and behavior will bring down the entire system of male dominance and compulsory heterosexuality.

If lesbians are established as threats to the status quo, as outcasts who must be punished, homophobia can wield its power over all women through lesbian baiting. Lesbian baiting is an attempt to control women by labeling us as lesbians because our behavior is not acceptable, that is, when we are being independent, going our own way, living whole lives, fighting for our rights, demanding equal pay, saying no to violence, being self-assertive, bonding with and loving the company of women, assuming the right to our bodies, insisting upon our own authority, making changes that include us in society's decision-making; lesbian baiting occurs when women are called lesbians because we resist male dominance and control. And it has little or nothing to do with one's sexual identity.

To be named as lesbian threatens all women, not just lesbians, with great loss. And any woman who steps out of role risks being called a lesbian. To understand how this is a threat to all women, one must understand that any woman can be called a lesbian and there is no real way she can defend herself: there is no way to credential one's sexuality. ("The Children's Hour," a Lillian Heilman play, makes this point when a student asserts two teachers are lesbians and they have no way to disprove it.) She may be married or divorced, have children, dress in the most feminine manner, have sex with men, be celibate—but there are lesbians who do all those things. *Lesbians look like all women and all women look like lesbians.* There is no guaranteed method of identification, and as we all know, sexual identity can be kept hidden. (The same is true for men. There is no way to prove their sexual identity, though many go to extremes to prove heterosexuality.) Also, women are not necessarily born lesbian. Some seem to be, but others become lesbians later in life after having lived heterosexual lives. Lesbian baiting of heterosexual women would not work if there were a definitive way to identify lesbians (or heterosexuals.)

We have yet to understand clearly how sexual identity develops. And this is disturbing to some people, especially those who are determined to discover how lesbian and gay identity is formed so that they will know where to start in eliminating it. (Isn't it odd that there is so little concern about discovering the causes of heterosexuality?) There are many theories: genetic makeup, hormones, socialization, environment, etc. But there is no conclusive evidence that indicates that heterosexuality comes from one process and homosexuality from another.

We do know, however, that sexual identity can be in flux, and we know that sexual identity means more than just the gender of people one is attracted to and has sex with. To be a lesbian has as many ramifications as for a woman to be heterosexual. It is more than sex, more than just the bedroom issue many would like to make it: it is a woman-centered life with all the social interconnections that entails. Some lesbians are in long-term relationships, some in short-term ones, some date, some are celibate, some are married to men, some remain as separate as possible from men, some have children by men, some by alternative insemination, some seem "feminine" by societal standards, some "masculine," some are doctors, lawyers and ministers, some laborers, housewives and writers: what all share in common is a sexual/affectional identity that focuses on women in its attractions and social relationships.

If lesbians are simply women with a particular sexual identity who look and act like all women, then the major difference in living out a lesbian sexual identity as opposed to a heterosexual identity is that as lesbians we live in a homophobic world that threatens and imposes damaging loss on us for being who we are, for choosing to live whole lives. Homophobic people often assert that homosexuals have the choice of not being homosexual; that is, we don't have to act out our sexual identity. In that case, I want to hear heterosexuals talk about their willingness not to act out their sexual identity, including not just sexual activity but heterosexual social interconnections and heterosexual privilege. It is a question of wholeness. It is very difficult for one to be denied the life of a sexual being, whether expressed in sex or in physical affection, and to feel complete, whole. For our loving relationships with humans feed the life of the spirit and enable us to overcome our basic isolation and to be interconnected with humankind.

If, then, any woman can be named a lesbian and be threatened with terrible losses, what is it she fears? Are these fears real? Being vulnerable to a homophobic world can lead to these losses:

- *Employment.* The loss of job leads us right back to the economic connection to sexism. This fear of job loss exists for almost every lesbian except perhaps those who are self-employed or in a business that does not require societal approval. Consider how many businesses or organizations you know that will hire and protect people who are openly gay or lesbian.
- *Family.* Their approval, acceptance, love.
- *Children.* Many lesbians and gay men have children, but very, very few gain custody in court challenges, even if the other parent is a known abuser. Other children may be kept away from us as though gays and lesbians are abusers. There are written and unwritten laws prohibiting lesbians and gays from being foster parents or from adopting children. There is an irrational fear that children in contact with lesbians and gays will become homosexual through influence or that they will be sexually abused. Despite our knowing that 95 percent of those who sexually abuse children are heterosexual men, there are no policies keeping heterosexual men from teaching or working with children, yet in almost every school system in America, visible gay men and lesbians are not hired through either written or unwritten law.
- *Heterosexual privilege and protection.* No institutions, other than those created by lesbians and gays—such as the Metropolitan Community Church, some counseling centers, political organizations such as the National Gay and Lesbian Task Force, the National Coalition of Black Lesbians and Gays, the Lambda Legal Defense and Education Fund, etc.,— affirm homosexuality and offer protection. Affirmation and protection cannot be gained from the criminal justice system, mainline churches, educational institutions, the government.
- *Safety.* There is nowhere to turn for safety from physical and verbal attacks because the norm presently in this country is that it is acceptable to be overtly homophobic. Gay men are beaten on the streets; lesbians are kidnapped and "deprogrammed?" The National Gay and Lesbian Task Force, in an extended study, has documented violence against lesbians and gay men and noted the inadequate response of the criminal justice system. One of the major differences between homophobia/heterosexism and racism and sexism is that because of the Civil Rights Movement and the women's movement racism and sexism are expressed more covertly (though with great harm); because there has not been a major, visible lesbian and gay movement, it is permissible to be overtly homophobic in any institution or public forum. Churches spew forth homophobia in the same way they did racism prior to the Civil Rights Movement. Few laws are in place to protect lesbians and gay men, and the criminal justice system is wracked with homophobia.
- *Mental health.* An overtly homophobic world in which there is full permission to treat lesbians and gay men with cruelty makes it difficult for lesbians and gay men to maintain a strong sense of well-being and self-esteem. Many lesbians and gay men are beaten, raped, killed, subjected to aversion therapy, or put in mental institutions. The impact of such hatred and negativity can lead one to depression and, in some cases, to suicide. The toll on the gay and lesbian community is devastating.
- *Community.* There is rejection by those who live in homophobic fear, those who are afraid of association with lesbians and gay men. For many in the gay and lesbian community, there is a loss of public acceptance, a loss of allies, a loss of place and belonging.
- *Credibility.* This fear is large for many people: the fear that they will no longer be respected, listened to, honored, believed. They fear they will be social outcasts.

The list goes on and on. But any one of these essential components of a full life is large enough to make one deeply fear its loss. A black woman once said to me in a workshop, "When I fought for Civil Rights, I always had my family and community to fall back on even when they didn't fully understand or accept what I was doing. I don't know if I could have borne losing them. And you people don't have either with you. It takes my breath away?"

What does a woman have to do to get called a lesbian? Almost anything, sometimes nothing at all, but certainly anything that threatens the status quo, anything that steps out of role, anything that asserts the rights of women, anything that doesn't indicate submission arid subordination. Assertiveness, standing up for oneself, asking for more pay, better working conditions, training for and accepting a non-traditional (you mean a man's?) job, enjoying the company of women, being financially independent, being in control of one's life, depending first and foremost upon oneself, thinking that one can do whatever needs to be done, but above all, working for the rights and equality of women.

In the backlash to the gains of the women's liberation movement, there has been an increased effort to keep definitions man-centered. Therefore, to work on behalf of women must mean to work against men. To love women must mean that one hates men. A very effective attack has been made against the word *feminist* to make it a derogatory word. In current backlash usage, *feminist* equals *man-hater* which equals *lesbian*. This formula is created in the hope that women will be frightened away from their work on behalf of women. Consequently, we now have women who believe in the rights of women and work for those rights while from fear deny that they are feminists, or refuse to use the word because it is so "abrasive."

So what does one do in an effort to keep from being called a lesbian? She steps back into line, into the role that is demanded of her, tries to behave in such a way that doesn't threaten the status of men, and if she works for women's rights, she begins modifying that work. When women's organizations begin doing significant social change work, they inevitably are lesbian-baited; that is, funders or institutions or community members tell us that they can't work with us because of our "man-hating attitudes" or the presence of lesbians. We are called too strident, told we are making enemies, not doing good.

The battered women's movement has seen this kind of attack: the pressure has been to provide services only, without analysis of the causes of violence against women and strategies for ending it. To provide only services without political analysis or direct action is to be in an approved "helping" role; to analyze the causes of violence against women is to begin the work toward changing an entire system of power and control. It is when we do the latter that we are threatened with the label of man-hater or lesbian. For my politics, if a women's social change organization has not been labeled lesbian or communist, it is probably not doing significant work; it is only "making nice."

Women in many of these organizations, out of fear of all the losses we are threatened with, begin to modify our work to make it more acceptable and less threatening to the male-dominated society which we originally set out to change. The work can no longer be radical (going to the root cause of the problem) but instead must be reforming, working only on the symptoms and not the cause. Real change for women becomes thwarted and stopped. The word *lesbian* is instilled with the power to halt our work and control our lives. And we give it its power with our fear.

In my view, homophobia has been one of the major causes of the failure of the women's liberation movement to make deep and lasting change. (The other major block has been racism.) We were fierce when we set out but when threatened with the loss of heterosexual privilege, we began putting on brakes. Our best-known nationally distributed women's magazine was reluctant to print articles about lesbians, began putting a man on the cover several times a year, and writing articles about women who succeeded in a man's world. We worried about our image, our being all right, our being "real women" despite our work. Instead of talking about the elimination of sexual gender roles, we stepped back and talked about "sex role stereotyping" as the issue. Change around the edges for middleclass white women began to be talked about as successes. We accepted tokenism and integration, forgetting that equality for all women, for all people—and not just equality of white middleclass women with white men—was the goal that we could never put behind us.

But despite backlash and retreats, change is growing from within. The women's liberation movement is beginning to gain strength again because there are women who are talking about liberation for all women. We are examining sexism, racism, homophobia, classism, anti-Semitism, ageism, ableism, and imperialism, and we see everything as connected. This change in point of view represents the third wave of the women's liberation movement, a new direction that does not get mass media coverage and recognition. It has been initiated by women of color and lesbians who were marginalized or rendered invisible by the white heterosexual leaders of earlier efforts. The first wave was the 19th and early 20th century campaign for the vote; the second, beginning in the 1960s, focused on the Equal Rights Amendment and abortion rights. Consisting of predominantly white middleclass women, both failed in recognizing issues of equality and empowerment for all women. The third wave of the movement, multi-racial and multi-issued, seeks the transformation of the world for us all. We know that we won't get there until everyone gets there; that we must move forward in a great strong line, hand in hand, not just a few at a time.

We know that the arguments about homophobia originating from mental health and Biblical/religious attitudes can be settled when we look at the sexism that permeates religious and psychiatric history. The women of the third wave of the women's liberation movement know that *without the existence of sexism, there would be no homophobia.*

Finally, we know that as long as the word lesbian can strike fear in any woman's heart, then work on behalf of women can be stopped; the only successful work against sexism must include work against homophobia.

INDEX